W9-AQS-034

THIRD EDITION

Organizational Behavior

CONCEPTS, CONTROVERSIES, AND APPLICATIONS

Stephen P. Robbins

San Diego State University

PRENTICE-HALL, Englewood Cliffs, New Jersey 07632

Library of Congress Cataloging-in-Publication Data

ROBBINS, STEPHEN P.
  Organizational behavior.

  Includes bibliographies and indexes.
  1. Organizational behavior. I. Title.
HD58.7.R62 1986   158.7   85-17028
ISBN 0-13-641549-0

Editorial/production supervision: Eve Mossman
Interior and cover design: Christine Gehring-Wolf
Manufacturing buyer: Ed O'Dougherty

Printed in the United States of America
10 9 8 7 6 5 4 3 2 1

ISBN 0-13-641549-0   01

Prentice-Hall International (UK) Limited, *London*
Prentice-Hall of Australia Pty. Limited, *Sydney*
Prentice-Hall Canada Inc., *Toronto*
Prentice-Hall Hispanoamericana, S.A., *Mexico*
Prentice-Hall of India Private Limited, *New Delhi*
Prentice-Hall of Japan, Inc., *Tokyo*
Prentice-Hall of Southeast Asia Pte. Ltd., *Singapore*
Editora Prentice-Hall do Brasil, Ltda., *Rio de Janeiro*
Whitehall Books Limited, *Wellington, New Zealand*

For Joan G. Rapp—
my "in-house" library resource

Contents

PART TWO

THE INDIVIDUAL

3   Foundations of Individual Behavior   48

PART THREE

THE GROUP

6 Foundations of Group Behavior 168

PART IV

THE ORGANIZATION SYSTEM

11 Foundations of Organization Structure   328

PART FIVE

EPILOGUE

16 Summary and Selected Special Topics   488

Preface

The third edition of this text continues my commitment to present readers with a balanced, integrative, and highly readable introduction to the field of organizational behavior (OB). I want to use the next couple of pages to explain how I've tried to achieve this and also to describe the major changes since the last edition.

BALANCED TOPIC COVERAGE

This edition has been streamlined to 16 chapters from 19. Essentially this has been achieved by reducing the number of chapters on individual behavior. There is now a minimal degree of overlap with concepts typically covered in introductory psychology courses. I think I've further improved the text's balance by reorganizing the group material and integrating organizational politics into the chapter on power.

The entire research base for the book has been revised and updated since the previous edition. This activity brought to light a number of topics that needed to be added or significantly expanded. The following list represents some of the topics that are new to this edition:

- research methods in organizational behavior
- biographical characteristics (age, sex, tenure, etc.)
- self-perception theory
- ability's effect on performance
- decision making (individual and group)
- group demography
- stages of group development
- impact of unions on employee behavior
- Hersey and Blanchard's situational leadership theory

- the physical work setting (temperature, noise, work space, and so forth.)
- career development
- evaluating OD effectiveness
- impact of retrenchment on employee behavior
- two-tier pay systems
- dual career couples
- OB in an international context

INTEGRATIVE FRAMEWORK

This book makes use of two unique devices for helping you to integrate and synthesize its contents. The first is a building-block model, presented in Chapter 2, that explains why the topics are organized as they are and the interrelationships between them. The second is a set of four comprehensive models, included in the last chapter, that shows you how it all fits together and what it means.

The building-block model originated with the first edition and has proven to be an effective framework for overviewing the field of organizational behavior. It describes OB as focusing on three levels—the individual, the group, and the organization system—and defines the objectives of OB as explaining and predicting four outcomes—employee productivity, absence, turnover, and satisfaction.

I came to realize, however, that the building-block framework didn't go far enough in helping readers integrate OB concepts. So, for this edition, I've developed a set of comprehensive models that isolate and prioritize the key OB variables. In Chapter 16, you'll find a separate model for explaining and predicting each of the four outcome objectives. These four integrative models represent my best efforts at summarizing literally thousands of research studies.

READABILITY

Students and instructors have described earlier editions of this book in such terms as "lively," "interesting," "logical," and "conversational." But writing style is difficult to measure objectively. I think you'll find this revision maintains the high readability of the previous editions—with special care given to explaining concepts fully and making extensive use of examples—but only you can judge the accuracy of this claim.

PEDAGOGICAL FEATURES

An effective textbook is a comprehensive learning system. It should be designed to facilitate understanding and application. I've included a number of features in this book to help you better assimilate its contents.

- *Key terms and concepts*—Each chapter opens with a set of terms and concepts that you should be able to define and understand after reading the material.
- *Implications for performance and satisfaction*—Each of the core chapters ends with a section where that chapter's concepts are summarized in terms of their relevance to explaining and predicting employee performance and satisfaction.
- *Chapter wrap-ups*—All chapters end with a set of discussion questions and references for further reading.

- *"Point-Counterpoint" debates*—A unique pedagogical component in this text is the inclusion of "Point-Counterpoint" debates. They present interesting and current controversies in OB. My experience is that these debates are excellent for stimulating class discussion. For the third edition, the "Point-Counterpoint" sections have been shortened and rewritten to be more lively and focused.
- *Cases and exercises*—To assist in the transition from theory to practice, you'll find cases at the end of each major part and self-assessment exercises at the conclusion of the Individual, Group, and Organization System sections. Both the cases and exercises have been expanded by 30 percent. There are now 26 cases and 12 exercises included in the book.

ACKNOWLEDGMENTS

Every author has a long list of individuals to whom he is indebted. I appreciate the comments and suggestions made by the outside reviewers: Mark Miller, Pennsylvania State University; Douglas T. Hall, Boston University; Robert H. Drumm, the University of Texas at San Antonio; and Ronald Fry, Case Western Reserve University. I am also appreciative of the ideas offered by my colleagues at San Diego State, particularly Penny Wright, Alan Omens, Jim Lackritz, and Jim Beatty. My typist, Sharon Dillon, did an excellent job of translating my "hen scratchings" into a neatly typed manuscript.

There are dozens of people at Prentice-Hall who contributed to this book. To acknowledge all of them is impossible. Special thanks, however, are directed to Alison Reeves; Alison's assistant, Linda Siebert; Gerry Johnson; my production editor, Eve Mossman; and designer, Christine Wolf.

On a more personal note, I want to recognize the three women in my life. My daughters Dana and Jennifer make me look as if I knew what I were doing in my role as a father. My "friend," Joan, has opened my eyes to how good a relationship can be.

Oh, one last comment before I close. It's appropriate for authors to claim full responsibility for any errors or omissions in their text. I've often thought how nice it would be to veer from this tradition and to place the blame for any such mistakes somewhere else. Maybe my graduate assistant could have overlooked an important piece of research, my typist may have unintentionally left out a sentence or two, the copy editor may have had her mind somewhere else, the proofreader might have "hung one on" the night before reviewing these pages. . . . Unfortunately, such excuses won't work. If you find any errors or omissions, there's only one person to hold accountable. His name is on the cover!

San Diego, California

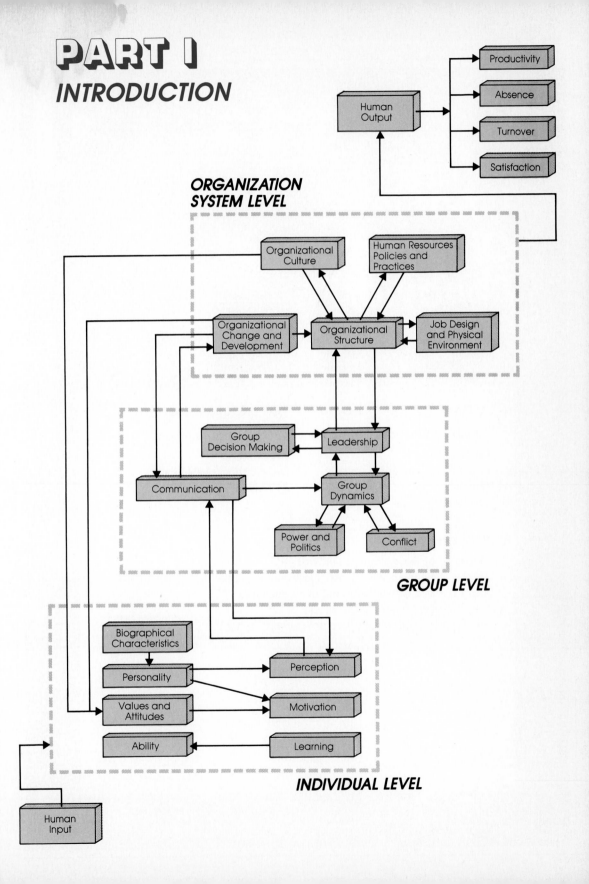

PART I
INTRODUCTION

Human Output
- Productivity
- Absence
- Turnover
- Satisfaction

ORGANIZATION SYSTEM LEVEL

- Organizational Culture
- Human Resources Policies and Practices
- Organizational Change and Development
- Organizational Structure
- Job Design and Physical Environment

GROUP LEVEL

- Group Decision Making
- Leadership
- Communication
- Group Dynamics
- Power and Politics
- Conflict

INDIVIDUAL LEVEL

- Biographical Characteristics
- Personality
- Perception
- Values and Attitudes
- Motivation
- Ability
- Learning

Human Input

What Is Organizational Behavior?

1

AFTER STUDYING THIS CHAPTER, YOU SHOULD BE ABLE TO:

Define and explain the following key terms and concepts:

Caused behavior
Contingency variables
Intuition
Management

Organization
Organizational behavior
Systematic study

Understand:

The value of the systematic study of OB
The contributions made by major behavioral science disciplines to OB
The difference between OB and management
Why managers require a knowledge of OB
The need for a contingency approach for studying OB

I'm not smart. I try to observe. Millions saw the apple fall but Newton was the one who asked why.

—B. BARUCH

*E*ach of us is a student of behavior. Since our earliest years, we have watched the actions of others and have attempted to interpret what we see. Whether or not you have explicitly thought about it before, you have been "reading" people almost all your life. You watch what others do and try to explain why they have engaged in their behavior. Additionally, you've attempted to predict what they might do under different sets of conditions.

You have already developed some generalizations that you find helpful in explaining and predicting what people do and will do. But how did you arrive at these generalizations? By observing, sensing, asking, listening, and reading. That is, your understanding comes either directly, from your own experience with things in the environment, or secondhand, through the experience of others.

How accurate are the generalizations that you hold? Some may represent extremely sophisticated appraisals of behavior and prove highly effective in explaining and predicting the behavior of others. However, most of us also carry about with us a number of beliefs that frequently fail to explain why people do what they do. To illustrate, consider the following half-dozen statements:

1. People are basically lazy.
2. Everyone is motivated by money.
3. You can't teach an old dog new tricks.
4. A job is just a means of survival.
5. Everyone wants a challenging job.
6. Happy workers are productive workers.

How many of these statements are true? For the most part, they are all false, and we shall touch on each at points later in this book. But whether these statements are true or false is not really important at this time. What is important is to make you aware that many of the views you hold concerning human behavior are based on intuition rather than fact. As a result, a systematic approach to the study of behavior can improve your explanatory and predictive abilities.

REPLACING INTUITION WITH SYSTEMATIC STUDY

The use of casual or commonsense approaches for obtaining knowledge about human behavior is inadequate. In reading this book you will discover that a systematic approach will uncover important facts and relationships and provide a base from which more accurate predictions of behavior can be made.

Underlying this systematic approach is the belief that behavior is not random. It is caused and directed toward some end that the individual believes, rightly or wrongly, is in his or her best interest.

> Behavior generally is predictable if we know how the person perceived the situation and what is important to him or her. While people's behavior may not appear to be rational to an outsider, there is reason to believe it usually is *intended* to be rational and it is seen as rational by them. An observer often sees behavior as nonrational because the observer does not have access to the same information or does not perceive the environment in the same way.[1]

Certainly there are differences between individuals. Placed in similar situations, all people do not act alike. However, there are certain fundamental consistencies underlying the behavior of all individuals that can be identified and used to alter conclusions based on individual differences.

The fact that there are these fundamental consistencies is very important. Why? Because it allows predictability. When you get into your car, you make some definite and usually highly accurate predictions about how other people will behave. You predict that other drivers will stop at stop signs and red lights, drive on the right side of the street, pass on your left, and not cross the solid double line on mountain roads. Notice that your predictions about the behavior of people behind the wheel of their cars is almost always correct. Obviously, the rules of driving make predictions about driving behavior fairly easy. What may be less obvious is that there are rules (written and unwritten) in every setting. Therefore, it can be argued that it is possible to predict behavior (obviously, not always with 100 percent accuracy) in supermarkets, classrooms, doctors' offices, and elevators and in most structured situations. To illustrate further, do you turn around and face the doors when you get into an elevator? Almost everyone does, yet did you ever read that you're supposed to do this? Probably not! Just as I make predictions about automobile drivers (where there are definite rules of the road), I can make predictions about the behavior of people in elevators (where there are few written rules). In a class of sixty students, if you wanted to ask a question of the instructor, I would predict that you would raise your hand. Why don't you clap, stand up, raise your leg, cough, or yell "Hey, over here!" The reason is that you have learned that raising your hand is appropriate behavior in school. These examples support a major contention in this book: Behavior is generally predictable and the systematic study of behavior is a means to making reasonably accurate predictions.

When we use the phrase "systematic study," we mean looking at relationships, attempting to attribute causes and effects, and basing our conclusions on scientific evidence, that is, on data gathered under controlled conditions and measured and interpreted in a reasonably rigorous manner.

Systematic study replaces intuition or those "gut feelings" about "why I do what I do" and "what makes others tick." Of course, a systematic approach does not mean that those things you have come to believe in an unsystematic way are necessarily incorrect. Some of the conclusions we make in this book, based on reasonably substantive research findings, will only support what you always knew was true. But you will also be exposed to research evidence that runs counter to what you may have thought was common sense. In fact, one of the challenges to teaching a subject like organizational behavior is to overcome the notion, held by many, that "it's *all* common sense."[2] You will find that many of the so-called "commonsense" views you hold about human behavior are, on closer examination, wrong. Moreover, what one person considers "common sense" frequently runs counter to another's version of "common sense." Are leaders born or made? Is conflict in a group always a bad sign or can conflict increase group performance? You probably have answers to such questions, and individuals who have not reviewed the research are likely to differ on their answers. Our point is that one of the objectives of this book is to encourage you to move away from your intuitive views of behavior toward a systematic analysis, in the belief that the latter will enhance your effectiveness in accurately explaining and predicting behavior.

PUTTING THE "ORGANIZATION" INTO ORGANIZATIONAL BEHAVIOR

This chapter's title asks, "What is organizational behavior?" To this point, we have addressed only the general subject of behavior, which concerns itself with the actions people do that can be observed or measured. Now, let us turn our attention to the "organizational" context.

First, what is an *organization?* An organization is a consciously coordinated social unit, composed of two or more people, that functions on a relatively continuous basis to achieve a common goal or set of goals. Manufacturing and service firms clearly meet this definition, as do schools, hospitals, churches, military units, retail stores, police departments, and local, state, and federal government agencies.

What, then, is *organizational behavior?* Organizational behavior (frequently abbreviated as OB) is a *field of study that investigates the impact that individuals,* groups, and structure have on behavior within organizations for the purpose of applying such knowledge toward improving an organization's effectiveness. That's a mouthful of words, so let's break it down.

Organizational behavior is a field of study. This means that it is a distinct area of expertise with a common body of knowledge. What does it study? It studies three determinants of behavior in organizations: individuals, groups, and structure. Additionally, OB is an applied field. It applies the knowledge gained about individuals, groups, and the effect of structure on behavior toward the end of making organizations work more effectively.

To sum up our definition, OB is concerned with the study of what people do in an organization and how that behavior affects the performance of the organization. And because OB is specifically concerned with employment-related environments, you should not be surprised to find that it gives emphasis to behavior as related to jobs, work, absenteeism, employment turnover, productivity, human performance, and management.

In addition to our definition, OB has been characterized in the broad sense as a way of thinking and in a narrower sense as a body of knowledge covering a relatively specific set of core topics. Let us briefly elaborate on these two points.

When we view OB as a way of thinking, we acknowledge that it can be systematically studied. Organizational behavior can be conceptualized as the systematic study of nonrandom cause and effect phenomena. It also directs one's thinking toward viewing behavior in a performance-related context, that is, as it leads to effectiveness or success in achieving organizationally desirable outcomes.

There is increasing agreement as to the components or topics that comprise the subject area of OB. While there continues to be considerable debate as to the relative importance of each, there appears to be general agreement that OB includes the core topics of motivation, leader behavior and power, interpersonal communication, group structure and process, learning, attitude development and perception, change processes, and conflict.

IS OB WORTH STUDYING?

So far, we have only *assumed* that there is value in being able to explain and predict behavior in an organizational setting. Therefore, we need to consider some specific reasons why the study of OB is deserving of your attention and effort.

Many people are interested in learning about OB for the sake of curiosity alone. They seek to understand behavior. They have no intention of ever applying their knowledge; rather, they merely seek an answer to why people behave the way they do in organizations with which they are familiar.

Beyond this understanding lies a desire to be able to predict what others will do. You may want to develop your skills to make valid predictions; that is, if *X*, then *Y*. The study of OB will help you to develop this predictive skill as it relates to behavior within organizations.

Probably the most popular reason for studying OB is that the reader is interested in pursuing a career in management and wants to learn how to predict

FIGURE 1–1
Source: Copyright 1960 by United Feature Syndicate, Inc. With permission.

behavior and apply it in some meaningful way to make organizations more effective. Having good ''people skills''—which includes the ability to understand your employees and to use this knowledge to get them to work efficiently and effectively for you—is a vital requirement if you are going to succeed as a manager.

Our final reason for studying OB may not be very exciting, but it is pragmatic—it may be a requirement for a particular degree or certificate you are seeking. In other words, you may be a captive in a required course and learning OB in your opinion may offer no obvious end that has value to you. In that case, the studying of OB is only a means toward that end. It is hoped that one of our first three reasons holds more relevance to *you*.

CONTRIBUTING DISCIPLINES TO THE OB FIELD

Organizational behavior is applied behavioral science and, as a result, is built upon contributions from a number of behavioral disciplines. The predominant areas are psychology, sociology, social psychology, anthropology, and political science. As we shall learn, contributions of the psychologists have been mainly at the individual or micro level of analysis, while the latter disciplines have contributed to our understanding of macro concepts—group processes and organization. Figure 1–2 overviews the contributions made toward a distinct field of study: organizational behavior.

Psychology

Psychology is the science that seeks to measure, explain, and sometimes change the behavior of humans and other animals. Psychologists concern themselves with studying and attempting to understand *individual* behavior. Those who have contributed and continue to add to the knowledge of OB are learning theorists, personality theorists, counseling psychologists, and, most important, organizational psychologists.

Early organizational psychologists concerned themselves with problems of fatigue, boredom, and any other factor relevant to working conditions that could impede efficient work performance. More recently, their contributions have been

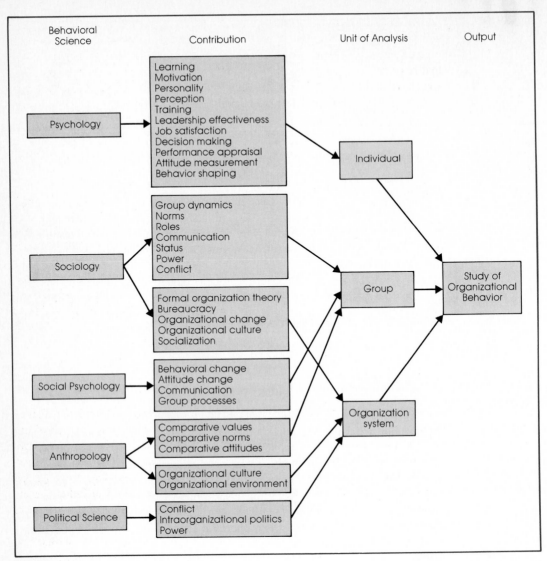

FIGURE 1–2
Toward an OB Discipline

expanded to include learning, perception, personality, training, leadership effectiveness, needs and motivational forces, job satisfaction, decision-making processes, performance appraisals, and attitude measurement.

Sociology

Whereas psychologists focus their attention on the individual, sociologists study the social system in which individuals fill their roles; that is, sociology studies people in relation to their fellow human beings. Specifically, sociologists have made their greatest contribution to OB through their study of group behavior in organizations, particularly formal and complex organizations. Areas within OB that have received valuable input from sociologists include group dynamics, the socialization process. organizational culture, formal organization theory and structure, bureaucracy, communications, status, power, and conflict.

Social Psychology

A relatively new field in its own right, social psychology examines interpersonal behavior. Whereas psychology and sociology attempt to explain individual and group behavior, respectively, social psychology seeks to explain how and why individuals behave as they do in group activities. One of the major areas receiving considerable investigation by social psychologists has been *change*—how to implement it and how to reduce barriers to its acceptance. Additionally, we find social psychologists making significant contributions in measuring, understanding, and changing attitudes, communication patterns, and the ways in which group activities can satisfy individual needs.

Anthropology

Anthropologists study societies, particularly primitive ones, to learn about human beings and their activities. Recognition that how we behave is a function of our culture, for example, dramatizes the contribution social anthropologists have made to OB. Differences in fundamental values, attitudes, and norms of acceptable behavior affect the way people act and explain to a considerable degree differences in behavior between, for example, Americans and East Indians, New Englanders and Southerners, or urbanites and those who were raised and have spent all their lives in rural or farm communities.

Our individual value systems—that is, our priorities and sense of right and wrong—will affect our attitudes and behavior on the job. Additionally, the work that anthropologists have done with animals, especially in the ape family, has been valuable in drawing generalizations about individual and group behavior.

Political Science

Although frequently overlooked, the contributions of political scientists are significant to the understanding of behavior in organizations. Political scientists study the behavior of individuals and groups within a political environment. Specific topics of concern to political scientists include structuring of conflict, allocation of power, and how people manipulate power for individual self-interest.

ARE "OB" AND "MANAGEMENT" SYNONYMOUS TERMS?

Many academics, practitioners, and students confuse the subject matter in OB and that in management or administration. While there is some overlap, management and OB have different means and ends.

Organizational behavior, as noted previously, is concerned with how people, individually and in groups, act in organizations. Management is concerned with the optimum attainment of organizational goals. However, since these goals are unattainable without human input, OB is a significant subset or segment of management.

The subject of OB is intended to support the knowledge necessary to be a manager. The understanding of individual and group behavior is important for what it can contribute toward the education and development of one's managerial talents. When managers perform managerial functions—planning, organizing, leading, and controlling—they need to know how their actions will impact on people. Since managers work with and get things done through other people, an understanding of people is critical to being a successful manager. But, of course, since managers also work with physical inputs (e.g., equipment, inventories) and financial inputs, a manager requires knowledge of subjects that go beyond human behavior to include, but are not limited to, accounting, finance, marketing, production systems, purchasing, forecasting, strategy and policy formation, economics, and computer science.

THERE ARE FEW ABSOLUTES IN OB

There are few, if any, simple and universal principles that explain organizational behavior. There are laws in the physical sciences—chemistry, astronomy, physics—that are consistent and apply in a wide range of situations. They allow scientists to generalize about the pull of gravity or confidently send astronauts into space to repair satellites. But as one noted behavioral researcher aptly concluded, "God gave all the *easy* problems to the physicists." Human beings are very complex. They are not alike, which limits the ability to make simple, accurate, and sweeping generalizations. Two people often act very differently in the same situation and the same person's behavior changes in different situations. For instance, not everyone is motivated by money, and you behave differently at church on Sunday than you did at the beer party the night before.

That doesn't mean, of course, that we can't offer reasonably accurate explanations of human behavior or make valid predictions. It does mean, however, that OB concepts must reflect situational or contingency conditions. We can say that *x* leads to *y,* but only under conditions specified in *z* (the contingency variables). The science of OB was developed by using general concepts and then altering their application to the particular situation. So, for example, OB scholars would avoid stating that effective leaders should always seek the ideas of their subordinates before making a decision. Rather, we shall find that in some situations, a participative style is clearly superior, but in other situations, an autocratic decision style is more effective. In other words, the effectiveness of a particular leadership style is *contingent* upon the situation in which it is utilized.

As you proceed through this book, you'll encounter a wealth of research-based theories about how people behave in organizations. But don't expect to find a lot of straightforward cause-effect relationships. There aren't many! Organizational behavior theories mirror the subject matter with which they deal. People are complex and complicated, and so too must be those theories developed to explain their actions.

POINT

OB IS A SOCIAL SCIENCE

OB has grown out of at least two older fields in business schools: human relations and management. It also includes significant ideas from psychology and sociology, although other social sciences such as economics, anthropology, and political science have certainly contributed to OB's development. In the past fifteen years, OB has received substantial inputs from a younger generation of scholars who have received their training in business schools under the label of Organizational Behavior itself (or some related term). If one, however, were required to select a single discipline that has most influenced the content of OB and its research methodologies, there is little disagreement over the answer: psychology. In second place, and closing slowly on the leader, is sociology.

Any study of the OB field would be generally acknowledged as incomplete without a discussion of the following ten topics: attitudes, job satisfaction, personality, perception, motivation, learning, job design, leadership, communication, and group dynamics. With the exception of the last two, the major work on each of these topics has been done by individuals whose primary training has been in psychology. The study of groups has belonged to the social psychologist and the sociologist. The interest in the past decade in power and conflict in organizations has also generally been furthered by individuals with sociological training. But the topics of power, conflict, and other interests of sociologists—including organizational culture and structure—suffer in contrast to the previously mentioned psychologically based concepts by failing to achieve unanimity among OB scholars as to their legitimacy.

Based on contributions from researchers in psychology, sociology, and other social sciences, we have made substantial progress in our search to be able to explain and predict the behavior of people at work. We have, for example, identified a number of factors that contribute to employees voluntarily quitting their jobs. More important, we have also developed models that show how these factors interact.

Does this imply that we now have a science of OB that can consistently and perfectly predict behavior? No! We have made substantial progress, but our knowledge is far from complete. There are many questions that remain unanswered. There is also considerable research that is inconsistent and, in some cases, even contradictory. Unfortunately, understanding human behavior is not as simple as the understnding of, say, polio. The latter led to a vaccine that effectively eliminated polio in North America. Further research on polio is not necessary. The understanding of human behavior, in contrast to polio, will never be fully understood. Research will continue, leading old theories to be replaced with new ones. We have come a great distance in our understanding of human behavior, but the road is long and we still have distance to cover.

COUNTERPOINT

BEHAVIOR IS GENETICALLY DETERMINED

Harvard zoologist Edward O. Wilson has, for over a decade now, been developing his argument that social behavior is substantially biologically based. He would claim that the study of human behavior is not the sole province of social scientists. Human beings are not born with a blank slate as social scientists claim, with their behavior being totally a response to their environment. Wilson views a large part of human behavior—why we organize ourselves as we do, act as we do, and perhaps even think as we do—as a result of a gene-culture co-evolution. Genetic makeup helps to guide and create culture, whereas culture in turn operates directly on the genes. Wilson believes that the future to understanding and changing behavior may lie in sociobiology—the study of the biological basis of social behavior.

Sociobiology began innocently enough as an attempt to understand the social behavior of animals, in particular insects. Wilson focused on their population structure, castes, and communication, together with all the physiology underlying the social adaptations. For instance, he found that the incest taboo, which prohibits sexual relations between close relatives, has been deterred in the animal world by natural selection. In some animal social systems, males are programmed to leave home and find a new colony or herd when they reach puberty. And in a specialized form of programmed learning known as "imprinting," many young animals, birds as well as mammals, memorize the appearance, voice, or odor of their siblings and parents and use the resulting image to make later mating decisions. They will go to great lengths in adulthood to avoid mating with a sibling with whom they have been raised.

Of course, it is one thing to talk about insects and another to talk bout human beings. Not surprisingly, it's been Wilson's extension of sociobiological concepts to humans that has generated the most discussion and criticism. He is suggesting some heavy-duty ideas—such as the possibility of social engineering that touches the deepest level of human motivation and moral reasoning. By selectively controlling the gene makeup in our society, we could significantly increase SAT scores, produce employees with high internal motivation, and eradicate racial divisiveness and wars. But who would decide this "ideal" society?

Wilson is not proposing that sociobiology will replace the social sciences. Rather, he sees disciplines such as psychology and sociology in some future time—probably a hundred or more years from now—being encompassed within the physical sciences. The study of topics like stress, perception, learning, and creativeness would then be analyzed in physiological terms. Stress would be evaluated in terms of the neurophysiological perturbations and their relaxation times. Perception would be translated into brain circuitry. Learning and creativeness would be defined as the alteration of specific portions of the cognitive machinery regulated by input from the motive centers.

For those who think Wilson's ideas too abstract, you might look at the progress made this century in chemistry. Psychopharmacology currently provides us with a wealth of drugs that can change and control behavior. Have you taken a valium lately?

FOR DISCUSSION

1. Contrast an intuitive approach to studying behavior with a systematic approach. Is intuition always inaccurate?

2. What does the phrase "behavior is caused" mean?

3. Define organizational behavior. How does this compare with management?

4. What is an organization? Is the family unit an organization?

5. Give four reasons for studying OB.

6. In what areas has psychology contributed to OB? Sociology? Social psychology? Anthropology? Political science? What other academic disciplines may have contributed to OB?

7. "The best way to view OB is through a contingency approach." Build an argument to support this statement.

8. "Since behavior is generally predictable, there is no need to formally study OB." Why is this statement wrong?

9. Some authors have defined the purpose of OB as being "to explain, predict, and *control* behavior." Do you agree or disagree? Discuss.

10. Why do you think the subject of OB might be criticized as being "only common sense" when one would rarely hear such a criticism of a course in physics or statistics?

11. Can the behavioral sciences such as psychology, sociology, and organizational behavior ever reach the precision of predictability that exists in the physical sciences? Support your position.

12. Give some examples of problems a manager might face for which a knowledge of organizational behavior might prove beneficial for finding solutions.

FOR FURTHER READING

ASTLEY, W. G., and A. H. VAN DEVEN, "Central Perspectives and Debates in Organization Theory," *Administrative Science Quarterly,* June 1983, pp. 245–73. The diverse schools of organizational thought are classified into four perspectives which are then systematically juxtaposed to create six theoretical debates.

CUMMINGS, L. L., "Organizational Behavior in the 1980s," *Decision Science,* July 1981, pp. 365–77. Presents two divergent but complementary views on the future of OB research and theory.

GREINER, L., "A Recent History of Organizational Behavior." In S. Kerr (ed.), *Organizational Behavior,* pp. 3–14. Columbus, Ohio: Grid, 1979. Reviews, in an historical context, the major contributions to the field of OB.

LORSCH, J. W., "Making Behavioral Science More Useful," *Harvard Business Review,* March–April 1979, pp. 171–80. Discusses the advantages of using a contingency view in studying behavior in organizations.

MOHR, L. B., *Explaining Organizational Behavior*. San Francisco: Jossey-Bass, 1982. Offers a critical appraisal of efforts to develop explanatory theories about organizational behavior.

VAN DEVEN, A. H., and W. G. ASTLEY, "A Commentary on Organizational Behavior in the 1980s," *Decision Science,* July 1981, pp. 388–98. Evaluates Cummings' article by noting points of agreement and conflicts. Argues for a broader definition of OB and the need to understand behavior across levels of organizational analysis.

NOTES FOR CHAPTER 1

1. E. E. Lawler III and J. G. Rhode, *Information and Control in Organizations* (Pacific Palisades, Calif.: Goodyear, 1976), p. 22.
2. R. Weinberg and W. Nord, "Coping with 'It's All Common Sense,'" *Exchange: The Organizational Behavior Teaching Journal,* Vol. 7, no. 2 (1982), pp. 29–33.

2

Toward Explaining and Predicting Behavior

AFTER STUDYING THIS CHAPTER, YOU SHOULD BE ABLE TO:

Define and explain the following key terms and concepts:

Absenteeism
Causality
Correlation coefficient
Correlational design
Dependent variable
Effectiveness
Efficiency
Experimental design
Field setting
Hawthorne effect
Independent variable

Job satisfaction
Laboratory setting
Models
Moderating variables
Observational design
Productivity
Reliability
Research
Rigor
Turnover

Understand:

The purpose of research
The criteria by which to evaluate research
The research designs most used by OB researchers
The individual advantages of laboratory and field settings
The value of models to students of OB
The three universal components in a model
The three levels of analysis in OB

*T*he purpose of this chapter is essentially to answer two questions. This book will introduce hundreds of research studies in support of a number of behavioral theories. But theories are only as good as the research presented to support them. So our first question is: *How do you, as a consumer of OB theories, evaluate the individual research studies presented in this text?* Second, there are many topics that are included within the discipline of OB. If you're going to understand what OB's about, you need to understand how the topics fit together. Therefore, the other question to be answered in this chapter is: *How do you structure the topics within OB into an integrative whole?* These two questions may, at first glance, seem somewhat unrelated. However, by the time you get to the end of this chapter, it should become obvious that the answers to these questions form the foundation upon which the rest of this book is built.

RESEARCH IN ORGANIZATIONAL BEHAVIOR

A friend of your author was lecturing on the value of long-distance running. He claimed that there was no record of anyone who had finished a twenty-six mile marathon ever having died of a heart attack (this, incidentally, took place well before the untimely heart attack that took the life of running guru Jim Fixx). While I questioned this fact, I also took issue with the assumption of causation he was making. He was of the opinion the research demonstrated that if we could just get people to run long distances—to the point where they could finish a marathon we could abolish heart attacks. My friend was somewhat perturbed when I suggested the possibility that certain types of individuals are more likely to run marathons—for instance, people who don't smoke; tend to be thin with low body fat; and have a low pulse rate—people who possess characteristics that minimize their exposure to heart attacks regardless of whether they run or not.

My friend was guilty of misusing research data. Of course, he is not alone. We are all continually bombarded with reports of experiments that link certain substances to cancer in mice and surveys that show changing attitudes toward sex among college students, for example. Many of these studies are carefully designed, with great caution taken to note the implications and limitations of the findings. But some studies are poorly designed, making their conclusions at best, suspect, and at worst, just plain meaningless.

Rather than attempting to make you a researcher, the purpose of this section is to increase your awareness as a consumer of behavioral research. A knowledge of research methods allows you to appreciate more fully the care in data collection that underlies the information and conclusions that will be presented in this book. Moreover, an understanding of research methods will make you a more skilled evaluator of those OB studies you will encounter in business and professional journals. So an appreciation of behavioral research is important because it (1) is the foundation upon which the theories in this book are built and (2) will benefit you, in future years, when you read reports of research and attempt to assess their value.

Purpose of Research

Research is concerned with the systematic gathering of information. Its purpose is to help us in our search for the truth. While we will never find ultimate truth—in our case, that would be to know precisely how any person would behave in any organizational context—ongoing research adds to our body of OB knowledge by supporting some theories, contradicting others, and suggesting new theories to replace those that fail to gain support.

Evaluating Research

The ultimate criterion by which we evelate the research process is its rigor. "Rigorousness is to a researcher what efficiency is to an executive: an ideal state that is always aspired to, never reached, and continually revered."[1]

How does a researcher achieve rigor? The answer to that question is easy, but implementing it is far more difficult. To achieve rigor, the researcher needs to define the problem and the relevant variables in unambiguous terms and then institute tight control over the variables. The more control the researcher has over the variables, the more rigorous the research.

One of the more perplexing problems in behavioral research is the willingness of some researchers to achieve rigor through triviality. That is, the research is trivial in terms of importance and in furthering the development of our understanding of human behavior, but it is high in rigor. Of course, the reverse also occurs—important issues are studied in a nonrigorous fashion—but such studies are far less likely to be published in prestigious journals and integrated into the common body of OB knowledge. There are many interesting questions that researchers have sought to analyze, but because of poor problem definition, poor choice of measurement techniques, inappropriate selection of subjects, and the like, the conclusions are questionable.

The foregoing discussion suggests that research should be judged on the basis of both its rigor and importance. Be aware of studies of important problems that fail the rigorousness test. Similarly, be aware of "little" studies conducted with great precision. We want to know, for example, how to improve employee satisfaction. But how generalizable is a study that assesses the job satisfaction of parking lot attendants, between 10 P.M. and 2 A.M. on Saturdays, in Bloomington, Indiana? It also would be valuable to understand the impact of changes in pay on employee productivity. But if such a study is done by using college students as proxies for employees and substitutes a highly controlled artificial laboratory setting for the complex workings of the real job world, you should be openly wary of the study's conclusions.

Research Design

The three designs most used by OB researchers are observation, correlation, and experimentation. As shown in Figure 2–1, experimental designs are the most rigorous and precise. Observational designs, on the other hands, are more loosely controlled and, hence, less rigorous. In this section, we will discuss all three designs. Before we begin, however, keep in mind that just because experimental designs are the most rigorous of the three does not mean they are always preferred. Some problems do not readily lend themselves to controlled experimentation. Maybe more relevant is the fact that, as you move to the right along the continuum in Figure 2–1, the information obtained tends to be more narrow and limited in terms of generalizability. So, again, rigor is now without costs. In terms of the three designs we'll discuss, the observational approach may be the least rigorous, but it tends to be an excellent source of rich and varied data.

FIGURE 2–1
Research Designs and Degree of Rigor
Source: Adapted from Gary Johns, *Organizational Behavior: Understanding Life at Work* (Glenview, Ill.: Scott, Foresman and Co., 1983), p. 34.

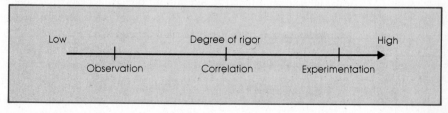

OBSERVATION

You have probably experienced one or more courses in college where you read and analyzed case studies of business practices. These cases, drawn from real-life situations, are the result of the case writers using an observational research design. They watched what others did and wrote it up in the form of a case.

The advantage of observation as a research technique is quickly evident when you read a well-written and well-documented case. It is rich in information and detail. But the quality of the information obtained depends completely on the perceptual skills of the observers. Since we all have perceptual biases, important facts may be overlooked. What one observer perceives as a critical interaction, another may see as inconsequential. This adversely affects the *reliability* of the information or the consistency of its measurement. High reliability is sought in any data. This ensures that the results can be accurately replicated by the researcher or another researcher. But because of perceptual bias, reliability often suffers in observation designs. Other problems with observational data are the possibility of delays between the observation and recording of data that adversely affects accuracy and the fact that, if the subjects are aware that they are being observed, they may alter their actions.

The more unobtrusive the researcher, the less likely that the subjects of the research will alter their behavior to look better in the eyes of the observer. So you should be more suspect of findings obtained where the subjects were aware that they were being watched. Of course, factors like time and who is doing the observing could modify this conclusion. If the observation takes place every day for many months, it is less likely to be contaminated by the subjects "looking good" for the observer than if the observation covered just a few hours. Similarly, an outsider is likely to be seen as more of a threat than an insider. Where the observer is an unobtrusive participant in the study—as when researchers actually become one of the workers—the impact of observation is minimized.

Several of the most frequently cited studies in OB are observational designs. For instance, in the famous Hawthorne studies, the productivity of women telephone assemblers was directly observed as changes were made in the amount of illumination.[2] To the surprise of the researchers, the assemblers' productivity rose as light intensity was both increased and *decreased*. Obviously, the level of illumination was not related to productivity, as the researchers theorized. This led to the so-called Hawthorne effect—that is, workers respond positively to special attention (like being observed by researchers)! In another study, Henry Mintzberg spent a week each with the chief executive of five different organizations.[3] His observations are important because they contradicted the notion of the manager as a thoughtful and reflective decision maker. Mintzberg found the executives he observed to engage in a variety of short-duration activities. His typical executive examined three dozen pieces of mail, attended eight meetings, and had five telephone conversations each day. Half of these activities lasted less than nine minutes. Mintzberg's research has contributed to a reevaluation of the manager's job—from one of thoughtful reflection to one characterized by action.

In summary, observational designs provide data that suffer in rigor but are rich in breadth and detail. Where the researcher minimizes the time between ob-servation and recording of data and keeps distortion low by making observations unobtrusive, the results can be enlightening. But care must always be taken when attempting to generalize to large populations of individuals or organizations from a limited set of observations.

CORRELATION

A more precise research technique is to use data from questionnaires, inter-views, or organizational records to assess potential relationships that may exist between two or more specific variables. We call this approach a correlation design.

For instance, a researcher might survey a group of employees to determine the satisfaction of each with his or her job. Then, using company productivity reports, the researcher could correlate the job-satisfaction scores against individ-ual productivity records to determine whether employees who are more satisfied with their jobs are more productive than their counterparts who indicated lower job satisfaction. The results would be expressed as a correlation coefficient.

Correlation coefficients range from -1.00 (a perfect negative relationship) to $+1.00$ (a perfect positive correlation). When two variables vary directly with one another, the correlation will be expressed as a positive number. When they vary inversely—that is, one increasing as the other decreases—the correlation will be expressed as a negative number. If the two variables vary absolutely indepen-dently of each other, we say that the correlation between them is zero. Usually one factor is called the independent variable and denoted by X, while the outcome is denoted by Y and called the dependent variable. If Y tends to increase as X increases, or Y tends to decrease as X decreases, then we have a positive corre-lation. If X and Y change in opposite directions, then we have a negative correlation.

In our example, suppose the researcher found a correlation coefficient be-tween satisfaction (the independent variable) and productivity (the dependent var-iable) of $+.50$. Would that be a strong association? There is, unfortunately, no precise numerical cutoff separating strong and weak relationships. A standard sta-tistical test would need to be applied to determine whether or not the relationship was a significant one. Obviously, we would like to see coefficients close to either $+1.00$ or -1.00.

Correlation designs are more precise than are observational designs, but their findings tend to be more narrow. What does that mean? Essentially, we tend to have more confidence in the results produced by correlation studies because controls are tighter, but the results tend to say less. Confidence in results, of course, is also a function of the quality of data used. And, very importantly, a correlation does not prove causation. Let us elaborate on these two points.

In the job satisfaction example mentioned, the value of the researcher's re-sults depend heavily on the quality of the instrument used to measure job satis-faction and upon the company's data on employee productivity. If the instrument is not valid—that is, if it does not measure what it purports to measure—then the results may not be what they appear to be. Similarly, if the productivity records are not accurate measurements of employees' actual productivity, the meaning of the correlation coefficient is questionable.

It's easy to assume that because a statistical relationship is found between two variables in a correlation study that a cause and effect relationship exists. This would be an incorrect assumption. Correlation studies cannot tell us whether the values of *X cause* the values of *Y*. There may be a cause and effect relationship, but not necessarily. The correlation may be due to the interaction of *X* and *Y* with an external factor common to both variables, or rather than *X* causing *Y*, *Y* may be causing *X*. Our point is simply that correlational designs only show association; they do not imply causation. Two examples may clarify this statement.

Married men and women live longer than their unmarried counterparts. This statement is true, corroborated by a wealth of statistical data. Is it correct to conclude, however, that marriage *causes* longer life? The answer is a qualified "No." Evidence suggests that people who are unlikely to live longer are also unlikely to marry or stay married, and since most people consider marriage desirable, those who do not marry are considered odd, which puts them under social pressures and stress that can wear them down physically and reduce their life expectancy. In other words, it is one thing to determine a relationship between marriage and longevity but another to attribute causality. Statistics also clearly show that college graduates earn substantially more money during their working lives than do individuals who have not attended college. It is tempting to conclude that the college experience *caused* the higher earnings. While higher educational institutions might wish this to be true, the statistical correlation does not prove causation. It could just as easily be argued that individuals who are bright and ambitious are more likely than their less bright, less ambitious peers to choose to go to college and that these brighter and more ambitious types would probably earn more than their peers, regardless of whether they went to college or not. The college experience, therefore, may have little, in fact, to do with the higher earnings.

So what can we conclude about correlation designs? Generally speaking, we can say that correlation designs, conducted with valid measurement instruments, will provide results regarding relationships with which we should have relatively high confidence.

EXPERIMENTATION

The major advantage of experimental research over a correlation design is the ability to imply causation. This is because in experimental designs the researcher manipulates the independent variable under controlled conditions. Then, assuming that all other things are equal, the researcher is able to conclude that any change in the dependent variable is due to the manipulation or change imposed on the independent variable. An example might make this clearer.

Assume that the management of a large company is interested in determining the impact that a four-day workweek would have on employee absenteeism. To be more specific, they want to know if employees working four ten-hour days have lower absence rates than similar employees working the traditional five-day week of eight hours each day. This question can be examined in an experimental design. Because the company is large, it has a number of manufacturing plants that employ essentially similar work forces. Two of these are chosen for the experiment, ideally in locations that are quite alike. Obviously, it's not appropriate to compare two similar-sized plants where one is in rural Mississippi and the other is in downtown Boston. Factors such as transportation and weather, in a comparison, might more likely explain any differences found than changes in the number of days worked per week.

In this example, the company's absence records become the dependent variable. In one plant, the experiment is put into place—workers begin the four-day week. At the other plant, which becomes the control group, no changes are made in their employees' five-day week. Absence data are gathered in both locations for a specified length of time—probably for a period in excess of a year to ensure that the results are not distorted by the mere novelty of changes being implemented in the experimental plant. The results from a study such as this, assuming tight controls are maintained, allow for the conclusion that any change found in the dependent variable at the experimental site (and not found in the control group) is due to the change introduced in the independent variable.

Why should you typically have more confidence in the results from a well-designed experimental study than from a similarly well-designed observation or correlation study? The answer lies in tighter control, which, in turn, translates into greater rigor. Control is enhanced by the researcher manipulating the independent variable and by maintaining a unit of comparison to ensure that the result wasn't caused by something else. In our shorter workweek example, let's say that the experiment resulted in a significant drop in employee absences. But what if I told you that there was a similar drop in the control group? This could happen. How? If the period in which the study was done happened to parallel a decline in the economy and a large increase in the unemployment rate, the drop in absenteeism may have been due entirely to employees' fear of losing their job. Without having set up a control group, we would have incorrectly concluded that the experiment alone was responsible for the reduction in absences.

Research Settings

The last research issue we want to take up is *where* the research is conducted. Our confidence in generalizing from a research study varies with the location where it is done. In very simple terms, research is conducted in either laboratory or field settings. On balance, field studies tend to have higher generalizability because they take place with real employees in real-life settings.

LABORATORY
Laboratory settings are artificial environments in which subjects work at "jobs" created by the researcher. The most typical laboratory studies are ones in which researchers hire individuals for a short period of time (from a few hours to several months) and have them perform jobs in an artificial work situation that simulates a real work environment. Because the researcher can tightly control the

laboratory setting and manipulate "working conditions," this setting is most often associated with experimental designs.

The experimental design provides a high degree of control, but it is limited by the antiseptic characteristics inherent in any simulated work situation. It tends to ignore the small, but certainly not inconsequential, nuances that full-time employees experience in the real world—things like long-term job boredom or internal political maneuverings. For those of you who have had to do a group paper in a college class, you may have already experienced the limitations of the laboratory setting. One or more of the group members frequently fails to do his or her share of the work, which increases the burden on the others. As my students are fond of reminding me, when faced with a "slacker" in their group, "in the real world, there'd be a boss and this loafer would be fired!"

FIELD

All things being equal, field settings are preferable because they tap the richness and detail inherent in the real world. Of course, all things aren't always equal! Control is less, and, hence, the potential for extraneous influences to distort the research findings increases.

Field settings are appropriate for any type of design. Case studies represent the result of observations made in the real world. Questionnaires or interview data obtained from employees are frequently used in correlational studies. Even experimental designs can be conducted in the field by defining experimental and control groups in the natural work setting.

Summary

The subject of organizational behavior is composed of a large number of theories that are research based. Research studies, when cumulatively integrated, become theories; and theories are proposed, followed by research studies designed to validate them. The concepts that make up OB, therefore, are only as valid as the research that supports them.

As you review the topics and issues introduced in this book, keep in mind that they are—for the most part—largely research derived. They represent the result of systematic information gathering rather than merely hunch, intuition, or opinion. But this does not mean that we have all the answers to OB issues. Many require far more corroborating evidence. The generalizability of others is limited by the research methods used. As we proceed through the topics in this book and as the research is reviewed, every effort will be made to point out limitations to the findings that relate to the quality or quantity of its supporting research.

DEVELOPING AN OB MODEL

The second part of this chapter has a more ambitious set of objectives. We will develop a general framework to define the field of OB, stake out its parameters, and present a model to show how key variables relate. The end result will be a "coming attraction" of the topics making up the remainder of this book. Let's begin by assessing what a model does.

What Is a Model?

A model is an abstraction of reality, a simplified representation of some real-world phenomenon. A mannequin in a retail store is a model. So, too, is the accountant's formula: assests = liabilities + owner's equity. Students of management are familiar with organization charts, those pyramid-shaped figures that hang on walls of personnel departments throughout the world. These charts are used by managers to represent the organization's hierarchy. But they are also models. Most of us are aware that decision influence within an organization is not always shown by its organization chart. In reality, there are informal processes that, even though not shown on the chart, are important influences on decision patterns. For example, one should not assume that all those in an organization who have similar titles, and who are at the same level in the formal organization structure, are equally influential. Who knows who, who owes who, and who has the "clout" are not depicted on organization charts. Yet organization charts help us to simplify complex relationships in a way that minimizes the loss of understanding.

Models can also be a useful tool for writers in their effort to clarify complex topics. With that in mind, your author believes that an OB model can help you to put together the contents of this book and assist you in explaining and predicting real-life behavior in organizations.

Key Components in a Model

All models have certain common elements. If something *is* a model, it will contain three universal components: an objective, variables, and relationships.

OBJECTIVE
The formulation of a model begins with determining what it is that we want the model to do. Is the model attempting to predict turnover, explain motivation, select the best job applicant, ascertain the most effective leadership style, or explain why productivity within a certain department has dropped off dramatically? Once the objective is known, the key variables that may affect this objective can be identified, their order classified, and relationships defined.

VARIABLES
General characteristics that can be measured and that change in either amplitude and/or intensity are called variables. You encountered the term previously in our discussion of research methods.

Variables are critical or key elements that affect the objective we have stated. In behavior modeling, the discussion usually centers on three types of variables: dependent, independent, and moderating. While we have briefly mentioned the first two types, elaboration is still necessary.

A *dependent variable* is a response that is affected by an independent variable. In behavioral research, popular dependent behaviors are productivity, absenteeism, and turnover. However, attitudes such as job satisfaction and organizational commitment are also used as dependent variables.

Independent variables affect the dependent variables. "An *independent variable* is the *presumed* cause of the *dependent variable,* the *presumed* effect."[4] Popular independent variables studied by OB researchers include intelligence, personality, attitudes, experience, motivation, reinforcement patterns, leadership style, reward allocations, selection methods, and organization design. By specifying the amplitude or intensity of an independent variable, for example, identifying close, moderate, and loose supervision, we can measure different levels in a dependent variable, for example, absenteeism. In this specific case, we would have three levels of the independent variable.

A third variable is one you encountered in the previous chapter's discussion of contingency conditions. This is the *moderating variable*. It abates the effect of the independent variable on the dependent variable. It increases complexity by saying: If X (independent variable), then Y (dependent variable) will occur, but only under conditions Z (moderating variable). To translate this into a real-life example, we might say that if we increase the amount of direct supervision in the work area *(X),* then there will be a change in worker productivity *(Y),* but this effect will be moderated by the complexity of the tasks being performed *(Z).*

This discussion of variables should not be interpreted to mean that certain variable characteristics are always dependent, always independent, or always moderating. Whether a characteristic is treated as a dependent, independent, or moderating variable depends on the objective of the model. Job satisfaction, for example, would be an independent variable if the objective were to ascertain how different levels of satisfaction influence turnover. However, if the objective were to determine the impact of various pay schedules on job satisfaction, job satisfaction would become a dependent variable.

RELATIONSHIPS

What is the relationship among variables in our model? What is the *cause* and what is the *effect?*

Our concern with causality—that is, implying presumed cause and effect—which we have discussed as it relates to research design, is just as critical in our development of an OB model. Why? Because an OB model, which purports to explain and predict, implies causation between its independent and dependent variables. In the model that we shall be using in this book, we shall articulate both types of variables and draw conclusions based on their implied relationship.

SUMMARY

At this point, it may be helpful to summarize and synthesize. You may be asking, "Who cares about causality?" "So what?" "What have models, objectives, variables, and relationships to do with understanding organizational behavior?'' Ah, but there is method in this madness!

The answer is really quite simple: OB is a complex field and an OB model can help us to attain our objective—to explain and predict the way in which people behave in organizations. Our OB model will be our road map through the vast OB maze (and through the approximately six hundred pages of this book). Since, like all models, it consists of an objective, variables, and relationships, it is important to understand these concepts in order to understand the organizational behavior that is represented by the model.

OB Model Components

We have stated the objective of an OB model: to explain and predict the way people behave in organizations. Our model makes many simplified assumptions and explicitly excludes moderating variables (they will be added as we go along), but it should help you to understand the key components of OB.

Our model begins by analyzing individual behavior. Using the knowledge gained at the individual level, we move on to a more complex topic, the group. Finally, we add a third level of complexity, the formal organization structural system, to arrive at our final destination: an understanding of organizational behavior. Figure 2–2 presents a skeleton on which we will construct our OB model. It proposes that there are three levels of analysis in OB and that as we move from the individual level through to the organizational systems level, we add systematically to our understanding of behavior in organizations. The three basic levels are analogous to building blocks—each level is constructed upon the previous level. Group concepts grow out of the foundation laid in the individual section; we overlay structural constraints on the individual and group in order to arrive at organizational behavior.

THE DEPENDENT VARIABLES

What are the primary dependent variables in OB? Scholars tend to emphasize productivity, absenteeism, turnover, and job satisfaction. Because of their

FIGURE 2–2
Basic OB Model, Stage I

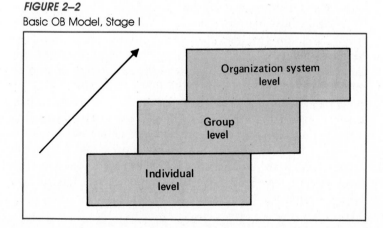

wide acceptance, we shall use these four as the critical determinants of an organization's human resources effectiveness. However, there is nothing magic about these variables. They essentially reflect the fact that OB research has strongly reflected managerial interests over those of individuals or of society as a whole. Of course, in years to come, new dependent variables may be added to, or may replace, those that currently dominate the OB field. For instance, one author has argued for the growing importance of job stress, individual dissent, and innovation as dependent variables.[5] In defense of innovation, he argues, "As a greater percentage of work becomes highly skilled and professionalized, the criteria of performance will likely become more ambiguous and subject to change. Therefore, questions of [employee] productivity may become translated into inquiries about working smarter rather than harder. . . . Where there is rapid change or competition is fierce, innovation may be the organization's most important outcome variable."[6] The fact remains, however, that productivity, absenteeism, turnover, and job satisfaction currently dominate the field. So let's review these terms to ensure that we understand what they mean and why they have achieved the distinction of being OB's primary dependent variables. We'll begin with the concept of productivity.

An organization is productive if it achieves its goals and does so by transferring inputs to outputs at the lowest cost. As such, *productivity* implies a concern for both effectiveness and efficiency.

A hospital, for example, is *effective* when it successfully meets the needs of its clientele. It is *efficient* when it can do this at a low cost. If a hospital manages to achieve higher output from its present staff by reducing the average number of days a patient is confined to a bed or by increasing the number of staff-patient contracts per day, we can say that the hospital has gained productive efficiency. Similarly, a school may be effective when a certain percentage of students achieve a specified score on standardized achievement tests. The school can improve its efficiency if these higher test scores can be secured by a smaller teaching and support staff. A business firm is effective when it attains its sales or market share goals, but its productivity also depends on achieving these goals efficiently. Measures of such efficiency may include return on investment, profit per dollar of sales, and output per hour of labor.

We can also look at productivity from the perspective of the individual employee. Take the cases of Mike and Al, who are both long-distance truckers. If Mike is supposed to haul his fully loaded rig from New York to its destination in Los Angeles in seventy-five hours or less, he is effective if he makes the 3,000-mile trip within this time period. But measures of productivity must take into account the costs incurred in reaching the goal. That is where efficiency comes in. Let us assume that Mike made the New York to Los Angeles run in sixty-eight hours and averaged 7 miles per gallon. Al, on the other hand, made the trip in sixty-eight hours also but averaged 9 miles per gallon (rigs and loads are identical). Both Mike and Al were effective—they accomplished their goal—but Al was more efficient than Mike because his rig consumed less gas and, therefore, he achieved his goal at a lower cost.

In summary, one of OB's major concerns is productivity. We want to know what factors will influence the effectiveness and efficiency of individuals, of groups, and of the overall organization.

The annual cost of *absenteeism* to U.S. organizations has been put as high as $26.4 billion when estimated days lost are multiplied by hourly wage rates.[7] When we add in the costs of rescheduling, overtime, and lower productivity that absenteeism creates, the figure is probably closer to $50 billion a year. At the job level, the direct cost to an employer of a single absence has been computed at approximately $145.00.[8] These figures indicate the importance to an organization of keeping absenteeism low.

It is obviously difficult for an organization to operate smoothly and to attain its objectives if employees fail to report to their jobs. The work flow is disrupted and often important decisions must be delayed. In organizations that rely heavily upon assembly-line technology, absenteeism can be considerably more than a disruption—it can result in a drastic reduction in quality of output, or, in some cases, it can bring about a complete shutdown of the production facility. Examples abound, for example, of the problems that the major U.S. Automobile manufacturers have with alarmingly large increases in absences on Mondays and Fridays, especially in summer months and at the onset of the hunting and fishing seasons. Certainly, levels of absenteeism beyond the normal range have a direct impact on an organization's effectiveness and efficiency.

Are *all* absences bad? Probably not! While most absences impact negatively on the organization, we can conceive of situations where the organization may benefit by an employee voluntarily choosing not to come to work. For instance, fatigue or excess stress can significantly decrease an employee's productivity. In jobs where an employee needs to be alert—surgeons and airline pilots are obvious examples—it may well be better for the organization if the employee does not report to work rather than show up and perform poorly. The cost of an accident in such jobs could be prohibitive. Even in managerial jobs, where mistakes are less spectacular, performance may be improved when incumbents absent themselves from work rather than make a poor decision under stress. But these examples are clearly atypical. For the most part, we can assume that organizations benefit when employee absenteeism is reduced.

A high rate of *turnover* in an organization means increased recruiting, selection, and training costs. It can also mean a disruption in the efficient running of an organization when knowledgeable and experienced personnel leave and replacements must be found and prepared to assume positions of responsibility. All organizations, of course, have some turnover. And if the right people are leaving the organization—the marginal and submarginal employees—turnover can be positive. It may create the opportunity to replace an individual with someone with higher skills or motivation, open up increased opportunities for promotions, and add new and fresh ideas to the organization.[9] But when turnover is excessive or when it is confined to the superior performers, it can be a major disruptive factor, hindering the organization's effectiveness.

The final dependent variable we will look at is *job satisfaction*—defined very generally as the difference between the amount of rewards workers receive and the amount they believe they should receive. Unlike the previous three variables, job satisfaction is unique because it represents an attitude rather than a behavior. Why is it then that it has become a primary dependent variable? Because of its demonstrated relationship to performance factors and the value preferences held by many OB researchers.

The belief that satisfied employees are more productive than dissatisfied employees has been a basic tenet among managers for years. While the evidence questions this assumed causal relationship, it can be argued that a wealthy nation should not only be concerned with the quantity of life but also with improving its quality. Those researchers with strong humanistic values argue that satisfaction should be a legitimate objective of an organization. Not only is satisfaction negatively related to absenteeism and turnover, but, they argue, organizations have a responsibility that goes beyond dollars and cents to provide employees with jobs that are challenging and intrinsically rewarding. Therefore, although job satisfaction represents an attitude rather than a behavior, OB researchers typically consider job satisfaction an important dependent variable.

THE INDEPENDENT VARIABLES

What are the major determinants of productivity, absenteeism, turnover, and job satisfaction? Our answer to that question brings us to the indepedent variables. Consistent with our belief that organizational behavior can best be understood when viewed essentially as a set of increasingly complex building blocks, the base or first level of our model lies in understanding individual behavior.

It has been said that "managers, unlike parents, must work with used, not new, human beings—human beings whom other people have gotten to first."[10] When individuals enter an organization, they're a bit like used cars. Each is different. Some are "low mileage"—they have been treated carefully and have limited exposure to the realities of the elements. Others are "well worn," having experienced a number of rough roads. This metaphor is meant to indicate that people enter organizations with certain characteristics that will influence their behavior at work. The more obvious of these are personal or biographical characteristics such as one's age, sex, and marital status; one's personality characteristics; one's values and attitudes; and one's basic ability levels. These characteristics are essentially intact when an individual enters the work force, and, for the most part, there is little management can do to alter them. Yet they have a very real impact on employee behavior. Therefore, each of these factors—biographical characteristics, personality, values and attitudes, and ability—will be discussed as independent variables in Chapters 3 through 5.

There are three other individual-level variables that have been shown to directly affect employee behavior: perception, learning, and motivation. These topics will be introduced and discussed in Chapters 3 and 5.

Figure 2–3 describes the individual level in our OB model. The variables that make up this figure are the subject matter of Chapters 3 through 5.

The behavior of people in groups is something more than the sum total of each individual acting in his or her own way. The complexity of our model is increased when we acknowledge that people's behavior when they are in groups is different from their behavior when they are alone. Therefore, the next step in the development of an understanding of OB is the study of group behavior.

Chapter 6 lays the foundation for an understanding of the dynamics of group behavior by presenting independent variables such as roles, norms, status, and group cohesiveness. This chapter discusses how individuals in groups are influenced by the patterns of behavior they are expected to exhibit, what the group considers to be acceptable standards of behavior, the status hierarchy established by the group, and the degree to which group members are attracted to each other. Chapters 7 through 10 then demonstrate how communication patterns, group decision-making processes, leadership styles, power and politics, and levels of conflict affect group behavior. Figure 2–4 describes how these concepts interact and form the group level in our OB model.

Organizational behavior reaches its highest level of sophistication when we add formal structure to our previous knowledge of individual and group behavior. Just as groups are more than the sum of their individual members, organizations are not necessarily merely the summation of the behavior of a number of groups. The structural design of the formal organization, the way in which jobs are designed and the physical environment laid out, the organization's culture, human resource policies used for evaluation and reward decisions, and the systems used for bringing about change must be added to our model to determine the impact that the structural system and organizationwide change processes have on the dependent variables.

Figure 2–5 describes the organization systems level variables in our model. These are discussed in detail in Chapters 11 through 15.

FIGURE 2–3
The Individual Level in the OB Model

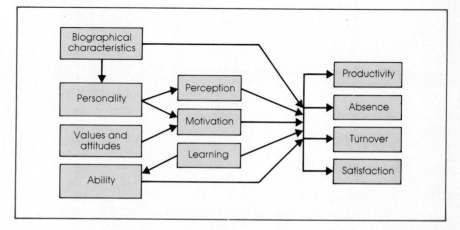

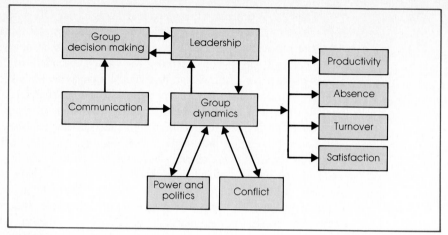

FIGURE 2–4
The Group Level in the OB Model

Toward a Contingency OB Model

Our final model is shown in Figure 2–6. It portrays the four key dependent variables and a large number of independent variables that research suggests have varying impacts on the former. Of course, the model does not do justice to the complexity of the OB subject matter. But for the purpose of helping to explain and predict behavior, it should prove valuable.

FIGURE 2–5
The Organization Systems Level in the OB Model

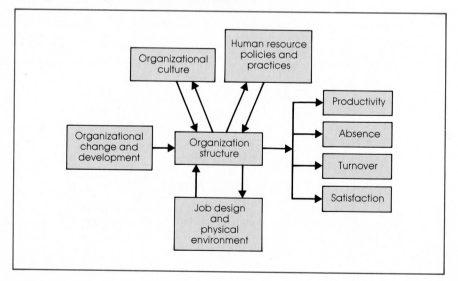

FIGURE 2–6
Basic OB Model, Stage II

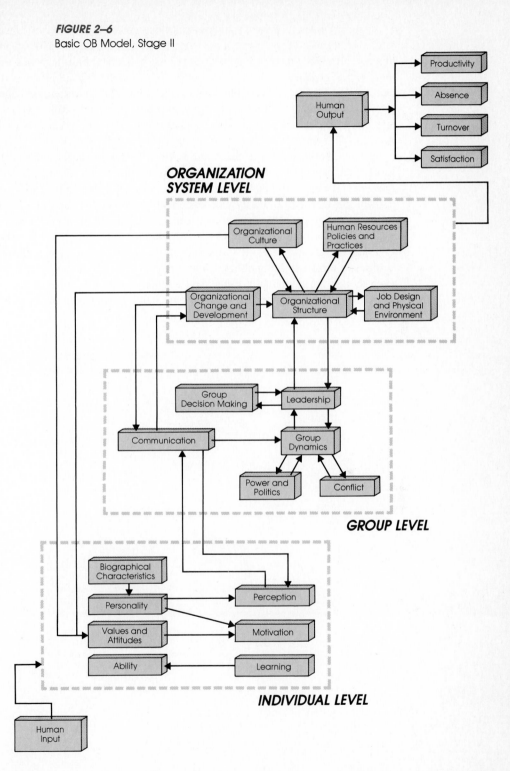

As we noted previously, our model does not explicitly identify moderating variables because of the tremendous complexity that would be involved in such a diagram. Rather, as you advance through this book, we shall introduce important moderating variables that will improve the explanatory linkage between the independent and dependent variables. Thus, the book will follow a contingency approach—identifying independent variables, isolating moderating variables, and attempting to explain why in certain situations A causes B, yet in other situations A causes C.

You should also note that Figure 2–6 includes linkages between the three levels that were not mentioned in the previous discussion of independent variables. For instance, organization structure is linked to leadership. This is meant to convey the fact that authority and leadership are related—management exerts its influence on group behavior through leadership. Similarly, communication is the means by which individuals transmit information; thus, it is the link between individual and group behavior. Communication is also central to organizational development efforts to bring about change. Finally, Figure 2–6 conveys the fact that even though an individual's values and attitudes tend to be substantially set prior to joining an organization, they can be modified by changes in organizational culture or through organizational development techniques.

POINT

EMPLOYEE TURNOVER IS DYSFUNCTIONAL TO AN ORGANIZATION

This book presents employee turnover as one of the four primary dependent variables in OB. This is consistent with the view—held by executives, personnel managers, and researchers in OB—that turnover has negative consequences for organizational performance. When an employee quits and has to be replaced, the organization incurs some very real and tangible costs. These can range from a few hundred dollars to train a counter clerk at McDonald's to several hundred thousand dollars for a nuclear power engineer or Air Force fighter pilot. Turnover costs to a firm for a typical job is probably at least several thousand dollars, as evidenced by research in a bank that found every instance of turnover by a teller costing approximately $2,800.

Every turnover incidence includes both direct and indirect costs. A review of these costs goes a long way in explaining why management should be concerned with minimizing employee turnover.

When an employee leaves, a replacement needs to be found. If inadequate notice is given, management will not have time to find and train the replacement, and a temporary employee will need to fill in. The result in this case is typically a drop in productivity. Where sufficient notice is given, the organization incurs the costs of recruiting, selecting, and training the replacement. In many cases, there may be a period of a few weeks or months where two people are on the payroll to do one job—the departing employee staying on to train his or her replacement.

The recruitment and training costs for almost any job quickly amounts to a sizable dollar figure. These costs include advertisements, maintaining a college recruitment staff, employment agency fees, travel and accommodation expenses for recruits, screening tests, background investigations, and the time spent by executives in interviewing. The departure of a middle-level manager may result in replacement costs exceeding $50,000, as the following suggests:

Search fees and expenses	$20,000
Interviewing time and expenses	3,000
Administrative costs (reference checks, psychological tests, medical exams)	3,000
Reimbursement associated with selling old home and purchasing new one	15,000
Travel and temporary living expenses	6,000
Moving expenses	8,000
Signing bonus	10,000
	$65,000

This list considers only the direct costs attributable to employee turnover. To these we have to add indirect costs such as training the replacement, loss in productivity incurred while the replacement develops his or her proficiency, loss in work group cohesiveness and morale, and the general organizational disruption caused by turnover (i.e., scheduling difficulties).

Given the direct and indirect costs associated with turnover, it is obvious that a management team that is concerned with maintaining effectiveness and efficiency will want to keep employee turnover to a minimum.

COUNTERPOINT

EMPLOYEE TURNOVER CAN BE FUNCTIONAL

All turnover is not bad for an organization. Discussions on the subject tend to stress the costs side of the ledger. But turnover also provides benefits to the organization. In fact, healthy levels of employee turnover may be a virtual windfall—in hard dollar terms—for the organization.

To consider all turnover negatively overstates its impact. Why? Well, first we need to look only at voluntary turnover. Involuntary turnover—where management initiates the departure—is functional, if we assume the decision is for a cause. Second, there are people who voluntarily leave the organization that benefit it. They may have been poor or, at best, marginal performers. But because of institutionalized employment security (labor unions, appeal boards, etc.), sympathetic bosses, the desire to maintain group morale, or similar factors, these people are not terminated. Finally, all voluntary quits are not controllable by management. That is, there are situations in which no reasonable action by management could have prevented it. It's a waste of organizational resources to try to reduce this element of turnover. In summary, any discussion of turnover should be concerned only with voluntary quits, and from that number we need to subtract all functional turnover plus the portion that, while dysfunctional, is unavoidable.

Now let's turn to a neglected issue: Turnover has a positive "dollar and cents" impact on the organization. In support of this position, we need to recognize that turnover may be reduced, but at a cost that exceeds its benefits, and new hires are not as costly to maintain in terms of salary and fringe benefits as are more senior employees.

A number of jobs have characteristically high levels of turnover—for instance, waitresses and bank clerks—that could be significantly reduced by merely raising their wage rates. But management has chosen not to pay the wages that would be necessary to keep these people. In cost-effectiveness terms, management's strategy has been to trade off higher turnover for lower labor costs.

An overlooked fact in organizations is that there are a number of jobs where wage rates increase with time, but there is no comparable increase in productivity. For instance, at one large public utility, entry-level employees receive $5.82 per hour and then move through the wage progression to $10.45 in their fifth year. The job remains the same, only the hourly wage cost nearly doubles. While employee productivity will increase over this five-year period, the increase is more likely to be in the 10 to 20 percent range. Additionally, given the fact that fringe benefit costs tend to be a percentage of direct labor costs, these too go up significantly as employee seniority increases. The result: Recent hires cost the organization less.

There are relatively large economies to be realized by employee turnover. To the extent that turnover is not excessive, that is, its costs do not exceed its benefits, a large amount of money might be saved each year by reasonable levels of turnover. Vigorous programs by organizations to reduce the incidence of employee turnover may be thoroughly shortsighted. This caveat may be particularly appropriate for organizations in which training requirements are minimal and experience may not lead to appreciably higher levels of performance.

Adapted from D. R. Dalton, W. D. Todor, and D. M. Krackhardt, "Turnover Overstated: The Functional Taxonomy," Academy of Management Review, January 1982, pp. 117–23; and Dalton and Todor, "Turnover: A Lucrative Hard Dollar Phenomenon," Academy of Management Review, April 1982, pp. 212–18.

FOR DISCUSSION

1. Why should students of OB spend time to develop an elementary understanding of research methods?
2. What factors might reduce the rigor of a research study?
3. What are the advantages and disadvantages to (a) observation, (b) correlation, and (c) experimentation designs?
4. What is reliability? Validity? What is the relevance of each to research?
5. Define a model and give several examples to illustrate your definition.
6. Describe three types of variables. Explain their relationship.
7. What does "causality" have to do with studying OB?
8. What are the three levels of analysis in our OB model? Are they related? If so, how?
9. If job satisfaction is not a behavior, why is it considered as an important dependent variable?
10. What are "effectiveness" and "efficiency," and how are they related to organizational behavior?
11. What are the four dependent variables in the OB model? Why have they been chosen over, for instance, percent return on investment?
12. Why are individual-, group-, and organization systems–level behaviors each described as increasingly more complex?

FOR FURTHER READING

DAFT, R. L., "Learning the Craft of Organizational Research," *Academy of Management Review,* October 1983, pp. 539–46. Proposes that scholarly research is a craft and that significant research outcomes are associated with the master of craft elements in the research process.

PINDER, C. C., and L. F. MOORE, "The Resurrection of Taxonomy to Aid the Development of Middle Range Theories of Organizational Behavior," *Administrative Science Quarterly,* March 1979, pp. 99–118. Argues that we should move away from systems or general models toward middle-range theories that explain a lot within a more narrow framework.

SHEPARD, J. M., and J. G. HOUGLAND, JR., "Contingency Theory: 'Complex Man' or 'Complex Organization'?" *Academy of Management Review,* July 1978, pp. 413–27. Compares the "individual differences" approach to contingency theory with the "organizational differences" approach and argues for an integration.

STAW, B. M., and G. R. OLDHAM, "Reconsidering Our Dependent Variables: A Critique and Empirical Study," *Academy of Management Journal,* December 1978, pp. 539–59. Reviews the prominent dependent variables, how they came to be, and the importance of determining whose perspective we are considering when defining dependent variables.

STONE, E. F., *Research Methods in Organizational Behavior.* Glenview, Ill.: Scott, Foresman, 1978. Reviews the research process, measurement methods, sampling, research design, and ethical issues.

THOMAS, K. W., and W. G. TYMON, JR., "Necessary Properties of Relevant Research: Lessons from Recent Criticisms of the Organizational Sciences," *Academy of Management Review,* July 1982, pp. 345–52. Responds to concerns about doing research that is relevant to both academics and practitioners.

NOTES FOR CHAPTER 2

1. C. Argyris, "Some Unintended Consequences of Rigorous Research," *Psychological Bulletin,* March 1968, p. 185.
2. E. Mayo, *The Human Problems of an Industrial Civilization* (New York: Macmillan, 1933); and F. J. Roethlisberger and W. J. Dickson, *Management and the Worker* (Cambridge, Mass.: Harvard University Press, 1939).
3. H. Mintzberg, *The Nature of Managerial Work* (New York: Harper & Row, 1973).
4. F. Kerlinger, *Foundations of Behavioral Research* (New York: Holt, Rinehart and Winston, 1965), p. 39. (Italics added.)
5. B. M. Staw, "Organizational Behavior: A Review and Reformulation of the Field's Outcome Variables," in M. R. Rosenzweig and L. W. Porter (eds.), *Annual Review of Psychology,* Vol. 35 (Palo Alto, Calif.: Annual Reviews, 1984), pp. 627–66.
6. Ibid., pp. 655–56.
7. R. M. Steers an S. R. Rhodes, "Major Influences on Employee Attendance: A Process Model," *Journal of Applied Psychology,* August 1978, p. 391.
8. P. H. Mirvis and E. E. Lawler III, "Measuring the Financial Impact of Employee Attitudes," *Journal of Applied Psychology,* February 1977, pp. 1–8. Dollar figures have been updated to reflect inflation.
9. D. R. Dalton and W. D. Todor, "Functional Turnover: An Empirical Assessment," *Journal of Applied Psychology,* December 1981, pp. 716–21.
10. H. J. Leavitt, *Managerial Psychology,* rev. ed. (Chicago: University of Chicago Press, 1964), p. 3.

CASE IA

DO ACCOUNTANTS NEED PEOPLE SKILLS?

Martha Altus and Gene White were both in their junior year, majoring in accounting, at State College. They sat in a study corner of the business building on a late April afternoon with their college catalogs and next fall's class schedule spread out before them.

"You know," interrupted Martha, "we wouldn't have so much trouble getting a decent schedule if it weren't for this conflict between Advanced Accounting Problems and Organizational Behavior."

"I know," replied Gene, "my emphasis is auditing. What's yours?"

"Tax."

"All right," began Gene, "explain something to me. Why the devil do we have to waste our time taking a course in organizational behavior? I can understand the finance courses, the quantitative methods course, and the classes in information systems. But why do they load us down with courses like marketing and organizational behavior? I doubt we'll get anything out of them. Even if I give these courses the benefit of the doubt—maybe there's something of value in them for us—look at the opportunity costs. If we weren't required to take these classes, we could take more advanced courses in tax, cost, and auditing!"

"You're absolutely right," agreed Martha. "I want to take all the tax courses I can. It's a tough field. Lots of specialized laws to know. And how are we going to pass the CPA exam if they make us take irrelevant course work? Accounting is a profession. It's based on technical skills, just like law and medicine. You don't see lawyers and doctors taking courses in marketing or organizational behavior! Of course not! Their faculty understands the need to develop a high level of specialization. But accounting programs somehow got intertwined with business degrees, so we have to take all these other courses."

As both struggled with finding an acceptable class schedule, Gene summed up his frustration: "I challenge the dean to explain how a course in organizational behavior is important to us. I expect to join a Big Eight accounting firm's auditing staff, and you will be in the tax department of some large corporation. What can this course offer us?"

Questions

1. What value, in general, could a course in OB be to accounting students?
2. What specific value could an OB course offer an auditor with a large accounting firm? A tax specialist with a large corporation?
3. Would an OB course be less relevant if each of their career goals were to run a one-person accounting practice, offering advisory services to individuals and small businesses?
4. What value would a marketing course offer to accounting students?
5. How valid is their "opportunity costs" argument?

CASE IB

"I'M NOT ALWAYS RIGHT, BUT I'M RIGHT MOST OF THE TIME"

Frank Doherty is fifty-six years old. He dropped out of high school in the tenth grade to support his widowed mother and three younger brothers. At nineteen, he borrowed $200 from his uncle to buy a couple of used cars, which he hoped to resell at a profit. The rest is history. Today, Frank owns five new car dealerships. A recent article in *Automotive News* described Frank Doherty as the largest new car dealer in Texas and among the top ten in the United States. It's estimated that his five dealerships sell better than 2,500 cars a month!

John Doherty, Frank's son, has been in the business with his dad for less than a year. A recent graduate of the University of Texas, John hoped to put what he learned while earning his B.S. and M.B.A. to work in the car business. But it was obvious to Frank that he and John had some definite differences of opinion on a number of issues. John told this case writer that the root of the problem is that "My dad is so damn dogmatic. He's been extremely successful. I mean, hell, it's hard to criticize someone who started with nothing and was a millionaire at age thirty. But, you gotta admit a lot of his success was due to being in the right place at the right time. It would have been pretty hard to lose money in Dallas with a Chevy dealership in the 1950s. And getting the VW franchise in 1961 and the Honda dealership in 1976 wasn't exactly bad timing! Sure, Dad had the foresight to see what the customer wanted, but that's part of the problem. Everything he's touched has turned to gold. He thinks he's infallible. You name the problem and he's instantly got the answer. Nothing burns me up more than his ideas on managing our staff.

"You know we've got about 120 salespeople working for us. We've got another 150 in the shop, and our office staff numbers better than 35. I mean, we're a pretty big operation. But Dad makes personnel decisions based on a bunch of his notions about people.

"For instance, he won't hire college graduates. He says college kids expect too much, too fast. He says they don't have patience and that they want to run the show right out of school. When that doesn't happen, they get frustrated and quit.

"Go out on the sales floor of any of our dealerships. Notice anything unusual? Did our salesmen all look like linebackers for the Dallas Cowboys? That's the result of another of Dad's crazy beliefs. He says the best salesmen are big. There's no use trying to argue with him. He thinks big guys are more aggressive and self-confident. And that results in more sales. As I said, you can't argue with him. All he says is 'Look at my track record.'

"In the office, Dad demands that the office manager keep a close eye on everybody. Dad says people are basically goof-offs. 'You leave them alone for a few minutes and they'll stop working and start playing.' The result is that our office looks like a Gestapo camp. Employees are always under close supervision.

"Everytime I try to talk with Dad about his attitudes, I get the same response. 'Listen, John. Maybe my ideas aren't *always* right, but they're right *most* of the time. You may not agree with the way I run the dealerships, but you can't argue with the fact that it works.'"

Questions

1. Compare intuition and systematic study as they relate to Frank Doherty's view of human behavior.
2. What factors could explain the radical differences between father and son in their attitudes and approaches to dealing with people?
3. Do you think John can change his father's style of management? Discuss.
4. "Frank's right. College kids *do* expect too much! The best salesmen are big! People *are* basically goof-offs! It is just this type of generally valid insights that have made Frank the success that he is." Discuss.
5. What is the impact of Frank's attitudes on (a) employee selection and (b) organizational effectiveness at his dealerships?

CASE IC

AN AFTERNOON TALK AT THE OLD LION TAVERN

Mike, Jenny, Molly, and Sean have over thirty years of experience, between them, with R. J. Reynolds Industries. It was 5:30 one Friday evening and the four had gotten together after work at their favorite watering hole, the Old Lion Tavern, to share a few drinks.

For the record, their backgrounds are quite varied. Currently, Mike is assistant to the vice-president of manufacturing operations, in the consumer products group. Jenny is a marketing brand manager in the tobacco group. Molly is a staff analyst in corporate finance. Sean is director of personnel for the consumer products group. The discussion among the four turned to the question of what determines whether their department is successful.

"In the operations area," began Mike, "I think the key factor is efficiency. We want to get the product out at the lowest cost. We have to maintain quality standards with a minimum of breakdowns in the production flow. Take our Hawaiian Punch division. As operations' people, we have to ensure that our high standards for the drink are maintained. We also have to be able to implement changes—like the new Hawaiian Punch carton containers—with minimal disturbances to our output goals."

"In marketing, I think we have two goals against which our effectiveness is measured," said Jenny. "Those are market share and rate of growth in sales. Sure, we have to develop new products. If we don't, the long-term viability of my brand is in jeopardy. But the name of the game is market share. I'm always watching how my brand does against my big rivals—Winston, True, and Marlboro. A change of 1 percent in market share is the difference between my being an also-ran around here or being a superstar."

"It's strange," commented Molly. "In the financial area, there is one bottom line—return on investment. In fact, everything you people are talking about could be subsumed under R.O.I. After all, isn't that why the company exists?"

"I don't know, Molly," said Sean. "I'm not so sure that the only thing R. J. Reynolds exists for is to get the highest return possible for our investors. Don't we have a responsibility to society? Or how about our employees? In my area, personnel, I'm judged by the degree to which I'm able to acquire and keep good people, maintain high morale, and ensure that we're developing people for the future."

Mike was becoming irritated by Molly's apparent arrogance. "Molly, what makes you think R.O.I. is so damn important? You make it sound like finance is more important than the rest of our areas. You know, I said efficiency was our top priority. It probably should be all of yours, too. Marketing efficiency relates to getting the most sales for the fewest marketing dollars. Financial efficiency is your R.O.I. number. And personnel efficiency is getting the most output per employee."

Questions

1. How do *you* measure an organization's effectiveness?
2. Is R.O.I. a universal measure of organizational effectiveness? How about efficiency?
3. Relate the objectives of OB to your introductory courses in marketing and finance. Are they the same? If not, are they reconcilable?
4. Relate OB's dependent variables to this debate.
5. How, if at all, could a knowledge of OB help each of these four individuals in their jobs?

CASE ID

ARNIE BENTLEY—HOUSEHUSBAND

October in southern California can be warm. It was, in fact, about ninety degrees on the Tuesday afternoon that I first spoke with the familiar bearded face in the supermarket checkout line.

"Hi," I began. "Seems like every time I'm in this place I see you."

"Yeah," he responded, "you retired, too?"

"No, afraid not. I'm a professor over at State. I teach on Mondays and Wednesdays, and the rest of the time I research and write at home. I try to hit the market during the day to avoid the crowds."

The bearded face, who had now introduced himself as Arnie Bentley, told me that he, too, liked to shop when most people were working.

"Are you retired?" I inquired "Hell, you can't be thirty-five years old!"

"I'm thirty-three to be exact," began Arnie. "I graduated from State in 1974, with a degree in computer science. Worked for San Diego Gas and Electric for six years but hated it. So I retired."

Arnie's story fascinated me. How did he make ends meet? What did he do with himself every day? I really wanted to get to know more about Arnie Bentley. I asked him if I could buy him a cold soda, and the two of us spent the next couple of hours sitting in a small restaurant—Arnie doing most of the talking and me listening.

Arnie's "retirement" was, in actuality, a voluntary decision not to have a real job. Married, with two children, Arnie is far from well fixed. His wife is an elementary school teacher and earns $24,000 a year.

"When I left the gas company in 1981, I was making $29,000 a year. If I stayed I'd be probably making $36,000 now. But I'd be a nervous wreck. No, I'm perfectly convinced that making more money is not so all important. We're now in a time where society offers new alternatives to working for a living. I'm not into the work ethic thing. So I've chosen to stay home and take care of the house. I guess you could say I'm a househusband. I see the kids off to school, cook, clean, do the laundry, shop, and maintain the house. I also do the typical husband chores like taking care of the yard and doing repairs."

When I asked Arnie how his wife felt about his life-style choice, he became quite serious. "At first Maggie was really upset. During the first six or nine months, I thought it was going to break up our marriage. But I held my ground. Maggie is a career woman. She's studying for her master's degree at night and she fully expects to be a school principal within five years. I really respect her ambition, but the career thing isn't for me. I think Maggie finally understood where I was coming from when I put it into the framework of the liberation movement. We talk a whole lot about women's lib. Well, I'm into male liberation! Just as women want to be free to choose, so do I! Women say they want to have the option of being physicians, lawyers, and construction workers, as well as housewives, teachers, or librarians. Well, I want those same options and I'm reaching for them. I've opted for a life-style that makes me happy, and I don't care what others think."

Questions

1. If Arnie had had the option at SDG&E of working a three-day week or to be on flexible work hours (which would have allowed him to arrive and leave when he wanted to as long as he put in his eight hours), do you think he might still be working? Discuss.

2. Given Arnie's choice of life-style, what do you think caused him to leave SDG&E? What could the company have done to retain someone like Arnie?
3. Could Arnie's life-style be the beginning of a new trend in North America? Explain.
4. Might Maggie approach her job differently because of Arnie's decision to be a house-husband, than if Arnie were earning $36,000 a year as a computer specialist?
5. Using the model presented in Chapter 2, which variables might help explain the differences between Arnie's and Maggie's orientation toward working in an organization?

CASE IE

"I LOVE MY WORK"

Stacey Friedman has been a literary agent with one of the largest literary agencies in New York for four years. Her job entails matching up authors and their manuscripts with book publishers. She has about two dozen established authors whom she represents in negotiations with the publishing houses. Stacey also regularly reviews manuscripts of new or less established authors who want her firm to represent them.

"I live and breathe this job. I'm up at 5:30 in the morning and in the office by 7:00. I either skip lunch or use lunch as an excuse to meet with publishing editors, with one of my established authors, or to talk with a prospective client. I'm never out of the office before 7:30 P.M., and it's usually closer to 9:00. When I get home, I spend an hour or two lying in bed reading manuscripts. I only wish I could find another five hours a day so I could squeeze in more things. God, I love my work."

You might be correct in calling Stacey a workaholic. She approaches her work almost compulsively. In college, she was in a sorority, played on her school's soccer team, and dated regularly. But Stacey's job is now her whole life. She told me she hadn't been on a date in five months, although she had had several dozen offers. She had no social life, except for that which rotated around her work. Stacey even admitted that she hadn't had time to dust or run the vacuum cleaner over the rugs in her apartment in six weeks.

"But don't get the wrong impression when I say my apartment is a mess," interjected Stacey. "I don't care. Every morning I pop out of bed and just thank the Lord for having a job that makes me so happy. When I run into people who complain about their work, I just shake my head. How lucky I am! I'd rather be negotiating with an editor, making manuscript suggestions, discussing strategy with one of my authors, or reading some unknown author's first book than be cleaning the house, jogging around Central Park, or for that matter, making love with Tom Selleck. I mean it when I say I've got a great job."

Stacey Friedman's enthusiasm appears to have had a very positive impact on her job performance. Her boss says she is the best young agent in the office. "She gives a hundred percent. But, of course, she's smart, too. Stacey has a bright future in this industry."

Questions

1. If you were to learn that Stacey made only $18,000 a year in her job, would you be surprised? Explain.
2. Since Stacey makes only $18,000, one can safely conclude that money is not her main source of motivation. What types of individual, organizational, and job-related factors might account for her high level of motivation?
3. Build a model showing the relationships among the factors that help explain Stacey's high level of performance and motivation.
4. Can you see any possible negative aspects of managing someone like Stacey?

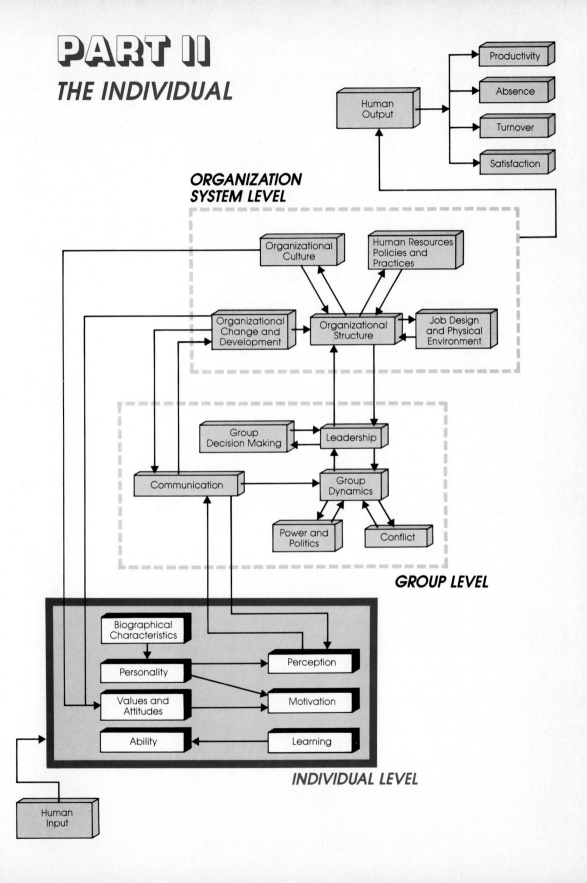

Foundations of Individual Behavior

3

AFTER STUDYING THIS CHAPTER, YOU SHOULD BE ABLE TO:

Assumed similarity
Attribution theory
Authoritarianism
Biographical characteristics
Classical conditioning
Continuous reinforcement
Externals
Fixed-interval schedule
Fixed-ratio schedule
Halo effect
Intermittent reinforcement
Internals
Learning
Locus of control

Machiavellianism
nAch
Operant conditioning
Perception
Personality
Personality traits
Realistic job previews
Selective perception
Shaping behavior
Social learning theory
Stereotyping
Variable-interval schedule
Variable-ratio schedule

The key biographical characteristics
The factors that determine an individual's personality
The impact of job typology on the personality–job performance
    relationship
The difference between perception and reality in determining behavior
Why we see what we want to see
Three determinants of attribution
How perception impacts on decision making
How shortcuts can assist or distort our judgment of others
How learning theories provide insights into changing behavior
The four schedules of reinforcement
The role of punishment in learning

I ain't much, baby—but I'm all I've got.

—J. LAIR

Are older workers more likely to remain with an organization than their younger counterparts? Do certain personality types make better employees? Why is it that many people tend to attribute their successes to their own actions but blame their failures on factors outside their control? Do employees learn better by having their desirable behaviors rewarded or their undesirable behaviors punished? These questions deal with four variables: biographical characteristics, personality, perception, and learning. In this chapter, we'll answer such questions and many more by reviewing how these four individual variables affect employee performance and satisfaction.

BIOGRAPHICAL CHARACTERISTICS

As discussed in the last chapter, this book is essentially concerned with finding and analyzing those variables that impact on employee productivity, absence, turnover, and satisfaction. The list of these variables—as was shown in Figure 2–6—is long and contains a number of complicated concepts. Many of these concepts—like motivation level, group norms, or organizational culture—are hard to assess. It might be valuable, then, to begin by looking at factors that are easily definable and readily available; data that can be obtained, for the most part, simply from information available in an employee's personnel file. What factors would this include? Obvious characteristics would be an employee's age, sex, marital status, number of dependents, and length of service with an organization. Fortunately, there is a sizable amount of research that has specifically analyzed many of these biographical characteristics.

Age

The older you get, the less likely you are to quit your job. That is the overwhelming conclusion based on studies of the age-turnover relationship.[1] Of course, this conclusion should not be too surprising. It's consistent with the reality that as workers get older they have fewer alternative job opportunities. It also reflects that older workers are less likely to resign because their longer tenure tends to provide them with higher wage rates, longer paid vacations, and more attractive pension benefits.

It's tempting to assume that age would also be inversely related to absenteeism. After all, if older workers are less likely to quit, wouldn't they also demonstrate higher stability by coming to work more regularly? Not necessarily! Most studies *do* show an inverse relationship, but closer examination finds that the age-absence relationship is partially a function of whether the absence is avoidable or unavoidable.[2] Generally, older employees have lower rates of avoidable absence than do younger employees. However, they have higher rates of unavoidable absence. This is probably due to poorer health associated with aging and the longer recovery period that older workers need when injured.

How does age affect productivity? Here the evidence is very mixed.[3] Whether age is beneficial, detrimental, or neutral in impacting on an employee's productivity seems to depend on the demands of the job. Where the job requires speed, agility, strength, hand-eye coordination, and similar skills that tend to decline with age, employee productivity should fall. But generally speaking, the demands of most jobs are not extreme enough for these declines in skill levels to have an effect on job productivity.

Our final concern is the relationship between age and job satisfaction. There is overwhelming evidence indicating a positive association between age and satisfaction, at least up to age sixty.[4] However, current changes taking place in technology may alter this. In jobs where workers are subject to dramatic changes causing their skills to become obsolete, such as those affected by the computer, the satisfaction of older workers is likely to be lower than is that of younger employees.

Sex

Few issues initiate more debates, myths, and unsupported opinions than whether females perform as well on jobs as do males. In this section, we want to review the research on this issue.

The evidence suggests that the best place to begin is with the recognition that there are few, if any, important differences between males and females that will affect their job performance. There are, for instance, no consistent male-female differences in problem-solving ability, analytical skills, competitive drive, motivation, leadership, sociability, or learning ability.[5] While psychological studies[6] have found that women are more willing to conform to authority, and that men are more aggressive and more likely than women to have expectations of success, these differences are minor. Given the significant changes that have taken place in the last dozen years in terms of increasing female participation rates in the work force and rethinking of what constitutes male and female roles, you should operate from the assumption that there is no significant difference as to job productivity between males and females. Similarly, there is no evidence indicating that an employee's sex affects job satisfaction.[7]

But what about absence and turnover rates? Are females less stable employees than males? First, on the question of turnover, the evidence is mixed.[8] Some have found females to have higher turnover rates, while others have found no difference. There doesn't appear to be enough information from which to draw meaningful conclusions. The research on absence, however, is a different story. The evidence consistently indicates that women have higher rates of absenteeism than do men.[9] The most logical explanation for this finding is that our society has historically placed home and family responsibilities on the female. When a child is ill or someone needs to stay home to await the plumber, it has been the woman who has traditionally taken time off work. However, this research is probably time-bound. The historical role of the woman in child caring and as secondary breadwinner is definitely changing in the 1980s.

Marital Status

There are not enough studies to draw any conclusions as to the effect of marital status on productivity. But we do have consistent research that indicates that married employees have fewer absences, undergo less turnover, and are more satisfied with their jobs.[10]

Marriage imposes increased responsibilities that may make a steady job more valuable and important. Of course, the results represent correlational studies; therefore, the causation issue is not clear. It may very well be that conscientious and satisfied employees are more likely to be married. Another offshoot of this issue that research has not pursued is other statuses besides single or married. Does being divorced impact on an employee's performance and satisfaction? What about couples who live together without being married? These are questions in need of investigation.

Number of Dependents

Again, we don't have enough information relating to employee productivity, but quite a bit of research has been done on the relationship between the number of dependents an employee has and absence, turnover, and satisfaction.

There is very strong evidence that the number of children an employee has is positively correlated with absence, especially among females.[11] Similarly, the evidence seems to point to a positive relationship between number of dependents and job satisfaction.[12] In contrast, studies relating number of dependents and turnover produce a mixed bag of results.[13] Some indicate that children increase turnover, while others show that they result in lower turnover. At this point, the evidence regarding turnover is just too contradictory to permit us to draw conclusions.

Tenure

The last biographical characteristic we'll look at is tenure. With the exception of the concern about male-female differences, there is probably no other issue that is more subject to myths and speculations than the impact of seniority on job performance.

Extensive reviews of the seniority-productivity relationship have been conducted.[14] While past performance tends to be related to output in a new position, seniority by itself is not a good predictor of productivity. In other words, holding all other things equal, there is no reason to believe that people who have been on a job longer are more productive than are thos with less seniority.

The research relating tenure with absence is quite straightforward. Studies consistently demonstrate seniority to be negatively related to absenteeism.[15] In fact, in terms of both absence frequency and total days lost at work, tenure is the single most important explanatory variable.[16]

As with absence, tenure is also a potent variable in explaining turnover. "Tenure has consistently been found to be negatively related to turnover and has been suggested as one of the single best predictors of turnover."[17]

PERSONALITY

Why are some people quiet and passive, while others are loud and aggressive? Are certain personality types better adapted for certain job types? What do we know from theories of personality that can help us to explain and predict the behavior of individuals in organizations? In this section we will attempt to answer such questions.

What Is Personality?

When we talk of personality, we do not mean that a person has charm, a positive attitude toward life, and a smiling face or is a finalist for "Happiest and Friendliest" in this year's Miss America contest. When psychologists talk of personality, they mean a dynamic concept describing the growth and development of a person's whole psychological system. Rather than looking at parts of the person, personality looks at some aggregate whole that is greater than the sum of the parts.

The most frequently used definition of personality was produced by Gordon Allport nearly fifty years ago. He said personality is "the dynamic organization within the individual of those psychophysical systems that determine his unique adjustments to his environment."[18] For our purposes, you should think of *personality* as the sum total of ways in which an individual reacts and interacts with others. This is most often described in terms of measurable personality traits that a person exhibits.

Personality Determinants

An early argument in personality research was whether an individual's personality was the result of heredity or environment. Was the personality predetermined at birth, or was it the result of the individual's interaction with his or her environment? Clearly, there is no simple "black-or-white" answer. Personality appears to be a result of both influences. Additionally, there has recently been an increased interest in a third factor—the situation. Thus, an adult's personality is now generally considered to be made up of both hereditary and environmental factors, moderated by situational conditions.

HEREDITY

Heredity refers to those factors that were determined at conception. Physical stature, facial attractiveness, sex, temperament, muscle composition and reflexes, energy level, and biological rhythms are characteristics that are generally considered to be either completely or substantially influenced by who your parents were; that is, by their biological, physiological, and inherent psychological makeup. The heredity approach argues that the ultimate explanation of an individual's personality is the molecular structure of the genes, located in the chromosomes. "In fact, much of the early work in personality could be subsumed under the series: Heredity is transmitted through the genes; the genes determine the hormone balance; hormone balance determines physique; and physique shapes personality."[19]

The heredity argument can be used to explain why Veronica's nose looks like her father's or why her chin resembles her mother's. It may explain why Diane is a "gifted athlete" when both her parents were similarly gifted. More controversy would surround the conclusion, by those who advocate the heredity approach, that Michael is lethargic as a result of inheriting this characteristic from his parents.

If all personality characteristics were completely dictated by heredity, they would be fixed at birth and no amount of experience could alter them. If you were relaxed and easygoing, for example, that would be the result of your genes, and it would not be possible for you to change these characteristics. While this approach may be appealing to the bigots of the world, it is an inadequate explanation of personality.

ENVIRONMENT

Among the factors that exert pressures on our personality formation are the culture in which we are raised; our early conditioning; the norms among our family, friends, and social groups; and other influences that we experience. The environment we are exposed to plays a critical role in shaping our personalities.

For example, culture establishes the norms, attitudes, and values that are passed along from one generation to the next and create consistencies over time. An ideology that is fostered in one culture may have only moderate influence in another. For instance, we in North America have had the themes of industriousness, success, competition, independence, and Protestant ethic constantly instilled in us through books, the school system, family, and friends. North Americans, as a result, tend to be ambitious and aggressive relative to individuals raised in cultures that have emphasized getting along with others, cooperation, and the priority of family over work and career.

An interesting area of research linking environmental factors and personality has focused on the influence of birth order. It has been argued that sibling position is an important psychological variable "because it represents a microcosm of the significant social experiences of adolescence and adulthood."[20] Those who see birth order as a predictive variable propose that while personality differences between children are frequently attributed to heredity, the environment in which the children are raised is really the critical factor that creates the differences. And the environment that a firstborn child is exposed to is different from that of later-born children.

The research indicates that firstborns are more prone to schizophrenia, more susceptible to social pressure, and more dependent than the later-born.[21] The firstborn are also more likely to experience the world as more orderly, predictable, and rational than later-born children. Of course, there is much debate as to the differing characteristics of first- versus later-born children, but the evidence does indicate that firstborns of the same sex "should be more concerned with social acceptance and rejection, less likely to break the rules imposed by authority, more ambitious and hard-working, more cooperative, more prone to guilt and anxiety, and less openly aggressive."[22]

Careful consideration of the arguments favoring either heredity or environment as the primary determinant of personality forces the conclusion that both are important. Heredity sets the parameters or outer limits, but an individual's full potential will be determined by how well he or she adjusts to the demands and requirements of the environment.

SITUATION

A third factor, the situation, further influences the effects of heredity and environment on personality. An individual's personality, while generally stable and consistent, does change in different situations. Different demands in different situations call forth different aspects of one's personality. We should not, therefore, look at personality patterns in isolation.

While it seems only logical to suppose that situations will influence an individual's personality, a neat classification scheme that would tell us the impact of various types of situations has so far eluded us. "Apparently we are not yet close to developing a system for clarifying situations so that they might be systematically studied."[23] However, we do know that certain situations are more relevant than others in influencing personality.

What is of interest taxonomically is that situations seem to differ substantially in the constraints they impose on behavior, with some situations—e.g. church, an employment interview—constraining many behaviors and others—e.g. a picnic in a public park—constraining relatively few.[24]

Furthermore, although certain generalizations can be made about personality, there are significant individual differences. As we shall see, the study of individual differences has come to receive greater emphasis in personality research, which originally sought out more general, universal patterns.

Personality Traits

The early work in the structure of personality revolved around attempts to identify and label enduring characteristics that describe an individual's behavior. Popular characteristics include shy, aggressive, submissive, lazy, ambitious, loyal, or timid. These characteristics, when they are exhibited in a large number of situations, are called traits. The more consistent the characteristic and the more frequently it occurs in diverse situations, the more important that trait is in describing the individual.

Efforts to isolate traits have been hindered by the fact that there are so many of them. In one study, 17,953 individual traits were identified.[25] However, it is virtually impossible to predict behavior when such a large number of traits must be taken into account. As a result, attention has been directed toward reducing these thousands to a more manageable number—to ascertain the source or primary traits.

One researcher isolated 171 surface traits but concluded that they were superficial and lacking in descriptive power.[26] What he sought was a reduced set of traits that would identify underlying patterns. The result was the identification of sixteen personality factors, which he called source or primary traits, that are the basic underlying causes of surface traits. They are shown in Table 3–1. These sixteen traits have been found to be generally steady and constant sources of behavior, allowing prediction of an individual's behavior in specific situations by weighing the characteristics for their situational relevance.

FIGURE 3–1

Source: Copyright © 1959 by United Feature Syndicate, Inc. with permission

TABLE 3–1
Sixteen Source Traits

1. Reserved	Outgoing
2. Less intelligent	More intelligent
3. Affected by feelings	Emotionally stable
4. Submissive	Dominant
5. Serious	Happy-go-lucky
6. Expedient	Conscientious
7. Timid	Venturesome
8. Tough-minded	Sensitive
9. Trusting	Suspicious
10. Practical	Imaginative
11. Forthright	Shrewd
12. Self-assured	Apprehensive
13. Conservative	Experimenting
14. Group-dependent	Self-sufficient
15. Uncontrolled	Controlled
16. Relaxed	Tense

Traits can additionally be grouped to form personality types. Instead of looking at specific characteristics, we can group those qualities that go together into a single category. For example, ambition and aggression tend to be highly correlated. Efforts to reduce the number of traits into common groups tend to isolate introversion-extroversion and something approximating high anxiety-low anxiety as the underlying interconnecting characteristics.[27] As depicted in Figure 3–2, these dimensions suggest four personality types.[28] For example, an individual with high anxiety and extroversion would be tense, excitable, unstable, warm, sociable, and dependent.

Should you put a lot of weight on personality traits as explanatory devices or predictors of employee behavior across a broad spectrum of situations? Probably not! This is because traits ignore situational contexts. They are not contingency oriented and, therefore, largely ignore the dynamic interchange that occurs

FIGURE 3–2
Four-Type Thesis

	High Anxiety	Low Anxiety
Extrovert	Tense, excitable, unstable, warm, sociable, and dependent	Composed, confident, trustful, adaptable, warm, sociable and dependent
Introvert	Tense, excitable, unstable, cold, and shy	Composed, confident, trustful, adaptable, calm, cold, and shy

in an individual's personality as a result of interaction with his or her environment. As a result, personality traits tend to be most valuable only with individuals who hold a trait at its extreme (see Figure 3–3). We might be able to predict some common behaviors among *extreme* extroverts or individuals who are *highly* anxious. But since the majority of people are in the vast middle range on most trait characteristics, personality traits must be considered in their situational context.

Major Personality Attributes Influencing OB

A number of specific personality attributes have been isolated as having potential for predicting behavior in organizations. The first of these is related to where one perceives the locus of control in one's life. The others are achievement orientation, authoritarianism, Machiavellianism, and propensity for risk taking. In this section, we shall briefly introduce these attributes and summarize what we know as to their ability to explain and predict employee behavior.

LOCUS OF CONTROL

Some people believe that they are masters of their own fate. Other people see themselves as pawns of fate, believing that what happens to them in their lives is due to luck or chance. The first type, those who believe that they control their destinies, have been labeled *internals,* whereas the latter, who see their lives as being controlled by outside forces, have been called *externals.*[29]

A large amount of research comparing internals with externals has consistently shown that individuals who rate high in externality are less satisfied with their jobs, have higher absenteeism rates, are more alienated from the work setting, and are less involved on their jobs than are internals.[30]

Why are externals more dissatisfied? The answer is probably because they perceive themselves as having little control over those organizational outcomes that are important to them. Internals, facing the same situation, attribute organi-

FIGURE 3–3

Predictive Validity of Personality Traits

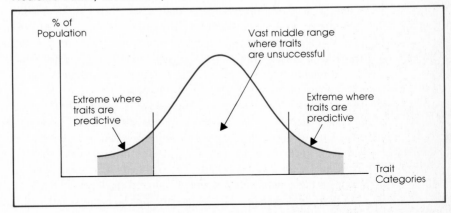

zational outcomes to their own actions. If the situation is unattractive, they believe that they have no one else to blame but themselves. Also, the dissatisfied internal is more likely to quit a dissatisfying job.

The impact of locus of control on absence is an interesting one. Internals believe that health is substantially under their own control through proper habits, so they take more responsibility for their health and have better health habits. This leads to lower incidences of sickness and, hence, lower absenteeism.[31]

We shouldn't expect any clear relationship between locus of control and turnover. The reason is that there are opposing forces at work. "On the one hand, internals tend to take action and thus might be expected to quit jobs more readily. On the other hand, they tend to be more successful on the job and more satisfied, factors associated with less individual turnover."[32]

The overall evidence indicates that internals generally perform better on their jobs but that conclusion should be moderated to reflect differences in jobs. Internals search more actively for information before making a decision, are more motivated to achieve, and make a greater attempt to control their environment. Externals, however, are more compliant and willing to follow directions. Therefore, internals do well on sophisticated tasks—which includes most managerial and professional jobs—that require complex information processing and learning. Additionally, internals are more suited to jobs that require initiative and independence of action. In contrast, externals should do well on jobs that are well structured and routine and where success depends heavily on complying with the direction of others.

ACHIEVEMENT ORIENTATION

We have noted that internals are motivated to achieve. This achievement orientation has also been singled out as a personality characteristic that varies among employees and that can be used to predict certain behaviors.

Research has centered around the need to achieve (nAch). People with a high need to achieve can be described as continually striving to do things better. They want to overcome obstacles, but they want to feel that their success (or failure) is due to their own actions. This means they like tasks of intermediate difficulty. If a task is very easy, it will lack challenge. High achievers receive no feeling of accomplishment from doing tasks that fail to challenge their abilities. Similarly, they avoid tasks that are so difficult that the probability of success is very low. Even if they succeed, it is more apt to be due to luck than ability. Given the high achiever's propensity for tasks where the outcome can be attributed directly to his or her efforts, the high-nAch person looks for challenges having approximately a 50-50 chance of success.

What can we say about high achievers on the job? In jobs that provide intermediate difficulty, rapid performance feedback, and allow the employee control over his or her results, the high nAch individual will perform well.[33] This implies, though, that high achievers will do better in sales, professional sports, or in management than on an assembly line or in clerical tasks. That is, those individuals with a high nAch will not always outperform those who are low or intermediate in this characteristic. The tasks that high achievers undertake must provide the challenge, feedback, and responsibility they look for if the high-*nAch* personality is to be positively related to job performance.

AUTHORITARIANISM

There is evidence that there is such a thing as an authoritarian personality, but its relevance to job behavior is more speculation than fact. With that qualification, let us examine authoritarianism and consider how it might be related to employee performance.

Authoritarianism refers to a belief that there should be status and power differences among people in organizations.[34] The extremely high-authoritarian personality is intellectually rigid, judgmental of others, deferential to those above and exploitative of those below, distrustful, and resistant to change. Of course, few people are extreme authoritarians, so conclusions must be guarded. It seems reasonable to postulate, however, that possessing a high-authoritarian personality would be related negatively to performance where the job demanded sensitivity to the feelings of others, tact, and the ability to adapt to complex and changing situations.[35] On the other hand, where jobs are highly structured and success depends on close conformance to rules and regulations, the high-authoritarian employee should perform quite well.

MACHIAVELLIANISM

Closely related to authoritarianism is the characteristic of Machiavellianism (Mach), named after Niccolo Machiavelli who wrote in the sixteenth century on how to gain and manipulate power. An individual high in Machiavellianism is pragmatic, maintains emotional distance, and believes that ends can justify means. "If it works, use it" is consistent with a high-Mach perspective.

A considerable amount of research has been directed toward relating high- and low-Mach personalities to certain behavioral outcomes.[36] High Machs manipulate more, win more, are persuaded less, and persuade others more than do low Machs.[37] Yet these high-Mach outcomes are moderated by situational factors. It has been found that high Machs flourish (1) when they interact face to face with others rather than indirectly; (2) when the situation has a minimum number of rules and regulations, thus allowing latitude for improvisation; and (3) where emotional involvement with details irrelevant to winning distracts low Machs.[38]

Should we conclude that high Machs make good employees? That answer depends on the type of job and whether you consider ethical implications in evaluating performance. In jobs that require bargaining skills (such as labor negotiation) or where there are substantial rewards for winning (as in commissioned sales), high Machs will be productive. But if ends can't justify the means, if there are *absolute* standards of behavior, or if the three situational factors noted in the previous paragraph are not in evidence, our ability to predict a high Mach's performance will be severely curtailed.

RISK TAKING

People differ in their willingness to take chances. This propensity to assume or avoid risk has been shown to impact on how long it takes managers to make a decision and how much information they require before making their choice. For instance, seventy-nine managers worked on simulated personnel exercises that required them to make hiring decisions.[39] High-risk-taking managers made more rapid decisions and used less information in making their choices than did the low-risk-taking managers. Interestingly, the decision accuracy was the same for both groups.

While it is generally correct to conclude that managers in organizations are risk aversive,[40] there are still individual differences on this dimension.[41] As a result, it makes sense to recognize these differences and even to consider aligning risk-taking propensity with specific job demands. For instance, a high-risk-taking propensity may lead to more effective performance for a stock trader in a brokerage firm. This type of job demands rapid decision making. On the other hand, this personality characteristic might prove a major obstacle to accountants performing auditing activities. This latter job might be better filled by someone with a low-risk-taking propensity.

Matching Personality and Jobs

In our discussion of locus of control, authoritarianism, Machiavellianism, and risk taking, our conclusions were qualified to recognize that the requirements of the job moderated the relationship between possession of the personality characteristic and job performance. This concern with matching the job requirements with personality characteristics has recently received increased attention. It is best articulated in John Holland's personality–job fit theory.[42] The theory presents six personality types and then proposes that satisfaction and the propensity to leave a job depends on the degree to which individuals successfully match their personalities with a congruent occupational environment.

Each one of the six personality types has a matching occupational environment. Listed next is a description of the six types and examples of congruent occupations:

Type	Occupations
1. *Realistic*—involves aggressive behavior, physical activities requiring skill, strength, and coordination	Forestry, farming, architecture
2. *Investigative*—involves activities requiring thinking, organizing, and understanding rather than feeling or emotion	Biology, mathematics, news reporting
3. *Social*—involves interpersonal rather than intellectual or physical activities	Foreign service, social work, clinical psychology
4. *Conventional*—involves rule-regulated activities and sublimation of personal needs to an organization or person of power and status	Accounting, finance, corporate management

5. *Enterprising*—involves verbal activities to influence others, to attain power and status

Law, public relations, small-business management

6. *Artistic*—involves self-expression, artistic creation, or emotional activities

Art, music, writing

Holland has developed a Vocational Preference Inventory questionnaire that contains 160 occupational titles. Respondents indicate which of these occupations they like or dislike, and these answers are used to form personality profiles. Utilizing this procedure, research strongly supports the hexagonal diagram in Figure 3–4.[43] This figure shows that the closer two fields or orientations are in the hexagon, the more compatible they are. Adjacent categories are quite similar, while those diagonally opposite are highly dissimilar.

What does all this mean? The theory argues that satisfaction is highest and turnover lowest where personality and occupation are in agreement. Social individuals should be in social jobs, conventional people in conventional jobs, and so forth. A realistic person in a realistic job is in a more congruent situation than is a realistic person in an investigative job. A realistic person in a social job is in the most incongruent situation possible. The key points of this model are that (1) there do appear to be intrinsic differences in personality among individuals, (2)

FIGURE 3–4

Relationships Among Occupational Personality Types

Source: John L. Holland, *Making Vocational Choices: A Theory of Careers* (Englewood Cliffs, N.J.: Prentice-Hall, Inc., 1973), p. 23. Used by permission. This model originally appeared in J. L. Holland et al., "An Empirical Occupational Classification Derived from a Theory of Personality and Intended for Practice and Research," ACT Research Report No. 29 Iowa City: The American College Testing Program, 1969.

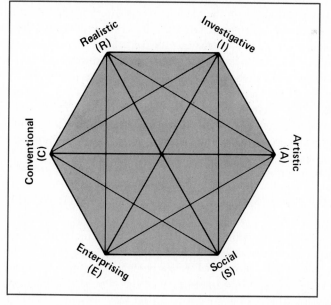

there are different types of jobs, and (3) people in job environments congruent with their personality types should be more satisfied and less likely to voluntarily resign than should people in incongruent jobs.

PERCEPTION

Any discussion of perception begins with the realization that the way in which we see the outside world need not be the same as the world really is. We tend to see the world as we want to perceive it. For supporting evidence, we need go no farther than the perception of how effective a college instructor is in the classroom. It is not unusual for an instructor to be rated "excellent" by some students and "unsatisfactory" by other students in the same class. The instructor's teaching behavior, of course, is a constant. Even though all the students see the same instructor, they perceive his or her effectiveness differently. This ilustration confirms that we do not see reality; rather, we interpret what we see and call it reality.

When distortions are low—for example, when you and I both agree that the bank robbery we just witnessed was carried out by a Caucasian male, approximately 5 feet, 10 inches tall, 170 pounds, with dark brown hair, and wearing jeans and a light blue nylon jacket with a white patch on the right shoulder—it means that we not only saw the same thing but that our base of interpretation was similar.

A frequently cited case of how perceptions distort reality derives from a study conducted with representatives from both management and labor.[44] Each group was given a photograph of an ordinary-looking man and was asked to describe the individual in the photograph using a long list of personality characteristics. The only difference was that for half the cases the man in the photograph was labeled a plant manager and for the other half he was described as a union official. The results confirmed that impressions were radically different and depended on whether the man in the photograph was seen as "union" or "management" and, of course, whether the evaluator represented "union" or "management." Management and labor representatives formed significantly different impressions, each viewing the other as less dependable and more intolerant of diverse points of view than members of their own group. Apparently, perception is like beauty in that it lies "in the eye of the beholder."

What Is Perception and Why Is It Important?

Perception can be defined as a process by which individuals organize and interpret their sensory impressions in order to give meaning to their environment. However, as we have noted, what one perceives can be substantially different from objective reality. It need not be, but there is often disagreement. For example, it is possible that all employees in a firm may view it as a great place to work—favorable working conditions, interesting job assignments, good pay, an understanding and responsible management—but, as most of us know, it is very unusual to find such consistencies.

Why is perception important in the study of OB? Simply, because people's behavior is based on their perceptions of what reality is, not reality itself. The world as it is perceived is the world that is behaviorally important.

Factors Influencing Perception

How do we explain the fact that individuals may look at the same thing, yet perceive it differently? A number of factors operate to shape and sometimes distort perception. These factors can reside in the *perceiver,* in the object or *target* being perceived, or in the context of the *situation* in which the perception is made.

THE PERCEIVER

When an individual looks at a target and attempts to interpret what he or she sees, that interpretation is heavily influenced by personal characteristics of the individual perceiver. Have you ever bought a new car and then suddenly noticed a large number of cars like yours on the road? It's unlikely that the number of such cars suddenly expanded. Rather, your own purchase has influenced your perception so that you are now more likely to notice them. This is an example of how factors related to the perceiver influence what he or she perceives. Among the more relevant personal characteristics affecting perception are attitudes, motives, interests, past experience, and expectations.

Sandy likes small classes because she enjoys asking a lot of questions of her teachers. Scott, on the other hand, prefers large lectures. He rarely asks questions and likes the anonymity that goes with being lost in a sea of bodies. On the first day of classes this term, Sandy and Scott find themselves walking into the university auditorium for their introductory course in psychology. They both recognize that they will be among some eight hundred students in this class. But given the different attitudes held by Sandy and Scott, it shouldn't surprise you to find that they interpret what they see differently. Sandy sulks, while Scott's smile does little to hide his relief in being able to blend unnoticed into the large auditorium. They both see the same thing, but they interpret it differently. A major reason is that they hold divergent *attitudes* concerning large classes.

Unsatisfied needs or *motives* stimulate individuals and may exert a strong influence on their perceptions. This was dramatically demonstrated in research on hunger.[45] Individuals in the study had not eaten for varying numbers of hours. Some had eaten an hour earlier, while others had gone as long as 16 hours without food. These subjects were shown blurred pictures, and the results indicated that the extent of hunger influenced the interpretation of the blurred pictures. Those who had not eaten for 16 hours perceived the blurred images as pictures of food far more frequently than did those subjects who had eaten only a short time earlier.

This same phenomenon has application in an organizational context as well. It would not be surprising, for example, to find that a boss who is insecure perceives a subordinate's efforts to do an outstanding job as a threat to his or her own position. Personal insecurity can be transferred into the perception that others are out to "get your job," regardless of the intention of the subordinates. Likewise, people who are devious are prone to see others in the same context.

It should not surprise you that a plastic surgeon is more likely to notice an imperfect nose than is a plumber. The supervisor who has just been reprimanded by her boss for the high level of lateness among her staff is more likely to notice lateness by an employee tomorrow than she was last week. If you are preoccupied with a personal problem, you may find it hard to be attentive in class. If you are hungry, you are more apt to notice that the person next to you in class is nibbling French fries than if you had just eaten. The focus of our attention appears to be influenced by our *interests*. Because our individual interests differ considerably, what one person notices in a situation can differ from what others perceive.

Just as interests narrow one's focus, so do one's *past experiences*. You perceive those things to which you can relate. However, in many instances, your past experiences will act to nullify an object's interest.

Those objects or events that have been experienced are less unusual or unique than are new experiences. As a result, you are more likely to notice a machine that you have never observed before than a standard typewriter that is exactly like a thousand others you have previously seen. Similarly, you are more likely to notice the operations along an assembly line if this is the first time you have seen an assembly line. In the late 1960s and early 1970s, women and minorities in managerial positions were highly visible, if for no other reason than historically these positions were the province of white males. Today, these groups are more widely represented in the managerial ranks, so we are less likely to take notice that a manager is female, black, or Chicano.

Finally, *expectations* can distort your perceptions in that you will see what you expect to see. If you expect police officers to be authoritative, young people to be unambitious, personnel directors to "like people," or individuals holding public office to be "power hungry," you may perceive them this way regardless of their actual traits.

THE TARGET

Characteristics in the target that is being observed can affect what is perceived. Loud people are more likely to be noticed in a group than are quiet ones. So, too, are extremely attractive or unattractive individuals. Motion, sounds, size, and other attributes of a target shape the way we see it.

Because targets are not looked at in isolation, the relationship of a target to its background influences perception, as does our tendency to group close things and similar things together.

What we see is dependent on how we separate a figure from its general background. For instance, what you see as you read this sentence is black letters on a white page. You do not see funny-shaped patches of black and white because you recognize these shapes and organize the black shapes against the white background. Figure 3–5 dramatizes this effect. The figure on the left may at first look like a white vase. However, if white is taken as the background, we see two gray profiles. At first observation, the figure on the right appears to be some gray modular figures against a white background. Closer inspection will reveal the word "FLY" once the background is defined as gray.

Objects that are close to each other will tend to be perceived together rather than separately. As a result of physical or time proximity, we often put together objects or events that are unrelated. Employees in a particular department are seen as a group. If, in a department of four members, two suddenly resign, we tend to assume that their departures were related when, in fact, they may be totally unrelated. Timing may also imply dependence when, for example, a new sales manager is assigned to a territory and, soon after, sales in that territory skyrocket. The assignment of the new sales manager and the increase in sales may not be related—the increase may be due to an introduction of a new product line or to one of many other reasons—but there is a tendency to perceive the two occurrences as related.

Persons, objects, or events that are similar to each other also tend to be grouped together. The greater the similarity, the greater the probablility that we will tend to perceive them as a common group. Women, blacks, or any other group that has clearly distinguishable characteristics in terms of features or color will tend to be perceived as alike in other, unrelated characteristics as well.

THE SITUATION

The context in which we see objects or events is important. Elements in the surrounding environment influence our perceptions.

I may not notice a twenty-five-year-old female in an evening gown and heavy makeup at a nightclub on Saturday night. Yet that same woman, so attired for my Monday morning management class, would certainly catch my attention (and that of the rest of the class). Neither the perceiver nor the target changed between Saturday night and Monday morning, but the situation was different. Similarly, you are more likely to notice your employees goofing off if your boss

FIGURE 3–5
Figure-Ground Illustrations

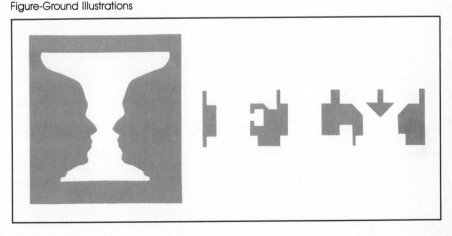

from head office happens to be in town. Again, the situation affects your perception. The time at which an object or event is seen can influence attention, as can location, light, heat, or any number of situational factors.

Perception and Individual Decision Making

Individuals in organizations make decisions. Top managers, for instance, determine their organization's goals, what products or services to offer, how best to organize corporate headquarters, or where to locate a new manufacturing plant. Middle- and lower-level managers determine production schedules, select new employees, and decide how pay raises are to be allocated. Of course, the making of decisions is not the sole province of managers. Nonmanagerial employees also make decisions that affect their jobs and the organizations they work for. The more obvious of these decisions might include whether to come to work or not on any given day, how much effort to put forward once at work, and whether to comply with a request made by the boss. Individual decision making, therefore, is an important part of organizational behavior. But how individuals in organizations *should* make decisions and how they *actually* make decisions can largely be explained by the presence of cognitive limitations and their impact on the decision maker's perceptions.

CLASSICAL VIEW OF DECISION MAKING
   The classical view of decision making (also called the optimizing or rational approach) owes its origin to the economists' notion of the optimizing individual. First, the decision maker clearly defines the problem. Second, all the viable alternatives that could possibly succeed in resolving the problem are identified. Third, the alternatives are critically evaluated. Finally, the optimum or best alternative is selected and implemented.[46]
   Sounds simple enough, right? Wrong! Inherent in these steps is a set of assumptions that make this process nearly impossible to follow. It assumes that the decision maker is fully objective and logical, that he or she has a singular goal that guides his or her choice, that all options are known, and that all preferences can be ranked in a preferential order that will be consistent over time.
   These assumptions obviously aren't very realistic. Problems are rarely clearly defined. It isn't feasible for a person to search for all possible alternatives. Individuals cannot always list their preferences in a rank order from most preferred to least preferred. Even when they can, the order tends to fluctuate over time. Recognition of these weaknesses in the classical view led to an alternative approach to describe how individuals make decisions.

BEHAVIORAL VIEW OF DECISION MAKING
   Individuals cannot optimize their decisions. How, then, do they make them? They *satisfice*; that is, they seek a solution that is satisfactory and sufficient.[47] They don't select the best alternative; they select one that is good enough. They respond to the complexity of their task by reducing problems to a level at which

they can readily be understood. That is, they create a simplified framework that extracts the essential features from problems without capturing all their complexity. Instead of developing an exhaustive list of alternatives, decision makers identify the more conspicuous choices. If a satisfactory choice isn't found in this list, then they look for additional alternatives in an incremental fashion. The first alternative that is acceptable ends the search.

Why do individuals satisfice rather than optimize when they make decisions? Because the information processing capabilities of human beings are limited. The classical view assumes the decision maker to be "all knowing and all seeing." Even if individuals had such knowledge, the classical view implies that decision makers could somehow assimilate and understand all this information. We know they can't. Human beings have a limited capacity for comprehending the inherent complexity in decision making. Cognitive limitations impair the decision maker's ability to define problems clearly, identify alternatives, and select the best choice among alternatives. So perception acts as a filter to simplify what would, otherwise, be a nearly impossible task.

Person Perception: Making Judgments About Others

Now we want to turn to the most relevant application of perception concepts to OB. This is the issue of person perception.

ATTRIBUTION THEORY

Our perceptions of people differ from our perceptions of inanimate objects like desks, machines, or buildings because we make inferences about the actions of people that we don't make about inanimate objects. Nonliving objects are subject to the laws of nature, but they have no beliefs, motives, or intentions. People do. The result is that when we observe people, we attempt to develop explanations of why they behave in certain ways. Our perception and judgment of a person's actions, therefore, will be significantly influenced by the assumptions we make about the person's internal state.

Attribution theory has been proposed to develop explanations of how we judge people differently depending on what meaning we attribute to a given behavior.[48] Basically the theory suggests that when we observe an individual's behavior, we attempt to determine whether it was internally or externally caused. That determination, however, depends on three factors: (1) distinctiveness, (2) consensus, and (3) consistency. First, let's clarify the differences between internal and external causation and then elaborate on each of the three determining factors.

Internally caused behaviors are those that are believed to be under the personal control of the individual. Externally caused behavior is seen as resulting from outside causes; that is, the person is seen as forced into the behavior by the situation. If one of your employees were late for work, you might attribute his lateness to his partying into the wee hours of the morning and then oversleeping. This would be an internal interpretation. But if you attributed his arriving late to a major automobile accident that tied up traffic on the road that your employee regularly uses, then you are making an external attribution. As observers, we have a tendency to assume that others' behavior is internally controlled, while we tend to exaggerate the degree to which our own behavior is externally determined. But this is a broad generalization. There still exists a considerable amount of deviation in attribution, depending on how we interpret the distinctiveness, consensus, and consistency of the actions.

Distinctiveness refers to whether an individual displays different behaviors in different situations. Is the employee who arrives late today also the source of complaints by co-workers for being a "goof-off"? What we want to know is if this behavior is unusual or not. If it is, the observer is likely to give the behavior an external attribution. If this action is not unique, it will probably be judged as internal.

If everyone who is faced with a similar situation responds in the same way, we can say the behavior shows *consensus*. Our late employee's behavior would meet this criterion if all employees who took the same route to work were also late. From an attribution perspective, if consensus is high you would be expected to give an external attribution to the employee's tardiness, whereas if other employees who took the same route made it into work on time, your conclusion as to causation would be internal.

Finally, an observer looks for *consistency* in a person's actions. Does the person respond the same way over time? Coming in ten minutes late for work is not perceived in the same way if for one employee it represents an unusual case (she hasn't been late for several months), while for another it is part of a routine pattern (she is regularly late two or three times a week). The more consistent the behavior, the more the observer is inclined to attribute it to internal causes.

This explains what you have seen operating for years. All similar behaviors are not perceived similarly. We look at actions and judge them within their situtional context. If you have a reputation as a good student yet blow one test in a course, the instructor is more likely to disregard the poor exam. Why? He or she will attribute the cause of this unusual performance to external conditions. It may not be your fault! But for the student who has a consistent record of being a poor performer, it is unlikely the teacher will ignore the low test score. Similarly, if everyone in class blew the test, the instructor may attribute the outcome to external causes (maybe the questions were poorly written, the room was too warm, students didn't have the prerequisites that he assumed) rather than to causes under the students' own control.

Attribution theory becomes extremely relevant when we consider how people judge others. We noted at the beginning of this section that when we observe people, in contrast to inanimate objects, we develop explanations for why they behave the way they do. These attributions, then, impact on how we interpret and judge the behavior we see. This will become clearer when we discuss how perceptions influence processes like the employment interview or performance appraisals.

Attribution theory is important because an individual's interpretations of actions will contribute to his or her behavioral responses to those actions and form a basis for the prediction of future events. We look for meaning in the behavior of others. Unfortunately, though, the reasons why people do what they do are very complex. Yet, because we still attempt to attribute causation, we end up basing our attribution on a simplification of what we see. Our ability to comprehend and store perceptual information is limited, so we reduce our observations into simple cause and effect sequences. As we shall demonstrate, this can bias how we judge others in organizations.

SPECIFIC APPLICATIONS IN ORGANIZATIONS

People in organizations are always judging each other. Managers must appraise their subordinates' performance. We evaluate how much effort our co-workers are putting into their jobs. When a new person joins a department, he or she is immediately "sized up" by the other department members. In many cases, these judgments have important consequences for the organization. Let us briefly look at a few of the more obvious applications.

A major input into who is hired or rejected is the *employment interview*. It's fair to say that few people are hired without an interview. But the evidence indicates that interviewers make perceptual judgments that are often inaccurate. Additionally, interrater agreement among interviewers is often poor; that is, different interviewers see different things in the same candidate and thus arrive at different conclusions about the applicant.

Interviewers generally draw early impressions that become very quickly entrenched. If negative information is exposed early in the interview, it tends to be more heavily weighted than if that same information were conveyed later.[49] Studies indicate that most interviewers' decisions change very little after the first four or five minutes of the interview. As a result, information elicited early in the interview carries greater weight than does information elicited later, and a "good applicant" is probably characterized more by the absence of unfavorable characteristics than by the presence of favorable characteristics.

Importantly, who you think is a good candidate and who I think is one may differ markedly. Because interviews usually have so little consistent structure and interviewers vary in terms of what they consider a good candidate, judgments of the same candidate can vary widely. If the employment interview is an important input into the hiring decision, and it usually is, you should recognize that perceptual factors influence who is hired and eventually the quality of an organization's labor force.

Another perceptual issue related to hiring new employees is the problem of unrealistic expectations. Every applicant acquires, during the selection process, a set of expectations about the organization and about the specific job the applicant is hoping to be offered. It is not unusual for these expectations to be excessively inflated as a result of receiving almost uniformly positive information. There is evidence that now demonstrates that these inaccurate perceptions lead to premature resignations but that *realistic job previews* can lead to lower turnover rates.[50] A realistic job preview includes both unfavorable and favorable information about the job. Research leads us to conclude that applicants who have been given a realistic job preview hold lower and more realistic expectations about the job they'll be doing and are better prepared for coping with the job and its frustrating elements. The result is fewer unexpected resignations by new employees.

Although the impact of *performance evaluations* on behavior will be discussed fully in Chapter 13, it should be pointed out here that an employee's performance appraisal is very much dependent on the perceptual process. An employee's future is closely tied to his or her appraisal—promotions, pay raises, and continuation of employment are among the most obvious outcomes. The performance appraisal represents an assessment of an employee's work. While this can be objective (e.g., a salesperson is appraised on how many dollars of sales she generates in her territory), most jobs are evaluated in subjective terms. Subjective measures are easier to implement, they provide managers with greater discretion, and many jobs do not readily lend themselves to objective measures. Subjective measures are, by definition, judgmental. The evaluator forms a general impression of an employee's work. To the degree that managers use subjective measures in appraising employees, what the evaluator perceives to be "good" or "bad" employee characteristics/behaviors will significantly influence the appraisal outcome.

An individual's future in an organization is usually not dependent on performance alone. In many organizations, the level of an employee's *effort* is given high importance. Just as teachers frequently consider how hard you try in a course as well as how you perform on examinations, so often do managers. And assessment of an individual's effort is a subjective judgment susceptible to perceptual distortions and bias. If it is true, as some claim, that "more workers are fired for poor attitudes and lack of discipline than for lack of ability,"[51] then appraisal of an employee's effort may be a primary influence on his or her future in the organization.

Another important judgment that managers make about employees is whether they are loyal to the organization. Few organizations appreciate employees, especially those in the managerial ranks, disparaging the firm. Further, in some organizations, if the word gets around that an employee is looking at other employment opportunities outside the firm, that employee may be labeled as disloyal, cutting off all future advancement opportunities. The issue is not whether organizations are right in demanding loyalty but that many do and that assessment of an employee's *loyalty* or commitment is highly judgmental. What is perceived as loyalty by one decision maker may be seen as excessive conformity by another. An employee who questions a top management decision may be seen as disloyal by some, yet caring and concerned by others. When evaluating a person's attitude, which loyalty assessment is, we must recognize that we are again involved with person perception.

FREQUENTLY USED SHORTCUTS IN JUDGING OTHERS

One last topic we should discuss is the fact that we use a number of shortcuts when we judge others. Perceiving and interpreting what others do is burdensome. As a result, individuals develop techniques for making the task more manageable. These techniques are frequently valuable—they allow us to make accurate perceptions rapidly and provide valid data for making predictions. However, they are not foolproof. They can and do get us into trouble. An understanding of these shortcuts can be helpful toward recognizing when they can result in significant distortions.

Any characteristic that makes a person, object, or event stand out will increase the probability that it will be perceived. Why? Because it is impossible for us to assimilate everything we see—only certain stimuli can be taken in. This explains why, as we noted earlier, you're more likely to notice cars like your own or why some people may be reprimanded by their boss for doing something that when done by another employee goes unnoticed. Since we can't observe everything going on about us, we engage in *selective perception*. A classic example shows how vested interests can significantly influence what problems we see.

Dearborn and Simon[52] performed a perceptual study in which twenty-three business executives read a comprehensive case describing the organization and activities of a steel company. Six of the twenty-three executives were in the sales function, five in production, four in accounting, and eight in miscellaneous functions. Each manager was asked to write down the most important problem he found in the case. Eighty-three percent of the sales executives rated sales important, while only 29 percent of the others did so. This, along with other results of the study, led the researchers to conclude that the participants perceived aspects in a situation that related specifically to the activities and goals of the unit to which they were attached. A group's perception of organizational activities is selectively altered to align with the vested interest they represent. In other words, where the stimuli are ambiguous, as in the steel company case, perception tends to be influenced more by an individual's base of interpretation (i.e., attitudes, interests, and background) than by the stimulus itself.

But how does selectivity work as a shortcut in judging other people? Simply, since we cannot assimilate all that we observe, we take in bits and pieces. But these bits and pieces are not chosen randomly; rather, they are selectively chosen depending on the interests, background, experience, and attitudes of the observer. Selective perception allows us to "speed read" others, but not without the risk of drawing an inaccurate picture. Because we see what we want to see, we can draw unwarranted conclusions from an ambiguous situation. If there is a rumor going around the office that your company's sales are down and that large layoffs may be coming, a routine visit by a senior executive from headquarters might be interpreted as the first step in management's identification of people to be fired, when in reality such an action may be the farthest thing from the mind of the senior executive.

It is easy to judge others if we assume they are similar to us. Sometimes called the "like me" effect, *assumed similarity* means, for instance, that if you want challenge and responsibility in your job, you assume that others want the same. This assumption clouds judgments made of others.

If a person evaluates another's personality as more similar to himself than the other actually is, he distorts the other's personality to make it more like his own. When this shortcut is extensively used by a person, his observations and appraisals of others will correspond more to his own personality (as he sees it) than to the other's personality (as the other sees it).

What this means in practice is that among people who assume similarity, their perception of others is influenced more by what the observer is like than by what the person being observed is like. When observing others who actually are like them, these observers are quite accurate—not because they are more perceptive but only because they always judge people as being similar to themselves, so when they finally find one who is, they are naturally correct.

When we judge someone on the basis of our perception of the group to which he or she belongs, we are using the shortcut called *stereotyping*. William Faulkner engaged in stereotyping in his reported conversation with Ernest Hemingway, when he said, "The rich are different from you and me." Hemingway's reply, "Yes, they have more money," indicated that other than the required difference (you need money to be rich), he refused to stereotype or generalize characteristics about people based on their wealth.

Generalizations, of course, are not without their advantages. It makes assimilating easier since it permits us to maintain consistency. It is less difficult to deal with an unmanageable number of stimuli if we use stereotypes. But the problem occurs when we inaccurately stereotype. All accountants are *not* quiet and introspective in the same way that all salespeople are *not* aggressive and outgoing.

In an organizational context, we frequently hear comments that represent stereotyped representation of certain groups: "Married people are more stable employees"; "Managers don't give a damn about their people, only getting the work out"; or "Union people expect something for nothing." Clearly, these phrases represent stereotypes, but if people expect these perceptions, that is what they will see, whether it represents reality or not.

Obviously, one of the problems of stereotypes is that they are so widespread, in spite of the fact that they may not contain a shred of truth, or may be irrelevant. Their being widespread may only mean that many people are making the same, inaccurate perception based on a false premise about a group. The movement of women into managerial positions has been a major source of perceptual distortion. Studies indicate that male and female managers alike hold negative stereotypes about the ability of women to manage effectively.[53] Successful managers—whether male or female—tend to be perceived as having personality traits and skills associated with men. But, unfortunately, the same aggressive behavior that is judged positively when exhibited by a male manager is often appraised negatively when exhibited by a female manager. As one female executive confided to the author, "When I'm forceful and direct, I'm accused of being too aggressive. When I'm thoughtful or considerate, I'm told that I'm too weak. No matter what I do, I can't win!" Such negative stereotypes create conflicts for women in, and aspiring to, managerial positions. And, of course, they suboptimize the organization's effectiveness when they prevent the selection or promotion of the most qualified applicant.

When we draw a general impression about an individual based on a single characteristic such as intelligence, sociability, or appearance, a *halo effect* is operating. This phenomenon frequently occurs when students appraise their classroom instructor. Students may isolate a single trait such as enthusiasm and allow their entire evaluation to be tainted by how they judge the instructor on this one trait. Thus, an instructor may be quiet, assured, knowledgeable, and highly qualified, but if his style lacks zeal, he will be rated lower on a number of other characteristics.

The reality of the halo effect was confirmed in a classic study where subjects were given a list of traits like intelligent, skillful, practical, industrious, determined, and warm and asked to evaluate the person to whom these traits applied.[54] Based on these traits, the person was judged to be wise, humorous, popular, and imaginative. When the same list was modified to substitute cold for warm in the trait list, a completely different set of perceptions was obtained. Clearly, the subjects were allowing a single trait to influence their overall impression of the person being judged.

The propensity for the halo effect to operate is not random. Research suggests that it is likely to be most extreme when the traits to be perceived are ambiguous or unclear in behavioral terms, when the traits have moral overtones, and when the perceiver is judging traits with which he or she has had limited experience.[55]

In organizations, the halo effect is important in understanding an individual's behavior, particularly when judgment and evaluation must be made. It is not unusual for the halo effect to occur in selection interviews or at performance appraisal time. A sloppily dressed candidate for a marketing research position may be perceived by an interviewer as an irresponsible person with an unprofessional attitude and marginal abilities, when in fact the candidate may be highly responsible, professional, and competent. What has happened is that a single trait—appearance—has overridden other characteristics in the interviewer's general perception about the individual. The halo effect can have a similarly distorting impact on performance evaluation, causing the full appraisal to be biased by a single trait.

LEARNING

The last topic we will introduce in this chapter is learning. It is included for the obvious reason that almost all complex behavior is learned. If we want to explain and predict behavior, we need to understand how people learn.

A Definition of Learning

What is learning? A psychologist's definition is considerably broader than the layperson's view that "it's what we did when we went to school." In actuality, each of us is continuously going "to school." Learning is going on all the time. A generally accepted definition of learning is, therefore, *any relatively permanent change in behavior that occurs as a result of experience.* Ironically, we can say that changes in behavior indicate that learning has taken place and that learning is a change in behavior.

Obviously, the foregoing definition suggests that we shall never see some-one "learning." We can see changes, but not the learning itself. The concept is theoretical and hence not directly observable:

> You have seen people in the process of learning, you have seen people who behave in a particular way as a result of learning and some of you (in fact, I guess the majority of you) have "learned" at some time in your life. In other words, we infer that learning has taken place if an individual behaves, reacts, responds as a result of experience in a manner different from the way he formerly behaved.[56]

Our definition has several components that deserve clarification. First, learning involves change. This may be good or bad from an organizational point of view. People can learn unfavorable behaviors—to hold prejudices or to restrict their output, for example—as well as favorable behaviors. Second, the change must be relatively permanent. Temporary changes may be only reflexive and fail to represent any learning. Therefore, this requirement rules out behavioral changes caused by fatigue or temporary adaptations. Third, our definition is concerned with behavior. Learning takes place where there is a change in actions. A change in an individual's thought process or attitudes, if accompanied by no change in behavior, would not be learning. Finally, some form of experience is necessary for learning. This may be acquired directly through observation or prac-tice. Or it may result from indirect experiences, such as that acquired through reading. The crucial test still remains: Does this experience result in a relatively permanent change in behavior? If the answer is "Yes," we can say that learning has taken place.

Theories of Learning

How do we learn? Three theories have been offered to explain the process by which we acquire patterns of behavior. These are classical conditioning, operant conditioning, and social learning.

CLASSICAL CONDITIONING

Classical conditioning grew out of experiments to teach dogs to salivate in response to the ringing of a bell, conducted at the turn of the century by a Russian physiologist, Ivan Pavlov.[57]

A simple surgical procedure allowed Pavlov to measure accurately the amount of saliva secreted by a dog. When Pavlov presented the dog with a piece of meat, the dog exhibited a noticeable increase in salivation. When Pavlov with-held the presentation of meat and merely rang a bell, the dog had no salivation. Then, Pavlov proceeded to link the meat and the ringing of the bell. After re-peatedly hearing the bell before getting the food, the dog began to salivate as soon as the bell rang. After awhile, the dog would salivate merely at the sound of the bell, even if no food was offered. In effect, the dog had learned to respond—that is, to salivate—to the bell. Let's review this experiment to introduce the key con-cepts in classical conditioning.

The meat was an *unconditioned stimulus;* it invariably caused the dog to react in a specific way. The reaction that took place whenever the unconditioned stimulus occurred was called the *unconditioned response* (or the noticeable increase in salivation, in this case). The bell was an artificial stimulus, or what we call the *conditioned stimulus.* While it was originally neutral, when the bell was paired with the meat (an unconditioned stimulus), it eventually produced a response when presented alone. The last key concept is the *conditioned response.* This describes the behavior of the dog salivating in reaction to the bell alone.

Using these concepts, we can summarize classical conditioning. Essentially, learning a conditioned response involves building up an association between a conditioned stimulus and an unconditioned stimulus. Using the paired stimuli, one compelling and the other one neutral, the neutral one becomes a conditioned stimulus and, hence, takes on the properties of the unconditioned stimulus.

Classical conditioning can be used to explain why Christmas carols often bring back pleasant memories of childhood—the songs being associated with the festive Christmas spirit and initiating fond memories and feelings of euphoria. In an organizational setting, we can also see classical conditioning operating. For example, at one manufacturing plant, every time the top executives from the head office would make a visit, the plant management would clean up the administrative offices and wash the windows. This went on for years. Eventually, employees would turn on their best behavior and look prim and proper whenever the windows were cleaned—even in those occasional instances when the cleaning was not paired with the visit from the top brass. People had learned to associate the cleaning of the windows with the visit from the head office.

Classical conditioning is passive. Something happens and we react in a specific way. It is elicited in response to a specific, identifiable event. As such it can explain simple reflexive behaviors. But most behavior—particularly the complex behavior of individuals in organizations—is emitted rather than elicited. It is voluntary rather than reflexive. For example, employees choose to arrive at work on time, ask their boss for help with problems, or "goof off" when no one is watching. The learning of these behaviors is better understood by looking at operant conditioning.

OPERANT CONDITIONING

Operant conditioning argues that behavior is a function of its consequences. People learn to behave so they get something they want or avoid something they don't want. Operant behavior means voluntary or learned behavior in contrast to reflexive or unlearned behavior. The tendency to repeat such behavior is influenced as a result of the reinforcement or lack of reinforcement brought about by the consequences of the behavior. Reinforcement, therefore, strengthens a behavior and increases the likelihood that it will be repeated.

What Pavlov did for classical conditioning, noted Harvard psychologist B. F. Skinner has done for operant conditioning.[58] Building on earlier work in the field, Skinner's research has extensively expanded our knowledge of operant conditioning. Even his staunchest critics, who represent a sizable group, admit that his operant concepts work.

Behavior is assumed to be determined from without—that is, learned—rather than from within (reflexive or unlearned). Skinner argues that by creating pleasing consequences to follow specific forms of behavior, the frequency of that behavior will increase. People will most likely engage in desired behaviors if they are positively reinforced for doing so. Rewards, for example, are most effective if they immediately follow the desired response. Additionally, behavior that is not rewarded, or is punished, is less likely to be repeated.

You see illustrations of operant conditioning everywhere. For example, any situation in which it is either explicitly stated or implicitly suggested that reinforcements are contingent on some action on your part involves the use of operant learning. Your instructor says that if you want a high grade in the course you must supply correct answers on the test. A commissioned salesperson wanting to earn a sizable income finds that it is contingent on generating high sales in her territory. Of course, the linkage can also work to teach the individual to engage in behaviors that work against the best interests of the organization. Assume your boss tells you that if you will work overtime during the next three-week busy season, you will be compensated for it at the next performance appraisal. However, when performance appraisal time comes you find that you are given no positive reinforcement for your overtime work. The next time your boss asks you to work overtime, what will you do? You will probably decline! Your behavior can be explained by operant conditioning: If a behavior fails to be positively reinforced, the probability that the behavior will be repeated declines.

SOCIAL LEARNING

Individuals can also learn by observing what happens to other people and just by being told about something, as well as by direct experiences. So, for example, much of what we have learned comes from watching models—parents, teachers, peers, motion picture and television performers, bosses, and so forth. This view that we can learn both through observation and direct experience has been called social learning theory.[59]

While social learning theory is an extension of operant conditioning, that is, it assumes that behavior is a function of consequences, it also acknowledges the existence of observational learning and the importance of perception in learning. People respond to how they perceive and define consequences, not to the objective consequences themselves.

The influence of models is central to the social learning viewpoint. Four processes have been found to determine the influence that a model will have on an individual. As we'll show later in this chapter, the inclusion of the following processes when management sets up employee training programs will significantly improve the likelihood that the programs will be successful:

1. *Attentional processes.* People only learn from a model when they recognize and pay attention to its critical features. We tend to be most influenced by models that are attractive, repeatedly available, and we think are important, or we see as similar to us.

2. *Retention processes.* A model's influence will depend on how well the individual remembers the model's action, even after the model is no longer readily available.

3. *Motor reproduction processes.* After a person has seen a new behavior by observing the model, the watching must be converted to doing. This process then demonstrates that the individual can perform the modeled activities.

4. *Reinforcement processes.* Individuals will be motivated to exhibit the modeled behavior if positive incentives or rewards are provided. Behaviors that are reinforced will be given more attention, learned better, and performed more often.

Shaping: A Managerial Tool

Because learning takes place on the job as well as prior to it, managers will be concerned with how they can teach employees to behave in ways that most benefit the organization. When we attempt to mold individuals by guiding their learning in graduated steps, we are shaping behavior.

Consider the situation in which an employee's behavior is significantly different from that sought by management. If management only reinforced the individual when he or she showed desirable responses, there might be very little reinforcement taking place. In such a case, shaping offers a logical approach toward achieving the desired behavior.

We *shape* behavior by systematically reinforcing each successive step that moves the individual closer to the desired response. If an employee who has been chronically a half-hour late for work comes in only 20 minutes late, we can reinforce this improvement. Reinforcement would increase as responses more closely approximate the desired behavior.

METHODS OF SHAPING BEHAVIOR

There are four ways in which to shape behavior: through positive reinforcement, negative reinforcement, punishment, or extinction. When a response is followed with something pleasant, it is called *positive reinforcement*. This would describe, for instance, the boss who praises an employee for a job well done. When a response is followed by the termination or withdrawal of something unpleasant, it is called *negative reinforcement*. If your college instructor asks a question and you don't know the answer, looking through your lecture notes is likely to preclude your being called on. This is a negative reinforcement because you have learned that looking busily through your notes terminates being called on by the instructor. *Punishment* is causing an unpleasant condition in an attempt to eliminate an undesirable behavior. An employee who receives a two-day suspension from work, without pay, for showing up drunk is an example of punishment. Eliminating any reinforcement that is maintaining an unwanted behavior is called *extinction*. When the behavior is not reinforced, it tends to gradually be extinguished. College instructors who wish to discourage students from asking questions in class can eliminate this behavior in their students by ignoring those who raise their hands to ask questions. Hand-raising will become extinct when it is invariably met with an absence of reinforcement.

Both positive and negative reinforcement result in learning. They strengthen a desired response and increase the probability of repetition. In the preceding illustrations, praise strengthens and increases the behavior of doing a good job because praise is desired. The behavior of "looking busy" is similarly strengthened and increased by its terminating the undesirable consequence of being called on by the teacher. Both punishment and extinction, however, weaken behavior and tend to decrease its subsequent frequency.

Reinforcement, whether it is positive or negative, has an impressive record as a shaping tool. Our interest, therefore, is in reinforcement rather than punishment or extinction. A review of research findings on the impact of reinforcement upon behavior in organizations concluded that

1. Some type of reinforcement is necessary to produce a change in behavior.
2. Some types of rewards are more effective for use in organizations than others.
3. The speed with which learning takes place and the lasting of its effects will be determined by the timing of reinforcement.[60]

Point 3 is extremely important and deserves considerable elaboration.

SCHEDULES OF REINFORCEMENT

The two major types of reinforcement schedules are *continuous* and *intermittent*. A continuous schedule reinforces the desired behavior each and every time it is demonstrated. For example, in the case of someone who has historically had trouble being at work on time, every time he is *not* tardy his manager might compliment him on his desirable behavior. In an intermittent schedule, on the other hand, not every instance of the desirable behavior is reinforced, but reinforcement is given often enough to make the behavior worth repeating. This latter schedule can be compared to the workings of a gambling slot machine, which people will continue to play even when they know that it is adjusted to give a considerable return to the gambling house. The intermittent payoffs occur just often enough to reinforce the behavior of slipping in quarters and pulling the handle. Evidence indicates that the intermittent or varied form of reinforcement tends to promote more resistance to extinction than does the continuous form.[61]

An intermittent reinforcement can be of a ratio or interval type. Ratio schedules depend upon how many responses the subject makes. The individual is reinforced after giving a certain number of specific types of behavior. Interval schedules depend upon how much time has passed since the last reinforcement. With interval schedules, the individual is reinforced on the first appropriate behavior after a particular time has elapsed. A reinforcement can also be classified as fixed or variable. Intermittent techniques for administering rewards can, therefore, be placed into four categories, as shown in Figure 3–6.

In a *fixed-ratio* schedule, after a fixed or constant number of responses are given, a reward is initiated. For example, a piece-rate incentive plan is a fixed-ratio schedule—the employee receives a reward based on the number of work pieces generated. If the piece rate for a zipper installer in a dressmaking factory

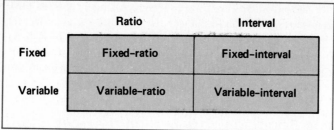

	Ratio	Interval
Fixed	Fixed-ratio	Fixed-interval
Variable	Variable-ratio	Variable-interval

FIGURE 3–6
Schedules of Reinforcement

is $5.00 a dozen, the reinforcement (money in this case) is fixed to the number of zippers sewn into garments. After every dozen is sewn in, the installer has earned another $5.00.

When rewards are spaced at uniform time intervals, the reinforcement schedule is of the *fixed-interval* type. The critical variable is time, and it is held constant. This is the predominant schedule for almost all salaried workers in North America. When you get your paycheck on a weekly, semi-monthly, monthly, or other predetermined time basis, you are rewarded on a fixed-interval reinforcement schedule.

When the reward varies relative to the behavior of the individual, he or she is said to be reinforced on a *variable-ratio* schedule. Salespeople on commission represent examples of individuals on such a reinforcement schedule. On some occasions, they may make a sale after only two calls on potential customers. On other ocasions, they might need to make twenty or more calls to secure a sale. The reward, then, is variable in relation to the number of sucessful calls the salesperson makes.

If rewards are distributed in time so that reinforcements are unpredictable, the schedule is of the *variable-interval* type. When an instructor advises her class there will be a number of pop quizzes given during the term (the exact number of which is unknown to the students), and the quizzes will account for 20 percent of the term grade, she is using such a variable-interval schedule. Similarly, a series of randomly timed unannounced visits to a company office by the corporate audit staff is an example of a variable-interval schedule.

REINFORCEMENT SCHEDULES AND BEHAVIOR

Continuous reinforcement schedules can lead to early satiation, and, under this schedule, behavior tends to weaken rapidly when reinforcers are withheld. However, continuous reinforcers are appropriate for newly emitted, unstable, or low-frequency responses. In contrast, intermittent reinforcers preclude early satiation because they don't follow every response. They are appropriate for stable or high-frequency responses.

In general, variable schedules tend to lead to higher performance than fixed schedules. For example, as noted previously, most employees in organizations are paid on fixed-interval schedules. But such a schedule does not clearly link performance and rewards. The reward is given for time spent on the job rather than for a specific response (performance). In contrast, variable-interval schedules generate high rates of response and more stable and consistent behavior because of a high correlation between performance and reward and because of the uncertainty involved—the employee tends to be more alert since there is a surprise factor.

Some Specific Organizational Applications

We have alluded to a number of situations where learning theory could be helpful to managers. In this section, we will briefly look at three specific applications: reducing absenteeism through use of lotteries, substituting well pay for sick pay, and developing effective employee training programs.

USING LOTTERIES TO REDUCE ABSENTEEISM

Management can design programs to reduce absenteeism by utilizing learning theory. For example, one firm created a poker game lottery for part of its organization whereby employees who came to work on time got to choose a card from a deck of playing cards.[62] At the end of the five-day week, the employee whose five cards made up the highest poker hand won $20. Obviously, anyone who was late or absent didn't get a card and couldn't participate in that week's lottery. Eight departments were chosen to participate in the lottery experiment, and a $20 prize was given to the best poker hand in each department. Several other sections within the organization were used as control groups—their attendance was monitored, but no lottery was implemented.

The poker game lottery followed a variable-ratio schedule. Prompt attendance increased an employee's probability of winning, yet just because an employee obtained five cards was no assurance that he or she would be reinforced by winning the $20. Consistent with the research on reinforcement schedules, this lottery resulted in lower absence rates. Over a four-month period, attendance among employees who participated in the lottery improved by 18 percent, while the attendance rate for employees in the control group actually decreased a little.

WELL PAY VS. SICK PAY

Most organizations provide their salaried employees with paid sick leave as part of the employee's fringe benefit program. But ironically, organizations with paid sick leave programs experience almost twice the absenteeism of organizations without such a program.[63] The reality is that sick leave reinforces the wrong behavior—absence from work. Organizations should have programs that encourage employees to be on the job by discouraging unnecessary absences. When an employee receives ten paid sick days a year, it is the unusual employee who doesn't make sure that all his or her days are consumed, regardless of whether he or she is sick or not. This suggests that organizations should reward attendance, not absence. As a case in point, one Midwest organization implemented a well-pay program that paid a bonus to employees who had no absence for any given four-week period and then only paid for sick leave after the first eight hours of absence.[64] Evaluation of the well-program found that it produced increased savings to the organization, reduced absenteeism, increased productivity, and improved employee satisfaction.

DEVELOPING TRAINING PROGRAMS

Most large organizations are actively involved with employee training. Can these organizations draw from our discussion of learning in order to improve the effectiveness of their training programs? The answer is a resounding "Yes!"

Social learning theory offers such a guide. It tells us that training should provide a model; it needs to grab the trainee's attention; provide motivational properties; help the trainee to file away what he or she has learned for later use; provide opportunities to practice new behaviors; offer positive rewards for accomplishments; and if the training has taken place off the job, allow the trainee some opportunity to transfer what he or she has learned to the job.

IMPLICATIONS FOR PERFORMANCE AND SATISFACTION

Let's try to summarize what we've found in terms of how biographical characteristics, personality, perception, and learning impact on an employee's performance and satisfaction.

Biographical Characteristics

Biographical characteristics enjoy the advantage of being readily available to management. For the most part, they represent data that are contained in almost every employee's personnel file.

A review of the research allows some noteworthy conclusions. First, it is difficult, if not impossible, to make accurate predictions about an employee's productivity based on biographical data. However, absence rates, turnover, and job satisfaction *are* influenced by some of these characteristics.

The strongest evidence stacks up behind an employee's age and seniority in the organization. Older workers are less likely to resign and tend to be more satisfied with their jobs. Similarly, tenure is negatively related to both absence and turnover; that is, employees with longer service have better attendance records and are less likely to quit.

Investigation of two other variables—sex and marital status—also produced significant findings. Women demonstrate poorer attendance records than do men. However, this statistic is undoubtedly dated. It tends to reflect the historical role of women in our culture. As more women work and pursue long-term careers in organizations, any difference between males and females in terms of absenteeism will undoubtedly disappear. Finally, the evidence indicates that married employees show greater stability and higher satisfaction than do their single counterparts.

Personality

A review of the personality literature offers suggestions on the characteristics that will make for effective job performance. As such, it can improve hiring, transfer, and promotion decisions. Because personality characteristics create the parameters for people's behavior, they give us a framework for predicting behavior. For example, individuals who are shy, introverted, and uncomfortable in social situations would probably be ill-suited as salespeople. Individuals who are submissive and conforming might not be effective as advertising ''idea'' people.

Can we predict which people will perform satisfactorily in sales, research, or assembly-line work based on their personality characteristics? The answer is a qualified ''Yes.'' We can look at certain characteristics that tend to be related to job success, test for these traits, and use these data to make selection more effective. A person who accepts rules, conformity, and dependence and rates high on authoritarianism is likely to feel more comfortable in a structured assembly-line job, as an admittance clerk in a hospital, or as an administrator in a large public agency than as a researcher or an employee whose job requires a high degree of creativity. This is exactly why personality tests are used in screening job candidates—to avoid potential mismatches!

Perception

Individuals behave in a given way based not on the way their external environment actually is but, rather, on what they see or believe it to be. Because individuals act on their interpretations of reality rather than reality itself, it is clear that perception must be a critical determinant of our dependent variables.

An organization may spend millions of dollars to create a pleasant work environment for its employees. However, in spite of these expenditures, if an employee believes that her job is lousy, she will behave accordingly. It is her perception of a situation that becomes the basis on which she behaves. The employee who perceives her supervisor as a hurdle-reducer and an aid to help her do a better job and the employee who sees the same supervisor as ''big brother, closely monitoring every motion, to ensure that I keep working'' will differ in their behavioral responses to their supervisor. The difference has nothing to do with the reality of the supervisor's role; the difference in behavior is due to different perceptions.

The evidence suggests that what individuals *perceive* from their work situation will influence their productivity more than will the situation itself. Whether a job is actually interesting or challenging is irrelevant. Whether a manager successfully plans and organizes the work of his subordinates and actually helps them to structure their work more efficiently and effectively is far less important than how his subordinates perceive his efforts. Similarly, issues like fair pay for work performed, the validity of performance appraisals, and the adequacy of the work conditions are not judged by employees in a way that assures common perceptions, nor can we be assured that individuals will interpret conditions about their jobs in a favorable light. Therefore, to be able to influence productivity, it is necessary to assesss how workers perceive their jobs.

It is unacceptable for a sales manager to argue that "John should be selling far more of our products in his territory. His territory is a gold mine. It has unlimited potential." When John is interviewed, we find that he believes he is getting as much as possible out of his territory. Whether the salesman is right or wrong is irrelevant. The fact is that he *perceives his view to be right*. If the manager hopes to improve sales in John's territory, he must first succeed in changing John's perceptions.

As with productivity, absenteeism, turnover, and job satisfaction are reactions to the individual's perceptions. Dissatisfaction with work conditions or the belief that there is a lack of promotion opportunities in the organization are judgments based on attempts to make some meaning out of one's job. Since there can be no such thing as a "bad job," only the perception that the job is bad, managers must spend time to understand how each individual interprets reality and, where there is a significant difference between what is seen and what exists, try to eliminate the distortions. Failure to deal with the differences when individuals perceive the job in negative terms will result in increased absenteeism and turnover and lower job satisfaction.

Learning

Any observable change in behavior is, by definition, prima facie evidence that learning has taken place. What we want to do, of course, is ascertain if learning concepts provide us with any insights that would allow us to explain and predict behavior. The evidence suggests that conditioning and shaping offer important tools for explaining levels of productivity, absenteeism rates, lateness, and the quality of employees' work. These concepts also can be valuable for giving insight into how undesirable work behaviors can be modified.

Positive reinforcement is a powerful tool for modifying behavior. By identifying and rewarding performance-related behaviors, management increases the likelihood that they will be repeated.

Our knowledge about learning further suggests that reinforcement is a more effective tool than punishment. Punished behavior tends to be only temporarily suppressed rather than permanently changed, and the recipients of punishment tend to become resentful of the punisher. Although punishment eliminates undesired behavior more quickly than negative reinforcement does, its effect is only temporary and it may later produce unpleasant side effects such as lower morale and higher absenteeism or turnover. Managers, therefore, are advised to use reinforcement rather than punishment.

POINT

TRAINING CAN IMPROVE PERCEPTUAL ACCURACY

PROSPER is a self-guided training program, sponsored by the Xerox Corporation, that seeks to stimulate awareness of racial issues. It is intended to increase the awareness of white managers to their racial biases and how those beliefs affect their on-the-job relationships with blacks. Further, the program helps white managers to become sensitive to the racial stereotypes in American institutions. PROSPER assumes that as managers become more aware of key factors that generate racial bias, they will be better able to understand their own feelings and improve their effectiveness in dealing with minorities, particularly blacks. The following describes the PROSPER program and its impact on the perceptions of white managers.

First, the domain and dimensions of the relevant attitudes had to be determined. Several large surveys were conducted, factor analyzed, and subsequently modified in a series of trials and refactorings, finally yielding five factors of importance: (1) the system is biased, (2) implementation of affirmative action policies is limited, (3) black employees are competent, (4) black employees need real inclusion, and (5) black employees need to build self-esteem. It was felt that these five factors would adequately profile a trainee's awareness and could serve as building blocks for the scenario and role play to follow.

The self-guided program was then constructed around the five awareness factors. The program developed was a 4-hour learning experience to increase managers' awareness of racially discriminating beliefs that reduce the effective utilization of black employees. Successive pilot programs were run to refine the learning experience, to minimize cost, and to maximize standardization of the change approach. The entire PROSPER program was then reduced to a single, simple work booklet.

Participants were tested to create a point of reference, followed by the PROSPER program—inbasket memos, role plays, and messages dealing with the five factors. Participants then addressed the awareness questionnaire to see what changes, if any, had occurred. The factors provided a meaningful structure for managers to talk about their understanding and feeling about black employees.

Results with over two thousand participants show that there was a significant increase in awareness on all five factors from beginning to end of PROSPER. Merely showing up at the start of the PROSPER program was associated with a more aware position on the five factors in contrast to a group that had not yet been enrolled. Awareness was greater still at the end of PROSPER. Three to five months afterward, awareness did decline in a sample selected for follow-up, but only about half-way back to where the larger sample had been at the beginning of the administration of PROSPER.

Adapted from B. M. Bass, W. F. Cascio, J. W. McPherson, and H. Tragash, ''PROSPER—Training and Research for Increasing Awareness of Affirmative Action in Race Relations,'' Academy of Management Journal, *September 1976, pp. 353–69.*

COUNTERPOINT

TRAINING DOESN'T ALWAYS IMPROVE PERCEPTUAL ACCURACY

Training doesn't always improve perceptual accuracy as the following study affirms.

This study had two objectives. First, it sought to investigate the effects of a training program upon interpersonal perception. Second, it sought to test a hypothesis for the relationship between accuracy and one component of the interpersonal perception situation—the amount of variability in the subjects' estimations: If the subject increases the variability of his or her judgments from one time to another and his or her ability to make accurate judgments does not increase correspondingly, then the subject will make greater errors the second time than the first. It also follows that whenever a judgmental task is very difficult or the objects are very low in ability, subjects with little variability in their estimations will make small errors, and subjects with high variability will make large errors. Stated otherwise, accuracy and variability will be negatively correlated when the task is difficult or the subject is very inaccurate.

To accomplish these purposes, interpersonal perception measures were administered at the beginning, during, and after the senior year to a class of medical students whose members were divided into experimental and control groups. The experimental group was instructed in physician-patient relationships and was provided with the opportunity to establish such relationships through more prolonged contact with patients than was possible for the control group. It was expected (1) that the students in the experimental group would become more accurate in interpersonal perception than students in the control group and (2) that variability in estimation would be negatively related to accuracy of judgment.

Contrary to expectation, the group that received more training in interpersonal relations (the experimental group) did not improve in accuracy of interpersonal perception more than did the group without such special training (control group). In fact, the results support the opposite conclusion: namely, that, as a result of their special training, the experimental group became less accurate than did the control group.

The results indicate that training programs devoted to increasing accuracy of interpersonal perception (as in medical education and in the training of teachers, clinical psychologists, and similar specialists) run the risk of decreasing accuracy when they increase the trainees' responsiveness to individual differences. Since very little is known about how to train people to make more accurate judgments about others, training programs frequently utilize a procedure of "exposure" and little else. The belief that placing the trainee in a position to observe others and to make judgments will produce desirable results is challenged by these findings. Such experience may lead the trainee to differentiate among people far beyond his or her capacity to do so accurately. In the absence of dependable measures of his or her accuracy, the trainee lacks knowledge of his or her errors and may continue inappropriate overdifferentiation long after the training has ceased.

Adapted from W. J. Crow, "The Effect of Training upon Accuracy and Variability in Interpersonal Perception," Journal of Abnormal and Social Psychology, Vol. 55, September 1957, pp. 355–59. Copyright © by the American Psychological Association. Reprinted by permission.

FOR DISCUSSION

1. Which biographical characteristics best predict *absenteeism? Turnover? Satisfaction?*

2. How does *heredity* influence personality? Environment? The situation?

3. What constrains the ability of personality traits to predict behavior?

4. What behavioral predictions might you make if you knew that an employee had (a) an external locus of control? (b) a high *nAch?* (c) a low Mach score?

5. "The type of job an employee does moderates the relationship between personality and job productivity." Do you agree or disagree with this statement? Discuss.

6. One day your boss comes in and he's nervous, edgy, and argumentative. The next day he is calm and relaxed. Does this suggest that personality traits aren't consistent from day to day?

7. "Everyone is a trait theorist. If one really believed that situations determined behavior, then there would be no reason to test or interview prospective employees for jobs—it would only be necessary to structure the situation properly." Do you agree or disagree? Discuss.

8. "The fact that you and I agree on what we see suggests that we have similar backgrounds and experiences." Do you agree or disagree? Discuss.

9. How might perceptual factors be involved when an employee receives a poor performance appraisal?

10. Give some positive results from using shortcuts when judging others.

11. Learning theory can be used to *explain* behavior and to *control* behavior. Can you distinguish between the two objectives? Can you give any ethical or moral arguments why managers should not seek control over other's behavior? How valid do you think these arguments are?

12. What have you learned about "learning" that could help you to explain the behavior of students in a classroom if (a) the instructor gives only one test—a final examination at the end of the course? (b) the instructor gives four exams during the term, all of which are announced on the first day of class? (c) the student's grade is based on the results of numerous exams, none of which are announced by the instructor ahead of time?

FOR FURTHER READING

DICKINSON, A. M., and M. P. ROSOW (eds.), *Industrial Behavior Modification: A Management Handbook.* Elmsford, N.Y.: Pergamon Press, 1982. Describes the use of operant conditioning concepts to sales, training, and other business applications.

EPSTEIN, S., "The Stability of Behavior: On Predicting Most of the People Much of the Time," *Journal of Personality and Social Psychology,* July 1979, pp. 1097–126. Reviews personality studies, indicating that while personality characteristics may not permit prediction of single instances of behavior, they are effective for predicting behavior averaged over a range of situations.

JACKSON, D. N., A. C. PEACOCK, and J. P. SMITH, "Impressions of Personality in the Employment Interview," *Journal of Personality and Social Psychology,* August 1980, pp. 294–307. Reports on research study that supports the importance of congruence of personality to the job in ratings of suitability and expected performance.

KELLEY, H. H., and J. L. MICHELA, "Attribution Theory and Research." In M. R. Rosenzweig and L. W. Porter (eds.), *Annual Review of Psychology,* Vol. 31, pp. 457–501. Palo Alto, Calif.: Annual Reviews, 1980. Presents several attribution "theories" illustrating both antecedents and consequences of attributions for behavior.

MITCHELL, T. R., "Attributions and Actions: A Note of Caution," *Journal of Management,* Spring 1982, pp. 65–74. Presents a critical overview of attribution theory. Argues that attributions are only moderately good predictors of behavior.

RORER, L. G., and T. A. WIDIGER, "Personality Structure and Assessment." In M. R. Rosenzweig and L. W. Porter (eds.), *Annual Review of Psychology,* Vol. 34, pp. 431–63. Palo Alto, Calif.: Annual Reviews, 1983. Reviews recent research on personality.

NOTES FOR CHAPTER 3

1. L. W. Porter and R. Steers, "Organizational, Work and Personal Factors in Employee Turnover and Absenteeism," *Psychological Bulletin,* January 1973, pp. 151–76; W. H. Mobley, R. W. Griffin, H. H. Hand, and B. M. Meglino, "Review and Conceptual Analysis of the Employee Turnover Process," *Psychological Bulletin,* May 1979, pp. 493–522; and S. R. Rhodes, "Age-Related Differences in Work Attitudes and Behavior: A Review and Conceptual Analysis," *Psychological Bulletin,* March 1983, pp. 328–67.

2. Rhodes, "Age-Related Differences," pp. 347–49.

3. Ibid., p. 340.

4. Ibid., p. 331–32; and A. L. Kalleberg and K. A. Loscocco, "Aging, Values, and Rewards: Explaining Age Differences in Job Satisfaction," *American Sociological Review,* February 1983, pp. 78–90.

5. J. B. Miner and M. G. Miner, *Personnel and Industrial Relations,* 3rd ed. (New York: Macmillan, 1977), p. 69.

6. E. Maccoby and C. Nagy Jacklin, *The Psychology of Sex Differences* (Stanford, Calif.: Stanford University Press, 1974), pp. 154, 211.

7. R. P. Quinn, G. L. Staines, and M. R. McCullough, *Job Satisfaction: Is There a Trend?* (Washington, D.C.: U.S. Government Printing Office, Document 2900-00195, 1974).

8. T. W. Mangione, "Turnover—Some Psychological and Demographic Correlates," in R. P. Quinn and T.W. Mangione (eds.), *The 1969–70 Survey of Working Conditions* (Ann Arbor: University of Michigan, Survey Research Center, 1973); and R. Marsh and H. Mannari, "Organizational Commitment and Turnover: A Predictive Study," *Administrative Science Quarterly,* March 1977, pp. 57–75.

9. R. J. Flanagan, G. Strauss, and L. Ulman, "Worker Discontent and Work Place Behavior," *Industrial Relations,* May 1974, pp. 101–23; K. R. Garrison and P. M. Muchinsky, "Attitudinal and Biographical Predictors of Incidental Absenteeism," *Journal of Vocational Behavior,* April 1977, pp. 221–30; G. Johns, "Attitudinal and Nonattitudinal Predictors of Two Forms of Absence from Work," *Organizational Behavior and Human Performance,* December 1978, pp. 431–44; and R. T. Keller, "Predicting Absenteeism from Prior Absenteeism, Attitudinal Factors, and Nonattitudinal Factors," *Journal of Applied Psychology,* August 1983, pp. 536–40.

10. Garrison and Muchinsky, "Attitudinal and Biographical Predictors"; C. J. Watson, "An Evaluation and Some Aspects of the Steers and Rhodes Model of Employee Attendance," *Journal of Applied Psychology,* June 1981, pp. 385–89; Keller, "Predicting Absenteeism"; J. M. Federico, P. Federico, and G. W. Lundquist, "Predicting Women's Turnover as a Function of Extent of Met Salary Expectations and Biodemographic Data," *Personnel Psychology,* Winter 1976, pp. 559–66; and Marsh and Mannari, "Organizational Commitment."

11. Porter and Steers, "Organizational, Work, and Personal Factors"; N. Nicholson and P. M. Goodge, "The Influence of Social, Organizational and Biographical Factors on Female Absence," *Journal of Management Studies,* October 1976, pp. 234–54; P. M. Muchinsky, "Employee Absenteeism: A Review of the Literature," *Journal of Vocational Behavior,* June 1977, pp. 316–40; and R. M. Steers and S. R. Rhodes, "Major Influences on Employee Attendance: A Process Model," *Journal of Applied Psychology,* August 1978, pp. 391–407.

12. Porter and Steers, "Organizational, Work, and Personal Factors"; Federico, Federico, and Lundquist, "Predicting Women's Turnover"; and Marsh and Mannari, "Organizational Commitments."

13. A. S. Gechman and Y. Wiener, "Job Involvement and Satisfaction as Related to Mental Health and Personal Time Devoted to Work," *Journal of Applied Psychology,* August 1975, pp. 521–23.

14. M. E. Gordon and W. J. Fitzgibbons, "Empirical Test of the Validity of Seniority as a Factor in Staffing Decisions," *Journal of Applied Psychology,* June 1982, pp. 311–19; and M. E. Gordon and W. A. Johnson, "Seniority: A Review of Its Legal and Scientific Standing," *Personnel Psychology,* Summer 1982, pp. 255–80.

15. Garrison and Muchinsky, "Attitudinal and Biographical Predictors"; N. Nicholson, C. A. Brown, and J. K. Chadwick-Jones, "Absence from Work and Personal Characteristics," *Journal of Applied Psychology,* June 1977, pp. 319–27; and Keller, "Predicting Absenteeism."

16. P. O. Popp and J. A. Belohlav, "Absenteeism in a Low Status Work Environment," *Academy of Management Journal,* September 1982, p. 681.

17. H. J. Arnold and D. C. Feldman, "A Multivariate Analysis of the Determinants of Job Turnover," *Journal of Applied Psychology,* June 1982, p. 352.

18. G. W. Allport, *Personality: A Psychological Interpretation* (New York: Holt, Rinehart and Winston, 1937), p. 48.

19. J. Kelly, *Organizational Behavior,* rev. ed. (Homewood, Ill.: Richard D. Irwin, 1974), p. 243.

20. I. Janis, G. F. Mahl, J. Kagan, and R. P. Holt, *Personality: Dynamics, Development and Assessment* (New York: Harcourt, Brace & World, 1969), p. 555.

21. J. R. Warren, "Birth Order and Social Behavior," *Psychological Bulletin,* January 1966, pp. 38–49.

22. Janis et al., *Personality,* p. 552.

23. L. Sechrest, "Personality," in M. R. Rosenzweig and L. W. Porter (eds.), *Annual Review of Psychology,* Vol. 27 (Palo Alto, Calif.: Annual Reviews, 1976), p. 10.

24. Ibid.

25. G. W. Allport and H. S. Odbert, "Trait Names, A Psycholexical Study," *Psychological Monographs,* No. 47, (1936).

26. R. B. Cattell, "Personality Pinned Down," *Psychology Today,* July 1973, pp. 40–46.

27. R. B. Cattell, *The Scientific Analysis of Personality* (Chicago: Aldine, 1965); and H. J. Eysenck, *The Structure of Human Personality* (London: Methuen, 1953).

28. S. R. Maddi, *Personality Theories* (Homewood, Ill.: Dorsey, 1968).

29. J. B. Rotter, "Generalized Expectancies for Internal Versus External Control of Reinforcement," *Psychological Monographs,* Vol. 80, no. 609 (1966).

30. P. E. Spector, "Behavior in Organizations as a Function of Employee's Locus of Control," *Psychological Bulletin,* May 1982, pp. 482–97.

31. Keller, "Predicting Absenteeism."

32. Spector, "Behavior in Organizations," p. 493.

33. J. B. Miner, *Theories of Organizational Behavior* (Hinsdale, Ill.: Dryden Press, 1980), pp. 46–75.

34. T. Adorno et al., *The Authoritarian Personality* (New York: Harper & Brothers, 1950).

35. H. Gough, "Personality and Personality Assessment," in M. D. Dunnette (ed.), *Handbook of Industrial and Organizational Psychology* (Chicago: Rand McNally, 1976), p. 579.

36. R. G. Vleeming, "Machiavellianism: A Preliminary Review," *Psychological Reports,* February 1979, pp. 295–310.

37. R. Christie and F. L. Geis, *Studies in Machiavellianism* (New York: Academic Press, 1970), p. 312.

38. Ibid.

39. R. N. Taylor and M. D. Dunnette, "Influence of Dogmatism, Risk-Taking Propensity, and Intelligence on Decision-Making Strategies for a Sample of Industrial Managers," *Journal of Applied Psychology,* August 1974, pp. 420–23.

40. I. L. Janis and L. Mann, *Decision Making: A Psychological Analysis of Conflict, Choice, and Commitment* (New York: Free Press, 1977).

41. N. Kogan and M. A. Wallach, "Group Risk Taking as a Function of Members' Anxiety and Defensiveness," *Journal of Personality,* March 1967, pp. 50–63.

42. J. L. Holland, *Making Vocational Choices: A Theory of Careers* (Englewood Cliffs, N.J.: Prentice-Hall, 1973).

43. See, for instance, L. S. Gottfredson, "Construct Validity of Holland's Occupational Typology in Terms of Prestige, Census, Department of Labor, and Other Classification Systems," *Journal of Applied Psychology,* December 1980, pp. 697–714; D. J. Prediger, "Dimensions Underlying Holland's Hexagon: Missing Link Between Interests and Occupations?" *Journal of Vocational Behavior,* October 1982, pp. 259–87; and B. J. Eberhardt and P. M. Muchinsky, "Structural Validation of Holland's Hexagonal Model: Vocational Classification Through the Use of Biodata," *Journal of Applied Psychology,* February 1984, pp. 174–81.

44. M. Haire, "Role Perceptions in Labor-Management Relations: An Experimental Approach," *Industrial and Labor Relations Review,* January 1955, pp. 204–16.

45. D. C. McClelland and J. W. Atkinson, "The Projective Expression of Needs: The Effect of Different Intensities of the Hunger Drive on Perception," *Journal of Psychology,* Vol. 25 (1948), pp. 205–22.

46. For a comprehensive review of the decision-making literature, see E. F. Harrison, *The Managerial Decision Making Process,* 2nd ed. (Boston: Houghton Mifflin, 1981).

47. H. A. Simon, *Administrative Behavior,* 3rd ed. (New York: Free Press, 1976).

48. H. H. Kelley, "Attribution in Social Interaction," in E. Jones et al. (eds.), *Attribution: Perceiving the Causes of Behavior* (Morristown, N.J.: General Learning Press, 1972).

49. See, for example, E. C. Webster, *Decision Making in the Employment Interview* (Montreal: McGill University, Industrial Relations Center, 1964).

50. J. P. Wanous, *Organizational Entry: Recruitment, Selection and Socialization of Newcomers* (Reading, Mass.: Addison-Wesley, 1980); and P. Popovich and J. P. Wanous, "The Realistic Job Preview as a Persuasive Communication," *Academy of Management Review,* October 1982, pp. 570–78.

51. D. Kipnis, *The Powerholders* (Chicago: University of Chicago Press, 1976).

52. D. C. Dearborn and H. A. Simon, "Selective Perception: A Note on the Departmental Identifications of Executives," *Sociometry,* June 1958, pp. 140–44.

53. See, for example, G. E. Stephens and A. S. Denisi, "Women as Managers: Attitudes and Attributions for Performance by Men and Women," *Academy of Management Journal,* June 1980, pp. 355–61; and A. S. Baron and K. Abrahamsen, "Will He—Or Won't He—Work with a Female Manager?" *Management Review,* November 1981, pp. 48–53.

54. S. E. Asch, "Forming Impressions of Personality," *Journal of Abnormal and Social Psychology,* July 1946, pp. 258–90.

55. J. S. Bruner and R. Tagiuri, "The Perception of People," in E. Lindzey (ed.), *Handbook of Social Psychology* (Reading, Mass.: Addison-Wesley, 1954), p. 641.

56. W. McGehee, "Are We Using What We Know About Training?—Learning Theory and Training," *Personnel Psychology,* Spring 1958, p. 2.

57. I. P. Pavlov, *The Work of the Digestive Glands,* trans. W. H. Thompson (London: Charles Griffin, 1902).

58. B. F. Skinner, *Contingencies of Reinforcement* (East Norwalk, Conn.: Appleton-Century-Crofts, 1971).

59. A. Bandura, *Social Learning Theory* (Englewood Cliffs, N.J.: Prentice-Hall, 1977).

60. T. W. Costello and S. S. Zalkind, *Psychology in Administration* (Englewood Cliffs, N.J.: Prentice-Hall, 1963), p. 193.

61. F. Luthans and R. Kreitner, *Organizational Behavior Modification* (Glenview, Ill.: Scott, Foresman, 1975) pp. 49–52.

62. E. Pedalino and V. U. Gamboa, "Behavior Modification and Absenteeism: Intervention in One Industrial Setting," *Journal of Applied Psychology,* December 1974, pp. 694–98.

63. D. Willings, "The Absentee Worker," *Personnel and Training Management,* December 1968, pp. 10–12.

64. B. H. Harvey, J. F. Rogers, and J. A. Schultz, "Sick Pay vs. Well Pay: An Analysis of the Impact of Rewarding Employees for Being on the Job," *Public Personnel Management Journal,* Summer 1983, pp. 218–24.

4

Values, Attitudes, and Job Satisfaction

AFTER STUDYING THIS CHAPTER, YOU SHOULD BE ABLE TO:

Define and explain the following key terms and concepts:

Attitudes
Attitude surveys
Cognitive dissonance
Conformity values
Egocentrism values
Existential values
Job involvement
Manipulative values

Organizational commitment
Reactive values
Self-perception theory
Sociocentric values
Tribalistic values
Values
Value system

Understand:

The source of an individual's value system
The impact of changing values
The three primary job-related attitudes
The relationship between attitudes and behavior
The role consistency plays in attitudes
How individuals reconcile inconsistencies
How to measure job satisfaction
What determines job satisfaction
The relationship between job satisfaction and behavior

When you prevent me from doing anything I want to do, that is persecution; but when I prevent you from doing anything you want to do, that is law, order and morals.

—G. B. SHAW

"*M*anagers should never socialize with their employees." "A little conflict in this place is good—it keeps everyone on their toes." "I don't think there's any justification for the president of this company to make a million dollars a year." "To me, the best boss is one who just leaves me alone!"

Statements such as these are regularly expressed by people at work. Importantly, these opinions—which we call values and attitudes—are not meaningless. They are often related to behavior. In this chapter, we will discuss values and attitudes and then look closely at the topic of job satisfaction.

VALUES

Is capital punishment right or wrong? How about engaging in sexual relations before marriage—is it right or wrong? If a person likes power, is that good or bad? The answers to these questions are value laden. Some might argue, for example, that capital punishment is right because it is an appropriate retribution for crimes like murder or treason. However, others may argue, just as strongly, that no government has the right to take anyone's life.

Values represent basic convictions that "a specific mode of conduct or end-state of existence is personally or socially preferable to an opposite or converse mode of conduct or end-state of existence."[1] They contain a judgmental element in that they carry an individual's ideas as to what is right, good, or desirable. Values have both content and intensity attributes. The content attribute says that a mode of conduct or end-state of existence *is important*. The intensity attribute specifies *how important* it is. When we rank an individual's values in terms of their intensity, we obtain that person's *value system*. All of us have a hierarchy of values that forms our value system. This system is identified by the relative importance we assign to such objects of values as freedom, pleasure, self-respect, honesty, obedience, equality, and so forth.

Importance of Values

Values are important to the study of organizational behavior because they lay the foundation for the understanding of attitudes and motivation as well as influencing our perceptions. Individuals enter an organization with preconceived notions of what "ought" and what "ought not" to be. Of course, these notions are not value free. On the contrary, they contain interpretations of right and wrong. Further, they imply that certain behaviors or outcomes are preferred over others. As a result, values cloud objectivity and rationality.

Values generally influence attitudes and behavior. Suppose that you enter an organization with the view that allocating pay on the basis of performance is right, whereas allocating pay on the basis of seniority is wrong or inferior. How are you going to react if you find that the organization you have just joined rewards seniority and not performance? You're likely to be disappointed—and this can lead to job dissatisfaction and the decision not to exert a high level of effort since "it's probably not going to lead to more money, anyway." Would your attitudes and behavior be different if your values aligned with the organization's pay policies? Most likely!

Sources of Our Value Systems

When we were children, why did many of our mothers tell us "you should always clean your dinner plate"? Why is it that, at least historically in our society, achievement has been considered good and being lazy has been considered bad? The answer is that, in our culture, certain values have developed over time and are continuously reinforced. Peace, cooperation, harmony, equity, and democracy are societal values that are considered desirable in our culture. These values are not fixed, but when they change, they do so very slowly.

The values we hold are essentially established in our early years—from parents, teachers, friends, and others. Your early ideas of what is right and wrong were probably formulated from the views expressed by your parents. Think back to your early views on such topics as education, sex, and politics. For the most part, they were the same as those expressed by your parents. As you grew up, and were exposed to other value systems, you may have altered a number of your values. For example, in high school, if you desired to be a member of a social club whose values included the conviction that "every person should carry a knife," there is a good probability that you changed your value system to align with members of the club, even if it meant rejecting your parents' value that "only hoodlums carry knives, and hoodlums are bad."

Interestingly, values are relatively stable and enduring. This has been explained as a result of the way in which they are originally learned.[2] As children, we are told that a certain behavior or outcome is *always* desirable or *always* undesirable. There were no gray areas. You were told, for example, that you should be honest and responsible. You were never taught to be just a little bit honest or a little bit responsible. It is this absolute or "black-or-white" learning of values that more or less assures their stability and endurance.

The process of questioning our values, of course, may result in a change. We may decide that these underlying convictions are no longer acceptable. More often, our questioning merely acts to reinforce those values we are holding.

Types of Values

At this point, we might rightfully inquire if it is possible to identify certain value "types." The most important early work in categorizing values was done by Allport and his associates.[3] They identified six types of values:

1. *Theoretical*—places high importance on the discovery of truth through a critical and rational approach
2. *Economic*—emphasizes the useful and practical
3. *Aesthetic*—places the highest value on form and harmony
4. *Social*—assigns the highest value to the love of people
5. *Political*—places emphasis on acquisition of power and influence
6. *Religious*—is concerned with the unity of experience and understanding of the cosmos as a whole

Allport and his associates developed a questionnaire that describes a number of different situations and asks respondents to preference rank a fixed set of answers. Based on the respondents' replies, the researchers can rank individuals in terms of the importance they give to each of the six types of values. The result is a value system for a specific individual.

Using this approach, it has been found, not surprisingly, that people in different occupations place different importance on the six value types.

Table 4–1 shows the responses from ministers, purchasing agents, and industrial scientists. As expected, religious leaders consider religious values most important and economic values least important. Economic values, on the other hand, are of highest importance to the purchasing executives.

More recent research suggests that there is a hierarchy of levels that are descriptive of personal values and life-styles. One such study identified seven levels:[4]

Level 1. *Reactive.* These individuals are unaware of themselves or others as human beings and react to basic physiological needs. Such individuals are rarely found in organizations. This is most descriptive of newborn babies.

TABLE 4–1
Ranking of Values by Importance Among Three Groups

MINISTERS	PURCHASING EXECUTIVES	SCIENTISTS IN INDUSTRY
1. Religious	1. Economic	1. Theoretical
2. Social	2. Theoretical	2. Political
3. Aesthetic	3. Political	3. Economic
4. Political	4. Religious	4. Aesthetic
5. Theoretical	5. Aesthetic	5. Religious
6. Economic	6. Social	6. Social

Source: R. Tagiuri, "Purchasing Executive: General Manager or Specialist?" *Journal of Purchasing,* August 1967, pp. 16–21.

Level 2. *Tribalistic*. These individuals are characterized by high dependence. They are strongly influenced by tradition and the power exerted by authority figures.

Level 3. *Egocentrism*. These persons believe in rugged individualism. They are aggressive and selfish. They respond primarily to power.

Level 4. *Conformity*. These individuals have a low tolerance for ambiguity, have difficulty in accepting people whose values differ from their own, and desire that others accept their values.

Level 5. *Manipulative*. These individuals are characterized by striving to achieve their goals by manipulating things and people. They are materialistic and actively seek higher status and recognition.

Level 6. *Sociocentric*. These individuals consider it more important to be liked and to get along with others than to get ahead. They are repulsed by materialism, manipulation, and conformity.

Level 7. *Existential*. These individuals have a high tolerance for ambiguity and people with differing values. They are outspoken on inflexible systems, restrictive policies, status symbols, and arbitrary use of authority.

This hierarchy has been used to analyze the problem of disparate values in organizations.[5] The research indicates that most people in today's organizations operate on levels 2 through 7. But, whereas historically organizations were run by level 4 and 5 managers, there is currently a rapid movement of level 6 and 7 types into influential positions in organizations. Although probably still a minority, the number of individuals holding existential and sociocentric values is increasing. They are being heard in their fight to improve the quality rather than the material quantity of life, in their refusal to accept promotions that would require a move to another community, and in their convictions that decision making should be shared by all organizational members and not just those in managerial positions.

The seven-level categorization of values also contributes toward explaining why individuals have different attitudes and engage in varying behaviors. Tribalistic values place a high importance on acceptance of authority while existential values do not. We can, therefore, expect individuals holding these divergent values to react differently to authoritarian directions. Similarly, conformity values are consistent with achievement and Protestant ethic behavior while sociocentric values find such behavior to be undesirable. Our conclusion, then, is that values impact on behavior and, therefore, knowledge of an individual's value type should assist us in explaining and predicting his or her behavior.

Changing Employee Values

We have noted that there is a significant increase in levels 6 and 7 types at the managerial level. Recent studies suggest that levels 6 and 7 values may becoming descriptive of employees in general. Although values are stable and enduring, they are not rigid. More important, new generations can bring with them a new set of values.

Among the old work values were those implied by the following statements: (1) a woman's place is in the home, not on a paid job; (2) if a job offers economic stability, you stay with it even if it is personally unpleasant; and (3) the incentives of money and status motivate most people. The new work values put an increased importance on (1) leisure, (2) a fulfilling and meaningful paid job, and (3) control over one's activities on the job.[6]

Other studies have found age to be a major differentiator of employee values.[7] Younger workers today place a higher importance on personal freedom, short-run gratification, individualism, and openness than their parents and grandparents do. These younger workers also place less value on competition, long-term returns, and formal authority. In other words, younger employees are forsaking levels 4 and 5 values for levels 6 and 7.

Comparisons of Gallup polls taken in 1955 and 1980 further confirm the impact of age on work values.[8] In 1955, 40 percent of a cross section of American adults valued the hours on their job more than the hours off. In 1980, the percentage had fallen to 24 percent. These changes were similar for both men and women respondents. The only group that was sampled in both surveys—people ages fifty to sixty-four in 1980 (who were twenty-five to thirty-nine in 1955)—was also the only group who continued to place a high value on work. The researchers concluded that these changes in work values over twenty-five years were not due so much to changes in the nature of work as to the retirement of people who learned to value work in the days when they were growing up on farms—an environment with a high work orientation.

What are the implications of these changes in values? Clearly, younger employees are bringing a different set of values to the workplace than their older peers. This means that management will need to respond to these new values if younger workers are to remain with the organization as productive members. Reliance by management on authority systems and job structures built around levels

2 through 5 values can be expected to result in reduced employee satisfaction and increased absenteeism and turnover.

ATTITUDES

Attitudes are evaluative statements—either favorable or unfavorable—concerning objects, people, or events. They reflect how one feels about something. When I say "I like my job," I am expressing my attitude about work.

Attitudes are not the same as values. Values are the broader and more encompassing concept. So attitudes are more specific than values. Values also contain a moral flavor of rightness or desirability. The statement that "discrimination is bad" reflects one's values. "I favor the implementation of an affirmative action program to recruit and develop women for managerial positions in our organization" is an attitude.

While attitudes and values are different, they are closely related. One comprehensive study took a cross section of heterogeneous value issues—including rights of blacks and the poor, family security, salvation, cleanliness, imaginativeness, obedience—and found values and attitudes to be significantly correlated.[9] The researcher concluded that virtually any attitude will be significantly associated with some value set. The evidence allows us to say that the values people hold can explain their attitudes and, in many cases, the behaviors they engage in, but unfortunately, we cannot yet say which values underlie which attitudes and behaviors.

Sources of Attitudes

Attitudes, like values, are acquired from parents, teachers, and peer group members. In our early years, we begin modeling our attitudes after those we admire, respect, or maybe even fear. We observe the way family and friends behave and we shape our attitudes and behavior to align with theirs. People imitate the attitudes of popular individuals or those they admire and respect. If the "right thing" is to favor eating at McDonald's, you are likely to hold that attitude. If it is popular to oppose busing, you may express that view.

In contrast to values, your attitudes are less stable. Advertising messages, for example, attempt to alter your attitudes toward a certain product or service: If the people at Ford can get you to hold a favorable opinion toward their cars, that attitude may lead to a desirable behavior (for them)—the purchase of a Ford product.

In organizations, attitudes are important because they affect job behavior. If workers believe, for example, that supervisors, auditors, bosses, and time and motion engineers are all in conspiracy to make the employee work harder for the same or less money, then it makes sense to try to understand how these attitudes were formed, their relationship to actual job behavior, and how they can be made more favorable.

Types of Attitudes

A person can have thousands of attitudes, but OB focuses our attention on a very limited number of job-related attitudes. These job-related attitudes tap positive or negative evaluations that employees hold about aspects of their work environment. Typically, there are three primary attitudes that are of concern to us: job satisfaction, job involvement, and organizational commitment.

Job satisfaction refers to an individual's general attitude toward his or her job. A person with a high level of job satisfaction holds positive attitudes toward the job, while a person who is dissatisfied with his or her job holds negative attitudes about the job. When people speak of employee attitudes, more often than not they mean job satisfaction. In fact, the two are frequently used interchangeably. We'll consider job satisfaction, in some detail, later in this chapter.

The term *job involvement* is a more recent addition to the OB literature.[10] While there is no complete agreement over what the term means, a workable definition states that job involvement measures the degree to which a person identifies with his or her job, actively participates in it, and considers his or her performance important to his or her self-worth.[11] It has been assumed by OB researchers that individuals who express high involvement in their jobs are likely to be more productive, have higher satisfaction, and be less likely to resign than employees with low involvement.

The third job attitude we shall discuss is *organizational commitment*. This attitude expresses an individual's orientation toward the organization by tapping his or her loyalty to, identification with, and involvement in the organization.[12] Individuals who are highly committed to the organization are likely to stay with their jobs and feel psychologically attached to them, regardless of whether they are satisfying or not. Given this definition, we should expect a strong negative relationship between organizational commitment and turnover rates, and this is precisely what the evidence indicates.[13] An individual's level of commitment is also an excellent barometer of his or her future likelihood of quitting in that reductions in commitment tend to precede actual resignations.[14]

In summary, when we talk about job attitudes and their impact on behavior, we are referring to the positive or negative appraisals that people make about their jobs or organizations. Job satisfaction is the most popular attitude measured in organizations, but more recently there has been increased attention given to job involvement and organizational commitment. For the most part, these attitudes are measured so that they can be used to predict behaviors like productivity, absenteeism, and turnover.

Attitudes and Consistency

Did you ever notice how people change what they say so it doesn't contradict what they do? Perhaps a friend of yours has consistently argued that American cars are poorly built and that he'd never own anything but a foreign import. But his dad gives him a late-model American-made car, and suddenly they're not so bad. Or, when going through sorority rush, a new freshman believes that sororities are good and that pledging a sorority is important. If she fails to make a sorority, however, she may say: "I recognized that sorority life isn't all it's cracked up to be, anyway!"

Research has generally concluded that people seek consistency among their attitudes and between their attitudes and behavior. This means that individuals seek to reconcile divergent attitudes and align their attitudes and behavior so they appear rational and consistent. When there is an inconsistency, forces are initiated to return the individual to an equilibrium state where attitudes and behavior are again consistent. This can be done by altering either the attitudes or the behavior or by developing a rationalization for the discrepancy.

For example, a recruiter for the ABC Company, whose job it is to visit college campuses, isolate qualified job candidates, and sell them on the advantages of ABC as a place to work, would be in conflict if he personally believes the ABC Company has poor working conditions and few opportunities for new college graduates. This recruiter could, over time, find his attitudes toward the ABC Company becoming more positive. He may, in effect, brainwash himself by continually articulating the merits of working for ABC. Another alternative would be for the recruiter to become overtly negative about ABC and the opportunities within the firm for prospective candidates. The original enthusiasm that the recruiter may have shown would dwindle, probably to be replaced by open cynicism toward the company. Finally, the recruiter might acknowledge that ABC is an undesirable place to work, but as a professional recruiter his obligation is to present the positive sides of working for the company. He might further rationalize that no place is perfect to work at; therefore, his job is not to present both sides of the issue, but rather to present a "rosy" picture of the company.

Cognitive Dissonance Theory

Can we additionally assume from this consistency principle that an individual's behavior can always be predicted if we know his or her attitude on a subject? If Mr. Jones views the company's pay level as too low, will a substantial increase in his pay change his behavior; that is, make him work harder? The answer to this question is, unfortunately, more complex than merely a "Yes" or "No."

Leon Festinger, in the late 1950s, proposed the theory of cognitive dissonance.[15] This theory sought to explain the linkage between attitudes and behavior.

Dissonance means an inconsistency. Cognitive dissonance refers to any incompatibility that an individual might perceive between two or more of his attitudes, or between his behavior and his attitudes. Festinger argued that any form of inconsistency is uncomfortable and that individuals will attempt to reduce dissonance and, hence, the discomfort. Therefore, individuals will seek a stable state where there is a minimum of dissonance.

Of course, no individual can completely avoid dissonance. You know prejudice is wrong, but you fear the economic impact on housing prices should your neighborhood become socially mixed. Or you tell your children to brush after every meal, but *you* don't. So how do people cope? Festinger would propose that the desire to reduce dissonance would be determined by the importance of the elements creating the dissonance, the degree of influence the individual believes he or she has over the elements, and the rewards that may be involved in dissonance.

If the elements creating the dissonance are relatively unimportant, the pressure to correct this imbalance will be low. However, say that a corporate manager—Mrs. Smith, who has a husband and several children—believes strongly that no company should pollute the air or water. Unfortunately, Mrs. Smith, because of the requirements of her job, is placed in the position of having to make decisions that would trade off her company's profitability against her attitudes on pollution. She knows that dumping the company's sewage into the local river (which we shall assume is legal) is in the best economic interest of her firm. What will she do? Clearly, Mrs. Smith is experiencing a high degree of cognitive dissonance. Because of the importance of the elements in this example, we cannot expect Mrs. Smith to ignore the inconsistency. There are several paths that she can follow to deal with her dilemma. She can change her behavior (stop polluting the river). Or she can reduce dissonance by concluding that the dissonant behavior is not so important after all ("I've got to make a living, and in my role as a corporate decision maker, I often have to place the good of my company above that of the environment or society"). A third alternative would be for Mrs. Smith to change her attitude ("There is nothing wrong in polluting the river"). Still another choice would be to seek out more consonant elements to outweigh the dissonant ones ("The benefits to society from our manufacturing our products more than offset the cost to society of the resulting water pollution").

The degree of influence that individuals believe they have over the elements will impact on how they will react to the dissonance. If they perceive the dissonance to be an uncontrollable result—something over which they have no choice—they are less likely to be receptive to attitude change. If, for example, the dissonance-producing behavior was required as a result of the boss's directive, the pressure to reduce dissonance would be less than if the behavior was performed voluntarily. While dissonance exists, it can be rationalized and justified.

Rewards also influence the degree to which individuals are motivated to reduce dissonance. High dissonance, when accompanied by high rewards, tends to reduce the tension inherent in the dissonance. The reward acts to reduce dissonance by increasing the consistency side of the individual's balance sheet. Since people in organizations are given some form of reward or remuneration for their services, employees often can deal with greater dissonance on their jobs than off their jobs.

These moderating factors suggest that just because individuals experience dissonance does not necessarily mean that they will directly move toward consistency; that is, toward reduction of this dissonance. If the issues underlying the dissonance are of minimal importance, if an individual perceives that the dissonance is externally imposed and is substantially uncontrollable by him or her, or if rewards are significant enough to offset the dissonance, the individual will not be under great tension to reduce the dissonance.

What are the organizational implications of the theory of cognitive dissonance? It can help to predict the propensity to engage in attitude and behavioral change. If individuals are required, for example, by the demands of their job, to say or do things that contradict their personal attitude, they will tend to modify their attitude in order to make it compatible with the cognition of what they have said or done. Additionally, the greater the dissonance—after it has been moderated by importance, choice, and reward factors—the greater the pressures to reduce the dissonance.

Measuring the A-B Relationship

We have maintained throughout this chapter that attitudes affect behavior. The early research work on attitudes assumed that they were causally related to behavior; that is, the attitudes that people hold determine what they do. Common sense, too, suggests a relationship. Is it not logical that people watch television programs that they say they like or that employees try to avoid assignments they find distasteful?

However, in the late 1960s, this assumed relationship between attitudes and behavior (A-B) was challenged by a review of the research.[16] Based on an evaluation of a number of studies that investigated the A-B relationship, the reviewer concluded that attitudes were unrelated to behavior or, at best, only slightly related.[17] More recent research has demonstrated that the A-B relationship can be improved by taking into consideration moderating contingency variables.

MODERATING VARIABLES

One thing that improves our chances of finding significant A-B relationships is the use of both specific attitudes and specific behaviors.[18] It is one thing to talk about a person's attitude toward "preserving the environment" and another to speak of his or her attitude toward "purchasing unleaded gasoline" (which generates less air pollution in the environment). The more specific the attitude we are measuring and the more specific we are in identifying a related behavior, the greater the probability that we can show a relationship between A and B. As a case in point, in the early 1970s, the laws did not yet require late-model cars to operate only on unleaded gas. In those days, people were free to choose between regular and unleaded gas. The unleaded variety typically cost a few cents more, but it did less environmental damage. Several researchers drew samples of drivers using unleaded and regular gas and then asked the drivers four levels of questions ranging from items about general interest in the environment issues to a specific question about the degree of personal obligation the individual felt to buy unleaded gasoline. The A-B relationship increased from +.12 to +.59 as the questions went from the least to the most specific level.[19] That is, the more specific the question, the closer the response related to actual gasoline purchasing behavior.

Another moderator is social constraints on behavior. Discrepancies between attitudes and behavior may occur because the social pressures on the individual to behave in a certain way may hold exceptional power.[20] Group pressures, for instance, may explain why an employee who holds strong anti-union attitudes attends pro-union organizing meetings.

Still another moderating variable is experience with the attitude in question.[21] The A-B relationship is likely to be much stronger if the attitude being evaluated refers to something about which the individual has experience. For instance, most of us will respond to a questionnaire on most any issue. But is my attitude toward starving fish in the Amazon any indication of whether I'd donate to a fund to save these fish? Probably not! Asking college students, with no work experience, their views on job factors that are important in determining whether they would stay put in a job is an example of an attitude response that is unlikely to predict much in terms of actual turnover behavior.

SELF-PERCEPTION THEORY

While most A-B studies yield positive results[22]—that attitudes do influence behavior—the relationship tends to be weak before adjustments are made for moderating variables. But requiring specificity, an absence of social constraints, and experience in order to get a meaningful correlation imposes severe limitations on making gneralizations about the A-B relationship. This has prompted some researchers to take another direction—to look at whether behavior influences attitudes. This view, called self-perception theory, has generated some encouraging findings.[23] Let's briefly review the theory.

When asked about an attitude toward some object, individuals recall their behavior relevant to that object and then infer their attitude from the past behavior. So if an employee were asked about her feelings about being a payroll clerk at Exxon, she would likely think, "I've had this same job at Exxon as a payroll clerk for ten years, so I must like it!" Self-perception theory, therefore, argues that attitudes are used, after the fact, to make sense out of the action that has already occurred rather than devices that precede and guide action.

Self-perception theory has been well supported.[24] While the traditional attitude-behavior relationship is generally positive, it is also weak. In contrast, the behavior-attitude relationship is quite strong. So what can we conclude? It seems that we are very good at finding reasons for what we do, but not so good at doing what we find reasons for.[25]

An Application: Attitude Surveys

The preceding review should not discourage us from using attitudes to predict behavior. In an organizational context, most of the attitudes management would seek to inquire about would be ones with which employees have some experience. If the attitudes in question are specifically stated, management should obtain information that can be valuable in guiding their decisions relative to these employees. But how does management get information about employee attitudes? The most popular method is through the use of attitude surveys.

Table 4–2 illustrates what an attitude survey might look like. Typically, attitude surveys present the employee with a set of statements or questions. Ideally, the items will be tailor made to obtain the specific information that management desires. An attitude score is achieved by summing up responses to individual questionnaire items. These scores can then be averaged for job groups, departments, divisions, or the organization as a whole.

Results from attitude surveys frequently surprise management. Why? Consistent with our discussion of perceptions in the previous chapter, the policies and practices that management views as objective and fair may be seen as inequitable by employees in general or among certain groups of employees. The fact that these distorted perceptions have led to negative attitudes about the job and organization should be important to management. This is because employee behaviors are based on perceptions, not reality. Remember, the employee who quits because she believes she is underpaid—when in fact management has objective data to support that her salary is highly competitive—is just as gone as if she had actually

TABLE 4–2
Sample Attitude Survey

Please answer each of the following statements using the following rating scale:

     5 = Strongly agree
     4 = Agree
     3 = Undecided
     2 = Disagree
     1 = Strongly disagree

STATEMENT	RATING
1. This company is a pretty good place to work.	_____
2. I can get ahead in this company if I make the effort.	_____
3. This company's wage rates are competitive with those of other companies.	_____
4. Employee promotion decisions are handled fairly.	_____
5. I understand the various fringe benefits the company offers.	_____
6. My job makes the best use of my abilities.	_____
7. My work load is challenging but not burdensome.	_____
8. I have trust and confidence in my boss.	_____
9. I feel free to tell my boss what I think.	_____
10. I know what my boss expects of me.	_____

---

been underpaid. The use of regular attitude surveys can alert management to potential problems and employees' intentions early so that action can be taken to prevent repercussions.

JOB SATISFACTION

We have already discussed job satisfaction briefly—earlier in this chapter as well as in Chapter 2. In this section we want to dissect the concept more carefully. How do we measure job satisfaction? Are most workers today satisfied with their jobs? What determines job satisfaction? What is its effect on employee productivity, absenteeism, and turnover rates? We'll answer each of these questions in this section.

Measuring Job Satisfaction

We've previously defined job satisfaction as an individual's general attitude toward his or her job. This definition is clearly a very broad one. Yet this is inherent in the concept. Remember, a person's job is more than just the obvious activities of shuffling papers, waiting on customers, or driving a truck. Jobs require interaction with co-workers and bosses, following organizational rules and policies, meeting performance standards, living with working conditions that are often less than ideal, and the like. This means that an employee's assessment of how satisfied or dissatisfied he is with his job is a complex summation of a number of discrete job elements. So how then do we measure the concept?

The two most widely used approaches are a single global rating and a summation score made up of a number of job facets. The single global rating method is nothing more than asking individuals to respond to one question, such as "All things considered, how satisfied are you with your job?" Respondents then reply by circling a number between 1 and 5 that corresponds with answers from "Highly Satisfied" to "Highly Dissatisfied." The other approach—a summation of job facets—is more sophisticated. It identifies key elements in a job and asks for the employee's feelings about each. Typical factors that would be included are the nature of the work, control over work, quality of the physical environment, supervisory support, and job rewards.[26] Each of these factors, in turn, is broken down into specific issues—such as time pressures, career opportunities, and pay equity—that are rated on a scale from 1 to 5 and then are added up to create an overall job satisfaction score.

Is one of the foregoing approaches superior to the other? Intuitively, it would seem that summing up responses to a number of job factors would achieve a more accurate evaluation of job satisfaction. The research, however, doesn't support such intuition.[27] This is one of those rare instances in which simplicity wins out over complexity. Comparisons of one-question global ratings with the more lengthy summation of job factors method indicate that the former is more valid. The best explanation for this outcome is that the concept of job satisfaction is inherently so broad that the single question actually becomes a more inclusive measure.

Job Satisfaction in the Workplace Today

If we accept the notion that a satisfied work force is desirable, one is led to the question: How satisfied *are* employees today with their jobs? This question has implications for you personally, even if you have no intention of being a manager. You will probably spend forty hours a week for forty or more years of your life at work, and you would undoubtedly like to find that time personally satisfying.

The answer to this question, as you might expect, depends on the precise way in which the question is worded. For instance, the Gallup poll regularly asks samples of American workers, "On the whole, would you say that you are satisfied or dissatisfied with the work you do?" Based on responses to this question, between 10 to 15 percent of the work force indicate dissatisfaction with their jobs.[28] But our knowledge of cognitive dissonance leads us to suspect that undoubtedly many alienated workers do not report being dissatisfied. A better test, therefore, might be to ask employees whether, given the opportunity, they would again choose the same kind of work; or whether they would want their children to follow in their footsteps. Answers to questions such as these generally show that less than half of the respondents see their jobs as attractive enough to choose again or recommend to their children.[29]

While the evidence is sketchy, it seems reasonable to speculate that satisfaction is also probably strongly influenced by economic conditions. For instance, during the 1960s and 1970s, there was a significant decline in satisfaction for most occupational groups.[30] But this time period was one of generally uninterrupted prosperity. In recessionary times, when unemployment rates move up to 10 percent and beyond—as occurred in 1981 and 1982—it's very likely that satisfaction levels in the work force rise. When those all about you are being laid off or losing their jobs, what previously seemed dissatisfying may be perceived less negatively.

Job Satisfaction as a Dependent Variable

We now turn to considering job satisfaction as a dependent variable. That is, we seek an answer to the question: *What* determines job satisfaction? An extensive review of the literature indicates that the more important factors conducive to job satisfaction include mentally challenging work, equitable rewards, supportive working conditions, and supportive colleagues.[31]

MENTALLY CHALLENGING WORK

Employees tend to prefer jobs that give them opportunities to use their skills and abilities and offer a variety of tasks, freedom, and feedback on how well they are doing. These characteristics make work mentally challenging. Jobs that have too little challenge create boredom. But too much challenge creates frustration and feelings of failure. Under conditions of moderate challenge, most employees will experience pleasure and satisfaction.

EQUITABLE REWARDS

Employees want pay systems and promotion policies that they perceive as being just, unambiguous, and in line with their expectations. When pay is seen as fair based on job demands, individual skill level, and community pay standards, satisfaction is likely to result. Of course, not everyone seeks money. Many people willingly accept less money to work in a preferred location or in a less demanding job or to have greater discretion in the work they do and the hours they work. But the key in linking pay to satisfaction is not the absolute amount one is paid; rather, it is the perception of fairness. Similarly, employees seek fair promotion policies and practices. Promotions provide opportunities for personal growth, more responsibilities, and increased social status. Individuals who perceive that promotion decisions are made in a fair and just manner, therefore, are likely to experience satisfaction from their job.

SUPPORTIVE WORKING CONDITIONS

Employees are concerned with their work environment for both personal comfort and facilitating doing a good job. Studies demonstrate that employees prefer physical surroundings that are not dangerous or uncomfortable. Temperature, light, noise, and other environmental factors should not be at either extreme—for example, having too much heat or too little light. Additionally, most employees prefer working relatively close to home, in clean and relatively modern facilities, and with adequate tools and equipment.

SUPPORTIVE COLLEAGUES

People get more out of work than merely money or tangible achievements. For most employees, work also fills the need for social interaction. Not surprisingly, therefore, having friendly and supportive co-workers leads to increased job satisfaction. The behavior of one's boss also is a major determinant of satisfaction. Studies generally find that employee satisfaction is increased when the immediate supervisor is understanding and friendly, offers praise for good performance, listens to the employee's opinions, and shows a personal interest in his or her employees.

Job Satisfaction as an Independent Variable

Managers' interest in job satisfaction tends to center on its effect on employee performance. Researchers have recognized this interest—so we find a large number of studies that have been designed to assess the impact of job satisfaction on employee productivity, absenteeism, and turnover. Let's look at the current state of our knowledge.

SATISFACTION AND PRODUCTIVITY

A number of reviews were done in the 1950s and 1960s, covering dozens of studies that sought to establish the relationship between satisfaction and productivity.[32] These reviews could find no consistent relationship. In the mid-1980s, though the studies are far from unambiguous, we can make some sense out of the evidence.

The early views on the satisfaction-performance relationship can be essentially summarized in the statement "a happy worker is a productive worker." Much of the paternalism shown by managers in the 1930s, 1940s, and 1950s—forming company bowling teams and credit unions, having company picnics, providing counseling services for employees, training supervisors to be sensitive to the concerns of subordinates—was done to make workers happy. But belief in the happy worker thesis was based more on wishful thinking than hard evidence. A careful review of the research indicates that if there is a positive relationship between satisfaction and productivity, the correlations are consistently low—in the vicinity of .14.[33] However, introduction of moderating variables has improved the relationship.[34] For example, the relationship is stronger when the employee's behavior is not constrained or controlled by outside factors. An employee's productivity on machine-paced jobs, for instance, is going to be much more influenced by the speed of the machine than his or her level of satisfaction. Similarly, a stockbroker's productivity is largely constrained by the general movement of the stock market. When the market is moving up and volume is high, both satisfied and dissatisfied brokers are going to ring up lots of commissions. Conversely, when the market is in the doldrums, the level of broker satisfaction is not likely to mean much.

Another point of concern in the satisfaction-productivity issue is the direction of the causal arrow. Most of the studies on the relationship used research designs that could not prove cause and effect. Studies that have controlled for this possibility indicate that the more valid conclusion is that productivity leads to satisfaction rather than the other way around.[35] If you do a good job, you intrinsically feel good about it. Additionally, assuming that the organization rewards productivity, your higher productivity should increase verbal recognition, your pay level, and probabilities for promotion. These rewards, in turn, increase your level of satisfaction with the job.

SATISFACTION AND ABSENTEEISM

We find a consistent negative relationship between satisfaction and absenteeism, but the correlation isn't high—usually less than .40.[36] While it certainly makes sense that dissatisfied employees are more likely to miss work, other factors impact on the relationship and reduce the correlation coefficient. For example, remember our discussion of sick pay versus well pay in the last chapter. Organizations that provide liberal sick leave benefits are encouraging all their employees—including those who are highly satisfied—to take days off. Assuming that you have a reasonable degree of varied interests, you can find work satisfying and yet still take off work to enjoy a three-day weekend, tan yourself on a warm summer day, or watch the World Series on television if those days come free with no penalties. Also, as with productivity, outside factors can act to reduce the correlation.

An excellent illustration of how satisfaction directly leads to attendance, where there is a minimum impact from other factors, is a study done at Sears, Roebuck.[37] Satisfaction data were available on employees at Sears' two headquarters in Chicago and New York. Additionally, it is important to note that Sears' policy was not to permit employees to be absent from work for avoidable reasons without penalty. The occurrence of a freak April 2 snowstorm in Chicago created the opportunity to compare employee attendance at the Chicago office with personnel in New York where the weather was quite nice. The interesting dimension in this study is that the snowstorm gave the Chicago employees a built-in excuse not to come to work. The storm crippled the city's transportation, and individuals knew they could miss work this day with no penalty. This natural experiment permitted the comparison of attendance records for satisfied and dissatisfied employees at two locations—one where you were expected to be at work (with normal pressures for attendance) and the other where you were free to choose with no penalty involved. If satisfaction leads to attendance, where there is an absence of outside factors, the more satisfied employees should have come to work in Chicago, while dissatisfied employees should have stayed home. The study found that, on this April 2 day, absenteeism rates in New York (the control group) were just as high for satisfied groups of workers as for dissatisfied groups. But in Chicago, the workers with high satisfaction scores had much higher attendance than did those with lower satisfaction levels. These findings are exactly what we would have expected if satisfaction is negatively correlated with absenteeism.

SATISFACTION AND TURNOVER

Satisfaction is also negatively related to turnover, but the correlation is stronger than what we found for absenteeism.[38] Yet, again, other factors such as labor market conditions, expectations about alternative job opportunities, and length of tenure with the organization are important constraints on the actual decision to leave one's current job.

Evidence indicates that an important moderating variable on the satisfaction-turnover relationship is the employee's level of performance.[39] Specifically, level of satisfaction is less important in predicting turnover for superior performers. Why? The organization typically makes considerable efforts to keep these people. They get pay raises, praise, recognition, increased promotional opportunities, and so forth. Just the opposite tends to apply to poor performers. Few attempts are made by the organization to retain them. There may even be subtle pressures to encourage them to quit. We would expect, therefore, that job satisfaction is more important in influencing poor performers to stay than for superior performers. Regardless of level of satisfaction, the latter are more likely to remain with the organization because the receipt of recognition, praise, and other rewards gives them more reasons for staying.

IMPLICATIONS FOR PERFORMANCE AND SATISFACTION

What's the importance of knowing about an individual's values? Although they don't directly impact behavior, values strongly influence a person's attitudes. So knowledge of an individual's value system can provide insight into his or her attitudes.

Given that people's values differ, managers can use the seven-level hierarchy to characterize potential employees and determine if their values align with the dominant values of the organization. An employee's performance and satisfaction are likely to be higher if his or her values fit well with the organization. For instance, the egocentric individualist is poorly matched with an organization that seeks conformity from its employees. Managers are more likely to appreciate, evaluate positively, and allocate rewards to employees who "fit in," and employees are more likely to be satisfied if they perceive that they "fit in."

Managers should be interested in their employee's attitudes because attitudes give warnings of potential problems and because they influence behavior. Satisfied and committed employees, for instance, have lower rates of turnover and absenteeism. Given that managers want to keep resignations and absences down—especially among their more productive employees—they will want to do those things that will generate positive job attitudes.

Managers should also be aware that employees will try to reduce cognitive dissonance. More important, dissonance can be managed. If employees are required to engage in activities that appear inconsistent to them or that are at odds with their attitudes, the pressures to reduce the resulting dissonance are lessened when the employee perceives that the dissonance is externally imposed and is beyond his or her control or if the rewards are significant enough to offset the dissonance.

POINT

THE IMPORTANCE OF HIGH JOB SATISFACTION

The importance of job satisfaction is obvious. Managers should be concerned with the level of job satisfaction in their organizations for at least three reasons: (1) there is clear evidence that dissatisfied employees skip work more often and are more likely to resign; (2) it has been demonstrated that satisfied employees have better health and live longer; and (3) satisfaction on the job carries over to the employee's life outside the job.

We reviewed the evidence between satisfaction and withdrawal behaviors in this chapter. That evidence was fairly clear: satisfied employees have lower rates of both turnover and absenteeism. If we consider the two withdrawal behaviors separately, however, we can be more confident about the influence of satisfaction on turnover. Specifically, satisfaction is strongly and consistently negatively related to an employee's decision to stay or leave the organization. Although satisfaction and absence are also negatively related, conclusions regarding the relationship should be more guarded.

An often overlooked dimension of job satisfaction is its relationship to employee health. Several studies have shown that employees who are dissatisfied with their jobs are prone to health setbacks—ranging from headaches to heart disease. Some research even indicates that job satisfaction is a better predictor of length of life than is physical condition or tobacco use. These studies suggest that dissatisfaction is not solely a psychological phenomenon. The stress that results from dissatisfaction apparently increases one's susceptibility to heart attacks and the like. For managers, this means that even if satisfaction didn't lead to less voluntary turnover and absence, the goal of a satisfied work force might be justifiable because it would reduce medical costs and the premature loss of valued employees by way of heart disease or strokes.

Our final point in support of job satisfaction's importance is the spin-off effect that job satisfaction has for society as a whole. When employees are happy with their jobs, it improves their lives off the job. In contrast, the dissatisfied employee carries that negative attitude home. In wealthy countries, such as the United States, doesn't management have a responsibility to provide jobs from which employees can receive high satisfaction? There are benefits, after all, that accrue to every citizen in our society. Satisfied employees contribute toward being satisfied citizens. These people will hold a more positive attitude toward life in general and make for a society of more psychologically healthy people.

The evidence is impressive. Job satisfaction is important. For management, a satisfied work force translates into higher productivity due to fewer disruptions caused by absenteeism or good employees quitting; and lower medical and life insurance costs. Additionally, there are benefits for society in general. Satisfaction on the job carries over to the employee's off-the-job hours. So the goal of high job satisfaction for employees can be defended in terms of both dollars and cents and social responsibility.

COUNTERPOINT

JOB SATISFACTION HAS BEEN OVEREMPHASIZED

Few issues have been more blown out of proportion than the importance of job satisfaction at work. Let's look closely at the evidence.

There is no consistent relationship indicating that satisfaction leads to productivity. And, after all, isn't productivity the name of the game? Organizations are not altruistic institutions. Management's obligation is to efficiently use the resources that it has available. It has no obligation to create a satisfied work force if the costs exceed the benefits. As one executive put it, "I don't care if my people are happy or not! Do they produce?"

It would be naive to assume that satisfaction alone would be a major impact on employee behavior. As a case in point, consider the issue of turnover. Certainly there are a number of other factors that have an equal or greater impact on whether an employee decides to remain with an organization or take a job somewhere else—length of time on the job, one's financial situation, availability of other jobs, and so on. If I'm fifty-five years old, have been with my company twenty-five years, perceive few other opportunities in the job market, and have no other source of income other than my job, does the fact that I'm unhappy likely to have much impact on my decision to stay with the organization? No!

Did you ever notice who seems to be most concerned with improving employee job satisfaction? It's usually college professors and researchers! They've chosen careers that provide them considerable freedom and opportunities for personal growth. They place a very high value on job satisfaction.

The problem is that they also impose their values on others. Because job satisfaction is important to them, they suppose that it's important to everyone. To a lot of people, a job is merely a means by which to get the money they want to do the things they desire during their nonworking hours. Assuming you work forty hours a week and sleep eight hours a night, you still have seventy hours or more a week to achieve fulfillment and satisfaction in off-the-job activities. So the importance of job satisfaction may be oversold when you recognize that there are other sources—outside the job—where the dissatisfied employee can find satisfaction.

A final point against overemphasizing job satisfaction is to consider the issue in a contingency framework. Even if satisfaction were significantly related to performance, it is unlikely that the relationship would hold consistently across all segments of the work force. In fact, evidence demonstrates that people differ in terms of the importance that work plays in their lives. To some, the job is their central life interest. But for the majority of people, their primary interests are off the job. Nonjob-oriented people tend not to be emotionally involved with their work. This relative indifference allows them to accept frustrating conditions at work more willingly. Importantly, the majority of the work force probably falls into this nonjob-oriented category. So while job satisfaction might be important to lawyers, surgeons, and other professionals, it may be irrelevant to the average worker because he or she is generally apathetic toward the job's frustrating elements.

FOR DISCUSSION

1. "Thirty years ago, young employees we hired were ambitious, conscientious, hard-working, and honest. Today's young workers don't have the same values." Do you agree or disagree with this manager's comments? Support your position.

2. Do you think the decline in the importance of work values will continue through the end of this century?

3. "Job candidates for a sales position are more likely to be successful if they hold egocentric values." Discuss.

4. Do you think there might be any positive and significant relationship between the possession of certain personal values and successful career progression in organizations like E. F. Hutton & Co., the AFL-CIO, or the City of Cleveland's Police Department? Discuss.

5. What is cognitive dissonance and how is it related to attitudes?

6. What is self-perception theory? Does it increase our ability to predict behavior?

7. What contingency factors can improve the statistical relationship between attitudes and behavior?

8. Why does job satisfaction receive so much attention by OB researchers? Do you think this interest is shared by practicing managers?

9. What determines job satisfaction?

10. What is the relationship between job satisfaction and productivity?

11. What is the relationship between job satisfaction and absenteeism? Turnover? Which is the stronger relationship?

12. What actions might management take if it wanted to change a specific employee attitude—for example, a negative view toward introduction of a new information system that requires many of the office personnel to make significant changes in the forms they use and the reports they fill out?

FOR FURTHER READING

CALDER, B. J., and P. H. SCHURR, "Attitudinal Processes in Organizations." In L. L. Cummings and B. M. Staw (eds.), *Research in Organizational Behavior,* Vol. 3, pp. 283–302. Greenwich, Conn.: JAI Press, 1981. Presents an information processing view of attitudes that reconciles the attitude-guides-behavior position versus the situational position.

COOPER, J., and R. R. CROYLE, "Attitudes and Attitude Change." In M. R. Rosenzweig and L. W. Porter (eds.), *Annual Review of Psychology,* Vol. 35, pp. 395–426. Palo Alto, Calif.: Annual Reviews, 1984. Updates the research on the attitude-behavior relationship, cognitive dissonance, and other advances in the literature on attitudes.

Cooper, M. R., B. S. Morgan, P. M. Foley, and L. B. Kaplan, "Changing Employee Values: Deeping Discontent?" *Harvard Business Review,* January–February 1979, pp. 117–25. Presents survey data over twenty-five years that indicates that there has been a major shift in the attitudes and values of the U.S. work force.

Fazio, R. H., M. C. Powell, and P. M. Herr, "Toward a Process Model of the Attitude-Behavior Relation: Assessing One's Attitude upon Mere Observation of the Attitude Object," *Journal of Personality and Social Psychology,* July 1983, pp. 724–35. Presents a model that demonstrates how and when particular attitudes are brought into play.

Kesselman, G. A., "The Attitude Survey: Does It Have a Bearing on Productivity?" *S.A.M. Advanced Management Journal,* Winter 1984, pp. 18–24. Describes attitude surveys conducted at four different companies, the changes that were implemented, and the results achieved.

Posner, B. Z., and J. M. Munson, "The Importance of Values in Organizational Behavior," *Human Resource Management,* Fall 1979, pp. 9–14. Describes values and how they are measured, and argues that values are important to study and important for managers to know about.

NOTES FOR CHAPTER 4

1. M. Rokeach, *The Nature of Human Values* (New York: Free Press, 1973), p. 5.
2. Ibid., p. 6.
3. G. W. Allport, P. E. Vernon, and G. Lindzey, *Study of Values* (Boston: Houghton Mifflin, 1951).
4. C. W. Graves, "Levels of Existence: An Open System Theory of Values," *Journal of Humanistic Psychology,* Fall 1970, pp. 131–55.
5. M. S. Myers and S. S. Myers, "Toward Understanding the Changing Work Ethic," *California Management Review,* Spring 1974, pp. 7–19.
6. D. Yankelovich, "The New Psychological Contracts at Work," *Psychology Today,* May 1978, pp. 46–50.
7. See, for instance, D. J. Cherrington, S. J. Condie, and J. L. England, "Age and Work Values," *Academy of Management Journal,* September 1979, pp. 617–23.
8. J. C. Horn, "The Last of Happy Workers," *Psychology Today,* April 1982, pp. 17–18.
9. Rokeach, *Human Values,* pp. 95–121.
10. S. Rabinowitz and D. T. Hall, "Organizational Research on Job Involvement," *Psychological Bulletin,* March 1977, pp. 265–88.
11. S. D. Saleh and J. Hosek, "Job Involvement: Concepts and Measurements," *Academy of Management Journal,* June 1976, p. 223.
12. B. Buchanan II, "Building Organizational Commitment: The Socialization of Managers in Work Situations," *Administrative Science Quarterly,* December 1974, pp. 533–46.

13. R. T. Mowday, L. W. Porter, and R. M. Steers, *Employee-Organization Linkages* (New York: Academic Press, 1982).

14. C. E. Rusbult and D. Farrell, "A Longitudinal Test of the Investment Model: The Impact on Job Satisfaction, Job Commitment, and Turnover of Variations in Rewards, Costs, Alternatives, and Investments," *Journal of Applied Psychology,* August 1983, pp. 429–38.

15. L. Festinger, *A Theory of Cognitive Dissonance* (Stanford, Calif.: Stanford University Press, 1957).

16. A. W. Wicker, "Attitude Versus Action: The Relationship of Verbal and Overt Behavioral Responses to Attitude Objects," *Journal of Social Issues,* Autumn 1969, pp. 41–78.

17. Ibid., p. 65.

18. T. A. Heberlein and J. S. Black, "Attitudinal Specificity and the Prediction of Behavior in a Field Setting," *Journal of Personality and Social Psychology,* April 1976, pp. 474–79.

19. Ibid.

20. H. Schuman and M. P. Johnson, "Attitudes and Behavior," in Alex Inkeles (ed.), *Annual Review of Sociology,* (Palo Alto, Calif.: Annual Reviews, 1976), pp. 161–207.

21. D. Regan and R. Fazio, "On the Consistency Between Attitudes and Behavior: Look to the Method of Attitude Formation," *Journal of Experimental Social Psychology,* January 1977, pp. 28–45.

22. Schuman and Johnson, "Attitudes and Behavior," p. 199; and L. R. Kahle and H. J. Berman, "Attitudes Cause Behaviors: A Cross-Lagged Panel Analysis," *Journal of Personality and Social Psychology,* March 1979, pp. 315–21.

23. D. J. Bem, "Self-Perception Theory," in L. Berkowitz (ed.), *Advances in Experimental Social Psychology,* Vol. 6 (New York: Academic Press, 1972), pp. 1–62.

24. See, for example, C. A. Kiesler, R. E. Nisbett, and M. P. Zanna, "On Inferring One's Belief from One's Behavior," *Journal of Personality and Social Psychology,* April 1969, pp. 321–27.

25. R. Abelson, "Are Attitudes Necessary?" in B. T. King and E. McGinnies (eds.), *Attitudes, Conflicts, and Social Change* (New York: Academic Press, 1972), p. 25.

26. See, for example, D. J. Weiss, R. V. Davis, G. W. England, and L. H. Lofquist, *Manual for the Minnesota Satisfaction Questionnaire: Minnesota Studies in Vocational Rehabilitation* (Minneapolis: University of Minnesota, Vocational Psychology Research, 1967).

27. V. Scarpello and J. P. Campbell, "Job Satisfaction: Are All the Parts There?" *Personnel Psychology,* Autumn 1983, pp. 577–600.

28. See, for example, H. L. Sheppard and N. Q. Herrick, *Where Have All the Robots Gone?* (New York: Free Press, 1972); and Studs Terkel, *Working* (New York: Pantheon, 1974).

29. See, for example, R. L. Kahn, "The Meaning of Work: Interpretation and Proposals for Measurement," in A. Campbell and P. E. Converse (eds.), *The Human Meaning of Social Change* (New York: Russell Sage Foundation, 1972).

30. G. L. Staines and R. P. Quinn, "American Workers Evaluate the Quality of Their Jobs," *Monthly Labor Review* January 1979, pp. 3–12.

31. E. A. Locke, "The Nature and Causes of Job Satisfaction," in M. D. Dunnette (ed.), *Handbook of Industrial and Organizational Psychology* (Chicago: Rand McNally, 1976), pp. 1319–28.

32. A. H. Brayfield and W. H. Crockett, "Employee Attitudes and Employee Performance," *Psychological Bulletin,* September 1955, pp. 396–428; F. Herzberg, B.

Mausner, R. O. Peterson, and D. F. Capwell, *Job Attitudes: Review of Research and Opinion* (Pittsburgh: Psychological Service of Pittsburgh, 1957); V. H. Vroom, *Work and Motivation* (New York: John Wiley, 1964); G. P. Fournet, M. K. Distefano, Jr., and M. W. Pryer, "Job Satisfaction: Issues and Problems," *Personnel Psychology,* Summer 1966, pp. 165–83.

33. Vroom, *Work and Motivation.*

34. See, for example, J. B. Herman, "Are Situational Contingencies Limiting Job Attitude-Job Performance Relationship?" *Organizational Behavior and Human Performance,* October 1973, pp. 208–24.

35. C. N. Greene, "The Satisfaction-Performance Controversy," *Business Horizons,* February 1972, pp. 31–41; and E. E. Lawler III, *Motivation in Organizations* (Monterey, Calif.: Brooks/Cole, 1973).

36. Locke, "The Nature and Causes of Job Satisfaction," p. 1331.

37. F. J. Smith, "Work Attitudes as Predictors of Attendance on a Specific Day," *Journal of Applied Psychology,* February 1977, pp. 16–19.

38. Brayfield and Crockett, "Employee Attitudes"; Vroom, *Work and Motivation*; J. Price, *The Study of Turnover* (Ames: Iowa State University Press, 1977); and W. H. Mobley, R. W. Griffin, H. H. Hand, and B. M. Meglino, "Review and Conceptual Analysis of the Employee Turnover Process," *Psychological Bulletin,* May 1979, pp. 493–522.

39. D. G. Spencer and R. M. Steers, "Performance as a Moderator of the Job Satisfaction–Turnover Relationship," *Journal of Applied Psychology,* August 1981, pp. 511–14.

Ability and Motivation

5

AFTER STUDYING THIS CHAPTER, YOU SHOULD BE ABLE TO:

Define and explain the following key terms and concepts:

Ability	Lower-order needs
Affiliation need	Motivation
Cognitive evaluation theory	Motivation-hygiene theory
Equity theory	Physical abilities
ERG theory	Power need
Expectancy theory	Reinforcement theory
Goal-setting theory	Self-actualization
Hierarchy of needs theory	Theory X
Higher-order needs	Theory Y
Intellectual abilities	Three needs theory

Understand:

Two types of ability
The motivation process
The best known theories of motivation
The characteristics that high achievers prefer in a job
Why high achievers don't make good managers
The types of goals that increase performance
The impact from underrewarding employees
The key relationships in expectancy theory

Set me anything to do as a task, and it is inconceivable the desire I have to do something else.

—G. B. SHAW

A popular, although arguably simplistic, way to think of employee performance is as a function of the interaction of ability and motivation; that is, performance $= f$ (ability $\times$ motivation). If either is inadequate, performance will be negatively affected. We've all seen examples of this interaction in the classroom and on the athletic field. The most gifted students often do not earn the highest grades in school. Similarly, who among us doesn't know someone of average abilities who, because he or she studies so hard, consistently earns outstanding grades? In sport, coaches regularly encounter the superathlete who just won't ''pay the price'' necessary to reach his or her full potential; and many of the best high school teams are composed of players who excel more because of their desire than their innate talent. These illustrations from the classroom and the athletic field also have their counterparts in the workplace. In this chapter, we will demonstrate the important role that ability and motivation each plays in explaining and predicting behavior in organizations.

ABILITY

Contrary to what we were taught in grade school, we weren't all created equal. Most of us are to the left of the median on some normally distributed ability curve. Regardless of how motivated you are, it is unlikely that you can write as well as James Michener, run as fast as Carl Lewis, tell jokes as well as Joan Rivers, or do improvisation as well as Robin Williams. Of course, just because we aren't all equal in abilities does not imply that some individuals are generally inferior to others. What we're acknowledging is that everyone has strengths and weaknesses in terms of ability that make him or her relatively superior or inferior to others in performing certain tasks or activities.[1] From management's standpoint, the issue isn't whether or not people differ in terms of their abilities. They do! The issue is *how* people differ in abilities and *using* that knowledge to increase the likelihood that an employee will perform his or her job well.

What does *ability* mean? As we'll use the term, ability refers to an individual's capacity to perform the various tasks in a job. It is a current assessment of what one *can* do. An individual's overall abilities are essentially made up of two sets of skills: intellectual and physical.

Intellectual Abilities

Intellectual abilities are those needed to perform mental activities. I.Q. tests, for example, are designed to ascertain one's intellectual abilities. So, too, are popular college admission tests like the SAT and ACT and graduate admission tests in business (GMAT), law (LSAT), and medicine (MCAT). Some of the more relevant dimensions making up intellectual abilities include number aptitude, verbal comprehension, perceptual speed, and inductive reasoning. Table 5–1 describes these dimensions.

Jobs differ in the demands they place on incumbents to use their intellectual abilities. Generally speaking, the higher an individual rises in an organization's hierarchy, the more that general intelligence and verbal abilities will be necessary to perform the job successfully. Strong intellectual skills, therefore, are not a prerequisite for all jobs. In fact, for many jobs—where employee behavior is highly routine and there exists little or no opportunities to exercise discretion—strong intellectual abilities should be unrelated to performance.

TABLE 5–1
Dimensions of Intellectual Ability

DIMENSION	DESCRIPTION	JOB EXAMPLE
Number aptitude	Ability to do speedy and accurate arithmetic computations	Accountant: Determining the sales tax on a set of items
Verbal comprehension	Ability to understand what is read or heard and the relationship of words to each other	Plant Manager: Following corporate policies
Perceptual speed	Ability visually to identify similarities and differences quickly and accurately	Fire Investigator: Identifying clues to support a charge of arson
Inductive reasoning	Ability to identify a logical sequence in a problem and then solve the problem	Market Researcher: Forecasting demand for a product in the next time period

Given that a job requires certain mental skills, management will rely on psychological tests to assess an employee's, or a potential employee's, abilities. Popular intelligence tests include Stanford-Binet and the Wechsler Adult Intelligence Scale. Of course, use of these tests for selection, placement, transfer, or promotion decisions automatically call into question whether there is a direct relationship between performance on the test and performance on the job. For instance, if management promotes one individual over another because the first scored 125 on a standardized I.Q. test versus 105 by the other, the law requires that management be able to demonstrate that higher I.Q. scores are directly related to higher job performance on this particular job. Otherwise, management is vulnerable to charges of discriminatory practices.[2] Nothing in the law makes the use of intellectual tests illegal; but employers who use such tests must document that the test is a valid predictor. The use of mental ability tests, for example, for determining who should or should not be put into most unskilled jobs is likely to be found discriminatory, if challenged in the courts, because there is little evidence to indicate a high correlation between mental abilities and performance on these jobs.

Physical Abilities

To the same degree that intellectual abilities play a larger role in performance as individuals move up the organizational hierarchy, specific physical abilities gain importance for successfully doing less skilled and more standardized jobs in the lower part of the organization. Jobs where success demands stamina, manual dexterity, leg strength, or similar talents require management to identify an employee's physical capabilities.

Research on the requirements needed in hundreds of jobs has identified nine basic abilities involved in the performance of physical tasks.[3] These are described in Table 5–2. Individuals differ in the amount to which they hold each of these abilities. Not surprisingly, there is also little relationship between them: a high score on one is no assurance of a high score on others. High employee performance is likely to be achieved when management has ascertained the extent to which a job requires each of the nine abilities and then ensures that employees in that job have those abilities.

The Ability-Job Fit

Our concern is with explaining and predicting the behavior of people at work. In this section, we have demonstrated that jobs make differing demands on people and that people differ in the abilities they possess. Employee performance, therefore, is enhanced when there is a high ability-job fit.

TABLE 5–2
Nine Basic Physical Abilities

Strength Factors

1. Dynamic strength	Ability to exert muscular force repeatedly or continuously over time
2. Trunk strength	Ability to exert muscular strength using the trunk (particularly abdominal) muscles
3. Static strength	Ability to exert force against external objects
4. Explosive strength	Ability to expend a maximum of energy in one or a series of explosive acts

Flexibility Factors

5. Extent flexibility	Ability to move the trunk and back muscles as far as possible
6. Dynamic flexibility	Ability to make rapid, repeated flexing movements

Other Factors

7. Body coordination	Ability to coordinate the simultaneous actions of different parts of the body
8. Balance	Ability to maintain equilibrium despite forces pulling off balance
9. Stamina	Ability to continue maximum effort requiring prolonged effort over time

Source: Reprinted from the June 1979 issue of *Personnel Administrator,* copyright 1979, The American Society for Personnel Administration; 606 North Washington Streeet; Alexandria, Virginia 22314. pp. 82–92.

The specific intellectual or physical abilities required for adequate job performance depend on the ability requirements of the job. Directing attention at only the employee's abilities or the ability requirements of the job ignores the fact that employee performance depends on the interaction of the two.

What predictions can we make when the fit is poor? As alluded to previously, if employees lack the required abilities, they are likely to fail. If you're hired as a typist and you can't meet the job's basic typing requirements, your performance is going to be poor irrespective of a positive attitude, the right personality-job match, or your high level of motivation. When the ability-job fit is out of sync because the employee has abilities that far exceed the requirements of the job, our predictions would be very different. Job performance is likely to be adequate, but there will be organizational inefficiencies and possible declines in employee satisfaction. Given that employee pay tends to reflect the highest skill level that they possess, if their abilities far exceed those necessary to do the job, management will be paying them more than they need to. Abilities significantly above those required can also reduce the employee's job satisfaction when the employee's desire to use his or her ability is particularly strong but that desire is frustrated by the limitations of the job.

MOTIVATION

In the study of individual behavior, probably no concept has received more attention than motivation. A cursory look at any organization quickly suggests that some people work harder than others. An individual with outstanding abilities may consistently be outperformed by someone with obviously inferior talents. Why do people exert different levels of effort in different activities? Why do some people appear to be "highly motivated," whereas others are not? These are questions we wish to answer in this section.

What Is Motivation?

Maybe the place to begin is to say what motivation isn't. Many people incorrectly view motivation as a personal trait—that is, some have it and others don't. In practice, this would characterize the manager who labels a certain employee as lazy. Such a label assumes that an individual is always lazy or is lacking in motivation. Our knowledge of motivation tells us that this just isn't true. What we know is that motivation is the result of the interaction of the individual and the situation. Certainly, individuals differ in their basic motivational drive. But the same employee who is quickly bored when pulling the lever on his drill press may pull the lever on a slot machine in Las Vegas for hours on end without the slightest hint of boredom. You may read a complete novel at one sitting, yet find it difficult to stay with a textbook for more than twenty minutes. It's not necessarily you—it's the situation. So as we analyze the concept of motivation, keep in mind that level of motivation both varies between individuals and within individuals at different times.

We'll define *motivation* as the willingness to exert high levels of effort toward organizational goals, conditioned by the effort's ability to satisfy some individual need. While general motivation is concerned with effort toward *any* goal, we'll narrow the focus to *organizational* goals in order to reflect our singular interest in work-related behavior. The three key elements in our definition are effort, organizational goals, and needs.

The effort element is a measure of intensity. When someone is motivated, he or she tries hard. But high levels of effort are unlikely to lead to favorable job performance outcomes unless the effort is channeled in a direction that benefits the organization.[4] Therefore, we must consider the quality of the effort as well as its intensity. Effort that is directed toward, and consistent with, the organization's goals is the kind of effort that we should be seeking. Finally, we will treat motivation as a need-satisfying process. This is depicted in Figure 5–1.

A need, in our terminology, means some internal state that makes certain outcomes appear attractive. An unsatisfied need creates tension that stimulates drives within the individual. These drives generate a search behavior to find par-

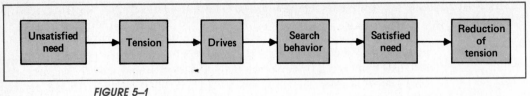

FIGURE 5–1
The Motivation Process

ticular goals that, if attained, will satisfy the need and lead to the reduction of tension.

So we can say that motivated employees are in a state of tension. To relieve this tension, they exert effort. The greater the tension, the higher the effort level. If this effort successfully leads to the satisfaction of the need, tension is reduced. But since we are interested in work behavior, this tension-reduction effort must also be directed toward organizational goals. Therefore, inherent in our definition of motivation is the requirement that the individual's needs are compatible and consistent with the organization's goals. Where this does not occur, we can have individuals exerting high levels of effort that actually run counter to the interests of the organization. This, incidentally, is not so unusual. Some employees regularly spend a lot of time talking with friends at work in order to satisfy their social needs. There is a high level of effort, only it's being unproductively directed.

Early Theories of Motivation

The 1950s were a fruitful period in the development of motivation concepts. Three specific theories were formulated during this period, which, though heavily attacked and now questionable in terms of validity, are probably the best known explanations for employee motivation. These are the hierarchy of needs theory, Theories X and Y, and the motivation-hygiene theory. As you'll see later in this chapter, we have since developed more valid explanations of motivation, but you should know these early theories for at least two reasons: (1) they represent a foundation from which contemporary theories have grown, and (2) practicing managers regularly use these theories and their terminology in explaining employee motivation.

HIERARCHY OF NEEDS THEORY

It's probably safe to say that the most well-known theory of motivation is Abraham Maslow's hierarchy of needs.[5] He hypothesized that within every human being there exists a hierarchy of five needs. These needs are:

1. *Physiological*—includes hunger, thirst, shelter, sex, and other bodily needs
2. *Safety*—includes security and protection from physical and emotional harm
3. *Love*—includes affection, belongingness, acceptance, and friendship
4. *Esteem*—includes internal esteem factors such as self-respect, autonomy, and achievement and external esteem factors such as status, recognition, and attention

5. *Self-actualization*—is represented by the drive to become what one is capable of becoming; includes growth, achieving one's potential, and self-fulfillment

As each of these needs becomes substantially satisfied, the next need becomes dominant. In terms of Figure 5–2, the individual moves up the hierarchy. From the standpoint of motivation, the theory would say that although no need is ever fully gratified, a substantially satisfied need no longer motivates.

Maslow separated the five needs into higher and lower levels. Physiological and safety needs were described as lower-order and love, esteem, and self-actualization as higher-order needs. The differentiation between the two orders was made on the premise that higher-order needs are satisfied internally to the person, whereas lower-order needs are predominantly satisfied externally (by such things as money wages, union contracts, and tenure). In fact, the natural conclusion to be drawn from Maslow's classification is that in times of economic plenty, almost all permanently employed workers have had their lower-order needs substantially met.

Maslow's need theory has received wide recognition, particularly among practicing managers. This can be attributed to the theory's intuitive logic and ease of understanding. Unfortunately, however, research does not generally validate

FIGURE 5–2

Maslow's Hierarchy of Needs

Source: By permission of the Modular Project of Organizational Behavior and Instructional Communications Centre. McGill University, Montreal, Canada.

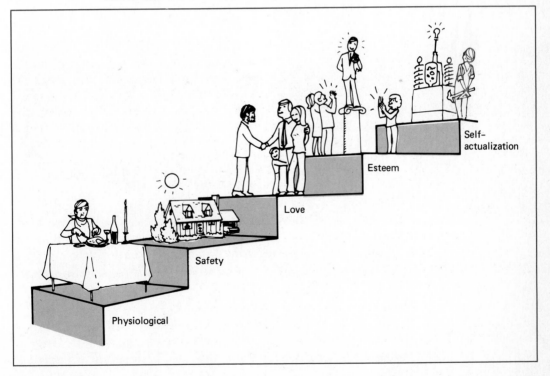

the theory. Maslow provided no empirical substantiation, and several studies that sought to validate the theory found no support.[6]

Old theories, especially ones that are intuitively logical, apparently die hard. One researcher reviewed the evidence and concluded that "although of great societal popularity, need hierarchy as a theory continues to receive little empirical support."[7] Further, the researcher stated that the "available research should certainly generate a reluctance to accept unconditionally the implication of Maslow's hierarchy."[8] Another review came to the same conclusion.[9] Little support was found for the prediction that need structures are organized along the dimensions proposed by Maslow, the prediction of a negative relationship between the level of need gratification and the activation of that need, or the prediction of a positive relationship between the level of need gratification and the activation level of the next higher need. But remember that there is a difference between finding "insufficient evidence" for a theory and labeling it "invalid." "It is clear that the available research does not support the Maslow theory to any significant degree. This does not imply that the theory is wrong, merely that it has not been supported."[10]

THEORY X AND THEORY Y

Douglas McGregor proposed two distinct views of human beings: one basically negative, labeled Theory X, and the other basically positive, labeled Theory Y.[11] After viewing the way in which managers dealt with employees, McGregor concluded that a manager's view of the nature of human beings is based on a certain grouping of assumptions and that he or she tends to mold his or her behavior toward subordinates according to these assumptions.

Under Theory X, the four assumptions held by managers are

1. Employees inherently dislike work and, whenever possible, will attempt to avoid it.
2. Since employees dislike work, they must be coerced, controlled, or threatened with punishment to achieve goals.
3. Employees will shirk responsibilities and seek formal direction whenever possible.
4. Most workers place security above all other factors associated with work and will display little ambition.

In contrast to these negative views toward the nature of human beings, McGregor listed four other assumptions that he called Theory Y:

1. Employees can view work as being as natural as rest or play.
2. People will exercise self-direction and self-control if they are committed to the objectives.
3. The average person can learn to accept, even seek, responsibility.
4. Creativity—that is, the ability to make innovative decisions—is widely dispersed throughout the population and is not necessarily the sole province of those in management positions.

What are the motivational implications if you accept McGregor's analysis? The answer is best expressed in the framework presented by Maslow. Theory X assumes that lower-order needs dominate individuals. Theory Y assumes that higher-order needs dominate individuals. McGregor, himself, held to the belief that Theory Y assumptions were more valid than Theory X. Therefore, he proposed such ideas as participation in decision making, responsible and challenging jobs, and good group relations as approaches that would maximize an employee's job motivation.

Unfortunately, there is no evidence to confirm that either set of assumptions is valid or that acceptance of Theory Y assumptions and altering one's actions accordingly will lead to more motivated workers. As will become evident later in this chapter, either Theory X or Theory Y assumptions may be appropriate in a particular situation.

MOTIVATION-HYGIENE THEORY Dual- Factor Theory

The motivation-hygiene theory was proposed by psychologist Frederick Herzberg.[12] In the belief that an individual's relation to his or her work is a basic one and that his or her attitude toward this work can very well determine the individual's success or failure, Herzberg investigated the question, "What do people want from their jobs?" He asked people to describe, in detail, situations when they felt exceptionally good or bad about their jobs. These responses were tabulated and categorized. Factors affecting job attitudes as reported in twelve investigations conducted by Herzberg are illustrated in Figure 5–3.

From the categorized responses, Herzberg concluded that the replies people gave when they felt good about their jobs were significantly different from the replies given when they felt bad. As seen in Figure 5–3, certain characteristics tend to be consistently related to job satisfaction (factors on the right side of the figure), and others to job dissatisfaction (the left side of the figure). Intrinsic factors, such as achievement, recognition, the work itself, responsibility, advancement, and growth seem to be related to job satisfaction. When those questioned felt good about their work, they tended to attribute these characteristics to themselves. On the other hand, when they were dissatisfied, they tended to cite extrinsic factors, such as company policy and administration, supervision, interpersonal relations, and working conditions.

The data suggest, says Herzberg, that the opposite of satisfaction is not dissatisfaction, as was traditionally believed. Removing dissatisfying characteristics from a job does not necessarily make the job satisfying. As illustrated in Figure 5–4, Herzberg proposes that his findings indicate the existence of a dual continuum: The opposite of "Satisfaction" is "No Satisfaction," and the opposite of "Dissatisfaction" is "No Dissatisfaction."

According to Herzberg, the factors leading to job satisfaction are separate and distinct from those that lead to job dissatisfaction. Therefore, managers who seek to eliminate factors that create job dissatisfaction can bring about peace, but not necessarily motivation. They will be placating their work force rather than motivating them. As a result, such characteristics as company policy and administration, supervision, interpersonal relations, working conditions, and salary have been characterized by Herzberg as hygiene factors. When they are adequate, people will not be dissatisfied; however, neither will they be satisfied. If we want to motivate people on their jobs, Herzberg suggests emphasizing achievement, rec-

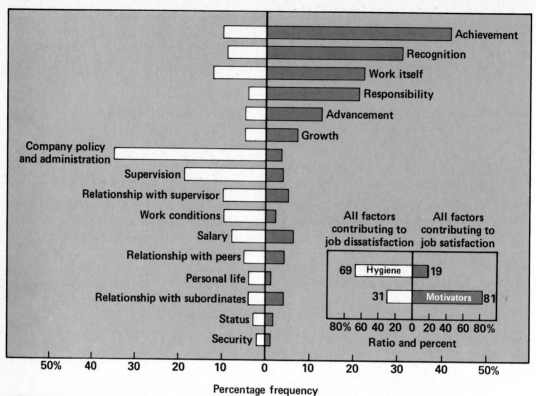

FIGURE 5–3

Comparison of Satisfiers and Dissatisfiers

ognition, the work itself, responsibility, and growth. These are the characteristics that people find intrinsically rewarding.

The motivation-hygiene theory is not without its detractors. The criticisms of the theory include the following:

1. The procedure that Herzberg used is limited by its methodology. When things are going well, people tend to take credit themselves. Contrarily, they blame failure on the extrinsic environment.

2. The reliability of Herzberg's methodology is questioned. Since raters have to make interpretations, it is possible that they may contaminate the findings by interpreting one response in one manner while treating another similar response differently.

3. No overall measure of satisfaction was utilized. In other words, a person may dislike part of his or her job, yet still think the job is acceptable.

4. The theory is inconsistent with previous research. The motivation-hygiene theory ignores situational variables.

5. Herzberg assumes that there is a relationship between satisfaction and productivity. But the research methodology he used looked only at satisfaction, not at productiv-

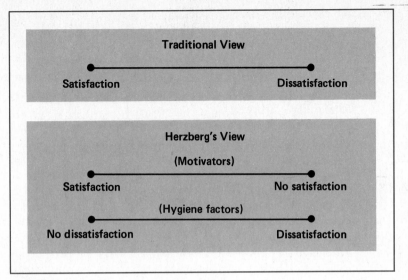

FIGURE 5–4

Contrasting Views of Satisfaction-Dissatisfaction

ity. To make such research relevant, one must assume a high relationship between satisfaction and productivity.[12]

Regardless of criticisms, Herzberg's theory has been widely read and few managers are unfamiliar with his recommendations. The increased popularity since the mid-1960s of vertically expanding jobs to allow workers greater responsibility in planning and controlling their work can probably be largely attributed to Herzberg's findings and recommendations.

From another perspective, Herzberg's findings appear consistent with general surveys made of workers' opinions about what they want from their job. Nationwide polls conducted by the National Opinion Research Center, for example, indicate that "more than half of the white, male work force in the United States believes that the most important characteristic of a job is that it involve work that is important and provides a sense of accomplishment."[13] Meaningful work is rated "most important" three times more frequently than are "opportunities for advancement" and "high income" and seven times more frequently than is the desire for "shorter work hours and much free time."

Contemporary Theories of Motivation

The previous theories are well known but, unfortunately, have not held up well under close examination. However, all is not lost. There are a number of contemporary theories that have one thing in common—each has a reasonable degree of valid supporting documentation. Of course, this doesn't mean that the theories we are about to introduce are unquestionably "right." What they do represent is the current "state of the art" in explaining employee motivation.

ERG THEORY

Clayton Alderfer of Yale University has reworked Maslow's need hierarchy to align it more closely with the empirical research. His revised need hierarchy is labeled ERG theory.[14]

Alderfer argues that there are three groups of core needs—existence, relatedness, and growth—hence the label: ERG theory. The existence group is concerned with providing our basic material existence requirements. They include the items that Maslow considered as physiological and safety needs. The second group of needs are those of relatedness—the desire we have for maintaining important interpersonal relationships. These social and status desires require interaction with others if they are to be satisfied, and they align with Maslow's love need and the external component of Maslow's esteem classification. Finally, Alderfer isolates growth needs—an intrinsic desire for personal development. These include the intrinsic component from Maslow's esteem category and the characteristics included under self-actualization.

Besides substituting three needs for five, how does Alderfer's ERG theory differ from Maslow? In contrast to Maslow, the ERG theory demonstrates that (1) more than one need may be operative at the same time and (2) if the gratification of a higher-level need is stifled, the desire to satisfy a lower-level need increases.

Maslow's need hierarchy is a rigid steplike progression. ERG theory does not assume that there exists a rigid hierarchy where a lower need must be substantially gratified before one can move on. A person can, for instance, be working on growth even though existence or relatedness needs are unsatisfied; or all three need categories could be operating at the same time.

ERG theory also contains a frustration-regression dimension. Maslow, you'll remember, argued that an individual would stay at a certain need level until that need was satisfied. ERG theory counters by noting that when a higher-order need level is frustrated, the individual's desire to increase a lower-level need takes place. Inability to satisfy a need for social interaction, for instance, might increase the desire for more money or better working conditions. So frustration can lead to a regression to a lower need.

In summary, ERG theory argues, like Maslow, that satisfied lower-order needs lead to the desire to satisfy higher-order needs; but multiple needs can be operating as motivators at the same time, and frustration in attempting to satisfy a higher-level need can result to regression to a lower-level need.

ERG theory is more consistent with our knowledge of individual differences among people. Variables such as education, family background, and cultural environment can alter the importance or driving force that a group of needs hold for a particular individual. The evidence demonstrating that people in other cultures rank the need categories differently—for instance, natives of Spain and Japan place social needs before their physiological requirements[15]—would be consistent with the ERG theory. Several studies have supported the ERG theory,[16] but there is also evidence that it doesn't work in some organizations.[17] Overall, however, ERG theory represents a more valid version of the need hierarchy.

THREE NEEDS THEORY

In Chapter 3, we introduced the need to achieve as a personality characteristic. It is also one of three needs proposed by David McClelland and others as being important in organizational settings for understanding motivation.[18] These three needs are achievement, power, and affiliation. They are identified as follows:

Need for achievement—the drive to excel, to achieve in relation to a set of standards, to strive to succeed

Need for power—the need to make others behave in a way that they would not have behaved otherwise

Need for affiliation—the desire for friendly and close interpersonal relationships

As described previously, some people who have a compelling drive to succeed are striving for personal achievement rather than the rewards of success per se. They have a desire to do something better or more efficiently than it has been done before. This drive is the achivement need *(nAch)*. From research into the achievement need, McClelland found that high achievers differentiate themselves from others by their desire to do things better.[19] They seek situations where they can attain personal responsibility for finding solutions to problems, where they can receive rapid feedback on their performance so they can tell easily whether they are improving or not, and where they can set moderately challenging goals. High achievers are not gamblers; they dislike succeeding by chance. They prefer the challenge of working at a problem and accepting the personal responsibility for success or failure rather than leaving the outcome to chance or the actions of others. Importantly, they avoid what they perceive to be very easy or very difficult tasks.

Again as noted in Chapter 3, high achievers perform best when they perceive their probability of success as being .5, that is, where they estimate that they have a 50-50 chance of success. They dislike gambling with high odds because they get no achievement satisfaction from happenstance success. Similarly, they dislike low odds (high probability of success) because then there is no challenge to their skills. They like to set goals that require stretching themselves a little. When there is an approximately equal chance of success or failure, there is the optimum opportunity to experience feelings of accomplishment and satisfaction from their efforts.

The need for power *(nPow)* is the desire to have impact, to be influential, and to control others. Individuals high in *nPow* enjoy being "in charge," strive for influence over others, prefer to be placed into competitive and status-oriented situations, and tend to be more concerned with gaining influence over others and prestige than with effective performance.

The third need isolated by McClelland is affiliation *(nAff)*. This need has received the least attention of researchers. Affiliation can be viewed as a Dale

Carnegie–type of need—the desire to be liked and accepted by others. Individuals with a high affiliation motive strive for friendship, prefer cooperative situations rather than competitive ones, and desire relationships involving a high degree of mutual understanding.

How do you find out if someone is, for instance, a high achiever? All three needs are typically measured through a projective test in which subjects respond to a set of pictures. Each picture is briefly shown to a subject and then he or she writes a story based on the picture. As an example, the picture may show a male sitting at a desk in a pensive positive, looking at a picture of a woman and two children that sits at the corner of the desk. The subject will then be asked to write a story describing what is going on, what preceded this situation, what will happen in the future, and so on. The stories become, in effect, projective tests that measure unconscious motives. Each story is scored and a subject's rating on each of the three needs is obtained.

Based on an extensive amount of research, some reasonably well-supported predictions can be made based on the relationship between achievement need and job performance. Although less research has been done on power and affiliation needs, there are consistent findings here, too.

First, as shown in Figure 5–5, individuals with a high need to achieve prefer job situations with personal responsibility, feedback, and an intermediate degree of risk. When these characteristics are prevalent, high achievers will be strongly motivated. The evidence consistently demonstrates, for instance, that high achievers are successful in entrepreneurial activities such as running their own businesses, managing a self-contained unit within a large organization, and serving in a variety of sales positions.[20]

Second, a high need to achieve does not necessarily lead to being a good manager, especially in large organizations. People with a high achievement need are interested in how well they do personally and not in influencing others to do well. High-*nAch* sales people do not necessarily make good sales managers, and the good manager in a large organization does not typically have a high need to achieve.[21]

Third, the needs for affiliation and power tend to be closely related to managerial success. The best managers are high in their need for power and low in their need for affiliation.[22] In fact, a high power motive may be a requirement for

FIGURE 5–5
Matching Achievers and Jobs

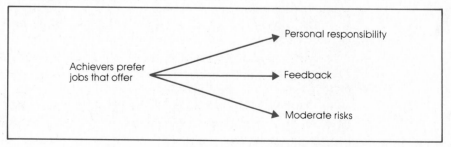

managerial effectiveness.[23] Of course, what is the cause and what is the effect is arguable. It has been suggested that a high power need may occur simply as a function of one's level in a hierarchical organization.[24] This latter argument proposes that the higher the level an individual rises to in the organization, the greater is the incumbent's power motive. As a result, powerful positions would be the stimulus to a high power motive.

Lastly, employees have been successfully trained to stimulate their achievement need. If the job calls for a high achiever, management can select a person with a high *nAch* or develop its own candidate through achievement training.[25]

COGNITIVE EVALUATION THEORY

In the late 1960s, one researcher proposed that the introduction of extrinsic rewards, such as pay, for work effort that had been previously intrinsically rewarding due to the pleasure associated with the content of the work itself, would tend to decrease the overall level of motivation.[26] This proposal—which has come to be called the cognitive evaluation theory—has been extensively researched, and a large number of studies have been supportive.[27] The importance of this theory cannot be understated because, as we'll show, it has major implications for the way in which people are paid in organizations.

Historically, motivation theorists have generally assumed that intrinsic motivators such as achievement, responsibility, and competence were independent from extrinsic motivators like high pay, promotions, good supervisor relations, and pleasant working conditions. That is, the stimulation of one would not affect the other. But the cognitive evaluation theory suggests otherwise. It argues that when extrinsic rewards are used by organizations as payoffs for superior performance, the intrinsic rewards, which are derived from individuals doing what they like, are reduced. In other words, when extrinsic rewards are given to someone for performing an interesting task, it causes intrinsic interest in the task itself to decline.

Why would such an outcome occur? The popular explanation is that the individual experiences a loss of control over his or her own behavior so that the previous intrinsic motivation diminishes. Further, the elimination of extrinsic rewards can produce a shift—from an external to an internal explanation—in an individual's perception of causation of why he works on a task. If you're reading a novel a week because your English literature instructor requires you to, you can attribute your reading behavior to an external source. However, after the course is over, if you find yourself continuing to read a novel a week, your natural inclination is to say, "I must enjoy reading novels, because I'm still reading one a week!"

If the cognitive evaluation theory is valid, it should have major implications for managerial practices. It has been a truism among compensation specialists for years that if pay or other extrinsic rewards are to be effective motivators, they should be made contingent on an individual's performance. But, cognitive evaluation theorists would argue, this will only tend to decrease the internal satisfaction that the individual receives from doing the job. We have substituted an external stimulus for an internal stimulus. In fact, if cognitive evaluation theory is correct, it would make sense to make an individual's pay *non*contingent on performance in order to avoid decreasing intrinsic motivation.

We noted earlier that the cognitive evaluation theory has been supported in a number of studies. Yet it has also met with attacks, specifically on the methodology used in these studies[28] and in the interpretation of the findings.[29] But where does this theory stand today? Can we say that when organizations use extrinsic motivators like pay and promotions to stimulate workers' performance that they do so at the expense of reducing intrinsic interest and motivation in the work being done? The answer is not a simple "Yes" or "No."

While further research is needed to clarify some of the current ambiguity, the evidence does lead us to conclude that the nonadditivity of extrinsic and intrinsic rewards is a real phenomenon.[30] But its impact on employee motivation at work, in contrast to motivation in general, may be considerably less than originally thought. First, many of the studies testing the theory were done with students, not paid organizational employees. The researchers would observe what happens to a student's behavior when a reward that had been allocated is stopped. This is interesting, but it does not represent the typical work situation. In the real world, when extrinsic rewards are stopped it usually means the individual is no longer part of the organization. Second, evidence indicates that very high intrinsic motivation levels are strongly resistant to the detrimental impacts of extrinsic rewards.[31] Even when a job is inherently interesting, there still exists a powerful norm for extrinsic payment.[32] At the other extreme, on dull tasks extrinsic rewards appear to increase intrinsic motivation.[33] Therefore, the theory may have limited applicability to work organizations because most low-level jobs are not inherently satisfying enough to foster high intrinsic interest and many managerial and professional positions offer intrinsic rewards. Cognitive evaluation theory may be relevant to that set of organizational jobs that falls in between—those that are neither extremely dull nor extremely interesting.

GOAL-SETTING THEORY

Gene Broadwater, coach of the Hamilton High School cross-country team, gave his squad these last words before they approached the line for the league championship race: "Each one of you is physically ready. Now, get out there and do your best. No one can ever ask more of you than that."

You've heard the phrase a number of times yourself: "Just do your best. That's all anyone can ask for." But what does "do your best" mean? Do we ever know if we've achieved that vague goal? Would the cross-country runners have recorded faster times if Coach Broadwater had given each a specific goal to shoot for? Might you have done better in your high school English class if your parents had said, "You should strive for 85 percent or higher on all your work in English" rather than telling you to "do your best"? The research on goal setting addresses these issues, and the findings, as you will see, are impressive in terms of the impact specific and challenging goals have on performance.

In the late 1960s, it was proposed that intentions to work toward a goal are a major source of work motivation.[34] The evidence strongly supports this thesis.

More to the point, we can say that specific goals increase performance; that difficult goals, when accepted, result in higher performance than do easy goals; and that feedback leads to higher performance than does nonfeedback.[35]

Specific hard goals produce a higher level of output than does a generalized goal of "do your best." The specificity of the goal itself acts as an internal stimulus. For instance, when a trucker commits to making eighteen round-trip hauls between Baltimore and Washington, D.C., each week, this intention gives him a specific objective to reach for. We can say that, all things being equal, the trucker with a specific goal will outperform his counterpart operating with no goals or the generalized goal of "do your best."

If factors like ability and acceptance of the goals are held constant, we can also state that the more difficult the goals, the higher the level of performance. However, it's logical to assume that easier goals are more likely to be accepted. But once an employee accepts a hard task, he or she will exert a high level of effort until it is achieved, lowered, or abandoned.

People will do better when they get feedback on how well they are progressing toward their goals. Why? Because feedback helps to identify discrepancies between what they have done and what they want to do; that is, feedback acts to guide behavior. But all feedback is not equally potent. Self-generated feedback—where the employee is able to monitor his or her own progress—has been shown to be a more powerful motivator than externally generated feedback.[36]

If employees have the opportunity to participate in the setting of their own goals, will they try harder? The evidence is mixed regarding the superiority of participation over assigned goals.[37] In some cases, participatively set goals elicit superior performance, while in other cases individuals performed best when assigned goals by their boss. But a major advantage of participation may be in increasing acceptance of the goal, itself, as a desirable one to work toward. As we noted, resistance is greater when goals are difficult. If people participate in goal setting, they are more likely to accept even a difficult goal than if they are arbitrarily assigned it by their boss. The reason is that individuals are more committed to choices in which they have a part. Thus, although participative goals may have no superiority over assigned goals when acceptance is taken as a given, participation does increase the probability that more difficult goals will be agreed to and acted upon.

Our overall conclusion is that intentions—as articulated in terms of hard and specific goals—are a potent motivating force. They do lead to higher performance. However, there is no evidence that such goals are associated with increased job satisfaction.[38]

REINFORCEMENT THEORY

A counterpoint to goal-setting theory is reinforcement theory. The former is a cognitive approach, proposing that an individual's purposes direct his or her action. In reinforcement theory we have a behavioristic approach, which argues that reinforcement conditions behavior. The two are clearly at odds philosophically. Reinforcement theorists see behavior as being environmentally caused. You need not be concerned, they would argue, with internal cognitive events; what controls behavior are reinforcers—any consequence that, when immediately following a response, increases the probability that the behavior will be repeated.

Reinforcement theory ignores the inner state of the individual and concentrates solely on what happens to a person when he or she takes some action. Because it does not concern itself with what initiates behavior, it is not, strictly speaking, a theory of motivation. But it does provide a powerful means of analysis of what controls behavior, and it is for this reason that it is typically considered in discussions of motivation.[39]

We discussed the reinforcement process in detail in Chapter 3. We showed how using reinforcers to condition behavior gives us considerable insight into how people learn. Yet we cannot ignore the fact that reinforcement has a wide following as a motivational device. In its pure form, however, reinforcement theory ignores feelings, attitudes, expectations, and other cognitive variables that are known to impact behavior. In fact, some researchers look at the same experiments that reinforcement theorists use to support their position and interpret the findings in a cognitive framework.[40]

Reinforcement is undoubtedly an important influence on behavior, but few scholars are prepared to argue that it is the *only* influence. The behaviors you engage in at work and the amount of effort you allocate to each task *is* affected by the consequences that follow from your behavior. If you are consistently reprimanded for outproducing your colleagues, you will likely reduce your productivity. But your lower productivity may also be explained in terms of goals, inequity, or expectancies.

EQUITY THEORY

Jane Pearson graduated last year from the State University with a degree in accounting. After interviews with a number of organizations on campus, she accepted a position with one of the nation's largest public accounting firms and was assigned to their Boston office. Jane was very pleased with the offer she received: challenging work with a prestigious firm, an excellent opportunity to gain important experience, and the highest salary any accounting major at State was offered last year—$2,100 a month. But Jane was the top student in her class; she was ambitious and articulate and fully expected to receive a commensurate salary.

Twelve months have passed since Jane joined her employer. The work has proved to be as challenging and satisfying as she had hoped. Her employer is extremely pleased with her performance; in fact she recently received a $100-a-month raise. However, Jane's motivational level has dropped dramatically in the past few weeks. Why? Her employer has just hired a fresh college graduate out of State University, who lacks the one-year experience Jane has gained, for $2,250 a month—$50 more than Jane now makes! It would be an understatement to describe Jane in any other terms than livid. Jane is even talking about looking for another job.

Jane's situation illustrates the role that equity plays in motivation. Employees make comparisons of their job inputs and outcomes relative to those of others. We perceive what we get from a job situation (outcomes) in relation to what we put into it (inputs), and then we compare our input-outcome ratio with the input-outcome ratio of relevant others. This is shown in Table 5–3. If we perceive our ratio to be equal to the relevant others with whom we compare ourselves, a state of equity is said to exist. We perceive our situation as fair—that justice prevails. If the ratios are unequal, inequity exists; that is, we tend to view ourselves as underrewarded or overrewarded. It has been proposed that an equity process takes place in which people who view any inequity as aversive will attempt to correct it.[41]

The referent than an employee selects adds to the complexity of equity theory. Evidence suggests that the reference chosen is an important variable in equity theory.[42] The three referent categories have been classified as "other," "system," and "self." The "other" category includes other individuals with similar jobs in the same organization and also includes friends, neighbors, or professional associates. Based on information that employees receive through word of mouth, newspapers, and magazines on such issues as executive salaries or a recent union contract, employees can compare their pay to that of others.

The "system" category considers organizational pay policies and procedures, and the administration of this system. It considers organizationwide pay policies, both implied and explicit. Precedents by the organization in terms of allocation of pay would be a major determinant in this category.

The "self" category refers to input-outcome ratios that are unique to the individual and differ from the individual's current input-outcome ratio. This category is influenced by such criteria as past jobs or commitments that must be met in terms of family role.

The choice of a particular set of referents is related to the information available about referents as well as to their perceived relevance. Based on equity the-

TABLE 5–3
Equity Theory

RATIO COMPARISONS	PERCEPTION
$\dfrac{O}{I_A} < \dfrac{O}{I_B}$	Inequity due to being underrewarded
$\dfrac{O}{I_A} = \dfrac{O}{I_B}$	Equity
$\dfrac{O}{I_A} > \dfrac{O}{I_B}$	Inequity due to being overrewarded
where $\dfrac{O}{I_A}$ represents the employee and	
$\dfrac{O}{I_B}$ represents relevant others	

ory, we might suggest that when employees envision an inequity, they may take one or more of five choices:

1. Distort either their own or others inputs or outcomes
2. Behave in some way so as to induce others to change their inputs or outcomes
3. Behave in some way so as to change their own inputs or outcomes
4. Choose a different comparison referent
5. Leave the field (quit their job)

Equity theory recognizes that individuals are concerned not only with the absolute amount of rewards they receive for their efforts; but also with the relationship of this amount to what others receive. They make judgments as to the relationship between their inputs and outcomes and the inputs and outcomes of others. Based on one's inputs, such as effort, experience, education, and competence, one compares outcomes such as salary levels, raises, recognition, and other factors. When people perceive an imbalance in their input-outcome ratio relative to others, tension is created. This tension provides the basis for motivation, as people strive for what they perceive as equity and fairness.

Specifically, the theory establishes four propositions relating to inequitable pay:

1. *Given payment by time, overrewarded employees will produce more than will equitably paid employees.* Hourly and salaried employees will generate high quantity or quality of production in order to increase the input side of the ratio and bring about equity.

2. *Given payment by quantity of production, overrewarded employees will produce fewer, but higher-quality, units than will equitably paid employees.* Individuals paid on a piece-rate basis will increase their effort to achieve equity, which can result in greater quality or quantity. However, increases in quantity will only increase inequity since every unit produced results in further overpayment. Therefore, effort is directed toward increasing quality rather than increasing quantity.

3. *Given payment by time, underrewarded employees will produce less or poorer quality of output.* Effort will be decreased, which will bring about lower productivity or poorer-quality output than equitably paid subjects.

4. *Given payment by quantity of production, underrewarded employees will produce a large number of low-quality units in comparison with equitably paid employees.* Employees on piece-rate pay plans can bring about equity because trading off quantity of output for quality will result in an increase in rewards with little or no increase in contributions.

These propositions have generally been supported,[43] although inequities created by overpayment do not seem to have a very significant impact on behavior in most work situations. Apparently, people have a great deal more tolerance of overpayment inequities or are better able to rationalize them than of underpayment inequities. Nevertheless, the evidence indicates that employee motivation is influenced significantly by relative rewards as well as by absolute rewards.[44] Employees will try to correct perceived inequities, which might result in lower or higher productivity, improved or reduced quality of output, increased absenteeism, or voluntary resignation.

Of course, equity theory is not without problems. The theory leaves some key issues still unclear.[45] For instance, how do employees select who is included in the "other" referent category? How do they handle conflicting equity signals, such as when unions point to other employee groups who are substantially *better off*, while management argues how much things have *improved?* How do employees define inputs and outputs? How do they combine and weigh their inputs and outcomes to arrive at totals? When and how do the factors change over time? Yet, regardless of these problems, equity theory continues to offer us some important insights into employee motivation.

EXPECTANCY THEORY

Currently, the most widely accepted explanation of motivation is the expectancy theory.[46] Although it has its critics,[47] most of the research evidence is supportive of the theory.[48]

Essentially, the expectancy theory argues that the strength of a tendency to act in a certain way depends on the strength of an expectation that the act will be followed by a given outcome and on the attractiveness of that outcome to the individual. It includes three variables.[49]

1. *Attractiveness*—the importance that the individual places on the potential outcome or reward that can be achieved on the job. This considers the unsatisfied needs of the individual.
2. *Performance-reward linkage*—the degree to which the individual believes that performing at a particular level will lead to the attainment of a desired outcome.
3. *Effort-performance linkage*—the perceived probability by the individual that exerting a given amount of effort will lead to performance.

While this may sound pretty complex, it really is not that difficult to visualize. Whether one has the desire to produce at any given time depends on one's particular goals and one's perception of the relative worth of performance as a path to the attainment of these goals.

Figure 5–6 is a considerable simplification of expectancy theory, but it expresses its major contentions. The strength of a person's motivation to perform (effort) depends on how strongly she believes that she can achieve what she attempts. If she achieves this goal (performance), will she be adequately rewarded and, if she is rewarded by the organization, will the reward satisfy her individual

FIGURE 5–6
Simplified Expectancy Model

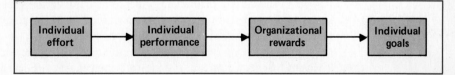

goals? Let us consider the four steps inherent in the theory and then attempt to apply it.

First, what perceived outcomes does the job offer the employee? Outcomes may be positive: pay, security, companionship, trust, fringe benefits, a chance to use talent or skills, congenial relationships. On the other hand, employees may view the outcomes as negative: fatigue, boredom, frustration, anxiety, harsh supervision, threat of dismissal. Importantly, reality is not relevant here; the critical issue is what the individual employee *perceives* the outcome to be, regardless of whether or not her perceptions are accurate.

Second, how attractive do employees consider these outcomes? Are they valued positively, negatively, or neutrally? This obviously is an internal issue to the individual and considers her personal values, personality, and needs. The individual who finds a particular outcome attractive—that is, positively valued—would prefer attaining it to not attaining it. Others may find it negative and, therefore, prefer not attaining it to attaining it. Still others may be neutral.

Third, what kind of behavior must the employee produce in order to achieve these outcomes? The outcomes are not likely to have any effect on the individual employee's performance unless the employee knows, clearly and unambiguously, what she must do in order to achieve them. For example, what is "doing well" in terms of performance appraisal? What are the criteria the employee's performance will be judged on?

Fourth and last, how does the employee view her chances of doing what is asked of her? After the employee has considered her own competencies and her ability to control those variables that will determine her success, what probability does she place on successful attainment?[50]

Let us use the classroom organization as an illustration of how one can use expectancy theory to explain motivation.

Most students prefer an instructor who tells them what is expected of them in the course. They want to know what the assignments and examinations will be like, when they are due or to be taken, and how much weight each carries in the final term grade. They also like to think that the amount of effort they exert in attending classes, taking notes, and studying will be reasonably related to the grade they will make in the course. If we assume that the above describes you, consider that five weeks into a class you are really enjoying (we'll call it B.A. 301), an exam is given back. You have studied hard for this exam. You have consistently scored A's and B's on exams in other courses where you have expended similar effort. And the reason you work so hard is to make top grades, which you believe are important for getting a good job upon graduation. Also, you are not sure, but you may want to go on to graduate school. Again, you think grades are important for getting into a good graduate school.

Well, the results of that five-week exam are in. The class median was 72. Ten percent of the class scored an 85 or higher and got an A. Your grade was 46; the minimum passing mark was 50. You're mad. You're frustrated. Even more, you're perplexed. How could you have possibly done so poorly on the exam when you usually score among the top grades in other classes by preparing as you had for this exam? Several interesting things are immediately evident in your behavior. Suddenly, you no longer are driven to attend B.A. 301 classes regularly. You find you do not study for the course either. When you do attend classes, you daydream a lot—the result is an empty notebook instead of several pages of notes. One would probably be correct in describing you as "lacking motivation" in B.A. 301. Why did your motivational level change? You know and I know, but let's explain it in expectancy terms.

If we use Figure 5–6 to understand this situation, we might say the following: Studying and preparation in B.A. 301 (effort) is conditioned by it resulting in answering the questions on the exam correctly (performance), which will produce a high grade (reward), which you believe will lead to the security, prestige, and other benefits that accrue from obtaining a good job (individual goal).

The attractiveness of the outcome—which in this case is a good grade—is high. But what about the performance-reward linkage? Do you feel that the grade you received truly reflects your knowledge of the material? In other words, did the test fairly measure what you know? If the answer is "Yes," then this linkage is strong. If the answer is "No," then at least part of the reason for your reduced motivational level is your belief that the test was not a fair measure of your performance. If the test was of an essay type, maybe you believe the instructor's grading method was poor. Was too much weight placed on a question that you thought was trivial? Maybe the instructor does not like you and was biased in grading your paper. These are examples of perceptions that influence the performance-reward linkage and your level of motivation.

Another possible demotivating force may be the effort-performance relationship. If, after you took the exam, you believed that you could not have passed it regardless of the amount of preparation you had done, then your desire to study will drop. Possibly the instructor wrote the exam under the assumption that you had had a considerably broader background in the course's subject matter. Maybe the course had several prerequisites that you did not know about, or possibly you had the prerequisites but took them several years ago. The end result is the same: You place a low value on your effort leading to answering the exam questions correctly, and hence there is a reduction in your motivational level and you lessen your effort.

The key to expectancy theory, therefore, is the understanding of an individual's goals and the linkage between effort and performance, between performance and rewards, and, finally, between the rewards and individual goal satisfaction. As a contingency model, expectancy theory recognizes that there is no universal principle for explaining everyone's motivations. Additionally, just because we understand what needs a person seeks to satisfy does not ensure that the individual himself perceives high performance as necessarily leading to the satisfaction of these needs. If you desire to take B.A. 301 in order to meet new people and make social contacts, but the instructor organizes the class on the assumption that you want to make a good grade in the course, the instructor may be personally disappointed should you perform poorly on the exams. Unfortunately, most instructors assume that their ability to allocate grades is a potent force in motivating students. But it will only be so if students place a high importance on grades, if students know what they must do to achieve the grade desired, and if the students consider there is a high probability of their performing well should they exert a high level of effort.

Let us summarize some of the issues expectancy theory has brought forward. First, it emphasizes payoffs or rewards. As a result, we have to believe that the rewards the organization is offering align with what the employee wants. It is a theory based on self-interest wherein each individual seeks to maximize her expected satisfaction: "Expectancy theory is a form of calculative, psychological *hedonism* in which the ultimate motive of every human act is asserted to be the maximization of pleasure and/or the minimization of pain."[51] Second, we have to be concerned with the attractiveness of rewards, which requires an understanding and knowledge of what value the individual puts on organizational payoffs. We shall want to reward the individual with those things she values positively. Third, expectancy theory emphasizes expected behaviors. Does the person know what is expected of her and how she will be appraised? Finally, the theory is concerned with expectations. It is irrelevant what is realistic or rational. An individual's own expectations of performance, reward, and goal satisfaction outcomes will determine her level of effort, not the objective outcomes themselves.

Does expectancy theory work? The space we have devoted to it suggests that it is important; yet, as we have seen before, few theories are irrefutable, without critics, or devoid of contradictory findings. Expectancy theory is no exception. Attempts to validate the theory have been complicated by methodological, criterion, and measurement problems. As a result, many published studies that purport to support or negate the theory must be viewed with caution. Importantly, most studies have failed to replicate the methodology as it was originally proposed. For example, the theory proposes to explain different levels of effort within the same person under different circumstances, but almost all replication studies have looked at different people. By correcting for this flaw, support for the validity of expectancy theory has been greatly improved.[52] Some critics suggest that the theory has only limited use, arguing that it tends to be more valid for predicting in situations where effort-performance and performance-reward linkages are clearly perceived by the individual.[53] Since few individuals perceive a high correlation between performance and rewards in their jobs, the theory tends to be idealistic. If organizations actually rewarded individuals for performance, rather than criteria such as seniority, effort, skill level, or job difficulty, then the theory's validity might be considerably greater. However, rather than invalidating expectancy theory, this criticism can be used in support of the theory and for explaining why a large segment of the work force exerts a minimal level of effort in carrying out their job responsibilities.

Integrating Contemporary Theories of Motivation

We've looked at a lot of motivation theories in this chapter. The fact that a number of these theories have been supported only complicates the matter. How simple it would have been if, after presenting half-a-dozen theories, only one was found valid. So the challenge is now to tie these theories together to help you understand their interrelationship.

Figure 5–7 presents a model that integrates much of what we know about motivation. Its basic foundation is the simplified expectancy model shown in Figure 5–6. Let's work through Figure 5–7, beginning at the extreme left.

The individual effort box has an arrow leading into it. This arrow flows out of the individual's goals. Consistent with goal-setting theory, this goals-effort loop is meant to remind us that goals direct behavior.

Expectancy theory predicts that an employee will exert a high level of effort if he or she perceives that there is a strong relationship between effort and performance, performance and rewards, and rewards and satisfaction of personal goals. Each of these relationships, in turn, is influenced by certain factors. For effort to lead to good performance, the individual must have the requisite ability to perform, and the performance evaluation system that measures the individual's performance must be perceived as being fair and objective. The performance-reward relationship will be strong if the individual perceives that it is performance (rather than seniority, personal favorites, or other criteria) that is rewarded. If cognitive evaluation theory were fully valid in the actual workplace, we would predict here that basing rewards on performance should decrease the individual's intrinsic motivation. The final link in expectancy theory is the rewards-goals relationship.

FIGURE 5–7

Integrating Contemporary Theories of Motivation

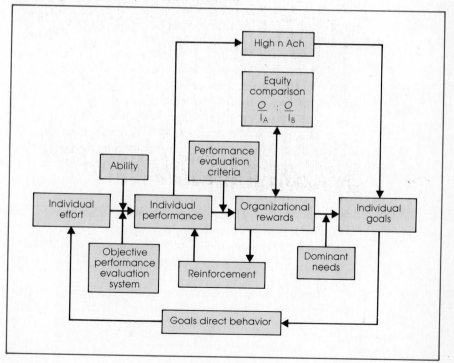

ERG theory would come into play at this point. Motivation would be high to the degree that the rewards an individual received for his or her high performance satisfied the dominant needs consistent with his or her individual goals.

A closer look at Figure 5–7 will also reveal that the model considers the achievement need and reinforcement and equity theories. The higher achiever is not motivated by the organization's rewards, hence, the jump from performance to individual goals for those with a high *nAch*. Remember, high achievers are internally driven as long as the jobs they are doing provide them with personal responsibility, feedback, and moderate risks. So they are not concerned with the performance-reward or rewards-goal linkages.

Reinforcement theory enters our model by recognizing that the organization's rewards reinforce the individual's performance. If management has designed a reward system that is seen by employees as "paying off" for good performance, the rewards will reinforce and encourage continued good performance.

Finally, rewards also play the key part in equity theory. Individuals will compare the rewards (outcomes) they receive from the inputs they make with the reward-input ratio of relevant others ($O/I_A:O/I_B$), and inequities may influence the effort expended.

IMPLICATIONS FOR PERFORMANCE AND SATISFACTION

We don't need to dwell on our earlier statement that ability directly influences an employee's level of performance and satisfaction through the ability-job fit. Given management's desire to get a compatible fit, what can be done? First, an effective selection process will improve the fit. A job analysis will provide information about jobs currently being done and the abilities that individuals need to perform the jobs adequately. Applicants can then be tested, interviewed, and evaluated as to the degree to which they possess the necessary abilities. Second, promotion and transfer decisions affecting individuals already in the organization's employment should reflect the abilities of candidates. As with new employees, care should be taken to assess critical abilities that incumbents will need in the job and matching those requirements with the organization's human resources. Third, the fit can be improved by fine-tuning the job to better match an incumbent's abilities. Often modifications can be made in the job that, while not significantly impacting the job's basic activities, better adapts it to the specific talents of a given employee. Examples of this might include changing some of the equipment used or reorganizing tasks within a group of employees. A final alternative is to provide training for employees. This is applicable to both new workers and present job incumbents. For the latter, training can keep their abilities current or provide new skills as times and conditions change.

The implications of motivation theories for higher-performing and more satisfied employees can best be summed up by listing some suggestions that tap the essence of what we know about motivation:

Recognize individual differences. Employees have different needs. Don't treat them all alike. Moreover, spend the time to understand what's important to each employee. This will allow you to individualize rewards to align with individual needs.

Match people to jobs. For example, if a job involves running a small business or an autonomous unit within a larger business, high achievers should be sought. If the job is a managerial slot in a large corporation, the best individual is likely to score high in *nPow* and low in *nAff*. Similarly, only put high achievers in jobs that will meet the requirements that will stimulate and satisfy their achievement need.

Use goals and feedback. Employees should have hard, specific goals as well as feedback on how well they are doing in pursuit of those goals.

Link rewards to performance. Consistent with reinforcement theory and expectancy theory, rewards should be contingent on performance. Importantly, employees must perceive a clear linkage. Regardless of how closely rewards are actually correlated to performance criteria, if individuals perceive this correlation to be low, we can expect low performance, a decrease in job satisfaction, and an increase in turnover and absenteeism statistics.

Check the system for equity. Rewards should also be perceived by employees as equating with the inputs they give. At a simplistic level, this should mean that experience, abilities, effort, and other obvious inputs should explain differences in performance and, hence, pay, job assignments, and other obvious rewards.

POINT

MONEY MOTIVATES!

The importance of money as a motivator has been consistently downgraded by most behavioral scientists. They prefer to point out the value of challenging jobs, goals, participation in decision making, feedback, cohesive work groups, and other nonmonetary factors as stimulants to employee motivation. We will argue otherwise here—that money is *the* crucial incentive to work motivation. As a medium of exchange, it is the vehicle by which employees can purchase the numerous need-satisfying "things" they desire. Further, money also performs the function of a "scorecard" by which employees assess the value that the organization places on their services and by which employees can compare their "value" to others.

Money's value as a medium of exchange is obvious. People may not work *only* for money, but take the money away and how many people would come to work? For the vast majority of the work force, a regular paycheck is absolutely necessary in order to meet their basic physiological and safety needs.

As equity theory suggests, money has symbolic value in addition to its exchange value. We use pay as the primary outcome against which we compare our inputs to determine if we are being treated equitably. The fact that an organization pays one executive $60,000 a year and another $75,000 means more than the latter merely earning $15,000 a year more. It is a message, from the organization to both employees, of how much it values the contribution of each. We see this every year in professional sports. A professional basketball player is making $750,000 a year but wants his contract renegotiated because another player, whose statistics are less impressive, signs a million-dollar-a-year contract. The case is never made that the player demanding a new contract *needs* an extra $250,000

a year to maintain his standard of living. It's not the exchange value of money at issue. It's the principle of the thing, which, in this case, is the message and symbolic value that pay carries.

In addition to equity theory, both reinforcement and expectancy theories attest to the value of money as a motivator. In the former, if pay is contingent on performance, it will encourage workers to high levels of effort. Consistent with expectancy theory, money will motivate to the extent that it is seen as being able to satisfy an individual's personal goals and is perceived as being dependent upon performance criteria.

The best case for money as a motivator is a review of studies done by Edwin Locke of the University of Maryland.[1] Locke looked at four methods of motivating employee performance: money, goal setting, participation in decision making, and redesigning jobs to give workers more challenge and responsibility. He found that the average improvement from money was 30 percent; goal setting increased performance 16 percent; participation improved performance by less than 1 percent; and job redesign positively impacted performance by an average of 17 percent. Moreover, every study Locke reviewed that used money as a method of motivation resulted in some improvement in employee performance. Such evidence demonstrates that money may not be the *only* motivator, but it is difficult to argue that it *doesn't* motivate!

[1] *E. A. Locke et al, "The Relative Effectiveness of Four Methods of Motivating Employee Performance," in* Changes in Working Life, *eds. K. D. Duncan, M. M. Gruneberg, and D. Wallis (London: John Wiley, Ltd., 1980), pp. 363–83.*

COUNTERPOINT

MONEY DOESN'T MOTIVATE MOST EMPLOYEES TODAY!

Money can motivate *some* people under *some* conditions. So the issue isn't really whether or not money *can* motivate. The answer to that is: It can! The more relevant question is: Does money motivate most employees in the work force today to higher performance? The answer to this question, we'll argue, is "No!"

For money to motivate an individual's performance, certain conditions must be met. First, money must be important to the individual. Second, money must be perceived by the individual as being a direct reward for performance. Third, the marginal amount of money offered for the performance must be perceived by the individual as being significant. Finally, management must have the discretion to reward high performers with more money. Let's take a look at each of these conditions.

Money is not important to all employees. High achievers, for instance, are intrinsically motivated. Money should have little impact on these people. Similarly, money is relevant to those individuals with strong lower-level needs; but for most of the work force, their lower-level needs are substantially satisfied.

Money would motivate if employees perceived a strong linkage between performance and rewards in organizations. Unfortunately, pay increases are far more often determined by community pay standards, the national cost-of-living index, and the organization's current and future financial prospects than by each employee's level of performance.

For money to motivate, the marginal difference in pay increases between a high performer and an average performer must be significant. In practice, it rarely is. For instance, a high-performing employee who currently is earning $30,000 a year is given a $200 a month raise. After taxes, that amounts to about $35 a week. But this employee's $30,000 a year co-worker, who is an average performer, is rarely passed over at raise time. Instead of getting an 8 percent raise, he or she is likely to get half of that. The net difference in their weekly paychecks is probably less than $20. How much motivation is there in knowing that if you work really hard you're going to end up with $20 a week more than someone who is doing just enough to get by? For a large number of people, not much!

Our last point relates to the degree of discretion that managers have in being able to reward high performers. Where unions exist, that discretion is almost zero. Pay is determined through collective bargaining and is allocated by job title and seniority, not level of performance. In nonunionized environments, the organization's compensation policies will constrain managerial discretion. Each job typically has a pay grade. So a systems analyst III can earn between $2,725 and $3,140 a month. No matter how good a job that analyst does, her boss cannot pay her more than $3,140 a month. Similarly, no matter how poorly someone does in that job, he will earn at least $2,725 a month. In most organizations, managers have a very small area of discretion within which they can reward their higher-performing employees. So money might be theoretically capable of motivating employees to higher levels of performance, but most managers aren't given enough flexibility to do much about it.

FOR DISCUSSION

1. How are ability and motivation interrelated?
2. Describe the specific steps you would take to ensure that an individual has the appropriate abilities to satisfactorily do a given job.
3. Define motivation. Describe the motivation process.
4. What are the implications of Theories X and Y to motivation practices?
5. Compare and contrast Maslow's hierarchy of needs theory with (a) Alderfer's ERG theory and (b) Herzberg's motivation-hygiene theory.
6. Describe the three needs isolated by McClelland. How are they related to worker behavior?
7. "The cognitive evaluation theory is contradictory to reinforcement and expectancy theories." Do you agree or disagree? Explain.
8. "Goal setting is part of both reinforcement and expectancy theories." Do you agree or disagree? Explain.
9. Reconcile equity and expectancy theories.
10. Do you think workaholics and high achievers are the same thing? Discuss.
11. Explain Figure 5–7 in your own words.
12. Can an individual be *too* motivated, so that his or her performance declines as a result of excessive effort? Discuss.

FOR FURTHER READING

CARRELL, M. R., and J. E. DITTRICH, "Equity Theory: The Recent Literature, Methodological Considerations, and New Directions," *Academy of Management Review,* April 1978, pp. 202–10. Reviews primary areas in which equity concepts have centered, notes findings and discusses significant theoretical and methodological issues.

LAWLER, E. E., III, *Motivation in Work Organizations.* Monterey, Calif.: Brooks/Cole, 1973. Reviews the literature in work motivation and satisfaction.

LOCKE, E. A., and G. P. LATHAM, *Goal Setting: A Motivational Technique That Works!* Englewood Cliffs, N.J.: Prentice-Hall, 1984. Reviews the literature on goal-setting theory and demonstrates how goals are recognized, explicitly or implicitly, in virtually every major theory of work motivation.

MINER, J. B., *Theories of Organizational Behavior.* Hinsdale, Ill.: Dryden Press, 1980, Chaps. 2, 3, 4, 5, 6, 7, and 10. Contains a comprehensive review and evaluation of major motivation theories: need hierarchy, achievement motivation, motivation-hygiene, equity, expectancy, goal setting, and Theories X and Y.

MITCHELL, T. R., "Motivation: New Directions for Theory, Research and Practice," *Academy of Management Review,* January 1982, pp. 80–88. Reviews current state of motivation theory; considers the circumstances under which the various theories are most effective.

STEERS, R. M., and L. W. PORTER, eds. *Motivation and Work Behavior,* 2nd ed. New York: McGraw-Hill, 1979. Reprints some of the major articles in the study of work motivation.

NOTES FOR CHAPTER 5

1. L. E. Tyler, *Individual Differences: Abilities and Motivational Directions* (Englewood Cliffs, N.J.: Prentice-Hall, 1974).
2. For a discussion of job-related testing, see S. P. Robbins, *Personnel: The Management of Human Resources,* 2nd ed. (Englewood Cliffs, N.J.: Prentice-Hall, 1982), Chaps. 6 and 7.
3. E. A. Fleishman, "Evaluating Physical Abilities Required by Jobs," *Personnel Administrator,* June 1979, pp. 82–92.
4. R. Katerberg and G. J. Blau, "An Examination of Level and Direction of Effort and Job Performance," *Academy of Management Journal,* June 1983, pp. 249–57.
5. A. Maslow, *Motivation and Personality* (New York: Harper & Row, 1954).
6. See for example, E. E. Lawler III and J. L. Suttle, "A Causal Correlational Test of the Need Hierarchy Concept," *Organizational Behavior and Human Performance,* April 1972, pp. 265–87; and D. T. Hall and K. E. Nongaim, "An Examination of Maslow's Need Hierarchy in an Organizational Setting," *Organizational Behavior and Human Performance,* February 1968, pp. 12–35.
7. A. K. Korman, J. H. Greenhaus, and I. J. Badin, "Personnel Attitudes and Motivation," in M. R. Rosenzweig and L. W. Porter (eds.), *Annual Review of Psychology* (Palo Alto, Calif.: Annual Reviews, 1977), p. 178.
8. Ibid., p. 179.
9. M. A. Wahba and L. G. Bridwell, "Maslow Reconsidered: A Review of Research on the Need Hierarchy Theory," *Organizational Behavior and Human Performance,* April 1976, pp. 212–40.
10. J. B. Miner, *Theories of Organizational Behavior* (Hinsdale, Ill.: Dryden Press, 1980), p. 41.
11. D. McGregor, *The Human Side of Enterprise* (New York: McGraw-Hill, 1960).
12. R. J. House and L. A. Wigdor, "Herzberg's Dual-Factor Theory of Job Satisfaction and Motivations: A Review of the Evidence and Criticism," *Personnel Psychology,* Winter 1967, pp. 369–89; and D. P. Schwab and L. L. Cummings, "Theories of Performance and Satisfaction: A Review," *Industrial Relations,* October 1970, pp. 403–30.
13. C. N. Weaver, "What Workers Want from Their Jobs," *Personnel,* May–June 1976, p. 49.
14. C. P. Alderfer, "An Empirical Test of a New Theory of Human Needs," *Organizational Behavior and Human Performance,* May 1969, pp. 142–75.
15. M. Haire, E. E. Ghiselli, and L. W. Porter, "Cultural Patterns in the Role of the Manager," *Industrial Relations,* February 1963, pp. 95–117.
16. C. P. Schneider and C. P. Alderfer, "Three Studies of Measures of Need Satisfaction

in Organizations," *Administrative Science Quarterly,* December 1973, pp. 489–505.

17. J. P. Wanous and A. Zwany, "A Cross-Sectional Test of Need Hierarchy Theory," *Organizational Behavior and Human Performance,* May 1977, pp. 78–97.

18. D. C. McClelland, *The Achieving Society* (New York: Van Nostrand Reinhold, 1961); J. W. Atkinson and J. O. Raynor, *Motivation and Achievement* (Washington, D.C.: Winston, 1974); and D. C. McClelland, *Power: The Inner Experience* (New York: Irvington, 1975).

19. McClelland, *The Achieving Society.*

20. D. C. McClelland and D. G. Winter, *Motivating Economic Achievement* (New York: Free Press, 1969).

21. McClelland, *Power;* and McClelland and D. H. Burnham, "Power Is the Great Motivator," *Harvard Business Review,* March–April 1976, pp. 100–10.

22. Ibid.

23. J. B. Miner, *Studies in Management Education* (New York: Springer, 1965).

24. D. Kipnis, "The Powerholder," in J. T. Tedeschi (ed.), *Perspectives in Social Power* (Chicago: Aldine, 1974), pp. 82–123.

25. D. Miron and D. C. McClelland, "The Impact of Achievement Motivation Training on Small Businesses," *California Management Review,* Summer 1979, pp. 13–28.

26. R. de Charms, *Personal Causation: The Internal Affective Determinants of Behavior* (New York: Academic Press, 1968).

27. E. L. Deci, *Intrinsic Motivation* (New York: Plenum, 1975); R. D. Pritchard, K. M. Campbell, and D. J. Campbell, "Effects of Extrinsic Financial Rewards on Intrinsic Motivation," *Journal of Applied Psychology,* February 1977, pp. 9–15; and R. D. Pritchard and E. L. Deci, "The Effects of Contingent and Noncontingent Rewards and Controls on Intrinsic Motivation," *Organizational Behavior and Human Performance,* October 1972, pp. 217–29.

28. W. E. Scott, "The Effects of Extrinsic Rewards on 'Intrinsic Motivation': A Critique," *Organizational Behavior and Human Performance,* February 1976, pp. 117–19; B. J. Calder and B. M. Staw, "Interaction of Intrinsic and Extrinsic Motivation: Some Methodological Notes," *Journal of Personality and Social Psychology,* January 1975, pp. 76–80; and K. B. Boal and L. L. Cummings, "Cognitive Evaluation Theory: An Experimental Test of Processes and Outcomes," *Organizational Behavior and Human Performance,* December 1981, pp. 289–310.

29. G. R. Salancik, "Interaction Effects of Performance and Money on Self-Perception of Intrinsic Motivation," *Organizational Behavior and Human Performance,* June 1975, pp. 339–51; and F. Luthans, M. Martinko, and T. Kess, "An Analysis of the Impact of Contingency Monetary Rewards on Intrinsic Motivation," *Proceedings of the Nineteenth Annual Midwest Academy of Management,* St. Louis, 1976, pp. 209–21.

30. Miner, *Theories of Organizational Behavior,* p. 157.

31. H. J. Arnold, "Effects of Performance Feedback and Extrinsic Reward upon High Intrinsic Motivation," *Organizational Behavior and Human Performance,* December 1976, pp. 275–88.

32. B. M. Staw, "Motivation in Organizations: Toward Synthesis and Redirection," in B. M. Staw and G. R. Salancik (eds.), *New Directions in Organizational Behavior* (Chicago: St. Clair, 1977), p. 76.

33. B. J. Calder and B. M. Staw, "Self-Perception of Intrinsic and Extrinsic Motivation," *Journal of Personality and Social Psychology,* April 1975, pp. 599–605.

34. E. A. Locke, "Toward a Theory of Task Motivation and Incentives," *Organizational Behavior and Human Performance,* May 1968, pp. 157–89.

35. G. P. Latham and G. A. Yukl, "A Review of Research on the Application of Goal

Setting in Organizations," *Academy of Management Journal,* December 1975, pp. 824–45; and E. A. Locke, K. N. Shaw, L. M. Saari, and G. P. Latham, "Goal Setting and Task Performance," *Psychological Bulletin,* January 1981, pp. 125–52.

36. J. M. Ivancevich and J. T. McMahon, "The Effects of Goal Setting, External Feedback, and Self-Generated Feedback on Outcome Variables: A Field Experiment," *Academy of Management Journal,* June 1982, pp. 359–72.

37. Latham and Yukl, "A Review of Research"; Locke, Shaw, Saari, and Latham, "Goal Setting"; and G. Shing-Yung Chang and P. Lovenzi, "The Effects of Participative Versus Assigned Goal Setting on Intrinsic Motivation," *Journal of Management,* Spring–Summer 1983, pp. 55–64.

38. J. C. Anderson and C. A. O'Reilly, "Effects of an Organizational Control System on Managerial Satisfaction and Performance," *Human Relations,* June 1981, pp. 491–501.

39. R. M. Steers and L. W. Porter, *Motivation and Work Behavior,* 2nd ed. (New York: McGraw-Hill, 1979), p. 13.

40. E. A. Locke, "Latham vs. Komaki: A Tale of Two Paradigms," *Journal of Applied Psychology,* February 1980, pp. 16–23.

41. J. S. Adams, "Inequity in Social Exchanges," in L. Berkowitz (ed.), *Advances in Experimental Social Psychology* (New York: Academic Press, 1965), pp. 267–300.

42. P. S. Goodman, "An Examination of Referents Used in the Evaluation of Pay," *Organizational Behavior and Human Performance,* October 1974, pp. 170–95.

43. P. S. Goodman and A. Friedman, "An Examination of Adams' Theory of Inequity," *Administrative Science Quarterly,* September 1971, pp. 271–88.

44. See, for example, M. R. Carrell, "A Longitudinal Field Assessment of Employee Perceptions of Equitable Treatment," *Organizational Behavior and Human Performance,* February 1978, pp. 108–18; R. G. Lord and J. A. Hohenfeld, "Longitudinal Field Assessment of Equity Effects on the Performance of Major League Baseball Players," *Journal of Applied Psychology,* February 1979, pp. 19–26; and J. E. Dittrich and M. R. Carrell, "Organizational Equity Perceptions, Employee Job Satisfaction, and Departmental Absence and Turnover Rates," *Organizational Behavior and Human Performance,* August 1979, pp. 29–40.

45. P. S. Goodman, "Social Comparison Process in Organizations," in B. M. Staw and G. R. Salancik (eds.), *New Directions in Organizational Behavior* (Chicago: St. Clair, 1977), pp. 97–132.

46. V. H. Vroom, *Work and Motivation* (New York: John Wiley, 1964).

47. See, for example, H. G. Heneman III and D. P. Schwab, "Evaluation of Research on Expectancy Theory Prediction of Employee Performance," *Psychological Bulletin,* July 1972, pp. 1–9; T. R. Mitchell, "Expectancy Models of Job Satisfaction, Occupational Preference and Effort: A Theoretical, Methodological and Empirical Appraisal," *Psychological Bulletin,* November 1974, pp. 1053–77; and L. Reinharth and M. A. Wahba, "Expectancy Theory as a Predictor of Work Motivation, Effort Expenditure, and Job Performance," *Academy of Management Journal,* September 1975, pp. 502–37.

48. See, for example, L. W. Porter and E. E. Lawler III, *Managerial Attitudes and Performance* (Homewood, Ill.: Richard D. Irwin, 1968); D. F. Parker and L. Dyer, "Expectancy Theory as a Within-Person Behavioral Choice Model: An Empirical Test of Some Conceptual and Methodological Refinements," *Organizational Behavior and Human Performance,* October 1976, pp. 97–117; and H. J. Arnold, "A Test of the Multiplicative Hypothesis of Expectancy-Valence Theories of Work Motivation," *Academy of Management Journal,* April 1981, pp. 128–41.

49. Vroom refers to these three variables as *valence, instrumentality,* and *expectancy,* respectively.

50. This four-step discussion was adapted from K. F. Taylor, "A 'Valence-Expectancy' Approach to Work Motivation," *Personnel Practice Bulletin,* June 1974, pp. 142–48.

51. E. A. Locke, "Personnel Attitudes and Motivation," in M. R. Rosenzweig and L. W. Porter (eds.), *Annual Review of Psychology,* (Palo Alto, Calif.: Annual Reviews, 1975), p. 459.

52. P. M. Muchinsky, "A Comparison of Within- and Across-Subjects Analyses of the Expectancy-Valence Model for Predicting Effort," *Academy of Management Journal,* March 1977, pp. 154–58.

53. R. J. House, H. J. Shapiro, and M. A. Wahba, "Expectancy Theory as a Predictor of Work Behavior and Attitudes: A Re-evaluation of Empirical Evidence," *Decision Sciences,* January 1974, pp. 481–506.

CASE IIA

IS THERE AN ACCOUNTING PERSONALITY?

Dana Maher was in the last semester of her senior year at California State University. Mindful that her father was planning to discontinue her $600-a-month allowance upon her graduation and the fact that she did like to eat regularly, Dana began to search for a full-time job.

The market for accounting majors, which was what Dana was, seemed pretty good. A number of companies were visiting the university's placement center and were looking for young graduates like Dana. She signed up for campus interviews, sent out a couple of dozen resumes to major companies, and began spreading the word through friends and relatives that she was soon to be "available."

Dana's friends had frequently teased her about her choice of an accounting major. The standard line was, "Dana, you just don't strike me as an accountant." Dana seemed different from most of her peers. She was extremely outgoing, talkative, and always in motion. She was active in her sorority and had at least two hundred "best" friends. Her mother frequently described her as having the "metabolism of a hummingbird." Her friends stereotyped her as being in a sales or personnel job rather than sitting quietly in some isolated office preparing accounting reports.

About six weeks prior to graduation, the job offers began to crystallize. She narrowed her choices to a trainee position with a San Francisco mortgage broker and a staff accounting job in Los Angeles with a prestigious national hotel chain. She accepted the accounting position, excited about the opportunity to work in the hotel business.

After six months on the job, Dana looked back on her experience. "I really enjoy my job. I spent the first six weeks in a general training program doing all kinds of different activities. I worked in the kitchen, in housekeeping, behind the check-in desk, and as a night auditor. Then I settled into the controller's office as a general accountant. I'm involved with accounts payable, preparing monthly financial statements, and doing special projects as they're needed. I think I'm doing a good job; at least everything Jim [her boss] has told me is positive. Yet I can't ignore the constant comments by the people I work with in accounting, and some of my friends in other areas of the hotel, that I'd be happier and have better career opportunities if I was in marketing or operations. They say I'm too outgoing for being an accountant. I think that's nonsense! Sure, I'd be interested in getting into operations. It would be a real challenge to someday be running my own hotel. But the job vacancy was in accounting and that's what I studied in school."

Questions

1. Using the hierarchy of values and the six personality types model, is there any discrepancy between Dana's values or personality and her job?
2. Is there such a thing as an "accounting personality" or a "marketing personality"?
3. Can you relate this case to learning theory?
4. If you had been Jim, would you have hired Dana? Support your position.
5. Would you expect Dana's level of job satisfaction to increase, decrease, or stay about the same if she were in this same job after three years? Support your position.

CASE IIB

THE HI-TECH DISASTER

Business has been awful at Hi-Tech Toys for nearly two years. In the late 1970s and early 1980s, the company grew from sales of less than $200,000 a year to over $10 million solely on its innovative video game business. But the video games market became saturated by Christmas 1983. Those that live by the sword, die by the sword—and so it was for Hi-Tech Toys. Between 1982 and 1984, the company's sales dropped more than 70 percent. In 1982, Hi-Tech made $1.7 million before taxes. In 1984, the firm lost a staggering $3.1 million!

Hi-Tech's management has not been sitting by idly watching the decline. They've tried, so far unsuccessfully, introducing new product lines. They've also cut their work force down from 350 to 120. Now management is concerned that this massive retrenchment, along with the company's uncertain future, is a threat to keeping the good people that are left. If Hi-Tech is to survive and flourish, it will need to hold on to its best product design, marketing, and management talent. To reduce the likelihood of any mass exodus among the remaining 120 people, Hi-Tech's president has called in his three most senior executives to consider their options.

Questions

1. One executive has suggested the need to cut salaries across the board by 15 percent if the company is to survive. What are the pros and cons to such an action? Would the addition of a profit-sharing plan soften the pay cut?
2. Another executive has suggested that if any additional overstaffing is identified that everyone's workweek should be reduced rather than firing any more people. In this way, everyone would share equally. Would you favor such a proposal? Explain.
3. The president favors administering an employee attitude survey to identify problems and solutions. You have been charged with developing the survey. How would you go about it and what would it look like?

CASE IIC

BUSINESS IS GOOD AT CONSOLIDATED— CHECK IT OUT!

Consolidated Printers is not a household name, yet it is the largest firm in its industry. For thirty-seven years, it has specialized in making checks. When you sit down to pay your monthly bills, odds are that you write your payments on checks printed by Consolidated.

The check-printing business has proven recessionproof. For Consolidated, sales have increased in each and every one of its thirty-seven years. Located in the small beach community of Seaside, about 100 miles north of Los Angeles, the company dominates the $200 million-a-year check-printing industry. Recent estimates indicate that Consolidated controls better than 70 percent of the market. However, because Consolidated is a family-held company, exact figures are not available. What is known is that Randall Phillips and his children, who own Consolidated, are extremely wealthy. The Phillips Foundation, for instance, regularly distributes several million dollars a year for charitable purposes. It is also well known in Seaside that the company has been allocating large sums of surplus funds for land and venture capital investments.

Consolidated Printers is the dominant employer in Seaside. Though non-union, its employees are well paid. Hourly wages range from a low of $8.24 an hour, to as high as $18.40 for some of the skilled engravers and machine engineers. But because of recent high demand for checks, most employees have been working overtime. Last month, for instance, the *average* production worker grossed more than $2,700. Randall Phillips, in a recent interview in the *Seaside Sentinel,* commented that "Consolidated people don't lack for motivation. They're currently the highest-paid employees in the county. But it's going to get better. Within sixty days, we will be putting into place a new productivity incentive plan that will allow selected employees to earn sizable annual bonuses based on a sophisticated productivity formula that has been developed by our cost accounting staff. All in all, the future is bright for Consolidated Printing and we expect to share this good fortune with our employees who make it all possible."

It came as quite a shock to Mr. Phillips when he received a letter from a group of a half-dozen anonymous employees, in which they outlined a long list of grievances. Among their complaints were the following:

"We're sick of all this overtime. You and the other honchos in the administrative offices might like working nights and Saturdays, but we enjoy being with our families and friends and having time to kick back and live a little.

"The new bonus plan is a sham. None of us can figure out how it works. As usual, it will be those people that kiss up to management that'll benefit. Stop manipulating us. We have no intention of working harder for something we don't have any chance of getting.

"How can you talk as if we're one big happy family and at the same time be preparing to throw us all out of work? It's common knowledge in town that the company has bought land in the Phoenix area and everyone says that you're going to close this plant and move the company to Arizona. Why should we give a damn about Consolidated Printers when you're abandoning us?''

Questions

1. From the standpoint of employee perceptions, what is happening here?
2. Judging by what you know about the need hierarchy theory, why are these half-dozen employees unhappy?
3. What role does expectancy theory play in this case?
4. What might the company have done to prevent these negative reactions?

CASE IID

TOM'S MIDLIFE CRISIS

Until last year, Tom Rapp's life was a classic American success story. He grew up in East St. Louis, Illinois. His father was an alcoholic and his mother waitressed to pay the bills. But Tom was a good student and an exceptional basketball player. He attended Stanford on an athletic scholarship, then went on to earn an M.B.A. at the Harvard Business School. He joined General Electric as a sales representative in 1968 and rose rapidly through the corporate ranks to become a vice-president by age 40. In 1983, an article in *Forbes* magazine named Tom as one of five candidates who might someday be heading up General Electric. But something happened to Tom after his fortieth birthday. Maybe the stress of the fast track finally got to him. Or maybe his wife's decision to leave him and file for divorce initiated the change in Tom.

In March, Tom's wife left their sprawling home in a well-to-do Fairfield, Connecticut, suburb. She took their three children with her. In May, at the request of his boss, Tom checked himself into an alcoholic rehabilitation center. Six weeks later he was back at his job, only it was not the same Tom Rapp that his colleagues had known. He was 15 pounds thinner. He had his teeth capped. He'd replaced his conservative Brooks Brothers clothes with expensive European-cut suits. Gone was Tom's Volvo sedan, replaced by a red Ferrari 308 GTS.

Tom's boss summarized his concern: ''Tom is one of the most talented people we have. He has an innate talent to ask the right question, at the right time, to the right person. A couple of years back, he single-handedly saved our division between $50 million and $100 million by seeing a flaw in our strategy that would have had us going head to head against General Motors with an overpriced, underdesigned diesel engine. He just kept asking questions and analyzing answers until the problem became obvious to everyone. I also understand the pressures he's been under since Barbara and the kids left. I even understand his attempt to create a new image. We've had others around here go through the midlife crisis. Tom just never had the time in his twenties to play around. He was too busy with his career. But I won't tolerate his lackadaisical attitude. He doesn't seem to give a damn anymore. He comes in late. In fact, in the past week, for two days he just didn't show up here at all. Never called in, and no one knew where he was. He takes two or three hours for lunch. He's missing important meetings. The morale among his people is really suffering. I don't know what to do. Here's a guy who was a winner for fifteen years and now, given what's happened in the past year, I'm actually thinking I'm going to have to fire the guy.''

Questions

1. Explain Tom's behavior in terms of motivation theory.
2. If personalities are generally stable, how is it that Tom's personality seems to have changed?
3. If you were Tom's boss, what options do you see yourself having in dealing with Tom? What specific action(s) would you take?

CASE IIE

MONEY ISN'T EVERYTHING, I GUESS!

Mike Brady has been with the National Broadcasting Company in New York for six years. After graduating from college, he joined NBC in the programming department and has risen to the position of assistant director for daytime programming. Twenty-eight years old and single, Mike appears to enjoy his job and has consistently received good performance appraisals by his bosses. But about six months ago, the programming offices were abuzz with the rumor that Mike would be leaving NBC. It appears the source of this rumor was Mike's current boss, Linda Lawrence.

You see, Mike Brady is the grandson of J. D. Brady, the founder and owner of the Brady Oil Company. The elder Brady, who died about a year ago, left an estate valued at over $300 million. It included oil properties, a 50,000-acre ranch, property holdings in ten states, and assorted other assets. While Mike was never close to J.D.—Mike's mother and father divorced when he was a baby, both of his parents remarried, and he was raised by his mother and stepdad in very middle-class surroundings—his grandfather apparently had not forgotten him. As one of J.D.'s five grandchildren, he was awarded 8 percent of the estate by his grandfather's will, or what would amount to more than $15 million after taxes.

Apparently, when Linda read in the newspaper that Mike was inheriting the millions from his grandfather's estate, she just assumed that Mike would be leaving his job. After all, his salary at NBC was less than $38,000 a year. And he was young, handsome, single, and well educated. As a multimillionaire, with the world at his feet, you couldn't expect Mike to continue working at a regular job, with regular hours, and three weeks of vacation a year. At least, that's what Linda thought.

But the months have passed and Mike appears as committed to his job as ever. The money he inherited has been invested and is supervised by a professional investment firm. Mike, however, continues to show up for work early, often works late when necessary, and appears to be totally unaffected by his new wealth. One of his close friends commented that Mike told him he had no intention of leaving his job. "I really like my work. Just because I came into some money doesn't change anything. What am I supposed to do? Become a jet-setter and spend my time commuting between homes in Paris, London, New York, and Beverly Hills? Come on, that's not for me. My grandfather worked hard for what he got. I don't know any idle rich. Both my real dad and stepdad went to work every day. I was brought up to value hard work and thrift. I guess that's the way I'll always be."

Linda Lawrence was puzzled. She knew if she inherited $15 million, she couldn't turn in her resignation fast enough.

Questions

1. If you inherited $15 million, would it change *your* life? Would you work? At what?
2. From a motivation viewpoint, can you explain Mike's behavior?
3. How do Mike's values influence his behavior?
4. How can the principles of operant conditioning be used to explain Mike's behavior?
5. Based on what you know about personality, examine potential reasons for the difference in Mike and Linda's attitudes toward work.
6. What percentage of the work force do you think would say they would continue to work if they got enough money to live comfortably for the rest of their lives? Explain.

CASE IIF

THE GREEN BAY LEGEND

Vince Lombardi is a legend in football. He single-handedly turned the Green Bay Packers from a mediocre pro team in the mid-1950s into a football dynasty in the 1960s. It was generally agreed that there were half a dozen other pro coaches who knew as much strategically and tactically as Lombardi, but what set him apart and made his team winners was his ability to motivate his players. He was able to get the extra 10 percent that other coaches couldn't. How did he get that extra 10 percent?

For one thing, he used participation. He'd put in a new play on a given morning, have his players practice it all afternoon, and come by the rooms of players he respected that night and ask, "Well, what do you think? Will it work?"

He also was excellent at figuring out what would motivate each individual player. Some guys needed to be driven, some needed a friendly pat on the rear, while others needed to be just left alone.

One player told how, after playing an excellent game, he had been totally ignored by Lombardi. Not a kind word, not anything. At workouts on the following Tuesday and Wednesday, Lombardi chewed him up and down. The player couldn't understand it. He so desperately wanted recognition from his coach. After Wednesday's practice, in the locker room, as the players were leaving for their cars, Lombardi singled out this player, walked up to him, hit him on the rear, and said, "I just want you to know that you're the best damn offensive tackle in pro football." The player remarked how that one sentence inspired him for months.

Frank Gifford, the premier receiver, said about Lombardi, "I was always trying to please him. When we played a game, I couldn't care less about the headlines on Monday. All I wanted was to be able to walk into the meeting Tuesday morning and have Vinny give me that big grin and pat me on the fanny and let me know that I was doing what he wanted me to do. A lot of our guys felt that way. We had guys who would run through a stadium wall for him—and then maybe cuss him in the next breath. . . ."

Lombardi knew how to challenge his teams. After his team broke a two-game winning streak, Lombardi walked into the locker room to find the players laughing and clowning around. Lombardi didn't think anything was funny. "Nobody wants to pay the price," he said. "I'm the only one here that's willing to pay the price. You guys don't care. You don't want to win."

The team was stunned. Nobody knew what to do, but the silence was broken when one player stood up and said, "My God, I want to win," and then somebody else said, "Yeah, I want to win," and pretty soon there were forty guys standing, all shouting, "I want to win." Lombardi had succeeded in making them ashamed and angry.

All-Pro defensive lineman Willie Davis gave an example of how Lombardi could make you feel important and, by doing so, get you around to his way of thinking.

I guess maybe my worst days in football were the days I tried to negotiate my contracts with the old man. I'd get myself all worked up before I went in to see him. I'd drive up from my home in Chicago, and all the way, I'd keep building up my anger, telling myself I was going to draw a hard line and get just as much money as I deserved.

One year, I walked into his office feeling cocky, you know, 'Roll out the cash, Jack, I got no time for small change.' All he had to do was say one harsh word, and I was really going to let him have it. I never got a word in. Soon as he saw me, he jumped up and began hugging me and patting me and telling me, 'Willie, Willie, Willie, it's so great to see you. You're the best trade I ever made. You're a leader. We couldn't have won without you, Willie. You had a beautiful year. And, Willie, I need your help. You see, I've got this budget problem. . . .'

He got me so off balance, I started feeling sorry for him. He had me thinking, 'Yeah, he's right, he's gotta save some money for the Kramers and the Greggs and the Jordans,' and the next thing I knew, I was saying, 'Yes, sir, that's fine with me,' and I ended up signing for about half what I was going to demand. When I got out of that office and started driving back to Chicago, I was so mad at myself, I was about to drive off the highway.

Questions

1. Analyze Lombardi's motivational style by using cognitive evaluation theory, equity theory, and goal-setting theory.
2. What motivation theory best describes Lombardi's approach to motivating his players? Explain.
3. Could Lombardi's approach be used in industry? Explain.

Adapted from J. Kramer and D. Schaap, *Lombardi: Winning Is the Only Thing* (New York: World Publishing, 1970). Reprinted by permission of The Sterling Lord Agency, Inc. Copyright © 1970 by Jerry Kramer and Dick Schaap.

EXERCISE IIA

Value Assessment Test

Directions. Read each statement in turn then circle both the *number* and *letter* appearing next to either Yes or No that best indicate your feeling of like or dislike for the activity described. *Be sure to answer each question.* A sample response is a follows:

"Enjoy eating ice cream"	2A	Yes	2A	No
1. Meet new people and get acquainted with them.	5D	Yes	5D	No
2. Take a carload of children for an outing.	6D	Yes	6D	No
3. Serve as a companion to an elderly person.	7D	Yes	7D	No
4. Like to be with people despite their physical deformities.	8D	Yes	8D	No
5. Work with a group to help the unemployed.	9D	Yes	9D	No

6.	Work with labor and management to help solve their conflicts.	(10D)	Yes	10D	No
7.	Go with friends to a movie.	(4D)	Yes	4D	No
8.	Help distribute food at a picnic.	3D	Yes	(3D)	No
9.	Play checkers with members of your family.	(2D)	Yes	2D	No
10.	Make a phone call for movie reservations.	1D	Yes	(1D)	No
11.	Collect specimens of small animals for a zoo or museum.	5A	Yes	(5A)	No
12.	Do algebra problems.	6A	Yes	(6A)	No
13.	Develop a foreign language.	(7A)	Yes	7A	No
14.	Do an experiment with the muscle and nerve of a frog.	8A	Yes	(8A)	No
15.	Study the various methods used in scientific investigations.	9A	Yes	(9A)	No
16.	Do research on the relation of brainwaves to thinking.	10A	Yes	(10A)	No
17.	Visit a research laboratory in which small animals are being tested in a maze.	(4A)	Yes	4A	No
18.	Plan the defense and offense you are to use before a tennis game.	3A	Yes	(3A)	No
19.	Read the biography of Louis Pasteur.	2A	Yes	(2A)	No
20.	See moving pictures in which scientists are heroes.	1A	Yes	(1A)	No
21.	Judge entries in a photo contest.	(5C)	Yes	5C	No
22.	Sketch action scenes on a drawing pad.	(6C)	Yes	(6C)	No
23.	Participate in a summer theater group.	(7C)	Yes	7C	No
24.	Compare the treatment of a classical work as given by two fine musicians.	8C	Yes	(8C)	No
25.	Mold a statue in clay.	9C	Yes	(9C)	No
26.	Be a ballet dancer.	(10C)	Yes	10C	No
27.	Be a sign painter.	4C	Yes	(4C)	No
28.	Plant flowers and shrubbery around a home.	3C	Yes	(3C)	No
29.	Listen to jazz records.	(2C)	Yes	2C	No
30.	Play the jukebox.	(1C)	Yes	1C	No
31.	Lead a round-table discussion.	(5B)	Yes	5B	No
32.	Be chairman of an organizing committee.	6B	Yes	(6B)	No
33.	Buy a run-down business and make it grow.	7B	Yes	(7B)	No
34.	Borrow money in order to put over a business deal.	8B	Yes	(8B)	No
35.	Run for political office.	9B	Yes	(9B)	No
36.	Own and operate a bank.	10B	Yes	(10B)	No
37.	Be a bank teller.	4B	Yes	(4B)	No
38.	Take a course in Business English.	(3B)	Yes	3B	No
39.	Major in business subjects in school.	(2B)	Yes	2B	No
40.	Collect lunch money at the end of a school cafeteria line.	1B	Yes	(1B)	No
41.	Send a letter of condolence to a neighbor.	5D	Yes	(5D)	No
42.	Help people to be comfortable when traveling.	6D	Yes	(6D)	No
43.	Belong to several social agencies.	(7D)	Yes	7D	No
44.	Treat wounds to help people get well.	(8D)	Yes	8D	No

45. Help an agency locate living places for evicted families.	9D	Yes	9D	No
46. Be a medical missionary to a foreign country.	10D	Yes	10D	No
47. Attend a dance.	4D	Yes	4D	No
48. Dine with classmates in the school cafeteria.	3D	Yes	3D	No
49. Play checkers.	2D	Yes	2D	No
50. Ride in a bus to San Francisco or a neighboring city.	1D	Yes	1D	No
51. Be a laboratory technician.	5A	Yes	5A	No
52. Be a scientific farmer.	6A	Yes	6A	No
53. Develop new kinds of flowers in a small greenhouse.	7A	Yes	7A	No
54. Solve knotty legal problems.	8A	Yes	8A	No
55. Develop improved procedures in a scientific experiment.	9A	Yes	9A	No
56. Develop new mathematical formulas for research.	10A	Yes	10A	No
57. Look at the displays on astronomy in an observatory exhibit.	4A	Yes	4A	No
58. Visit the fossil display at a museum.	3A	Yes	3A	No
59. Keep a chemical storeroom or physical laboratory.	2A	Yes	2A	No
60. Sell scientific books.	1A	Yes	1A	No
61. Judge window displays in a contest.	5C	Yes	5C	No
62. Collect rare and old recordings.	6C	Yes	6C	No
63. Be an interior decorator.	7C	Yes	7C	No
64. Make a comparative study of architecture.	8C	Yes	8C	No
65. Write a new arrangement for a musical theme.	9C	Yes	9C	No
66. Paint a mural.	10C	Yes	10C	No
67. Visit a flower show.	4C	Yes	4C	No
68. Make and trim household accessories like lamp shades, etc.	3C	Yes	3C	No
69. Dance to a fast number.	2C	Yes	2C	No
70. Paint the kitchen with colors of your choice.	1C	Yes	1C	No
71. Install improved office procedures in a big business.	5B	Yes	5B	No
72. Plan business and commercial investments.	6B	Yes	6B	No
73. Be an active member of a political group.	7B	Yes	7B	No
74. Address a political convention.	8B	Yes	8B	No
75. Operate a race track.	9B	Yes	9B	No
76. Become a U.S. senator.	10B	Yes	10B	No
77. Purchase supplies for a picnic.	4B	Yes	4B	No
78. Live in a large city rather than a small town.	3B	Yes	3B	No
79. Work at an information desk.	2B	Yes	2B	No
80. Be a private secretary.	1B	Yes	1B	No

Turn to page 519 for scoring directions and key.

Source: J. Shorr, "The Development of a Test to Measure Intensity of Values," *Journal of Educational Psychology,* Vol. 44 (1953), pp. 266–74.

EXERCISE IIB

Determining Your Locus of Control

Read each statement carefully. Then indicate the extent to which you agree or disagree by circling the number following each statement. The numbers and their meanings are indicated below:

If you agree strongly: circle +3
If you agree somewhat: circle +2
If you agree slightly: circle +1

If you disagree slightly: circle −1
If you disagree somewhat: circle −2
If you disagree strongly: circle −3

First impressions are usually best. Read each statement, decide if you agree or disagree and the strength of your opinion, and then circle the appropriate number.

	STRONGLY DISAGREE	DISAGREE SOMEWHAT	SLIGHTLY DISAGREE	SLIGHTLY AGREE	AGREE SOMEWHAT	STRONGLY AGREE
1. Whether or not I get to be a leader depends mostly on my ability.	(−3)	−2	−1	+1	+2	+3
2. To a great extent my life is controlled by accidental happenings.	−3	−2	−1	+1	(+2)	+3
3. I feel like what happens in my life is mostly determined by powerful people.	−3	−2	−1	(+1)	+2	+3
4. Whether or not I get into a car accident depends mostly on how good a driver I am.	(−3)	−2	−1	+1	+2	+3
5. When I make plans, I am almost certain to make them work.	−3	−2	−1	+1	(+2)	+3
6. Often there is no chance of protecting my personal interests from bad luck happenings.	−3	−2	−1	(+1)	+2	+3

7. When I get what I want, it's usually because I'm lucky.   −3   −2   −1   (+1)   (+2)   +3

8. Although I might have good ability, I will not be given leadership responsibility without appealing to those in positions of power.   −3   (−2)   −1   +1   +2   +3

9. How many friends I have depends on how nice a person I am.   −3   −2   −1   (+1)   +2   +3

10. I have often found that what is going to happen will happen.   −3   −2   −1   (+1)   +2   +3

11. My life is chiefly controlled by powerful others.   −3   −2   −1   +1   (+2)   +3

12. Whether or not I get into a car accident is mostly a matter of luck.   −3   −2   (−1)   +1   +2   +3

13. People like myself have very little chance of protecting our personal interests when they conflict with those of strong pressure groups.   −3   −2   −1   (+1)   +2   +3

14. It's not always wise for me to plan too far ahead because many things turn out to be a matter of good or bad fortune.   −3   (−2)   −1   +1   +2   +3

15. Getting what I want requires pleasing those people above me.   −3   −2   (−1)   (+1)   +2   +3

16. Whether or not I get to be a leader depends on whether I'm lucky enough to be in the right place at the right time.   (−3)   −2   −1   +1   +2   +3

17. If important people were to decide they didn't like me, I probably wouldn't make many friends.   −3   −2   −1   (+1)   +2   +3

18. I can pretty much determine what will happen in my life.

-3	(-2)	-1	$+1$	$+2$	$+3$

19. I am usually able to protect my personal interests.

-3	-2	-1	$+1$	$(+2)$	$(+3)$

20. Whether or not I get into a car accident depends mostly on the other driver.

-3	-2	-1	$+1$	$(+2)$	$+3$

21. When I get what I want, it's usually because I worked hard for it.

-3	-2	-1	$+1$	$(+2)$	$+3$

22. In order to have my plans work, I make sure that they fit in with the desires of people who have power over me.

-3	-2	-1	$(+1)$	$+2$	$+3$

23. My life is determined by my own actions.

-3	-2	-1	$(+1)$	$+2$	$+3$

24. It's chiefly a matter of fate whether or not I have a few friends or many friends.

(-3)	-2	-1	$+1$	$+2$	$+3$

Turn to page 520 for scoring directions and key.

Source: Adapted from J. B. Rotter, "Generalized Expectancies for Internal Versus External Control of Reinforcement," *Psychological Monographs,* Vol. 80, no. 609 (1966). With permission.

EXERCISE IIC

Needs Test

Indicate how important each of the following is in the job you would like to get. Write the numbers 1, 2, 3, 4, or 5 on the line after each item.

1 = Not important
2 = Slightly important
3 = Moderately important
4 = Very important
5 = Extremely important

1. Cooperative relations with my co-workers. __4__
2. Developing new skills and knowledge at work. __4__
3. Good pay for my work. __5__
4. Being accepted by others. __4__
5. Opportunity for independent thought and action. __3__
6. Frequent raises in pay. __5__
7. Opportunity to develop close friendships at work. __4__
8. A sense of self-esteem. __5__
9. A complete fringe benefit program. __4__
10. Openness and honesty with my co-workers. __3__
11. Opportunities for personal growth and development. __4__
12. A sense of security from bodily harm. __5__

Turn to page 521 for scoring directions and key.

Source: Adapted from Clayton P. Alderfer, *Existence, Relatedness, and Growth: Human Needs in Organizational Settings*. Copyright © 1972 by The Free Press, a Division of Macmillan Publishing Co., Inc.

EXERCISE IID

Supervisory Attitude Scale

Instructions.   Check off the level of agreement or disagreement that you feel personally toward each of the ten statements below.

	STRONGLY AGREE	AGREE	UNCERTAIN	DISAGREE	STRONGLY DISAGREE
1. Most employees want to be told clearly and in specific detail exactly what to do and how to do it.	☐	☐	☑	☐	☐
2. Workers generally want more responsibility for their own work activities.	☐	☐	☑	☐	☐
3. Most workers must be pushed and pressured by the boss to get them to "put out" on the job.	☐	☐	☐	☑	☐
4. Employees perform best when rewarded with recognition for their achievements, in addition to monetary or other rewards.	☐	☑	☐	☐	☐
5. People are best coaxed into productive activity by gentle prodding rather than by threats or force.	☐	☑	☐	☐	☐

6. Most people want jobs that give them the leeway to figure out on their own how to do the job best.

7. Workers will naturally try to do the minimum they can get away with, and this is why supervisors need to keep a close and constant watch.

8. Most employees enjoy work that is challenging and that gives them a realistic opportunity for achievement.

9. Effective supervision requires that one be willing to follow up on threats with actions, when a worker fails to perform.

10. Most workers are far more capable of outstanding performance than is realized or than they have the chance to demonstrate.

Turn to page 521 for scoring directions and key.
Source: M. Sashkin and W. C. Morris, *Organizational Behavior: Concepts and Experiences* (Reston, Va.: Reston Publishing Co., 1984), p. 84. With permission.

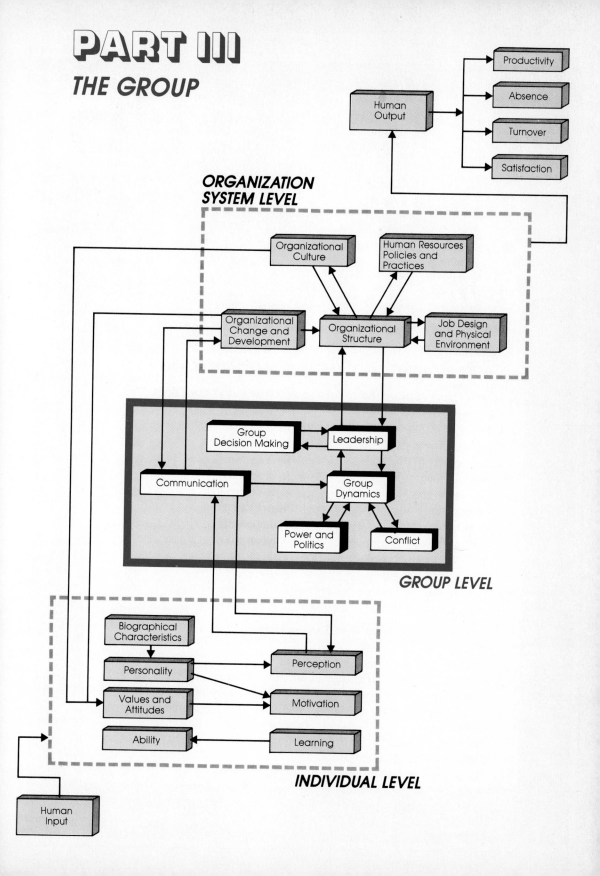

PART III
THE GROUP

ORGANIZATION
SYSTEM LEVEL

Human
Output

Productivity

Absence

Turnover

Satisfaction

Organizational
Culture

Human Resources
Policies and
Practices

Organizational
Change and
Development

Organizational
Structure

Job Design
and Physical
Environment

Group
Decision Making

Leadership

Communication

Group
Dynamics

Power and
Politics

Conflict

GROUP LEVEL

Biographical
Characteristics

Personality

Perception

Values and
Attitudes

Motivation

Ability

Learning

INDIVIDUAL LEVEL

Human
Input

Foundations of Group Behavior

AFTER STUDYING THIS CHAPTER, YOU SHOULD BE ABLE TO:

Define and explain the following key terms and concepts:

Cohesiveness
Cohorts
Command group
Conformity
Formal group
Friendship group
Group
Group demography
Informal group
Interest group
Norms

Psychological contract
Role
Role conflict
Role expectations
Role identity
Role perception
Social loafing
Status equity
Status hierarchy
Task group

Understand:

The difference between formal and informal groups
Why people join groups
The four stages of group development
How role requirements change in different situations
How norms exert influence on an individual's behavior
The importance of the Hawthorne studies to the understanding of
   behavior
The need for status
The sources of status
The benefits and disadvantages of cohesive groups

One Supreme Court Justice to another: "This daily metamorphosis never fails to amaze me. Around the house I'm a perfect idiot. I come to court, put on a black robe, and, by God, I'm IT!"

—M. HANDELSMAN

Groups are a relatively new way of looking at organizational behavior. Fifty years ago it was acceptable to say that organizations were composed of individuals and leave it at that. It was not really until the 1930s and 1940s that contemporary ideas about groups came along: awareness that the behavior of individuals in groups is something more than the sum total of each acting in his or her own way. In other words, when individuals are in groups, they act differently from when they are alone. Today, we recognize the vital role an understanding of groups plays in explaining the larger phenomena of organizational behavior.

DEFINING AND CLASSIFYING GROUPS

A group is defined as two or more individuals, interacting and interdependent, who come together to achieve particular objectives. Groups can be either formal or informal. By formal, we mean defined by the organization's structure, with designated work assignments establishing tasks and work groups. In formal groups, the behaviors that one should engage in are stipulated by and directed toward organizational goals. In contrast, informal groups are alliances that are neither formally structured nor organizationally determined. These groups are natural formations in the work environment, which appear in response to the need for social contact.

It is possible to subclassify groups further as command, task, interest, or friendship groups.[1] Command and task groups are dictated by the formal organization, whereas interest and friendship groups are informal alliances.

The *command group* is determined by the organization chart. It is composed of the subordinates who report directly to a given manager. An elementary school principal and her twelve teachers form a command group, as do the director of postal audits and his five inspectors.

Task groups, also organizationally determined, represent those working together to complete a job task. However, a task group's boundaries are not limited to its immediate hierarchical superior. It can cross command relationships. For instance, if a college student is accused of a campus crime, it may require communication and coordination among the Dean of Academic Affairs, the Dean of Students, the Registrar, the Director of Security, and the student's advisor. Such a formation would constitute a task group. It should be noted that all command groups are also task groups, but because task groups can cut across the organization, the reverse need not be true.

People who may or may not be aligned into common command or task groups may affiliate to attain a specific objective with which each is concerned. This is an *interest group.* Employees who band together to have their vacation schedule altered, to support a peer who has been fired, or to seek increased fringe benefits represent the formation of a united body to further their common interest.

Groups often develop because the individual members have one or more common characteristics. We call these formations *friendship groups.* Social allegiances, which frequently extend outside the work situation, can be based on similar age, support for "Big Red" Nebraska football, having attended the same college, or the holding of similar political views, to name just a few such characteristics.

Informal groups provide a very important service by satisfying their members' social needs. Because of interactions that result from the close proximity of workstations or task interactions, we find workers playing golf together, riding to and from work together, lunching together, and spending their breaks around the water cooler together. We must recognize that these types of interactions among individuals, even though informal, deeply affect their behavior and performance.

WHY DO PEOPLE JOIN GROUPS?

There is no single reason why individuals join groups. Since most people belong to a number of groups, it is obvious that different groups provide different benefits to their members. The most popular reasons for joining a group are related to our needs for security, status, interaction, power, and goal achievement.

Security

"There's strength in numbers," By joining a group, we can reduce the insecurity of "standing alone"—we feel stronger, have fewer self-doubts, and are more resistant to threats. New employees are particularly vulnerable to a sense of isolation and turn to the group for guidance and support. However, whether we are talking about new employees or those with years on the job, we can state that few individuals like to stand alone. We get reassurances from interacting with others and being part of a group. This often explains the appeal of unions —if management creates an environment in which employees feel insecure, they are likely to turn to unionization to reduce their feelings of insecurity.

Status and Self-esteem

"I'm proud to be a member of the Blue Angels," commented a Navy pilot. He was acknowledging the role that a group can have in giving prestige. Group membership means "I'm somebody." It can fulfill extrinsic needs by giving an individual status and recognition. For new freshmen in college, fraternities, sororities, the gymnastics team, or the pep club represent groups in which membership may be sought in order to reinforce feelings of worth. The move from high school to college often means going from being a "wheel" to being a "nobody." Membership in one or more college groups can help to reassure us that we are important. Similarly, many employees in organizations place a high value on meeting their esteem needs and look to membership in both formal and informal groups for satisfaction of these needs.

Groups can also fulfill intrinsic needs. Our self-esteem is bolstered when we are accepted by a highly valued group. Being assigned to a task force whose purpose is to review and make recommendations for the location of the company's new corporate headquarters can fulfill one's intrinsic needs for competence and growth, as well as one's extrinsic needs for status and influence.

Interaction and Affiliation

"I'm independently wealthy, but I wouldn't give up my job. Why? Because I really like the people I work with!" This quote, from a $25,000-a year purchasing agent who inherited several million dollars' worth of real estate, verifies that groups can fulfill our social needs. People enjoy the regular interaction that comes with group membership. For many people, these on-the-job interactions are their primary source for fulfilling their need for affiliation. For almost all people, work groups significantly contribute to fulfilling their need for friendships and social relations.

Power

"I tried for two years to get the plant management to increase the number of female restrooms on the production floor to the same number as the men have. It was like talking to a wall. But I got about fifteen other women who were production employees together and we jointly presented our demands to management. The construction crews were in here adding female restrooms within ten days!''

This episode demonstrates that one of the appealing aspects of groups is that they represent power. What often cannot be achieved individually becomes possible through group action. Of course, this power may not be sought only to make demands on others. It may be desired merely as a countermeasure. In order to protect themselves from unreasonable demands by management, individuals may align with others.

Informal groups additionally provide opportunities for individuals to exercise power over others. For individuals who desire to influence others, groups can offer power without a formal position of authority in the organization. As a group leader, you may be able to make requests of group members and obtain compliance without any of the responsibilities that traditionally go with formal managerial positions. So, for people with a high power need, groups can be a vehicle for fulfillment.

Goal Achievement

''I'm part of a three-person team studying how we can cut our company's transportation costs. They've been going up at over 30 percent a year for several years now so the corporate controller assigned representatives from cost accounting, shipping, and marketing to study the problem and make recommendations.''

This task group was created to achieve a goal that would be considerably more difficult if pursued by a single person. There are times when it takes more than one person to accomplish a particular task—there is a need to pool talents, knowledge, or power in order to get a job completed. In such instances, management will rely on the use of a formal group.

STAGES OF GROUP DEVELOPMENT

Group development is a dynamic process. Most groups are in a continual state of change. But just because groups probably never reach complete stability doesn't mean that there isn't some general pattern that describes how most groups evolve. There is strong evidence that groups pass through a standard sequence of four stages.[2] As shown in Figure 6–1, these four stages have been labeled forming, storming, norming, and performing.

The first stage—*forming*—is characterized by a great deal of uncertainty about the group's purpose, structure, and leadership. Members are ''testing the waters''—to determine what types of behavior are acceptable. This stage is complete when members have begun to think of themselves as part of a group.

The *storming* stage is one of intragroup conflict. Members accept the existence of the group, but there is resistance to the control that the group imposes on individuality. Additionally, there is conflict over who will control the group.

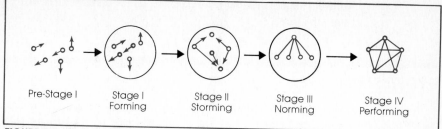

FIGURE 6–1
Stages of Group Development

When stage II is complete, there will be a relatively clear hierarchy of leadership within the group.

The third stage is one in which close relationships develop and the group demonstrates cohesiveness. There is now a strong sense of group identity and comaraderie. This *norming* stage is complete when there is a continuing structure for the group and the group has assimilated a common set of expectations of what defines correct member behavior.

The final stage is *performing*. The structure at this point is fully functional and accepted. Group energy has moved from getting to know and understand each other to the job of task performance.

Most of you have probably encountered each of these stages when you have had to do a group term project for a class. Group members are selected and then you meet for the first time. There is a "feeling out" to assess what the group is going to do and how it is going to do it. This is usually rapidly followed by the battle for control: Who is going to lead us? Once this is resolved and a hierarchy is agreed upon, the group moves to identifying specific activities of what needs to be done, who is going to do it, and dates by which the parts need to be completed. General expectations become set and agreed upon for each member. This forms the foundation for what you hope will be a coordinated group effort culminating in a project that group members and the instructor agree is a job well done. Of course, groups occasionally don't get much beyond the first or second stage, which frequently results in projects and grades that are disappointing.

Should one assume from the foregoing that group effectiveness improves as progression is made through the four stages? While some argue that effectiveness of work units increases at advanced stages,[3] it is not that simple. While this assumption may be generally true, what makes a group effective is a complex issue. Under some conditions, high levels of conflict are conducive to high group performance. So we might expect to find situations where groups in stage II outperform those in stages III or IV. Similarly, movement through stages is not always clear. Sometimes, in fact, several stages are going on simultaneously—as when groups are storming and performing at the same time. Groups even occasionally regress to previous stages. Therefore, to assume that this developmental process is followed precisely by all groups or that stage IV is always the most preferable is likely to prove incorrect. It is better to think of this four-stage model as a general framework. It reminds you that groups are dynamic entities and can help you to understand better the problems and issues that are most likely to surface during a group's life.

GROUP STRUCTURE

A basic understanding of group structure can be found in three concepts—roles, norms, and status. We have all heard these words before. They may even be a standard part of your vocabulary. But if you expect to be able to analyze groups, you are going to have to feel comfortable with these concepts and understand the theory that underlies them. This section seeks to achieve that end.

Roles

Shakespeare said, "All the world's a stage, and all the men and women merely players." Using the same metaphor, all group members are actors, each playing a *role*. By this term, we mean a set of expected behavior patterns attributed to someone occupying a given position in a social unit. The understanding of role behavior would be dramatically simplified if each of us chose one role and "played it out" regularly and consistently. Unfortunately, we are required to play a number of diverse roles, both on and off our jobs. As we shall see, one of the tasks in understanding behavior is grasping the role that a person is currently playing.

For example, on his job, Bill Patterson is a plant manager with Electrical Industries, a large electrical equipment manufacturer in Phoenix. He has a number of roles that he fulfills on that job—for instance, Electrical Industries employee, member of middle management, electrical engineer, and the primary company spokesperson in the community. Off the job, Bill Patterson finds himself in still more roles: husband, father, Catholic, Rotarian, tennis player, member of the Thunderbird Country Club, and president of his homeowners' association. Many of theses roles are compatible; some create conflicts. For instance, how does his religious involvement influence his managerial decisions regarding layoffs, expense account padding, or providing accurate information to government agencies? A recent offer of promotion requires Bill to relocate, yet his family very much wants to stay in Phoenix. Can the role demands of his job be reconciled with the demands of husband and father roles?

The issue should be clear: Like Bill Patterson, we all are required to play a number of roles, and our behavior varies with the role we are playing. Bill's behavior when he attends church on Sunday morning is different from his behavior on the golf course later that same day. You, too, act differently in the role of student than you do when you play husband or wife, or boyfriend or girlfriend. In fact, I personally find it humorous to think of the student role and how it totally fails to simulate the managerial environment that we like to think we, in academia, are preparing students for. We want to prepare students to be articulate decision makers. Yet, look at most testing procedures. It will be indeed the rare boss who calls you into his office, invites you to sit down, requests that you take out a piece of paper, asks you half-a-dozen questions, and tells you to write up these answers and turn them in in 50 minutes. Is it surprising, then, that many students have a difficult time moving out of the role of student (passive, note-taking regurgitator) to the role of employee in a real organization?

ROLE IDENTITY

There are certain attitudes and actual behaviors consistent with a role, and they create the role identity. People have the ability to shift roles rapidly when they recognize that the situation and its demands clearly require major changes. For instance, when union stewards were promoted to supervisory positions, it was found that their attitudes changed from pro-union to pro-management within a few months of their promotion. When these promotions had to later be rescinded because of economic difficulties in the firm, it was found that the demoted supervisors had once again adopted their pro-union attitudes.[4]

When the situation is more vague and the role one is to play less clear, people often revert to old role identities. An investigation of high school reunions verified this view.[5] At the reunions studied, even though participants had been away from high school and their peers for five, ten, or twenty or more years, they reverted back to their old roles. The "ins" replayed their former roles, as did the "outs." Even though entirely new criteria were being used in the real world for success, the former "jocks," student officers, and the cheerleaders acted as "ins" and the others expected them to. In spite of the fact that some of the former losers were now winners by society's standards, they found it very difficult to deal with the winner's role when placed in an environment in which they had always been losers. With the role requirements ill-defined, identities became clouded, and individuals reverted back to old patterns of behavior.

ROLE PERCEPTION

One's view of how one is supposed to act in a given situation is a role perception. Based on an interpretation of how we believe we are supposed to behave, we engage in certain types of behavior.

Where do we get these perceptions? From stimuli all around us—friends, books, movies, television. Undoubtedly many of today's young surgeons formed their role identities from their perception of Hawkeye on "M.A.S.H.," while college instructors may be emulating the character of Professor Kingsfield in *The Paper Chase*. It also seems reasonable to conclude that many current police officers learned their roles from *Serpico* or "Starsky and Hutch" and tomorrow's officers will have been influenced by "Hill Street Blues." Of course, the primary reason that apprenticeship programs exist in many trades and professions is to allow individuals to watch an "expert" so they can learn to act as they are supposed to.

ROLE EXPECTATIONS

Role expectations are defined as how others believe you should act in a given situation. How you behave is determined, to a large part, by the role defined in the context in which you are acting. The role of a U.S. senator is viewed as having propriety and dignity, whereas a football coach is seen as aggressive, dynamic, and inspiring to his players. In the same context, we might be surprised to learn that the neighborhood priest moonlights during the week as a bartender. Why? Because our role expectations of priests and bartenders tend to be considerably different. When role expectations are concentrated into generalized categories, we have role stereotypes.

During the last several decades we have seen a major change in the general population's role stereotypes of females. In the 1950s, a woman's role was to stay home, take care of the house, raise children, and generally care for her husband. Today, most of us no longer hold this stereotype. Boys *can* play with Barbie Dolls and girls *can* play with G.I. Joes. Girls can aspire to be doctors, lawyers, and astronauts as well as the more traditional activities of nurse, school teacher, secretary, or housewife. In other words, many of us have changed our role expectations of women, and, similarly, many women carry new role perceptions.

In the workplace, it can be helpful to look at the topic of role expectations through the perspective of the *psychological contract*. There is an unwritten agreement that exists between employees and their employer. This psychological contract sets out mutual expectations—what management expects from workers, and vice versa.[6] In effect, this contract defines the behavioral expectations that go with every role. Management is expected to treat employees justly, provide acceptable working conditions, clearly communicate what is a fair day's work, and give feedback on how well the employee is doing. Employees are expected to respond by demonstrating a good attitude, following directions, and showing loyalty to the organization.

What happens when role expectations as implied in the psychological contract are not met? If management is derelict in keeping up its part of the bargain, we can expect negative repercussions on employee performance and satisfaction. When employees fail to live up to expectations, the result is usually some form of disciplinary action up to and including firing.

The psychological contract should be recognized as a "powerful determiner of behavior in organizations."[7] It points out the importance of communicating accurately role expectations. In Chapter 14, we shall discuss how organizations socialize employees in order to get them to play out their roles in the way management desires.

ROLE CONFLICT

When an individual is confronted by divergent role expectations, the result is role conflict. It exists when an individual finds that compliance with one role requirement may make more difficult the compliance with another. At the extreme it would include situations in which two or more role expectations are mutually contradictory.

Many believe that the topic of role conflict is the most critical role concept in attempting to explain behavior. This, for example, is one of the classic problems of college presidents, a fact which became highly evident in the late 1960s. The college president is forced to reconcile diverse role expectations by faculty, students, board members, alumni, and other admimistrators. The behavior expectations that are perceived as acceptable by one group are often totally in disagreement with the expectations of other groups.[8]

Our previous discussion of the many roles Bill Patterson had to deal with included several role conflicts—for instance, Bill's attempt to reconcile the expectations placed on him as head of his family and as an executive with Electrical Industries. The former emphasizes stability and concern for the desire of his wife and children, as you will remember, to remain in Phoenix. Electrical Industries, on the other hand, expects its employees to be responsive to the needs and requirements of the company. Although it might be in Bill's financial and career interests to accept a relocation, the conflict comes down to choosing between family and career role expectations.

The issue of ethics in business demonstrates a well-publicized area of role conflict among corporate executives. For example, one study found that 57 percent of *Harvard Business Review* readers had experienced the dilemma of having to choose between what was profitable for their firms and what was ethical.[9]

All of us have faced and will continue to face role conflicts. The critical issue, from our standpoint, is how conflicts, imposed by divergent expectations within the organization, impact on behavior. Certainly they increase internal tension and frustration. There are a number of behavioral responses one may engage in. For example, one can give a formalized bureaucratic response. The conflict is then resolved by relying on the rules, regulations, and procedures that govern organizational activities. For example, a worker faced with the conflicting requirements imposed by the corporate controller's office and his own plant manager decides in favor of his immediate boss—the plant manager. Similarly, many college professors create a formal environment in class by calling their students "Mr." and "Ms.," and expecting to be called "Professor"—to avoid allowing friendships to interfere with the objective requirements of the professorial role. Other behavioral responses may include withdrawal, stalling, negotiation or, as we found in our discussion of dissonance in Chapter 4, redefining the facts or the situation to make them appear congruent.

AN EXPERIMENT: ZIMBARDO'S SIMULATED PRISON

One of the more illuminating role experiments was done by Stanford University psychologist Philip Zimbardo and his associates.[10] They created a "prison" in the basement of the Stanford psychology building; hired at $15 a day two dozen emotionally stable, physically healthy, law-abiding students who scored "normal average" on extensive personality tests; randomly assigned them the role of either "guard" or "prisoner"; and established some basic rules. The experimenters then stood back to see what would happen.

At the start of the planned two-week simulation, there were no measurable differences between those individuals assigned to be guards and those chosen to be prisoners. Additionally, the guards received no special training in how to be prison guards. They were told only to "maintain law and order" in the prison and not to take any nonsense from the prisoners: physical violence was forbidden. To simulate further the realities of prison life, the prisoners were allowed visits from relatives and friends, but while the mock guards worked eight-hour shifts, the mock prisoners were kept in their cells around the clock and were allowed out only for meals, exercise, toilet privileges, head count lineups, and work details.

It took the mock guards little time to adjust to their new authority roles or for the "prisoners" to accept the authority positions of the guards. The guards' primary forms of interaction with the prisoners were commands, insults, degrading references, verbal and physical aggression, and threats. Every guard, at some time during the simulation, engaged in abusive, authoritarian behavior. And after an initial rebellion was crushed by the guards, the prisoners played out their passive roles, even as the guards daily escalated their aggression. But the simulation actually proved *too* successful in demonstrating how quickly individuals learn new roles. The researchers had to stop the experiment after only six days because of the pathological reactions that the participants were demonstrating. And, remember, these were individuals chosen precisely for their normalcy and emotional stability.

What should you conclude from this prison simulation? The participants in this prison simulation had, like the rest of us, learned stereotyped conceptions of guard and prisoner roles from the mass media and their own personal experiences in power and powerlessness relationships gained at home (parent-child), in school (teacher-student), and in other situations. This, then, allowed them easily and rapidly to assume roles that were very different from their inherent personalities. In this case, we saw that people with no prior personality pathology or training in their roles could execute extreme forms of behavior consistent with the roles they were playing.

Norms

Tens of millions of women put on eye shadow, rouge, lipstick, earrings, and an attractive dress every day. They then go to work, play, or whatever, with a minimal amount of attention. However, when a man does the same thing—such as rock star Boy George—he is sure to attract interest on most streets in most cities. Why? Norms!!

All groups have established norms, that is, acceptable standards of behavior that are shared by the group's members. Norms tell members what they ought or ought not to do under certain circumstances. From an individual's standpoint, they tell what is expected of you in certain situations. When agreed to and accepted by the group, norms act as a means of influencing the behavior of group members with a minimum of external controls. Norms differ among groups, communities, and societies, but they all have them.

Formalized norms are written up in organizational manuals, setting out rules and procedures for employees to follow. By far, the majority of norms in organizations are informal. You do not need someone to tell you that throwing paper airplanes or engaging in prolonged bull sessions at the water cooler are unacceptable behaviors when the "big boss from New York" is touring the office. Similarly, we all know that when we are in an employment interview discussing what we did not like about our previous job, there are certain things we should not talk about (difficulty in getting along with co-workers or our supervisor), while it is very appropriate to talk about other things (inadequate opportunities for advancement or unimportant and meaningless work). Evidence suggests that even high school students recognize that in such interviews certain answers are more socially desirable than others.[11]

Students learn how to quickly assimilate classroom norms. Depending upon the environment created by the instructor, the norms may support unequivocal acceptance of the material suggested by the instructor, or, at the other extreme, students may be expected to question and challenge the instructor on any point that is unclear. For example, in most classroom situations, the norms dictate that one not engage in loud, boisterous discussion that makes it impossible to hear the lecturer or humiliate the instructor by pushing him or her "too far," even if one has obviously located a weakness in something the instructor has said. Should some in the classroom group behave in such a way as to violate these norms, we can expect pressure to be applied against the deviant members so as to bring their behavior into conformity with group standards.

THE HAWTHORNE STUDIES

It is generally agreed among behavioral scientists that full-scale appreciation of the importance norms play in influencing worker behavior did not occur until the early 1930s. This enlightenment grew out of a study undertaken at Western Electric Company's Hawthorne Works in Chicago between 1927 and 1932.[12] Conducted under the direction of Harvard psychologist Elton Mayo, the Hawthorne studies concluded that a worker's behavior and sentiments were closely related, that group influences were significant in affecting individual behavior, that group standards were highly effective in establishing individual worker output, and that money was less a factor in determining worker output than group standards, sentiments, and security. Let us briefly review the Hawthorne investigations and demonstrate the importance of these findings in explaining group behavior.

The Hawthorne researchers began by examining the relation between the physical environment and productivity. Illumination, temperature, and other working conditions were selected to represent this physical environment. The researchers' initial findings contradicted their anticipated results.

They began with illumination experiments with various groups of workers. The researchers manipulated the intensity of illumination upward and downward, while at the same time noting changes in group output. Results varied, but one thing was clear: In no case was the increase or decrease in output in proportion to the increase or decrease in illumination. So the researchers introduced a control group: An experimental group was presented with varying intensity of illumination, while the controlled unit worked under a constant illumination intensity. Again, the results were bewildering to the Hawthorne researchers. As the light level was increased in the experimental unit, output rose for each group. But to the surprise of the researchers, as the light level was dropped in the experimental group, productivity continued to increase in both. In fact, a productivity decrease was observed in the experimental group only when the light intensity had been reduced to that of moonlight. Mayo and his associates concluded that illumination intensity was only a minor influence among the many influences that affected an employee's productivity, but they could not explain the behavior they had witnessed.

As a follow-up to the illumination experiments, the researchers began a second set of experiments in the relay assembly test room at Western Electric. A small group of women were isolated from the main work group so that their behavior could be more carefully observed. They went about their job of assembling small telephone relays in a room laid out similar to their normal department. The only difference was the placement in the room of a research assistant who acted as an observer—keeping records of output, rejects, working conditions, and a daily log sheet describing everything that happened. Over a two-and-a-half-year period, this small group's output increased steadily as did its morale. The number of personal absences and those due to sickness were approximately one-third of those recorded by women in the regular production department. What became evident was that this group's performance was significantly influenced by its status of being a "special" group. The women in the test room thought that being in the experimental group was fun, that they were in sort of an elite group, and that management was concerned with their interest by engaging in such experimentation.

A third experiment in the bank wiring observation room was similar in design to the experiment in the relay test room, except that male workers were used. Additionally, a sophisticated wage incentive plan was introduced on the assumption that individual workers will maximize their productivity when they see that it is directly related to economic rewards. The most important finding coming out of this experiment was that employees did not individually maximize their outputs. Rather, their output became controlled by a group norm that determined what was a proper day's work. Output was not only being restricted, but individual workers were giving erroneous reports. The total for a week would check with the total week's output, but the daily reports showed a steady, level output regardless of actual daily production. What was going on?

Interviews determined that the group was operating well below its capability and was leveling output in order to protect itself. Members were afraid that if they significantly increased their output, the unit incentive rate would be cut, the expected daily output would be increased, layoffs might occur, or slower men would be reprimanded. So the group established its idea of a fair output—neither too much nor too little. They helped each other out to ensure that their reports were nearly level.

The norms that the group established included a number of "don'ts." *Don't* be a rate-buster, turning out too much work. *Don't* be a chisler, turning out too little work. *Don't* be a squealer on any of your peers.

How did the group enforce these norms? Their methods were neither gentle nor subtle. They included sarcasm, name calling, ridicule, and even physical punches to the upper arm of members who violated the group's norms. Members would also ostracize individuals whose behavior was against the group's interest.

The Hawthorne studies made an important contribution to our understanding of group behavior—particularly the significant place that norms have in determining individual work behavior.

COMMON NORMS IN ORGANIZATIONS

An organization's norms are like an individual's fingerprints—each is unique. Yet there are still some common classes of norms that appear in most organizations.[13]

Probably the most widespread norms, as demonstrated in the Hawthorne studies, relate to levels of *effort* and *performance*. Work groups typically provide their members with very explicit cues on how hard they should work, their level of output, when to look busy, when it's acceptable to goof off, and the like. These norms are extremely powerful in affecting an individual employee's performance—capable of significantly modifying a performance prediction based solely on the employee's ability and level of personal motivation.

Some organizations have formal *dress* codes. However, even in their absence, norms frequently develop to dictate the kind of clothing that should be worn to work. College seniors, interviewing for their first postgraduate job, pick up this norm quickly. Every spring on college campuses throughout the country, you can usually spot those interviewing for jobs—they're the ones walking around in the dark gray or blue pinstriped suits. They are enacting the dress norms they have learned are expected in professional positions. Of course, what connotes acceptable dress in one organization may be very different from another. Faculty members in the Graduate Schools of Business at Harvard and U.C.L.A. may teach the same subject matter, but the social norms at Harvard dictate a much more formal dress attire than exists at the West Coast school.

Few managers appreciate employees who disparage the organization. Similarly, professional employees and those in the executive ranks recognize that most employers view with a great deal of disfavor those who visibly "look" for another job. If such people are unhappy, they know to keep their job search secret. These examples demonstrate that *loyalty* norms are widespread in organizations. This concern for demonstrating loyalty, by the way, often explains why ambitious aspirants to top management positions in an organization willingly take work home at night, come in on weekends, and accept transfers to cities they would otherwise not prefer to live in.

THE "HOW" AND "WHY" OF NORMS

How do norms develop? *Why* are they enforced? A review of the research can allow us to answer these questions.[14]

Norms typically develop gradually as group members learn what behaviors are necessary for the group to function effectively. Of course, critical events in the group might short-circuit the process and act quickly to solidify new norms. Most norms develop in one or more of the following four ways: (1) *Explicit statements made by a group member*—often the group's supervisor or a powerful member. The group leader might, for instance, specifically say that no personal phone calls are allowed during working hours or that coffee breaks are to be kept to ten minutes. (2) *Critical events in the group's history.* These set important precedents. A bystander is injured while standing too close to a machine, and, from that point on, members of the work group regularly monitor each other to ensure that no one other than the operator gets within 5 feet of any machine. (3) *Primacy.* The first behavior pattern that emerges in a group frequently sets group expectations. Friendship groups of students often stake out seats near each other on the first day of class and become perturbed if an outsider takes "their" seats in a later class. (4) *Carry-over behaviors from past situations.* Group members bring expectations with them from other groups of which they have been members. This can explain why work groups typically prefer to add new members who are similar to current ones in background and experience. This is likely to increase the probability that the expectations they bring are consistent with those already held by the group.

But groups do not establish or enforce norms for every conceivable situation. The norms that the group will enforce tend to be those that are important to it. But what makes a norm important? (1) *If it facilitates the group survival.* Groups don't like to fail, so they look to enforce those norms that increase their chances for success. This means that they will try to protect themselves from interference from other groups or individuals. (2) *If it increases the predictability of group members' behaviors.* Norms that increase predictability enable group members to anticipate each other's actions and to prepare appropriate responses. (3) *If it reduces embarrassing interpersonal problems for group members.* Norms are important that ensure the satisfaction of their members and prevent as much interpersonal discomfort as possible. (4) *If it allows members to express the central values of the group and clarify what is distinctive about the group's identity.* Norms that encourage expression of the group's values and distinctive identity help to solidify and maintain the group.

CONFORMITY

As a member of a group, you desire acceptance by the group. Because of your desire for acceptance, you are susceptible to conforming to the group's norms. There is considerable evidence that groups can place strong pressures on individual members to change their attitudes and behaviors to conform to the group's standard.[15]

Do individuals conform to the pressures of all the groups they belong to? Obviously not, because people belong to many groups and their norms vary. In some cases, they may even have contradictory norms. So what do people do? They conform to the important groups to which they belong or hope to belong. The important groups have been referred to as *reference* groups and are characterized as ones where the person is aware of the others, the person defines himself or herself as a member, or would like to be a member, and the person feels that the group members are significant to him or her.[16] The implication, then, is that *all* groups do not impose equal conformity pressures on their members.

The impact that group pressures for conformity can have on an individual member's judgment and attitudes was demonstrated in the now classic studies by

Solomon Asch.[17] Asch made up groups of seven or eight people, who sat in a classroom and were asked to compare two cards held by the experimenter. One card had one line, the other had three lines of varying length. As shown in Figure 6–2, one of the lines on the three-line card was identical to the line on the one-line card. Also, as shown in Figure 6–2, the difference in line length was quite obvious; under ordinary conditions, subjects made fewer than 1 percent errors. The object was to announce aloud which of the three lines matched the single line. But what happens if all the members in the group begin to give incorrect answers? Will the pressures to conform result in the unsuspecting subject (USS) altering his or her answer to align with the others? That was what Asch wanted to know. So he arranged the group so only the USS was unaware that the experiment was "fixed." The seating was prearranged: The USS was placed so as to be the last to announce his or her decision.

The experiment began with several sets of matching exercises. All the subjects gave the right answers. On the third set, however, the first subject would give an obviously wrong answer—for example, saying "C" in Figure 6–2. The next subject gave the same wrong answer, and so did the others until it got to the unknowing subject. He knew "B" was the same as "X," yet everyone had said "C." The decision confronting the USS is this: Do you state a perception publicly that differs from the preannounced position of the others? Or do you give an answer that you strongly believe is incorrect in order to have your response agree with the other group members?

The results obtained by Asch demonstrated that over many experiments and many trials, subjects conformed in about 35 percent of the trials; that is, the subjects gave answers that they knew were wrong but that were consistent with the replies of other group members.

What can we conclude from this study? The results suggest that there are group norms that press us toward conformity. We desire to be one of the group and avoid being visibly different. We can generalize further to say that when an individual's opinion of objective data differs significantly from that of others in the group, he or she feels extensive pressure to align his or her opinions to conform with that of the others.

FIGURE 6–2
Examples of Cards Used in Asch Study

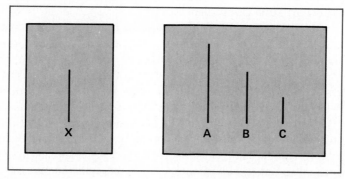

Status

While teaching a college course on adolescence a few years ago, the instructor asked the class to list things that contributed to status when they were in high school. The list was long, including such activities as being a "jock," being able to cut class without getting caught, and dating a cheerleader. Then the instructor asked the students to list things that didn't contribute to status. Again, it was easy for the students to create a long list—getting straight A's, having your mother drive you to school, and so forth. Finally, the students were asked to develop a third list—those things that didn't matter one way or the other. There was a long silence. Finally, a young woman in the back row volunteered, "In high school, nothing didn't matter."[18]

Status permeates far beyond the walls of high school. It would not be incorrect to rephrase the quotation to read, "In the status hierarchy of life, nothing doesn't matter." In spite of the fact that most of us are quick to declare how unimportant status is, most of us are greatly concerned with acquiring status symbols. Fortunately, or unfortunately, depending on your predilections, we live in a class-structured society. In spite of attempts to make our world more egalitarian, we have made little movement toward a classless society. As far back as scientists have been able to trace human groupings, we have had chiefs and Indians, nobility and peasants, the haves and the have-nots. This continues to be the case today. Even the smallest group will develop roles, rights, and rituals to differentiate its members. Status is an important factor in understanding behavior because it is a significant motivator and has major behavioral consequences when individuals perceive a disparity between what they perceive their status to be and what others perceive it to be.

Status is a prestige grading, position, or rank within a group. It may be formally imposed by a group, that is, organizationally imposed, through titles or amenities. This is the status that goes with being crowned "the heavyweight champion of the world" or being elected "most congenial." We are all familiar with the trappings that are associated with high organizational status—large offices with thick carpeting on the floor and an adjoining bathroom with a shower, impressive titles, high pay and fringe benefits, preferred work schedules, and so on. Whether management acknowledges the existence of a status hierarchy, organizations are filled with amenities that are not uniformly available to everyone and hence, carry status value.

More often, we deal with status in an informal sense. Status may be informally acquired by such characteristics as education, age, sex, skill, or experience. Anything can have status value if others in the group evaluate it as such. But just because status is informal does not mean that it is less important or that there is less agreement on who has it or who does not. This was supported when individuals were asked to rank the status of their high school classmates a number of years following graduation.[19] The respondents were able to place former classmates into a status hierarchy and the rankings were almost identical. We can and do place people into status categories and there appears to be high agreement among members as to who is high, low, and in the middle.

"Do you know who you're talking to, Buster? You're talking to the guy with the biggest desk, biggest chair, longest drapes, and highest ceiling in the business!"

FIGURE 6–3

Source: Drawing by Dana Fradon; © 1981. The New Yorker Magazine, Inc. With permission.

In his classic restaurant study, William F. Whyte demonstrated the importance of status.[20] Whyte proposed that people work more smoothly if high-status personnel customarily originate action for lower-status personnel. He found a number of instances where, when those of lower status were initiating action, this created a conflict between formal and informal status systems. For example, he cited one instance in which waitresses passed their customers' orders on to counterworkers—and thus low-status servers were initiating action for high-status cooks. By the simple addition of an aluminum spindle to which the order could be hooked, a buffer was created, thus allowing the counterworkers to initiate action on orders when they felt ready.

Whyte also noted that in the kitchen, supply people secured food supplies from the chefs. This was, in effect, a case of low-skilled employees initiating action upon the high skilled. Conflict was stimulated when several supply people explicitly and implicitly urged the chefs to "get a move on." However, Whyte observed that one supply man had little trouble. He gave the chef the order and asked that the chef call him when it was ready, thus reversing the initiating process. In Whyte's analysis, he suggested several changes in procedures, which aligned interactions more closely with the accepted status hierarchy and resulted in substantial improvements in worker relations and effectiveness.

SOURCES OF STATUS

Status is given by the group and, as such, is a value perception. It varies by time and place. It may mean being Catholic, Protestant, white, black, Puerto Rican, young, old, male, female, an "Ivy Leaguer," or a third-generation resident in the community or possessing some physical characteristic. Among professional wrestlers, high weight is valued and therefore possesses status. Among professional jockeys or members of Weight Watchers, low weight carries status. In Montreal, speaking English with a French accent has a different status connotation than it does in Houston. Being able to dunk a basketball means a lot among a group of young boys putting together a basketball team in New York City but nothing to a group of young boys fishing off the Atlantic City pier. Whether what you have, know, or can do has status depends on who is doing the evaluating.

Among most middle-class North Americans, certain things appear to have universal status: being the author of a best-selling book, being interviewed by Johnny Carson on the "Tonight Show," having dinner at the White House. Why is it, though, that some things tend to have universal status recognition while others are highly localized? The answer appears to lie in the scarceness of the activity and its visibility. Johnny Carson will interview fewer than five hundred people on his show this year and more than ten million people will be in attendance by way of their television sets for each interview. In contrast, there will be about twenty thousand young men this year who will be captains of their high school football team and the extent of visibility each receives will be highly restricted. So Jack Winthrop, captain of the Burlington (Vermont) High School football team, has high status in northern Vermont and is unknown throughout the rest of the world. On the other hand, astronaut Sally Ride attracts the admiration of most of the Western world.

Basically, organizations give status through one of four ways: through organizational association—"I'm with the FBI"; occupation—"He's a Supreme Court Justice"; organizational level—"He holds the position of executive director"; or salary—"I make a hundred thousand dollars a year." Additionally, status may be a personal attribute valued by others, such as age, education, sex, race, religion, physical appearance, communicative skills, experience, or competence. Table 6–1 lists some examples of items that can carry high status in organizations. Obvious ones include large offices, thick carpeting on the floor, impressive titles, and high pay. For example, one oil company's regional executives have the four prestige corner offices on the "executive" floor of the firm's building. Though the offices are of equal size, the quality of the views are unequal and are allocated by rank. The better views go to those with higher status.

Illustrations abound of status trappings in industry. Bank of America executives know that they have made it when they are given stationery with the bank's logo in gold rather than black ink. At Ford Motor Company, low-level executives' perks are limited to little more than an outside parking space. Middle-management positions come with larger offices, windows, plants, an intercom system, and a secretary. Senior executives get an office with a private lavatory, signed Christmas cards from the chairman, an indoor parking space, and their company cars washed and gassed on request.[21] Western Electric, has its complement of status symbols that relate to rank, one of the more obvious being telephones. As junior managers move up through the company, they typically first have a black Touch-Tone telephone. They then progressively move up to a colored Touch-Tone phone, a Touch-Tone desk set with a "hands-free" device, a Touch-Tone model with a set of insertable programmed cards that dial the desired number, an electronic preset dialing system requiring only the touch of one button to dial a specific number, and—for the president and executive vice-presidents—a Picturephone.[22]

Even work loads have status connotations. Among college professors, a frequent measure of prestige is teaching load. Paradoxically, the status of teachers

TABLE 6–1
Examples of What May Connote Formal Status

Titles
- Director
- Manager
- Chief
- Head
- Senior

Relationships
- Work for an important individual
- Job requires you to work with high-ranking organizational members
- Work in a critical group or on an important assignment

Pay and Fringe Benefits
- Expense account
- Liberal travel opportunities
- Reserved parking space with your name on it
- Company-paid car
- Key to executive washroom

Work Schedule
- Day work rather than evening or shift
- Freedom from punching a time clock
- Freedom to come and go as one pleases

Office Amenities
- Large office
- Large desk with high-back chair
- Windows with attractive view
- Private secretary to screen visitors

among their peers is directly related to how little they teach! Teaching four or five courses a week is viewed as a lot of work and is considered low status. Three is more than competitive and suggests that the teacher is being given some release time to engage in research. Two courses is better yet. Teaching only one course a semester is very infrequent and hence carries very high status. Of course, the eminent status position is reserved for the "teacher" who has succeeded in achieving the ultimate—no teaching load!

A recent survey of office workers confirmed much of the speculation surrounding status in the office.[23] As shown in Table 6–2, the workspaces of higher-status employees were different from lower-status employees in the amount and quality of furnishings, the capacity for personalization, the control over access, and the amount of space. High-status employees were characterized by superior furnishings, room to display personal items, privacy, and spacious surroundings.

FUNCTIONS OF STATUS

Status symbols have been found to provide several functions in an organization. They serve as rewards, incentives, and communication facilitators.[24]

Status trappings operate as rewards for achievements earned through hard work or superior ability. They also act as incentives for future performance for individuals motivated by the trappings that go with higher rank. But the value of status to the organization may be most important as a vehicle for facilitating and defining communication. It defines who initiates communications, to whom, and

---

TABLE 6–2
Status Factors in the Office

Furnishings
- Number of work surfaces
- Desk size
- Number of chairs
- Amount of storage capacity

Capacity for Personalization
- Space to display personal items

Control over Access
- Private office
- Office door
- Screening capability for visitors or callers
- Number of people who can observe worker
- Number of people working in the office

Space
- Proximity to nearest neighboring worker
- Space to work with someone across one's work surface

Source: Adapted from E. Konar, E. Sundstrom, C. Brady, D. Mandel, and R. W. Rice, "Status Demarcation in the Office," *Environment and Behavior,* September 1982, p. 571. Reprinted by permission of Sage Publications, Inc.

the amount of information transmitted. Status symbols further aid communications by signaling an individual's authority and hierarchical position to others within the organization and by signaling formal rank to important constituencies outside the organization. Of course, on this last point, status can act to distort communications between groups or organizations when the status criteria are not similar. For instance, one U.S. manager in Japan offended a high-ranking Japanese executive by failing to give him the respect his position commanded.[25] The manager was introduced to the Japanese executive in the latter's office. The American manager assumed that the executive was a low-level decision maker and paid him little attention because of the small and sparsely furnished office he occupied. He did not know that the offices of Japanese executives do not flaunt the status accoutrements of their American counterparts.

STATUS EQUITY

It is important for group members to believe that the status hierarchy is equitable. When inequity is perceived, it creates disequilibrium resulting in various types of corrective behavior.

The concept of equity presented in Chapter 5 applies to status. Individuals expect rewards to be proportionate to costs incurred. If Sally and Betty are the two finalists for the head nurse position in a hospital, and it is clear that Sally has more seniority and better preparation for assuming the promotion, Betty will view the selection of Sally to be equitable. However, if Betty is chosen because she is the daughter-in-law of the hospital director, Sally will believe there is an injustice.

The trappings that go with formal positions are also important elements in maintaining equity. If we believe there is an inequity between the perceived ranking of an individual and the status accoutrements he or she is given by the organization, we are experiencing status incongruence. Some examples of incongruence are the supervisor earning less than her subordinates, the more desirable office location being held by a lower-ranking individual, or paid country club membership being provided by the company for division managers but not for vice-presidents. Employees expect the things an individual has and receives to be congruent with his or her status.

In spite of our acknowledgment that groups generally agree within themselves on status criteria and hence tend to rank individuals fairly closely, individuals can find themselves in a conflict situation when they move between groups whose status criteria are different or where groups are formed of individuals with heterogeneous backgrounds. Business executives may use income, total wealth, or size of the companies they run as determinants. Government bureaucrats might use the size of their agencies. Academics may use the number of grants received or articles published. Blue-collar workers may use years of seniority, job assignments, or bowling scores. Where groups are made up of heterogeneous individuals or where heterogeneous groups are forced to be interdependent, there is a potential for status differences to initiate conflict as the group attempts to reconcile and align the differing hierarchies.

CONTINGENCY VARIABLES THAT AFFECT GROUP BEHAVIOR

A number of contingency variables have been identified that improve our ability to explain and predict group behavior. Among these variables are the personality characteristics of members, the size of the group, and the degree of heterogeneity among members.

Personality Characteristics of Members

There has been a great deal of research on the relationship between personality traits and group attitudes and behavior. The general conclusion is that attributes that tend to have a positive connotation in our culture tend to be positively related to group productivity, morale, and cohesiveness. These include traits such as sociability, self-reliance, and independence. In contrast, negatively evaluated characteristics such as authoritarianism, dominance, and unconventionality tend to be negatively related to the dependent variables.[26]

Is any one personality characteristic a good predictor of group behavior? The answer is "No." The magnitude of the effect of any *single* characteristic is small, but taken *together,* the consequences for group behavior are of major significance. We can conclude, therefore, that personality characteristics of group members play an important part in determining behavior in groups.

Group Size

Does the size of a group affect the group's overall behavior? The answer to this question is a definite "Yes," but the effect depends on what dependent variables you look at.[27]

The evidence indicates, for instance, that smaller groups are faster at completing tasks than are larger ones. However, if the group is engaged in problem solving, large groups consistently get better marks than their smaller counterparts. Translating these results into specific numbers is a bit more hazardous, but we can offer some parameters. Large groups—with a dozen or more members—are good for gaining diverse input. So if the goal of the group is fact-finding, larger groups should be more effective. On the other hand, smaller groups are better at doing something productive with that input. Groups of approximately seven members, therefore, tend to be more effective for action taking.

One of the most important findings related to the size of a group has been labeled "social loafing." It directly challenges the logic that the productivity of the group as a whole should at least equal the sum of the productivity of each individual in that group.

A common stereotype about groups is that the sense of team spirit spurs individual effort and enhances the group's overall productivity. In the late 1920s, a German psychologist named Ringelmann compared the results of individual and group performance on a rope-pulling task.[28] He expected that the group's effort would be equal to the sum of the efforts of individuals within the group. That is, three people pulling together should exert three times as much pull on the rope as one person, and eight people should exert eight times as much pull. Ringelmann's results, however, did not confirm his expectations. Groups of three people exerted a force only two-and-a-half times the average individual performance. Groups of eight collectively achieved less than four times the solo rate.

Replications of Ringelmann's research with similar tasks have generally supported his findings.[29] Increases in group size are inversely related to individual performance. More may be better in the sense that the total productivity of a group of four is greater than one or two, but the individual productivity of each group member declines.

What causes this social loafing effect? It may be due to a belief that others in the group are not pulling their own weight. If you see others as lazy or inept, you can reestablish equity by reducing your effort. Another explanation is the dispersion of responsibility. Because the results of the group cannot be attributed to any single person, the relationship between an individual's input and the group's output is clouded. In such situations, individuals may be tempted to become "free riders" and coast on the group's efforts. In other words, there will be a reduction in efficiency where individuals think that their contribution cannot be measured.

The implications for OB of this effect on work groups are significant. Where managers utilize collective work situations to enhance morale and teamwork, they must also provide means by which individual efforts can be identified. If this is not done, management must weigh the potential losses in productivity against any possible gains in worker satisfaction.[30]

The research on group size also leads us to two additional conclusions: (1) Groups with an odd number of members tend to be preferred over those with an even number, and (2) groups made up of five or seven members do a pretty good job of extracting the best elements of both small and large groups.[31] The preference for an odd number of members eliminates the possibility of ties. Groups made up of five or seven members are large enough to form a majority and allow for diverse input yet avoid the negative outcomes often associated with large groups such as domination by a few members, development of subgroups, inhibited participation by some members, and excessive time taken to reach a decision.

Heterogeneity of Members

Most group activities require a variety of skills and knowledge. Given this requirement, it would be reasonable to conclude that heterogeneous groups—those made up of dissimilar individuals—would be more likely to have diverse abilities and information and should be more effective. Research studies substantiate this conclusion.[32]

When a group is heterogeneous in terms of personality, opinions, abilities, skills, and perspectives, there is an increased probability that the group will possess the needed characteristics to complete its tasks effectively.[33] The group may be more conflict laden and less expedient as diverse positions are introduced and assimilated, but the evidence generally supports the conclusion that heterogeneous groups perform more effectively than do those that are homogeneous.

A more specific offshoot of the heterogeneity issue has recently received a great deal of attention by group researchers. This is the degree to which members of a group share a common demographic attribute such as age, sex, race, educational level, or length of service in the organization and the impact of these attributes on turnover. We'll call this variable "group demography."[34]

We discussed individual demographic factors in Chapter 3. Here we consider the same type of factors but in a group context. That is, it is not whether a person is male or female, or has been employed with the organization a year rather than ten years. What now becomes our focus of attention is the individual's attribute in relationship to the others with whom he or she works. Let's work through the logic of group demography, review the evidence, and then consider the implications.

Groups and organizations are composed of cohorts, which we define as individuals who hold a common attribute. For instance, everyone in a group born in 1960 is of the same age. This means they also have shared common experiences. People born in 1960 have experienced the women's movement but not the Korean conflict. People born in 1945 shared the Vietnam war but not the Great Depression. Women in organizations today who were born prior to 1945 matured prior to the women's movement and have substantially different experiences from women born after 1960. Group demography, therefore, suggests that such attributes as age or the date that someone joins a specific work group or organization should help us to predict turnover. How would this occur? Essentially the logic would go like this: Turnover will be greater among those with dissimilar experiences because communication is more difficult; conflict and power struggles more likely, and more severe when they occur. The increased conflict makes group membership less attractive, so employees are more likely to quit. Similarly, the losers in a power struggle are more apt to leave voluntarily or be forced out.

Several studies have sought to test this thesis, and the evidence is quite encouraging.[35] For example, in departments or separate work groups where a large portion of members entered at the same time, there is considerably more turnover among those outside this cohort. Also, where there are large gaps between cohorts, turnover is higher. People who enter together or at approximately the same time are more likely to associate with one another, have a similar perspective of the group or organization, and thus are more likely to stay. On the other hand, discontinuities or bulges in the group's date-of-entry distribution is likely to result in a higher turnover rate within that group.

The implications from this line of inquiry is that the composition of a group may be an important predictor of turnover. Differences, per se, may not predict turnover. But large differences in similarity within a single group will lead to turnover. If everyone is moderately dissimilar from everyone else in a group, the feelings of being an outsider are reduced. So, it's the degree of dispersion on an attribute, rather than the level, that matters most. We can speculate that variance within a group in respect to other attributes, such as social background, sex differences, or levels of education, might similarly create discontinuities or bulges in the distribution that will encourage some members to leave. To extend this even farther, the fact that a group member is a female, in itself, may mean little in predicting turnover. In fact, if the work group is made up of ten members, nine of which are women, we'd be more likely to predict that the lone male would leave. In the executive ranks of organizations, where females are the minority, we would predict this minority status to increase the likelihood that female managers would quit.

CHARACTERISTICS OF EFFECTIVE GROUPS

What makes a group effective? One reviewer has attempted to answer this question by summarizing the research studies on group effectiveness. We will share his findings in this section.[36] Of course, any assessment of effectiveness is going to be somewhat subjective. What may be perceived as effective by one analyst can be seen as ineffective by another. The characteristics offered here have a strong humanist orientation. They assume that group members should achieve and maintain a sense of importance and personal worth from the group. Additionally, they place a strong emphasis on the role of leadership and supportive relationships.

With these caveats made explicit, the major properties and performance characteristics of the ideal highly effective group are as follows:

1. Members are skilled in all the various leadership and membership roles and functions required for interaction between leaders and members and between members and other members.

2. The group has well-established and relaxed working relationships among all its members.

3. Members of the group are attracted to it and are loyal to its members, including the leaders.

4. The values and goals of the group are a satisfactory integration and expression of the relevant values and needs of its members.

5. Each member is motivated to all that he or she can reasonably do to help the group achieve its central objectives.

6. All the interaction, problem-solving, and decision-making activities of the group occur in a supportive atmosphere. While members accept that there are real and important differences of opinion, the focus is on arriving at sound solutions and not on exacerbating and aggravating conflicts.

7. The group is eager to help each member develop his or her full potential.

8. Each member accepts willingly and without resentment the goals and expectations that the group has established.

9. Members provide mutual help, when necessary or advisable, so that each can successfully accomplish his or her goals.

10. The supportive atmosphere stimulates creativity.

11. The group knows the value of "constructive" conformity and knows when to use it and for what purposes.

12. There is high motivation on the part of each member to initiate and receive communications openly.

13. Members are flexible and adaptable in regard to their goals and attitudes.

14. Individual members feel secure in making decisions that seem appropriate to them because the goals and philosophy of operation are clearly understood by each member.

SHOULD MANAGEMENT SEEK COHESIVE GROUPS?

Many of the previously listed characteristics of effective groups imply the value of cohesiveness. In this section we want to detemine whether cohesiveness, as a group characteristic, is desirable. More specifically, should management actively seek to create work groups that are highly cohesive?

Intuitively, it would appear that groups in which there is a lot of internal disagreement and a lack of cooperative spirit would be relatively less effective in completing their tasks than would groups in which individuals generally agree and cooperate and where members like each other. Research to test this intuition has focused on the concept of group cohesiveness, defined as the degree to which members are attracted to one another and share the group's goals. That is, the more that members are attracted to each other and the more that the group's goals align with their individual goals, the greater the group's cohesiveness. In the following pages, we'll review the factors that have been found to influence group cohesiveness and then look at the effect of cohesiveness on group productivity.[37]

Determinants of Cohesiveness

What factors determine whether group members will be attracted to one another? Cohesiveness can be affected by such factors as time spent together, the severity of initiation, group size, external threats, and previous successes.

TIME SPENT TOGETHER

If you rarely get an opportunity to see or interact with other people, you're unlikely to be attracted to them. The amount of time that people spend together, therefore, influences cohesiveness. As people spend more time together, they become more friendly. They naturally begin to talk, respond, gesture, and engage in other interactions. These interactions typically lead to the discovery of common interests and increased attraction.[38]

The opportunity for group members to spend time together is dependent on their physical proximity. We would expect more close relationships among members who are located close to one another rather than far apart. People who live on the same block, ride the same car pool, or share a common office are more likely to become a cohesive group because the physical distance between them is minimal. For instance, among clerical workers in one organization it was found that the distance between their desks was the single most important determinant of the rate of interaction between any two of the clerks.[39]

SEVERITY OF INITIATION

The more difficult it is to get into a group, the more cohesive that group becomes. The hazing through which fraternities typically put their pledges is meant to screen out those who don't want to "pay the price" and to intensify the desire of those who do to become fraternity actives. But group initiation needn't be as blatant as hazing. The competition to be accepted to a good medical school results in first-year medical school classes that are highly cohesive. The common initiation rites—applications, test taking, interviews, and the long wait for a final decision—all contribute to creating this cohesiveness. Similarly, the months or often years that an apprentice trade worker must put in to developing his or her skills before being advanced to journeyman status results in union journeymen generally being a cohesive group.

GROUP SIZE

If group cohesiveness tends to increase with the time members are able to spend together, it seems logical that cohesiveness should decrease as group size increases, since it becomes more difficult for a member to interact with all the members. This is generally what the research indicates.[40] As group size expands, interaction with all members becomes more difficult, as does the ability to maintain a common goal. Not surprisingly, too, as a single group's size increases, the likelihood of cliques forming also increases. The creation of groups within groups tends to decrease overall cohesiveness.

Evidence suggests that these size-cohesiveness conclusions may be moderated by the gender of the group members.[41] In experiments comparing groups of four and sixteen members, some made up of males only, some with females only, and others mixed, the small groups proved to be more cohesive than large ones as long as all the members were of the same sex. But when the groups were made up of both males and females, the larger groups were more cohesive. Members of both sexes liked the mixed groups more than the single-sex groups, and apparently the opportunity to interact with a larger set of both sexes increased cohesiveness. While it is dangerous to generalize from this study, we should nevertheless be aware of the possible moderating effect of sex on the size-cohesiveness relationship, especially nowadays as the work force becomes more equally divided between males and females.

EXTERNAL THREATS

Most of the research supports the proposition that a group's cohesiveness will increase if the group comes under attack from external sources.[42] Management threats frequently bring together an otherwise disarrayed union. Efforts by management unilaterally to redesign even one or two jobs or to discipline one or two employees occasionally grab local headlines when the entire work force walks out in support of the abused few. These examples illustrate a cooperative phenomenon that can develop within a group when it is attacked from outside.

While a group generally moves toward greater cohesiveness when threatened by external agents, this does not occur under all conditions. If group members perceive that their group may not meet an attack well, then the group becomes less important as a source of security, and cohesiveness will not necessarily increase. Additionally, if members believe the attack is directed at the group merely because of its existence and that it will cease if the group is abandoned or broken up, there is likely to be a decrease in cohesiveness.[43]

PREVIOUS SUCCESSES

Everyone loves a winner! If a group has a history of previous successes, it builds an esprit de corps that attracts and unites members. Successful firms find it easier to attract and hire new employees. The same holds true for successful research groups, well-known and prestigious universities, and winning athletic teams. When Bill Bowerman was head track coach at the University of Oregon during the 1960s, he never had trouble attracting the country's top track and field athletes to his campus. The best athletes wated to come to Oregon because of Bowerman's highly successful program. In fact, Bowerman claims to never have initiated contact with an athlete. In contrast to track coaches at other major universities, if an athlete wanted to compete at Oregon, he had to prove his interest by taking the first step. Continuing with another university example, for those readers who harbor ambitions of attending a top-quality graduate school of business, you should recognize that the success of these schools attracts large numbers of aspiring candidates—many have twenty or more applicants for every vacancy. Again, everyone loves a winner!

Effects of Cohesiveness on Group Productivity

The previous section indicates that, generally speaking, group cohesiveness is increased when members spend time together and undergo a severe initiation, when the group size is small, when external threats exist, and when the group has a history of previous successes. But is increased cohesiveness always desirable from the point of view of management? Is it related to increased productivity?

Research has generally shown that highly cohesive groups are more effective than those with less cohesiveness,[44] but the relationship is more complex than merely allowing us to say high cohesiveness is good. First, high cohesiveness is both a cause and outcome of high productivity. Second, the relationship is moderated by the degree to which the group's attitude aligns with its formal goals or those of the larger organization of which it is a part.

Cohesiveness influences productivity and productivity influences cohesiveness. Camaraderie reduces tension and provides a supportive environment for the successful attainment of group goals. But as already noted, the successful attainment of group goals, and the members' feelings of having been a part of a successful unit, can serve to enhance the commitment of members. Basketball coaches, for example, are famous for their endearment of teamwork. They believe that if the team is going to win games, members have to learn to play together. Popular coaching phrases include, "There are no individuals on this team" and "We win together, or we lose together." The other side of this view, however, is that winning reinforces camaraderie and leads to increased cohesiveness; that is, successful performance leads to increased intermember attractiveness and sharing.

More important has been the recognition that the relationship of cohesiveness and productivity depends on the alignment of the group's attitude with its formal goals, or for work groups, those of the larger organization of which it is a part.[45] The more cohesive a group, the more its members will follow its goals. If these attitudes are favorable (i.e., high output, quality work, cooperation with individuals outside the group), a cohesive group will be more productive than a less cohesive group. But if cohesiveness is high and attitudes unfavorable, there will be decreases in productivity. If cohesiveness is low and there is support of goals, productivity increases but less than in the high cohesiveness—high support situation. Where cohesiveness is low and attitudes are not in support of the organization's goal, there seems to be no significant effect of cohesiveness upon productivity. These conclusions are summarized in Figure 6–4.

FIGURE 6–4
Relationship of Cohesiveness to Productivity

		Cohesiveness	
		High	Low
Alignment of Group and Organizational Goals	High	Strong increase in productivity	Moderate increase in productivity
	Low	Decrease in productivity	No significant effect on productivity

The title of this section was: "Should Management Seek Cohesive Groups?" Based on the previous discussion, our answer is a qualified "Yes." The qualification lies in the degree of alignment between the group and organization's goals. Management should attempt to create work groups whose goals are consistent with those of the organization. If this is achieved, then high group cohesiveness will make a positive contribution to the group's productivity.

IMPLICATIONS FOR PERFORMANCE AND SATISFACTION

We've covered a lot of territory in this chapter. Now it's necessary to extract those group characteristics that have the most significant impact on performance and satisfaction.

Performance

A number of factors show a relationship to performance. Among the more prominent are role perception, norms, the size of the group, its demographic makeup, and its degree of cohesiveness.

There is a positive relationship between role perception and an employee's performance evaluation.[46] The degree of congruence that exists between an employee and his or her boss, in the perception of the employee's job, influences the degree to which that employee will be judged as an effective performer by the boss. To the extent that the employee's role perception fulfills the boss's role expectation, the employee will receive a higher performance evaluation.

Norms control group member behavior by establishing standards of right or wrong. If we know the norms of a given group, it can help us to explain the behaviors of its members. Where norms support high output, we can expect individual performance to be markedly higher than where group norms aim to restrict output. Similarly, acceptable standards of absence will be dictated by the group norms.

The impact of size on a group's performance depends upon the type of task in which the group is engaged. Larger groups are more effective in fact-finding activities. Smaller groups are more effective in action-taking tasks. Our knowledge of social loafing suggests that if management uses larger groups, efforts should be made to provide measures of individual performance within the group.

We found the group's demographic composition to be a key determinant of individual turnover. Specifically, the evidence indicates that group members who share a common age or date of entry into the work group are less prone to resign.

Cohesiveness can play an important function in influencing a group's level of productivity. Whether or not it does depends on the degree of coalignment that exists between the group's attitude or goals and the goals of the larger organization of which it is a part.

Satisfaction

Several of the same group variables that impact performance also influence employee satisfaction. These include role perception and group size. Additionally, role conflict and status show strong relationships with satisfaction.

As with the role perception–performance relationship, high congruence between a boss and employee, as to the perception of the employee's job, shows a significant association with high employee satisfaction.[47] Similarly, role conflict is associated with job-induced tension and job dissatisfaction.[48]

Status inequities create frustrations for employees and adversely affect satisfaction levels.[49] There also appears to be a strong correlation between the prestige of an occupation and members' satisfaction with their job.[50] The higher an occupation's status, the more satisfied are those people who engage in it. In North America, professionals have the highest occupational prestige, and they also have the highest level of work satisfaction. Among three thousand workers in sixteen industries polled, higher satisfaction scores were recorded by professional and white-collar occupations such as university professors, mathematicians, physicists, chemists, lawyers, and school superintendents. In contrast, significantly lower scores were made by skilled tradespeople and blue-collar workers.[51]

The group size–satisfaction relationship is what one would intuitively expect: Larger groups are associated with lower satisfaction.[52] As size increases, opportunities for participation and social interaction decrease, as does the ability for members to identify with the group's accomplishments. At the same time, having more members also prompts dissension, conflict, and the formation of subgroups, which all act to make the group a less pleasant entity to be a part of.

POINT

DESIGNING JOBS AROUND GROUPS

It's time to take small groups seriously, that is, to use groups, rather than individuals, as the basic building blocks for an organization. I propose that we can design organizations from scratch around small groups rather than the way we have always done it—around individuals.

Why would management want to do such a thing? At least seven reasons can be identified. First, small groups seem to be good for people. They can satisfy important membership needs. They can provide a moderately wide range of activities for individual members. They can provide support in times of stress and crisis. They are settings in which people can learn not only cognitively but empirically to be reasonably trusting and helpful to one another. Second, groups seem to be good problem-finding tools. They seem to be useful in promoting innovation and creativity. Third, in a wide variety of decision situations, they make better decisions than individuals do. Fourth, they are great tools for implementation. They gain commitment from their members so that group decisions are likely to be willingly carried out. Fifth, they can control and discipline individual members in ways that are often extremely difficult through impersonal quasi-legal disciplinary systems. Sixth, as organizations grow large, small groups appear to be useful mechanisms for fending off many of the negative effects of large size. They help to prevent communication lines from growing too long, the hierarchy from growing too steep, and the individual from getting lost in the crowd.

There is a seventh, but altogether different, kind of argument for taking groups seriously. Groups are natural phenomena, and facts of organizational life. They can be created, but their spontaneous development cannot be prevented.

Operationally, how would an organization function that was designed around groups? One answer to this question is merely to take the things that organizations do with individuals and apply them with groups. The idea would be to raise the level from the atom to the molecule and *select* groups rather than individuals, *train* groups rather than individuals, *pay* groups rather than individuals, *promote* groups rather than individuals, *design jobs* for groups rather than for individuals, *fire* groups rather than individuals, and so on down the list of activities that organizations have traditionally carried on in order to use human beings in their organizations.

In the past, the human group has been primarily used for patching and mending organizations that were built around the individual. The time is rapidly approaching, and it may already be here, for management to begin redesigning organizations around groups.

Adapted from H. J. Leavitt, "Suppose We Took Groups Seriously," in E. L. Cass and F. G. Zimmer (eds.), Man and Work in Society *(New York: Van Nostrand Reinhold, 1975), pp. 67–77.*

COUNTERPOINT

JOBS SHOULD BE DESIGNED AROUND INDIVIDUALS

The argument that organizations can and should be designed around groups might hold in a socialistic society, but not in the United States. The following response directly relates to the United States and American workers, although it is probably generalizable to other economically advanced capitalistic countries. In fact, given China's and Russia's recent successes in isolated experiments with profit-motivated businesses, the case for the individually oriented organization may be applicable throughout the world.

America was built on the individual ethic. This ethic has been pounded into us from birth. The result is that it is deeply embedded in the psyche of every American. We strongly value individual achievement. We praise competition. Even in team sports, we want to identify individuals for recognition. Sure, we enjoy group interaction. We like being part of a team, especially a winning team. But it is one thing to be a member of a work group while maintaining a strong individual identity and another to sublimate your identity to that of the group. The latter is inconsistent with the values of American life.

The American worker likes a clear link between his or her individual effort and a visible outcome. It is not happenstance that the United States, as a nation, has a considerably larger proportion of high achievers than exists in socialistic countries. America breeds achievers, and achievers seek personal responsibility. They would be frustrated in job situations where their contribution is commingled and homogenized with the contributions of others.

Americans want to be hired based on their individual talents. They want to be evaluated on their individual efforts. They also want to be rewarded with pay raises and promotions based on their individual performance. Americans believe in an authority and status hierarchy. They accept a system where there are bosses and subordinates. They are not likely to accept a group's decision on such issues as their job assignments and wage increases.

One of the more interesting illustrations of America's commitment to the individualistic ethic is research that has assessed the public's views on the American tax structure. We'd expect the rich to favor low tax rates on individuals with high incomes— $60,000 a year or more. But studies consistently find that Americans below the government's defined "poverty level" also strongly favor lower tax rates for high-income earners. A reasonable interpretation of these findings is that there is a very strong belief, held across the full range of economic levels, that anyone can make it in America. And when they make it, they don't want to be saddled with a heavy tax burden! Isn't this consistent with the stereotype of the individualistic American, motivated by his or her self-interest? Yes! Is this a worker who would be satisfied and reach his or her full productive capacity, in a group-centered organization? Not likely!

FOR DISCUSSION

1. Compare and contrast command, task, interest, and friendship groups.
2. What might motivate you to join a group?
3. How could you use the four-stage group development model to better understand group behavior?
4. Identify five roles you play. What behaviors do they require? Are any of these roles in conflict? If so, in what way? How do you resolve these conflicts?
5. How would it help you to know that a woman has to reconcile her roles of mother, Methodist, Democrat, Councilwoman, and warden of the Michigan State Penitentiary for Women?
6. What is the relationship between the psychological contract and role expectations?
7. "The imposition of group norms is enforced via management authority rather than by group acceptance." Do you agree or disagree? Discuss.
8. Describe the Hawthorne studies. What is the importance of this research to understanding group behavior?
9. How do norms develop?
10. How can a group's demography help you to predict turnover?
11. What factors influence the degree to which group members will be attracted to each other?
12. "High cohesiveness in a group leads to higher group productivity." Do you agree or disagree? Explain.

FOR FURTHER READING

CUMMINGS, T. G., "Designing Effective Work Groups." In P. C. Nystrom and W. H. Starbuck (eds.), *Handbook of Organizational Design*, Vol. 2, pp. 250–71. New York: Oxford University Press, 1981. Reviews our knowledge about controllable variables that can alter group outcomes, how outcomes translate into performance, and our understanding of group design processes.

HACKMAN, J. R., "Group Influences on Individuals." In M. D. Dunnette (ed.), *Handbook of Industrial and Organizational Psychology*, pp. 1455–1525. Chicago: Rand McNally, 1976. Analyzes how groups influence individual behavior and attitudes.

HOMANS, G. C., *The Human Group*. New York: Harcourt Brace Jovanovich, 1950. Offers a classic presentation of a group behavior model that predicts the group's productivity, its level of satisfaction, and its ability to develop, change, and innovate.

JEWELL, L. N., and H. J. REITZ, *Group Effectiveness in Organizations*. Glenview, Ill.: Scott, Foresman, 1981. Discusses group processes, and how they influence organizational effectiveness, and presents a comprehensive group behavior model.

WILSON, S., *Informal Groups: An Introduction*. Englewood Cliffs, N.J.: Prentice-Hall, 1978. Describes the creation and operations of informal groups; an introductory text.

ZANDER, A., *Making Groups Effective*. San Francisco: Jossey-Bass, 1982. Summarizes how to make groups effective, by one of the founders of group dynamics.

NOTES FOR CHAPTER 6

1. L. R. Sayles, "Work Group Behavior and the Larger Organization," in C. Arensburg et al. (eds.), *Research in Industrial Relations* (New York: Harper & Row, 1957), pp. 131–45.

2. B. W. Tuckman, "Developmental Sequence in Small Groups," *Psychological Bulletin*, May 1965, pp. 384–99.

3. L. N. Jewell and H. J. Reitz, *Group Effectiveness in Organizations* (Glenview, Ill.: Scott, Foresman, 1981).

4. S. Lieberman, "The Effects of Changes in Roles on the Attitudes of Role Occupants," *Human Relations*, November 1956, pp. 385–402.

5. R. Keyes, *Is There Life After High School?* (New York: Warner Books, 1976).

6. See, for example, J. P. Kotter, "The Psychological Contract," *California Management Review*, Spring 1973, pp. 91–99.

7. E. H. Schein, *Organizational Psychology*, 3rd ed. (Englewood Cliffs, N.J.: Prentice-Hall, 1980), p. 24.

8. S. P. Robbins, *Positional Authority of Selected College and University Presidents as Perceived by Their Interacting Publics*, doctoral dissertation, University of Arizona, Tucson, 1971.

9. S. N. Brenner and E. A. Molander, "Is the Ethics of Business Changing?" *Harvard Business Review*, January–February 1977, pp. 57–71.

10. P. G. Zimbardo, C. Haney, W. C. Banks, and D. Jaffe, "The Mind Is a Formidable Jailer: A Pirandellian Prison," *The New York Times*, April 8, 1973, pp. 38–60.

11. A. Harlan, J. Kerr, and S. Kerr, "Preference for Motivator and Hygiene Factors in a Hypothetical Interview Situation: Further Findings and Some Implications for the Employment Interview," *Personnel Psychology*, Winter 1977, pp. 557–66.

12. Much of this description was adapted from "The Hawthorne Studies: A Synopsis," reported in E. L. Cass and F. G. Zimmer (eds.), *Man and Work in Society* (New York: Van Nostrand Reinhold, 1975), pp. 278–306.

13. This section is adapted from G. Johns, *Organizational Behavior: Understanding Life at Work* (Glenview, Ill.: Scott, Foresman, 1983), pp. 259–60.

14. D. C. Feldman, "The Development and Enforcement of Group Norms," *Academy of Management Journal*, January 1984, pp. 47–53.

15. C. A. Kiesler and S. B. Kiesler, *Conformity* (Reading, Mass.: Addison-Wesley, 1969).

16. Ibid., p.27.
17. S. E. Asch, "Effects of Group Pressure upon the Modification and Distortion of Judgments," in H. Guetzkow (ed.), *Groups, Leadership and Men* (Pittsburgh: Carnegie Press, 1951), pp. 177–90.
18. Keyes, *Is There Life After High School?*
19. Ibid.
20. W. F. Whyte, "The Social Structure of the Restaurant," *American Journal of Sociology*, January 1954, pp. 302–8.
21. "Top Dollar Jobs," *Time*, June 2, 1980, p. 60.
22. S. P. Robbins, *Personnel: The Management of Human Resources* (Englewood Cliffs, N.J.: Prentice-Hall, 1978), p. 294.
23. E. Konar, E. Sundstrom, C. Brady, D. Mandel, and R. W. Rice, "Status Demarcation in the Office," *Environment and Behavior,* September 1982, pp. 561–80.
24. Ibid., pp. 564–65.
25. D. A. Ricks, M. Y. C. Fu, and J. S. Arpas, *International Business Blunders* (Columbus, Ohio: Grid, 1974).
26. M. E. Shaw, *Contemporary Topics in Social Psychology* (Morristown, N.J.: General Learning Press, 1976), pp. 350–51.
27. E. J. Thomas and C. F. Fink, "Effects of Group Size," *Psychological Bulletin*, July 1963, pp. 371–84; A. P. Hare, *Handbook of Small Group Research* (New York: Free Press, 1976); and M. E. Shaw, *Group Dynamics: The Psychology of Small Group Behavior*, 3rd ed. (New York: McGraw-Hill, 1981).
28. W. Moede, "Die Richtlinien der Leistungs-Psychologie," *Industrielle Psychotechnik*, Vol. 4 (1927), pp. 193–207.
29. A. G. Ingham, G. Levinger, J. Graves, and V. Peckham, "The Ringelmann Effect: Studies of Group Size and Group Performance," *Journal of Experimental Social Psychology*, July 1974, pp. 371–84; B. Latane, K. Williams, and S. Harkins, "Many Hands Make Light the Work: The Causes and Consequences of Social Loafing," *Journal of Personality and Social Psychology*, November 1979, pp. 822–32; and K. Williams, S. Harkins, and B. Latane, "Identifiability as a Determinant to Social Loafing: Two Cheering Experiments," *Journal of Personality and Social Psychology*, February 1981, pp. 303-11.
30. B. Latane, K. Williams, and S. Harkins, "Social Loafing," *Psychology Today*, October 1979, p. 110.
31. Thomas and Fink, "Effects of Group Size"; Hare, *Handbook;* Shaw, *Group Dynamics*; and P. Yetton and P. Bottger, "The Relationships Among Group Size, Member Ability, Social Decision Schemes, and Performance," *Organizational Behavior and Human Performance,* October 1983, pp. 145–59.
32. See, for example, R. L. Hoffman, "Homogeneity of Member Personality and Its Effect on Group Problem Solving," *Journal of Abnormal and Social Psychology*, January 1959, pp. 27–33; and R. L. Hoffman and N. R. F. Maier, "Quality and Acceptance of Problem Solutions by Members of Homogeneous and Heterogeneous Groups," *Journal of Abnormal and Social Psychology*, March 1961, pp. 401–07.
33. Shaw, *Contemporary Topics*, p. 356.
34. Adapted from J. Pfeffer, "Organizational Demography," in L. L. Cummings and B. M. Staw (eds.), *Research in Organizational Behavior*, Vol. 5 (Greenwich, Conn.: JAI Press, 1983), pp. 299–357.
35. B. E. McCain, C. A. O'Reilly III, and J. Pfeffer, "The Effects of Departmental Demography on Turnover: The Case of a University," *Academy of Management Journal*, December 1983, pp. 626–41; and W. G. Wagner, J. Pfeffer, and C. A. O'Reilly III,

"Organizational Demography and Turnover in Top-Management Groups," *Administrative Science Quarterly,* March 1984, pp. 74–92.

36. Adapted from R. Likert, "The Nature of Highly Effective Groups," in D. A. Kolb, I. M. Rubin, and J. M. McIntyre (eds.), *Organizational Psychology: Readings on Human Behavior in Organizations,* 4th ed. (Englewood Cliffs, N.J.: Prentice-Hall, 1984), pp. 153–66.

37. For an excellent review of the group cohesiveness literature, see A. J. Lott and B. E. Lott, "Group Cohesiveness as Interpersonal Attraction: A Review of Relationships with Antecedent and Consequent Variables," October 1965, pp. 259–309.

38. C. Insko and M. Wilson, "Interpersonal Attraction as a Function of Social Interaction," *Journal of Personality and Social Psychology,* December 1977, pp. 903–11.

39. J. T. Gullahorn, "Distance and Friendship as Factors in the Gross Interaction Matrix," *Sociometry,* February–March 1952, pp. 123–34.

40. E. J. Thomas and C. F. Fink, "Effects of Group Size," *Psychological Bulletin,* July 1963, pp. 371–84.

41. L. Libo, *Measuring Group Cohesiveness* (Ann Arbor: University of Michigan, Institute of Social Research, 1953).

42. A. Stein, "Conflict and Cohesion: A Review of the Literature," *Journal of Conflict Resolution,* March 1976, pp. 143–72.

43. A. Zander, "The Psychology of Group Processes," in M. R. Rosenzweig and L. W. Porter (eds.), *Annual Review of Psychology,* Vol 30 (Palo Alto, Calif.: Annual Reviews, 1979), p. 436.

44. See, for example, L. Berkowitz, "Group Standards, Cohesiveness, and Productivity," *Human Relations,* November 1954, pp. 509–19.

45. S. E. Seashore, *Group Cohesiveness in the Industrial Work Group* (Ann Arbor: University of Michigan, Survey Research Center, 1954).

46. T. P. Verney, "Role Perception Congruence, Performance, and Satisfaction," in D. J. Vredenburgh and R. S. Schuler (eds.), *Effective Management: Research and Application,* Proceedings of the 20th Annual Eastern Academy of Management, Pittsburgh, Pa., May 1983, pp. 24–27.

47. Ibid.

48. M. Van Sell, A. P. Brief, and R. S. Schuler, "Role Conflict and Role Ambiguity: Integration of the Literature and Directions for Future Research," *Human Relations,* January 1981, pp.43–71; and A. G. Bedeian and A. A. Armenakis, "A Path-Analytic Study of the Consequences of Role Conflict and Ambiguity," *Academy of Management Journal,* June 1981, pp. 417–24.

49. Konar et al., "Status Demarcation in the Office."

50. Reported by R. L. Kahn in "The Work Module," *Psychology Today,* February 1973, p. 39.

51. Ibid.

52. Thomas and Fink, "Effects of Group Size"; Hare, *Handbook*; and Shaw, *Group Dynamics.*

7

Communication and Group Decision Making

AFTER STUDYING THIS CHAPTER, YOU SHOULD BE ABLE TO:

Define and explain the following key terms and concepts:

Active listening	Filtering
Brainstorming	Grapevine .
Channel	Groupshift
Communication	Groupthink
Communication networks	Informational cues
Communication process	Interacting groups
Decoding	Kinesics
Delphi technique	Message
Encoding	Nominal group technique
Feedback loop	Nonverbal communication

Understand:

The process of communication
Barriers to effective communication
Techniques for overcoming the barriers
The relationship of perception to communication
The benefits and disadvantages of each communication network
Factors affecting the use of the grapevine
The advantages and disadvantages to group decision making

Every improvement in communication makes the bore more terrible.

—F. M. COLBY

Probably the most frequently cited source of interpersonal conflict is poor communication.[1] Because we spend nearly 70 percent of our waking hours communicating—writing, reading, speaking, listening—it seems reasonable to conclude that one of the most inhibiting forces to successful group performance is a lack of effective communication.

No group can exist without communication: the transference of meaning among its members. It is only through transmitting meaning from one person to another that information and ideas can be conveyed. Communication, however, is more than merely imparting meaning. It must also be understood. In a group where one member speaks only German and the others do not know German, the individual speaking German will not be fully understood. Therefore, communication must include both the *transference and understanding* of meaning.

An idea, no matter how great, is useless until it is transmitted and understood by others. Perfect communication, if there were such a thing, would exist when a thought or idea was transmitted so that the mental picture perceived by the receiver was exactly the same as that envisioned by the sender. Although elementary in theory, perfect communication is never achieved in practice, for reasons we shall expand upon later.

Before making too many generalizations concerning communication and problems in communicating effectively, we need to review briefly the functions that communication performs and describe the communication process.

FUNCTIONS OF COMMUNICATION

Communication serves four major functions within a group or organization: control, motivation, emotional expression, and information.[2]

Communication acts to *control* member behavior in several ways. Organizations have authority hierarchies and formal guidelines that employees are required to follow. When employees, for instance, are required to first communicate any job-related grievance to their immediate boss, to follow their job description, or to comply with company policies, communication is performing a control function. But informal communication also controls behavior. The Hawthorne experiments, discussed in the previous chapter, showed how the group maintained control by communicating—sometimes very explicitly—the norms that were to be followed.

Communication fosters *motivation* by clarifying to employees what is to be done, how well they are doing, and what can be done to improve performance if it's subpar. We saw this operating in our review of goal-setting and reinforcement theories in Chapter 5. The formation of specific goals, feedback on progress toward the goals, and reinforcement of desired behavior all stimulate motivation and require communication.

For many employees, their work group is a primary source for social interaction. The communication that takes place within the group is a fundamental mechanism by which members show their frustrations and feelings of satisfaction. Communication, therefore, provides a release for the *emotional expression* of feelings and for fulfillment of social needs.

The final function that communication performs relates to its role in facilitating decision making. It provides the *information* that individuals and groups need to make decisions by transmitting the data to identify and evaluate alternative choices.

No one of these four functions should be seen as being more important than the others. For groups to perform effectively, they need to maintain some form of control over members, stimulate members to perform, provide a means for emotional expression, and make decision choices. You can assume that almost every communication interaction that takes place in a group or organization performs one or more of these four functions.

THE COMMUNICATION PROCESS

Communication can be thought of as a process or flow. Communication problems occur when there are deviations or blockages in that flow. In this section, we will describe the process in terms of a communication model and then consider how distortions can disrupt the process.

A Communication Model

Before communication can take place, a purpose, expressed as a message to be conveyed, is needed. It passes between a source (the sender) and a receiver. The message is encoded (converted to symbolic form) and is passed by way of some medium (channel) to the receiver, who retranslates (decodes) the message initiated by the sender. The result is a transference of meaning from one person to another.[3]

Figure 7–1 depicts the communication process. This model is made up of seven parts: (1) the communication source, (2) encoding, (3) the message, (4) the channel, (5) decoding, (6) the receiver, and (7) feedback.

The source initiates a message by encoding a thought. Four conditions have been described that affect the encoded message: skill, attitudes, knowledge, and the social-cultural system.

My success in communicating to you is dependent upon my writing skills; in the writing of textbooks, if the authors are without the requisite skills, their message will not reach students in the form desired. One's total communicative success includes speaking, reading, listening, and reasoning skills as well. As we discussed in Chapter 4, our attitudes influence our behavior. We hold predisposed ideas on numerous topics, and our communications are affected by these attitudes. Further, we are restricted in our communicative activity by the extent of our knowledge on the particular topic. We cannot communicate what we do not know, and should our knowledge be too extensive, it is possible that our receiver will not understand our message. Clearly, the amount of knowledge the source holds about his or her subject will affect the message he or she seeks to transfer. And, finally, just as attitudes influence our behavior, so does our position in the social-cultural system in which we exist. Your beliefs and values, all part of your culture, act to influence you as a communicative source.

The message is the actual physical product from the source encoding. "When we speak, the speech is the message. When we write, the writing is the message. When we paint, the picture is the message. When we gesture, the movements of our arms, the expressions on our face are the message."[4] Our message is affected by the code or group of symbols we use to transfer meaning, the content of the message itself, and the decisions that the source makes in selecting and arranging both codes and content.

The channel is the medium through which the message travels. It is selected by the source, who must determine which channel is formal and which one is informal. Formal channels are established by the organization and transmit messages that pertain to the job-related activities of members. They traditionally follow the authority network within the organization. Other forms of messages, such as personal or social, follow the informal channels in the organization.

FIGURE 7–1
The Communication Process Model

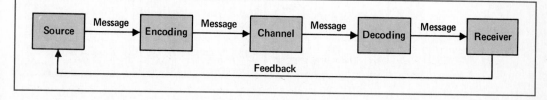

The receiver is the object to whom the message is directed. But before the message can be received, the symbols in it must be translated into a form that can be understood by the receiver. This is the decoding of the message. Just as the encoder was limited by his or her skills, attitudes, knowledge, and social-cultural system, so is the receiver equally restricted. Just as the source must be skillful in writing or speaking, the receiver must be skillful in reading or listening, and both must be able to reason. One's level of knowledge, attitudes, and cultural background influences one's ability to receive, just as it does the ability to send.

The final link in the communicative process is a feedback loop. "If a communication source decodes the message that he encodes, if the message is put back into his system, we have feedback."[5] Feedback is the check on how successful we have been in transferring our messages as originally intended. It determines whether understanding has been achieved.

Sources of Distortion

Unfortunately, most of the seven components in the process model have the potential to create distortion and, therefore, impinge upon the goal of communicating perfectly. These sources of distortion explain why the message that is decoded by the receiver is rarely the exact message that the sender intended.

If the encoding is done carelessly, the message decoded by the sender will have been distorted. The message itself can also cause distortion. The poor choice of symbols and confusion in the content of the message are frequent problem areas. Of course, the channel can distort a communication if a poor one is selected or if the noise level is high. The receiver represents the final potential source for distortion. His or her prejudices, knowledge, perceptual skills, attention span, and care in decoding are all factors that can result in interpreting the message somewhat differently than envisioned by the sender.

FIGURE 7–2

Source: Berke Breathed, *Toons for our Times: Bloom County* (Boston: Little, Brown, 1984). Copyright © 1984 by The Washington Post Company. By permission of Little, Brown and Company in association with the Atlantic Monthly Press.

BARRIERS TO EFFECTIVE COMMUNICATION

We have noted the potential for distortion in the communication process. As illustrated in Table 7–1, what managers say can be different from what they mean and still different from a subordinate's interpretation. What causes such communication breakdown? In addition to the general distortions previously identified in the communication process, there are other barriers to effective communication of which you should be aware.

TABLE 7–1
How Communications Break Down

WHAT THE MANAGER SAID	WHAT THE MANAGER MEANT	WHAT THE SUBORDINATE HEARD
I'll look into hiring another person for your department as soon as I complete my budget review.	We'll start interviewing for that job in about three weeks.	I'm tied up with more important things. Let's forget about hiring for the indefinite future.
Your performance was below par last quarter. I really expected more out of you.	You're going to have to try harder, but I know you can do it.	If you screw up one more time, you're out.
I'd like that report as soon as you can get to it.	I need that report within the week.	Drop that rush order you're working on and fill out that report today.
I talked to the boss but at the present time, due to budget problems, we'll be unable to fully match your competitive salary offer.	We can give you 95 percent of that offer, and I know we'll be able to do even more for you next year.	If I were you, I'd take that competitive offer. We're certainly not going to pay that kind of salary to a person with your credentials.
We have a job opening in Los Angeles that we think would be just your cup of tea. We'd like you to go out there and look it over.	If you'd like that job, it's yours. If not, of course you can stay here in Denver. You be the judge.	You don't have to go out to L.A. if you don't want to. However, if you don't, you can kiss good-bye to your career with this firm.
Your people seem to be having some problems getting their work out on time. I want you to look into this situation and straighten it out.	Talk to your people and find out what the problem is. Then get with them and jointly solve it.	I don't care how many heads you bust, just get me that ouput. I've got enough problems around here without you screwing things up too.

Source: R. M. Hodgetts and S. Altman. *Organizational Behavior* (New York: Holt, Rinehart and Winston, 1979), p. 305. With permission.

Filtering

Filtering refers to a sender manipulating information so that it will be seen more favorably by the receiver. For example, when a manager tells his boss what he feels his boss wants to hear, he is filtering information. Does this happen much in organizations? Sure! As information is passed up to senior executives, it has to be condensed and synthesized by underlings so those on top don't become overloaded with information. The personal interests and perceptions of what is important by those doing the synthesizing is going to result in filtering. As a former group vice-president of General Motors described it, the filtering of communications through levels at GM made it impossible for senior managers to get objective information because "lower-level specialists . . . provided information in such a way that they would get the answer they wanted. I know. I used to be down below and do it."[6]

The major determinant of filtering is the number of levels in an organization's structure. The more vertical levels in the organization's hierarchy, the more opportunities there are for filtering.

Selective Perception

We have mentioned selective perception before in this book. It appears again because the receivers, in the communication process, selectively see and hear based on their needs, motivations, experience, background, and other personal characteristics. Receivers also project their interests and expectations into communications as they decode them. The employment interviewer who *expects* a female job applicant to put her family ahead of her career is likely to *see* that in female applicants, regardless of whether the applicants feel that way or not. As we said in Chapter 3, we don't see reality; rather, we interpret what we see and call it reality.

Emotions

How the receiver feels at the time of receipt of a communication message will influence how he or she interprets it. The same message received when you're angry or distraught is likely to be interpreted differently when you're in a neutral disposition. Extreme emotions—such as jubilation or depression—are most likely to hinder effective communication. In such instances, we are most prone to disregard our rational and objective thinking processes and substitute emotional judgments.

Language

Words mean different things to different people. "The meanings of words are *not* in the words; they are in us."[7] Age, education, and cultural background are three of the more obvious variables that influence the language a person uses and the definitions they give to words. The language of William F. Buckley, Jr., is clearly different from that of the typical high school–educated Burger King employee. The latter, in fact, would undoubtedly have trouble understanding much of Buckley's vocabulary (but then so do a lot of people with graduate degrees!). The language problem, of course, goes both ways. Try your hand at the quiz in Table 7–2. If you are a black who was raised in an urban environment, you should be able to get ten or more of the items right. For rural whites, a score of three or four would be typical.

In an organization, employees usually come from diverse backgrounds. Additionally, the grouping of employees into departments creates specialists who develop their own jargon or technical language. In large organizations, members are also frequently widely dispersed geographically—even operating in different countries—and individuals in each locale will use terms and phrases that are unique to their area.

The existence of vertical levels can also cause language problems. For instance, differences in meaning with regard to words such as *incentives* and *quotas* have been found at different levels in management. Top managers often speak about the need for incentives and quotas, yet these terms imply manipulation and create resentment among many lower managers.

The point is that while you and I both speak a common language—English—our usage of that language is far from uniform. If we knew how each of us modified the language, communication difficulties would be minimized. The problem is that members in an organization usually don't know how others, with whom they interact, have modified the language. Senders tend to assume that the words and terms they use mean the same to the receiver as they do to them. This, of course, is often incorrect, thus creating communication difficulties.

TABLE 7–2
Test Your Ability to Understand Black Street Language

What is:		
1. Bad?	6. Hanging?	11. A natural?
2. A crib?	7. Humbuggin?	12. An oreo?
3. Fat-mouthing?	8. A jackleg?	13. Racking?
4. A fox?	9. Later?	14. A splib?
5. A grey-boy?	10. A Mack man?	15. Stepping?

ANSWERS: (1) Good, strong, or brave. (2) Where one lives; place of domicile. (3) Talking too much. (4) An attractive woman. (5) A white male. (6) Doing nothing. (7) Fighting. (8) An amateur. (9) Goodbye. (10) A pimp. (11) An Afro haircut. (12) A black person who thinks or acts like a white. (13) Studying. (14) A black person. (15) Dancing.

Source: Adapted from T. Kochman, "'Rapping' in the Black Ghetto." *TransAction*, February 1969, pp. 26–34: *Rappin' and Stylin' Out: Communication in Urban Black America,* ed. T. Kochman (Urbana: University of Illinois Press, 1972); and W. Safire, "Getting Down," *The New York Times Magazine,* January18, 1981, pp. 6, 8.

OVERCOMING THE BARRIERS

Given that there are barriers to communciation, what can individuals do to minimize problems and attempt to overcome these barriers? The following suggestions should be helpful in making communication more effective.

Use Feedback

Many communication problems can be attributed directly to misunderstandings and inaccuracies. These are less likely to occur if you ensure that the feedback loop is utilized in the communication process. We'll elaborate using verbal feedback as an illustration, but keep in mind that feedback can also be written or nonverbal.

If you ask a receiver, "Did you understand what I said?" the response to this question represents feedback. But the "yes" or "no" type of feedback can definitely be improved upon. A sender can ask a set of questions relating to the message in order to determine whether or not it was received as intended. Better yet, a sender can ask the receiver to restate the message, in his or her own words. If the sender then hears what was intended, understanding and accuracy should be enhanced. Feedback can also be more subtle than the direct asking of questions or the summarizing of the message by the receiver. General comments made by the receiver can give the sender a sense of the reaction to a message. Additionally, organizational processes and rewards—such as performance appraisals, salary reviews, job assignments, and promotion decisions—represent important, but more subtle, forms of feedback.

Simplify Language

Since language can be a barrier, the sender should seek to structure messages in ways that will make them clear and understandable. Words should be chosen carefully. The sender needs to simplify his or her language and consider the audience to whom a message is directed, so that the language will be compatible with the receiver. Remember, effective communication is achieved when a message is both received and *understood*. Understanding is improved by simplifying the language used in relation to the audience intended. This means, for example, that a hospital administrator should always try to communicate in clear and easily understood terms and that the language used for conveying messages to the surgical staff should be purposely different from that used with employees in the admission's office. Specialized vocabularies—jargon—can facilitate understanding when it is used with other group members who speak that "language," but it can cause innumerable problems when used outside that group. "Antecedent conditions," "beta weights," "single zero-order correlations," and "unstandardized regression coefficients'' are examples of terms that facilitate communication among social scientists but are only likely to create confusion when used among those untrained in research and statistics.

Listen Actively

When someone talks, we hear. But, too often, we don't listen. Listening is an active search for meaning, whereas hearing is passive. When you listen, two people are thinking—the receiver and the sender.

Many of us are poor listeners. Why? Because it's difficult and because it's usually more satisfying to be on the offensive. Listening, in fact, is often more tiring than talking. It demands intellectual effort. Unlike hearing, active listening demands total concentration. The average person speaks at a rate of about 150 words per minute, whereas we have the capacity to listen at the rate of over 1,000 words per minute. The difference creates idle brain time and opportunities for mind wandering.

Active listening is enhanced when the receiver develops empathy with the sender, that is, when the receiver tries to place himself or herself in the sender's position. Since senders differ in attitudes, interests, needs, and expectations, empathy makes it easier to understand the actual content of a message. An empathetic listener reserves judgment on the message's content and carefully listens to what is being said. The goal is to improve one's ability to receive the full meaning of a communication, without having it distorted by premature judgments or interpretations. Other suggestions for effective listening are offered in Table 7–3.

Constrain Emotions

It would be naive to assume that we always communicate in a fully rational manner. Yet we know that emotions can severely cloud and distort the transference of meaning. If we're emotionally upset over an issue, we're more likely to misconstrue incoming messages, and we may fail to express our outgoing messages clearly and accurately. What can you do? The best approach is to defer from further explicit communication until your composure is regained.

COMMUNICATION PATTERNS

Communication patterns encompass the directions that communications take in groups and organizations, as well as the channels by which communications flow. In this section, we'll describe downward, upward, and lateral communications; identify the five most common formal communication networks and assess the advantages of each; and conclude with a discussion of the informal network.

TABLE 7–3
Suggestions for Effective Listening

1. **Stop talking!**
   You cannot listen if you are talking.
   Polonius *(Hamlet)*: "Give every man thine ear, but few thy voice."
2. **Put the talker at ease.**
   Help a person feel free to talk.
   This is often called a permissive environment.
3. **Show a talker that you want to listen.**
   Look and act interested. Do not read your mail while someone talks.
   Listen to understand rather than to oppose.
4. **Remove distractions.**
   Don't doodle, tap, or shuffle papers.
   Will it be quieter if you shut the door?
5. **Empathize with talkers.**
   Try to help yourself see the other person's point of view.
6. **Be patient.**
   Allow plenty of time. Do not interrupt a talker.
   Don't start for the door or walk away.
7. **Hold your temper.**
   An angry person takes the wrong meaning from words.
8. **Go easy on argument and criticism.**
   These put people on the defensive, and they many "clam up" or become angry.
   Do not argue: Even if you win, you lose.
9. **Ask questions.**
   This encourages a talker and shows that you are listening.
   It helps to develop points further.
10. **Stop talking!**
    This is first and last, because all other guides depend on it.
    You cannot do an effective listening job while you are talking.

- Nature gave people two ears but only one tongue,
  which is a gentle hint that they should listen more than they talk.
- Listening requires two ears,
  one for meaning and one for feeling.
- Decision makers who do not listen
  have less information for making sound decisions.

Source: *Human Behavior at Work: Organizational Behavior,* Sixth Edition, by Keith Davis © 1981 by McGraw-Hill, Inc. With permission.

Directions of Communication

Communications can flow vertically or laterally. The vertical dimension can be further divided into downward and upward directions.[8]

DOWNWARD
Communciations that flow from one level of a group or organization to a lower level is a downward communication. When we think of managers commu-

nicating with subordinates, the downward pattern is the one we usually think of. It is used by group leaders and managers to assign goals, provide job instructions, inform underlings of policies and procedures, point out problems that need attention, and offer feedback about performance. But downward communication doesn't have to be oral or face-to-face contact. When management sends letters to employees' homes to advise them of the organization's new sick leave policy, it is using downward communication.

Is downward communication an effective method for transmitting information? Its major problem lies in filtering. The more levels a message must go through to get to the bottom of the hierarchy, the more likely that a sizable portion of the original information will be lost or substantially distorted. This effect, however, can be substantially offset by relying on feedback provided by upward communication.

UPWARD

Upward communication flows to a higher level in the group or organization. It is used to provide feedback to higher-ups, inform them of progress toward goals, and relay current problems. Upward communication keeps managers aware of how employees feel about their jobs, co-workers, and the organization in general. Managers also rely on upward communication for ideas on how things can be improved.

Some organizational examples of upward communication include performance reports prepared by lower management for review by middle and top management, suggestion boxes, employee attitude surveys, grievance procedures, superior-subordinate discussions, and informal ''gripe'' sessions where employees have the opportunity to identify and discuss problems with their boss or representatives of higher management.

LATERAL

When communication takes place among members of the same work group, among members of work groups at the same level, among managers at the same level, or among any horizontally equivalent personnel, we describe it as lateral communications.

Why would there be a need for horizontal communciations if a group or organization's vertical communications are effective? The answer is that horizontal communications are often necessary to save time and facilitate coordination. In some cases, these lateral relationships are formally sanctioned. Often, they are informally created to short-circuit the vertical hierarchy and expedite action. So lateral communications can, from management's viewpoint, be good or bad. Since strict adherence to the formal vertical structure for all communications can impede the efficient and accurate transfer of information, lateral communications can be beneficial. In such cases, they occur with the knowledge and support of superiors. But they can create dysfunctional conflicts when the formal vertical channels are breached, when members go above or around their superiors to get things done, or when bosses find out that actions have been taken or decisions made without their knowledge.

Communication Networks

The three directions just described can be combined into a variety of communication networks. Most studies of communication networks have taken place in groups created in a laboratory setting. As a result, the research conclusions have limited application because of the artificial settings and the small groups used. Five common networks are shown in Figure 7–3; these are the chain, "Y," wheel, circle, and all-channel. For our discussion purposes, let's think in an organizational context and assume that the organization has only five members. While this obviously is a simplistic assumption, it will permit us to translate readily the networks in Figure 7–3 into their organizational equivalent.

The chain would represent a five-level hierarchy where communications cannot move laterally, only upward and downward. In a formal organization, this type of network would be found in direct-line authority relations with no deviations. For example, the payroll clerk reports to the payroll supervisor, who in turn reports to the general accounting manager, who reports to the plant controller, who reports to the plant manager. These five individuals would represent a chain network.

If we turn the "Y" network upside down, we can see two subordinates reporting to a supervisor, with two levels of hierarchy still above the supervisor. This is, in effect, a four-level hierarchy.

If we look at the wheel diagram in Figure 7–3 as if we were standing above the network, it becomes obvious that the wheel represents a supervisor with four subordinates. However, there is no interaction between the subordinates. All communications are channeled through the supervisor.

The circle network allows members to interact with adjoining members, but no farther. It would represent a three-level hierarchy in which there is communication between superiors and subordinates and lateral communication at the lowest level.

FIGURE 7–3
Common Communication Networks

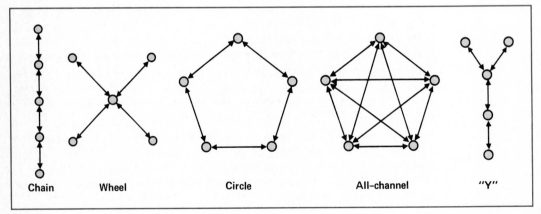

Chain   Wheel   Circle   All-channel   "Y"

Finally, the all-channel network allows each of the subjects to communicate freely with the other four. Of the networks discussed, it is the least structured. While it is like the circle, in some respects, the all-channel network has no central position. However, there are no restrictions; all members are equal. This network is best illustrated by a committee, where no one member either formally or informally assumes a dominant or take-charge position. All members are free to share their viewpoints.

EVALUATING NETWORK EFFECTIVENESS

Is any one network better than the others? The answer to that depends on the dependent variable you are concerned about.

Table 7–4 summarizes the effectiveness of the various networks against four criteria—speed, accuracy, the probability that a leader will emerge, and level of satisfaction among members. One observation is immediately apparent: No single network will be best for all occasions. If speed is important, the wheel and all-channel networks are preferred. The chain, "Y," and wheel score high on accuracy. The structure of the wheel facilitates the emergence of a leader. The circle and all-channel networks are best if you are concerned with having high employee satisfaction.

THE INFORMAL NETWORK

The previous discussion of networks emphasized formal communication patterns, but the formal system is not the only communication system in a group or organization. Let us, therefore, now turn our attention to the informal system—where information flows along the well-known grapevine and rumors can flourish.

A classic study of the grapevine was reported over thirty years ago.[9] The researcher investigated the communication pattern among sixty-seven managerial personnel in a small manufacturing firm. The basic approach used was to learn from each communcation recipient how he first received a given piece of information and then trace it back to its source. It was found that, while the grapevine was an important source of information, only 10 percent of the executives acted as liaison individuals, that is, passed the information on to more than one other

TABLE 7–4
Networks and Evaluation Criteria

CRITERIA	NETWORKS				
	Chain	**Y**	**Wheel**	**Circle**	**All-Channel**
Speed	Moderate	Moderate	Fast	Slow	Fast
Accuracy	High	High	High	Low	Moderate
Emergence of leader	Moderate	Moderate	High	None	None
Satisfaction	Moderate	Moderate	Low	High	High

Source: Adapted from A. Bavelas and D. Barrett, "An Experimental Approach to Organizational Communication," *Personnel*, March 1951, p. 370.

person. For example, when one executive decided to resign to enter the insurance business, 81 percent of the executives knew about it, but only 11 percent transmitted this information on to others.

Two other conclusions from this study are also worth noting. Information on events of general interest tended to flow between the major functional groups (i.e., production, sales) rather than within them. Also, no evidence surfaced to suggest that any one group consistently acted as liaisons; rather, different types of information passed through different liaison persons.

An attempt to replicate this study among employees in a small state government office also found that only 10 percent act as liaison individuals.[10] This is interesting since the replication contained a wider spectrum of employees—including rank-and-file as well as managerial personnel. However, the flow of information in the government office took place within rather than between functional groups. It was proposed that this discrepancy might be due to comparing an executive-only sample against one which also included rank-and-file workers. Managers, for example, might feel greater pressure to stay informed and thus cultivate others outside their immediate functional group. Also, in contrast to the findings of the original study, the replication found that a consistent group of individuals acted as liaisons by transmitting information in the government office.

Is the information that flows along the grapevine accurate? The evidence indicates that about 75 percent of what is carried is accurate.[11] But what conditions foster an active grapevine? What gets the rumor mill rolling?

It is frequently assumed that rumors start because they make titillating gossip. Such is rarely the case. Rumors have at least four purposes: to structure and reduce anxiety; to make sense of limited or fragmented information; to serve as a vehicle to organize group members, and possibly outsiders, into coalitions; and to signal a sender's status ("I'm an insider and, with respect to this rumor, you're an outsider") or power ("I have the power to make you into an insider").[12] Research indicates that rumors emerge as a response to situations that are *important* to us, where there is *ambiguity,* and under conditions that arouse *anxiety.*[13] Work situations frequently contain these three elements, which explains why rumors flourish in organizations. The secrecy and competition that typically prevail in large organizations—around such issues as the appointment of new bosses, the relocation of offices, and the realignment of work assignments—create conditions that encourage and sustain rumors on the grapevine. A rumor will persist either until the wants and expectations creating the uncertainty underlying the rumor are fulfilled or until the anxiety is reduced.

What can we conclude from this discussion? Certainly the grapevine is an important part of any group or organization's communication network and well worth understanding. It identifies for managers those confusing issues that employees consider important and anxiety provoking. It acts, therefore, as both a filter and a feedback mechanism, picking up the issues that employees consider relevant. Maybe more important, again from a managerial perspective, it seems possible to analyze grapevine information and to predict its flow, given that only a small set of individuals (around 10 percent) actively passes on information to more than one other person. By assessing which liaison individuals will consider

TABLE 7–5

Suggestions for Reducing the Negative Consequences of Rumors

1. Announce timetables for making important decisions.
2. Explain decisions and behaviors that may appear inconsistent or secretive.
3. Emphasize the downside, as well as the upside, risks of current decisions and future plans.
4. Openly discuss worst case possibilities—it is almost never as anxiety provoking as the unspoken fantasy.

Source: Adapted from L. Hirschhorn, ''Managing Rumors,'' in L. Hirschhorn, *Cutting Back* (San Francisco: Jossey-Bass, 1983), pp. 54–56. With permission.

a given piece of information to be relevant, we can improve our ability to explain and predict the pattern of the grapevine.

Can management entirely eliminate rumors? ''No!'' What management *can do,* however, is minimize the negative consequences of rumors by limiting their range and impact. Table 7–5 offers a few suggestions for minimizing those negative consequences.

NONVERBAL COMMUNICATION

Anyone who has ever paid a visit to a singles bar or a nightclub is aware that communication need not be verbal in order to convey a message. A glance, a stare, a smile, a frown, a provocative body movement—they all convey meaning. This example illustrates that no discussion of communication would be complete without a discussion of nonverbal messages. These include body movements, the intonations or emphasis we give to words, facial expressions, and the physical distance between the sender and receiver.

The academic study of body motions has been labeled *kinesics*. It refers to gestures, facial configurations, and other movements of the body But it is a relatively new field, and it has been subject to far more conjecture and popularizing than the research findings support. Hence, while we acknowledge the fact that body movement is an important segment of the study of communciation and behavior, conclusions must be necessarily guarded. Recognizing this qualification, let us briefly consider the ways in which body motions convey meaning.

It has been argued that every *body movement* has a meaning and that no movement is accidental.[14] For example, through body language,

> We say, ''Help me, I'm lonely. Take me, I'm available. Leave me alone, I'm depressed.'' And rarely do we send our messages consciously. We act out our state of being with nonverbal body language. We lift one eyebrow for disbelief. We rub our noses for puzzlement. We clasp our arms to isolate ourselves or to protect ourselves. We shrug our shoulders for indifference, wink one eye for intimacy, tap our fingers for impatience, slap our forehead for forgetfulness.[15]

While we may disagree with the specific meaning of these movements, body language adds to and often complicates verbal communication. A body position or movement does not by itself have a precise or universal meaning, but when it is linked with spoken language, it gives fuller meaning to a sender's message.

If you read the verbatim minutes of a meeting, you could not grasp the impact of what was said in the same way you could if you had been there or saw the meeting on film. Why? There is no record of nonverbal communication. The emphasis given to words or phrases is missing. To illustrate how *intonations* can change the meaning of a message, consider the student in class who asks the instructor a question. The instructor replies, "What do you mean by that?" The student's reaction will be different depending on the tone of the instructor's response. A soft, smooth tone creates a different meaning from an intonation that is abrasive with strong emphasis placed on the last word.

The facial expression of the instructor will also convey meaning. A snarled face says something different from a smile. Facial expressions, along with intonations, can show arrogance, aggressiveness, fear, shyness, and other characteristics that would never be communicated if you read a transcript of what had been said.

The way individuals space themselves in terms of *physical distance* also has meaning. What is considered proper spacing is largely dependent on cultural norms. For example, what is "businesslike" distance in some European countries would be viewed as "intimate" in many parts of North America. If someone stands closer to you than is considered appropriate, it may indicate aggressiveness or sexual interest. If farther away than usual, it may mean disinterest or displeasure with what is being said.

It is important for the receiver to be alert to these nonverbal aspects of communication. You should look for nonverbal cues as well as listen to the literal meaning of a sender's words. You should particularly be aware of contradictions between the messages. The boss may say that she is free to talk to you about that raise you have been seeking, but you may see nonverbal signals that suggest that this is *not* the time to discuss the subject. Regardless of what is being said, an individual who frequently glances at her wristwatch is giving the message that she would prefer to terminate the conversation. We misinform others when we express one emotion verbally, such as trust, but nonverbally communicate a contradictory message that reads, "I don't have confidence in you." These contradictions often suggest that "actions speak louder (and more accurately) than words."

PERCEPTION AND THE CREATION OF MEANING

We have been looking at communication as a process subject to a number of potential distortions. A more recent approach to communication is one that emphasizes the impact of perception on the transference of meaning.[16] The central theme of this viewpoint is that meanings are not *transferred* from one person to another. Rather, receivers of the message *create* their own meanings from incoming sensory cues.[17] As we shall show, there is an increasing body of evidence that demonstrates that the way a person perceives and interprets communications will have a significant impact on his or her job satisfaction.

Think about this for a moment: "One cannot NOT communicate."[18] Every word, action, silence or inaction carries meaning. Regardless of intention, meaning is attached to others' behaviors. So you have communicated as soon as someone has derived meaning from your actions or inactions. What does this mean in terms of interpersonal behavior? Simply, that people will create their own meanings to cues they receive from others and this interpretation is a major determinant of their satisfaction or dissatisfaction. Two areas of investigation have applied this perspective.

Applying Equity Theory to Communication

In Chapter 5, we introduced equity theory as a partial explanation of an individual's motivation. When employees perceive an inequity between their input-outcome ratio and those of relevant others, they will attempt to correct this inequity. We can look at this same concept from a communication perspective.

What is communicated is perceived and evaluated. But not all individuals are privy to all information. If your boss confides information to you that is withheld from others, that information in effect is seen as a reward. Communications, therefore, have a reward value that is subject to social comparisons. More specifically, it has been proposed that the communication process is modified as follows:[19] First, attention is paid to information to establish whether communication has actually taken place. Second, if communication has occurred, meaning must be attached in order to create a message. Third, the meaning must be evaluated in terms of importance; that is, is it relevant and does it have high saliency for the receiver? Finally, if it is relevant and has high saliency, an outcome is established. If equity exists, the message provides the receiver with a reward that serves his or her personal needs and enhances job satisfaction. Perceived inequity, on the other hand, is likely to lead to job dissatisfaction. So the fact that someone possesses information that you don't is only pertinent if you see that information as important and relevant. Then, and only then, will you compare the messages you receive with what you expect to receive in order to assess whether equity exists.

Although there is no substantive research to support the process we have described, propositions have been offered concerning four outcomes: (1) quantity of salient messages, (2) timeliness of salient messages, (3) interaction conditions, and (4) the opportunity to initiate salient messages. In terms of predicting satisfaction, the following four hypotheses are made:

1. Employees who perceive they do not receive as many salient messages as others in relation to their inputs (i.e., effort, ability, experience, education) to the group or organization will feel "less in the know" and will tend to be less satisfied on the job.

2. Employees who see themselves as the "last to know" some important information are likely to be less satisfied than ones who get this information at earlier times.

3. Employees who get a message under positive interaction conditions (e.g., the boss comes into their office and tells them) will be more satisfied than if they receive the same message under less positive conditions (e.g., it is overheard in the restroom).

4. Employees who see themselves as having fewer opportunities to initiate actions which result in the reception of important messages (e.g., opportunities to question or participate in decision making) will be more dissatisfied.[20]

Looking for Informational Cues

Another way in which perception enters into communication is related to informational cues and their impact on how people perceive their jobs. The characteristics of a job are not fixed and objective; rather, they are socially constructed realities that are defined by signals or messages that an employee receives from others. Studies demonstrate that, if these cues are manipulated (i.e., a co-worker or boss comments on the existence or absence of features such as difficulty, challenge, or autonomy in the job), employees are more satisfied with their jobs when they receive positive informational cues.[21]

It was traditionally believed that people responded to the objective characteristics of the jobs that they were doing. For instance, as we'll discuss in Chapter 12, jobs that offer employees a variety of identifiable and relevant tasks, as well as autonomy and feedback, seem to lead to more motivated, satisfied, and productive employees.[22] But attributes like variety, identity, or autonomy are not fully objective. The same job may be perceived differently by different groups. Even the same attribute may be seen as positive in one setting and negative in another. It seems reasonable to suggest, therefore, that employees may respond to both informational influences and objective characteristics.

This is just what the research indicates. In one study, investigators manipulated both the task characteristics and information cues in a simulated selection task.[23] They found that informational cues had a greater impact on job satisfaction than the objective characteristics of the task itself. Similarly, when another set of investigators manipulated task characteristics and information cues in a simulated routine clerical task, they too found that the informational cues were the dominant force determining job satisfaction.[24]

These findings underline that an employee's attiitudes reflect both objective characteristics of the job or task and the informational influence of others. Moreover, the communciation that an employee receives from others in terms of informational cues may be a more powerful motivation force than the actual properties of the task. To generalize beyond the research, it may be that the informational cues that we get on our job from bosses, co-workers, and subordinates are as important as goal setting, equitable compensation, or intrinsically meaningful tasks in creating high motivation, high productivity, and favorable attitudes about our work.

GROUP DECISION MAKING

One of the more obvious applications of communciation concepts is in the area of group decision making. We communicate information, and information is used in the making of decisions. Moreover, group decisions require transmitting of messages between members, and the effectiveness of this communication process will significantly impact the quality of the group's decisions.

The belief—characterized by juries—that two heads are better than one, has long been accepted as a basic component of our legal system. This belief has expanded to the point that, today, many decisions in organizations are made by groups or committees. There are permanent executive committees that meet on a regular basis, special task forces created to analyze unique problems, temporary project teams used to develop new products, and "quality circles" made up of representatives from management and labor who meet to identify and solve production problems, to name a few of the more obvious examples.

Groups vs. the Individual

Decision-making groups may be widely used in organizations, but does that imply that group decisions are preferable to those made by an individual alone? The answer to this question depends on a number of factors. Let's begin by looking at the advantages and disadvantages that groups afford.[25]

ADVANTAGES OF GROUPS

Individual and group decisions each have their own set of strengths. Neither is ideal for all situations. The following identifies the major advantages that groups offer over individuals in the making of decisions:

1. *More complete information and knowledge*. By aggregating the resources of several individuals, we bring more input into the decision process.

2. *Increases diversity of views*. In addition to more input, groups can bring heterogeneity to the decision process. This opens up the opportunity for more approaches and alternatives to be considered.

3. *Increases acceptance of a solution*. Many decisions fail after the final choice has been made because people do not accept the solution. However, if people who will be affected by a decision and who will be instrumental in implementing it are able to participate in the decision itself, they will be more likely to accept it and encourage others to accept it. This translates into more support for the decision and higher satisfaction among those required to implement it.

4. *Increases legitimacy*. Our society values democratic methods. The group decision-making process is consistent with democratic ideals and, therefore, may be perceived as being more legitimate than decisions made by a single person. When an individual decision maker fails to consult with others before making a

decision, the fact that the decision maker has complete power can create the perception that the decision was made autocratically and arbitrarily.

DISADVANTAGES OF GROUPS

Of course, group decisions are not without drawbacks. Their major disadvantages include:

1. *Time consuming.* It takes time to assemble a group. The interaction that takes place once the group is in place is frequently inefficient. The result is that groups take more time to reach a solution than would be the case if an individual were making the decision. This can limit management's ability to act quickly and decisively when necessary.

2. *Pressures to conform.* As noted in the previous chapter, there are social pressures in groups. The desire by group members to be accepted and considered as an asset to the group can result in squashing any overt disagreement, thus encouraging conformity among viewpoints.

3. *Domination by the few.* Group discussion can be dominated by one or a few members. If this dominant coalition is also composed of low- and medium-ability members, the group's overall effectiveness will suffer.

4. *Ambiguous responsibility.* Group members share responsibility, but who is actually accountable for the final outcome? In an individual decision, it is clear who is responsible. In a group decision, the responsibility of any single member is watered down.

EFFECTIVENESS AND EFFICIENCY

Whether groups are more effective than individuals depends on the criteria you use for defining effectiveness. In terms of *accuracy,* group decisions will tend to be more accurate. The evidence indicates that, on the average, groups makes better quality decisions than individuals.[26] This doesn't mean, of course, that all groups will outperform *every* individual. Rather, group decisions have been found to be better than those that would be reached by the average individual in the group. However, they are seldom better than the performance of the best individual.

If decision effectiveness is defined in terms of *speed,* individuals are superior. If *creativity* is important, groups tend to be more effective than individuals. And if effectiveness means the degree of *acceptance* the final solution achieves, the nod again goes to the group.

But effectiveness cannot be considered without also assessing efficiency. In terms of efficiency, groups almost always stack up as a poor second to the individual decision maker. With few exceptions, group decision making consumes more work hours than if an individual were to tackle the same problem alone. The exceptions tend to be those instances where, to achieve comparable quantities of diverse input, the single decision maker must spend a great deal of time reviewing files and talking to people. Because groups can include members from diverse areas, the time spent searching for information can be reduced. However, as we noted, these advantages in efficiency tend to be the exception. Groups are generally less efficient than individuals. In deciding whether to use groups, then, consideration should be given to assessing whether increases in effectiveness are more than enough to offset the losses in efficiency.

SUMMARY

Groups offer an excellent vehicle for performing many of the steps in the decision-making process. They are a source of both breadth and depth of input for information gathering. If the group is composed of individuals with diverse backgrounds, the alternatives generated should be more extensive and the analysis more critical. When the final solution is agreed upon, there are more people in a group decision to support and implement it. These pluses, however, can be more than offset by the time consumed by group decisions, the internal conflicts they create, or the pressures they generate toward conformity. Table 7–6 briefly outlines the group's assets and liabilities. It allows you to evaluate the net advantage or disadvantage that would accrue in a given situation when you have to choose between an individual or group decision.

Groupthink and Groupshift

Two by-products of group decision making have received a considerable amount of attention by researchers in OB. As we'll show, these two phenomena have the potential to affect the group's ability to appraise alternatives objectively and arrive at decision solutions.

The first phenomenon, called *groupthink,* is related to norms. It describes situations in which group pressures for conformity deter the group from critically appraising unusual, minority, or unpopular views. Groupthink is a disease that attacks many groups and can dramatically hinder their performance. The second phenomenon we shall review is called *groupshift.* It indicates that in discussing a given set of alternatives and arriving at a solution, group members tend to exaggerate the initial positions that they held. In some situations, caution dominates, and there is a conservative shift. More often, however, the evidence indicates that groups tend toward a risky shift. Let's look at each of these phenomena in more detail.

TABLE 7–6
The Group Decision: Its Assets and Liabilities

ASSETS	LIABILITIES
Breadth of information	Time consuming
Diversity of information	Conformity
Acceptance of solution	Domination of discussion
Legitimacy of process	Ambiguous responsibility

GROUPTHINK

A number of years ago your author had a peculiar experience. During a faculty meeting that he attended, a motion was placed on the floor stipulating each faculty member's responsibilities in regard to counseling students. The motion received a second, and the floor was opened for questions. There were none. After about fifteen seconds of silence, the chairman asked if he could "call for the question" (fancy terminology for permission to take the vote). No objections were voiced. When the chairman asked for those in favor, a vast majority of the thirty-two faculty members in attendance raised their hands. The motion was passed, and the chairman proceeded to the next item on the agenda.

Nothing in the process seemed unusual, but the story is not over. About twenty minutes following the end of the meeting, a professor came roaring into my office with a petition. The petition said that the motion on counseling students had been rammed through and requested the chairman to replace the motion on the next month's agenda for discussion and a vote. When I asked this professor why he had not spoken up less than an hour earlier, he just gave me a frustrated look. He then proceeded to tell me that in talking with people after the meeting, he realized there actually had been considerable opposition to the motion. He didn't speak up, he said, because he thought he was the only one opposed. Conclusion: The faculty meeting we had attended had been attacked by the deadly groupthink "disease."

Have you ever felt like speaking up in a meeting, classroom, or informal group, but decided against it? One reason may have been shyness. On the other hand, you may have been a victim of groupthink, the phenomenon that occurs when group members become so enamoured with seeking concurrence that the norm for consensus overrides the realistic appraisal of alternative courses of action and the full expression of deviant, minority, or unpopular views. It describes a deterioration in an individual's mental efficiency, reality testing, and moral judgments as a result of group pressures.[27]

We have all seen the symptoms of the groupthink phenomenon:

1. Group members rationalize any resistance to the assumptions they have made. No matter how strongly the evidence may contradict their basic assumptions, members behave so as to reinforce those assumptions continually.

2. Members apply direct pressures on those who momentarily express doubts about any of the group's shared views or who question the validity of arguments supporting the alternative favored by the majority.

3. Those members who have doubts or hold differing points of view seek to avoid deviating from what appears to be group consensus by keeping silent about misgivings and even minimizing to themselves the importance of their doubts.

4. There appears to be an illusion of unanimity. If someone does not speak, it is assumed that he or she is in full accord. In other words, abstention becomes viewed as a "Yes" vote.[28]

In studies of American foreign policy decisions, these symptoms were found to prevail when government policymaking groups failed: unpreparedness at

Pearl Harbor in 1941, the U.S. invasion of North Korea, the Bay of Pigs fiasco, and the escalation of the Vietnam war by introduction of bombing during the Johnson administration. Importantly, these four groupthink characteristics could not be found where group policy decisions were successful: the Cuban missile crisis and the formulation of the Marshall Plan.[29]

Groupthink appears to be closely aligned with the conclusions Asch drew in his experiments with a lone dissenter. Individuals who hold a position that is different from the dominant majority are under pressure to suppress, withhold, or modify their true feelings and beliefs. As members of a group, we find it is more pleasant to be in agreement—to be a positive part of the group—than to be a disruptive force, even if disruption is necessary to improve the effectiveness of the group's decisions. All groups, to some degree, suffer from groupthink. It is a natural by-product of individual desire for consensus and agreement. However, it can have a significant destructive effect upon a group's performance.

GROUPSHIFT

In comparing group decisions with the individual decisions of members within the group, evidence suggests that there are differences.[30] In some cases, the group decisions are more conservative than the individual decision. More often, the shift is toward greater risk.[31]

What appears to happen in groups is that the discussion leads to a significant shift in the positions of members toward a more extreme position in the direction toward which they were already leaning before the discussion. So conservative types become more cautious and the more aggressive types take on more risk. The group discussion tends to *exaggerate* the initial position of the group.

The groupshift can be viewed as actually a special case of groupthink. The decision of the group reflects the dominant decision-making norm that develops during the group's discussion. Whether the shift in the group's decision is toward greater caution or more risk depends on the dominant prediscussion norm.

The greater occurrence of the shift toward risk has generated several explanations for the phenomena.[32] It's been argued, for instance, that the discussion creates familiarization among the members. As they become more comfortable with each other, they also become more bold and daring. Another argument is that our society values risk, that we admire individuals who are willing to take risks, and that group discussion motivates members to show that they are at least as willing as their peers to take risks. The most plausible explanation of the shift toward risk, however, seems to be that the group diffuses responsibility. Group decisions free any single member from accountability for the group's final choice. Greater risk can be taken because even if the decision fails, no one member can be held wholly responsible.

So how should you use the findings on groupshift? You should recognize that group decisions exaggerate the initial position of the individual members, that the shift has been shown more often to be toward greater risk, and that whether a group will shift toward greater risk or caution is a function of the member's prediscussion inclination.

Group Decision-Making Techniques

The most common form of group decision making takes place in face-to-face *interacting* groups. But as our discussion of groupthink demonstrated, interacting groups often censor themselves and pressure individual members toward conformity of opinion. Brainstorming, nominal group, and Delphi techniques have been proposed as ways to reduce many of the problems inherent in the traditional interacting group. We'll discuss each in this section.

BRAINSTORMING

Brainstorming is meant to overcome pressures for conformity in the interacting group that retard the development of creative alternatives.[33] It does this by utilizing an idea-generation process that specifically encourages any and all alternatives while withholding any criticism of those alternatives.

In a typical brainstorming session, a half-dozen to a dozen people sit around a table. The group leader states the problem in a clear manner so that it is understood by all participants. Members then "free wheel" as many alternatives as they can in a given length of time. No criticism is allowed, and all the alternatives are recorded for later discussion and analysis. The fact that one idea stimulates others and that judgment of even the most bizarre suggestions are withheld until later encourages group members to "think the unusual."

Brainstorming, however, is merely a process for generating ideas. The next two techniques go farther by offering techniques for actually arriving at a preferred solution.[34]

NOMINAL GROUP TECHNIQUE

The nominal group technique restricts discussion or interpersonal communication during the decision-making process, hence, the term *nominal*. Group members are all physically present, as in a traditional committee meeting, but members operate independently. Specifically, a problem is presented and then the following steps take place:

1. Members meet as a group but, before any discussion takes place, each member independently writes down his or her ideas on the problem.
2. This silent period is followed by each member presenting one idea to the group. Each member takes his or her turn, going around the table, presenting a single idea until all ideas have been presented and recorded (typically on a flip chart or chalkboard). No discussion takes place until all ideas have been recorded.
3. The group now discusses the ideas for clarity and evaluates them.
4. Each group member silently and independently rank orders the ideas. The final decision is determined by the idea with the highest aggregate ranking.

The chief advantage of the nominal group technique is that it permits the group to meet formally but does not restrict independent thinking as does the interacting group.

DELPHI TECHNIQUE

A more complex and time-consuming alternative is the Delphi technique. It is similar to the nominal group technique except that it does not require the physical presence of the group's members. In fact, the Delphi technique never allows the group members to meet face to face. The following steps characterize the Delphi techniques:

1. The problem is identified and members are asked to provide potential solutions through a series of carefully designed questionnaires.
2. Each member anonymously and independently completes the first questionnaire.
3. Results of the first questionnaire are compiled at a central location, transcribed, and reproduced.
4. Each member receives a copy of the results.
5. After viewing the results, members are again asked for their solutions. The results typically trigger new solutions or cause changes in the original position.
6. Steps 4 and 5 are repeated as often as necessary until consensus is reached.

Like the nominal group technique, the Delphi technique insulates group members from the undue influence of others. Because it does not require the physical presence of the participants, the Delphi technique can be used for decision making among geographically scattered groups. For instance, Sony could use the technique to query its managers in Tokyo, Brussels, Paris, London, New York, Toronto, Rio de Janeiro, and Melbourne as to the best worldwide price for one of the company's products. The cost of bringing the executives together at a central location is avoided. Of course, the Delphi technique has its drawbacks. Because the method is extremely time consuming, it is frequently not applicable where a speedy decision is necessary. Additionally, the method may not develop the rich array of alternatives that the interacting or nominal group technique does. The ideas that might surface from the heat of face-to-face interaction may never arise.

SUMMARY: EVALUATING EFFECTIVENESS

How do these various techniques stack up against the traditional interacting group? As we find so often, each technique has its own unique set of strengths and weaknesses. The choice of one technique over the others depends on the criteria you seek to emphasize. For instance, as Table 7–7 indicates, the interacting group is good for building group cohesiveness, brainstorming keeps social pressures to a minimum, and the Delphi technique minimizes interpersonal conflict. The "best" technique is defined by the criteria you use to evaluate the group.

IMPLICATIONS FOR PERFORMANCE AND SATISFACTION

A careful review of this chapter finds a common theme regarding the relationship between communication and employee satisfaction: The less the uncertainty, the greater the satisfaction. Distortions, ambiguities, and incongruities all increase uncertainty and, hence, negatively impact on satisfaction.

TABLE 7–7

Evaluating Group Effectiveness

EFFECTIVENESS CRITERIA	TYPE OF GROUP			
	Interacting	Brainstorming	Nominal	Delphi
Number of ideas	Low	Moderate	High	High
Quality of ideas	Low	Moderate	High	High
Social pressure	High	Low	Moderate	Low
Time/money costs	Moderate	Low	Low	High
Task orientation	Low	High	High	High
Potential for interpersonal conflict	High	Low	Moderate	Low
Feelings of accomplishment	High to low	High	High	Moderate
Commitment to solution	High	Not applicable	Moderate	Low
Builds group cohesiveness	High	High	Moderate	Low

Source: Reprinted by permission of the publisher from "Group Decision Making: What Strategies Should You Use?" J. K. Murnighan, *Management Review,* February 1981, p. 61. © AMACOM, a division of American Management Associations, New York. All rights reserved.

The less distortion that occurs in communication, the more that goals, feedback, and other management messages to employees will be received as they were intended. This, in turn, should reduce ambiguities and clarify the group's task. Extensive use of vertical, lateral, and informal channels will increase communication flow, reduce uncertainty, and improve group performance and satisfaction. We should also expect incongruities between verbal and nonverbal communiques to increase uncertainty and reduce satisfaction.

Many concepts that have been discussed in previous chapters embrace communication issues. Perception, motivation, roles, and norms are concepts that are intimately related to the communication process and are determinants of the effectiveness with which meaning is transmitted. Take the topic of perception. We know that people react to their perceptions rather than to reality. Job satisfaction, for instance, appears to be significantly influenced by an individual's judgments of equity or inequity in the receipt and evaluation of salient messages and by whether or not she receives positive or negative social cues about her job. This perceptual focus can be expanded further. If individuals perceive that a communication is threatening, they will behave accordingly, regardless of the sender's intent. The resulting behavior might be increased defensiveness, less compliance with directions, lower output, decreased job satisfaction, or an increase in the search for alternative employment opportunities.

A study of nearly seven hundred public utility employees confirms the importance of perception in communication.[35] It was found that processes that were seen to maximize important aspects and minimize unimportant aspects in communications were significantly correlated with the employees' satisfaction with work, satisfaction with supervision, and satisfaction with co-workers. However, processes that were seen as selectively withholding information were found to be negatively correlated with satisfaction. The problem, of course, is that what may be perceived as screening out unimportant information in one case may be perceived as the selective withholding of relevant information in another case.

We cited how different networks influence satisfaction and performance. The evidence suggests that job satisfaction is highest in the circle and all-channel networks, where democracy was most simulated. These networks also proved to generate more effective performance in the solution of complex problems. Where high performance requires close supervision and tight controls, the wheel was found to be most effective.

Findings in the chapter further suggest that the goal of perfect communication is unattainable. Yet, there is evidence that demonstrates a positive relationship between effective communication (which includes factors such as perceived trust, perceived accuracy, desire for interaction, top management receptiveness, and upward information requirements) and worker productivity.[36] Choosing the correct channel, clarifying jargon, and utilizing feedback may, therefore, make for more effective communication, but candidness requires the admission that the human factor generates distortions that can never be fully eliminated. The communication process represents an exchange of messages, but the outcome is meanings that may or may not approximate those that the sender intended. Whatever the sender's expectations, the decoded message in the mind of the receiver represents his or her reality. And it is this "reality" that will determine performance, along with the individual's level of motivation and his or her degree of satisfaction. The issue of motivation is critical, so we should briefly review how communication is central in assessing an individual's degree of motivation.

You will remember from expectancy theory that the degree of effort an individual exerts depends on his or her perception of the effort-performance, performance-reward, and reward–goal satisfaction linkages. If individuals are not given the data necessary to make the perceived probability of these linkages high, motivation will be less than it could be. If rewards are not made clear, if the criteria for determining and measuring performance are ambiguous, or if individuals are not relatively certain that their effort will lead to satisfactory performance, then effort will be reduced. So communication plays a significant role in determining the level of motivation.

A final implication from the communication literature relates to predicting turnover. The use of realistic job previews acts as a communication device for clarifying role expectations. Employees who have been exposed to a realistic job preview have more accurate information about that job. Comparisons of turnover rates between organizations that use the realistic job preview versus either no preview or only presentation of positive job information show that those *not* using the realistic preview have almost 29 percent higher turnover on the average.[37] This makes a strong case for management conveying honest and accurate information about a job to applicants during the recruiting and selection process.

MAKING JUDGMENTS IS THE MAJOR BARRIER TO COMMUNICATION

The major barrier to mutual interpersonal communication is our very natural tendency to judge, to evaluate, and to approve (or disapprove) the statements of the other person or the other group. Let me illustrate this view with a couple of simple examples. Suppose that someone, commenting on this discussion, says, "I didn't like what that man said." What will you respond? Almost invariably your reply will be either approval or disapproval of the attitude expressed. Either you respond, "I didn't either; I thought it was terrible," or else you tend to reply, "Oh, I thought it was really good." In other words, the primary reaction is to evaluate it from *your* point of view, your own frame of reference.

Or take another example. Suppose that I say with some feeling, "I think the Republicans are showing a lot of good sound sense these days." What is the response that arises in your mind? The overwhelming likelihood is that it will be evaluative. In other words, you will find yourself agreeing, or disagreeing, or making some judgment about me such as "He must be a conservative" or "He seems solid in his thinking."

Although the tendency to make evaluations is common in almost all interchange of language, it is greatly heightened in those situations where feelings and emotions are deeply involved. So the stronger our feelings, the more likely it is that there will be no mutual element in the communication. There will be just two ideas, two feelings, two judg-ments, missing each other in psychological space.

I am sure you recognize this from your own experience. When you have not been emotionally involved yourself and have listened to a heated discussion, you often go away thinking, "Well, actually they weren't talking about the same thing." And they were not. Each was making a judgment, an evaluation, from his or her own frame of reference. There was really nothing that could be called communication in any genuine sense. This tendency to react to any emotionally meaningful statement by forming an evaluation of it from our own point of view is, I repeat, the major barrier to interpersonal communication.

The solution to this evaluative tendency is to see the expressed idea and attitudes from the other person's point of view, to sense how it feels to him, or her, to achieve his or her frame of reference in regard to the thing about which he or she is talking. When each of the different parties comes to *understand* the other from the *other's* point of view rather than *judge* that point of view, the insincerities, the lies, and the "false fronts" drop away with astonishing speed.

Adapted from C. R. Rogers, in C. R. Rogers and F. J. Roethlisberger, ''Barriers and Gateways to Communication,'' Harvard Business Review, *August 1952, pp. 46–50.*

COUNTERPOINT

THE SEARCH FOR IMPROVED COMMUNICATION IS THE PROBLEM

The major barrier to communication is the naive assumption that individuals actually want to *improve* communication. Most of us seem to overlook a very basic fact: It is often in the sender's and/or receiver's best interest purposely to keep communication fuzzy.

"Lack of communication" seems to have replaced original sin as the explanation for the ills of the world. We're continually hearing that problems would go away if we could "just communicate better." Some of the basic assumptions underlying this view need to be looked at carefully.

One assumption is the way in which poor communication resembles original sin: Both tend to get tangled up with control of the situation. If one defines communication as mutual understanding, this does not imply control for either party and certainly not for both. However, equating good communication with control appears in the assumption that better communication will necessarily reduce strife and conflict. Each individual's definition of better communication, like his or her definition of virtuous conduct, becomes that of having the other party accept his or her views, which would reduce conflict at that party's expense. As long as both feel this way, the stroll can continue indefinitely, but strictly speaking, it has very little to do with communication difficulties per se. A better understanding of the situation might serve only to underline the differences rather than to resolve them. Indeed, many of the techniques thought of as poor communciation were apparently developed with the aim of bypassing or avoiding confrontation, and some of them continue to be reasonably successful in this aim.

Another assumption that grows from this view is that when a conflict has existed for a long time and shows every sign of continuing, lack of communication must be one of the basic problems. Usually if the ituation is examined more carefully, plenty of communication will be found; the problem is again one of equating communication with agreement.

Still a third asssumption, somewhat related but less squarely based on the equation of communication with controls, is that *it is always in the interest of at least one of the parties to an interaction and often of both to attain maximum clarity as measured by some more or less objective standard.* Aside from the difficulty of setting up this standard—whose standard? and doesn't this give *him* or *her* control of the situation?—there are some sequences, and perhaps many of them, in which it is to the interests of both parties to leave the situation as fuzzy, amorphous, and undefined as possible. This is notably true in culturally or personally sensitive and taboo areas involving prejudices, preconceptions, and so on, but it can, for similar reasons, also be true when the area is merely a new one that could be seriously distorted by using old definitions and old solutions.

Too often we forget that keeping organizational communications fuzzy cuts down on questions, permits faster decision making, minimizes objections, reduces opposition, makes it easier to deny one's earlier statements, preserves freedom to change one's mind, helps to preserve mystique and hide insecurities, allows one to say several things at the same time, permits one to say "no" diplomatically, and helps to avoid confrontation and anxiety.

Adapted from C. O. Kursh, "The Benefits of Poor Communication," The Psychoanalytic Review, Summer–Fall 1971, pp. 189–208. Through the courtesy of the editors and the publisher, National Psychological Association for Psychoanalysis, New York, N.Y.

FOR DISCUSSION

1. "Communication is the transference of meaning among group members." Discuss this definition and indicate what is missing from this definition to ensure that communications are effective.

2. Describe the functions that communication provides within a group or organization. Give an example of each.

3. Describe the communication process, identifying its key components. Give an example of how this process operates with both oral and written messages.

4. What is the importance of the statement that "people will create their own meanings to cues they receive from others"?

5. "Ineffective communication is the fault of the sender." Do you agree or disagree? Discuss.

6. Describe the advantages and disadvantages of each of these networks: (a) all-channel, (b) chain, (c) circle, (d) wheel, and (e) "Y."

7. For each of the networks, indicate the conditions under which it will be most effective.

8. What can you do to improve the likelihood that your communiques will be received and understood as you intend?

9. "Informal communication can facilitate a group's effectiveness." Do you agree or disagree? Discuss.

10. "Rumors start because something makes titillating gossip." Do you agree or disagree? Discuss.

11. What is groupthink? Is the concept applicable to the family unit as well as to organizations? Explain.

12. What can management do to improve group decision-making effectiveness?

FOR FURTHER READING

BASKIN, O. W., and C. E. ARONOFF, *Interpersonal Communication in Organizations*. Glenview, Ill.: Scott, Foresman, 1980. Presents an introduction to communication, the communication process, and the role of communication in decision making.

GUZZO, R. A. (ed.), *Improving Group Decision Making in Organizations: Approaches from Theory and Research*. New York: Academic Press, 1982. Brings together advances in understanding of decision-making groups and identifies ways of making them more effective.

HATFIELD, J. D., and R. C. HUSEMAN, "Perceptual Congruence About Communication as Related to Satisfaction: Moderating Effects of Individual Characteristics," *Academy of Management Journal*, June 1982, pp. 349–58. Shows how congruence about communication between supervisor and subordinate is significantly related to job satisfaction.

JOHNSON, B. M., *Communication: The Process of Organizing*. Boston: Allyn & Bacon, 1977. Argues that all organizations are created through communication. The book is about how people communicate to organize cooperative activities.

KLAUSS, R., and B. M. BASS, *Interpersonal Communications in Organizations*. New York: Academic Press, 1982. Presents a model that shows the extent to which received outcomes depend on the sender's credibility.

MCCASKEY, M. B., "The Hidden Messages Managers Send," *Harvard Businesss Review,* November–December 1979, pp. 135–48. Tells how managers convey messages about themselves in three ways: through their metaphors, office settings, and body language.

NOTES FOR CHAPTER 7

1. See, for example, K. W. Thomas and W. H. Schmidt, "A Survey of Managerial Interests with Respect to Conflict," *Academy of Management Journal,* June 1976, p. 317.
2. W. G. Scott and T. R. Mitchell, *Organization Theory: A Structural and Behavioral Analysis* (Homewood, Ill.: Richard D. Irwin, 1976).
3. D. K. Berlo, *The Process of Communication* (New York: Holt, Rinehart and Winston, 1960), pp.30–32.
4. Ibid., p. 54.
5. Ibid., p. 103.
6. J. DeLorean, quoted in S. P. Robbins, *The Administrative Process* (Englewood Cliffs, N.J.: Prentice-Hall, 1976), p. 404.
7. S. I. Hayakawa, *Language in Thought and Action* (New York: Harcourt Brace Jovanovich, 1949), p. 292.
8. R. L. Simpson, "Vertical and Horizontal Communication in Formal Organizations," *Administrative Science Quarterly,* September 1959, pp. 188–96; and B. Harriman, "Up and Down the Communications Ladder," *Harvard Business Review,* September–October 1974, pp. 143–51.
9. K. Davis, "Management Communication and the Grapevine," *Harvard Business Review,* September–October 1953, pp. 43–49.
10. H. Sutton and L. W. Porter, "A Study of the Grapevine in a Governmental Organization," *Personnel Psychology,* Summer 1968, pp. 223–30.
11. K. Davis, cited in R. Rowan, "Where Did *That* Rumor Come From?" *Fortune,* August 13, 1979, p. 134.
12. L. Hirschhorn, "Managing Rumors," in L. Hirschhorn (ed.), *Cutting Back* (San Francisco: Jossey-Bass, 1983), pp. 49–52.
13. R. L. Rosnow and G. A. Fine, *Rumor and Gossip: The Social Psychology of Hearsay* (New York: Elsevier, 1976).
14. R. L. Birdwhistell, *Introduction to Kinesics* (Louisville, Ky.: University of Louisville Press, 1952).

15. J. Fast, *Body Language* (Philadelphia: M. Evans, 1970), p. 7.

16. See, for example, W. C. Redding, *Communication Within the Organization* (New York: Industrial Communications Council, 1972).

17. P. L. Wilkens and P. R. Timm, "Perceived Communication Inequity: A Determinant of Job Dissatisfaction," *Journal of Management*, Spring 1978, pp. 107–19.

18. Ibid., p. 108.

19. Ibid., p. 114.

20. Ibid., p. 116.

21. J. Thomas and R. Griffin, "The Social Information Processing Model of Task Design: A Review of the Literature," *Academy of Management Review*, October 1983, pp. 672–82.

22. J. R. Hackman, "Work Design," in J. R. Hackman and J. L. Suttle (eds.), *Improving Life at Work* (Santa Monica, Calif.: Goodyear, 1977) pp. 96–162.

23. C. A. O'Reilly III and D. F. Caldwell, "Information Influence as a Determinant of Perceived Task Characteristics and Job Satisfaction,"*Journal of Applied Psychology*, April 1979, pp. 157–65.

24. S. E. White and T. R. Mitchell, "Job Enrichment Versus Social Cues: A Comparison and Competitive Test," *Journal of Applied Psychology*, February 1979, pp. 1–9.

25. N. R. F. Maier, "Assets and Liabilities in Group Problem Solving: The Need for an Integrative Function," *Psychological Review*, April 1967, pp. 239–49; and G. W. Hill, "Group Versus Individual Performance: Are $N+1$ Heads Better than One?" *Psychological Bulletin*, May 1982, pp. 517–39.

26. M. E. Shaw, *Group Dynamics*, 3rd ed. (New York: McGraw-Hill, 1981).

27. I. L. Janis, *Victims of Groupthink* (Boston: Houghton Mifflin, 1972).

28. Ibid.

29. Ibid.

30. D. G. Myers and H. Lamm, "The Group Polarization Phenomenon," *Psychological Bulletin*, July 1976, pp. 602–27.

31. See, for example, N. Kogan and M. A. Wallach, "Risk Taking as a Function of the Situation, the Person, and the Group,"in *New Directions in Psychology*, Vol. 3 (New York: Holt, Rinehart and Winston, 1967); and M. A. Wallach, N. Kogan, and D. J. Bem, "Group Influence on Individual Risk Taking," *Journal of Abnormal and Social Psychology*, Vol. 65 (1962), pp. 75–86.

32. R. D. Clark III, "Group-Induced Shift Toward Risk: A Critical Appraisal," *Psychological Bulletin*, October 1971, pp.251–70.

33. A. F. Osborn, *Applied Imagination: Principles and Procedures of Creative Thinking* (New York: Scribners, 1941).

34. The following discussion is based on A. L. Delbecq, A. H. Van deVen, and D. H. Gustafson, *Group Techniques for Program Planning: A Guide to Nominal and Delphi Processes* (Glenview, Ill.: Scott, Foresman, 1975).

35. P. M. Muchinsky, "Organizational Communication: Relationships to Organizational Climate and Job Satisfaction," *Academy of Management Journal*, December 1977, pp. 592–607.

36. S. A. Hellweg and S. L. Phillips, "Communication and Productivity in Organizations: A State-of-the-Art Review," in *Proceedings of the 40th Annual Academy of Management Conference*, Detroit, Michigan, 1980, pp. 188–92.

37. R. R. Reilly, B. Brown, M. R. Blood, and C. Z. Malatesta, "The Effects of Realistic Previews: A Study and Discussion of the Literature," *Personnel Psychology*, Winter 1981, pp. 823–34.

Leadership

8

AFTER STUDYING THIS CHAPTER, YOU SHOULD BE ABLE TO:

Define and explain the following key terms and concepts:

Autocratic leader	Leadership
Behavioral theories	LPC
Consideration	Managerial Grid
Democratic leader	Maturity
Employee-oriented leader	Position power
Initiating structure	Production-oriented leader
Leader-member relations	Task structure

Understand:

The nature of leadership
The conclusions of trait theories
The limitations of behavioral theories
Fiedler's contingency model
The path-goal theory
The situational leadership theory
The leader-participation model
Why no leadership style is ideal in all situations
The strengths and limitations in current contingency theories

Leadership is making people do what they don't want to do, and liking it.

—H. S. TRUMAN

*I*t has been accepted as a truism that good leadership is essential to business, to government, and to the countless groups and organizations that shape the way in which we live, work, and play.[1] If leadership is such an important factor, the critical issue is: What makes a great leader? The tempting answer to give is: Great followers! While there is some truth to this response, the issue is far more complex.

WHAT IS LEADERSHIP?

Leadership is the ability to influence a group toward the achievement of goals. The source of this influence may be formal, such as that provided by the possession of managerial rank in an organization. Since management positions come with some degree of formally designated authority, an individual may assume a leadership role as a result of the position he or she holds in the organization. But not all leaders are managers or, for that matter, are all managers leaders. Just because an organization provides its managers with certain rights is no assurance that they will be able to lead effectively. We find that nonsanctioned leadership, that is, the ability to influence that arises outside of the formal structure of the organization, is as important or more important than formal influence. In other words, leaders can emerge from within a group as well as being formally appointed.

FIGURE 8–1

Source: Reprinted by permission: Tribune Media Services, Inc.

TRANSITION IN LEADERSHIP THEORIES

The leadership literature is voluminous, and much of it is confusing and contradictory. In order to make our way through this "forest," we shall consider three basic approaches to explaining what makes an effective leader. The first sought to find universal personality traits that leaders had to some greater degree than nonleaders. The second tried to explain leadership in terms of the behavior that a person engaged in. Both approaches have been described as "false starts," based on their erroneous and oversimplified conception of leadership.[2] Most recently, we have looked to contingency models to explain the inadequacies of previous leadership theories in reconciling and bringing together the diversity of research findings. In this chapter, we shall present the contributions and limitations of each of the three approaches and conclude by attempting to ascertain the value of the leadership literature in explaining and predicting behavior.

TRAIT THEORIES

If we were to describe a leader based on the general connotations presented in today's media, we might list qualities such as intelligence, charisma, decisiveness, enthusiasm, strength, bravery, integrity, self-confidence, and so on—possibly eliciting the conclusion that effective leaders must be one part Boy Scout and two parts Jesus Christ. The search for characteristics such as those listed that would differentiate leaders from nonleaders occupied the early psychologists who studied leadership.

Is it possible to isolate one or more personality, social, physical, or intellectual characteristics in individuals we generally acknowledge as leaders—Napoleon, Hitler, Lincoln, Joan of Arc, Cezar Chavez, Martin Luther King, Jr., John F. Kennedy, Mahatma Gandhi—that nonleaders do not possess? We may agree that these individuals meet our definition of a leader, but they represent individuals with utterly different characteristics. If the concept of traits were to be proved valid, there had to be found specific characteristics that all leaders possess.

Research efforts at isolating these traits resulted in a number of dead ends. For instance, a review of twenty different studies identified nearly eighty leadership traits, but only five of these traits were common to four or more of the investigations.[3] If the search was to identify a set of traits that would always differentiate leaders from followers and effective from ineffective leaders, the search obviously failed. Perhaps it was a bit optimistic to believe that there could be consistent and unique traits that would apply across the board to all effective leaders no matter whether they were in charge of the Hell's Angels, the Mormon Tabernacle Choir, General Electric, the C.I.A., the Ku Klux Klan, or the Congress of Racial Equality.

If, however, the search was to identify traits that were consistently associated with leadership, the results can be interpreted in a more impressive light. For example, intelligence, dominance, self-confidence, high energy level, and task-relevant knowledge are five traits that show consistently positive correlations with leadership.[4] But ''positive correlations'' should not be interpreted to mean ''definitive predictors.'' The correlations between these traits and leadership have generally been in the range of $+.25$ to $+.35$[5]—interesting results, but not earth shattering!

The results represent the conclusions based on seventy years of trait research. These modest correlations coupled with the inherent limitations of the trait approach—it overlooks the needs of followers, generally fails to clarify the relative importance of various traits, doesn't separate cause from effect (i.e., are leaders self-confident or does success as a leader build self-confidence?), and ignores situational factors—naturally led researchers in other directions. Although there has been some resurgent interest in traits during the past decade,[6] a major movement away from traits began as early as the 1940s. Leadership research from the late 1940s through the mid-1960s emphasized the preferred behavioral styles that leaders demonstrated.

BEHAVIORAL THEORIES

The inability to strike ''gold'' in the trait mines led researchers to look at the behaviors that specific leaders exhibited. They wondered if there was something unique in the way that effective leaders behave. For example, do they tend to be more democratic than autocratic?

Not only, it was hoped, would the behavioral approach provide more definitive answers about the nature of leadership but, if successful, it would have practical implications quite different from those of the trait approach. If trait research had been successful, it would have provided a basis for *selecting* the ''right'' person to assume formal positions in groups and organizations requiring leadership.

In contrast, if behavioral studies were to turn up critical behavioral determinants of leadership, we could *train* people to be leaders. The difference between trait and behavioral theories, in terms of application, lies in their underlying assumptions. If trait theories were valid, then leaders are basically born: You either have it or you do not. On the other hand, if there were specific behaviors that identified leaders, then we could teach leadership—we could design programs that implanted these behavioral patterns in individuals who desired to be effective leaders. This was surely a more exciting avenue for it would mean that the supply of leaders could be expanded. If training worked, we could have an infinite supply of effective leaders.

There were a number of studies that looked at behavioral styles. We shall briefly review the two most popular: the Ohio State group and the University of Michigan group. Then we shall see how the concepts that these studies developed could be used to create a grid for looking at and appraising leadership styles.

Ohio State Studies

The most comprehensive and replicated of the behavioral theories resulted from research that began at Ohio State University in the late 1940s.[7] These studies sought to identify independent dimensions of leader behavior. Beginning with over a thousand dimensions, they eventually narrowed the list into two categories that substantially accounted for most of the leadership behavior described by subordinates. They called these two dimensions initiating structure and consideration.

Initiating structure refers to the extent to which a leader is likely to define and structure his or her role and those of subordinates in the search for goal attainment. It includes behavior that attempts to organize work, work relationships, and goals. The leader characterized as high in initiating structure could be described in terms such as assigns group members to particular tasks, expects workers to maintain definite standards of performance, and emphasizes the meeting of deadlines.

Consideration is described as the extent to which a person is likely to have job relationships that are characterized by mutual trust, respect for subordinates' ideas, and regard for their feelings. He shows concern for his followers' comfort, well-being, status, and satisfaction. A leader high in consideration could be described as one who helps subordinates with personal problems, is friendly and approachable, and treats all subordinates as equals.

Extensive research, based on these definitions, found that leaders high in initiating structure and consideration (a "high-high" leader) tended to achieve high subordinate performance and satisfaction more frequently than those who rated low on either consideration, initiating structure, or both. However, the "high-high" style did not always result in positive consequences. For example, leader behavior characterized as high on initiating structure led to greater rates of grievances, absenteeism, and turnover and lower levels of job satisfaction for workers performing routine tasks. Other studies found that high consideration was negatively related to performance ratings of the leader by his superior. In conclusion, the Ohio State studies suggested that the "high-high" style generally resulted in positive outcomes, but enough exceptions were found to indicate that situational factors needed to be integrated into the theory.

University of Michigan Studies

Leadership studies undertaken at the University of Michigan's Survey Research Center, at about the same time as those being done at Ohio State, had similar research objectives: to locate behavioral characteristics of leaders that appeared to be related to measures of performance effectiveness.

The Michigan group also came up with two dimensions of leadership behavior that they labeled *employee oriented* and *production oriented*.[8] Leaders who were employee oriented were described as emphasizing interpersonal relations; they took a personal interest in the needs of their subordinates and accepted individual differences among members. The production-oriented leaders, in contrast, tended to emphasize the technical or task aspects of the job—their main concern was in accomplishing their group's tasks and the group members were a means to that end.

The conclusions arrived at by the Michigan researchers strongly favored the leaders who were employee oriented in their behavior. Employee-oriented leaders were associated with higher group productivity and higher job satisfaction. Production-oriented leaders tended to be associated with low group productivity and lower work satisfaction.

The Managerial Grid

A graphic portrayal of a two-dimensional view of leadership style has been developed by Blake and Mouton.[9] They propose a Managerial Grid® based on the styles of "concern for people" and "concern for production," which essentially represent the Ohio State dimensions of consideration and initiating structure or the Michigan dimensions of employee oriented and production oriented.

The grid, depicted in Figure 8–2, has nine possible positions along each axis, creating eighty-one different positions in which the leader's style may fall. The grid does not show results produced but, rather, the dominating factors in a leader's thinking in regard to getting results.

Based on the findings of Blake and Mouton, managers perform best under a 9,9 style, as contrasted, for example, with a 9,1 (authority type) or the 1,9 (country-club type)) leader.[10] Unfortunately, the grid offers a better framework for conceptualizing leadership style than for presenting any tangible new information in clarifying the leadership quandary since there is little substantive evidence to support the conclusion that a 9,9 style is most effective in all situations.[11]

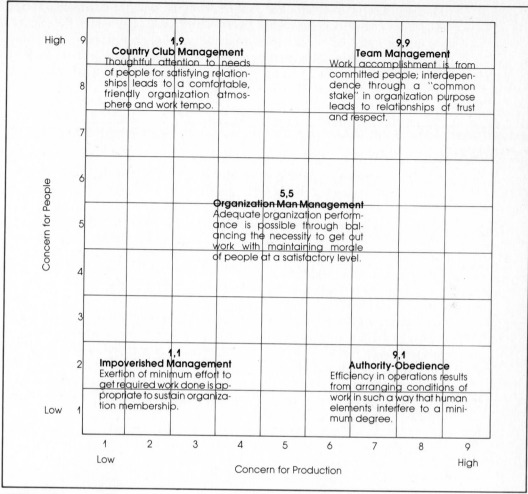

High 9 | **1,9**
Country Club Management
Thoughtful attention to needs of people for satisfying relation- ships leads to a comfortable, friendly organization atmos- phere and work tempo.

9,9
Team Management
Work accomplishment is from committed people; interdepen- dence through a "common stake" in organization purpose leads to relationships of trust and respect.

5,5
Organization Man Management
Adequate organization perform- ance is possible through bal- ancing the necessity to get out work with maintaining morale of people at a satisfactory level.

1,1
Impoverished Management
Exertion of minimum effort to get required work done is ap- propriate to sustain organiza- tion membership.

9,1
Authority-Obedience
Efficiency in operations results from arranging conditions of work in such a way that human elements interfere to a mini- mum degree.

Concern for People (vertical axis, 1–9, Low to High)

Concern for Production (horizontal axis, 1–9, Low to High)

FIGURE 8–2
The Managerial Grid®

Source: Robert R. Blake, Jane S. Mouton, Louis B. Barnes, and Larry E. Greiner, "Breakthrough in Organization Development," *Harvard Business Review,* November–December 1964, p. 136.
Copyright © by the President and Fellows of Harvard College; all rights reserved.

Summary of Behavioral Theories

We have described the most popular and important of the attempts to explain leadership in terms of the behavior exhibited by the leader. There were other ef- forts,[12] but they faced the same problem that confronted the Ohio State and Mich- igan findings: They had very little success in identifying consistent relationships between patterns of leadership behavior and group performance. General state- ments could not be made because results would vary over different ranges of cir- cumstances. What was missing was consideration of the situational factors that influence success or failure. For example, it seems unlikely that Martin Luther King, Jr., would have been a great leader of his people at the turn of the century, yet he was in the 1950s and 1960s. Would Ralph Nader have risen to lead a consumer activist group had he been born in 1834 rather than 1934, or in Costa Rica rather than Connecticut? It seems quite unlikely, yet the behavioral approaches we have described could not clarify these situational factors.

CONTINGENCY THEORIES

It became increasingly clear to those who were studying the leadership phenomenon that the predicting of leadership success was more complex than isolating a few traits or preferable behaviors. The failure to obtain consistent results led to a new focus on situational influences. The relationship between leadership style and effectiveness suggested that under condition *a,* style *x* would be appropriate, while style *y* would be more suitable for condition *b,* and style *z* for condition *c.* But what were the conditions *a, b, c,* and so forth? It was one thing to say that leadership effectiveness was dependent on the situation and another to be able to isolate those situational conditions.

There has been no shortage of studies attempting to isolate critical situational factors that affect leadership effectiveness. One author, in reviewing the literature, found that the task being performed (i.e., complexity, type, technology, size of the project) was a significant moderating variable but additionally uncovered studies that isolated situational factors such as style of the leader's immediate supervisor, group norms, span of control, external threat and stress, time demands, and organizational climate.[13]

Several approaches to isolating key situational variables have proven more successful than others and, as a result, have gained wider recognition. We shall consider five of these: the autocratic-democratic continuum and the Fiedler, Hersey-Blanchard, path-goal, and leader-participation models.

Autocratic-Democratic Continuum Model

If autocratic and democratic behavior were viewed only as two extreme positions, this model would be correctly labeled as a behavioral theory. However, they are merely two of many positions along a continuum. At one extreme the leader makes the decisions, tells his or her subordinates, and expects them to carry out that decision. At the other extreme, the leader fully shares his or her decision-making power with subordinates, allowing each member of the group to carry an equal voice—one person, one vote. Between these two extremes fall a number of leadership styles, with the style selected dependent upon forces in the leader, the operating group, and the situation. Although this represents a contingency theory, we shall find, upon investigating other contingency approaches, that it is quite primitive.

As depicted in Figure 8–3, there is a relationship between the degree of authority used and the amount of freedom available to subordinates in reaching decisions. This continuum is seen as a zero-sum game; as one gains, the other loses, and vice versa.[14] However, much of the research using this model has been concentrated on the extreme positions.

After reviewing eleven separate studies, Filley, House, and Kerr found seven to demonstrate that participative leadership has positive effects upon productivity while there were no significant effects in the other four. Although only three of the eleven investigations reported on participative leadership's effect on subordinate satisfaction, all showed positive results.[15]

Hamner and Organ reached a similar conclusion when they reviewed the research:

> Generally speaking, we find that participative leadership is associated with greater satisfaction on the part of subordinates than is nonparticipative leadership; or, at worst, that participation does not lower satisfaction. We cannot summarize so easily the findings with respect to productivity. Some studies find participative groups to

FIGURE 8–3
Leadership-Behavior Continuum

Source: Robert Tannenbaum and Warren H. Schmidt, "How to Choose a Leadership Pattern," *Harvard Business Review*, March–April 1958, p. 96. With permission. Copyright © 1958 by the President and Fellows of Harvard College; all rights reserved.

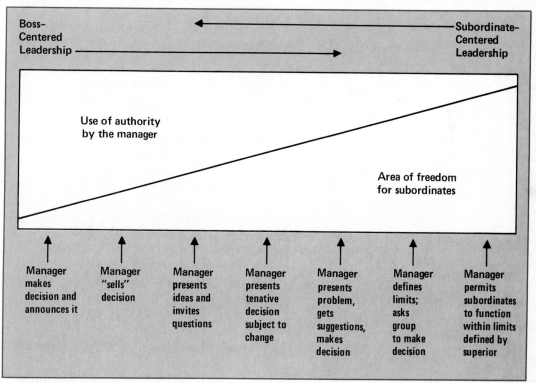

be more productive; some find nonparticipative groups to be more effective; and quite a few studies show no appreciable differences in productivity between autocratically versus democratically managed work groups.[16]

The previous suggests a clear link between participation or the democratic style of leadership and satisfaction, but the relationship of this style to productivity is less apparent. The research can be interpreted as saying that people like democracy, but that it will not necessarily result in higher productivity.

A contingency approach would recognize that neither the democratic nor autocratic extreme is effective in all situations. The following models more comprehensively appraise these situational characteristics.

Fiedler Model

The first comprehensive contingency model for leadership was developed by Fred Fiedler.[17] His model proposes that effective group performance depends upon the proper match between the leader's style of interacting with his or her subordinates and the degree to which the situation gives control and influence to the leader. Fiedler developed an instrument, which he called the least preferred co-worker (LPC) questionnaire, that purports to measure whether a person is task or relationship oriented. Further, he isolated three situational criteria—leader-member relations, task structure, and position power—that he believes can be manipulated so as to create the proper match with the behavioral orientation of the leader. In a sense, the Fiedler model is an outgrowth of trait theory, since the LPC questionnaire is a simple psychological test. However, Fiedler goes significantly beyond trait and behavioral approaches by attempting to isolate situations, relating his personality measure to his situational classification, and then predicting leadership effectiveness as a function of the two.

The description of the Fiedler model is somewhat abstract. Let us now look at the model more closely.

Fiedler believes a key factor in leadership success to be an individual's basic leadership style. So he begins by trying to find out what that basic style is. Fiedler created the LPC questionnaire for this purpose. It contains sixteen contrasting adjectives (such as pleasant-unpleasant, efficient-inefficient, open-guarded, supportive-hostile). The questionnaire then asks the respondent to think of all the co-workers they have ever had and to describe the one person they *least enjoyed* working with by rating him or her on a scale of 1 to 8 for each of the sixteen sets of contrasting adjectives. Fiedler believes that based on the respondents' answers to this LPC questionnaire, he can determine their basic leadership style. If the least preferred co-worker is described in relatively positive terms (a high LPC score), then the respondent is primarily interested in good personal relations with this co-worker. That is, if you essentially describe the person you are least able to work with in favorable terms, Fiedler would label you relationship oriented. In contrast, if the least preferred co-worker is seen in relatively unfavorable terms (a low LPC score), the respondent is primarily interested in productivity and thus would be labeled task oriented. Notice that the LPC results in placing every respondent into either one of two leadership styles—relationship or task oriented. Also take note that Fiedler assumes that an individual's leadership style is fixed. As we'll show in a moment, this is important because it means that if a situation requires a task-oriented leader and the person in that leadership position is relationship oriented, either the situation has to be modified or the leader removed and replaced if optimum effectiveness is to be achieved. Fiedler argues that leadership style is innate to a person—you *can't* change your style to fit changing situations!

After an individual's basic leadership style has been assessed through the LPC, it is necessary to match the leader with the situation. Fiedler has identified three contingency dimensions that, he argues, define the key situational factors that determine leadership effectiveness. These are leader-member relations, task structure, and position power. They are defined as follows:

1. *Leader-member relations*—the degree of confidence, trust, and respect subordinates have in their leader
2. *Task structure*—the degree to which the job assignments are procedurized (i.e., structured or unstructured)
3. *Position power*—the degree of influence a leader has over power variables such as hiring, firing, discipline, promotions, and salary increases

So the next step in the Fiedler model is to evaluate the situation in terms of these three contingency variables. Leader-member relations are either good or poor, task structure either high or low, and position power either strong or weak.

Fiedler states the better the leader-member relations, the more highly structured the job, and the stronger the position power, the more control or influence the leader has. For example, a very favorable situation (where the leader would have a great deal of control) might involve a payroll manager who is well respected and whose subordinates have confidence in her (good leader-member relations), where the activities to be done—such as wage computation, check writing, report filing—are specific and clear (high task structure), and the job provides considerable freedom for her to reward and punish her subordinates (strong position power). On the other hand, an unfavorable situation might be the disliked chairman of a voluntary United Way fund–raising team. In this job, the leader has very little control. Altogether, by mixing the three contingency variables, there are potentially eight different situations or categories in which a leader could find himself or herself.

With knowledge of an individual's LPC and an assessment of the three contingency variables, the Fiedler model proposes matching them up to achieve maximum leadership effectiveness. Based on Fiedler's study of over twelve hundred groups, where he compared relationship versus task-oriented leadership styles in each of the eight situational categories, he concluded that task-oriented leaders tend to perform better in situations that were *very favorable* to them and in situations that were *very unfavorable* (see Figure 8–4). So Fiedler would predict that when faced with a category I, II, III, VII or VIII situation, task-oriented leaders perform better. Relationship-oriented leaders, however, perform better in moderately favorable situations—categories IV through VI.

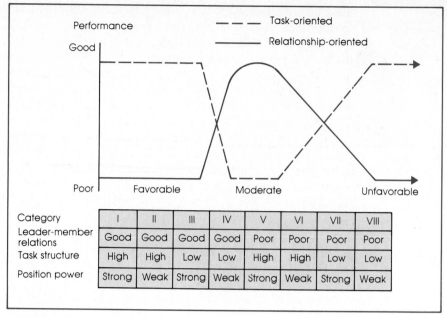

FIGURE 8–4
Findings from Fiedler Model

Given Fiedler's findings, how would you apply them? You would seek to match leaders and situations. Individuals' LPC scores would determine the type of situation for which they were best suited. That "situation" would be defined by evaluating the three contingency factors of leader-member relations, task structure, and position power. But remember that Fiedler views an individual's leadership style as being fixed. Therefore, there are really only two ways in which to improve leader effectiveness. First, you can change the leader to fit the situation. Analogous to a baseball game, management can reach into its "bullpen" and put in a right-handed pitcher or a left-handed pitcher, depending on the situational characteristics of the hitter. So, for example, if a group situation rates as highly unfavorable but is currently led by a relationship-oriented manager, the group's performance could be improved by replacing that manager with one who is task oriented. The second alternative would be to change the situation to fit the leader. That could be done by restructuring tasks or increasing or decreasing the power that the leader has to control factors such as salary increases, promotions, and disciplinary actions. To illustrate, assume a task-oriented leader were in a category IV situation. If this leader could increase his or her position power, then the leader would be operating in category III and the leader-situation match would be compatible for high group performance.

One should not surmise that Fiedler has closed all the gaps and put to rest all the questions underlying leadership effectiveness. Continued research strongly confirms that the Fiedler model predicts categories I and IV with relatively high consistency. Predictions for categories V and VIII are confirming, but at a more moderate level. Most pertinent, the model's predictions appear irrelevant to categories II, III, VI, and VII.[19]

The ability of the model to predict in several categories may mean that Fiedler has made some important insights into leadership. On the other hand, the model has a number of weaknesses.[20] First, the contingency variables are complex and difficult to assess. It's often difficult in practice to determine how good the leader-member relations are, how structured the task is, and how much position power the leader has. Second, the model gives little attention to the characteristics of the subordinates. Third, no attention is given to varying technical competencies of the leader or the subordinates. The model assumes that both the leader and subordinates have adequate technical competence. Fourth, the correlations Fiedler presents in defense of the model are relatively weak. Though generally in the right direction, they are often low and statistically nonsignificant. Finally, the LPC instrument is open to question. The logic underlying the LPC is not well understood, and studies have shown that respondents' LPC scores are not stable.[24]

In spite of these criticisms, the Fiedler model continues to be a dominant input in the development of a contingency explanation of leadership effectiveness. Its greatest contribution, however, may be in the direction it has taken leadership research, rather than in any definitive answers that it provides.

Hersey-Blanchard's Situational Theory

One of the most widely practiced leadership models is Paul Hersey and Ken Blanchard's situational leadership theory.[22] It has been used as a major training device at such *Fortune* 500 companies as Bank of America, Caterpillar, IBM, Mobil Oil, and Xerox; it has also been widely accepted in all the military services.[23] Although the theory has not undergone extensive evaluation to test its validity, we include it here becasuse of its wide acceptance and its strong intuitive appeal. Additionally, in defense of the theory, at this point in its development it's too early to dismiss it out of hand merely because researchers have not chosen to evaluate it more thoroughly.

Situational leadership is a contingency theory that focuses on the followers. Successful leadership is achieved by selecting the right leadership style, which Hersey and Blanchard argue is contingent on the level of the followers' maturity. Before we proceed, we should clarify two points: Why focus on the followers? and What is meant by the term *maturity*?

The emphasis on the followers in leadership effectiveness reflects the reality that it is they who accept or reject the leader. Regardless of what the leader does, effectiveness depends on the actions of his or her followers. This is an important dimension that has been overlooked or underemphasized in most leadership theories.

The term *maturity*, as defined by Hersey and Blanchard, is the ability and willingness of people to take responsibility for directing their own behavior. It has two components: job maturity and psychological maturity. The first encompasses one's knowledge and skills. Individuals who are high in job maturity have the knowledge, ability, and experience to perform their job tasks without direction from others. Psychological maturity relates to the willingness or motivation to do something. Individuals high in psychological maturity don't need much external encouragement; they are already intrinsically motivated.

Situational leadership uses the same two leadership dimensions that Fiedler identified: task and relationship behaviors. However, Hersey and Blanchard go a step farther by considering each as either high or low and then combining them into four specific leadership styles: telling, selling, participating, and delegating. They are described as follows:

Telling (high task–low relationship). The leader defines roles and tells people what, how, when, and where to do various tasks. It emphasizes directive behavior.

Selling (high task–high relationship). The leader provides both directive behavior and supportive behavior.

Participating (low task–high relationship). The leader and follower share in decision making, with the main role of the leader being facilitating and communicating.

Delegating (low task–low relationship). The leader provides little direction or support.

The final component in Hersey and Blanchard's theory is defining four stages of maturity:

M1. People are both unable and unwilling to take responsibility to do something. They are neither competent nor confident.

M2. People are unable but willing to do the necessary job tasks. They are motivated but currently lack the appropriate skills.

M3. People are able but unwilling to do what the leader wants.

M4. People are both able and willing to do what is asked of them.

Figure 8–5 integrates the various components into the situational leadership model. As followers reach high levels of maturity, the leader responds by not only continuing to decrease control over activiities, but also by continuing to decrease relationship behavior as well. At stage M1, followers need clear and specific directions. At stage M2, both high-task and high-relationship behavior is needed. The high-task behavior compensates for the followers' lack of ability, and the high-relationship behavior tries to get the followers psychologically to "buy into" the leader's desires. M3 creates motivational problems that are best solved by a supportive, nondirective, participative style. Finally, at stage M4, the leader doesn't have to do much because followers are both willing and able to take responsibility.

The astute reader might have noticed the high similarity between Hersey and Blanchard's four leadership styles and the four extreme "corners" in the Managerial Grid. The telling style equates to the 9,1 leader; selling equals 9,9; participating is equivalent to 1,9; and delegating is the same as the 1,1 leader. Is situational leadership, then, merely the Managerial Grid with one major difference—the replacement of the 9,9 ("one style for all occasions") contention with the recommendation that the "right" style should align with the maturity of the followers? Hersey and Blanchard say "No!"[24] They argue that the grid empha-

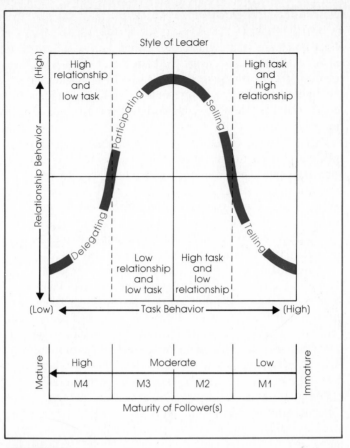

FIGURE 8–5
Situational Leadership Model

Source: Adapted from P. Hersey and K. Blanchard, *Management of Organizational Behavior: Utilizing Human Resources*, 4th ed. © 1982, p. 152. Reprinted by permission of Prentice-Hall, Inc., Englewood Cliffs, N.J.

sizes *concern* for production and people, which are attitudinal dimensions. Situational leadership, in contrast, emphasizes task and relationship *behavior*. In spite of Hersey and Blanchard's claim, this is a pretty minute differentiation. Understanding of the situational leadership theory is probably enhanced by considering it as a fairly direct adaptation of the grid framework to reflect four stages of follower maturity.

Finally, we come to the critical question: Is there evidence to support situational leadership theory? As noted earlier, the theory has received little attention by researchers. With a few exceptions,[25] the validation research has been done by Hersey, Blanchard, and their graduate students. Not surprisingly, their studies have been generally favorable. More research to test the theory is clearly necessary. Without additional, objective research to support the theory, any enthusiastic endorsement at this point should be cautioned against.

Path-Goal Theory

What situational leadership currently is to practicing managers, the path-goal theory of leadership is to academic researchers. Path-goal theory is currently *the* dominant focus of investigation by researchers in leadership.

Path-goal theory is a contingency model of leadership that builds on the Ohio State leadership research dealing with initiating structure and consideration.[26]

The essence of the theory is that it's the leader's job to assist his or her followers in attaining their goals and to provide the necessary direction and/or support to ensure that their goals are compatible with the overall objectives of the group or organization. The term "path-goal" is derived from the belief that effective leaders clarify the path to help their followers get from where they are to the achievement of their work goals and make the journey along the path easier by reducing roadblocks and pitfalls. Initiating structure acts to clarify the path, and consideration makes the path easier to travel.

According to path-goal theory, a leader's behavior is *acceptable* to subordinates to the degree that it is viewed by them as an immediate source of satisfaction or as a means of future satisfaction. A leader's behavior is *motivational* to the degree that it (1) makes subordinate need satisfaction contingent on effective performance and (2) provides the coaching, guidance, support, and rewards that are necessary for effective performance. In testing these statements about a leader's behavior, most studies have focused on two leadership styles: consideration and initiating structure.[27] When leaders demonstrate high consideration, subordinates are likely to experience greater satisfaction, whereas high initiating structure provides role clarity and should lead to higher performance. But there are contingency variables residing in the subordinate and the work environment that moderate the relationship between the leader's style and the subordinate's satisfaction and performance (see Figure 8–6). These include the degree of task structure in the job, the subordinate's perception of his or her own ability, and the subordinate's locus of control. Most of the research, however, has been directed at testing hypotheses relating to the degree of task structure. Let's briefly look at these predictions.

Path-goal theory proposes that consideration is most helpful to subordinates in structured situations and less helpful in unstructured ones, and that initiating structure will lead to greater satisfaction when the tasks are ambiguous or stressful than when they are highly sturctured and well laid out. Where the tasks to be done are not clear, subordinates appreciate the leader clarifying the path to goal achievement. High consideration, on the other hand, results in high employee satisfaction when subordinates are performing structured or routine tasks. In clearly defined and structured tasks, efforts by the leader to explain tasks that are already clear will be seen by the subordinates as redundant or even insulting.

There is no shortage of research studies testing propositions developed out of the path-goal theory.[28] What does the research indicate? The evidence generally supports the logic underlying the theory.[29] That is, initiating structure is more ef-

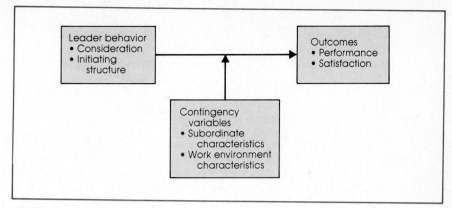

FIGURE 8–6
Simplified Model of Path-Goal Theory

fective when subordinates work on unstructured tasks, while consideration leads to higher satisfaction when the subordinate's job tasks are structured and unambiguous. Yet the findings are more consistent with predictions of satisfaction than with predictions of performance.

So, where does this leave us? The continued interest by researchers in evaluating and modifying the theory suggests confidence in its general framework. Problems relate to the need to clarify more fully the variables it includes, how the variables are measured, the inconsistent predictions of performance outcomes, and the growing complexity of the theory as new moderating variables are added. We can expect future research to contribute toward resolving these problems. However, it is becoming obvious from the numerous studies on leadership that we are a long way from being able to identify the definitive leadership styles or contingency variables that moderate the style-effectiveness relationship. Moreover, from a practical point of view, if that day ever comes, the result may be so complex that few managers will be willing to go to the trouble of understanding it.

Leader-Participation Model

The most recent addition to the contingency approach is the leadership-participation model proposed by Victor Vroom and Phillip Yetton.[30] It relates leadership behavior and participation to decision making. Recognizing that task structures have varying demands for routine or nonroutine activities, these researchers suggest that leader behavior must adjust to reflect the task sturcture. Vroom and Yetton's model is normative—it provides a sequential set of rules that should be followed in determining the form and amount of participation in decision making, as determined by different types of situations. As shown in Figure 8–7, the model is a decision tree incorporating seven contingencies and five alternative leadership styles.

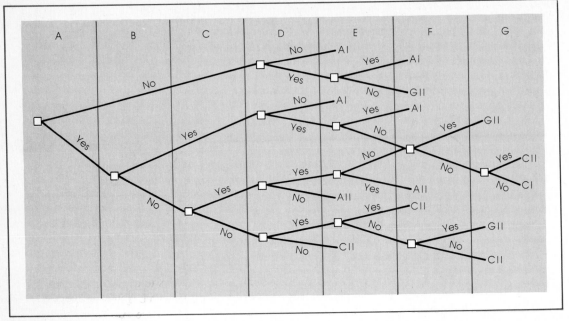

FIGURE 8–7
Leader-Participation Model

The model assumes that any of five behaviors may be feasible in a given situation—Autocratic I (AI), Autocratic II (AII), Consultative I (CI), Consultative II (CII), and Group II (GII):

AI. You solve the problem or make a decision yourself using information available to you at that time.

AII. You obtain the necessary information from subordinates and then decide on the solution to the problem yourself. You may or may not tell subordinates what the problem is in getting the information from them. The role played by your subordinates in making the decision is clearly one of providing the necessary information to you rather than generating or evaluating alternative solutions.

CI. You share the problem with relevant subordinates individually; getting their ideas and suggestions without bringing them together as a group. Then *you* make the decision that may or may not reflect your subordinates' influence.

CII. You share the problem with your subordinates as a group, collectively obtaining their ideas and suggestions. Then, you make the decision that may or may not reflect your subordinates' influence.

GII. You share the problem with your subordinates as a group. Together you generate and evaluate alternatives and attempt to reach an agreement (consensus) on a solution.

Although these five decision behaviors closely parallel the autocratic-democratic continuum depicted in Figure 8–3, the Vroom-Yetton model goes beyond that model by suggesting a specific way of analyzing problems by means of seven contingency questions. By answering "Yes" or "No" to these questions, the leader can arrive at which of the five decisions behaviors is preferred—that is, how much participation should be used.

The seven questions must be answered in order from A to G:

A. Is there a quality requirement?
B. Do I have sufficient information to make a high quality decision?
C. Is the problem structured?
D. Is acceptance of the decision by subordinates critical to its implementation?
E. If I were to make the decision by myself, is it reasonably certain that it would be accepted by my subordinates?
F. Do subordinates share the organizational goals to be obtained in solving this problem?
G. Is conflict among subordinates likely in obtaining the preferred solution?

Again, referring to Figure 8–7, based on the answers to questions A through G, the leader follows the decision tree until reaching its end. The designation at the end of the branch (either AI, AII, CI, CII, or GII) tells the leader what to do.

To date the research testing the leader-participation model has been encouraging,[31] but considerably more investigations are needed to test the model's normative propositions against effectiveness data. It does, however, confirm existing empirical evidence that leaders use participatory methods (1) when the quality of the decision is important, (2) when it is important that subordinates accept the decision and it is unlikely that they will do so unless they are allowed to take part in it, and (3) when subordinates can be trusted to pay attention to the goals of the group rather than simply to their own preferences.

This model has also confirmed that leadership research should be directed at the situation rather than the person. It probably makes more sense to talk about autocratic and participative *situations* rather than autocratic and participative *leaders*. This, importantly, is a fundamental deviation from Fiedler's viewpoint. The Fiedler model emphasizes changing the situation to match the inherent characteristics of the leader. The leader's style is basically assumed to be inflexible. Vroom and Yetton would disagree. They demonstrate that leaders are not rigid, but can adjust their style to different situations.

The cartoon in Figure 8–8 proposes adjusting the individual to the coat, rather than vice versa. We can think of the "coat" as analogous to the "situation." In terms of leadership, if an individual's leadership style range is very narrow, as Fiedler proposes, we are required to place individuals into the appropriate "size of coat" if they are to lead successfully. If Vroom and Yetton are right, then all the leader has to do is assess the "coat" that is available and adjust his or her style accordingly. Whether we adjust the coat to fit the person (à la Fiedler) or fix the person to fit the coat (à la Vroom and Yetton) is an issue requiring further investigation.

FIGURE 8–8

Source: Brant Parker and Johnny Hart, *Let There Be Reign* (Greenwich, Conn: Fawcett Books, 1972).

Sometimes Leadership Is Irrelevant!

In keeping with the contingency spirit, we want to conclude this section by offering this notion: the belief that *some* leadership style *will always* be effective *regardless* of the situation may not be true. Leadership may not always be important. Data from numerous studies collectively demonstrate that, in many situations, whatever behaviors leaders exhibit are irrelevant. Certain individual, job, and organizational variables can act as *substitutes* for leadership or *neutralize* the leader's effect to influence his or her subordinates.[32]

Neutralizers make it impossible for leader behavior to make any difference to subordinate outcomes. They negate the leader's influence. Substitutes, on the other hand, make a leader's influence not only impossible but also unnecessary. They act as a replacement for the leader's influence. For instance, characteristics of subordinates such as their experience, training, "professional" orientation, or need for independence can neutralize the effect of leadership. These characteristics can replace the need for a leader's support or ability to create structure and reduce task ambiguity. Jobs that are inherently unambiguous and routine or that are intrinsically satisfying may place less demands on the leadership variable. Organizational characteristics like explicit formalized goals, rigid rules and procedures, or cohesive work groups can act in the place of formal leadership.

This recent recognition that leaders don't always have an impact on subordinate outcomes should not be that surprising. After all, we have introduced a number of independent variables—attitudes, personality, ability, and group norms, to name but a few—that have been documented to impact on employee performance and satisfaction. Yet supporters of the leadership concept have tended to place an undue burden on this variable for explaining and predicting behavior. It is too simplistic to consider subordinates as guided to goal accomplishments based solely on the behavior of their leader. It is important, therefore, to recognize explicitly that leadership is merely another independent variable in our overall OB model. In some situations, it may contribute a lot to explaining employee productivity, absence, turnover, and satisfaction, but in other situations, it may contribute little toward that end.

LOOKING FOR COMMON GROUND: WHAT DOES IT ALL MEAN?

The topic of leadership certainly doesn't lack for theories. But from an overview perspective, what does it all mean? Let's try to identify commonalities among the leadership theories and attempt to determine what, if any, practical value the theories hold for application to organizations.

Careful examination discloses that the concepts of "task" and "people"—often expressed in more elaborate terms that hold substantially the same meaning—permeate most of the theories.[33] The task dimension is called just that by Fiedler, but it goes by the name of "initiating structure" for the Ohio State group and the path-goal supporters, "production orientation" by the Michigan researchers, and "concern for production" by Blake and Mouton. The people dimension gets similar treatment, going under such aliases as "consideration" and "employee-oriented" or "relationship-oriented" leadership. It seems clear that leadership behavior can be reduced to two dimensions—task and people—but researchers continue to differ as to whether the orientations are two ends of a single continuum (you could be high on one or the other but not both) or two independent dimensions (you could be high or low on both).

Although one well-known scholar argues that virtually every theory has also "wrestled with the question of how much a leader should share power with subordinates in decision making,"[34] there is far less support for this contention. The autocratic-participative continuum, the situational leadership theory, and the leadership-participation model address this issue, but the task-people dichotomy appears to be far more encompassing.

How should we interpret the findings presented in this chapter? Some traits have shown, over time, to be modest predictors of leadership effectiveness. But the fact that a manager possessed intelligence, dominance, self-confidence, or the like would by no means assure us that his or her subordinates would be productive and satisfied employees. The ability of these traits to predict leadership success is just not that strong.

The early task-people approaches (i.e., the Ohio State, Michigan, and Managerial Grid theories) also offer us little substance. The strongest statement one can make based on these theories is that leaders who rate high in people orientation should end up with satisfied employees. The research is too mixed to make predictions regarding employee productivity or the effect of a task orientation on productivity and satisfaction.

The wealth of research on the Fiedler model has failed to confirm the theory in its entirety, but parts of it are supported. When category I, IV, V, or VIII situations exist, the utilization of the LPC instrument to assess whether there is a leader-situation match and the use of that information to predict employee productivity and satisfaction outcomes seem warranted.

Hersey and Blanchard's situational leadership theory is straightforward, intuitively appealing, and important for its explicit recognition that the subordinate's ability and motivation are critical to the leader's success. Yet, in spite of its wide acceptance by practitioners, the lack of empirical support renders the theory, at least at this time, more speculative than substantive.

The autocratic-participative continuum and its modern-day equivalent, the Vroom-Yetton leadership-participation model, offer a diversity of leadership styles. Although studies to validate the Vroom-Yetton model are still scarce, the early results are encouraging. One investigation, for example, found that leaders who were high in agreement with the model had subordinates with higher productivity and higher satisfaction than did those leaders who were in low agreement with the model.[35] A major reservation, in addition to the need for more confirming studies, is the complexity of the model itself. With five styles, seven contingency variables, and eighteen possible outcomes, it would be difficult to use as a guide for practicing managers. One might additionally question whether, under the stress of day-to-day activities, managers could be expected to follow the rational, conscious process the model requires. Of course, from our descriptive perspective, we might answer, "It doesn't matter." What does matter is that where we find leaders who follow the model, we should expect also to find productive and satisfied employees.

Finally, the path-goal model represents an up-to-date task-people approach. Its use of task characteristics as moderating variables has met with reasonable success, especially in predicting satisfaction. Yet the theory itself is "relatively new to the literature of organizational behavior. Consequently, path-goal theory is offered more as a tool for directing research and stimulating insight than as a proven guide for managerial action."[36]

IMPLICATIONS FOR PERFORMANCE AND SATISFACTION

Leadership plays a central part in understanding group behavior, for it is the leader who usually provides the direction toward goal attainment. Therefore, a more accurate predictive capability should be valuable in improving group performance.

In this chapter we have described a transition in approaches to the study of leadership—from the simple trait orientation to increasingly complex and sophisticated models, such as the path-goal and leader-participation models. With the increase in complexity has also come an increase in our ability to explain and predict behavior.

Predictive ability increased as a result of the recognition that inclusion of situational factors was critical. Recent efforts have moved beyond mere recognition toward specific attempts to isolate these situational variables. We can expect further progress to be made with leadership models, but the last decade has seen us take several large steps—large enough that we now can make moderately effective predictions as to who can best lead a group and explain under what conditions a given approach (task oriented or people oriented) is likely to lead to high performance and satisfaction.

POINT

LEADERS MAKE A REAL DIFFERENCE!

There can be little question that the success of an organization, or any group within an organization, depends largely on the quality of its leadership. Whether in business, government, education, medicine, or religion, the quality of an organization's leadership determines the quality of the organization itself. Successful leaders anticipate change, vigorously exploit opportunities, motivate their followers to higher levels of productivity, correct poor performance, and lead the organization toward its objectives.

The importance relegated to the leadership function is well known. For example, a November 1976 issue of *Time* magazine allocated a dozen pages to an article entitled, "Leadership: The Biggest Issue." Rarely does a week go by that we don't hear or read about some leadership concern: "Jimmy Carter Fails to Provide the Leadership America Needs!" "Iacocca Leads the Turnaround at Chrysler!" "Boston Celtics Win NBA Title on Larry Bird's Leadership!" "The Democratic Party Searches for New Leadership!" "Polls Rate Reagan a Strong Leader."

Why is leadership so important to an organization's success? The answer lies in the need for coordination and control. Organizations exist to achieve objectives that are either impossible or extremely inefficient to achieve if done by individuals acting alone. The organization itself is a coordination and control mechanism. Rules, policies, job descriptions, and authority hierarchies are illustrations of devices created to facilitate coordination and control. But leadership, too, contributes toward integrating various job activities, coordinating communication between organizational subunits, monitoring activities, and controlling deviations from standard. No amount of rules and regulations can replace the experienced leader who can make rapid and decisive decisions.

The importance of leadership is not lost on those who staff organizations. Corporations, government agencies, school systems, and institutions of all shapes and sizes cumulatively spend billions of dollars every year to recruit, select, evaluate, and train individuals for leadership positions. The best evidence, however, of the importance organizations place on leadership roles is exhibited in salary schedules. Leaders are routinely paid ten, twenty, or more times the salary of those in nonleadership positions. The head of General Motors earns approximately $1 million annually. The highest skilled auto worker, in contrast, earns under $40,000 a year. The president of this auto worker's union makes better than $75,000 a year. Police officers typically make around $25,000 to $30,000 a year. Their boss probably earns 25 percent more, and his boss another 25 percent more. The pattern is well established. The more responsibility a leader has, as evidenced by his or her level in the organization, the more he or she earns. Would organizations voluntarily pay their leaders so much more than their nonleaders if they didn't strongly believe that leaders make a real difference?

COUNTERPOINT

LEADERS DON'T MAKE A DIFFERENCE!

Given the resources that have been spent on studying, selecting, and training leaders, you'd expect there to be clear evidence supporting the positive impact of leadership on a group or organization's performance. That evidence has failed to surface!

Analyses of leadership have frequently presumed that leadership style or leader behavior was an independent variable that could be selected or trained at will to conform to what research would find to be optimal. Even theorists who took a more contingent view of appropriate leadership behavior generally assumed that with proper training, appropriate behavior could be produced. Fiedler, noting how hard it is to change behavior, suggested changing the situational characteristics rather than the person, but this was an unusual suggestion in the context of prevailing literature that suggested that leadership style was something to be strategically selected according to the variables of the particular leadership theory.

But the leader is embedded in a social system, which constrains behavior. The leader has a role set, in which members have expectations for appropriate behavior and persons make efforts to modify the leader's behavior. Pressures to conform to the expectations of peers, subordinates, and superiors are all relevant in determining actual behavior.

Leaders, even in high-level positions, have unilateral control over fewer resources and fewer policies than might be expected. Investment decisions may require approval of others, while hiring and promotion decisions may be accomplished by committees. Leader behavior is contrained both by the demands of others in the role set and by organizationally prescribed limitations on the sphere of activity and influence.

Many factors that may affect organizational performance are outside a leader's control, even if he or she were to have complete discretion over major areas of organizational decision. For exam-

ple, consider the executive in a construction firm. Costs are largely determined by operation of commodities and labor markets, and demand is largely affected by interest rates, availability of mortgage money, and economic conditions that are affected by governmental policies over which the executive has little control. School superintendents have little control over birth rates and community economic development, both of which profoundly affect school system budgets. While the leader may react to contingencies as they arise, or may be a better or worse forecaster, in accounting for variation in organizational outcomes, he or she may account for relatively little compared to external factors.

The leader's success or failure may also be partly due to circumstances unique to the organization but still outside his or her control. Leader positions in organizations vary in terms of the strength and position of the organization. The choice of a new executive does not fundamentally alter a market and financial position that has developed over years and affects the leader's ability to make strategic changes and the likelihood that the organization will do well or poorly. Organizations have relatively enduring strengths and weaknesses. The choice of a particular leader for a particular position has limited impact on these capabilities.

There is a basic myth associated with leadership. We believe in attribution—when something happens, we believe something has *caused* it. Leaders play that role in organizations. They take the credit for successes and the blame for losses. A more realistic conclusion would probably be that except in times of rapid growth, change, or crisis, leaders don't make much of a difference in an organization's performance.

Much of this argument is based on J. Pfeffer, "The Ambiguity of Leadership," Academy of Management Review, January 1977, pp. 104–11.

FOR DISCUSSION

1. Trace the development of leadership research.
2. Discuss the strengths and weaknesses in the trait approach to leadership.
3. "Behavioral theories of leadership are static." Do you agree or disagree? Discuss.
4. What is the Managerial Grid? Contrast its approach to leadership with the Ohio State and Michigan groups.
5. What are the contingencies in Fiedler's contingency model?
6. Develop an example where you operationalize the Fiedler model.
7. Contrast the situational leadership theory with the Managerial Grid.
8. How do Hersey and Blanchard define *maturity*? Is this contingency variable included in any other contingency theory of leadership?
9. Develop an example where you operationalize path-goal theory.
10. Describe the leader-participation model. Using the model, what is the preferred leadership style for a prison guard? For a surgeon in the operating room? For a high school principal? For the manager of research and development at Eastman Kodak?
11. When might leaders be irrelevant?
12. Which leadership theories, or parts of theories, appear to demonstrate reasonable predictive capability? Can you integrate them into a single synthesized theory?

FOR FURTHER READING

BASS, B. M., *Stogdill's Handbook of Leadership*. New York: Free Press, 1978. Continues to be the definitive resource book on leadership research; contains over five thousand references.

BLAKE, R. R., and J. S. MOUTON, "Theory and Research for Developing a Science of Leadership," *Journal of Applied Behavioral Science,* Vol. 18, no. 3 (1982), pp. 275–91. Reviews the evidence surrounding the controversy that leadership has the leader changing his or her behavior to fit the situation versus another view holding that the leader changes the situation to make it congruous with his or her principles of behavior.

HUNT, J. G., U. SEKARAN, and C. A. SCHRIESHEIM, *Leadership: Beyond Establishment Views*. Carbondale: Southern Illinois University Press, 1982. Contains sixteen chapters on the latest thinking in leadership theory; Volume 6 in an ongoing leadership symposia series.

JAGO, A. G., "Leadership: Perspectives in Theory and Research," *Management Science,* March 1982, pp. 315–36. Contains a concise review and summary of the prominent theories in leadership, organized around a fourfold typology.

MINER, J. B. "The Uncertain Future of the Leadership Concept: Revisions and Clarifications," *Journal of Applied Behavioral Science,* Vol. 18, no. 3 (1982), pp. 293–307. Criticizes the limitations in the paradigm that has governed thinking and research on the leadership concept.

YUKL, G., *Leadership in Organizations.* Englewood Cliffs, N.J.: Prentice-Hall, 1981. Distills, blends, and integrates existing theoretical, conceptual, and research material on leadership.

NOTES FOR CHAPTER 8

1. F. E. Fiedler, "Style or Circumstance: The Leadership Enigma," *Psychology Today,* March 1969, p. 39.
2. V. H. Vroom, "The Search for a Theory of Leadership," in J. W. McGuire (ed.), *Contemporary Management: Issues and Viewpoints* (Englewood Cliffs, N.J.: Prentice-Hall, 1974), p. 396.
3. J. G. Geier, "A Trait Approach to the Study of Leadership in Small Groups," *Journal of Communication,* December 1967, pp. 316–23.
4. R. M. Stogdill, *Handbook of Leadership: A Survey of Theory and Research* (New York: Free Press, 1974).
5. Ibid.
6. See, for instance, D. A. Kenny and S. J. Zaccaro, "An Estimate of Variance due to Traits in Leadership," *Journal of Applied Psychology,* November 1983, pp. 678–85.
7. R. M. Stogdill and A. E. Coons (eds.), *Leader Behavior: Its Description and Measurement,* Research Monograph No. 88 (Columbus: Ohio State University, Bureau of Business Research, 1951). For an updated literature review of the Ohio State research, see S. Kerr, C. A. Schriesheim, C. J. Murphy, and R. M. Stogdill, "Toward a Contingency Theory of Leadership Based upon the Consideration and Initiating Structure Literature," *Organizational Behavior and Human Performance,* August 1974, pp. 62–82.
8. R. Kahn and D. Katz, "Leadership Practices in Relation to Productivity and Morale," D. Cartwright and A. Zander (eds.), *Group Dynamics: Research and Theory,* 2nd ed. (Elmsford, N.Y.: Row, Paterson, 1960.)
9. R. R. Blake and J. S. Mouton, *The Managerial Grid* (Houston: Gulf, 1964).
10. See, for example, R. R. Blake and J. S. Mouton, "A Comparative Analysis of Situationalism and 9,9 Management by Principle," *Organizational Dynamics,* Spring 1982, pp. 20–43.
11. See, for example, L. L. Larson, J. G. Hunt, and R. N. Osborn, "The Great Hi-Hi Leader Behavior Myth: A Lesson from Occam's Razor," *Academy of Management Journal,* December 1976, pp. 628–41; and P. C. Nystrom, "Managers and the Hi-Hi Leader Myth," *Academy of Management Journal,* June 1978, pp. 325–31.
12. See, for example, the three styles—autocratic, participative, and *laissez-faire*—proposed by K. Lewin and R. Lippitt, "An Experimental Approach to the Study of Autocracy and Democracy: A Preliminary Note," *Sociometry,* no. 1 (1938), pp. 292–380; or the more recent 3-D theory proposed by W. J. Reddin, *Managerial Effectiveness* (New York: McGraw-Hill, 1970).

13. J. C. Barrow, "The Variables of Leadership: A Review and Conceptual Framework," *Academy of Management Review*, April 1977, pp. 231–51.
14. R. Tannenbaum and W. H. Schmidt, "How to Choose a Leadership Pattern," *Harvard Business Review*, March–April 1958, pp. 95–101.
15. A. C. Filley, R. J. House, and S. Kerr, *Managerial Process and Organizational Behavior*, 2nd ed. (Glenview, Ill.: Scott, Foresman, 1976), p. 223.
16. W. C. Hamner and D. W. Organ, *Organizational Behavior: An Applied Psychological Approach* (Dallas: Business Publications, 1978), pp. 396–97.
17. F. E. Fiedler, *A Theory of Leadership Effectiveness* (New York: McGraw-Hill, 1967).
18. F. E. Fiedler, M. M. Chemers, and L. Mahar, *Improving Leadership Effectiveness: The Leader Match Concept* (New York: John Wiley, 1977).
19. J. B. Miner, *Theories of Organizational Behavior* (Hinsdale, Ill.: Dryden Press, 1980), pp. 307–9.
20. See E. H. Schein, *Organizational Psychology*, 3rd ed. (Englewood Cliffs, N.J.: Prentice-Hall, 1980), pp. 116–17; and B. Kabanoff, "A Critique of Leader Match and Its Implications for Leadership Research," *Personnel Psychology*, Winter 1981, pp. 749–64.
21. See, for instance, R. W. Rice, "Psychometric Properties of the Esteem for the Least Preferred Coworker (LPC Scale)," *Academy of Management Review*, January 1978, pp. 106–18; and C. A. Schriesheim, B. D. Bannister, and W. H. Money, "Psychometric Properties of the LPC Scale: An Extension of Rice's Review," *Academy of Management Review*, April 1979, pp. 287–90.
22. P. Hersey and K. H. Blanchard, "So You Want to Know Your Leadership Style?" *Training and Development Journal*, February 1974, pp. 1–15; and P. Hersey and K. H. Blanchard, *Management of Organizational Behavior: Utilizing Human Resources*, 4th ed. (Englewood Cliffs, N.J.: Prentice-Hall, 1982) pp. 150–61.
23. Hersey and Blanchard, *Management of Organizational Behavior*, p. 171.
24. P. Hersey and K. H. Blanchard, "Grid Principles and Situationalism: Both! A Response to Blake and Mouton," *Group and Organization Studies*, June 1982, pp. 207–10.
25. See R. K. Hambleton and R. Gumpert, "The Validity of Hersey and Blanchard's Theory of Leader Effectiveness," *Group and Organization Studies*, June 1982, pp. 225–42; and C. L. Graeff, "The Situational Leadership Theory: A Critical View," *Academy of Management Review*, April 1983, pp. 285–91.
26. R. J. House, "A Path-Goal Theory of Leader Effectiveness," *Administrative Science Quarterly*, September 1971, pp. 321–38; and R. J. House and T. R. Mitchell, "Path-Goal Theory of Leadership," *Journal of Contemporary Business*, Autumn 1974, p. 86.
27. House has expanded the original leadership styles to four—directive, supportive, achievement oriented, and participative—but most research continues to use initiating structure and consideration.
28. See, for example, C. A. Schriesheim and M. A. Von Glinow, "The Path-Goal Theory of Leadership: A Theoretical and Empirical Analysis," *Academy of Management Journal*, September 1977, pp. 398–405; C. N. Greene, "Questions of Causation in the Path-Goal Theory of Leadership," *Academy of Management Journal*, March 1979, pp. 22–41; J. F. Schriesheim and C. A. Schriesheim, "A Test of the Path-Goal Theory of Leadership and Some Suggested Directions for Future Research," *Personnel Psychology*, Summer 1980, pp. 349–70; and P. M. Podsakoff, W. D. Todor, and R. S. Schuler, "Leader Expertise as a Moderator of the Effects of Instrumental and

Supportive Leader Behaviors," *Journal of Management,* Vol. 9, no. 2 (1983), pp. 173–85.

29. See, for example, C. A. Schriesheim and A. S. DeNisi, "Task Dimensions as Moderators of the Effects of Instrumental Leadership: A Two-Sample Replicated Test of Path-Goal Leadership Theory,"*Journal of Applied Psychology,* October 1981, pp. 589–97; and J. Fulk and E. R. Wendler,"Dimensionality of Leader-Subordinate Interactions: A Path-Goal Investigation," *Organizational Behavior and Human Performance,* October 1982, pp. 241–64.

30. V. H. Vroom and P. W. Yetton, *Leadership and Decision-Making* (Pittsburgh: University of Pittsburgh Press, 1973).

31. See, for example, V. H. Vroom and A. G. Jago, "On the Validity of the Vroom-Yetton Model," *Journal of Applied Psychology,* April 1978, pp. 151–62; C. Margerison and R. Glube, "Leadership Decision-Making: An Empirical Test of the Vroom and Yetton Model," *Journal of Management Studies,* February 1979, pp. 45–55; and R. H. G. Field, "A Test of the Vroom-Yetton Normative Model of Leadership," *Journal of Applied Psychology,* October 1982, pp. 523–32.

32. S. Kerr and J. M. Jermier, "Substitutes for Leadership: Their Meaning and Measurement," *Organizational Behavior and Human Performance,* December 1978, pp. 375–403; J. P. Howell and P. W. Dorfman, "Substitutes for Leadership: Test of a Construct," *Academy of Management Journal,* December 1981, pp. 714–28; and P. W. Howard and W. F. Joyce, "Substitutes for Leadership: A Statistical Refinement," paper presented at the 42nd Annual Academy of Management Conference, New York, August 1982.

33. B. Karmel, "Leadership: A Challenge to Traditional Research Methods and Assumptions," *Academy of Management Review,* July 1978, pp. 477–79.

34. Schein, *Organizational Psychology,* p. 132.

35. Margerison and Glube, "Leadership Decision-Making."

36. House and Mitchell, "Path-Goal Theory," p. 94.

9

Power
and Politics

AFTER STUDYING THIS CHAPTER, YOU SHOULD BE ABLE TO:

Define and explain the following key terms and concepts:

Coalitions
Coercive power
Dependency
Elasticity of power
Expert power
Illegitimate political behavior
Knowledge power

Legitimate political behavior
Opportunity power
Personal power
Persuasive power
Political behavior
Power
Referent power

Understand:

Four bases of power
Four sources of power
Seven power tactics and their contingencies
How power is achieved
What creates dependency in power relationships
The importance of a political perspective
Those individual and organizational factors that stimulate political
  behavior

You can get much farther with a kind word and a gun than you can with a kind word alone.

—A. CAPONE

*P*ower has been described as the last dirty word. It is easier for most of us to talk about money or even sex than it is to talk about power. People who have it deny it; people who want it, try not to appear to be seeking it; and those who are good at getting it, are secretive about how they got it.[1]

Ten years ago, we knew little about power. That's no longer true. During the past decade, we've gained considerable insights into the topic.[2] We can now make some fairly accurate predictions, for example, about what one should do if he or she wants to have power in a group or organization. In this chapter, we'll demonstrate that the acquisition and distribution of power is a natural process in any group or organization. Power determines the goals to be sought and how resources will be distributed. These, in turn, have important implications for member performance and satisfaction.

A DEFINITION OF POWER

Power refers to a capacity that A has to influence the behavior of B, so that B does something he or she would not otherwise do. This definition implies (1) a *potential* that need not be actualized to be effective, (2) a *dependence* relationship, and (3) the assumption that B has some *discretion* over his or her own behavior. Let's look at each of these points more closely.

Power may exist but not be used. It is, therefore, a capacity or potential. Arthur Fonzarelli, appearing nightly in reruns of "Happy Days," has power. Everyone is afraid of "The Fonz," yet he has never actually had to use his power to get others to comply with his wishes. They respond in fear that he *might* use his physical force. Our point again is that one can have power but not impose it.

Probably the most important aspect of power is that it is a function of dependence. The greater B's dependence on A, the greater is A's power in the relationship. Dependence, in turn, is based on alternatives that B perceives and the importance that B places on the alternative(s) that A controls. A person can have power over you only if he or she controls something you desire. If you want a college degree, have to pass a certain course to get that degree, and your current instructor is the only faculty member in the college that teaches that course, he or she has power over you. Your alternatives are highly limited and you place a high degree of importance on obtaining a passing grade. Similarly, if you're attending college on funds totally provided by your parents, you probably recognize the power that they hold over you. You are dependent on them for financial support. But once you're out of school, have a job, and are making a solid income, your parents' power is reduced significantly. Who among us, though, has not known or heard of the rich relative who is able to control a large number of family members merely through the implicit or explicit threat of ''writing them out of the will''?

For A to get B to do something he or she otherwise would not do means that B must have the discretion to make choices. At the extreme, if B's job behavior is so programmed that he is allowed no room to make choices, he obviously is constrained in his ability to do something other than what he is doing. For instance, job descriptions, group norms, organizational rules and regulations, as well as community laws and standards constrain people's choices. As a nurse, you may be dependent on your supervisor for continued employment. But in spite of this dependence, you're unlikely to comply with her request to perform heart surgery on a patient or steal several thousand dollars from petty cash. Your job description and laws against stealing constrain your ability to make these choices.

FIGURE 9–1

Source: Berke Breathed, *Bloom County: "Loose Tails"* (Boston: Little, Brown, 1983). Copyright © 1983 by The Washington Post Company. By permission of Little, Brown and Company in association with the Atlantic Monthly Press.

CONTRASTING LEADERSHIP AND POWER

A careful comparison of our description of power with our description of leadership in the previous chapter should bring the recognition that the two concepts are closely intertwined. Leaders use power as a means of attaining group goals. Leaders achieve goals, and power is a means of facilitating their achievement.

What differences are there between the two terms? One difference relates to goal compatibility. Power does not require goal compatibility, merely dependence. Leadership, on the other hand, requires some congruence between the goals of the leader and the led. A second difference relates to the direction of influence. Leadership focuses on the downward influence on one's subordinates. It ignores lateral and upward influence patterns. Power does not. Still another difference deals with research emphasis. Leadership research, for the most part, emphasizes style. It seeks answers to such questions as: How supportive should a leader be? How much decision making should be shared with subordinates? In contrast, the research on power has tended to encompass a broader area and focus on tactics for gaining compliance. It has gone beyond the individual as exerciser because power can be used by groups as well as by individuals to control other individuals or groups.

BASES AND SOURCES OF POWER

Where does power come from? What is it that gives an individual or group influence over others? The early answer to these questions was a five-category classification scheme identified by French and Raven.[3] They proposed that there were five bases or sources of power that they termed coercive, reward, expert, legitimate, and referent power. Coercive power depends on fear; reward power derives from the ability to distribute anything of value (typically money, favorable performance appraisals, interesting work assignments, friendly colleagues, and preferred work shifts or sales territories); expert power refers to influence that derives from special skills or knowledge; legitimate power is based on the formal rights one receives as a result of holding an authoritative position or role in an organization; and referent power develops out of others' admiration for one and their desire to model their behavior and attitudes after that person. While French and Raven's classification scheme provided an extensive repertoire of possible bases of power, their categories created ambiguity because they confused bases of power with sources of power.[4] The result was much overlapping. We can improve our understanding of the power concept by separating bases and sources so as to develop clearer and more independent categories.

Bases of power refers to what the powerholder has that gives him or her power. Assuming that you're the powerholder, your bases are what you control that enables you to manipulate the behavior of others. There are four power bases—coercive power, reward power, persuasive power, and knowledge power.[5] We'll expand on each in a moment.

How are sources of power different from bases of power? The answer is that sources tell us where the power holder gets his or her power bases. That is, sources refer to how you come to control the bases of power. There are four sources—the position you hold, your personal characteristics, your expertise, and the opportunity you have to receive and obstruct information.[6] Each of these will also be discussed in a moment.

Let us now consider the four bases of power.

Bases of Power

COERCIVE POWER

The coercive base depends on fear. One reacts to this power out of fear of the negative ramifications that might result if one fails to comply. It rests on the application, or the threat of application, of physical sanctions such as infliction of pain, deformity, or death; the generation of frustration through restriction of movement; or the controlling through force of basic physiological or safety needs.

In the 1930s, when John Dillinger went into a bank, held a gun to the teller's head, and asked for the money, he was incredibly successful at getting compliance with his request. His power base? Coercive. A loaded gun gives its holder power because others are fearful that they will lose something that they hold dear—their lives.

> Of all the bases of power available to man, the power to hurt others is possibly most often used, most often condemned, and most difficult to control . . . the state relies on its military and legal resources to intimidate nations, or even its own citizens. Businesses rely upon the control of economic resources. Schools and universities rely upon their right to deny students formal education, while the church threatens individuals with loss of grace. At the personal level, individuals exercise coercive power through a reliance upon physical strength, verbal facility, or the ability to grant or withhold emotional support from others. These bases provide the individual with the means to physically harm, bully, humiliate, or deny love to others.[7]

At the organization level, A has coercive power over B if A can dismiss, suspend, or demote B, assuming that B values his or her job. Similarly, if A can assign B work activities that B finds upleasant or treat B in a manner that B finds embarrassing, A possesses coercive power over B.

REWARD POWER

The opposite of coercive power is the power to reward. People comply with the wishes of another because it will result in positive benefits; therefore, one who can distribute rewards that others view as valuable will have power over them. Our definition of rewards is here limited to only material rewards. This would include salaries and wages, commissions, fringe benefits, and the like.

PERSUASIVE POWER

Persuasive power rests on the allocation and manipulation of symbolic rewards. If you can decide who is hired, manipulate the mass media, control the allocation of status symbols, or influence a group's norms, you have persuasive power. For instance, when a teacher uses the class climate to control a deviant student, or when a union steward arouses the members to use their informal power to bring a deviant member into line, you are observing the use of persuasive power.

KNOWLEDGE POWER

Knowledge, or access to information, is the final base of power. We can say that when an individual in a group or organization controls unique information, and when that information is needed to make a decision, that individual has knowledge-based power.

To summarize, the bases of power refer to what the powerholder controls that enables him or her to manipulate the behavior of others. The coercive base of power is the control of punishment, the reward base is the control of material rewards, the persuasive base is the control of symbolic rewards, and the knowledge base is the control of information. Table 9–1 offers some common symbols that would suggest a manager has developed strong power bases.

Sources of Power

POSITION POWER

In formal groups and organizations, probably the most frequent access to one or more of the power bases is one's structural position. A teacher's position includes significant control over symbols, a secretary frequently is privy to important information, and the head coach of an NFL team has substantial coercive

TABLE 9–1
Common Symbols of a Manager's Power

To what extent a manager can

- Intercede favorably on behalf of someone in trouble with the organization
- Get a desirable placement for a talented subordinate
- Get approval for expenditures beyond the budget
- Get above-average salary increases for subordinates
- Get items on the agenda at policy meetings
- Get fast access to top decision makers
- Get regular, frequent access to top decision makers
- Get early information about decisions and policy shifts

Source: Reprinted by permission of the *Harvard Business Review*. An exhibit from "Power Failure in Management Circuits," by Rosabeth M. Kanter (July/August 1979). p 67. Copyright © 1979 by the President and Fellows of Harvard College; all rights reserved.

resources at his disposal. All of these bases of power are achieved as a result of the formal position each holds within their structural hierarchy.

PERSONAL POWER

Personality traits were discussed in Chapter 3 and again in the previous chapter on leadership. They reappear within the topic of power when we acknowledge the fact that one's personal characteristics can be a source of power. If you are articulate, domineering, physically imposing, or possessing of that mystical quality called "charisma," you hold personal characteristics that may be used to get others to do what you want.

EXPERT POWER

Expertise is a means by which the powerholder comes to control specialized information (rather than the control itself, which we have discussed as the knowledge base of power). Those who have expertise in terms of specialized information can use it to manipulate others. Expertise is one of the most powerful sources of influence, especially in a technologically oriented society. As jobs become more specialized, we become increasingly dependent on "experts" to achieve goals. So, while it is generally acknowledged that physicians have expertise and hence expert power—when your doctor talks, you listen—you should also recognize that computer specialists, tax accountants, solar engineers, industrial psychologists, and other specialists are able to wield power as a result of their expertise.

OPPORTUNITY POWER

Finally, being in the right place at the right time can give one the opportunity to exert power. One need not hold a formal position in a group or organization to have access to information that is important to others or to be able to exert coercive influence. An example of how one can use an opportunity to create a power base is the story of former U.S. President, Lyndon Johnson, when he was a student at Southwestern Texas State Teachers College. He had a job as special assistant to the college president's personal secretary.

> As special assistant, Johnson's assigned job was simply to carry messages from the president to the department heads and occasionally to other faculty members. Johnson saw that the rather limited function of messenger had possibilities for expansion; for example, encouraging recipients of the messages to transmit their own communications through him. He occupied a desk in the president's outer office, where he took it upon himself to announce the arrival of visitors. These added services evolved from a helpful convenience into an aspect of the normal process of presidential business. The messenger had become an appointments secretary, and, in time, faculty members came to think of Johnson as a funnel to the president. Using a technique which was later to serve him in achieving mastery over the Congress, Johnson turned a rather insubstantial service into a process through which power was exercised.[8]

Johnson eventually broadened his informal duties to include handling the president's political correspondence, preparing his reports for state agencies, and even regularly accompanying the college president on his trips to the state capi-

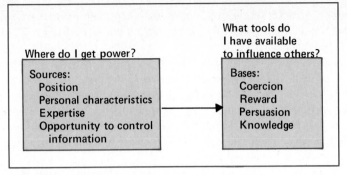

FIGURE 9–2

Sources and Bases of Power

tal—the president eventually relying on his young apprentice for political counsel. Certainly this represents an example of someone using an opportunity to redefine his job and to give himself power.

Summary

The foundation to understanding power begins by identifying where power comes from (sources) and, given that one has the means to exert influence, what it is that one manipulates (bases). Figure 9–2 visually depicts the relationship between sources and bases. Sources are the means. Individuals can use their position in the structure, rely on personal characteristics, develop expertise, or take advantage of opportunities to control information. Control of one or more of these sources allows the powerholder to manipulate the behavior of others via coercion, reward, persuasion, or knowledge bases. To reiterate, sources are *where* you get power. Bases are *what* you manipulate. Those who seek power must develop a source of power. Then, and only then, can they acquire a power base.

DEPENDENCY: THE KEY TO POWER

Earlier in this chapter it was said that probably the most important aspect of power is that it is a function of dependence. In this section, we'll show how an understanding of dependency is central to furthering your understanding of power itself.

The General Dependency Postulate

Let's begin with a general postulate: *The greater B's dependency on A, the greater power A has over B*. When you possess anything that others require but that you alone control, you make them dependent upon you and, therefore, you gain power over them.[9] Dependency, then, is inversely proportional to the alternative sources of supply. If something is plentiful, possession of it will not increase your power. If everyone is intelligent, intelligence gives no special advantage. Similarly, among the superrich, money is no longer power. But as the old saying goes, "in the land of the blind, the one-eyed man is king!" If you can create a monopoly by controlling information, prestige, or anything that others crave, they become dependent on you. Conversely, the more that you can expand your options, the less power you place in the hands of others. This explains, for example, why most organizations develop multiple suppliers rather than give their business to only one. It also explains why so many of us aspire to financial independence. Financial independence reduces the power that others can have over us.

An example of the role that dependency plays in a work group or an organization is the case of Mike Milken, the thirty-year-old head of the corporate bond department at a major New York City brokerage firm.[10] A native Californian, Milken grew disenchanted with New York and decided to return to southern California and a warmer climate. But Milken made so much money for his employer that the firm was not about to let him go. The solution: Rather than lose his trading skills to some competitor with West Coast connections, the company agreed to move its entire bond department to California. Milken and the staff of twenty people working for him were all moved to Los Angeles. The cost of setting up this office, moving employees and their families, and absorbing housing subsidies was all part of the price Mike Milken's employer was willing to pay to keep his skills.

Another example took place in professional basketball during the fall of 1981. Earvin "Magic" Johnson, the then twenty-two-year-old superstar on the Los Angeles Laker team, chose one Wednesday evening to blast his coach's system. He told the press that he could not continue to play under his coach, Paul Westhead, and demanded to be traded. Within twenty-four hours, the Lakers' owner fired Westhead.

Westhead's record was not in question. He had led the Lakers to the NBA championship during the 1979–80 season. At the time of his firing, the team was only half-a-game behind its conference leader with a 7–4 win-loss record. The issue really was: Who was dispensable? In the summer of 1981, Johnson had signed a twenty-five-year, $25 million contract with the Laker organization. Westhead, on the other hand, was operating under a far less lucrative four-year pact. Johnson was a major asset to the Laker team and his twenty-five-year contract made it almost impossible for him to be traded. No other team was willing to assume such a contractual obligation. The Laker owner had little choice but to fire the coach. Regardless of the fact that a professional coach is the formal "boss" over his team's members, this example dramatizes that a player or any employee (who has no legitimate position power) can still be extremely influential if the "team's" options are severely restricted.

What Creates Dependency?

Dependency is increased when the resource you control is *important, scarce,* and *nonsubstitutable.*[11]

IMPORTANCE

If nobody wants what you've got, it's not going to create dependency. To create dependency, therefore, the thing(s) you control must be perceived as being important. It's been found, for instance, that organizations actively seek to avoid uncertainty.[12] We should, therefore, expect that those individuals or groups who can absorb an organization's uncertainty will be perceived as controlling an important resource. For instance, a study of industrial organizations found that the marketing departments in these firms were consistently rated as the most powerful.[13] It was concluded by the researcher that the most critical uncertainty facing these firms was selling their products. This might suggest that during a labor strike, the organization's negotiating representatives have increased power or that engineers, as a group, would be more powerful at Apple Computers than at Procter & Gamble. These inferences appear to be generally valid. Labor negotiators do become more powerful within the personnel area and the organization as a whole during periods of labor strife. An organization such as Apple Computers, which is heavily technologically oriented, is highly dependent on its engineers to maintain its product quality. And, at Apple, engineers are clearly the most powerful group. At Procter & Gamble, marketing is the name of the game, and marketers are the most powerful occupational group. These examples support not only the view that the ability to reduce uncertainty increases a group's importance and, hence, its power but also that what's important is situational. It varies between organizations and undoubtedly also varies over time within any given organization.

SCARCITY

As noted previously, if something is plentiful, possession of it will not increase your power. A resource needs to be perceived as scarce to create dependency.

This can help to explain how low-ranking members in an organization, who have important knowledge not available to high-ranking members, gain power over the high-ranking members. Possession of a scarce resource—in this case, important knowledge—makes the high-ranking member dependent on the low-ranking member. This also helps to make sense out of behaviors of low-ranking members that, otherwise, might seem illogical, such as destroying the procedure manuals that describe how a job is done, refusing to train people in their job or even to show others exactly what they do, creating specialized language and terminology that inhibits others from understanding their jobs, or operating in secrecy so the activity will appear more complex and difficult than it really is.

The scarcity-dependency relationship can further be seen in the power of occupational categories. Individuals in occupations in which the supply of personnel is low relative to demand can negotiate compensation and benefit packages far more attractive than can those in occupations where there is an abundance of candidates. College administrators have no problem today finding English instructors. The market for business teachers, in contrast, is extremely tight—with demand high and the supply limited. The result is that the bargaining power of business faculty allows them to negotiate higher salaries, lighter teaching loads, and other benefits. Similarly, petroleum engineers were able to negotiate incredibly attractive deals with employers in the late 1970s. But by 1982, when the demand for oil dropped and exploration projects were shelved, those same petroleum engineers found their bargaining power greatly reduced. There is nothing inherently magic about the skills of a petroleum engineer that allowed new college graduates in the field to earn 30 percent more than other engineering graduates in 1979—scarcity had temporarily created dependency, which, in turn, increased the bargaining power of petroleum engineers.

NONSUBSTITUTABILITY

The more that a resource has no viable substitutes, the more power that control over that resource provides. This is illustrated in a concept we'll call the "elasticity of power."

In economics, considerable attention is focused on the elasticity of demand, which is defined as the relative responsiveness of quantity demanded to change in price. This concept can be modified to explain the strength of power.

Elasticity of power is defined as the relative responsiveness of power to change in available alternatives. One's ability to influence others is viewed as being dependent on how these others perceive their alternatives.

As shown in Figure 9–3, assume that there are two individuals. Mr. A's power elasticity curve is relatively inelastic. This would describe, for example, an employee who believed that he had a large number of employment opportunities outside his current organization. Fear of being fired would have only a moderate

FIGURE 9–3
Elasticity of Power

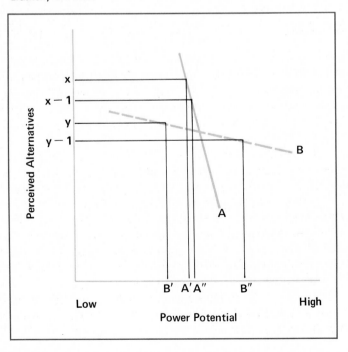

impact on Mr. A., for he perceives that he has a number of other alternatives. Mr. A's boss finds that threatening A with termination has only a minimal impact on influencing A's behavior. A reduction in alternatives (from X to $X-1$) only increases the power of A's boss slightly (A' to A''). However, Mr. B's curve is relatively elastic. He sees few other job opportunities. His age, education, present salary, or lack of contacts may severely limit his ability to find a job somewhere else. As a result, Mr. B is dependent on his present organization and boss. If B loses his job (Y to $Y-1$), he may face prolonged unemployment, and it shows itself in the increased power of B's boss. As long as B perceives his options as limited and B's boss holds the power to terminate his employment, B's boss will hold considerable power over him. In such a situation, it is obviously important for B to get his boss to believe that his options are considerably greater than they really are. If this is not achieved, B places his fate in the hands of his boss and makes him captive to almost any demands the boss devises.

Higher education provides an excellent example of how this elasticity concept operates. In universities where there are strong pressures for the faculty to publish, we can say that a department head's power over a faculty member is inversely related to that member's publication record. The more recognition the faculty member receives through publication, the more mobile he or she is. That is, since other universities want faculty who are highly published and visible, there is an increased demand for his or her services. Although the concept of tenure can act to alter this relationship by restricting the department head's alternatives, those faculty members with little or no publications have the least mobility and are subject to the greatest influence from their superiors.

POWER TACTICS

This section is a logical extension of our previous discussions. We've reviewed *where* power comes from and *what* it is that powerholders manipulate. Now, we go the final step—to power tactics. Tactics tell us *how* to manipulate the bases. The following discussion will show you how employees translate their power bases into specific actions.

One of the few elements of power that has gone beyond anecdotal evidence or armchair speculation is the topic of tactics. Recent research indicates that there are standardized ways by which powerholders attempt to get what they want.[14]

When 165 managers were asked to write essays describing an incident in which they influenced their bosses, co-workers, or subordinates, a total of 370 power tactics grouped into 14 categories were identified. These answers were condensed, rewritten into a 58-item questionnaire, and given to over 750 employees. These respondents were not only asked how they went about influencing others at work but also the possible reasons for influencing the target person. The results, which are summarized here, give us considerable insight into power tactics—how managerial employees influence others and the conditions under which one tactic is chosen over another.[15]

The findings identified seven tactical dimensions or strategies:

Reason—use of facts and data to make a logical or rational presentation of ideas

Friendliness—use of flattery, creation of goodwill, acting humble, and being friendly prior to making a request

Coalition—getting the support of other people in the organization to back up the request

Bargaining—use of negotiation through the exchange of benefits or favors

Assertiveness—use of a direct and forceful approach such as demanding compliance with requests, repeated reminders, ordering individuals to do what is asked, and pointing out that rules require compliance

Higher authority—gaining the support of higher levels in the organization to back up requests

Sanctions—use of organizationally derived rewards and punishments such as preventing or promising a salary increase, threatening to give an unsatisfactory performance evaluation, or withholding a promotion

The researchers found that employees do not rely on the seven tactics equally. However, as shown in Table 9–2, the most popular strategy was the use of reason, regardless of whether the influence was directed upward or downward. Additionally, the researchers uncovered four contingency variables that affect the selection of a power tactic: the manager's relative power, the manager's objectives for wanting to influence, the manager's expectation of the target person's willingness to comply, and the organization's culture.

A manager's relative power impacts the selection of tactics in two ways. First, managers who control resources that are valued by others, or who are perceived to be in positions of dominance, use a greater variety of tactics than do those with less power. Second, managers with power use assertiveness with

TABLE 9–2
Usage of Power Tactics: From Most to Least Popular

	WHEN MANAGERS INFLUENCED SUPERIORS*	WHEN MANAGERS INFLUENCED SUBORDINATES
Most Popular	Reason	Reason
	Coalition	Assertiveness
	Friendliness	Friendliness
	Bargaining	Coalition
	Assertiveness	Bargaining
Least Popular	Higher authority	Higher authority
		Sanctions

*Sanctions is omitted in the scale that measures upward influence.

Source: Reprinted, by permission of the publisher from "Patterns of Managerial Influence: Shotgun Managers, Tacticians, and Bystanders," by D. Kipnis et al. *Organizational Dynamics,* Winter 1984, p. 62. © 1984 Periodicals Division, American Management Associations, New York. All rights reserved.

greater frequency than do those with less power. Initially, we can expect that most managers will attempt to use simple requests and reason. Assertiveness is a backup strategy, used when the target of influence refuses or appears reluctant to comply with the request. Resistance leads to managers using more directive strategies. Typically, they shift from using simple requests to insisting that their demands be met. But the manager with relatively little power is more likely to stop trying to influence others when they encounter resistance. Why? Because they perceive the costs associated with assertiveness as unacceptable.

Managers vary their power tactics in relation to their objectives. When managers seek benefits from a superior, they tend to rely on kind words and the promotion of pleasant relationships; that is, they use friendliness. In comparison, managers attempting to persuade their superiors to accept new ideas usually rely on reason. This matching of tactics to objectives also holds true for downward influence. For example, managers use reason to sell ideas to subordinates and friendliness to obtain favors.

The manager's expectations of success guides his or her choice of tactics. When past experience indicates a high probability of success, managers use simple requests to gain compliance. Where success is less predictable, managers are more tempted to use assertiveness and sanctions to achieve their objectives.

Finally, we know that cultures within organizations differ markedly—for example, some are warm, relaxed, and supportive; others are formal and conservative. The organizational culture in which a manager works, therefore, will have a significant bearing on defining which tactics are considered appropriate. Some cultures encourage the use of friendliness, some encourage reason, and still others rely on sanctions and assertiveness. So the organization itself will influence which subset of power tactics is viewed as acceptable for use by managers.

POWER IN GROUPS: COALITIONS

Those "out of power" and seeking to be "in" will first try to increase their power individually. Why spread the spoils if one doesn't have to? But if this proves ineffective, the alternative is to form a coalition. There is strength in numbers.

The natural way to gain influence is to become a powerholder. Therefore, those who want power will attempt to build a personal power base. But, in many instances, this may be difficult, risky, costly, or impossible. In such cases, efforts will be made to form a coalition of two or more "outs" who, by joining together, can combine their resources to increase rewards for themselves.[16]

In the late 1960s, college students found that by joining together to form a "student power group," they could achieve ends that had been impossible individually. Historically, employees in organizations who were unsuccessful in bargaining on their own behalf with management resorted to labor unions to bargain for them. In recent years, even some managers have joined unions after finding it difficult to exert power individually to attain higher wages and greater job security.

What predictions can we make about coalition formation?[17] First, coalitions in organizations often seek to maximize their size. In political science theory, coalitions move the other way—they try to minimize their size. They tend to be just large enough to exert the power necessary to achieve their objectives. But legislatures are different from organizations. Specifically, decision making in organizations does not end with merely selection from among a set of alternatives. The decision must also be implemented. In organizations, the implementation of and commitment to the decision is at least as important as the decision itself. It's necessary, therefore, for coalitions in organizations to seek a broad constituency to support the coalition's objectives. This means expanding the coalition to encompass as many interests as possible. This coalition expansion to facilitate consensus building, of course, is more likely to occur in organizational cultures where cooperation, commitment, and shared decision making are highly valued. In autocratic and hierarchically controlled organizations, this search for maximizing the coalition's size is less likely to be sought.

Another prediction about coalitions relates to the degree of interdependence within the organization. More coalitions will likely be created where there is a great deal of task and resource interdependence. In contrast, there will be less interdependence among subunits and less coalition formation activity where subunits are largely self-contained or resources are abundant.

Finally, coalition formation will be influenced by the actual tasks that workers do. The more routine the task of a group, the greater the likelihood that coalitions will form. The more that the work that people do is routine, the greater their substitutability for each other and, thus, the greater their dependence. To offset this dependence, they can be expected to resort to a coalition. We see, therefore, that unions appeal more to low-skill and nonprofessional workers than to skilled and professional types. Of course, where the supply of skilled and professional employees is high relative to their demand or where organizations have standardized traditionally unique jobs, we would expect even these incumbents to find unionization attractive.

POLITICS: POWER IN ACTION

When people get together in groups, power will be exerted. People want to carve out a niche from which to exert influence, to earn awards, and to advance their careers.[18] When employees in organizations convert their power into action, we describe them as engaged in politics. Those with good political skills have the ability to use their bases of power effectively.[19]

Definition

There have been no shortages of definitions for organizational politics. Essentially, however, they have focused on the use of power to affect decision making in the organization or on behaviors by members that are self-serving and organizationally nonsanctioned.[20] For our purposes, we shall define political behavior in organizations as *those activities that are not required as part of one's formal role in the organization, but that influence, or attempt to influence, the distribution of advantages and disadvantages within the organization.*[21]

This definition encompasses key elements from what most people mean when they talk about organizational politics. Political behavior is *outside* one's specified job requirements. The behavior requires some attempt to use one's *power* bases. Additionally, our definition encompasses efforts to influence the goals, criteria, or processes used for *decision making* when we state that politics is concerned with "the distribution of advantages and disadvantages within the organization." Our definition is broad enough to include such varied political behaviors as withholding key information from decision makers, whistleblowing, filing of grievances, spreading rumors, leaking confidential information about organizational activities to the media, exchanging favors with others in the organization for mutual benefit, or lobbying on behalf of or against a particular individual or decision alternative.

A final comment relates to what has been referred to as the "legitimate-illegitimate" dimension in political behavior.[22] Legitimate political behavior refers to normal everyday politics—complaining to your supervisor, bypassing the chain of command, forming coalitions, obstructing organizational policies or decisions through inaction or excessive adherence to rules, and developing contacts outside the organization through one's professional activities. On the other hand, there are also illegitimate or extreme political behaviors that violate the implied"rules of the game." Those who pursue such activities are often described as individuals who "play hardball." Illegitimate actitvities include sabotage, whistleblowing, and symbolic protests such as unorthodox dress, wearing protest buttons, or groups of employees cumulatively calling in sick.

The vast majority of all organizational political actions are of the legitimate variety. The reasons are pragmatic: the extreme illegitimate forms of political behavior pose a very real risk of loss of organizational membership or extreme sanctions against those who use them and then fall short in having enough power to insure they work.

The Importance of a Political Perspective

Those who fail to acknowledge political behavior ignore the reality that organizations are political systems. It would be nice if all organizations or formal groups within organizations could be described in such terms as supportive, harmonious, trusting, collaborative, or cooperative. A nonpolitical perspective can lead one to believe that employees will always behave in ways consistent with the interests of the organization. In contrast, a political view can explain much of, what may seem to be, irrational behavior in organizations. It can help to explain, for instance, why employees withhold information, restrict output, attempt to "build empires," publicize their successes, hide their failures, distort performance figures to make themselves look better, and engage in similar activities that appear to be at odds with the organization's desire for effectiveness and efficiency.

Factors Contributing to Political Behavior

Recent research and observation has identified a number of factors that appear to be associated with political behavior. Some are individual characteristics, derived from the unique qualities of the people that the organization employs; others are a result of the organization's culture or internal environment.

INDIVIDUAL FACTORS

At the individual level, researchers have identified certain personality characteristics, needs, and other individual factors that are likely to be related to political behavior. Employees who are authoritarian, have a high-risking propensity, or possess an external locus of control have been shown to act politically with less regard for the consequences to the organization.[23] A high need for power, autonomy, security, or status has also been found to be a major contributor to an employee's tendency to engage in political behavior.[24]

Additionally, an individual's investment in the organization, perceived alternatives, and expectations of success will influence the degree to which he or she will pursue illegitimate means of political action.[25] The more that a person has invested in the organization in terms of expectations of increased future benefits, the more a person has to lose if forced out and the less likely he or she is to use illegitimate means. The more alternative job opportunities an individual has—due to a favorable job market, scarce skills or knowledge, prominent reputation, or influential contacts outside the organization—the more likely he or she is to risk illegitimate political actions. Last, if an individual places a low expectation of success in using illegitimate means, it is unlikely that he or she will attempt them. Conversely, high expectations of success—and use of illegitimate means—are most likely to be the province of experienced and powerful individuals with polished political skills and inexperienced and naive employees who misjudge their probabilities of success.

ORGANIZATIONAL FACTORS

Political activity is probably more a function of the organization's culture than of individual difference variables. Why? Because most organizations have a large number of employees with the characteristics we listed, yet the presence of political behavior varies widely.

While we acknowledge the role that individual differences can play in fostering politicking, the evidence more strongly supports that certian cultures promote politics. Cultures characterized by low trust, role ambiguity, unclear performance evaluation systems, zero-sum reward allocation practices, and democratic decision making will create opportunities for political activities to nurture.[26]

The less trust there is within the organization, the higher the level of political behavior and the more likely that the political behavior will be of the illegitimate kind. So high trust should suppress the level of political behavior in general and inhibit illegitimate actions in particular.

Role ambiguity means that the prescribed behaviors of the employee are not clear. There are fewer limits, therefore, to the scope and functions of the employee's political actions. Since political activities are defined as those not required as part of one's formal role, the greater the role ambiguity, the more one can engage in political activity with little chance of it being visible.

The practice of performance evaluation is far from a perfected science. The more that organizations use subjective criteria in the appraisal, emphasize a single outcome measure, or allow significant time to pass between the time of an action and its appraisal, the greater the likelihood that an employee can get away with politicking. Subjective performance criteria create ambiguity. The use of a single outcome measure encourages indivdiuals to do whatever is necessary to "look good" on that measure, but often at the expense of performing well on other important parts of the job that are being appraised. The amount of time that elapses between an action and its appraisal is also a relevant factor. The longer the time period, the more unlikely that the employee will be held accountable for his or her political behaviors.

The more that an organization's culture emphasizes the zero-sum or win-lose approach to reward allocations, the more employees will be motivated to engage in politicking. The zero-sum approach treats the reward "pie" as fixed so that any gain one person or group achieves has to come at the expense of another person or group. If I win, you must lose! If $10,000 in annual raises is to be distributed among five employees, then any employee who gets more than $2,000 takes money away from one or more of the others. Such a practice encourages making others look bad and increasing the visibility of what you do.

In the last twenty-five years there has been a general move in North America toward making organizations less autocratic. While much of this trend has been more in theory than in practice, it is undoubtedly true that in many organizations, managers are being asked to behave more democratically. Managers are told that they should allow subordinates to advise them on decisions and that they should rely to a greater extent on group input into the decision process. Such moves toward democracy, however, are not necessarily desired by individual managers. Many managers sought their positions in order to have legitimate power so as to be able to make unilateral decisions. They fought hard and often paid high personal costs to achieve their influential positions. Sharing their power with others runs directly against their desires. The result is that managers may use the required committees, conferences, and group meetings in a superficial way—as arenas for maneuvering and manipulating.

IMPLICATIONS FOR PERFORMANCE AND SATISFACTION

Knowledge-based power is the most strongly and consistently related to effective performance. For example, in a study of five organizations, knowledge was the most effective base for getting others to perform as desired.[27] Competence appears to offer wide appeal, and its use as a power base results in high performance by group members.

In contrast, position power does *not* appear to be related to performance differences. In spite of position being the most widely given reason for complying with a superior's wishes, it does not seem to lead to higher performance, though the findings are far from conclusive. Among blue-collar workers, one researcher found significantly positive relations between position power and four of six production measures. However, position power was not related with average earnings or performance against schedule.[28] Another study could find no relationship between the use of position power and high efficiency ratings.[29] One's position is effective for exacting compliance, but there is little evidence to suggest that it leads to higher levels of performance. This may be explained by the fact that position power tends to be fairly constant, especially within a given organization.

The use of reward and coercive power has a significant inverse relationship to performance. People hold a negative view of reward and coercion as reasons for complying with a superior's requests. This view is reflected in the finding that these bases are associated with lower performance.[30] Further, research finds the use of coercive power to be negatively related to group effectiveness.[31]

We find that knowledge power is also strongly and consistently related to satisfaction. The evidence overwhelmingly indicates that this base is most satisfying to subjects of the power.[32] Knowledge-based power obtains both public and private compliance and avoids the problem of making subjects comply merely because the powerholder has the "right" to request compliance. Additionally, our value system is built on the idea of merit and competence, and knowledge power appears to align most closely with these values. If individuals find knowledge power to be most compatible with American values, it should logically give the greatest satisfaction.

Finally, the use of coercive power is inversely related to individual satisfaction. Coercion not only creates resistance, it is generally disliked by individuals. Studies of college teachers and sales personnel found coercion the least preferred power base.[33] A study of insurance company employees also drew the same conclusion.[34]

POINT

SUCCESSFUL MANAGERS ARE POWER ORIENTED

What makes or motivates a good manager? This question is so enormous in scope that anyone trying to answer it has difficulty knowing where to begin. Some people might say that a good manager is one who is successful, and by now, most business researchers and business executives themselves know what motivates people who successfully run their own small businesses. The key to their success has turned out to be what psychologists call "the need for achievement," the desire to do something better or more efficiently than it has been done before.

But what does achievement motivation have to do with good management? There is no reason on theoretical grounds why a person who has a strong need to be more efficient should make a good manager. Rather, the manager's job seems to call more for someone who can influence people than for someone who does things better on his or her own. In motivational terms, then, we might expect the successful manager to have a greater "need for power" than a need to achieve.

To measure the motivations of managers, good and bad, we studied a number of individual managers from different U.S. corporations who were participating in management workshops designed to improve their managerial effectiveness. The general conclusion of these studies is that the top manager of a company must possess a high need for power, that is, a concern for influencing people. However, this need must be disciplined and controlled so that it is directed toward the benefit of the institution as a whole and not toward the manager's personal aggrandizement. Moreover, the top manager's need for power ought to be greater than his or her need for being liked by people.

In examining the motive scores of over fifty managers of both high- and low- morale units in all sections of the same large company, we found that most of the managers—over 70 percent—were high in power motivation compared with employees in general. This finding confirms the fact that power motivation is important for management. (Remember that as we use the term "power motivation," it refers not to dictatorial behavior, but to a desire to have impact, to be strong and influential.) The better managers, as judged by the morale of those working for them, tended to score even higher in power motivation. But the most important determining factor of high morale turned out not to be how their power motivation compared to their need to achieve but whether it was higher than their need to be liked. This relationship existed for 80 percent of the better sales managers as compared with only 10 percent of the poorer managers. And the same held true for other managers in nearly all parts of the company.

In summary, the good manager in a large company does not have a high need for achievement, as we define and measure that motive, although there must be plenty of that motive somewhere in the organization. The top managers shown here have a high need for power and an interest in influencing others, both greater than their interest in being liked by people. The manager's concern for power should be socialized—controlled so that the institution as a whole, not only the individual, benefits. People and nations with this motive profile are empire builders; they tend to create high morale and to expand the organizations they head.

Adapted by permission of the Harvard Business Review. *Excerpted from "Power Is the Great Motivator" by D. C. McClelland and D. H. Burnham* (Harvard Business Review, *March–April 1976).* *Copyright© 1976 by the President and Fellows of Harvard College; all rights reserved.*

COUNTERPOINT

THE CASE FOR THE RELATIONAL MANAGER

Data from contemporary research indicate that people who now get to the top in management are strongly power motivated. They do not typically show strong needs for affiliation—for close, cozy groups. But the organizational world is not fixed; it is slowly changing. So it seems quite possible that researchers will "discover" some years from now that successful managers are more relational than they had believed and less competitive or power oriented.

Some relevant questions we have been worrying about include these:

Do competitive, power-driven people now succeed because of the inherent nature of organized work or because that's the way we set up our organizations in the old days and changing now is very painful?

Does the direct, competitive, power image of the executive at least partly reflect the rigid old organization's effort to attract people like itself from the shrinking population of young people who still share those standards?

Let us elaborate on the assertion that times are indeed changing in a direction calling for more *relational* managerial styles.

Consider the following findings and current trends:

1. Despite the widespread macho mythology about competitiveness in the executive suite, research points out that competitiveness does not seem to be the key to success. Other, more "intrinsic" styles called "work" (preference for getting on with the work) and "mastery" (an interest in mastering skills and the like) seem to play a far bigger role.

2. Young people are shifting their values and interests (not radically, but incrementally) away from careers as their central life focus and toward a concern about general "life-style."

3. The hunger for warm, affectionate relationships appears to be growing in the United States. Many of the traditional institutions that provided people with a sense of membership and community have been declining. And faith in them has been declining more rapidly.

4. Firms using strongly relational styles often are successful in the United States. Recent studies of American companies, derived from earlier observations of Japanese organizations, suggest the advantages, including the cost-effectiveness, of a relational milieu.

5. Women are moving into management. Organizations now have access to a large number of people in our society who traditionally have been trained to a very high level of relational orientation and skill.

6. More and more, the tasks of contemporary organizations (particularly in high-technology industries) require teamwork. Buying collections of individual stars does not necessarily produce great team performance unless those stars can be bonded together with some strong relational glue.

Taken together, these forces seem to dictate a prescription for incremental, modest, but real shifts toward more relational strategies.

Adapted by permission of the publisher, from "A Case for the Relational Manager" by H. J. Leavitt and J. Lipman-Blumen, Organizational Dynamics, *Summer 1980 © 1980 by AMACOM, a division of American Management Associations, pp. 27–32. All rights reserved.*

FOR DISCUSSION

1. What is power? How is it different from leadership?
2. Contrast French and Raven's power classification to the bases and sources presented in this chapter.
3. What is the difference between a source of power and a base of power?
4. Contrast power tactics with power bases and sources. What are some of the key contingency variables that determine which tactic a powerholder is likely to use?
5. "Knowledge power and expert power are the same thing." Do you agree or disagree? Discuss.
6. What is a coalition? When is it likely to develop?
7. Based on the information presented in this chapter, what would you do as a new college graduate entering a new job to maximize your power and accelerate your career progress?
8. How are power and politics related?
9. "More powerful managers are good for an organization. It is the powerless, not the powerful, that are the ineffective managers." Do you agree or disagree with this statement? Discuss.
10. Define political behavior. Differentiate between legitimate and illegitimate political actions.
11. "Politicking in organizations is bad." Do you agree or disagree with this this statement? Discuss.
12. What factors contribute to political activity?

FOR FURTHER READING

CHRISTIE, R., and F. GEIS, *Studies in Machiavellianism*. New York: Academic Press, 1970. Undertakes in a scholarly fashion to define and measure Machiavellianism. Reports that high Machs manipulate more, win more, are persuaded less, and persuade others more.

GANDZ, J., and V. V. MURRAY, "The Experience of Workplace Politics," *Academy of Management Journal*, June 1980, pp. 237–51. Reports from recent graduates of a business school on the impact that politics has in their organizations.

KOTTER, J. P., "Power, Dependence, and Effective Management," *Harvard Business Review*, July–August 1977, pp. 125–36. Describes common characteristics of managers who have been successful at acquiring considerable power and using it to manage their dependence on others.

PETTIGREW, A. M., *The Politics of Organizational Decision-Making*. London: Tavistock, 1973. Reports in detail on the power and political factors involved in a computer equipment decision by a large British firm.

SCHEIN, V. E., "Individual Power and Political Behaviors in Organizations: An Inadequately Explored Reality," *Academy of Management Review,* January 1977, pp. 64–72. Looks at the bases of power and the intent and means of the powerholder to provide a starting point for research on political behaviors in organizations.

WRONG, D., *Power: Its Forms, Bases, and Uses.* New York: Harper & Row, 1979. Synthesizes the sociological and political perspectives toward power.

NOTES FOR CHAPTER 9

1. R. M. Kanter, "Power Failure in Management Circuits," *Harvard Business Review,* July–August 1979, p. 65.
2. See, for example, D. Kipnis, *The Powerholders* (Chicago: University of Chicago Press, 1976); S. B. Bacharach and E. J. Lawler, *Power and Politics in Organizations* (San Francisco: Jossey-Bass, 1980); J. Pfeffer, *Power in Organizations* (Mansfield, Mass.: Pitman, 1981); and H. Mintzberg, *Power In and Around Organizations* (Englewood Cliffs, N.J.: Prentice-Hall, 1983).
3. J. R. P. French, Jr., and B. Raven, "The Bases of Social Power,"in D. Cartwright (ed.), *Studies in Social Power* (Ann Arbor: University of Michigan, Institute for Social Research, 1959), pp.150–67.
4. Bachrach and Lawler, *Power and Politics,* pp. 34–36.
5. Adapted from Ibid., and A. Etzioni, *Comparative Analysis of Complex Organizations* (New York: Free Press, 1961).
6. Bachrach and Lawler, *Power and Politics,* pp. 34–36.
7. Kipnis, *Powerholders,* pp. 77–78.
8. D. Kearns, "Lyndon Johnson and the American Dream," *The Atlantic Monthly,* May 1976, p. 41.
9. R. E. Emerson, "Power-Dependence Relations,"*American Sociological Review,* Vol. 27 (1962), pp. 31–41.
10. S. Johnson, "Mohammed and the Mountain," *The New York Times,* January 29, 1978, p. F5.
11. Mintzberg, *Power In and Around Organizations,* p. 24.
12. R. M. Cyert and J. G. March, *A Behavioral Theory of the Firm* (Englewood Cliffs, N.J.: Prentice-Hall, 1963).
13. C. Perrow, "Departmental Power and Perspective in Industrial Firms," in M. N. Zald (ed.), *Power in Organizations* (Nashville, Tenn.: Vanderbilt University Press, 1970).
14. See, D. Kipnis, S. M. Schmidt, and I. Wilkinson, "Intraorganizational Influence Tactics: Explorations in Getting One's Way," *Journal of Applied Psychology,* August 1980, pp. 440–52; W. K. Schilit and E. A. Locke, "A Study of Upward Influence in Organizations," *Administrative Science Quarterly,* June 1982, pp. 304–16; and D. Kipnis, S. M. Schmidt, C. Swaffin-Smith, and I. Wilkinson, "Patterns of Managerial Influence: Shotgun Managers, Tacticians, and Bystanders," *Organizational Dynamics,* Winter 1984, pp. 58–67.
15. This section is adapted from Kipnis, Schmidt, Swaffin-Smith, and Wilkinson, "Patterns of Managerial Influence."
16. P. P. Poole, "Coalitions: The Web of Power," in D. J. Vredenburgh and R. S. Schuler (eds.), *Effective Management: Research and Application,* Proceedings of the 20th Annual Eastern Academy of Management, Pittsburgh, May 1983, pp. 79–82.

17. See Pfeffer, *Power in Organizations*, pp. 155–57.
18. S. A. Culbert and J. J. McDonough, *The Invisible War: Pursuing Self-interest at Work* (New York: John Wiley, 1980), p. 6.
19. Mintzberg, *Power In and Around Organizations*, p. 26
20. D. J. Vredenburgh and J. G. Maurer, "A Process Framework of Organizational Politics," *Human Relations*, January 1984, pp. 47–66.
21. D. Farrell and J. C. Petersen, "Patterns of Political Behavior in Organizations," *Academy of Management Review*, July 1982, p. 405.
22. Ibid., pp. 406–07.
23. See, for example, B. T. Mayes and R. W. Allen, "Toward a Definition of Organizational Politics," *Academy of Management Review*, October 1977, pp. 672–78; D. J. Moberg, "Factors Which Determine the Perception and Use of Organizational Politics," paper presented at the 38th Annual Academy of Management Conference, San Francisco, 1978; and L. W. Porter, R. W. Allen, and H. L. Angle, "The Politics of Upward Influence in Organizations," in L. L. Cummings and B. M. Staw (eds.), *Research in Organizational Behavior*, Vol. 3 (Greenwich, Conn.: JAI Press, 1981), pp. 121–22.
24. See, for example, J. E. Haas and T. E. Drabek, *Complex Organizations: A Sociological Perspective* (New York: Macmillan, 1973); R. T. Mowday, "The Exercise of Upward Influence in Organizations," *Administrative Science Quarterly*, March 1978, pp. 137–56; and D. L. Madison, R. W. Allen, L. W. Porter, P. A. Renwick, and B. T. Mayes, "Organizational Politics: An Exploration of Manager's Perceptions," *Human Relations*, February 1980, pp. 79–100.
25. Farrell and Petersen, "Patterns of Political Behavior," p. 408.
26. See, for example, Madison et al., "Organizational Politics"; Porter et al., "The Politics of Upward Influence in Organizations," pp. 113–20; Vredenburgh and Maurer, "A Process Framework of Organizational Politics"; and Farrell and Petersen, "Patterns of Political Behavior," p. 409.
27. J. G. Bachman, D. G. Bowers, and P. M. Marcus, "Bases of Supervisory Power: A Comparative Study in Five Organizational Settings," in A. S. Tannenbaum (ed.), *Control in Organizations* (New York: McGraw-Hill, 1968), p. 236.
28. K. Student, "Supervisory Influence and Work-Group Performance," *Journal of Applied Psychology*, June 1968, pp. 188–94.
29. J. Ivancevich, "An Analysis of Control, Bases of Control, and Satisfaction in an Organizational Setting," *Academy of Management Journal*, December 1970, pp. 427–36.
30. J. G. Bachman, "Faculty Satisfaction and the Dean's Influence: An Organizational Study of Twelve Liberal Arts Colleges," *Journal of Applied Psychology*, February 1968, pp. 55–61; and J. G. Bachman, C. G. Smith, and J. A. Slesinger, "Control, Performance and Satisfaction: An Analysis of Structure and Individual Effort," *Journal of Personality and Social Psychology*, August 1966, pp. 127–36.
31. Bachman, Bowers, and Marcus, "Bases of Supervisory Power."
32. Ibid.
33. See note 30.
34. Ivancevich, "Analysis of Control."

10

Conflict

AFTER STUDYING THIS CHAPTER, YOU SHOULD BE ABLE TO:

Define and explain the following key terms and concepts:

Accommodation	Dysfunctional conflict
Avoidance	Felt conflict
Behavioral view	Functional conflict
Collaboration	Interactionist view
Competition	Perceived conflict
Compromise	Traditional view
Conflict	

Understand:

The difference between the traditional, behavioral, and interactionist
  views
The conflict process
The difference between functional and dysfunctional conflict
The sources of conflict
Five methods for reducing conflicts
The benefits and disadvantages of conflict

Part of my job as a coach is to keep the five guys who hate me away from the five guys who are undecided.

—C. STENGEL

*I*t has been proposed that conflict is a theme that has occupied the thinking of man more than any other—with the exception of God and love.[1] It has been only recently, though, that conflict has become a major area of interest and research for students of organizational behavior. The evidence suggests that this interest has been well placed—the type and intensity of conflict *does* affect group behavior.

In this chapter we shall define conflict, review three different ways of looking at it, present a process model of conflict, and consider the impact of conflict on group behavior.

A DEFINITION OF CONFLICT

There has been no shortage of definitions for conflict.[2] In spite of the divergent meanings the term has acquired, several common themes underlie most definitions. Conflict must be *perceived* by the parties to it. Whether conflict exists or not is a perception issue. If no one is aware of a conflict, it is generally agreed that no conflict exists. Of course, conflicts perceived may not be real while many situations that otherwise could be described as conflictive are not because the group members involved do not perceive the conflict. For a conflict to exist, therefore, it must be perceived. Additional commonalities among most conflict definitions are the concepts of *opposition, scarcity,* and *blockage* and the assumption that there are two or more parties whose interests or goals appear to be incompatible. Resources—whether money, jobs, prestige, power, or whatever—are not unlimited, and their scarcity encourages blocking behavior. The parties are therefore in opposition. When one party blocks the goal achievement of another, a conflict state exists.

Differences between definitions tend to center on *intent* and whether conflict is a term limited only to *overt acts*. The intent issue is a debate over whether blockage behavior must be a determined action or whether it could occur as a result of fortuitous circumstances. As to whether conflict can only refer to overt acts, some definitions, for example, require signs of manifest fighting or open struggle as criteria for the existence of conflict.

Our definition of conflict acknowledges awareness (perception), opposition, scarcity, and blockage. Further, we assume it to be a determined action, which can exist at either the latent or overt level. We define conflict to be *a process in which an effort is purposely made by A to offset the efforts of B by some form of blocking that will result in frustrating B in attaining his or her goals or furthering his or her interests.*

While this definition may, at first glance, seem esoteric, the terms and concepts that are used will become increasingly clear later in this chapter when we describe the stages that lead to conflict.

TRANSITIONS IN CONFLICT THOUGHT

It is entirely appropriate to say that there has been "conflict" over the role of conflict in groups and organizations. One school of thought has argued that conflict must be avoided—that it indicates a malfunctioning within the group. We call this the *traditional* view. Another school of thought, the *behavioral* view, argues that conflict is a natural and inevitable outcome in any group and that it need not be evil, but rather has the potential to be a positive force in determining group performance. The third, and most recent perspective, proposes not only that conflict *can* be a positive force in a group but explicitly argues that some conflict is *absolutely necessary* for a group to perform effectively. We label this third school the *interactionist* approach. Let us take a closer look at each of these views.[3]

The Traditional View

The early approach to conflict assumed that conflict was bad. Conflict was viewed negatively, and it was used synonymously with such terms as violence, destruction, and irrationality to reinforce its negative connotation. Conflict, by definition, was viewed as being harmful and was to be avoided.

The traditional view was consistent with the attitudes that prevailed about group behavior in the 1930s and 1940s. From findings provided by studies like those done at Hawthorne, it was argued that conflict was a dysfunctional outcome resulting from poor communication, a lack of openness and trust between people, and the failure of managers to be responsive to the needs and aspirations of their employees.

The view that all conflict is bad certainly offers a simple approach to looking at the behavior of people who create conflict. Since all conflict is to be avoided, we need merely direct our attention to the causes of conflict and correct these malfunctionings in order to improve group and organizational performance. Although research studies now provide strong evidence to dispute that this approach to conflict reduction results in high group performance, most of us still evaluate conflict situations utilizing this outmoded standard.

The Behavioral View

The behavioral position argued that conflict was a natural occurence in all groups and organizations. Since conflict was inevitable, the behavioral school advocated acceptance of conflict. They rationalized its existence: It cannot be eliminated, and there are even times when conflict may benefit a group's performance. The behavioral view dominated conflict theory from the late 1940s through the mid-1970s.

The Interactionist View

The current view toward conflict is the interactionist perspective. While the behavioral approach *accepted* conflict, the interactionist approach *encourages* conflict on the grounds that a harmonious, peaceful, tranquil, and cooperative group is prone to becoming static, apathetic, and nonresponsive to needs for change and innovation. The major contribution of the interactionist approach, therefore, is encouraging group leaders to maintain an ongoing minimum level of conflict— enough to keep the group viable, self-critical, and creative.

Given the interactionist view, and it is the one we shall take in this chapter, it becomes evident that to say conflict is all good or all bad is inappropriate and naive. Whether a conflict is good or bad depends on the type of conflict. Specifically, it's necessary to differentiate between functional and dysfunctional conflicts.

FUNCTIONAL VERSUS DYSFUNCTIONAL CONFLICT

The interactionist view does not propose that *all* conflicts are good. Rather, some conflicts support the goals of the group and improve its performance; these are functional, constructive forms of conflict. Additionally, there are conflicts that hinder group performance; these are dysfunctional or destructive forms.

Of course, it is one thing to argue that conflict can be valuable for the group, but how does one tell if a conflict is functional or dysfunctional?

The demarcation between functional and dysfunctional is neither clear nor precise. No one level of conflict can be adopted as acceptable or unacceptable under all conditions. The type and level of conflict that creates healthy and positive involvement toward one group's goals may, in another group or in the same group at another time, be highly dysfunctional.

The important criterion is group performance. Since groups exist to attain a goal or goals, it is the impact that the conflict has on the group, rather than on any singular individual, that defines functionality. The impact of conflict on the individual and on the group is rarely mutually exclusive, so the ways that individuals perceive a conflict may have an important influence on its effect on the group. However, this need not be the case, and when it is not, our orientation will be to the group. For us to appraise the impact of conflict on group behavior—to consider its functional and dysfunctional effects—we shall consider whether the individual group members perceive the conflict as being good or bad to be irrelevant. A group member may perceive an action as dysfunctional, in that the outcome is personally dissatisfying to him or her. However, for our analysis, it would be functional if it furthers the objectives of the group.

THE CONFLICT PARADOX

If some conflict has been proven to be beneficial to a group's performance, why do most of us continue to look at conflict as undesirable? The answer is that we live in a society that has been built upon the traditional view. Tolerance of conflict is counter to most cultures in developed nations. In North America, the home, school, and church are generally the most influential institutions during the early years when our attitudes are forming. These institutions, for the most part, have historically reinforced anticonflict values and emphasized the importance of getting along with others.

The home has historically reinforced the authority pattern through the parent figure. Parents knew what was right and children complied. Conflict between children or between parents and children has generally been actively discouraged. The traditional school systems in developed countries reflected the structure of the home. Teachers had *the* answers and were not to be challenged. Disagreements at all levels were viewed negatively. Examinations reinforced this view: Students attempted to get their answers to agree with those the teacher had determined were right. The last major influencing institution, the church, also has supported anticonflict values. The religious perspective emphasizes peace, harmony, and tranquility. Church doctrines, for the most part, advocate acceptance rather than argument. This is best exemplified by the teachings of the Roman Catholic Church. According to its beliefs, when the pope speaks officially (ex cathedra) on religious matters, he is infallible. Such dogma has discouraged questioning the teachings of the Church.

Should we be surprised, then, that the traditional view of conflict continues to receive wide support in spite of the evidence to the contrary?

Let us now proceed to move beyond definitions and philosophy, to describe and analyze the evolutionary process leading to conflict outcomes.

CONFLICT PROCESS

The conflict process can be thought of as comprising four stages: potential opposition, cognition and personalization, behavior, and outcomes. The process is diagrammed in Figure 10–1.

Stage I: Potential Opposition

The first step in the conflict process is the presence of conditions that create opportunities for conflict to arise. They *need not* lead directly to conflict, but one of these conditions is necessary if conflict is to arise. For simplicity's sake, these conditions (which also may be looked at as causes or sources of conflict) have been condensed into three general categories: communication, structure, and personal variables.

COMMUNICATION

The communicative source represents those opposing forces that arise from semantic difficulties, misunderstandings, and "noise" in the communication channels. Much of this discussion can be related back to our comments on communication and communication networks in Chapter 7.

One of the major myths that most of us carry around with us is that poor communication is the reason for conflicts—"if we could just communicate with

FIGURE 10–1

The Conflict Process

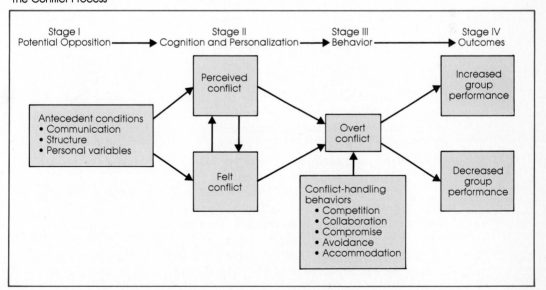

each other, we could eliminate our differences.'' Such a conclusion is not unreasonable, given the amount of time each of us spends communicating. But, of course, poor communication is certainly not the source of *all* conflicts, though there is considerable evidence to suggest that problems in the communication process act to retard collaboration and stimulate misunderstanding.

A review of the research suggests that semantic difficulties, insufficient exchange of information, and noise in the communication channel each are barriers to communication and potential antecedent conditions to conflict.[4] Specifically, evidence demonstrates semantic difficulties arise as a result of differences in training, selective perception, and inadequate information about others. Research has further demonstrated a surprising finding: The potential for conflict increases when either too little or too much communication takes place. Apparently, an increase in communication is functional up to a point, whereupon it is possible to overcommunicate with a resultant increase in the potential for conflict. Too much information as well as too little can lay the foundation for conflict. Further, the channel chosen for communicating can have an influence on stimulating opposition. The filtering process that occurs as information is passed between members and the divergence of communications from formal or previously established channels offer potential opportunities for conflict to arise.

STRUCTURE

The term structure is used, in this context, to include variables such as size, degree of specialization in the tasks assigned to group members, jurisdictional clarity, status consistencies, member goal compatibility, leadership styles, reward systems, and the degree of dependence between groups.

Research indicates that size and specialization act as forces to stimulate conflict. The larger the group and the more specialized its activities, the greater the likelihood of conflict. Tenure and conflict have been found to be inversely related. The potential for conflict tends to be greatest where group members are younger and where turnover is high.

The greater the ambiguity in precisely defining where responsibility for actions lies, the greater the potential for conflict to emerge. Such jurisdictional ambiguities increase intergroup fighting for control of resources and territory.

In Chapter 6, we discussed the importance of maintaining status equity. That discussion should lead us to the logical conclusion that inconsistencies between formal rank and status accoutrements will create ambiguity and foster conflict. Similarly, the status system itself tends to stimulate conflict. The fact that people higher in organizations have more freedom, amenities, and prerogatives can breed conflicts with those of lesser rank.

Groups within organizations have diverse goals. For instance, purchasing is concerned with the timely acquisition of inputs at low prices, marketing's goals concentrate on disposing of outputs and increasing revenues, quality control's attention is focused on improving quality and ensuring that the organization's products meet up to standard, and production units seek efficiency of operations by maintaining a steady production flow. This diversity of goals among groups is a major source of conflict. Where groups within an organization seek diverse ends, some of which—like sales and credit—are inherently at odds, there are increased opportunities for conflict.

There is some indication that a close style of leadership—tight and continuous observation with general control of the others' behaviors—increases conflict potential, but the evidence is not particularly strong. Too much reliance on participation may also stimulate conflict. Research tends to confirm that participation and conflict are highly correlated, apparently because participation encourages the promotion of differences. Reward systems, too, are found to create conflict when one member's gain is at another's expense. Finally, if a group is dependent on another group (in contrast to the two being mutually independent) or if interdependence allows one group to gain at another's expense, opposing forces are stimulated.[5]

PERSONAL VARIABLES

Personal factors include the individual value systems that each person has and the personality characteristics that account for individual idiosyncracies and differences.

The evidence indicates that certain personality types—for example, individuals who are highly authoritarian, and dogmatic and who demonstrate low esteem—lead to potential conflict. Most important, and probably the most overlooked variable in the study of social conflict, is differing value systems. Value differences, for example, are the best explanation of such diverse issues as prejudice, disagreements over one's contribution to the group and the rewards one deserves, or assessments of whether this particular book is any good. The fact that John dislikes blacks and Dana believes John's position indicates his ignorance, that an employee thinks he is worth $30,000 a year but his boss believes him to be worth $24,000, and that Ann thinks this book is interesting to read while Jennifer views it as a "crock of . . . " are all value judgments. And differences in value systems are important sources for creating the potential for conflict.

Stage II: Cognition and Personalization

If the conditions cited in Stage I generate frustration, then the potential for opposition becomes actualized in the second stage. The antecedent conditions can only lead to conflict when one or more of the parties are affected by, and cognitive of, the conflict.

As we noted in our definition of conflict, perception is required. Therefore, one or more of the parties must be aware of the existence of the antecedent conditions. However, because a conflict is perceived does not mean that it is personalized. In other words, "A may be aware that B and A are in serious disagreement . . . but it may not make A tense or anxious, and it may have no effect whatsoever on A's affection towards B."[6] It is at the felt level, when individuals become emotionally involved, that parties experience anxiety, tenseness, frustration, or hostility.

Stage III: Behavior

We are in the third stage of the conflict process when a member engages in action that frustrates the attainment of another's goals or prevents the furthering of the other's interests. This action must be intended; that is, there must be a knowing effort to frustrate another. At this juncture, the conflict is out in the open.

Overt conflict covers a full range of behaviors—from subtle, indirect, and highly controlled forms of interference to direct, aggressive, violent, and uncontrolled struggle. At the low range, this overt behavior is illustrated by the student who raises his or her hand in class and questions a point the instructor has made. At the high range, strikes, riots, and wars come to mind.

Stage III is also where most conflict-handling behaviors are initiated. Once the conflict is overt, the parties will develop a method for dealing with the conflict. This does not exclude conflict-handling behaviors from being initiated in Stage II, but in most cases, these techniques for reducing the frustration are used when the conflict has become observable rather than as preventive measures.

Figure 10–2 represents one author's effort at identifying the primary conflict-handling orientations. Using two dimensions—*cooperativeness* (the degree to which one party attempts to satisfy the other party's concerns) and *assertiveness* (the degree

FIGURE 10–2

Dimensions of Conflict-Handling Orientations

Source: K. Thomas, "Conflict and Conflict Management," in M. D. Dunnette (ed.), *Handbook of Industrial and Organizational Psychology*, p. 900. Copyright © 1976 Rand McNally. Reprinted by permission of John Wiley & Sons, Inc.

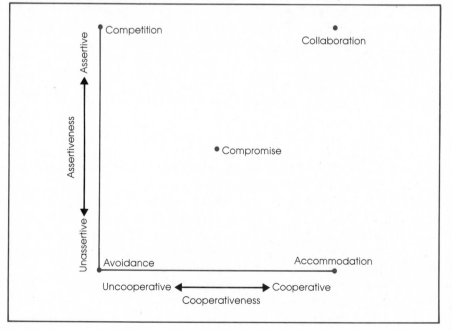

to which one party attempts to satisfy his or her own concerns)—five conflict-handling orientations can be identified: *competition* (assertive and uncooperative), *collaboration* (assertive and cooperative), *avoidance* (unassertive and uncooperative), *accommodation* (unassertive and cooperative), and *compromise* (midrange on both assertiveness and cooperativeness).[7]

COMPETITION

When one person seeks to achieve her goals or further her interests, regardless of the impact on the parties to the conflict, she competes and dominates. These win-lose struggles, in formal groups or in an organization, frequently utilize the formal authority of a mutual superior as the dominant force, and the conflicting individuals each will use their own power bases in order to resolve a victory in their favor.

COLLABORATION

When the parties to conflict each desire to satisfy fully the concern of all parties, we have cooperation and the search for a mutually beneficial outcome. In collaboration, the behavior of the parties is aimed at solving the problem, at clarifying the differences rather than accommodating various points of view. The participants consider the full range of alternatives, the similarities and differences in viewpoint become more clearly focused, and the causes or differences become outwardly evident. Because the solution sought is advantageous to all parties, collaboration is often thought of as a win-win approach to resolving conflicts. It is, for example, a frequent tool of marriage counselors. Behavioral scientists, who value openness, trust, authenticity, and spontaneity in relationships, are also strong advocates of a collaborative approach to resolving conflicts.

AVOIDANCE

A person may recognize that a conflict exists but react by withdrawing or by suppressing the conflict. Indifference or the desire to evade overt demonstration of disagreement can result in withdrawal: The individuals acknowledge physical separation and each stakes out a territory that is distinct from the other's. If withdrawal is not possible or desirous, the individuals may suppress, that is, withhold, their differences. When group members are required to interact because of the independence of their tasks, suppression is a more probable outcome than withdrawal.

ACCOMMODATION

When the parties seek to appease their opponent, they may be willing to place their opponent's interests above their own. In order that the relationship can be maintained, one party is willing to be self-sacrificing. We refer to this behavior as accommodation. When husbands and wives have differences, it is not uncommon for one to accommodate the other by placing their spouses's interest above their own.

COMPROMISE

When each party to the conflict must give up something, sharing occurs, resulting in a compromised outcome. In compromise, there is no clear winner or loser. Rather, there is a rationing of the object of the conflict or, where the object is not divisible, one rewards the other by yielding something of substitute value. The distinguishing characteristic of compromise, therefore, is that it requires each party to give up something. Negotiations between unions and management represent a situation where compromise is required in order to reach a settlement and agree upon a labor contract.

No one conflict resolution mode is appropriate in all situations. But when is one preferable over another? Table 10–1 lists situations that tend to favor each.

TABLE 10–1
When to Use the Five Conflict-Handling Orientations

CONFLICT-HANDLING ORIENTATION	APPROPRIATE SITUATIONS
Competition	1. When quick, decisive action is vital (e.g., in emergencies) 2. On important issues where unpopular actions need implementing (e.g., in cost cutting, enforcing unpopular rules, discipline). 3. On issues vital to organization's welfare when you know you're right 4. Against people who take advantage of noncompetitive behavior
Collaboration	1. To find an integrative solution when both sets of concerns are too important to be compromised 2. When your objective is to learn 3. To merge insights from people with different perspectives 4. To gain commitment by incorporating concerns into a consensus 5. To work through feelings that have interfered with a relationship
Avoidance	1. When an issue is trivial, or more important issues are pressing 2. When you perceive no chance of satisfying your concerns 3. When potential disruption outweighs the benefits of resolution 4. To let people cool down and regain perspective 5. When gathering information supersedes immediate decision 6. When others can resolve the conflict more effectively 7. When issues seem tangential or symptomatic of other issues

Accommodation	1. When you find you are wrong—to allow a better position to be heard, to learn, and to show your reasonableness
	2. When issues are more important to others than yourself—to satisfy others and maintain cooperation
	3. To build social credits for later issues
	4. To minimize loss when you are outmatched and losing
	5. When harmony and stability are especially important
	6. To allow subordinates to develop by learning from mistakes
Compromise	1. When goals are important, but not worth the effort or potential disruption of more assertive modes
	2. When opponents with equal power are committed to mutually exclusive goals
	3. To achieve temporary settlements to complex issues
	4. To arrive at expedient solutions under time pressure
	5. As a backup when collaboration or competition is unsuccessful

Source: K. W. Thomas, "Toward Multidimensional Values in Teaching: The Example of Conflict Behaviors," *Academy of Management Review,* July 1977, p. 487. With permission.

Stage IV: Outcomes

The interplay between the overt conflict behavior and conflict-handling behaviors result in consequences. As the model demonstrates, they may be functional in that the conflict has resulted in an improvement in the group's performance. Conversely, group performance may be hindered and we would describe the outcome as dysfunctional.

FUNCTIONAL OUTCOMES

How might conflict act as a force to increase group performance? It is hard to visualize a situation where open or violent aggression could be functional. But there are a number of instances where it is possible to envision how low or moderate levels of conflict could improve the effectiveness of a group. Because it is often difficult to think of instances where conflict can be constructive, let us consider some examples and then look at the research evidence.

Conflict is constructive when it improves the quality of decisions, stimulates creativity and innovation, encourages interest and curiosity among group members, provides the medium through which problems can be aired and tensions released, and fosters an environment of self-evaluation and change. The evidence suggests that conflict can improve the quality of decision making by allowing all points, particularly the ones that are unusual or held by a minority, to be weighed in important decisions. Conflict is an antidote for groupthink. It does not allow the group passively to "rubber stamp" decisions that may be based on weak assumptions, inadequate consideration to relevant alternatives, or other debilities. Conflict challenges the status quo and therefore furthers the creation of new ideas, promotes reassessment of group goals and activities, and increases the probability that the group will respond to change.

Research studies in diverse settings confirm the functionality of conflict. Consider the following findings.

The comparison of six major decisions during the administrations of four different U.S. presidents found that conflict reduced the chance that groupthink would overpower policy decisions. The comparisons demonstrated that conformity among presidential advisors was related to poor decisions, while an atmosphere of constructive conflict and critical thinking surrounded the well-developed decisions.[8]

The bankruptcy of the Penn Central Railroad has been generally attributed to mismanagement and a failure of the company's board of directors to question actions taken by management. The board was composed of outside directors who met monthly to oversee the railroad's operations. Few questioned the decisions made by the operating management, though there was evidence that several board members were uncomfortable with many decisions made by the management. Apathy and a desire to *avoid* conflict allowed poor decisions to stand unquestioned.[9] This, however, should not be surprising since a review of the relationship between bureaucracy and innovation has found that conflict encourages innovative solutions.[10] The corollary of this finding also appears true: Lack of conflict results in a passive environment with reinforcement of the status quo.

Not only do better and more innovative decisions result from situations where there is some conflict, but there is evidence indicating that conflict can be positively related to productivity. It was demonstrated that, among established groups, performance tended to improve more when there was conflict among members than when there was fairly close agreement. The investigators observed that when groups analyzed decisions that had been made by the individual members of that group, the average improvement among the high-conflict groups was 73 percent greater than was that of those groups characterized by low-conflict conditions.[11] Others have found similar results: Groups composed of members with different interests tend to produce higher-quality solutions to a variety of problems than do homogeneous groups.[12]

Similarly, studies of professionals—systems analysts and research and development scientists—support the constructive value of conflict. An investigation of twenty-two teams of systems analysts found that the more incompatible groups were likely to be more productive.[13] Research and development scientists have been found to be most productive where there is a certain amount of intellectual conflict.[14]

Conflict can even be constructive on sports teams and in unions. Studies of sports teams indicate that moderate levels of group conflict contribute to team effectiveness and provide an additional stimulus for high achievement.[15] An examination of local unions found that conflict between members of the local was positively related to the union's power and to member loyalty and participation in union affairs.[16] These findings might suggest that conflict within a group indicates strength rather than, in the traditional view, weakness.

DYSFUNCTIONAL OUTCOMES

The destructive consequences of conflict upon a group or organization's performance are generally well known. A reasonable summary might state: Uncontrolled opposition breeds discontent, which acts to dissolve common ties, and eventually leads to destruction of the group. And, of course, there is a substantial body of literature to document how conflict—the dysfunctional varieties—can reduce group effectiveness.[17] Among the more undesirable consequences are a retarding of communication, reductions in group cohesiveness, and subordination of group goals to the primacy of infighting between members. At the extreme, conflict can bring group functioning to a halt and potentially threaten the group's survival.

This discussion has again returned us to the issue of what is functional and what is dysfunctional. Research on conflict has yet to identify those situations where conflict is more likely to be constructive than destructive. However, the difference between functional and dysfunctional conflict is important enough for us to go beyond the substantive evidence and propose at least two hypotheses. The first is that extreme levels of conflict—exemplified by overt struggle or violence—are rarely, if ever, functional. Functional conflict is probably most often characterized by low to moderate levels of subtle and controlled opposition. Second, the type of group activity should be another factor determining functionality. We hypothesize that the more creative or unprogrammed the decision-making tasks of the group, the greater the probability that internal conflict is constructive. Groups that are required to tackle problems requiring new and novel approaches— as in research, advertising, and other professional activities—will benefit more from conflict than groups performing highly programmed activities—for instance, those of work teams on an automobile assembly line.

IMPLICATIONS FOR PERFORMANCE AND SATISFACTION

Many people assume that conflict is related to lower group and organizational performance. This chapter has demonstrated that this assumption is frequently fallacious. Conflict can be either constructive or destructive to the functioning of a group or unit. As shown in Figure 10–3, levels of conflict can be either too high or too low. Either extreme hinders performance. An optimal level is where there is enough conflict to prevent stagnation, stimulate creativity, allow tensions to be released, and initiate the seeds for change; yet not so much as to be disruptive or deter coordination of activities.

Inadequate or excessive levels of conflict can hinder the effectiveness of a group or an organization, resulting in reduced satisfaction of group members, increased absence and turnover rates, and eventually lower productivity. On the other hand, when conflict is at an optimal level, complacency and apathy should

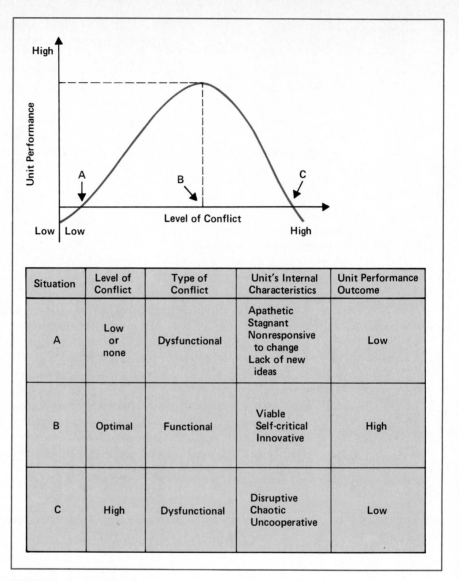

FIGURE 10–3
Conflict and Unit Performance

be minimized, motivation should be enhanced through the creation of a challenging and questioning environment with a vitality that makes work interesting, and there should be the needed turnover to rid the organization of misfits and poor performers.

POINT

CONFLICT IS GOOD FOR AN ORGANIZATION

We've made considerable progress in the last fifteen years toward overcoming the negative stereotype given to conflict. Most behavioral scientists and an increasing number of practitioners now accept that the goal of effective management is not to eliminate conflict. Rather, it is to create the right intensity of conflict so as to reap its functional benefits.

Since conflict can be good for an organization, it is only logical to acknowledge that there may be tiimes when managers will purposely want to increase its intensity. Let's briefly review how stimulating conflict can provide benefits to the organization.

Conflict is a means by which to bring about radical change. It is an effective device by which managment can change drastically the existing power structure, current interaction patterns, and entrenched attitudes.

Conflict facilitiates group cohesiveness. While conflict increases hostility between groups, external threats tend to cause a group to pull together as a unit. Intergroup conflicts raise the extent to which members identify with their own group and increase feelings of solidarity, while, at the same time, internal differences and irritations dissolve.

Conflict improves group and organizational effectiveness. The stimulation of conflict initiates the search for new means and goals and clears the way for innovation. The successful solution of a conflict leads to greater effectiveness, to more trust and openness, to greater attraction of members for each other, and to depersonalization of future conflicts. In fact, it has been found that as the number of minor disagreements increases, the number of major clashes decreases.

Conflict brings about a slightly higher, more constructive level of tension. This enhances the chances of solving the conflicts in a way satisfactory to all parties concerned. When the level of tension is very low, the parties are not sufficiently motivated to do something about a conflict.

These points are clearly not comprehensive. As noted in the chapter, conflict provides a number of benefits to an organization. However, groups or organizations devoid of conflict are likely to suffer from apathy, stagnation, groupthink, and other debilitating diseases.

The points presented here were influenced by E. Van de Vliert, "Escalative Intervention in Small-Group Conflicts," Journal of Applied Behavioral Science, Vol. 21, No. 1, 1985, pp. 19–36.

COUNTERPOINT

ALL CONFLICTS ARE DYSFUNCTIONAL!

It may be true that conflict is an inherent part of any group or organization. It may not be possible to eliminate it completely. However, just because conflicts exist is no reason to deify them. *All* conflicts are dysfunctional, and it is one of management's major responsibilities to keep conflict intensity as low as humanly possible. A few points will support my case.

The negative consequences from conflict can be devastating. The list of negatives associated with conflict are awesome. The most obvious include increased turnover, decreased employee satisfaction, inefficiencies between work units, sabotage, labor grievances and strikes, and physical aggression.

Effective managers build teamwork. A good manager builds a coordinated team. Conflict works against such an objective. A successful work group is like a successful sports team; each member knows his or her role and supports his or her teammates. When a team works well, the whole becomes greater than the sum of the parts. Management creates teamwork by minimizing internal conflicts and facilitating internal coordination.

Competition is good for an organization, but not conflict. Competition and conflict should not be confused with each other. *Conflict* is behavior directed against another party, whereas *competition* is behavior aimed at obtaining a goal without interference from another party. Competition is healthy; it is the source of organizational vitality. Conflict, on the other hand, is destructive.

Managers who accept and stimulate conflict don't survive in organizations. The whole argument on the value of conflict may be moot as long as senior executives in organizations view conflict from the traditional view. In the traditional view, *any* conflict will be seen as bad. Since the evaluation of a manager's performance is made by higher-level executives, those managers who do not succeed in eliminating conflicts are likely to be appraised negatively. This, in turn, will reduce opportunities for advancement. Any manager who aspires to move up in such an environment will be wise to follow the traditional view and eliminate any outward signs of conflict. Failure to follow this advice might result in the premature departure of the manager.

FOR DISCUSSION

1. Define conflict.
2. Do you think *conflict* and *competition* are synonymous terms?
3. Name, discuss, and contrast three views on conflict.
4. Under what conditions might conflict be beneficial to a group?
5. Identify various types of conflict.
6. What are the components in the conflict process model? From your own experiences, give an example of how a conflict proceeded through the four stages.
7. Discuss five conflict resolution techniques. What are the strengths and weaknesses of each.
8. "The larger the group, the greater the likelihood of conflict." Do you agree or disagree? Discuss.
9. "Units within an organization will always have divergent goals; therefore, all organizations will be characterized by the presence of conflict." Do you agree or disagree? Discuss.
10. "As an organization becomes more structured, it tends to eliminate creativity." Do you agree or disagree? Discuss.
11. "Participation is an excellent method for identifying differences and resolving conflicts." Do you agree or disagree? Discuss.
12. What is the difference between functional and dysfunctional conflict? What determines functionality?

FOR FURTHER READING

BERES, M. E., and S. M. SCHMIDT, "The Conflict Carousel: A Contingency Approach to Conflict Management." In G. B. J. Bomers and R. B. Peterson (eds.), *Conflict Management and Industrial Relations,* pp. 37–59. Boston: Kluwer-Nijhoff, 1982. Provides a unifying framework that accounts for differences among social, international, industrial, and organizational conflict research.

BLAKE, R. R., and J. S. MOUTON, *Solving Costly Organizational Conflicts.* San Francisco: Jossey-Bass, 1984. Describes a method for resolving conflicts and establishing trust and cooperation among groups, departments, and divisions that must work together.

FILLEY, A. C., *Interpersonal Conflict Resolution.* Glenview, Ill.: Scott, Foresman, 1975. Analyzes the conflict process and describes the integrative decision-making method of conflict resolution through problem solving.

KILMANN, R. H., and K. W. THOMAS, "Four Perspectives on Conflict Management: An Attributional Framework for Organizing Descriptive and Normative Theory," *Academy of Management Review,* January 1978, pp. 59–68.

Identifies four perspectives on conflict derived from the process versus structure distinction and the internal versus external attributions distinction.

KING, D., "Three Cheers for Conflict," *Personnel,* January–February 1981, pp.13–22. Provides detailed discussion of fifteen positive outcomes of constructive conflict in organizations.

ROBBINS, S. P., "'Conflict Management' and 'Conflict Resolution' Are Not Synonymous Terms," *California Management Review,* Winter 1978, pp. 67–75. Argues that conflict management encompasses both resolution and stimulation techniques.

NOTES FOR CHAPTER 10

1. R. D. Luce and H. Raiffa, *Games and Decisions* (New York: John Wiley, 1957).
2. C. F. Fink, "Some Conceptual Difficulties in the Theory of Social Conflict," *Journal of Conflict Resolution,* December 1968, pp. 412–60.
3. This section has been adapted from S. P. Robbins, *Managing Organizational Conflict: A Nontraditional Approach* (Englewood Cliffs, N.J.: Prentice-Hall, 1974), pp. 11–25.
4. Ibid., pp. 39–40.
5. Ibid., pp. 49–50.
6. L. R. Pondy, "Organizational Conflict: Concepts and Models," *Administrative Science Quarterly,* September 1967, p. 302.
7. K. W. Thomas, "Conflict and Conflict Management," in M. Dunnette (ed.), *Handbook of Industrial and Organizational Psychology,* (Chicago: Rand McNally, 1976), pp. 889–935.
8. I. L. Janis, *Victims of Groupthink* (Boston: Houghton Mifflin, 1972).
9. P. Binzen and J. R. Daughen, *Wreck of the Penn Central* (Boston: Little, Brown, 1971).
10. V. A. Thompson, "Bureaucracy and Innovation," *Administrative Science Quarterly,* March 1965, pp. 1–20.
11. J. Hall and M. S. Williams, "A Comparison of Decision-Making Performances in Established and Ad-Hoc Groups," *Journal of Personality and Social Psychology,* February 1966, p. 217.
12. R. L. Hoffman, "Homogeneity of Member Personality and Its Effect on Group Problem-Solving," *Journal of Abnormal and Social Psychology,* January 1959, pp. 27–32; and R. L. Hoffman and N. R. F. Maier, "Quality and Acceptance of Problem Solutions by Members of Homogeneous and Heterogeneous Groups," *Journal of Abnormal and Social Psychology,* March 1961, pp. 401–7.
13. R. E. Hill, "Interpersonal Compatibility and Work Group Performance Among Systems Analysts: An Empirical Study," *Proceedings of the Seventeenth Annual Midwest Academy of Management Conference,* Kent, Ohio, April 1974, pp. 97–110.
14. D. C. Pelz and F. Andrews, *Scientists in Organizations* (New York: John Wiley, 1966).
15. H. Lenk, "Konflikt und Leistung in Spitzensportmannschafter: Isozometrische Strukturen von WettKämpfachtern in Ruden," *Soziale Welt,* Vol.15 (1964), pp. 307–43.
16. A. Tannenbaum, "Control Structure and Union Functions," *American Journal of Sociology,* May 1956, pp. 127–40.
17. For an excellent source of studies that focus on the dysfunctional consequences of conflict, see the *Journal of Conflict Resolution.*

CASE IIIA

WELCOME TO THE SCHOOL BOARD

Vacaville is a small community in southern Texas. Its 22,000 residents are primarily farmers or operators of small businesses. The Vacaville School Board is made up of the mayor, two members of the city council, the superintendent of Vacaville schools, and eight members, at large, elected for four-year terms by Vacaville voters.

The school board is a relatively stable body. Paul Gomez has been the mayor of Vacaville for eleven years. A rancher, Gomez spends about ten hours a week on his mayoral duties, for which he is paid $5,000 a year. The two city council members have each been on the board for more than eight years. Jack deNuervo, the school superintendent, has held his same job for nearly twenty-six years, currently earns $36,000 annually, but has reached sixty-five years of age and has advised the board that he will be retiring. The remaining eight at-large members have staggered terms. Every year two come up for reelection.

In the November 1984 election, long-time at-large board member Mary Cardoza was defeated by a wealthy businessman, J. T. Thomas. The election campaign had been bitter. Thomas spent over $30,000 to defeat Cardoza. In contrast, Cardoza reported spending less than $2,000 on her campaign. Name calling had risen to unheard-of levels. Thomas' campaign was built almost exclusively on attacking what he referred to as "Cardoza's free-spending and liberal views on education" rather than selling himself. However, he did consistently tell the voters through his television, radio, and newspaper ads that, if elected, he was committed to "cutting truancy and getting tough with those students causing discipline problems."

It was obvious to everyone who attended the first meeting of 1985, which coincidentally was also the first one where Thomas sat as a board member, that the days of short and tranquil meetings were over. That January 12 meeting began at 7:00 P.M. and disbanded (a more appropriate term than adjourned) four-and-a-half hours later. For the record, no one who was there could remember any previous board meeting running longer than two hours.

The fireworks began almost immediately. Gomez and deNeurvo had expected Thomas to be trouble. They anticipated that he would propose some new and strict policies for governing the schools, and they certainly expected him to be active in the selection of deNuervo's successor. What they hadn't expected was the coalition Thomas had formed with the other at-large members. When Thomas spoke, it was obvious he was not speaking as a lonely voice. His comments were consistently echoed by the other at-large members.

The first item on the January 12 agenda had been a routine capital expenditure request. DeNuervo was requesting $4,200 to purchase three new IBM typewriters that would replace three old manual models. DeNuervo held little discussion on the request, assuming routine approval. He nearly fell out of his chair when the request was defeated 8 to 4.

The second item on the agenda was approval of a job offer to fill a vacancy in the fine arts department at the high school. Board members had had an opportunity to review the candidate's file earlier. But deNuervo was more cautious now. Rather than call for a quick vote, he wanted to hear from each member. It soon became obvious that while the candidate was fully qualified, one thing was bothering Thomas. It seems that in the late 1960s, when the candidate had been a college freshman, he had been arrested for participating in an antiwar demonstration. After nearly two hours of debate surrounding the candidate's character, deNeurvo realized that the battle was lost. All at-large members were dominated by Thomas. Whichever way he voted, so would the others. The final vote was predictable. The candidate was rejected 8 to 4.

At 11:15 P.M., deNuervo realized he was going to have to end the meeting, but he was determined to handle one last item—the appointments to the superintendent's screening and selection committee. This committee would be made up of three board members and their task would be to find deNuervo's replacement. Each of the board members was given a piece of paper and told to write three names on it. Those three board members with the highest votes would comprise the committee. Not surprisingly, the three highest vote-getters were Thomas and two other at-large members.

When deNuervo got home that night and related what had happened at the meeting to his wife, she replied, "I'm not surprised. I've heard that Thomas has promised all the at-large members that if they support him on the board, he will finance their reelection campaigns. He apparently has also told them that if they go against him—ever—he would actively support their opponents."

Questions

1. Describe the power interactions in this case.
2. There is conflict between the at-large members and the others. What is the source of this conflict? How could the conflict be resolved?
3. Use Fiedler's leadership model to explain Thomas' apparent success as a leader. Can Thomas be classified as a high- or low-LPC leader? Why?
4. If you were deNuervo, what could you do to counteract or defuse Thomas' power?

CASE IIIB

A MAN HAS GOT TO KNOW HIS PLACE

Scott Korman was not your ordinary doctoral student. At age thirty-five, he was ten years older than most other students in the Ph.D. program. Also unlike his contemporaries, he held no teaching assistantship. In fact, he made no secret that he did not need financial assistance as did his peers. Scott's Pierre Cardin shirts, Gucci loafers, and $50,000 Mercedes didn't do much toward helping him blend into the role of the struggling student.

Scott's background is well known around the university. He had his B.A. and M.A. degrees in English literature from Stanford University by the time he was twenty-three. Scott then took a job at a junior college in Virginia and taught English literature and creative writing. In his spare time, he wrote. His first novel was published when Scott was twenty-seven. It was favorably received by critics and the book-buying public. The book sold nearly 60,000 copies in hardback and over 2 million in paperback. At twenty-nine, Scott published his second novel. Selected by several major book clubs, this novel sold over 300,000 in hardback, and 3 million in paperback. It was also sold to Hollywood for $500,000, though it never was made into a film. His third novel, published last year, was on the best-seller list for twenty-two weeks. The paperback rights alone were purchased for $1.6 million.

Success to Scott was more than selling lots of books and making millions of dollars. Scott wanted the academic life. He dreamed of being a professor of creative writing at a quality eastern university and sharing his ideas with young people. But such a goal requires a doctoral degree—the Ph.D. So Scott has decided to go back to school to earn his doctorate.

The first semester back was difficult for Scott. It was not easy for him to sublimate a lot of his opinions on writing. Unfortunately, many of his ideas did not agree with those held by his professors. But he was learning to play the student role. The more pressing problem was something Scott couldn't control. That was the way the faculty reacted to him. Not surprisingly, they were not used to having a best-selling author around, especially as a lowly graduate student. One young assistant professor, who himself could not have been much over twenty-six years old, told Scott directly, "You don't belong here. You don't have any talent. Your books may sell a lot and you may be the darling of Madison Avenue, but I'm going to do everything I can to see that you never get your degree."

At one level, Scott felt like laughing. Why would these people—established academics with all the appropriate credentials—care that he had written three successful novels? He wasn't a novelist here; he was a student! At another level, Scott realized that whether he got a Ph.D. or not rested with the professors in his department, and they apparently didn't enjoy playing second fiddle, in reputation, to a graduate student.

Questions

1. Analyze Scott's dilemma in terms of the various types of role conflict and in relation to status incongruence.
2. Analyze Scott's situation in terms of interpersonal conflict and power.
3. Utilizing the material on power, explain why some professors are not excited by Scott's presence in the program.
4. What could Scott do to increase the likelihood of obtaining his Ph.D.?

CASE IIIC

TIP SAYS NO WAY

Marc Lattoni supervises an eight-member cost accounting department in a large metals fabricating plant in Albuquerque, New Mexico. He was promoted about six months ago to his supervisory position after only a year as an accountant. It was no secret that Marc got the promotion predominantly due to his education—he has an M.B.A., whereas no one else in the department has a college degree. The transition to supervisor went smoothly, and there was little in the way of problems until this morning.

Business had been prospering at the plant for some time, and the need for an additional cost accountant in the department to handle the increased work load was becoming increasingly apparent. In fact, it had been on Marc's mind for over a month. Department members were complaining about the heavy work load. Overtime had become commonplace, and the large amount of overtime was adversely affecting the department's efficiency statistics. Marc believed that he would have little or no trouble supporting his request for a new full-time position with his boss.

Marc believed the search for the new employee would be relatively hassle free. This was because he had already spotted an individual who he thought would fill the new slot nicely. The individual he had in mind was currently working in the production control department of the plant.

Unofficially, Marc had talked with the production control supervisor and the plant's personnel director, and the three had agreed that Ralph Simpson, a young black clerk in production, would be an excellent candidate to move into cost accounting. Ralph had been with the company for eight months, had shown above-average potential, and was only six units shy of his bachelor's degree (with a major in accounting) which he was earning at night at the state university.

Marc had met with Ralph earlier in the week and discussed the possibility that cost accounting might have a vacancy. Ralph told Marc that he would be very interested in pursuing the position. After further discussing the subject over lunch, all unofficially, Marc said that, although he could make no promises, he was prepared to recommend Ralph for the job. However, Marc emphasized that it would be a week to ten days before a final decision was made and the announcement made official.

But trouble was brewing. Rumors were spreading that Ralph was going to join the department. One of the cost accountants, Tip O'Malley, was openly challenging Ralph's addition to the department. Fifty-eight years old, raised in a small town in the Deep South, and working at the Albuquerque plant since its opening twenty-six years ago, Tip walked into Marc's office and told him: "The grapevine is saying that a black down in production control is coming up here. Let me tell you something! I've never worked with a black and I never will. We have a close-knit group here. You better not appoint *anybody* without talking with us first. And I can assure you, some other people in the department also think like I do about working with a black!''

Questions

1. Analyze the actions in this case in terms of formal and informal communication.
2. Analyze this case in terms of group dynamics.
3. Use the Vroom-Yetton model to determine how Marc should approach his decision.
4. Analyze the power relationship between Marc and Tip.
5. If Marc believes that Tip is the only department member who holds these strong negative attitudes toward blacks, what conflict resolution technique should he use?

CASE IIID

GETTING OFF TO A GOOD START

Sue Reynolds is twenty-two years old and will be receiving her B.S. degree in Human Resource Management from the University of Hartford at the end of this semester. She has spent the past two summers working for Connecticut Mutual, filling in on a number of different jobs while employees took their vacations. She has received and accepted an offer to join CM on a permanent basis upon graduation, as a supervisor in the policy renewal department.

Connecticut Mutual is a large insurance company. In the headquarters office alone, where Sue will work, they employ five thousand employees. The company believes strongly in the personal development of its employees. This translates into a philosophy, emanating from the top executive offices, of trust and respect for all CM employees.

The job Sue will be assuming requires her to direct the activities of twenty-two clerks. Their jobs require little training and are highly routine. A clerk's responsibility is to ensure that renewal notices are sent on current policies, to tabulate any changes in premium from a standardized table, and to advise the sales division if a policy is to be canceled as a result of nonresponse to renewal notices.

Sue's group is composed of all females, ranging from nineteen to sixty-two years of age, with a median age of twenty-three. For the most part, they are high school graduates with little prior working experience. The salary range for policy renewal clerks is $920 to $1,270 per month. Sue will be replacing a long-time CM employee, Mabel Fincher. Mabel is retiring after thirty-seven years with CM, the last fourteen spent as a policy renewal supervisor. Since Sue had spent a few weeks in Mabel's group last summer, she was familiar with Mabel's style and also knew most of the group members. She anticipated no problems from any of her soon-to-be employees, except possibly for Lillian Lantz. Lillian was well into her fifties, had been a policy renewal clerk for over a dozen years, and—as the "grand old lady"—carried a lot of weight with group members. Sue concluded that without Lantz' support, her job could prove very difficult.

Sue is determined to get her career off on the right foot. As a result, she has been doing a lot of thinking about the qualities of an effective leader.

Questions

1. What are the critical factors that will influence Sue's success as a leader? Would these factors be the same if success were defined as group satisfaction rather than group productivity?
2. Do you think that Sue can choose a leadership style? If so, describe the style you think would be most effective for her. If not, why?
3. What suggestions might you make to Sue to help her win over or control Lillian Lantz?

CASE IIIE

GAMES PEOPLE PLAY IN THE SHIPPING DEPARTMENT

The Science Fiction Book Club (SFBC) sells a large list of science fiction books, at discount prices, entirely by mail order. In 1985, the club shipped over 370,000 books and generated revenues of $5.4 million. Anyone familiar with the mail-order business realizes that it offers extremely high profit potential because, under careful management, inventory costs and overhead can be kept quite low. The biggest problems in mail-order businesses are filling orders, shipping the merchandise, and billing the customers. At SFBC, the Packing and Shipping (P&S) Department employs eight full-time people:

Ray, forty-four years old, has worked in P&S for seven years.

Al, forty-nine years old, has worked in P&S for nine years.

R.J., fifty-three years old, has worked in P&S for sixteen years. He had been head of the department for two years back in the late-1970s but stepped down voluntarily due to continuing stomach problems that doctors attributed to supervisory pressures.

Pearl, fifty-nine years old, was the original employee hired by the founder. She has been at SFBC for twenty-five years and in P&S for twenty-one years.

Margaret, thirty-one years old, is the newest member of the department. She has been employed less than a year.

Steve, twenty-seven years old, has worked in P&S for three years. He goes to college at nights and makes no effort to hide that he plans on leaving P&S and probably SFBC when he gets his degree next year.

George, forty-six years old, is currently head of P&S. He has been with SFBC for ten years, and in P&S for six.

Gary, twenty-five years old, has worked in P&S for two years.

The jobs in a shipping department are uniformly dull and repetitive. Each person is responsible for wrapping, addressing, and making the bills out on anywhere from 100 to 200 books a day. Part of George's responsibilities are to make allocations to each worker and to ensure that no significant backlogs occur. However, George spends less than 10 percent of his time in supervisory activities. The rest of the time he wraps, addresses, and makes out bills just like everyone else.

Apparently to deal with the repetitiveness of their jobs, the department members have created a number of games that they play among themselves. They seem almost childish, but it is obvious that the games mean something to these people. Importantly, each is played regularly. Some of the ones that will be described are played at least once a day. All are played a minimum of twice a week.

"The Stamp Machine Is Broken" is a game that belongs to Al. At least once a day, Al goes over to the postage meter in the office and unplugs it. He then proceeds loudly to attempt to make a stamp for a package. "The stamp machine is broken again," he yells. Either Ray or Gary, or both, will come over and spend thirty seconds or so trying to "fix it," then "discover" that it's unplugged. The one who finds it unplugged then says "Al, you're a mechanical spastic" and others in the office join in and laugh.

Gary is the initiator of the game "Steve, There's a Call for You." Usually played in the late afternoon, an hour or so before everyone goes home, Gary will pick up the phone and pretend that there is someone on the line. "Hey, Steve, it's for you," he'll yell out. "It's Mr. Big [the president of SFBC]. Says he wants you to come over to his office right away. You're going to be the new vice-president!" The game is an obvious sarcastic jab at Steve's going to college and his frequent comments about someday being a big executive.

At least two or three times a day, Ray will go out of his way to walk by Margaret's desk. As he walks by, he sensuously runs his hand down her back and blows in her ear. She always jumps, though she knows he's coming. Ray's desk is two ahead of Margaret's and to get behind her he has to walk by her. The irony of this little flirtatious game is that Margaret obviously loves the attention, though she always plays "upset" by Ray's actions. In fact, when Ray was on vacation for two weeks last month, everyone noticed how Margaret seemed depressed. Could she actually be missing Ray?

R.J., though fifty-three years old, has never married and lives with his mother. The main interests in his life are telling stories and showing pictures of last year's vacation and planning for this year's vacation. Without exception, everyone finds R.J.'s vacation talk boring. But that doesn't stop Pearl or George from "setting him up" several times a week. "Hey R.J., can we see those pictures you took last year in Oregon again?" That question always gets R.J. to drop whatever he's doing and pull 75 to 100 pictures from his top drawer. "Hey, R.J., what are you planning to do on your vacation this year?'' always gets R.J.'s eyes shining and invariably leads to the unfolding of maps he also keeps in his top drawer.

George's favorite game is "What's It Like to Be Rich?" which he plays with Pearl. Pearl's husband had been a successful banker and had died a half-dozen years earlier. He left her very well off financially. Pearl enjoys everyone knowing that she doesn't have to work, has a large lovely home, buys a new car every year, and includes some of the city's more prominent business people and politicians among her friends. George will mention the name of some big shot in town and Pearl never fails to take the bait. She proceeds to tell how he is a close friend of hers. George might also bring up money in some context in order to allow Pearl to complain about high taxes, the difficulty in finding good house-keepers, the high cost of traveling to Europe, or some other concern of the affluent.

Questions

1. Analyze the group dynamics going on in P&S.
2. How do these games affect the department's performance?
3. Does this department lack leadership?
4. Is the informal communication taking place in the department functional?

CASE IIIF

I DON'T MAKE DECISIONS!

I met Ted Kelly for the first time at a cocktail party. As things happen, we got to talking about our work. When he found out I taught organizational behavior, he understood my interest in his job. Ted was the plant manager at a large chemical refinery in town. About ten minutes or so into our conversation, I asked him what type of leadership style he used.

Ted: "I don't make decisions at my plant."

Author: "You mean you use democratic leadership?"

Ted: "No. I said I don't make decisions! My subordinates are paid to make decisions. No point in my doing their jobs."

Ted went on to say that about five years ago he decided that his subordinate managers had become too dependent on him. After some deliberation, he made a decision—as he tells it, it was the last one he made on his job. He decided never to make a decision again.

I didn't really believe what I was hearing. I guess Ted sensed that, so he offered me an invitation to visit his plant. I wasn't going to miss the opportunity. I asked him when I could come over. "Any time you like, except Mondays between 1 and 3 P.M." "Anytime?" I questioned. "Yeah," he replied. "Ever since I decided not to decide, I've got nothing to keep me busy."

The middle of the next week, I popped in on Ted unannounced. I found his office by following the signs. He had no secretary. He was lying on his sofa, half asleep. My arrival seemed to jar him awake. He seemed glad to see me. He offered me a seat.

Our conversation began by my inquiring exactly what he did everyday. "You're looking at it. I sleep a lot. Oh yeah, I read the four or five memos I get from the head office every week." I couldn't believe what I was hearing. Here was a fifty-year-old, obviously successful, executive, probably earning better than $85,000 a year, telling me he doesn't do anything. He could tell, however, that I wasn't buying his story.

"If you don't believe what I'm saying, check with my subordinates," he told me. He said he had six department managers working for him. I asked him to choose one I could talk with.

"No, I can't do that. First, I don't make decisions. Second, when the one I chose confirmed what I've been telling you, you'd think it was a setup. Here—these are the names and numbers of my department managers. You call them."

I did just that. I picked Peter Chandler, who headed up quality control. I dialed his number. He answered on the first ring. I told him that I wanted to talk to him about his boss's leadership style. He said "Come on over. I've got nothing to do anyway."

When I arrived at Pete's office, he was staring out the window. We sat down and he began to laugh. "I'll bet Ted's been telling you about how he doesn't make decisions." I concurred. "It's all true," he injected. "I've been here for almost three years and I've never seen him make a decision."

I couldn't figure out how this could be. "How many people do you have working here?" I asked.

Peter: "About 200."

Author: "How does this plant's operating efficiency stack up against the others?"

Peter: "Oh, we're number one out of the eighteen refineries. Been that way for years and years. Interesting thing is that this is the oldest refinery in the company, too. Our equipment may be outdated, but we're as efficient as they come."

Author: "What does Ted Kelly do?"

Peter: "Beats me. He attends the staff meetings on Monday afternoons from 1 to 3 P.M., but other than that, I don't know."

Author: "I get it. He makes all the decisions at that once-a-week staff meeting?"

Peter: "No. Each department head tells what key decisions he made last week. We then critique each other. Ted says nothing. The only thing he does at those meetings is listen and pass on any happenings up at headquarters."

I wanted to learn more, so I went back to Ted's office. I found him clipping his fingernails.

"I told you I was telling the truth," was the first thing he said. What followed was a long conversation in which I learned the following facts:

The two-hour weekly staff meeting is presided over by one of the department heads. They choose among themselves who will be their leader. It's a permanent position. Any problem that has come up during the week, if it can't be handled by a manager, will first be considered by several of the managers together. Only if the problem is still unresolved will it be taken to the leader. All issues are resolved at that level. They are never taken to Ted Kelly's level.

The performance record at Kelly's plant is well known in the company. Three of the last four plant managers have come out of Kelly's plant. When asked by the head office to recommend candidates for a plant management vacancy, Ted always selects the department head who presides over the staff meetings. The result is that there is a great deal of competition to lead the staff meetings. Additionally, because of Kelly's plant record for breeding management talent, whenever there is a vacancy for a department manager at Kelly's plant, the best people in the company apply for it. Of course, the decision as to who is hired is made by the existing heads at their weekly staff meeting.

The three plant managers who previously worked under Kelly have instituted a similar leadership style. Their plants have also shown significant improvement as measured by the companywide efficiency reports.

Even the department managers are practicing the Kelly method. They are forcing decision making down to their supervisors.

Questions

1. Why does Ted Kelly's "leadership style" work?
2. Is Ted Kelly abrogating his decision-making responsibilities? Are his department managers?
3. Would you like to work for Ted Kelly? Why?
4. Would you want Ted Kelly working for you? Why?
5. If Kelly's plant performance suddenly dropped off, what predictions would you make?

EXERCISE IIIA

Status-Ranking Task

Instructions: Rank the following occupations according to the prestige which is attached to them in the United States. Place a "1" in front of the occupation which you feel to be most prestigious, and so on, all the way to "16," least prestigious.

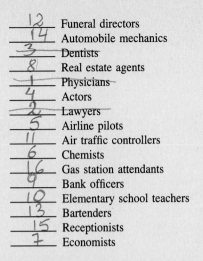

_12_ Funeral directors
_14_ Automobile mechanics
_3_ Dentists
_8_ Real estate agents
_1_ Physicians
_4_ Actors
_2_ Lawyers
_5_ Airline pilots
_11_ Air traffic controllers
_6_ Chemists
_16_ Gas station attendants
_9_ Bank officers
_10_ Elementary school teachers
_13_ Bartenders
_15_ Receptionists
_7_ Economists

Now form a group of from six to twelve participants. The objective of this group will be to create a consensus group ranking. The ranking of each occupation must be agreed upon by each member before it becomes a part of the group's decision. Members should try to make each ranking one with which *all* members agree at least partially. Two ground rules: no averaging and no "majority rule" votes. The group should take no more than 30 minutes to complete its task. When a group decision has been reached, turn to page 522 for the correct answer (based on studies of occupational prestige conducted in many countries and applied to 1970 U.S. Census classification) and further directions.

Source: D. J. Treiman, *Occupational Prestige in Comparative Prospective* (New York: Academic Press, 1977), pp. 306–15.

EXERCISE IIIB

Test Your Management Communication Skills

Circle the answer that best describes what you would do in each situation.

1. Your boss's immediate supervisor asks you to lunch. When you return, you sense your boss is curious. Do you . . .
   a. Give your boss a detailed description of the lunch?
   b. Avoid telling your boss anything?
   c. Mention the lunch casually—as though it really had no significance?
2. You're in the middle of an important meeting with your boss and there's a long-distance business call for you. Do you . . .
   a. Ask the boss's secretary to say you're out of the office?
   b. Accept the call and take as much time as it needs?
   c. Tell the person you're in a meeting and ask when you may call back?

3. As you're ready to leave for a hard-to-get job interview, you discover a spot on your shirt. Do you . . .
   a. Call to reschedule the interview?
   b. Rush to the nearest store and buy a new shirt?
   c. Decide that the spot is not very noticeable after all, and go to the interview "as is"?

4. You're conducting a staff meeting on new sales procedures. One employee keeps interrupting with questions not germane to the subject. Do you . . .
   a. Request all employees to hold their questions until you're finished?
   b. Accept the interruptions?
   c. Tell the employee that interruptions are out of order?

5. You're asked, by someone outside the company, to write a recommendation for a former employee whose work record was not very satisfactory. Do you . . .
   a. Write a letter that details your negative observations?
   b. Write a letter emphasizing one or two positive points?
   c. Decline the request?

6. A staff member comes to you to complain about the work habits of another. Do you say . . .
   a. "We'll have to discuss that later—there's too much else to do now"?
   b. "I'll be glad to talk with both of you—together, not separately"?
   c. "What's the problem . . . let's discuss it now"?

7. Your employees' Christmas party is underway when you arrive. Everybody seems well into the season's spirits—too well, in fact. Do you . . .
   a. Try to be a "good guy" and join in the fun?
   b. Leave immediately?
   c. Tell the person in charge that the party is out-of-hand and suggest it be ended as soon as possible.

8. For the fourth consecutive Friday, a staff member asks to leave early. Do you say . . .
   a. "I can't keep giving you permission like this—others resent it"?
   b. "Not today—there may be a staff meeting at 4 o'clock"?
   c. "You're important to us—I need you to put in a full day, especially on Fridays"?

9. You've been quoted correctly and favorably by the writer of a national magazine article. Do you now . . .
   a. Send the writer a gift?
   b. Call and thank the writer for the publicity?
   c. Write an appreciative note and offer to be of future help to the writer?

10. You've been hired from outside the company as director of a large department. You know several staff members thought they should have had the position. On the first day, do you . . .
    a. Initiate individual conversations with those individuals about the situation?
    b. Ignore the problem and hope it'll go away?
    c. Recognize the problem but concentrate on your job and on getting to know everyone?

11. An employee says to you, "I shouldn't tell you this, but have you heard . . .?" Do you say . . .
    a. "I don't want to hear any office gossip"?
    b. "I'm interested only if it concerns our business"?
    c. "What's the latest—let me in on it"?

12. Your boss, in a customer meeting, makes an inaccurate statement. Do you . . .
   a. Point out the mistake later to your boss—and expect him to correct the statement?
   b. Correct your boss in front of the customer?
   c. Try to handle it yourself with the customer—at another time?

Turn to page 522 for scoring directions and key.

Source: Communispond, Inc., as reproduced in Jacob's Ladder, *Baltimore Sun,* May 4, 1983, p. D1. With permission.

EXERCISE IIIC

Leadership Questionnaire

The following items describe aspects of leadership behavior. Respond to each item according to the way you would be most likely to act if you were the leader of a work group. Circle whether you would be likely to behave in the described way always (A), frequently (F), occasionally (O), seldom (S), or never (N).

If I were the leader of a work group . . .

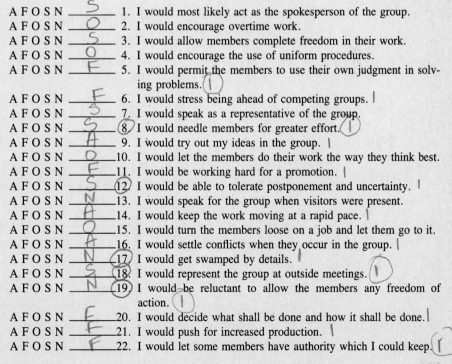

A F O S N ___S___ 1. I would most likely act as the spokesperson of the group.
A F O S N ___O___ 2. I would encourage overtime work.
A F O S N ___S___ 3. I would allow members complete freedom in their work.
A F O S N ___O___ 4. I would encourage the use of uniform procedures.
A F O S N ___F___ 5. I would permit the members to use their own judgment in solving problems.
A F O S N ___F___ 6. I would stress being ahead of competing groups.
A F O S N ___S___ 7. I would speak as a representative of the group.
A F O S N ___S___ 8. I would needle members for greater effort.
A F O S N ___A___ 9. I would try out my ideas in the group.
A F O S N ___O___ 10. I would let the members do their work the way they think best.
A F O S N ___F___ 11. I would be working hard for a promotion.
A F O S N ___S___ 12. I would be able to tolerate postponement and uncertainty.
A F O S N ___N___ 13. I would speak for the group when visitors were present.
A F O S N ___A___ 14. I would keep the work moving at a rapid pace.
A F O S N ___O___ 15. I would turn the members loose on a job and let them go to it.
A F O S N ___A___ 16. I would settle conflicts when they occur in the group.
A F O S N ___N___ 17. I would get swamped by details.
A F O S N ___S___ 18. I would represent the group at outside meetings.
A F O S N ___N___ 19. I would be reluctant to allow the members any freedom of action.
A F O S N ___F___ 20. I would decide what shall be done and how it shall be done.
A F O S N ___F___ 21. I would push for increased production.
A F O S N ___F___ 22. I would let some members have authority which I could keep.

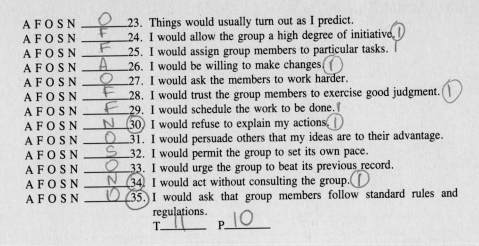

A F O S N ___O___ 23. Things would usually turn out as I predict.
A F O S N ___F___ 24. I would allow the group a high degree of initiative. ①
A F O S N ___F___ 25. I would assign group members to particular tasks. ⏐
A F O S N ___A___ 26. I would be willing to make changes. ①
A F O S N ___O___ 27. I would ask the members to work harder.
A F O S N ___F___ 28. I would trust the group members to exercise good judgment. ①
A F O S N ___F___ 29. I would schedule the work to be done. ⏐
A F O S N ___N___ ③0. I would refuse to explain my actions. ①
A F O S N ___O___ 31. I would persuade others that my ideas are to their advantage.
A F O S N ___S___ 32. I would permit the group to set its own pace.
A F O S N ___O___ 33. I would urge the group to beat its previous record.
A F O S N ___N___ ③4. I would act without consulting the group. ①
A F O S N ___O___ ③5. I would ask that group members follow standard rules and regulations.
T___11___ P__10__

Turn to page 523 for scoring directions and key.
Source: J. W. Pfeiffer and J. E. Jones (eds.), *A Handbook of Structured Experiences for Human Relations Training*, Vol. 1 (Revised), San Diego, CA: University Associates Press, 1974. Used with permission.

EXERCISE IIID

Power Orientation Test

Instructions.   For each statement, circle the number that most closely resembles your attitude.

STATEMENT	DISAGREE			AGREE	
	A lot	A little	Neutral	A little	A lot
1. The best way to handle people is to tell them what they want to hear.	1	②	③	4	5
2. When you ask someone to do something for you, it is best to give the real reason for wanting it rather than giving reasons that might carry more weight.	1	2	3	4	⑤
3. Anyone who completely trusts anyone else is asking for trouble.	1	2	③	4	5
4. It is hard to get ahead without cutting corners here and there.	1	2	③	4	5

5. It is safest to assume that all people have a vicious streak, and it will come out when they are given a chance.

    1   2   3   4   5

6. One should take action only when it is morally right.

    1   2   3   4   5

7. Most people are basically good and kind.

    1   2   3   4   5

8. There is no excuse for lying to someone else.

    1   2   3   4   5

9. Most people forget more easily the death of their father than the loss of their property.

    1   2   3   4   5

10. Generally speaking, people won't work hard unless they're forced to do so.

    1   2   3   4   5

Turn to page 524 for scoring directions and key.

Source: R. Christie and F. L. Geis, *Studies in Machiavellianism.* © Academic Press 1970. Reprinted by permission.

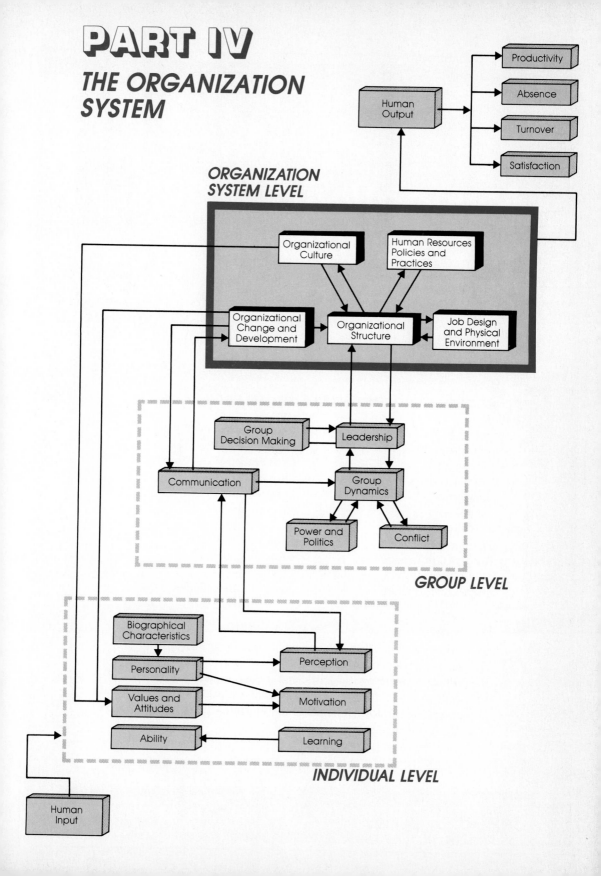

Foundations of Organization Structure

11

AFTER STUDYING THIS CHAPTER, YOU SHOULD BE ABLE TO:

Define and explain the following key terms and concepts:

Adhocracy	Organic structure
Bureaucracy	Organization size
Centralization	Organization structure
Complexity	Power-control
Environment	Product structure
Formalization	Simple structure
Functional structure	Spatial differentiation
Horizontal differentiation	Span of control
Matrix structure	Technology
Mechanistic structure	Vertical differentiation

Understand:

The three components that make up organization structure

The factors that determine structure

The difference between mechanistic and organic structures

The conditions that favor different organization structures

The moderating factors that influence the structure—performance/ satisfaction relationship

One man's red tape is another man's system.

—D. WALDO

Jerry Nichols has, what most people would call, a pretty good job. He's got an attractively furnished office on the top floor of a Houston skyscraper, a nice view, his own secretary, the prestige that goes with being a security analyst with a major brokerage firm, and a compensation package that brings him in better than $60,000 a year—not bad for a twenty-eight-year-old guy who has been out of graduate school for less than five years. In addition, Jerry's employer treats him as a professional. His work hours are relatively flexible. He comes and goes as he pleases. He's supposed to have an hour for lunch, but he frequently takes two. In contrast to most people's job, Jerry has a considerable amount of autonomy.

Jerry Nichols' job may provide him with more freedom and discretion than most employees enjoy, but he is far from unrestricted. He may not have to punch in and out on a time clock or contend with a boss who watches over his every move, but Jerry faces a number of restrictions on his behavior. Almost every employee in an organization, including professionals like Jerry Nichols, have job descriptions that outline what they are supposed to do. The organization also imposes policies, procedures, and rules that restrict an employee's freedom of choice. Further, an authority hierarchy exists that defines each member's boss and specifies the formal channels through which communications are to pass. These constraints represent examples of structural devices created to direct and control the behavior of employees. Every organization has them. For some employees, like Jerry Nichols, these structural constraints act more as general limits on discretion than as compelling controls that severely restrict what he can or cannot do. But *all* employees are constrained, in some degree, by their organization's structure. In this chapter, we want to demonstrate how an organization's structure can and does affect the attitudes and behavior of its members.

WHAT IS STRUCTURE?

Organizations create structure to facilitate the coordination of activities and to control the actions of its members. Structure, itself, is made up of three components. The first has to do with the degree to which activities within the organization are broken up or differentiated. We call this *complexity*. Second, is the degree to which rules and procedures are utilized. This component is referred to as *formalization*. The third component of structure is *centralization,* which considers where decision-making authority lies. Combined, these three components make up an organization's structure.[1] Some large organizations, like General Electric or the U.S. Department of Defense, are rigidly structured. They have lots of differentiated units, a great number of vertical levels between top management and the workers at the bottom, numerous rules and regulations that members are required to follow, and elaborate decision-making networks. At the other extreme are organizations that are loosely structured—few differentiated units, only a couple levels of management hierarchy, little in terms of formalized regulations to restrict employees, and a simple system for making decisions. Of course, in between these two extremes lie a number of structural combinations. The fact exists that organizations differ in the ways they are structured. What is of primary interest to us is how these structural differences impact on employee attitudes and behavior. First, however, let's briefly elaborate on the three components we have identified to ensure we have a common understanding of what is meant when we use the term *organization structure*.

Complexity

Complexity encompasses three forms of differentiation: horizontal, vertical, and spatial. *Horizontal differentiation* considers the degree of horizontal separation between units. We can state that the larger the number of different occupations within an organization that require specialized knowledge and skills, the more horizontally complex that organization is. Why? Because diverse orientations make it more difficult for organizational members to communicate and more difficult for management to coordinate their activities. When organizations have coordination problems because the cost accountants can't understand the priorities of the industrial engineers or because marketing and credit personnel have conflicting goals, the source of the problems is horizontal differentiation.

Vertical differentiation refers to the depth of the organizational hierarchy. The more levels that exist between top management and the operatives, the more complex the organization is. This is because there is a greater potential for communication distortion, it's more difficult to coordinate the decisions of managerial personnel, and it's harder for top management to oversee closely the actions of operatives where there are more vertical levels. It's a lot more likely that information having to go through eight or ten levels of management hierarchy will become distorted or misinterpreted than if that information had to move through only two or three levels.

Spatial differentiation encompasses the degree to which the location of an organization's physical facilities and personnel are geographically dispersed. As spatial differentiation increases so does complexity, because communication, coordination, and control become more difficult. Coordinating Sheraton's hundreds of hotels, located around the world, is a far more complex undertaking than coordinating the dozen New York City hotels that make up the Helmsley chain.

Formalization

Formalization refers to the degree to which jobs within the organization are standardized. If a job is highly formalized, then the job incumbent has a minimum amount of discretion over what is to be done, when it is to be done, and how he or she should do it. Employees can be expected always to handle the same input in exactly the same way, resulting in a consistent and uniform output. There are explicit job descriptions, lots of organizational rules, and clearly defined procedures covering work processes in organizations where there is high formalization. Where formalization is low, job behaviors are relatively nonprogrammed and employees have a great deal of freedom to exercise discretion in their work. Since an individual's discretion on the job is inversely related to the amount of behavior that is preprogrammed by the organization, the greater the standardization, the less input the employee has into how his or her work is to be done. Standardization not only eliminates the possibility of employees engaging in alternative behaviors, but it even removes the need for employees to consider alternatives.

The degree of formalization can vary widely between organizations and within organizations. Certain jobs, for instance, are well known to have little formalization. College book travelers—the representatives of publishers who call on professors to inform them of their company's new publications—have a great deal of freedom in their jobs. They have no standard sales "spiel," and the extent of rules and procedures governing their behavior may be little more than the requirement that they submit a weekly sales report and some suggestions on what to emphasize for the various new titles. At the other extreme, there are clerical and editorial positions in the same publishing houses where employees are required to "clock in" at their workstation by 8:00 A.M. or be docked a half-hour of pay and, once at that workstation, to follow a set of precise procedures dictated by management.

Centralization

In some organizations, top managers make all the decisions. Lower-level managers merely carry out top management's directives. At the other extreme, there are organizations where decision making is pushed down to those managers who are closest to the action. The former case is called centralization; the latter is decentralization.

The term centralization refers to the degree to which decision making is concentrated at a single point in the organization. The concept includes only formal authority, that is, the rights inherent in one's position. Typically, it is said that if top management makes the organization's key decisions with little or no input from lower-level personnel, then the organization is centralized. In contrast, the more that lower-level personnel provide input or are actually given the discretion to make decisions, the more decentralized the organization.

An organization characterized by centralization is an inherently different structural animal from one that is decentralized. In a decentralized organization, action can be taken more quickly to solve problems, more people provide input into decisions, and employees are less likely to feel alienated from those who make the decisions that affect their work lives.

CLASSIFYING ORGANIZATION STRUCTURES

Concepts like complexity, formalization, and centralization often seem abstract to the typical reader or, for that matter, the average employee in an organization. In this section, we want to develop a simple classification scheme that can help you to describe organizations better. Then, we will offer a more detailed discussion of four specific structural designs that are now widely utilized.

Mechanistic and Organic Structures

An organization's overall structure generally falls into one of two designs. One is the *mechanistic structure*. It's characterized by high complexity (especially a great deal of horizontal differentiation), high formalization, a limited information network (mostly downward communication), and little participation by low-level members in decision making. At the other extreme is the *organic structure*. It is low in complexity and formalization, it possesses a comprehensive information network (utilizing lateral and upward communication as well as downward), and it involves high participation in decision making. As Figure 11-1 depicts, mechanistic structures are rigid, relying on authority and a well-defined hierarchy to facilitate coordination. The organic structure, on the other hand, is flexible and adaptive. Coordination is achieved through constant communication and adjustment.

The mechanistic-organic dichotomy is a useful designation device for generalizing about organization structures. The world of organizations, of course, is not so neatly defined. We can, however, introduce two specific structural forms that capture the essential ingredients of mechanistic and organic designs. You've undoubtedly heard the term *bureaucracy* to describe certain organizations. The bureaucratic structure has most of the characteristics associated with the mechan-

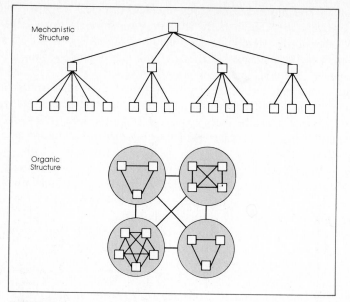

FIGURE 11-1

Two Diverse Structural Designs

istic model. *Adhocracy,* or the adhocratic structure, combines most of the features we've described in the organic model.

To many, the term bureaucracy conjures up a host of attributes implying inefficiency—red tape, paper shuffling, rigid application of rules, and redundance of effort. That is not what we mean by the term. When we talk of bureaucracy, we refer to a structural design that German sociologist Max Weber has described as having the following characteristics:

Division of labor—Each person's job is broken down into simple, routine, and well-defined tasks.

Well-defined authority hierarchy—There is a multilevel formal structure, with a hierarchy of positions or offices. Each lower office is under the supervision and control of a higher one.

High formalization—To ensure uniformity and to regulate the behavior of jobholders, there is heavy dependence on formal rules and procedures.

Impersonal nature—Sanctions are applied uniformly and impersonally to avoid involvement with individual personalities and personal preferences of members.

Employment decisions based on merit—Selection and promotion decisions are based on technical qualifications, competence, and performance of the candidate.

Career tracks for employees—Members are expected to pursue a career in the organization. In return for this career commitment, employees are given permanent employment; that is, they are retained even if they "burn out" or their skills become obsolete.

Distinct separation of members' organizational and personal lives—To prevent the demands and interests of personal affairs from interfering with the rational impersonal conduct of the organization's activities, the two are kept completely separate.[2]

While these characteristics represent the ideal or perfect bureaucracy, cumulatively they are a fairly accurate description of most large organizations. Whether you are describing the structure of Mobil Oil, the American Broadcasting Company, Bristol-Myers, the New York City school system, or the U.S. Army, these organizations and thousands of others substantially meet all the characteristics we attribute to bureaucracy. In structural terms, they are highly complex and highly formalized. Whether they are centralized or decentralized typically depends on the type of people they employ. If employees are professionals or hold specialized skills, the bureaucracy will be decentralized. Otherwise, authority is typically kept centralized.

What bureaucracy is to the mechanistic form, adhocracy is to the organic. The term ''adhocracy'' refers to any structure that is essentially a flexible, adaptive, responsive system organized around unique problems to be solved by groups of relative strangers with diverse professional skills. In terms of our structural dimensions, adhocracies would be characterized as having moderate to low complexity, low formalization, and decentralized decision making.

An adhocracy may be a temporary project group, a task force, or a committee. For instance, if Procter & Gamble wanted to develop and design a new product, say, a toothpaste, it would likely rely on an adhocratic structure. Personnel with expertise in finance, marketing, manufacturing, cost accounting, product design, research, and other relevant areas would be tapped from their functional departments and temporarily assigned the task of creating the product, designing its package, determining its market, computing its manufacturing costs, and assessing its profit margin. Once the problems had been fully worked out of the product and it was ready to be produced in quantity, the adhocratic structure would be disbanded and the toothpaste would be integrated into the permanent functional structure.

Let's now turn our attention to describing several of the more widely used structural designs.

FIGURE 11–2

Source: GOOSEMYER by Parker and Wilder. © 1983 News Group Chicago, Inc. Courtesy of News America Syndicate.

The Simple Structure

What do a small retail store, an electronics firm run by a hard-driving entrepreneur, and the reelection campaign office for a city councilman in Eugene, Oregon have in common? They probably all have simple structures.

Most small organizations, or new ones that are just starting out, utilize the simple structure. In terms of absolute number, most organizations in North America are probably simple structures.

Simple structures are characterized most by what they're not rather than what they are.[3] The simple structure is *not* elaborated. It is low in complexity, has little formalization, and has authority centralized in a single person. Overall, it is more organic than mechanistic.

Figure 11–3 shows an example of the simple structure: the Fashion Flair retail stores. Notice that this organization is flat or low on vertical differentiation. Decision making is basically informal—all important decisions are centralized in the hands of the senior executive who, because of the organization's low complexity, is able readily to obtain key information and can act rapidly when required. The senior executive is the owner-manager at Fashion Flair.

The Functional Structure

Pick up a copy of the organization chart for any *Fortune 500* company and take a close look at how the organization is designed. The probability is very high that the design will encompass the functional structure.

The distinguishing feature of the functional structure is that similar and related occupational specialties are grouped together. Activities such as marketing, accounting, manufacturing, and personnel are grouped under a functional head

FIGURE 11–3
Simple Structure of Fashion Flair Stores

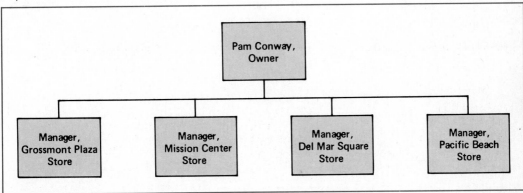

who reports to a central headquarters. Figure 11–4 shows a typical functional structure for a manufacturing firm.

The functional structure is extremely popular, undoubtedly due to its compatibility with the bureaucratic structure. That is, the functional structure maximizes the economies from specialization. Putting like specialties together affords economies of scale and reduces duplication of personnel and equipment, and employees are likely to feel comfortable and satisfied because they are part of a homogeneous group where their peers all talk "the same language."

The Product Structure

In addition to organizing by function, you can structure an organization around product lines. Figure 11–5 shows a simplified version of the product structure developed by General Motors for its North American Automotive Operations. Created in 1984, this structure has two integrated car groups, each operating as a self-contained business unit. Each car group is responsible for its own product, including engineering, manufacturing, assembly, and marketing.

The major advantage to the product form is accountability. The product manager is responsible for all facets surrounding the product. Instead of having the marketing manager oversee fifteen different product lines, each product structure will have its own marketing manager with sole responsibility for marketing his or her division's product. In this way, product control is centralized with the product manager. The drawbacks, of course, are the need to coordinate activities between product structures and the duplication of functions within the various structures. Whereas in the functional structure a department of five people might be able to handle the entire organization's purchasing activities, if that organization is structured around ten product divisions, each will probably require a purchasing agent, thus doubling the number of personnel engaged in purchasing.

FIGURE 11–4
Functional Structure in a Manufacturing Organization

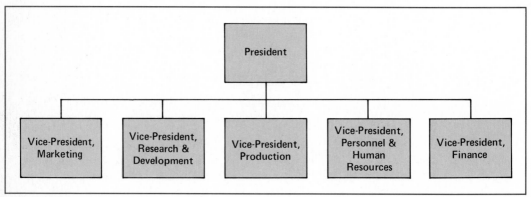

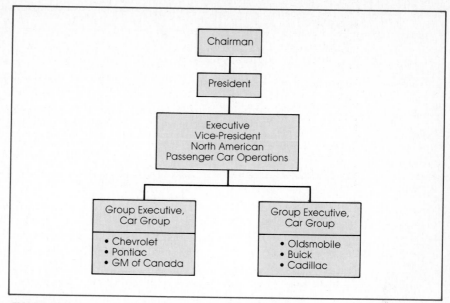

FIGURE 11–5

Product Structure for General Motors' North American Automotive Operations

Source: General Motors Corp., 1984 General Motors Public Interest Report (April 1984), p. 7. With permission.

The Matrix Structure

One of the more recent organizational design innovations is the matrix structure. Essentially, the matrix combines the functional and product structures. Ideally, it seeks to gain the strengths of each, while avoiding their weaknesses. That is, the strength of the functional structure lies in putting like specialists together, which minimizes the number necessary, and it allows the pooling and sharing of specialized resources across products. Its major disadvantage is the difficulty of coordinating the tasks of diverse functional specialists so that their activities are completed on time and within budget. The product structure, on the other hand, has exactly the opposite benefits and disadvantages. It facilitates the coordination among specialties to achieve on-time completion and meet budget targets. Further, it provides clear responsibility for all activities related to a product, but with duplication of activities and costs.

Figure 11–6 shows the matrix form as used in a College of Business Administration. The academic departments of accounting, economics, marketing, and so forth are functional units. Additionally, specific programs (i.e., products) are overlaid on the functions. In this way, members in a matrix structure have a dual assignment: to their functional department and to their product group. For instance, a professor of accounting teaching an undergraduate course reports to the director of undergraduate programs as well as to the chairman of the accounting department.

Programs Academic Departments	Undergraduate	Master's	Ph. D.	Research	Executive Programs	Community-Service Programs
Accounting						
Administrative Studies						
Economics						
Finance						
Marketing						
Organizational Behavior						
Quantitative Methods						

FIGURE 11-6

Matrix Structure for a College of Business Administration

WHY DO STRUCTURES DIFFER?

We've described two general structural designs—the mechanistic and organic—and their counterparts in practice—bureaucracy and adhocracy. Then we briefly described four specific structural designs that you're likely to encounter. But why are some organizations structured along more mechanistic lines while others follow organic characteristics? What are the forces that influence the form that is chosen? Management is the obvious decision-making body for choosing structure. But there are forces that limit management's choices. In the following pages, we shall present the major forces that researchers have identified as causes or determinants of an organization's structure.

Organization Size

A quick glance at the organizations we deal with regularly in our lives would lead most of us to conclude that size would have some bearing on an organization's structure. The more than 800,000 employees of the U.S. Postal Service, for example, do not neatly fit into one building, or into several departments supervised by a couple of managers. It's pretty hard to envision 800,000 people being organized in any manner other than one that contained a great deal of horizontal, vertical, and spatial differentiation, used a large number of procedures and regulations to ensure uniform practices, and followed a high degree of decentralized decision making. On the other hand, a local messenger service that employs ten people and generates less than $300,000 a year in service fees is not likely to need decentralized decision making or formalized procedures and regulations.

A little more thought suggests that the same conclusion—size influences structure—can be arrived at through a more sophisticated reasoning process. As an organization hires more operative employees, it will attempt to take advantage of the economic benefits from specialization. The result will be increased horizontal differentiation. Grouping like functions together will facilitate intragroup efficiencies, but will cause intergroup relations to suffer as each performs its different activities. Management, therefore, will need to increase vertical differentiation to coordinate the horizontally differentiated units. This expansion in size is also likely to result in spatial differentiation. All of this increase in complexity will reduce top management's ability to directly supervise the activities within the organization. The control achieved through direct surveillance, therefore, will be replaced by the implementation of formal rules and regulations. This increase in formalization may also be accompanied by still greater vertical differentiation as management creates new units to coordinate the expanding and diverse activities of organizational members. Finally, with top management further removed from the operating level, it becomes difficult for senior executives to make rapid and informative decisions. The solution is to substitute decentralized decision making for centralization. Following this reasoning, we see changes in size leading to major structural changes.

But does it actually happen this way? Does structure change directly as a result in a change in the total number of employees? A review of the evidence indicates that size has a significant influence on some but certainly not all elements of structure.

Size appears to impact on complexity at a decreasing rate.[4] That is, increases in organization size are accompanied by initially rapid and subsequently more gradual increases in differentiation. The biggest effect, however, is on vertical differentiation.[5] As organizations increase their number of employees, more levels are added, but at a decreasing rate.

The evidence is quite strong linking size and formalization.[6] There is a logical connection between the two. Management seeks to control the behavior of its employees. This can be achieved by direct surveillance or by the use of formalized regulations. While not perfect substitutes for each other, as one increases, the need for the other should decrease. Because surveillance costs should increase very rapidly as an organization expands in size, it seems reasonable to expect that it would be less expensive for management to substitute formalization for direct surveillance as size increases.

There is also a strong inverse relationship between size and centralization.[7] In small organizations, it's possible for management to exercise control by keeping decisions centralized. As size increases, management is physically unable to maintain control in this manner and, therefore, is forced to decentralize.

Technology

The term *technology* refers to how an organization transfers its inputs to outputs. Every organization has one or more technologies for converting financial, human, and physical resources into products or services. The Ford Motor Company, for instance, predominantly uses an assembly-line process to make its products. On the other hand, colleges may use a number of instruction technologies—the ever-popular formal lecture method, the case analysis method, the experiential exercise method, the programmed learning method, and so forth.

There is no agreement on a universal technology classification.[8] If there is a common denominator among those classifications that attempt to describe the processes or methods that organizations use to transform inputs into outputs, it is the *degree of routineness*. By this we mean that technologies tend toward either routine or nonroutine activities. The former are characterized by automated and standardized operations. This describes such diverse processes as mass-production assembly lines or repetitive clerical tasks. Nonroutine activities are customized. They include such varied operations as furniture restoring, custom shoemaking, or NASA's efforts at developing the space shuttle. As shown in Figure 11–7, we can think of all technologies as falling somewhere along a routine-nonroutine continuum.

Some researchers argue that there is a *technological imperative,* that is, that technology *causes* structure.[9] A more moderate position is that technology *constrains* managers. If managers have a considerable degree of choice over their organization's technology, then there is little basis for the imperative argument. Technology would only control structure to the degree that managers chose a technology that demanded certain structural dimensions. For instance, it has been argued that organizations choose the domain in which they will operate and, hence, the activities in which they will engage.[10] If an organization decides to offer consulting advice tailored to the needs of its clients, it is not likely to use the routine-oriented mass-production technology. Similarly, the fact that Honda of America chose to build a manufacturing facility in Ohio that could produce at least four hundred cars a day that could, in turn, retail in the $8,000–12,000 price range pretty well eliminated any technology other than one relying heavily on routinized mass-production activities. Had Honda decided to produce only four cars

FIGURE 11–7
Technology Classification with Representative Examples

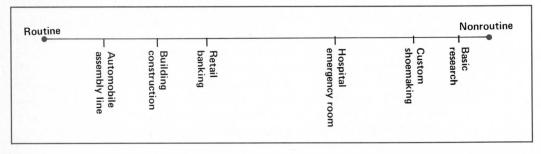

a day at that plant and charge $100,000 or more a piece for each car (which more accurately describes the production facility at Rolls Royce), then routine mass production might not be at all appropriate. The point is that "choice of domain, and a set of activities and tasks, tend to constrain the organization's technology, but the domain is still chosen."[11] The counterpoint, of course, is that even though domain is chosen, technology is still a major influence on structure. For instance, research laboratories are typically low in formalization, whereas claims departments in insurance companies are typically high on this structural dimension. A good part of this structural difference can be traced to the fact that research labs use nonroutine technologies and claims departments activities are standardized and routine.

What relationships have been found between technology and structure? Although the relationship is not overwhelmingly strong, we do find that routine technology is positively associated with low complexity. The greater the routineness, the fewer the number of occupational groups.[12] Similarly, as the work becomes more sophisticated, customized, and nonroutine, more problems occur that require management's attention. Closer supervision results and, with it, more vertical levels are necessary in the structure. So nonroutine technology is likely to lead to high complexity.

The technology-formalization relationship is stronger. Studies consistently show routineness to be associated with the presence of rule manuals, job descriptions, and other formalized documentation.[13]

Finally, the technology-centralization relationship is less straightforward. It seems logical that routine technologies would be associated with a centralized structure, whereas nonroutine technologies, which rely more heavily on the knowledge of specialists, would be characterized by delegated decision authority. This position has met with some support.[14] However, a more generalizable conclusion is that the technology-centralization relationship is moderated by the degree of formalization.[15] Formal regulations and centralized decision making are both control mechanisms and management can substitute them for each other. Routine technologies should be associated with centralized control if there is a minimum of rules and regulations. However, if formalization is high, routine technology can be accompanied by decentralization. So, we would predict that routine technology would lead to centralization, but only if formalization is low.

Environment

An organization's environment represents anything outside the organization itself. The problem of defining an organization's environment, however, is often quite difficult. "Nature has neatly packaged people into skins, animals into hides, and allowed trees to enclose themselves with bark. It is easy to see where the unit is and where the environment is. No so for social organizations."[16] We'll define the environment as composed of those institutions or forces that affect the performance of the organization, but over which the organization has little control. These typically include suppliers, customers, government regulatory agencies, and the like. But keep in mind that it is not always clear who or what is included in any specific organization's relevant environment.

The environment-structure relationship has received a large amount of attention. The reason for this attention is quite simple: Organizations must adapt to their environments if they are to succeed because organizations are dependent on their environments if they are to survive. They must identify and follow their environments, sense changes in those environments, and make appropriate adjustments as necessary. But changing environments produce uncertainty if management can't predict in what ways their environments are moving. And management doesn't like uncertainty. As a result, management will try to eliminate or at least minimize the impact of environmental uncertainty. Alterations in the organization's structural components are a major tool that management has for controlling environmental uncertainty. The environmental imperative would propose, therefore, that the degree of environmental uncertainty is *the* determinant of structure. If uncertainty is high, the organization will be designed along flexible lines in order to adapt to rapid changes, that is, as an organic structure. If uncertainty is low, management will opt for a structure that will be most efficient and offer the highest degree of managerial control—the mechanistic structure.

Does the evidence support these predictions? The answer is "Yes." Environmental uncertainty and organizational complexity are inversely related. This is particularly true for departments within organizations.[17] Those departments within the organization that are most dependent on the environment—such as marketing or research and development—are typically the lowest in complexity.

Similarly, formalization and environmental uncertainty are inversely related.[18] That is, certain and stable environments lead to high formalization. Why? Because stable environments create a minimal need for rapid response and economies exist for organizations that standardize their activities.

Centralization is also affected by the environment. If the environment is large and multifaceted, it becomes difficult for management to monitor. As a result, the structure tends to become decentralized.[19] This explains why the marketing function in organizations is typically decentralized. If a firm has a large number of customers and the needs of these customers are prone to rapid changes, management must be able to respond rapidly if it is to keep its customers satisfied. This can best be achieved by pushing key decisions down to the local marketing managers who are closest to the customer. Decentralization allows for more rapid response.

Power-Control

An increasingly popular and insightful approach to the question of what causes structure is to look to a political explanation. Size, technology, and environment—even when combined—can at best explain only 50 to 60 percent of the variability in structure.[20] There is a growing body of evidence that suggests that power and control can explain a good portion of the residual variance. More specifically, the power-control explanation states that an organization's structure is the result of a power struggle by internal constituencies who are seeking to further their interests.[21] Like all decisions in an organization, the structural decision is not fully rational. Managers do not necessarily choose those alternatives that will maximize the organization's interest. They choose criteria and weight them so that the "best choice" will meet the minimal demands of the organization, and also satisfy or enhance the interests of the decision maker. Size, technology, and environmental uncertainty act as constraints by establishing parameters and defining how much discretion is available. Almost always, within the parameters, there is a great deal of room for the decision maker to maneuver. The power-control position, therefore, argues that those in power will choose a structure that will maintain or enhance their control. Consistent with this perspective, we should expect structures to change very slowly, if at all. Significant changes would occur only as a result of a political struggle in which new power relations evolve. But this rarely occurs. Transitions in the executive suite are usually peaceful. They are evolutionary rather than revolutionary. However, major shake-ups in top management occasionally do occur. Not surprisingly, they are typically followed by major structural changes.

Predictions based on the power-control viewpoint differ from those based on the three previous approaches in that those approaches were basically contingency models: Structures change to reflect changes in size, technology, or environmental uncertainty. The power-control approach, however, is essentially noncontingent. It assumes little change within the organization's power coalition. Hence, it would propose that structures are relatively stable over time. More important, power-control advocates would predict that after taking into consideration size, technology, and environmental factors, those in power would choose a structure that would best serve their personal interests. What type of structure would that be? Obviously one that would be low in complexity, high in formalization, and centralized. These structural dimensions will most likely maximize control in the hands of senior management. A structure with these properties becomes the single "one best way" to organize. Of course, *best* in this context refers to "maintenance of control" rather than enhancement of organizational performance.

Is the power-control position an accurate description? The evidence suggests that it explains a great deal of why organizations are structured the way they are.[22] The dominant structural forms in organizations today are essentially mechanistic. Organic structures have received a great deal of attention by academicians, but the vast majority of real organizations, especially those that employ several hundred or more employees, are mechanistic. Even the simple structure, though low in formalization, maintains control by consolidating decision-making power in the hands of the senior executive.

Applying the Contingency Factors

Under what conditions would each of the contingency factors we've introduced— organization size, technology, and enviroment—be the dominant determinant of an organization's structure? More specifically, when should we expect to find mechanistic structures and when should organic structures be most prevalent?

ORGANIZATION SIZE

The larger an organization's size, in terms of the number of members it employs, the more likely it is to use the mechanistic structure. The creation of extensive rules and regulations only makes sense when there are a large number of people to be coordinated. Similarly, given the fact that a manager's ability to supervise a set of subordinates directly has some outside limit, as more people are hired to do the work, more managers will be needed to oversee these people. This creates increased complexity.

We should not, however, expect the size-structure relationship to be linear over a wide range. This is because once the organization becomes relatively large—having fifteen hundred to two thousand employees or more—it will tend to have already acquired most of the properties of a mechnistic structure. So the addition of five hundred employees to an organization that has only one hundred employees is likely to lead to significantly increased levels of complexity and formalization. Yet adding five hundred employees to an organization that already employs ten thousand is likely to have little or no impact on that organization's structure.

TECHNOLOGY

The evidence demonstrates that routine technologies are associated with mechanistic structures, whereas organic structures are best for dealing with the uncertainties inherent with nonroutine technologies. But we shouldn't expect technology to affect all parts of the organization equally.

The closer a department or unit within the organization is to the operating core, the more it will be affected by technology and, hence, the more technology will act to define structure. The primary activities of the organization take place at the operating core. State motor vehicle divisions, for example, process driver's license applications as well as distribute vehicle license plates and monitor the ownership of vehicles within their state. Those departments within the motor vehicle division that are at the operating core—giving out driver's tests, collecting fees for plates, and so on—will be significantly affected by technology. But as units become removed from this core, technology will play a less important role. The structure of the executive offices at the motor vehicle division, for instance, are not likely to be affected much by technology. So, to continue with the motor vehicle example, the use of routine technology at the operating core should result in the units at the core being high in both complexity and formalization. As units within the division move farther away from activities at the operating core, technology will become less of a constraint on structural choices.

ENVIRONMENT

Will a dynamic and uncertain environment always lead to an organic structure? Not necessarily! Whether environment is a major determinant of an organization's structure depends on the degree of dependence of the organization on its environment.

IBM operates in a highly dynamic environment—the result of a continual stream of new competitors introducing products to compete against theirs. But IBM's size, reputation for quality and service, and marketing expertise act as potent forces to lessen the impact of this uncertain environment on IBM's performance. This ability by IBM to lessen its dependence on its environment results in a structure that is much more mechanistic in design than would be expected given the uncertain environment within which it exists. In contrast, firms like Apple Computers and Digital Equipment Corporation have been far less successful in managing their dependence on their environment. Environment, therefore, is a much stronger influence on Apple and DEC's structure than at IBM.

KEY STRUCTURAL VARIABLES AND THEIR RELEVANCE TO OB

Now we move to the crux of our concern: relating structure to performance and satisfaction. This is no trivial task. The research on the structure-performance relationship, for instance, has been described as "among the most vexing and ambiguous in the field of management and organizational behavior."[23] Six structural variables have received the bulk of the attention. As a result, the following analysis reviews the evidence as it relates only to these variables.[24] This is not a major shortcoming, however, since these six include the essence of what we have called "organization structure."

Organization Size

If we look at the organization as a whole, there is increasing evidence to suggest that job satisfaction tends to decrease with size. This is intuitively logical since larger size results in fewer opportunities for individuals to participate in decision making, less proximity and identification with organizational goals, and less clarity between individual effort and an identifiable outcome. Increased organizational size also appears to lead to higher absenteeism, though not necessarily greater turnover. The larger size offers less opportunity for an employee to identify with his or her organization, but evidence suggests that larger organizations tend to pay better than smaller ones. The result is that individuals do not leave the larger organization but they do have a propensity to absent themselves more frequently from work. Interestingly, these findings may be moderated by the degree of decentralization. If increased size is accompanied by increased delegation of authority, the negative impact of size tends to be reduced.

The attention paid to the impact of size on performance and attitudes has not been focused solely at the level of the total organization. Concern has also been given to subunit size, that is, to the size of intraorganizational work units. There appears to be a definite positive relationship between subunit size and both absenteeism and turnover. This is in contrast to total organization size, which, as we noted, tends to be related only to absenteeism. Regarding job satisfaction, there seems to be no systematic and consistent relationship attributable to subunit size.

Organizational Level

Is satisfaction or performance affected by an employee's position in the vertical hierarchy? For instance, are senior executives more satisfied with their jobs than operatives or low-level supervisors?

In terms of structural variables, the most frequently investigated characteristic has been level in the organizational hierarchy. Although the evidence is far from conclusive, the bulk of the evidence finds that as we go up the hierarchy, we generally find more satisfied employees. Although one can debate causality, it seems unlikely that satisfied employees are getting more promotions than grumpy employees. It is far more logical to conclude that as one moves up in the organization, pay, formal authority, status accoutrements, and other rewards increase and, with them, job satisfaction.

Span of Control

The term "span of control" refers to the number of subordinates who report directly to a manager. Does this variable influence employee performance or satisfaction?

A review of the research indicates that it is probably safe to say that there is no evidence to support a relationship between span of control and performance. While it is intuitively attractive to argue that large spans might lead to higher employee performance because these spans provide more distant supervision, more opportunity for personal initiative, the research fails to support this notion. At this point it is impossible to state that any particular span of control is best for producing high performance or high satisfaction among subordinates. The most we can say is that there is some, but slight, evidence that a *manager*'s job satisfaction increases as the number of subordinates he or she supervises increases.

Horizontal Differentiation

There have not been many studies that have looked at the horizontal differentiation–performance relationship. The preponderance of evidence suggests a positive relationship—that is, the greater the specialization, the higher the performance—but because the measures of performance tend to be questionable and several studies find no association, a realistic conclusion would be that the relationship between horizontal differentiation and performance has not been clearly demonstrated.

Evidence for the impact of horizontal differentiation on satisfaction is only a little more encouraging. Horizontal differentiation has generally been regarded as leading to lower satisfaction in that a large segment of the work force is turned off and alienated by having to do narrowly defined and repetitive tasks. However, as we shall show in the next chapter's discussion on job design, this conclusion must be moderated by individual differences. Some people prefer structured and narrowly defined work tasks, while others value autonomy and freedom. Again, a clear relationship between horizontal differentiation and satisfaction has not been demonstrated.

Vertical Differentiation

Are there significant differences in terms of employee performance and satisfaction in tall organizations (with many vertical levels) versus flat organizations? There are mixed findings on the performance dimension. Both positive and negative relationships are reported in reviews of the research, making it difficult to generalize. On the satisfaction dimension, it appears that vertical differentiation does matter. High-level managers in tall organizations and lower-level managers in flat organizations experience more satisfaction than their opposites.

Centralization

The last independent variable we shall look at is centralization. Although we must qualify our generalizations, there do seem to be some meaningful relationships between centralization and our dependent variables.

The evidence supports the conclusion that centralization is negatively related with performance. Although these studies were done with managerial and professional personnel—therefore limiting our ability to generalize to blue-collar and nonprofessional employees—the evidence is nevertheless consistent.

There is limited evidence that—for a large segment of the work force—decentralization generates less job alienation, less dissatisfaction with work, greater satisfaction with supervision, and greater communication frequency among co-workers at the same level in the organization. Yet, even though centralization and satisfaction appear to be inversely related, this conclusion is likely to be moderated by individual differences and the type of tasks that employees perform. For instance, we would predict that this inverse relationship is likely to be stronger among professionals than among blue-collar workers.

ARE ORGANIZATION STRUCTURES REAL OR IN PEOPLE'S MINDS?

Complexity, formalization, and centralization are objective structural components that can be measured by organizational researchers. Every organization can be evaluated as to the degree to which it is high or low in all three. But employees don't objectively measure these components! They observe things around them in an unscientific fashion and then form their own implicit models of what the organization's structure is like. How many different people did they have to interview with before they were offered their job? How many people work in their department and building? How visible is the organization's policy manual, if one exists? Is everyone given a copy? If not, is one readily available? Is it referred to frequently? How is the organization and its top management described in newspapers and periodicals? Answers to questions such as these, when combined with an employee's past experiences and comments made by peers, leads members to form an overall subjective image of what their organization's structure is like. This image, though, may in no way resemble the organization's actual objective structural characteristics.

The importance of implicit models of organization structure should not be overlooked. As we noted in Chapter 3, people respond to their perceptions rather than to objective reality. We know that the relationship between many structural variables (i.e., span of control, horizontal differentiation, vertical differentiation) and subsequent levels of performance or job satisfaction are inconsistent. Some of this was explained as being attributable to individual preferences. Some employees, for instance, prefer narrowly defined and routine jobs; others abhor such characteristics. Additionally, however, a contributing cause to these inconsistent findings may be diverse perceptions of the objective characteristics. Researchers have focused on actual levels of the various structural components, but these may be irrelevant if people interpret similar components differently. The bottom line, therefore, is to understand how employees interpret their organization's structure. That should prove a more meaningful predictor of their behavior than the objective characteristics themselves.

IMPLICATIONS FOR PERFORMANCE AND SATISFACTION

This chapter has defined organization structure, explained its causes, presented a number of different ways in which structures may be designed, and then reviewed the evidence linking organization structure to performance and satisfaction. Our position is that an organization's internal structure contributes to explaining and predicting behavior. That is, in addition to individual differences and group factors, the structural relationships in which people work have an important bearing on employee attitudes and behavior.

What's the basis for our argument that structure impacts both attitudes and behavior? To the degree that an organization structure reduces ambiguity for an employee and clarifies concerns such as "What am I supposed to do?" "How am I supposed to do it?" "Who do I report to?" and "Who do I go to if I have a problem?" it shapes their attitudes and facilitates and motivates employees to higher levels of performance. Of course, structure also constrains employees to the extent that it limits and controls what they do.[25]

In spite of our claim that structure is important, much of the research from which we have drawn our conclusions has fatal flaws. For instance, measures of performance and satisfaction are frequently open to question, as are definitions and instruments used to measure such variables as size and centralization. Additionally, some studies include only professionals, while others include only blue-collar workers. It is not surprising, therefore, that we find conflicting results and qualified conclusions.

Figure 11–8 visually depicts what we have discussed in this chapter. Size, technology, environment, and power-control determine the type of structure an organization will have. Complexity, formalization, and centralization represent the structural components that can be mixed and matched to form various structural designs. For the most part, structural designs fall into one of two categories: mechanistic or organic. But common structural components do not necessarily impact on every employee's level of performance and satisfaction in a uniform way. The impact of objective structural characteristics on members of the organization is moderated by the employees' individual preferences and their subjective interpretation of the objective characteristics. Let us now offer some general thoughts.

For a large proportion of the population, high structure—that is, high complexity, high formalization, and centralization—leads to reduced job satisfaction. High vertical differentiation tends to alienate lower-level employees because vertical communication becomes more difficult and one can feel like "low man on the totem pole." On the other hand, upper management undoubtedly finds that the rewards that go with *their* positions enhance job satisfaction.

Specialization would also tend to be inversely related to satisfaction, especially where jobs have been divided into extremely minute tasks. This conclusion would have to be moderated to reflect individual differences among employees. While most prefer autonomy, not *all* do.

For individuals who value autonomy and self-actualization, large size, when accompanied by high centralization, results in lower satisfaction. As we have noted, there are fewer opportunities to participate in decision making, less proximity and identification with organizational goals, and less feeling that individual effort is linked to an identifiable outcome. In other words, the larger the organization, the more difficult it is for the individual to see the impact of his or her contribution to the final goods or service produced.

Organic structures increase cohesiveness among unit members and more closely aligns their authority with the responsibility for completion of a particular assignment. For certain types of activities, these structures are undoubtedly superior from management's standpoint. For instance, if tasks are nonroutine and there exists a great deal of environmental uncertainty, the organization can be

FIGURE 11–8
Organization Structure Model

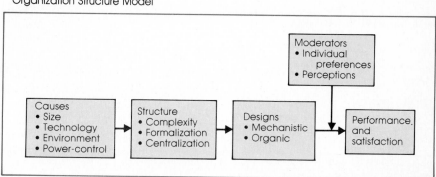

more responsive when structured along organic rather than mechanistic lines. But these more responsive structures provide both advantages and disadvantages to employees. They rarely have restrictive job descriptions or excessive rules and regulations, and they do not require workers to obey commands that are issued by distant executives. But they usually have overlapping layers of responsibility and play havoc with individuals who need the security of doing standardized tasks. To maximize employee performance and satisfaction, individual differences should be taken into account.[26] Individuals with a high degree of bureaucratic orientation tend to place a heavy reliance on higher authority, prefer formalized and specific rules, and prefer formal relationships with others on the job. These people are better suited to mechanistic structures. Those individuals with a low degree of bureaucratic orientation would be better suited to organic structures.[27]

POINT

BUREAUCRACIES ARE A DYING STRUCTURAL BREED

Every age develops an organizational form appropriate for its time. Bureaucracy was the most efficient form for the first two-thirds of this century. However, it is now fading fast from the scene.

The bureaucratic "machine model" was developed as a reaction against the personal subjugation, nepotism and cruelty, and the capricious and subjective judgments that passed for managerial practices during the early days of the Industrial Revolution. Bureaucracy emerged out of the organizations' need for order and precision and the workers' demands for impartial treatment. It was an organization ideally suited to the values and demands of the Victorian era. And just as bureaucracy emerged as a creative response to a radically new age, so today new organizational shapes are surfacing before our eyes.

There are at least four relevant threats to bureaucracy:

1. *Rapid and unexpected change.* Bureaucracy's strength is its capacity to manage efficiently the routine and predictable events in human affairs. Bureaucracy, with its nicely defined chain of command, its rules, and its rigidities, is ill adapted to the rapid change the environment now demands.

2. *Growth in size.* While, in theory, there may be no natural limit to the height of a bureaucratic pyramid, in practice the element of complexity is almost invariably introduced with great size.

3. *Increasing diversity.* Today's activities require persons of very diverse, highly specialized competence.

Hurried growth, rapid change, and increase in specialization pit these three factors against the components of the pyramid structure, and we should expect the pyramid of bureaucracy to begin crumbling.

4. *Change in managerial behavior.* There is a subtle but perceptible change in the philosophy underlying management behavior. Real change seems under way because of:

a. A new concept of human nature, based on increased knowledge of complex and shifting needs, which replaces an oversimplified, innocent, push-button idea of human nature.

b. A new concept of power, based on collaboration and reason, which replaces a model of power based on coercion and threat.

c. A new concept of organizational values, based on humanistic-democratic ideals, which replaces the depersonalized mechanistic value system of bureaucracy.

The real push for these changes stems from the need not only to humanize the organization, but to use it as a stimulus for personal growth and development of self-realization. Bureaucracies are a dying organizational form. They are, and will continue to be, replaced by adhocracies—adaptive, rapidly changing temporary structures—that more closely align with the tasks that today's organizations are attempting to achieve and the type of personnel they employ to accomplish those tasks.

Adapted from Warren G. Bennis, "The Coming Death of Bureaucracy," Think, November–December 1966, pp. 30–35. Reprinted by permission from Think Magazine, published by IBM. Copyright 1966 by International Business Machine Corp.

COUNTERPOINT

BUREAUCRACIES ARE ALIVE, WELL, AND FLOURISHING

There is no doubt that organizations are changing. But are these changes leaving bureaucracy behind? Nothing could be farther from the truth! Bureaucracies are alive, well, and flourishing.

The persepctive of all modern scholars on the subject of bureaucracy is probably conditioned by the extent of their exposure to the pioneering work of Max Weber. Genius though he was, Weber did not have a crystal ball. He could not have foreseen all the many forms that the essence of bureaucracy could take. His formulation of bureaucracy has provided an invaluable tool for the analysis of organizational problems in a society that is making the adjustment to industrialization. However, rather than making the superficial assumption that "postindustrial" means "postbureaucratic," it might be wiser for today's students to inquire whether bureaucracy can adjust to the new age that, so the sociologists and economists insist, we have recently entered. Some believe that the transition in administrative thought from mechanical to organic models will be fatal to bureaucracy. But is bureaucracy restricted to the mechanical? In many cases, it would appear that external bureaucratic constraints have simply been replaced by more subtle influences on the individual. The end result in either case is the same: a high degree of predictability about human behavior within the large complex organization.

For Weber, the essence of bureaucracy was to make affairs of individuals more amenable to rational calculation. Given the administrative technology of the nineteenth century and his familiarity with the authoritarian tendencies of the Germans, it is little wonder that Weber described the bureaucratic instrument as he did. He would hardly have been surprised, however, to learn that more sophisticated means of controlling behavior had been invented.

Weber's main scholarly concern, then, was with the progressive rationalization of the world and its impact on human relationships.

The current, postbureaucratic system is nothing more than the Weberian model with all the more sophisticated modifications. Despite all the contortions that management specialists have subjected themselves to in the twentieth century, the remarkable fact remains that there has been no substantial change in their basic premises. The guiding belief is still that regularities exist that, on one level or another, may be learned and acted upon. Whether the knowledge is embodied in the "bounded rationality" of a formal bureaucratic structure or in the professional's internalized determinants of behavior, administration is nothing more than the pursuit of a limited concept of rational discipline.

In reviewing the literature of a half-century of management science, one comes to the conclusion not that bureaucracy is dead but, rather, that the most controversial element of the Weberian model is gradually being replaced by a less artificial and more effective variation. To find specific elements of Weber's model of bureaucracy poorly adjusted to our times is a reasonable concession to the fact that conditions do change. But this is not the same as eliminating bureaucracy, for, in the most profound sense, bureaucracy will be with us as long as men insist that there is only one perception of reality by which rationality can be measured.

Adapted from Robert D. Miewald, "The Greatly Exaggerated Death of Bureaucracy." © 1970 by the Regents of the University of California. Reprinted from California Management Review, *Vol. 13, No. 2, pp. 65–69 by permission of the Regents.*

FOR DISCUSSION

1. What is meant by the term "organization structure"?
2. Describe the factors that determine how complex an organization is.
3. Which one of the following *most* determines structure: size, technology, environment, power-control? Explain.
4. Define and give examples of what is meant by the terms *technology* and *environment*.
5. Define a bureaucracy. Identify its key components. How prevalent do you think this structural form is?
6. Which one of the following structures is least centralized: simple, bureaucratic, product? Why?
7. Under what conditions would management likely choose (a) a mechanistic structure? (b) an organic structure?
8. What is a matrix structure? What are its advantages? Disadvantages?
9. "Employees prefer to work in flat, decentralized organizations." Do you agree or disagree? Discuss.
10. What is the relationship between each of the following and employee performance and satisfaction: (a) size? (b) organizational level? (c) span of control? (d) horizontal differentiation? (e) vertical differentiation? (f) centralization?
11. Do you think most employees prefer high formalization? Support your position.
12. What is the importance of the statement: "Employees form implicit models of organization structure"?

FOR FURTHER READING

CHILD, J., *Organization,* 2nd ed. London: Harper & Row Ltd., 1984. Reviews organization theory to offer advice to practitioners for solving management problems.

DAFT, R. L., *Organization Theory and Design.* St. Paul, Minn.: West, 1983. Gives a comprehensive review of key issues relating to organization structure and design.

KATZ, D., and R. L. KAHN, *The Social Psychology of Organizations,* 2nd ed. New York: John Wiley, 1978. Contains a highly sophisticated analysis of organizational design and processes from a systems perspective.

MILES, R. H., *Macro Organizational Behavior.* Glenview, Ill.: Scott, Foresman, 1980. Offers a sophisticated treatment of structure's impact on organizational behavior.

MINTZBERG, H., *Structure in Fives*. Englewood Cliffs, N.J.: Prentice-Hall, 1983. Describes the primary structural designs available to management and the strengths and weaknesses of each.

VAN DE VEN, A. H., and W. F. JOYCE (eds.). *Perspectives on Organization Design and Behavior*. New York: Wiley-Interscience, 1981. Contains separately written chapters that review contemporary issues in organization design.

NOTES FOR CHAPTER 11

1. S. P. Robbins, *Organization Theory: The Structure and Design of Organizations* (Englewood Cliffs, N.J.: Prentice-Hall, 1983), Chap. 3–5.
2. M. Weber, *The Theory of Social and Economic Organizations*, ed. T. Parsons and trans. A. M. Henderson and T. Parsons (New York: Free Press, 1947).
3. H. Mintzberg, "Structure in 5's: A Synthesis of the Research on Organization Design," *Management Science,* March 1980, p. 331.
4. P. M. Blau, "A Formal Theory of Differentiation in Organizations," *American Sociological Review,* April 1970, pp. 201–18.
5. D. S. Mileti, D. F. Gillespie, and J. E. Haas, "Size and Structure in Complex Organizations," *Social Forces,* September 1977, pp. 208–17.
6. W. A. Rushing, "Organizational Size, Rules, and Surveillance," in J. A. Litterer (ed.), *Organizations: Structure and Behavior,* 3rd ed. (New York: John Wiley, 1980), pp. 396–405; and Y. Samuel and B. F. Mannheim, "A Multidimensional Approach Toward a Typology of Bureaucracy," *Administrative Science Quarterly,* June 1970, pp. 216–28.
7. See, for example, P. M. Blau and R. A. Schoenherr, *The Structure of Organizations* (New York: Basic Books, 1971); and J. Child and R. Mansfield, "Technology, Size, and Organization Structure," *Sociology,* September 1972, pp. 369–93.
8. The most frequently referenced technology categories have been offered by J. Woodward, *Industrial Organization: Theory and Practice* (London: Oxford University Press, 1965); C. Perrow, "A Framework for the Comparative Analysis of Organizations," *American Sociological Review,* April 1967, pp. 194–208; and J. D. Thompson, *Organizations in Action* (New York: McGraw-Hill, 1967).
9. Woodward, *Industrial Organization;* and Perrow, *Framework.*
10. J. Pfeffer, *Organizational Design* (Arlington Heights, Ill.: AHM, 1978), p. 99.
11. Ibid.
12. J. Hage and M. Aiken, "Routine Technology, Social Structure, and Organizational Goals," *Administrative Science Quarterly,* September 1969, pp. 366–77.
13. D. Gerwin, "Relationships Between Structure and Technology at the Organizational and Job Levels," *Journal of Management Studies,* February 1979, pp. 70–79.
14. A. Van De Ven, A. Delbecq, and R. Koenig, Jr., "Determinants of Coordination Modes Within Organizations," *American Sociological Review,* April 1976, pp. 322–38.
15. J. Hage and M. Aiken, "Relationship of Centralization to Other Structural Properties," *Administrative Science Quarterly,* June 1967, pp. 72–92.
16. J. Pfeffer and G. R. Salancik, *The External Control of Organizations: A Response Dependence Perspective* (New York: Harper & Row, 1978), p. 29.

17. P. Lawrence and J. W. Lorsch, *Organization and Environment: Managing Differentiation and Integration* (Boston: Harvard Business School, Division of Research, 1967).

18. See, for example, R. B. Duncan, "Characteristics of Organizational Environments and Perceived Environmental Uncertainty," *Administrative Science Quarterly,* September 1972, pp. 313–27.

19. H. Mintzberg, *The Structuring of Organizations* (Englewood Cliffs, N.J.: Prentice-Hall, 1979), pp. 273–76.

20. J. Child, "Organization Structure, Environment and Performance: The Role of Strategic Choice," *Sociology,* January 1972, pp. 1–22; and D. S. Pugh, "The Management of Organization Structures: Does Context Determine Form?" *Organizational Dynamics,* Spring 1973, pp. 19–34.

21. Pfeffer, *Organizational Design.*

22. Ibid.

23. D. R. Dalton, W. D. Todor, M. J. Spendolini, G. J. Fielding, and L. W. Porter, "Organization Structure and Performance: A Critical Review," *Academy of Management Review,* January 1980, p. 60.

24. This section has drawn on the findings and insights provided in L. W. Porter and E. E. Lawler III, "Properties of Organization Structure in Relation to Job Attitudes and Job Behavior," *Psychological Bulletin,* July 1965, pp. 23–51; L. R. James and A. P. Jones, "Organization Structure: A Review of Structural Dimensions and Their Conceptual Relationships with Individual Attitudes and Behavior," *Organizational Behavior and Human Performance,* June 1976, pp. 74–113; C. J. Berger and L. L. Cummings, "Organizational Structure, Attitudes, and Behaviors," B. M. Staw (ed.), *Research in Organizational Behavior,* Vol. 1 (Greenwich, Conn.: JAI Press, 1979), pp. 169–208; Dalton et al., "Organization Structure," pp. 49–64; J. S. Ebeling and M. King, "Hierarchical Position in the Work Organization and Job Satisfaction: A Failure to Replicate," *Human Relations,* July 1981, pp. 567–72; G. Stephenson, C. Brotherton, G. Delafield, and M. Skinner, "Size of Organization, Attitudes to Work and Job Satisfaction," *Industrial Relations Journal,* Summer 1983, pp. 28–40; and W. Snizek and J. H. Bullard, "Perception of Bureaucracy and Changing Job Satisfaction: A Longitudinal Analysis," *Organizational Behavior and Human Performance,* October 1983, pp. 275–87.

25. D. A. Nadler, J. R. Hackman, and E. E. Lawler III, *Managing Organizational Behavior* (Boston: Little, Brown, 1979), pp. 182–84.

26. P. M. Nemiroff and D. L. Ford, Jr., "Task Effectiveness and Human Fulfillment in Organizations: A Review and Development of a Conceptual Contingency Model," *Academy of Management Review,* October 1976, pp. 69–82.

27. Ibid., p. 74.

12

Job Design, Work Settings, and Job Stress

AFTER STUDYING THIS CHAPTER, YOU SHOULD BE ABLE TO:

Define and explain the following key terms and concepts:

Autonomous work teams	Job sharing
Autonomy	Motivating potential score
Compressed workweek	Physical environment
Feedback	Quality circles
Flextime	Scientific management
Growth need strength	Skill variety
Integrated work teams	Sociotechnical systems
Job characteristics model	Stress
Job design	Task identity
Job enlargement	Type A behavior
Job enrichment	Type B behavior
Job redesign	Work modules
Job rotation	Workspace design

Understand:

What is job design
The evolution of job design
The characteristics that make jobs different
Current design options available to management
Key work setting factors that influence employee behavior
The relationship between status and workspace design
Requirements for potential stress to become actual stress
The sources of stress

On too many jobs, nine-to-five seems like five-to-life.

—S.P.R.

*D*awn Blackstone, Frank Greer, and Lynn Fleming all have something in common—they recently quit their jobs at a large northeastern newspaper. When asked why they resigned, each gave a different answer.

Dawn: "I was bored to death. At first, I found my job interesting, but, after about six months, I could do it with my brain turned off. I had to get out before *rigor mortis* set in."

Frank: "This may sound crazy, but I felt isolated at the paper. I was a proofreader. My office was stuck in a corner on the seventh floor. I really enjoyed my work, but I like to interact with people on my job. The location of my office and its privacy made it all but impossible for me to interact. I felt claustrophobic. I asked my boss if the four proofreaders could be put together in one office, but he said it would be too noisy for us to do a good job. I got an offer from a book publisher in town where I'm working closely with a dozen or so other proofers. My work is a lot more fun now."

Lynn: "I really loved my job as director of advertising. The pay was awesome and I had a great support staff. But I just couldn't take the pressure. Top management was constantly pushing me to increase our advertising revenues. The more I got, the more they wanted. I gave it my best for two years. Then my doctor told me I had ulcers. My stomach was hurting all the time. I was having trouble sleeping, too. Finally, I realized I had to get out. My new job has a lot less responsibility, and I'm making almost $10,000 a year less. But I'm sleeping nights again."

This chapter deals with the causes of Dawn, Frank, and Lynn's decisions to resign their jobs. Dawn complained of the boredom she found in her work. We'll show that the way a job is designed can contribute to, or reduce, an employee's satisfaction with that job. Frank's decision to quit was due to a feeling of isolation on his job. A positive work setting—a comfortable temperature level, the right amount of lighting, the proper layout of the workspace—can make employees perform better. Obviously, a poorly designed work setting can hinder performance. We'll consider in this chapter the major elements in the work setting that can impact on an employee's work performance. Finally, Lynn's resignation was due to job stress. The last part of this chapter will review the causes of stress and how it affects employee performance and job satisfaction variables.

JOB DESIGN

Jobs are different. On that point there can be little debate. It's also true that individuals perceive certain jobs as being more desirable than others. However, what *you* consider to be a routine and boring job, someone *else* is very likely to view as quite satisfying. So while jobs can be objectively differentiated, we cannot say that everyone would find the job of theater critic for the *Chicago Sun Times* interesting and challenging. Nor can we say that filing credit card applications alphabetically for eight hours a day, five days a week, at the American Express office in New York would be universally considered a dull job. As we learned in Part 2 of this book, individuals have different needs and preferences. This should show up in their preference for jobs. And, of course, it does. In fact, most organizations go to a great deal of trouble to select individuals who will fit smoothly into the organization and the job vacancy to be filled. The evidence indicates that certain individuals are attracted to and selected by certain types of organizations.[1] Those entrepreneurial individuals who like to see things happen fast, like to take risks, and are more loners than team players are typically turned off by large mechanistic organizations—and such organizations can be expected to be turned off by this type of individual. This is consistent with the literature on personnel selection. Organizations use tests, interviews, and other selection devices to find the right match between the organization's characteristics and an applicant's personal and background attributes. But additionally, research demonstrates that job characteristics mediate the relationship between organization structure and employee reactions.[2] That is, structural properties affect the characteristics of employees' jobs. So, for instance, organization structures that are highly formalized and centralized tend to be negatively associated with employee descriptions of the amount of autonomy, variety, and feedback in their jobs.[3]

The way jobs are designed, therefore, influences employee performance and satisfaction. But how? Given that jobs are different, what are these differences? And how do these differences affect employee performance and satisfaction? These are questions this section seeks to answer.

FIGURE 12–1
Source: Copyright 1973, G. B. Trudeau. Distributed by Universal Press Syndicate.

What Is Job Design?

The term *job design* refers to the way that tasks are combined to form complete jobs. Some jobs are routine because the tasks are standardized and repetitive; others are nonroutine. Some require a large number of varied and diverse skills; others are narrow in scope. Some jobs constrain employees by requiring them to follow very precise procedures; others allow employees substantial freedom in how they do their work. Our point is that jobs differ as to the way their tasks are combined.

A term closely aligned with jobs design is *job redesign*. When jobs are changed, job redesign takes place. More specifically, job redesign refers to any activities that involve the alteration of specific jobs (or interdependent systems of jobs) that seeks to increase both the quality of an employee's work experience and on-the-job productivity.[4] In the following pages, we shall discuss job design and then propose various redesign options available to management. Particular attention will be focused on how given redesign options affect employee productivity, absence, turnover, and satisfaction.

Historical Development of Job Design

It's very hard to pick up any recent business periodical and *not* find an article about some company or government agency introducing a four-day workweek, flexible work hours, Japanese-style participation groups, autonomous work teams, or some similar job redesign. This may lead you to think of job design as a relatively new topic. This is far from the case.

The content and design of jobs has interested engineers and economists for centuries. In its early years, job design was really nothing more than a synonym for job specialization. In 1776, for instance, Adam Smith articulated in his *Wealth of Nations* the economic efficiencies that could be achieved by dividing jobs into smaller and smaller pieces so each worker could perform a minute and specialized task. Undoubtedly one of the most important early efforts at job design was undertaken at the turn of this century by Frederick Taylor in what has become known as the scientific management movement.

SCIENTIFIC MANAGEMENT

In the early 1900s, Frederick Taylor proposed scientific management principles designed to maximize production efficiency. He sought to replace the seat-of-the-pants approach for determining each element of a worker's job with a scientific approach. The centerpiece of scientific management was the elimination of time and motion waste. How was this done? By carefully studying jobs to determine the most efficient way they could be completed. Jobs were partitioned into small and simple segments and the workers were given specific instructions on how each segment was to be done.

The results of Taylor's efforts—in economic terms—were nothing short of spectacular. He was consistently able to achieve productivity improvements in the range of 200 percent or more. Many workers, however, did not like the jobs designed according to the dictates of scientific management. They found the repetitive work depersonalized, boring, and unchallenging. Because their jobs often represented small "cogs" in a big "wheel," employees increasingly complained that their work was meaningless. To offset the boredom of their highly repetitive jobs, workers would do things that were not always in the best interest of the organization. They came to work late, they took three- or four-day weekends, and they quit to find more interesting work.

Probably one of the most publicized reactions to overspecialized jobs was the action by automobile assembly-line workers in the early 1970s at the Lordstown, Ohio, Chevrolet plant. Workers were found to be welding empty soda pop bottles inside doors, purposely gouging the paint on cars as they went by, and engaging in other dysfunctional behaviors. The Lordstown workers, it was said, were frustrated and looking for ways to overcome the dull, repetitive, and unchallenging tasks they were assigned. Welding a bottle inside a door or putting a deep scratch into a car's paint without getting caught provided a diversionary outlet.

The Lordstown events occurred in the early 1970s, but the recognition that a good thing—work simplification—could be carried too far began to get attention in the late 1940s and early 1950s. As a result of insights from psychologists, sociologists, and other social scientists, attention began to shift to the human needs of people. The jobs themselves had been engineered to be efficiently performed by robotlike workers. But people are not robots. They have needs and feelings. No matter how well engineered a job is, if the design fails to consider the human element, the economies of specialization could be more than offset by the diseconomies of employee dissatisfaction. And on many jobs, this is exactly what was happening. So attention became increasingly focused on job design approaches that would make work less routine and more meaningful.

JOB ENLARGEMENT

One of the first approaches was to expand jobs horizontally, or what we call *job enlargement*. Increasing the number and variety of tasks that an individual performed resulted in jobs with more diversity. Instead of only sorting the incoming mail by department, for instance, a mail sorter's job could be enlarged to include physically delivering the mail to the various departments or running outgoing letters through the postage meter.

Efforts at job enlargement met with less than enthusiastic results. As one employee who experienced such a redesign on his job remarked to your author, "Before I had one lousy job. Now, through enlargement, I have three!"

So, while job enlargement attacked the lack of diversity in overspecialized jobs, it did little to instill challenge or meaningfulness to a worker's activities. Job enrichment was introduced to deal with the shortcomings of enlargement.

JOB ENRICHMENT

Job enrichment refers to the vertical expansion of jobs. It increases the degree to which the worker controls the planning, execution, and evaluation of his or her job. An enriched job organizes tasks so as to allow workers to do a complete activity, increases the employee's freedom and independence, increases responsibility, and provides feedback so individuals will be able to assess and correct their own performance.

Reports of organizations implementing job enrichment programs have been well publicized, and the importance of the concept requires that it be given an expanded discussion. Such a discussion will be undertaken later in this chapter. From an historical perspective, it is sufficient to note that job enrichment essentially developed in the 1960s as a response to employee dissatisfaction and productivity problems that excessive specialization created. The interest it initiated continues through to today.

SOCIOTECHNICAL SYSTEMS

Another job design innovation of the 1960s was the concept of sociotechnical systems. Like job enlargement and enrichment, this approach represented a response to the overly narrow scientific management view of job design.

Sociotechnical systems is more a philosophy toward job design than a specific technique. Its central theme is that job design must address both the technical and the social aspects of the organization if work systems are to produce greater employee productivity and higher personal fulfillment for organization members. Every job has technological aspects. But technical tasks are performed in an environment influenced by a culture, a set of values, and generally acceptable organization practices. Redesign efforts that look only at the technical aspects of a job are likely to overlook critical factors that influence employee performance and satisfaction.

Advocates of sociotechnical systems provided no explicit guidance in exactly how the work, the social surroundings, and the organization interact. Their suggestions, however, did rely heavily on group-oriented approaches to work.

The idea of work teams, which we shall discuss later in this section, evolved out of the sociotechnical systems philosophy. The notion that there are a number of interrelated factors that eventually influence the success or failure of a job design effort—which we shall also discuss later in this section—undoubtedly is also rooted in sociotechnical systems.

Individual Redesign Options

The first set of options is concerned with redesigning individual tasks. Prominent examples of individual redesign options include job rotation, work modules, and job enrichment.

JOB ROTATION
Job rotation increases variety by permitting workers to shift jobs periodically. When an activity no longer is challenging, the employee would be rotated to another job, at the same level, that has similar skill requirements. The shifts can include as few as two people—the rotation being merely an exchange of jobs. However, the organization can provide much more elaborate rotation designs where a dozen or more employees are involved. The latter case would describe, for instance, the practices in the headquarters of some of the largest U.S. banks. New college graduates are hired with the idea that in three or four years they will be able to assume managerial positions in the bank. Their training consists of spending four to six months in all the key areas of the bank—operations, lending, trusts, and so forth. At about the time they have gained a reasonable understanding of an activity, they are rotated to a new area (see Figure 12–2).

The strength of job rotation is that it reduces boredom through diversifying the employee's activities. Of course, it can also have indirect benefits for the organization since employees with a wider range of skills give management more flexibility in scheduling work, adapting to changes, and filling vacancies. On the other hand, job rotation is not without its drawbacks. Training costs are increased, and productivity is reduced by moving a worker into a new position just when his or her efficiency at the prior job was creating organizational economies. Job rotation also creates disruptions. Members of the work group have to adjust to the new employee. The supervisor may also have to spend more time answering ques-

FIGURE 12–2
Job Rotation

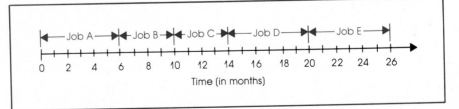

tions and monitoring the work of the recently rotated employee. Finally, job rotation can demotivate intelligent and ambitious trainees who seek specific responsibilities in their chosen specialty.

WORK MODULES

If you can conceive of extremely rapid job rotation, to the point where one would assume new activities every few hours, you can comprehend the use of work modules. The work modules concept has been suggested as a solution to meet the problem of fractioned, boring, and programmed work, at an acceptable price, with undiminished quality and quantity of output.[5]

Work modules are defined as a time task unit equal to approximately two hours of work at a given task. A normal forty-hour-a-week job would then be defined in terms of four modules a day, five days a week, for between forty-eight and fifty weeks a year (see Figure 12–3).

Through the use of modules, it would be possible to increase work diversity and give employees a greater opportunity to determine the nature of their jobs. Employees could request a set of modules that would together constitute a day's work. Additionally, those tasks that are characteristically seen as undesirable could be spread about, for example, by having everyone take a module or two each day. The result would be that people would change activities through changing work modules.

One benefit of work modules includes letting employees pick their work tasks, thus taking into account individual job preferences. Further, it provides a way for the more boring and undesirable tasks to get completed without totally demoralizing those people who must do them. Finally, since employees would be allowed some say in the choice of modules, the job would be constructed to meet the needs of the individual, rather than forcing people to fit a particularly defined job.

However, work modules would present the same cost and disruption obstacles as job rotation. Considerable time and money are involved in planning and executing the changeover. Bookkeeping and payroll computation costs increase. Conflicts can also develop over the question of equity and allocation of modules.

FIGURE 12–3

Example of a Work Module Schedule

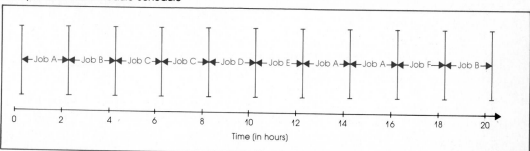

JOB ENRICHMENT

We introduced job enrichment earlier as the vertical expansion of jobs. In this section we shall discuss the concept at greater length.

Job enlargement, as we mentioned earlier, expands jobs horizontally. That is, it increases the job's scope or diversity (see Figure 12–4). In contrast, job enrichment increases job depth (see Figure 12–5). What this means is that employees gain greater control over their work. They assume some of the tasks typically done by their supervisor, such as planning and evaluating the job. An example can illustrate how job enrichment works.

Travelers Insurance was displeased with the performance of its keypunch operators.[6] Output seemed low, the error rate high, and absenteeism excessive. As a result, the following changes were introduced:

1. The random assignment of work was replaced by assigning to each operator continuing responsibility for certain accounts.
2. Some planning and control functions were combined with the central task of keypunching.
3. Each operator was given several channels of direct contact with clients. When problems arose, the operator, not the supervisor, took them up with the client.
4. Operators were given the authority to set their own schedules, plan their daily work, and correct obvious coding errors on their own.
5. Incorrect cards were returned by the computer department to the operators who punched them, and the operators corrected their own errors. Weekly computer printouts of errors and productivity were sent directly to the operator rather than the supervisor.

These enrichment efforts led to some impressive results. Fewer keypunch operators were needed, output increased, error rates and absenteeism were reduced, and job attitudes improved. The changes reportedly saved Travelers over $90,000 a year.

Any successful job enrichment program should ideally increase employee satisfaction. But since organizations do not exist to create employee satisfaction as an end, there must be direct benefits to the organization. There is evidence that

FIGURE 12–4

Job Enlargement Increases Job Scope

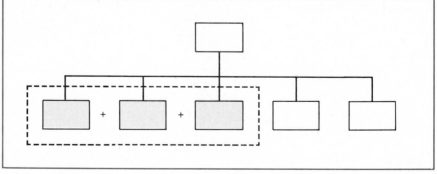

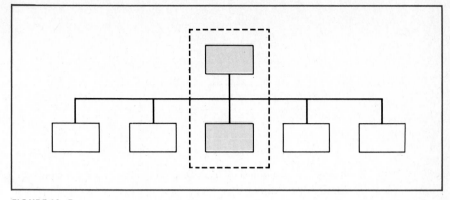

FIGURE 12–5
Job Enrichment Increases Job Depth

job enrichment produces lower absenteeism and reduced turnover costs, but on the critical issue of productivity, the evidence is inconclusive. In some situations, such as at Travelers, job enrichment has increased productivity; in others, productivity has decreased. However, even when it decreases, there does appear to be more consistently conscientious use of resources and a higher quality of product or service. In other words, in terms of efficiency, for the same input a higher quality of output is obtained.

Group Redesign Options

During the last ten to fifteen years, the focus on redesign options has shifted from the individual to the group. Integrated work teams, autonomous work teams, and quality circles are examples of redesign options developed around group tasks.

INTEGRATED WORK TEAMS

Job enlargement at the group rather than individual level results in integrated work teams. For jobs that require teamwork and cooperation, this approach can increase diversity for team members.

What would an integrated work team look like? Basically, instead of performing a single task, a large number of tasks would be assigned to a group. The group then would decide the specific assignments of members and be responsible for rotating jobs among the members as the tasks required. The team would still have a supervisor who would oversee the group's activities (see Figure 12–6). You see the frequent use of integrated work teams in such activities as building maintenance and construction. In the cleaning of a large office building, it is not unusual for the supervisor to identify the tasks to be completed and then to let the maintenance workers, as a group, choose how the tasks will be allocated. Similarly, a road construction crew frequently decides, as a group, how its various tasks are to be completed.

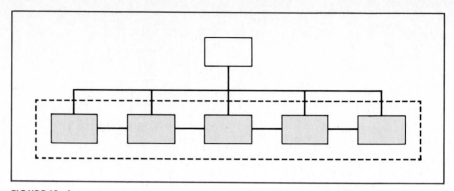

FIGURE 12–6
Integrated Work Teams

AUTONOMOUS WORK TEAMS

Autonomous work teams represent job enrichment at the group level. The work that the team does is deepened through vertical integration. The team is given a goal to achieve and then is free to determine work assignments, rest breaks, inspection procedures, and the like. Fully autonomous work teams even select their own members and have the members evaluate each other's performance. As a result, supervisory positions take on decreased importance and may even be eliminated (see Figure 12–7). The autonomous work team concept is in operation at the Oklahoma plant of Shaklee Corporation, where nutritional products, vitamins, and other pills are made.[7]

About 190 of the Oklahoma plant's production employees were organized into teams with 3 to 15 members. The team members set their own production schedules, decided what hours to work, selected new team members from a pool approved by the personnel department, and even initiated discharges if necessary. The results were impressive. The company reported that units produced per hour of labor went up nearly 200 percent over levels at other plants, two-thirds of which increase was attributed to the autonomous work team concept (the rest was explained by better equipment). Management stated that the Oklahoma plant could produce the same volume as the more traditional facilities at 40 percent of the labor costs.

The improvement at Shaklee is not isolated. There are other reports of favorable improvements in worker attitudes and performance when autonomous work teams have been implemented. For instance, a three-year study of coal mining crews found that creation of autonomous teams resulted in more positive attitudes toward work and a slight positive increase in performance.[8]

QUALITY CIRCLES

The most recent addition to job redesign alternatives has been the quality circle. Originally begun in the United States and exported to Japan in the 1950s, the quality circle has been imported back to the United States. As it developed in Japan, the quality circle concept is frequently mentioned as one of the techniques

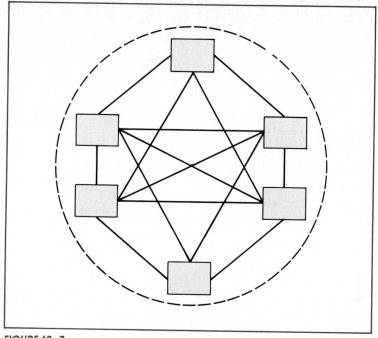

FIGURE 12–7
Autonomous Work Teams

that Japanese firms utilize that has allowed them to make better quality products at lower costs than their American counterparts can. In fact, this concept has grown so popular in Japan, one expert estimates that approximately one out of every nine Japanese workers is involved in a quality circle.[9]

What is a quality circle? It's a work group of eight to ten employees and supervisors who have a shared area of responsibility. They meet regularly—typically once a week, on company time and on company premises—to discuss their quality problems, investigate causes of the problems, recommend solutions, and take corrective actions. They take over the responsibility for solving quality problems, and they generate and evaluate their own feedback. But management typically retains control over the final decision regarding implementation of recommended solutions. Of course, it is not presumed that employees inherently have this ability to analyze and solve quality problems. Therefore, part of the quality circle concept includes teaching participating employees group communication skills, various quality strategies, and measurement and problem analysis techniques. Figure 12–8 describes a typical quality circle process.

Quality circles are in place in more than two thousand American companies.[10] Some of these companies have literally dozens of circles. For instance, General Electric has more than a thousand at plants across the United States.[11] But the success of quality circles has been far from overwhelming. For instance, one study of 176 companies that had adopted quality circles by 1981 found that the management at 60 percent were lukewarm or unhappy about what, if any-

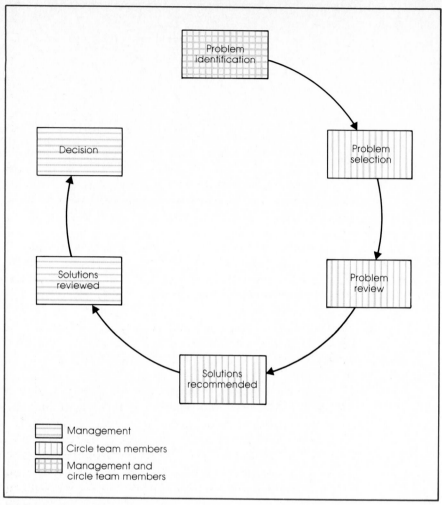

FIGURE 12–8
How a Typical Quality Circle Operates

thing, their circles were accomplishing, including 7 percent that had dropped them entirely.[12] Yet, in defense of the concept, undoubtedly much of this lack of enthusiasm is attributable to improper introduction of the technique, inadequate support for the circle concept, and/or unrealistic expectations in terms of productivity improvement.

Alternative Work Schedule Options

The four-day compressed workweek, flextime, and job sharing are scheduling innovations that have been introduced with the intent of reducing the problems of job dissatisfaction and worker discontent. Although they are not job design concepts in the strictest sense, we include them in our discussion of job design options.

THE COMPRESSED WORKWEEK

We define the compressed workweek as comprised of four 10-hour days. While there have been experiments with three-day weeks and other compressed workweek variants, we limit our attention to four-day, forty-hour (4–40) programs.

The 4–40 program was conceived to allow workers more leisure time and more shopping time and to permit them to travel to and from work at nonrush-hour times. It was suggested that such a program would increase employee enthusiasm, morale, and commitment to the organization; increase productivity and reduce costs; reduce machine downtime in manufacturing; reduce overtime, turnover, and absenteeism; and make it easier for the organization to recruit employees.

It has been proposed that the compressed workweek may positively affect productivity in situations in which the work process requires significant start-up and shutdown periods.[13] When start-up and shutdown times are a major factor, productivity standards take these periods into consideration in determining the time required to generate a given output. Consequently, in such cases, the compressed workweek will increase productivity even though performance of the workers is not affected, because the improved work scheduling reduces nonproductive time. Performance results under the 4–40 program, however, appears to be mixed.

An investigation of 470 clerical and supervisory employees in an accounting function found that 62 percent of the workers saw their jobs as more tiring under the 4–40 program, and managers complained about the difficulties of coordinating work loads. However, there was a 10 percent reduction in overtime, and 78 percent of the employees did not want to revert to the traditional five-day workweek once the program had been operating for six months. Although analysis of productivity figures indicated that they were unaffected either positively or negatively, supervisors were generally unenthusiastic about the program. Fifty-one percent of them saw it as detrimental to their work areas; only 18 percent saw it as beneficial.[14]

What is the effect of a compressed workweek when it has been established for at least a year? One study, taken over thirteen months, using experimental and controlled subjects, found that workers utilizing the four-day workweek were more satisfied with their personal worth, social affiliation, job security, and pay; experienced less anxiety and stress; and performed better with regard to productivity than did the control group members working the five-day week.[15] A study in a medium-sized pharmaceutical company employing over two hundred people found workers generally positive toward the compressed workweek, but these attitudes did change over time.[16] After one year, the effects of the four-day week on the workers' home lives were perceived as significantly less positive than when they were first reported.

While one must be careful in generalizing from such mixed findings, the evidence does indicate that the compressed workweek is effective in improving morale, reducing dissatisfaction, and reducing absenteeism and turnover figures in the early months after implementation. However, after approximately one year, some of these advantages may disappear. Employees begin to complain more frequently about increased fatigue and the difficulty of coordinating their jobs with their personal lives—the latter a problem more particularly for working mothers.

FLEXTIME

During the past dozen years, the introduction of flexible work hours—or flextime—has been widely practiced. Flextime is a scheduling system that allows employees some discretion over when they arrive at work and leave. Employees have to work a specific number of hours a week, but they are free to vary the hours of work within certain limits. As shown in Figure 12–9, each day consists of a common core, usually six hours, with a flexibility band surrounding the core. For example, exclusive of a one-hour lunch break, the core may be 9:00 A.M. to 3:00 P.M., with the office actually opening at 6:00 A.M. and closing at 6:00 P.M. All employees are required to be at their jobs during the common core period, but they are allowed to accumulate their other two hours before and/or after the core time. Some flextime programs allow extra hours to be accumulated and turned into a free day off each month.

The benefits claimed for flextime are numerous. They include reduced absenteeism, increased productivity, reduced overtime expenses, a lessening in hostility toward management, reduced traffic congestion around work sites, elimination of tardiness, and increased autonomy and responsibility for employees that may increase employee job satisfaction.[17] But beyond the claims, what's flextime's record?

Most of the performance evidence stacks up favorably. It tends to reduce absenteeism and frequently improves worker productivity.[18] Why? There are probably several reasons. Employees can schedule their work hours to align with personal demands, thus reducing tardiness and absences, and employees can adjust their work activities to those hours in which they are individually more productive. "Morning people" can come in early, whereas "night people" can come in later and stay later.

FIGURE 12–9
Example of a Flextime Schedule

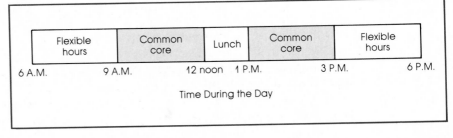

The negatives on flextime tend to be problems that could apply equally to the compressed workweek—dissipation of the change's effect over time, unrealistic employee expectations, and enhanced relative attractiveness of off-the-job activities. But flextime's biggest drawback may relate to its negative impact on managers and the organization in general.[19] Flextime increases the difficulty for managers to direct subordinates outside the common-core time period, causes confusion where there is shift work, increases difficulties when someone with particular skills or knowledge is not available, and makes planning and controlling work activities more cumbersome and costly. There is, for instance, a tendency (especially among nonprofessionals) for employees to report to work very early and leave early.[20] This creates a general shift to again concentrate beginning and leaving times, which counters some of the benefits of flextime—such as reduced traffic congestion and the heightened sense of freedom to choose one's work hours.

JOB SHARING

Lois Pattiz teaches two courses in psychology at the state university. So, too, does Russ Chandler. Both are considered permanent employees, although each teaches only halftime. They participate in faculty meetings; they also receive employee fringe benefits like their full-time colleagues. But Lois and Russ share a full professorship in the psychology department. Lois is a 35-year-old mother of two preschool children who has chosen to trade off half her salary for the time to spend at home. In contrast, Russ is 62 years old and formerly held a full-time position in the department. But he doesn't want to teach full time anymore. By sharing a position with Lois, he has a steady income and considerably more time to phase into his retirement. From the university's perspective, it has the services of two highly qualified academics for the price of one.

Job sharing is a recent work scheduling innovation. It allows two or more individuals to split a traditional forty-hour-a-week job. While the concept is new and is not widely practiced, it is consistent with the changing needs of the work force. For example, women with school-age children are a group that are returning to the work force. Many of these women don't want full-time jobs. An alternative to accepting a part-time job is a shared full-time position. Similarly, it is increasingly difficult for retirees to maintain their standard of living on their pensions and savings alone. Job sharing allows them to supplement their income, while allowing the organization to gain from having the skills of more than one individual.

The Job Characteristics Model

We've presented a number of redesign options in this section. Are some better than others? If management is concerned with designing jobs or sets of jobs to maximize employee performance, are there any guidelines available? Some redesign options *are* better in motivating employees, in stimulating their productivity, and in increasing their job satisfaction. The *job characteristics model (JCM)* can guide management in evaluating jobs and can help you to predict an employee's productivity and satisfaction. How? By identifying the five key job characteristics or core dimensions, their interrelationships, and their predicted impact on employee productivity, motivation, and satisfaction.[21]

CORE DIMENSIONS

According to the JCM, any job can be described in terms of five core job dimensions, defined as follows:

1. *Skill variety*—the degree to which a job requires a variety of different activities so the worker can use a number of different skills and talents
2. *Task identity*—the degree to which the job requires completion of a whole and identifiable piece of work
3. *Task significance*—the degree to which the job has a substantial impact on the lives or work of other people
4. *Autonomy*—the degree to which the job provides substantial freedom, independence, and discretion to the individual in scheduling the work and in determining the procedures to be used in carrying it out
5. *Feedback*—the degree to which carrying out the work activities required by the job results in the individual obtaining direct and clear information about the effectiveness of his or her performance.

Table 12–1 offers examples of job activities that rate high and low for each characteristic.

Figure 12–10 presents the model. Notice how the first three dimensions—skill variety, task identity, and task significance—combine to create meaningful work. That is, if these three characteristics exist in a job, we can predict that the incumbent will view the job as being important, valuable, and worthwhile. Notice, too, that jobs that possess autonomy give the job incumbent a feeling of personal responsibility for the results and that, if a job provides feedback, the employee will know how effectively he or she is performing. From a motivational standpoint, the model says that internal rewards are obtained by an individual when he *learns* (knowledge of results) that he *personally* (experienced responsibility) has performed well on a task that he *cares* about (experienced meaningfulness).[22] The more that these three psychological states are present, the greater will be the employee's motivation, performance, and satisfaction, and the lower his absenteeism and likelihood of leaving the organization. As Figure 12–10 shows, the links between the job dimensions and the outcomes are moderated or adjusted by the strength of the individual's growth need, that is, by the employee's desire for self-esteem and self-actualization. This means that individuals with a high growth need are more likely to experience the psychological states when their jobs are enriched than are their counterparts with a low growth need. Moreover, they will respond more positively to the psychological states, when they are present, than will low-growth-need individuals.

TABLE 12–1
Examples of High and Low Job Characteristics

Skill Variety	
High variety	The owner-operator of a garage who does electrical repair, rebuilds engines, does body work, and interacts with customers
Low variety	A body shop worker who sprays paint eight hours a day
Task Identity	
High identity	A cabinetmaker who designs a piece of furniture, selects the wood, builds the object, and finishes it to perfection
Low identity	A worker in a furniture factory who operates a lathe solely to make table legs
Task Significance	
High significance	Nursing the sick in a hospital intensive care unit
Low significance	Sweeping hospital floors
Autonomy	
High autonomy	A telephone installer who schedules his or her own work for the day, makes visits without supervision, and decides on the most effective techniques for a particular installation
Low autonomy	A telephone operator who must handle calls as they come according to a routine, highly specified procedure
Feedback	
High feedback	An electronics factory worker who assembles a radio and then tests it to determine if it operates properly
Low feedback	An electronics factory worker who assembles a radio and then routes it to a quality control inspector who tests it for proper operation and makes needed adjustments

Source: J. Richard Hackman and Greg R. Oldham, *Work Redesign.* © 1980, Addison-Wesley, Reading, Mass. (Adapted material from Fig. 4.2.) Reprinted with permission.

PREDICTIONS FROM THE MODEL

The core job dimensions can be combined into a single predictive index, called the motivating potential score (MPS). Its computation is shown in Figure 12–11.

Jobs that are high on motivating potential must be high on at least one of the three factors that lead to experiencing meaningfulness, and they must be high on both autonomy and feedback. If jobs score high on motivating potential, the model predicts that motivation, performance, and satisfaction will be positively affected, while the likelihood of absence and turnover is lessened.

RESEARCH EVIDENCE

The job characteristics model has been well researched.[23] While most of the evidence supports the general framework of the theory, some characteristics seem to be more potent than others and efforts to support growth-need strength as a moderating variable have demonstrated mixed results.

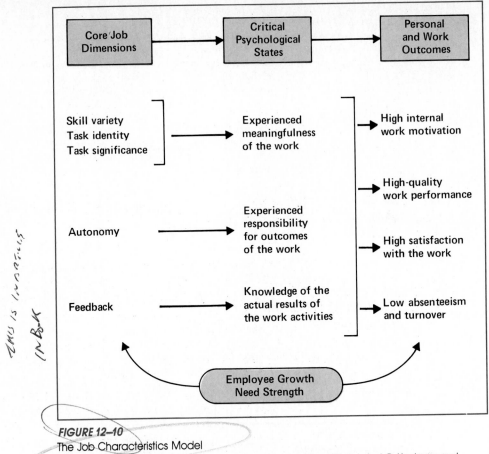

FIGURE 12-10

The Job Characteristics Model

Source: J. Richard Hackman, "Work Design," in *Improving Life at Work*, eds. J. R. Hackman and J. L. Suttle (Santa Monica, Calif.: Scott, Foresman and Company, 1977), p. 129.

There is, for instance, increasing evidence that task identity fails to add to the model's predictive ability, that skill variety may be redundant with autonomy, and that merely adding all the variables rather than adding some and multiplying by others may achieve equally predictive scores.[24]

While some studies have found growth-need strength to be a meaningful moderating variable,[25] most have not.[26] Given the current state of evidence, it would appear that growth-need strength is not a very strong moderating variable. At this point, given the mixed findings, it is probably best to minimize the importance of growth-need strength as moderating the core job dimensions–outcomes relationship.

Where does this leave us? Given the current state of evidence, we can make the following statements with relative confidence: (1) People who work on jobs with high-core job dimensions are more motivated, satisfied, and productive than are those who do not; and (2) job dimensions operate through the psychological

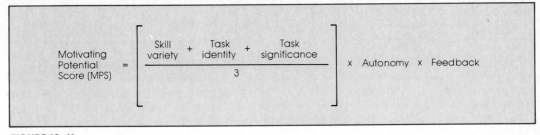

FIGURE 12–11
Computing a Motivating Potential Score

states in influencing personal and work outcome variables rather than influence them directly.[27]

THE SOCIAL CONSTRUCTION OF JOB CHARACTERISTICS

It has recently been suggested that part of the problem with the job characteristics model is the use of objective job components rather than perceptions.[28] Just as people tend to respond to their perceptions of organization structure, not its objective dimensions, individuals respond to their perception of their job's characteristics rather than their actual intensity.

Employees transform objective job characteristics into perceived job characteristics. A major influence on how tasks are perceived is the social context; that is, people develop their perception of their job in part from norms, roles, attitudes of friends at work and at home, and organizational messages from employers, labor unions, and relevant others. The result is that an individual's perception of his or her job is, in actuality, a socially constructed reality. So if you want to explain and predict an individual's behavior based on the JCM, you should not forget to assess the social context that acts to form that individual's perception of his or her job's core dimensions.

JOB REDESIGN OPTIONS AND JOB CHARACTERISTICS

Table 12–2 summarizes the redesign and work schedule options we have discussed in terms of their ability to meet the criteria identified in the job characteristics model. A quick glance tells us that there is a considerable degree of difference between the various options.

The compressed workweek and job sharing do not positively affect any of the five job characteristics. Flextime, at best, only enhances autonomy.

The other options all increase skill variety. Whether or not they increase task significance is difficult to assess without knowing more about the work content in question.

Table 12–2 indicates that job enrichment, autonomous work teams, and quality circles are significantly superior to the other options *in terms of the job characteristics model*. Of course, there are other reasons why management may decide to redesign jobs in addition to increasing their motivation potential, and

TABLE 12–2
Job Characteristics Provided by Various Redesign Options

REDESIGN OPTION	SKILL VARIETY	TASK IDENTITY	TASK SIGNIFICANCE	AUTONOMY	FEEDBACK
Job Rotation	X		?		
Work modules	X		?		
Job enlargement	X		?		
Job enrichment	X	X	?	X	X
Integrated work teams	X		?		
Autonomous work teams	X	X	?	X	X
Quality circles	X	X	?		X
Compressed workweek			?		
Flextime			?	X	
Job sharing			?		

there is nothing in Table 12–2 to indicate cost-benefit considerations. The various options we have proposed differ significantly in their implementation costs. Obviously, autonomous work teams must generate considerably more benefits than job rotation if they are to justify the greater time, effort, and cost to implement them. Nevertheless, an employee's performance and satisfaction should be higher when working in enriched jobs or on autonomous work teams or participating in quality circles.

WORK SETTINGS

Employees are affected by more than the characteristics in the jobs they do and the overall structure in which they work. They are also influenced by their physical work setting. Architects, production engineers, and office designers have known for decades that factors like temperature, noise level, and the physical layout of the work station impact on an employee's performance. It seems intuitively logical, for instance, that it is harder to do good work where noise levels are unusually high or that satisfaction will be higher for workers who are not physically isolated from others. But as we have learned throughout this book, intuition is not always a good guide. Behavioral scientists have recently recognized the potential impact of the work setting and have focused increased attention on examining its affect on employee performance and satisfaction. In this section, we'll review the results of their efforts.

Figure 12–12 outlines the essential theme in this section. Work setting factors can and do influence productivity, absence, turnover, and satisfaction. Except for satisfaction, however, these factors act as indirect influences.

When the work setting is poorly designed or uncomfortable for the worker, it can contribute to employee fatigue and hinder communication. Tired employees have difficulty in achieving both quantity and quality of output. Similarly, high

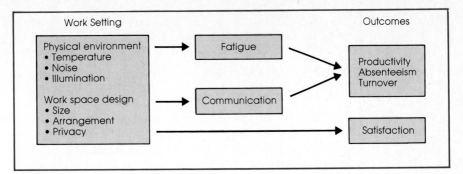

FIGURE 12–12

The Work Setting Influence

Source: From *Workspace: Creating Environments in Organizations* by F. D. Becker. Copyright © 1981 Praeger Publishers. Reprinted and adapted by permission of Praeger Publishers.

noise levels or physical partitions make it difficult for employees to engage in social interactions or form informal group ties. Our point, therefore, is that a knowledge of an employee's physical work setting should assist us in our search to explain and predict behavior.

Physical Environment

Most progressive organizations today provide a physical work environment conducive to high performance. This would include proper heating and air-conditioning equipment to maintain year-round temperature comfort, acoustics that minimize noise distractions, and light levels that allow for minimum eye strain. But what constitutes acceptable standards? What are the outside limits where performance levels might be adversely affected?

TEMPERATURE

We'll limit our discussion to the question of air temperature and avoid concerns such as humidity or ventilation. Essentially, our interest in in determining how hot or cold it has to get at the workplace before performance is affected.

The effects of heat on the performance of people performing heavy *physical* activities have been well documented.[29] But there are negative effects on employees doing *mental* tasks as well.[30] In contrasting individuals working in 95° (Fahrenheit) temperatures versus 70°, the former condition produced more errors, with the difference becoming especially great as the number of hours of exposure extended beyond three.

The effects of cold are not as severe. The performance of manual tasks is not affected until skin temperatures fall below 55°. On mental tasks, the available evidence suggests that cold is relatively unimportant.[31]

Appropriate clothing can dampen the impact of extreme heat or cold.[32] Light clothing in warm conditions and heavy clothing in cold lessens the impact of adverse temperatures. Of course, individuals vary in their personal preference to heat or cold. Those organizations whose dress codes are flexible enough to allow employees to dress according to their own physical needs will minimize the adverse effects from temperature preferences.

NOISE

Noise intensity or loudness is measured by decibels, which is a logarithmic scale. A 10-decibel difference in intensity is actually a tenfold difference in sound level. The evidence from noise studies indicates that noise does not *generally* cause deterioration in work performance.[33] If there is, it is at levels above 90 decibels, which is equivalent to the noise generated by a subway train at 20 feet. To put this in perspective, the typical decibel level in an accounting office is less than 60 decibels, and the noise levels in printing press plants are rarely in excess of 85 decibels.[34]

ILLUMINATION

You know how reading in the dark puts a strain on your eyes. You undoubtedly study better with good light rather than dim illumination. But what is the optimum illumination level?

The right light intensity depends upon task difficulty and required accuracy.[35] For difficult and critical tasks, illumination levels as high as 100 to 150 footcandles is typically appropriate. This would include activities like general office work and proofreading. Difficult inspection tasks might require 500 footcandles. Loading and unloading materials, on the other hand, can be done effectively with 20 footcandles of illumination.

A study of employees performing a difficult insurance office task under three levels of illumination—50, 100, and 150 footcandles—found that both productivity and accuracy increased at higher levels of illumination.[36] The employees rated the higher illumination levels as more satisfying and reported that they were under less stress, were more productive, and were more motivated in their work.

Workspace Design

Now we turn to the actual design of the employee's workspace. Specifically, we'll look at how the amount of that workspace, its arrangement or layout, and the degree of privacy it provides impact on communication and, eventually, an employee's performance and satisfaction.

SIZE

Size is defined by the square feet per employee. While you might think that the task to be accomplished would be the major factor in determining how much space is provided for an employee, this is not the case. Status is the most important determinant of space.[37] The higher an individual is in the organization's hierarchy, the more space he or she gets.

The fact that status and space are highly correlated demonstrates the symbolic value that the amount of space one controls plays. By merely walking into a manager's office and visually calculating his or her office size, you can immediately gauge this manager's authority and importance in the organization.

In the management ranks, office space may be the most cherished and fought over reward that the organization offers, after money and titles. Because it connotes achievement and rank, it is not unusual for organizations, especially large ones, to define square footage for each level in the hierarchy. Senior managers, for instance, may be assigned 800 square feet plus 300 square feet for a private secretary's office. A section manager may get 400 square feet, a unit manager 120, and supervisors only 80 square feet. Clerical personnel may be relegated to sharing an eight-person office. Again, there is no necessary relationship between the square footage required to do one's job and that assigned. And because status is the key determinant of workspace size, deviations from this pattern are likely to decrease job satisfaction for those individuals who perceive themselves on the short end of the discrepancy.

ARRANGEMENT

While size measures the amount of space per employee, arrangement refers to the distance between people and facilities. As we'll show, the arrangement of one's workplace is important, primarily because it significantly influences social interaction.

There is a sizable amount of research that supports that you are more likely to interact with those individuals who are physically close.[38] An employee's work location, therefore, is likely to influence the information to which one is privy and one's inclusion or exclusion from organization events. Whether you are on a certain grapevine network or not, for instance, will be largely determined by where you are physically located in the organization.

One area that has received a considerable amount of attention is office arrangements, specifically the placement of the desk and where the officeholder chooses to sit.[39] The arrangement of an office conveys nonverbal messages to visitors—some arrangements making people feel comfortable and at ease, others conveying formality and the authority of the officeholder.

The natural arrangement for people who seek to converse is to sit at right angles, as shown in Figure 12–13. In contrast, when people sit in opposite positions, as in Figure 12–14, a competitive or more structured situation is desired by one or both of the parties. Similarly, there are arrangements within an office that will emphasize structure (Figure 12–15) or reduce structure and its concomitant superior-subordinate relations (Figure 12–16). A desk between two parties creates structure, whereas the elimination of the desk is a move toward equality by the officeholder.

The importance of space arrangements was found in a study of faculty offices at a small, coeducational liberal arts college.[40] Two groups were identified: faculty whose office arrangements had desks between themselves and their students (db) and those who did not have a desk between the students and themselves (dnb). The researcher found that senior faculty members were significantly more

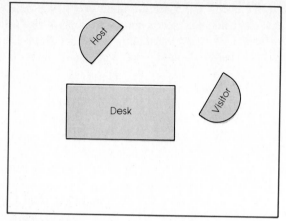

FIGURE 12–13
Natural Arrangement

likely to use the db design. Seventy-three percent of the senior faculty used the db design, compared with only 47 percent of the younger faculty. Of particular interest was the finding that dnb instructors were rated more positively on overall student ratings of the courses they taught and of themselves as instructors. The placement of a barrier (such as a desk) between an officeholder and visitor emphasizes a superior-subordinate relationship. Where visitors prefer to minimize the we-they distinction (which undoubtedly includes most students), barriers retard interaction and probably visitor satisfaction.

PRIVACY

Privacy is in part a function of the amount of space per person and the arrangement of that space. But it also is influenced by walls, partitions, and other

FIGURE 12–14
Structured Arrangement

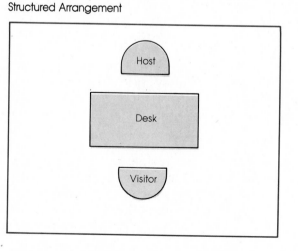

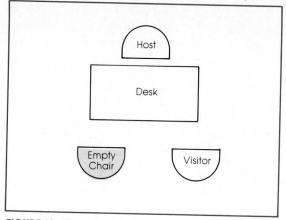

FIGURE 12–15
Formal Interaction Position

physical barriers. Most employees desire a large degree of privacy in their jobs (especially in managerial positions, where privacy is associated with status). Yet most employees also desire opportunities to interact with colleagues, which is restricted as privacy increases. A relevant illustration of the dilemma is the issue of how closed versus open offices impact on employee performance and satisfaction.[41]

The argument favoring the open office—one with internal walls and partitions removed—is that its flexible work environment facilitates contact between managers and subordinates, thereby improving all channels of communication, improving group cohesiveness, and increasing office efficiency and productivity. In practice, numerous problems affecting employee's work have been found, such

FIGURE 12–16
Informal Interaction Position

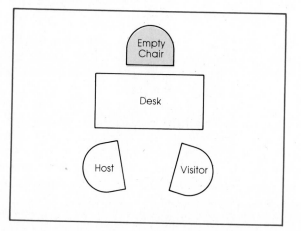

as lack of privacy and high levels of distractions and disturbances. While social cohesiveness does increase, there is no evidence that the open office design leads to any improvement in productivity. Most people seem to prefer privacy over accessibility—suggesting that the conventional closed office is more likely to be associated with high employee performance and satisfaction.

JOB STRESS

The last topic in this chapter is job stress. The medical profession has long been concerned about the effect of stress on health, but it is only recently that organizational researchers have begun to examine the impact of stress on worker behavior.

Why the recent concern with stress as an OB topic? First, stress appears to be linked to employee performance and satisfaction. So the topic is a relevant independent variable. Second, there is an implicit obligation of management to improve the quality of organizational life for employees. Because stress has been directly linked to coronary heart disease, a reduction in stress can increase both the general health and longevity of an organization's work force. Of course, this too can have performance implications.

One point of clarification is necessary before we proceed. The point is that the topic of stress has individual and group-level relevance as well as organization system implications. As we will show, an individual's stress level can be increased by such varied factors as his or her personality, role conflicts, or job's design. So job stress, while presented in this book's section on the organization system, is a multilevel concept.

What Is Stress?

Stress is a dynamic condition in which an individual is confronted with an opportunity, constraint, or demand related to what he or she desires and for which the outcome is perceived to be both uncertain and important.[42] This is a complicated definition. Let's look at its components more closely.

Stress is not necessarily bad in and of itself. While stress is typically discussed in a negative context, it also has positive value. It is an opportunity when it offers potential gain. Consider, for example, the superior performance that an athlete or stage performer gives in "clutch" situations. Such individuals often use stress positively to rise to the occasion and perform at or near their maximum.

More typically, stress is associated with constraints and demands. The former prevent you from doing what you desire. The latter refers to the loss of something desired. So when you take a test at school or you undergo your annual performance review at work, you feel stress because you confront opportunity, constraints, and demands. A good performance review may lead to a promotion, greater responsibilities, and a higher salary. But a poor review may prevent you from getting the promotion. An extremely poor review might even result in your being fired.

Two conditions are necessary for potential stress to become actual stress.[43] There must be uncertainty over the outcome and the outcome must be important. Regardless of the conditions, it is only when there is doubt or uncertainty regarding whether the opportunity will be seized, the constraint removed, or the loss avoided that there is stress. That is, stress is highest for those individuals who perceive that they are uncertain as to whether they will win or lose and lowest for those individuals who think that winning or losing is a certainty. But importance is also critical. If winning or losing is an unimportant outcome, there is no stress. If keeping your job or earning a promotion doesn't hold any importance to you, you have no reason to feel stress over having to undergo a performance review.

Facts About Stress and Work

The research on stress has uncovered several important facts. First, stress creates some very real costs to organizations. Second, stress is additive. Third, people react differently to stress situations. Each of these facts is relevant to our discussion.

Over one million Americans suffer heart attacks each year. Half of these attacks will be fatal.[44] One out of every five average, healthy, male Americans will suffer a heart attack before he reaches sixty-five years of age.[45] There is no doubt that organizational stress is a major contributor to coronary heart disease.[46] Beyond their significance for the quality of human life, these statistics have direct implications for organizations. Stress-induced heart disease increases both short- and long-term absenteeism and the need to replace employees due to premature retirements or death. While the linkage is less clear, stress also undoubtedly contributes to mental illness, alcoholism, drug abuse, and other work-related dysfunctional conditions and behaviors.

Stress is additive.[47] It builds up. Each new and persistent stressor adds to an individual's stress level. A single stressor, in and of itself, may seem relatively unimportant, but if it is added to an already high level of stress, it can be "the straw that breaks the camel's back." If we want to appraise the total amount of stress an individual is under, we have to sum up his or her opportunity stresses, constraint stresses, and demand stresses.

Another important fact about stress is that it does not necessarily follow from a stressor. Whether a potential stressor actually provokes a stress condition depends in large measure on the personality of the individual exposed to it. Individual differences moderate the relationship between a potential stress condition and the reaction to it.[48] Individuals react differently to common stress situations, and this difference can be substantially predicted by these individuals' personality characteristics. The relevant personality constructs will be elaborated upon later in this section.

Causes of Stress

Figure 12–17 summarizes the key causes and consequences of stress. As noted previously, individual-, group-, and organizational-level variables can influence stress. Based on research, examples of each variable are included in the model.[49] Whether factors like the work setting or one's personality create stress depends on whether the opportunity, constraint, or demand is perceived as uncertain and important. These are the stressors that turn potential stress into actual or felt stress. The consequences are changes in satisfaction, productivity, or turnover rates. High levels of stress will reduce productivity, lower job satisfaction, and increase the likelihood that the employee will voluntarily resign.

Symptoms of Stress

Stress shows itself in a number of ways. For instance, an individual who is experiencing a high level of stress may develop high blood pressure, ulcers, irritability, difficulty in making routine decisions, loss of appetite, accident proneness, and the like. These can be subsumed under three general categories: physiological, psychological, and behavioral symptoms.[50]

FIGURE 12–17

Causes and Consequences of Stress

Source: Adapted from S. Parasuraman and J. A. Alutto, "Sources and Outcomes of Stress in Organizational Settings: Toward the Development of a Structural Model," *Academy of Management Journal,* June 1984, p. 333. With permission.

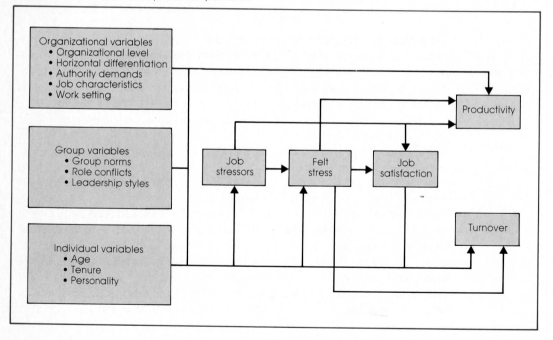

PHYSIOLOGICAL SYMPTOMS

Most of the early concern with stress was directed at physiological symptoms. This was predominately due to the fact that the topic was researched by specialists in the health and medical sciences. This research led to the conclusion that stress could create changes in metabolism, increase heart and breathing rates, increase blood pressure, bring on headaches, and induce heart attacks.

The link between stress and particular physiological symptoms is not clear. There are few, if any, consistent relationships.[51] This is attributed to the complexity of the symptoms and the difficulty of objectively measuring them. But of greater relevance is the fact that physiological symptoms have the least direct relevance to students of OB. Our concern is with behaviors and attitudes. Therefore, the two other symptoms of stress are more important to us.

PSYCHOLOGICAL SYMPTOMS

Stress can cause dissatisfaction. Job-related stress can cause job-related dissatisfaction. Job dissatisfaction, in fact, is "the simplest and most obvious psychological effect" from stress.[52] But stress shows itself in other psychological states—for instance, tension, anxiety, irritability, boredom, and procrastination.

The evidence indicates that when people are placed in jobs that make multiple and conflicting demands or in which there is a lack of clarity as to the incumbent's duties, authority, and responsibilities, both stress and dissatisfaction are increased.[53] Similarly, the less control people have over the pace of their work, the greater the stress and dissatisfaction. While more research is needed to clarify the relationship, the evidence suggests that jobs that provide a low level of variety, significance, autonomy, feedback, and identity to incumbents create stress and reduce satisfaction and involvement in the job.[54]

BEHAVIORAL SYMPTOMS

Behaviorally related stress symptoms include changes in productivity, absence, and turnover, as well as changes in eating habits, increased smoking or consumption of alcohol, rapid speech, fidgeting, and sleep disorders.

There has been a significant amount of research investigating the stress-performance relationship. Given our particular interest in factors that influence employee performance, this research is summarized in the following section.

Stress and Performance

The best known and most thoroughly documented pattern in the stress-performance literature is the inverted-U relationship.[55] This is shown in Figure 12–18.

The logic underlying the inverted-U is that low to moderate levels of stress stimulate the body and increase its ability to react. Individuals then often perform their tasks better, more intensely, or more rapidly. But too much stress places unattainable demands or constraints on a person, which results in lower performance. This inverted-U pattern may also describe the reaction to stress over time, as well as to changes in stress intensity. That is, even moderate levels of stress

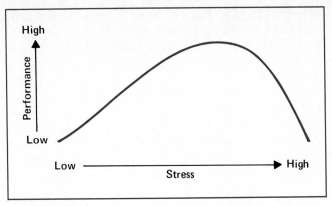

FIGURE 12–18
Relationship Between Stress and Job Performance

can have a negative influence on performance over the long term as the continued intensity of the stress wears down the individual and saps his or her energy resources. An athlete may be able to use the positive effects of stress to obtain a higher performance during every Saturday's game in the fall season. Or a sales executive may be able to psych herself up for her presentation at the annual national meeting. But moderate levels of stress experienced continually over long periods of time—as typified by the emergency room staff in a large urban hospital—can result in lower performance. This may explain why emergency room staffs at such hospitals are frequently rotated and why it is unusual to find individuals who have spent the bulk of their career in such an environment. In effect, to do so would expose the individual to the risk of "career burnout."

The inverted-U hypothesis is moderated by at least two important contingency factors: the type of job and the personality of the individual.

TYPE OF JOB

You don't have to be an insightful behavioral scientist to hypothesize that jobs differ in such a way that a given level of stress might effect performance positively in one job and negatively in another. Casual observation would lead most of us to assume that the stress level of a scriptwriter who has to turn out a fresh half-hour comedy show every week is probably quite high. A high state of arousal is probably necessary to get a quality script. Stress stimulates a nervousness and intensity that is functional. But would that same stress level be functional for a brain surgeon? Probably not. While the brain surgeon certainly works under stress, it is of a lower level. It is more controlled. Since the surgeon is typically performing precise yet routine procedures, extremely high levels of arousal are likely to lead to a lower level of surgical performance. But this extreme arousal level may be just what is necessary for the scriptwriter to do her best work.

The evidence suggests that high-stress jobs are those where incumbents have little control over their work, are under relentless time pressures, face threatening physical conditions, or have major responsibilities for financial or human resources.[56] Managers fall in this category, as do secretaries, supervisors, waiters, inspectors, and clinical lab technicians. In contrast, jobs rating low on stress include farm laborer, maid, stock handler, and college professor.[57]

PERSONALITY

There is an increasing amount of research to support the proposition that the effect of stress on an employee's behavior is moderated by his or her personality type. Personality traits that moderate an individual's response to stress at work include extroversion, rigidity, authoritarianism, dogmatism, locus of control, and tolerance for ambiguity.[58] The greatest interest, however, has been directed at what has come to be known as Type A and Type B personalities.[59]

The Type A personality is characterized by feeling a chronic sense of time urgency and by an *excessive* competitive drive. A Type A individual is "*aggressively* involved in a *chronic, incessant* struggle to achieve more and more in less and less time, and if required to do so, against the opposing efforts of other things or other persons."[60] In the North American culture, such characteristics tend to be highly prized and positively correlated with ambition and the successful acquisition of material goods. Type A's

1. Are always moving, walking, and eating rapidly
2. Feel impatient with the rate at which most events take place
3. Strive to think or do two or more things simultaneously
4. Cannot cope with leisure time
5. Are obsessed with numbers; success is measured in terms of how much of everything they acquire

In contrast to the Type A personality is the Type B, who is exactly opposite. Type B's are "rarely harried by the desire to obtain a wildly increasing number of things or participate in an endless growing series of events in an ever decreasing amount of time."[61] Type B's

1. Never suffer from a sense of time urgency with its accompanying impatience
2. Feel no need to display or discuss either their achievements or accomplishments unless such exposure is demanded by the situation
3. Play for fun and relaxation, rather than to exhibit their superiority at any cost
4. Can relax without guilt

The evidence links these two distinct personality types with diverse behaviors and different performance outcomes depending on the requirements of the job.

Before we review the research findings, it is interesting to note that Type A is the predominant personality type in North America. Without knowing anything about you, it would be statistically correct for me to assume that *you* are a Type A. About 50 percent of the population is Type A, approximately 40 percent is Type B, and the remaining 10 percent is a mix of both Type A and Type B characteristics. The fact that Type A personality characteristics are associated with two to three times greater risk of heart attack than Type B characteristics[62] can additionally help to explain the prevalence of heart disease in North America.

Type A's operate under moderate to high levels of stress. They subject themselves to more or less continuous time pressure, creating for themselves a life of deadlines. These characteristics result in some rather specific behavioral outcomes. For example, Type A's are fast workers. This is because they emphasize quantity over quality. In managerial positions, Type A's demonstrate their competitiveness by working long hours and, not infrequently, making poor decisions because they make them too fast. Type A's are also rarely creative. Because of their concern with quantity and speed, they rely on past experiences when faced with problems. They will not allocate the time that is necessary to develop unique solutions to new problems. They rarely vary in their responses to specific challenges in their milieu; hence their behavior is easier to predict than that of Type B's.

Are Type A's or Type B's more successful in organizations? In spite of the Type A's hard work, the Type B's are the ones who appear to make it to the top. Great salesmen are usually Type A's, while senior executives are usually Type B's. Why? The answer lies in the tendency of Type A's to trade off quality of effort for quantity:

> promotion and elevation, particularly in corporate and professional organizations, usually go to those who are wise rather than to those who are merely hasty, to those who are tactful rather than to those who are hostile, and to those who are creative rather than to those who are merely agile in competitive strife.[63]

The Type A–Type B dichotomy offers us some insight into the impact of personality characteristics on the stress-performance relationship. Where high energy alone is a major determinant in job success, Type A's should be highly effective. In those jobs where originality, thought, and care are important, the Type B personality should be more successful.

IMPLICATIONS FOR PERFORMANCE AND SATISFACTION

The job characteristics model demonstrates that for employees with a high growth need, jobs with a large degree of variety, identity, significance, autonomy, and feedback will lead to high employee performance and satisfaction. Job enrichment, autonomous work teams, and quality circles are three redesign options that rate strongly on these characteristics.

The physical work setting in which people do their jobs can hinder or enhance productivity. A poorly designed or uncomfortable work setting contributes to fatigue and retards communication. Tired employees have difficulty in achieving high levels of performance. Similarly, a poorly designed work area can restrict both formal and informal interactions.

Stress can be either a positive or negative influence on employee performance. Its impact on satisfaction, however, is typically only negative. Low levels of stress increase alertness and the ability to react. This can translate into a more intense and rapid work pace. But when moderate levels of stress are maintained over long periods of time or when high levels of stress are experienced, performance is likely to suffer.

POINT

A JOB DESIGN SCENARIO: ROUTE ONE

How will work be designed a decade from now? If you assume many individuals are presently underutilized and underchallenged at work, you get the "Route One" scenario. If people are underutilized by the work they do, it should lead to increases in the level of challenge that is built into jobs and in the degree of control jobholders have in managing their own work. Jobs would be changed to make them fit better for the people who do them.

For some unknown millions of people, work is neither a challenge nor a personally fulfilling part of life. And the organizations that employ them are obtaining only a portion of the contribution that these people could be making. The solution is to "fit jobs to people."

The core idea of Route One is to build increased challenge and autonomy into the work for the people who perform it. By creating job conditions that motivate employees *internally*, gains might be realized both in the productive effectiveness of the organization and in the personal satisfaction and well-being of the work force.

Specifically, the aspiration would be to design work so that employees experience the work as inherently meaningful, feel personal responsibility for the outcomes of the work, and receive, on a regular basis, trustworthy knowledge about the results of their work activities. When all three of these conditions are met, most people are internally motivated to do a good job—that is, they get a positive internal "kick" when they do well and feel bad when

they do poorly. Such feelings provide an incentive for trying to perform well and, when performance is excellent, leads to feelings of satisfaction with the work and with one's self.

Assuming that we follow Route One, and do so competently and successfully, here are some speculations about the future design and management of work.

1. Responsibility for work will be pegged clearly at the organizational level at which the work is done. No longer will employees experience themselves as people who merely execute activities that "belong" to someone else (such as a line manager). Instead, they will feel, legitimately, that they are both responsible and accountable for the outcomes of their own work.

2. Explicit consideration will be given to questions of employee motivation and satisfaction when new technologies and work practices are invented and engineered.

3. Organizations will be leaner, with fewer hierarchical levels and fewer managerial and staff personnel.

Adapted from J. R. Hackman, "The Design of Work in the 1980s," Organizational Dynamics, *Summer 1978 (New York: AMACOM, a division of American Management Associations, 1978), pp. 3–17. With permission.*

COUNTERPOINT

A JOB DESIGN SCENARIO: ROUTE TWO

If you assume that people are more adaptable than we traditionally give them credit for, you get "Route Two." If people gradually adapt and adjust to almost any work situation, even one that initially seems to underutilize their talents greatly, it should lead to greater control of work procedures and closer monitoring of work outcomes by management to increase the productive efficiency of the work force. This Route Two scenario proposes "fitting people to the jobs."

If we take Route Two, the idea is to design and engineer work for maximum economic and technological efficiency and then do whatever must be done to help people adapt and adjust in personally acceptable ways to their work experiences. No great flight of imagination is required to guess what work will be like if we follow Route Two; the sprouts of this approach are visible now. Work is designed and managed in a way that clearly subordinates the needs and goals of people to the demands and requirements of fixed jobs. External controls are employed to ensure that individuals do in fact behave appropriately on the job. These include close and directive supervision, financial incentives for correct performance, tasks that are engineered to minimize the possibility of human mistakes, and information and control systems that allow management to monitor the performance of the work system as closely and continuously as possible.

If we continue down Route Two, what might we predict about the future design and management of work?

1. Technological and engineering considerations will dominate decision making about the design of jobs. People will have substantially less discretion and challenge in their work activities used to select people and assign them to tasks, and only rarely will an individual be put into a job for which he or she is not fully qualified.

The result of all these developments will be a quantum improvement in the efficiency of most work systems, especially those that process physical materials or paper. And while employees will receive more pay for less work, they will also experience substantially less discretion and challenge in their work activities.

2. Work performance and organizational productivity will be closely monitored and controlled by managers using highly sophisticated information systems. And because managerial control of work will increase substantially, responsibility for work outcomes will lie squarely in the laps of managers, and the gap between those who do the work and those who control it will grow. There will be accelerated movement toward a two-class society of people who work in organizations, with the challenge and intrinsic interest of managerial and professional jobs increasing even as the work of rank-and-file employees becomes more controlled and less involving.

3. Desired on-the-job behavior will be elicited and maintained by extensive and sophisticated use of extrinsic rewards. Because many jobs will be routinized, standardized, and closely controlled by management, it is doubtful that employee motivation to perform appropriately can be created and maintained from intrinsic rewards (people working hard and effectively because they enjoy the tasks or because they obtain internal reinforcement from doing them well). So management will have to use extrinsic rewards (such as pay or supervisory praise) to motivate employees, providing such rewards for behavior that is in accord with the wishes of management.

Based on J. R. Hackman, "The Design of Work in the 1980s," Organizational Dynamics, *Summer 1978, pp. 3–17.*

FOR DISCUSSION

1. Contrast job design in 1906 and in 1986.
2. What is the job characteristics model?
3. Why must a job, to score high on motivating potential, have both high autonomy and feedback?
4. "Employees should have jobs that give them autonomy and diversity." Do you agree or disagree? Discuss.
5. Contrast job enlargement with job enrichment.
6. "Want to find out if a person likes his job? Ask him if he would stay with it if he inherited $5 million tomorrow!" What percentage of today's labor force do you think would continue working at their present jobs if they were suddenly independently wealthy? Do you see any common characteristics either in the persons or jobs of those who would choose to continue their present work?
7. How do work-setting factors affect productivity?
8. How are workspace design and status related?
9. What turns potential stress into actual stress?
10. Contrast Type A and Type B individuals. Are Type B's less effective employees than Type A's?
11. What are the symptoms of stress?
12. What is the relationship between stress and performance?

FOR FURTHER READING

COOPER, C., and R. PAYNE (eds.), *Current Concerns in Occupational Stress*. New York: John Wiley, 1980. Contains eleven articles focusing on the current status on our knowledge of stress.

HACKMAN, J. R., and G. R. OLDHAM, *Work Redesign*. Reading, Mass.: Addison-Wesley, 1980. Offers an excellent review of the job design literature and the job characteristics model.

KELLY, J. E., *Scientific Management, Job Redesign and Work Performance*. New York: Academic Press, 1982. Challenges many assumptions about job redesign and argues that many job redesign initiatives were achieved through changes in pay programs, control systems, and other traditional scientific management mechanisms rather than through changes in intrinsic motivation or worker attitudes.

NADLER, D. A., and E. E. LAWLER III, "Quality of Work Life: Perspectives and Directions," *Organizational Dynamics,* Winter 1983, pp. 20–30. Clarifies definition and assesses which factors predict why some quality of work life efforts are more successful than others.

NORTON, D. D., D. MASSENGIL, and H. L. SCHNEIDER, "Is Job Enrichment a Success or Failure?" *Human Resource Management,* Winter 1979, pp. 28–37. Reviews job enrichment and presents a contingency view of when it is related to success.

SHARIT, J., and G. SALVENDY, "Occupational Stress: Review and Reappraisal," *Human Factors,* April 1982, pp. 129–62. Reviews the measurement, sources, and management of stress as well as the relationship between stress and coronary heart disease.

NOTES FOR CHAPTER 12

1. See, for example, G. R. Oldham and J. R. Hackman, "Relationships Between Organizational Structure and Employee Reactions: Comparing Alternative Frameworks," *Administrative Science Quarterly,* March 1981, pp. 66–83.
2. Ibid.
3. J. L. Pierce and R. B. Dunham, "An Empirical Demonstration of the Convergence of Common Macro- and Micro-Organization Measures," *Academy of Management Journal,* September 1978, pp. 410–18.

4. J. R. Hackman, "Work Design," in J. R. Hackman and J. L. Suttle (eds.), *Improving Life at Work,* (Santa Monica, Calif.: Goodyear, 1977), p. 98.
5. R. L. Kahn, "The Work Module," *Psychology Today,* February 1973, pp. 35–39.
6. J. R. Hackman, G. R. Oldham, R. Janson, and K. Purdy, "A New Strategy for Job Enrichment," *California Management Review,* Summer 1975, pp. 57–71.
7. "The New Industrial Relations," *Business Week,* May 11, 1981, p. 96.
8. P. S. Goodman, *Assessing Organizational Change: The Rushton Quality of Work Experiment* (New York: Wiley-Interscience, 1979).
9. "A Quality Concept Catches on Worldwide," *Industry Week,* April 16, 1979, p. 125.
10. J. Main, "The Trouble with Managing Japanese-Style," *Fortune,* April 2, 1984, p. 50.
11. Ibid., p. 51.
12. Ibid., p. 50.
13. E. J. Calvasina and W. R. Boxx, "Efficiency of Workers on the Four-Day Workweek," *Academy of Management Journal,* September 1975, pp. 604–10.
14. J. C. Goodale and A. K. Aaagaard, "Factors Relating to Varying Reactions to the 4-Day Work Week," *Journal of Applied Psychology,* February 1975, pp. 33–38.
15. J. M. Ivancevich, "Effects of the Shorter Workweek on Selected Satisfaction and Performance Measures," *Journal of Applied Psychology,* December 1974, pp. 717–21.
16. W. R. Nord and R. Costigain, "Worker Adjustment to the Four-Day Week: A Longitudinal Study," *Journal of Applied Psychology,* August 1973, pp. 60–66.
17. W. F. Glueck, "Changing Hours of Work: A Review and Analysis of the Research," *The Personnel Administrator,* March 1979, pp. 44–47 and 62–66.
18. R. T. Golembiewski and C. W. Proehl, Jr., "A Survey of the Empirical Literature on Flexible Workhours: Character and Consequences of a Major Innovation," *Academy of Management Review,* October 1978, pp. 837–53; R. T. Golembiewski and C. W. Proehl, Jr., "Public Sector Applications of Flexible Workhours: A Review of Available Experience," *Public Administration Review,* January–February 1980, pp. 72–85;

J. S. Kim and A. F. Campagna, "Effects of Flextime on Employee Attendance and Performance: A Field Experiment," *Academy of Management Journal,* December 1981, pp. 729–41; J. L. Pierce and J. W. Newstrom, "Employee Responses to Flexible Work Schedules: An Inter-Organization, Inter-System Comparison," *Journal of Mangement,* Spring 1982, pp. 9–25; and M. Krausz and N. Freibach, "Effects of Flexible Working Time for Employed Women upon Satisfaction, Strains, and Absenteeism," *Journal of Occupational Psychology,* June 1983, pp. 155–59.

19. G. W. Rainey, Jr., and L. Wolf, "The Organizationally Dysfunctional Consequences of Flexible Work Hours: A General Overview," *Public Personnel Journal,* Summer 1982, pp. 165–75.

20. Ibid., p. 167.

21. J. R. Hackman and G. R. Oldham, "Development of the Job Diagnostic Survey," *Journal of Applied Psychology,* April 1975, pp. 159–70.

22. Hackman, "Work Design," p. 129.

23. For a review of the research, see "Job Characteristics Theory of Work Redesign," in J. B. Miner, *Theories of Organizational Behavior* (Hinsdale, Ill.: Dryden Press, 1980), pp. 231–66; and K. H. Roberts and W. Glick, "The Job Characteristics Approach to Task Design: A Critical Review," *Journal of Applied Psychology,* April 1981, pp. 193–217.

24. See R. B. Dunham, "Measurement and Dimensionality of Job Characteristics," *Journal of Applied Psychology,* August 1976, pp. 404–09; J. L. Pierce and R. B. Dunham, "Task Design: A Literature Review," *Academy of Management Review,* January 1976, pp. 83–97; and D. M. Rousseau, "Technological Differences in Job Characteristics, Employee Satisfaction, and Motivation: A Synthesis of Job Design Research and Sociotechnical Systems Theory," *Organizational Behavior and Human Performance,* October 1977, pp. 18–42.

25. See, for example, H. P. Sims, Jr., and A. D. Szilagyi, "Job Characteristic Relationships: Individual and Structural Moderators," *Organizational Behavior and Human Performance,* December 1976, pp. 211–30.

26. See, for example, J. K. White, "Individual Differences and the Job Quality-Worker-Response Relationship: Review, Integration, and Comments," *Academy of Management Review,* April 1978, pp. 267–80; and R. W. Griffin, A. Welsh, and G. Moorhead, "Perceived Task Characteristics and Employee Performance: A Literature Review," *Academy of Management Journal,* September 1981, pp. 655–64.

27. Hackman, "Work Design," pp. 132–33.

28. G. Salancik and J. Pfeffer, "A Social Information Processing Approach to Job Attitudes and Task Design," *Administrative Science Quarterly,* June 1978, pp. 224–53; and G. J. Blau and R. Katerberg, "Toward Enhancing Research with the Social Information Processing Approach to Job Design," *Academy of Management Review,* October 1982, pp. 543–50.

29. E. J. McCormick and D. Ilgen, *Industrial Psychology,* 7th ed. (Englewood Cliffs, N.J.: Prentice-Hall, 1980), p. 388.

30. B. J. Fine and J. L. Kobrick, "Effects of Altitude and Heat on Complex Cognitive Tasks," *Human Factors,* February 1978, pp. 115–22.

31. McCormick and Ilgen, *Industrial Psychology,* p. 390.

32. S. C. Vickroy, J. B. Shaw, and C. D. Fisher, "Effects of Temperature, Clothing, and Task Complexity on Task Performance and Satisfaction," *Journal of Applied Psychology,* February 1982, pp. 97–102.

33. McCormick and Ilgen, *Industrial Psychology,* p. 391.

34. Ibid.

35. J. D. Wineman, "Office Design and Evaluation: An Overview," *Environment and Behavior,* May 1982, p. 276.

36. J. F. Barnaby, "Lighting for Productivity Gains," *Lighting Design and Application,* February 1980, pp. 20–28.

37. J. Pfeffer, *Organizations and Organization Theory* (Boston: Pitman, 1982), p. 261.

38. See, for example, L. S. Festinger, S. Schacter, and K. Back, *Social Pressures in Informal Groups* (Stanford, Calif.: Stanford University Press, 1950).

39. See, for example, R. L. Zweigenhaft, "Personal Space in the Faculty Office Desk Placement and the Student-Faculty Interaction," *Journal of Applied Psychology,* August 1976, pp. 529–32; D. E. Campbell, "Interior Office Design and Visitor Response," *Journal of Applied Psychology,* December 1979, pp. 648–53; and P. C. Morrow and J. C. McElroy, "Interior Office Design and Visitor Response: A Constructive Replication," *Journal of Applied Psychology,* October 1981, pp. 646–50.

40. Zweigenhaft, "Personal Space."

41. See, for example, G. R. Oldham and D. J. Brass, "Employees' Reactions to an Open-Plan Office: A Natural Occurring Quasi-Experiment," *Administrative Science Quarterly,* June 1979, pp. 267–84; E. Sundstrom, R. E. Burt, and D. Kamp, "Privacy at Work: Architectural Correlates of Job Satisfaction and Job Performance," *Academy of Management Journal,* March 1980, pp. 101–17; A. Hedge, "The Open-Plan Office," *Environment and Behavior,* September 1982, pp. 519–42; and T. R. V. Davis, "The Influence of the Physical Environment in Offices," *Academy of Management Review,* April 1984, pp. 271–83.

42. Adapted from R. S. Schuler, "Definition and Conceptualization of Stress in Organizations," *Organizational Behavior and Human Performance,* April 1980, p. 189. Supported by P. G. Wilhelm, "An Exploratory Field Test of Selected Factors in Schuler's Stress Definition"; *Effective Management: Research and Applications,* D. J. Vredenburgh and R. S. Schuler (eds.), Proceedings of the 20th Annual Eastern Academy of Management, Pittsburgh, May 1983, pp. 16–19.

43. Schuler, "Definition and Conceptualization of Stress in Organizations," p. 191.

44. D. C. Glass, "Stress, Competition, and Heart Attacks," *Psychology Today,* December 1976, p. 54.

45. K. Albrecht, *Stress and the Manager* (Englewood Cliffs, N.J.: Prentice-Hall, 1979), p. 33.

46. See, for instance, C. L. Cooper and J. Marshall, "Occupational Sources of Stress: A Review of the Literature Relating to Coronary Heart Disease and Mental Ill Health," *Journal of Occupational Psychology,* Vol. 49, no. 1 (1976), pp. 11–28.

47. H. Selye, *The Stress of Life,* rev. ed. (New York: McGraw-Hill, 1956).

48. B. J. Mullin and R. L. Swinth, "Individual Differences in Perceived Stress and Performance in Response to Organizational Stressors," paper presented at the meeting of Western Academy of Management, Monterey, Calif., April 1981.

49. See, for example, A. Arsenault and S. Dolan, "The Role of Personality, Occupation, and Organization in Understanding the Relationship Between Job Stress, Performance, and Absenteeism," *Journal of Occupational Psychology,* September 1983, pp. 227–40; D. F. Parker and T. A. DeCotiis, "Organizational Determinants of Job Stress," *Organizational Behavior and Human Performance,* October 1983, pp. 160–77; and S. Parasuraman and J. A. Alutto, "Sources and Outcomes of Stress in Organizational Settings: Toward the Development of a Structural Model," *Academy of Management Journal,* June 1984, pp. 330–50.

50. Schuler, "Definition and Conceptualization of Stress," pp. 200–5.

51. T. A. Beehr and J. E. Newman, "Job Stress, Employee Health, and Organizational Effectiveness: A Facet Analysis, Model, and Literature Review," *Personnel Psychology,* Winter 1978, pp. 665–99.

52. Ibid., p. 687.

53. Cooper and Marshall, "Occupational Sources of Stress."

54. Hackman and Oldham, "Development of the Job Diagnostic Survey," pp. 159–70.

55. See, for instance, J. E. McGrath, "Stress and Behavior in Organizations," in M. D. Dunnette (ed.), *Handbook of Industrial and Organizational Psychology* (Chicago: Rand McNally, 1976); and R. T. Keller, "Job Stress and Employee Performance in a Manufacturing Plant," paper presented at the meeting of the National Academy of Management, San Diego, August 1981.

56. C. L. Cooper and R. Payne, *Stress at Work* (London: John Wiley, 1978).

57. As reported in *U.S. News and World Report,* March 13, 1978, pp. 80–81.

58. These traits are reviewed in A. P. Brief, R. S. Schuler and M. Van Sell, *Managing Job Stress* (Boston: Little, Brown, 1981), pp. 94–98.

59. M. Friedman and R. H. Rosenman, *Type A Behavior and Your Heart* (New York: Alfred A. Knopf, 1974).

60. Ibid., p. 84.

61. Ibid., pp. 84–85.

62. O. Behling and F. D. Holcombe, "Dealing with Employee Stress," *MSU Business Topics,* Spring 1981, p. 53.

63. Friedman and Rosenman, *Type A. Behavior,* p. 86.

Human Resource Policies and Practices

AFTER STUDYING THIS CHAPTER, YOU SHOULD BE ABLE TO:

Define and explain the following key terms and concepts:

Assessment centers
Career
Career stages
Extrinsic rewards
Intrinsic rewards
Job analysis

Job description
Job specification
Labor unions
Leniency error
Similarity error
Work sampling

Understand:

The purposes of job analysis
Popular job analysis methods
When to use interviews in selection
The advantages of performance simulation tests over written tests
The importance of performance evaluation
The purposes of performance evaluation
What should be evaluated
Potential problems in evaluation and actions that can correct these
    problems
The criteria by which rewards are distributed
The types of rewards
The four stages in a career
The activities in an effective career counseling program
How the existence of a union affects employee behavior

What's worth doing is worth doing for money.

—J. DONOHUE

Every organization has human resource policies that influence who is hired and, once employed, such personnel practices as evalution procedures, the size of pay increases, career development activities, and union-management relations. In all large and most medium-sized organizations, these policies are formally written down. In smaller organizations, they're more often informal. But all organizations have explicit or implicit human resource policies. In this chapter, we'll demonstrate that these policies and practices have a significant influence on employees by guiding and controlling their behavior.

SELECTION PRACTICES

The objective of effective selection is to match individual characteristics (ability, experience, etc.) with the requirements of the job. When management fails to get a proper match, both employee performance and satisfaction suffer. In this search to achieve the right individual-job fit, where does management begin? The answer is to assess the demands and requirements of the job. The process of assessing the activities within a job is called job analysis.

Job Analysis

Job analysis involves developing a detailed description of the tasks involved in a job, determining the relationship of a given job to other jobs, and ascertaining the knowledge, skills, and abilities necessary for an employee to successfully perform the job.

How is this information achieved? Table 13–1 describes the more popular job analysis methods.

Information gathered by using one or more of the job analysis methods results in the organization being able to create a job description and job specification. The former is a written statement of what a jobholder does, how it is done, and why it is done. It should accurately portray job content, environment, and conditions of employment. The job specification states the minimum acceptable qualifications that an employee must possess to perform a given job successfully. It identifies the knowledge, skills, and abilities needed to do the job effectively. So job descriptions identify characteristics of the job, while job specifications identify characteristics of the successful job incumbent.

The job description and specification are important documents for guiding the selection process. The job description can be used to describe the job to potential candidates. The job specification keeps the attention of those doing the selection on the list of qualifications necessary for an incumbent to perform a job and assists in determining whether or not candidates are qualified.

Selection Devices

What do application forms, interviews, employment tests, background checks, and personal letters of recommendation have in common? Each is a device for obtaining information about a job applicant that can help the organization determine whether the applicant's skills, knowledge, and abilities are appropriate for the job in question. In this section, we review the more important of these selection devices—interviews, written tests, and performance simulation tests.

INTERVIEWS

Do you know anyone who has gotten a job without at least one interview? You may have an acquaintance who got a part-time or summer job through a close friend or relative without having to go through an interview, but such instances

TABLE 13–1
Popular Job Analysis Methods

1. **Observation Method.** An analyst watches employees directly or reviews films of workers on the job.
2. **Individual Interview Method.** Selected job incumbents are extensively interviewed, and the results of a number of these interviews are combined into a single job analysis.
3. **Group Interview Method.** Same as individual except that a number of job incumbents are interviewed simultaneously.
4. **Structured Questionnaire Method.** Workers check or rate the items they perform in their jobs from a long list of possible task items.
5. **Technical Conference Method.** Specific characteristics of a job are obtained from "experts," who typically are supervisors with extensive knowledge of the job.
6. **Diary Method.** Job incumbents record their daily activities in a diary.

are rare. There is little doubt that the interview is the most widely used selection device that organizations rely upon to differentiate candidates. Few employees are hired without one or more interviews. With a bit less certainty, we can also say that the interview seems to carry a great deal of weight. That is, not only is it widely used, its results tend to carry a disproportionate amount of influence in the selection decision. The candidate who performs poorly in the employment interview is likely to be cut from the applicant pool, regardless of his or her experience, test scores, or letters of recommendation.

These findings are important because, to many people's surprise, the interview is a poor selection device for most jobs.[1] Why? Because the data gathered from interviews are often biased and unrelated to future job performance. Research indicates that prior knowledge about an applicant biases the interviewer's evaluation, that interviewers tend to favor applicants who share their attitudes, that the order in which applicants are interviewed influences evaluations, that negative information is given unduly high weight, and that an applicant's ability to do well in an interview is irrelevant in most jobs.[2] On this last point: What relevance does "good interviewing skills" have for successful performance as a bricklayer, drillpress operator, or data-entry operator? The answer is: "Little or none!" These jobs don't require this skill. Yet employers typically use the interview as a selection device for such jobs. The evidence suggests that interviews are good for assessing an applicant's intelligence, level of motivation, and interpersonal skills. Since these are attributes that are most likely to be relevant qualities for upper managerial positions, the interview makes sense for the selection of senior executives. Its use in identifying "good performers" for most lower-level jobs appears unfounded.

WRITTEN TESTS

Written tests include tests of intelligence, aptitude, ability, and interest. Long popular as selection devices, there has been a marked decline in their use during the past twenty years. The reason is that such tests have frequently been characterized as discriminating and not directly job relevant. To design and validate written tests for a broad spectrum of jobs is both time consuming and costly. For expediency sake, many employers have just chosen to drop such tests.

PERFORMANCE SIMULATION TESTS

What better way to find out if an applicant can do a job successfully than by having him or her do it? The logic of this question has resulted in increased usage of performance simulation tests. Undoubtedly the enthusiasm for these tests lies in the fact that they are based on job analysis data and, therefore, should more easily meet the requirement of job relatedness than do written tests. Performance simulation tests are made up of actual job behaviors rather than surrogates, as are written tests.

The two best known performance simulation tests are work sampling and assessment centers. The former is suited to routine jobs, whereas the latter is relevant for the selection of managerial personnel.

Work sampling is an effort to create a miniature replica of a job. Applicants demonstrate that they possess the necessary talents by actually doing the tasks.

By carefully devising work samples based on job analysis data, the knowledge, skills, and abilities needed for each job are determined. Then each work sample element is matched with a corresponding job performance element. For instance, a work sample for a job that involves computations on an adding machine would require the applicant to make similar computations.

The results from work sample experiments are impressive. One review of the literature showed that work samples have almost always yielded validities superior to those yielded by traditional tests.[3] Another review similarly found work samples to be better than written aptitude, personality, or intelligence tests.[4]

A more elaborate set of performance simulation tests, specifically designed to evaluate a candidate's managerial potential, is administered in *assessment centers*. In assessment centers, line executives, supervisors, and/or trained psychologists evaluate candidates as they go through two to four days of exercises that simulate real problems that they would confront on the job. Based on a list of descriptive dimensions that the actual job incumbent has to meet, activities might include interviews, inbasket problem-solving exercises, group discussions, and business decision games.

The evidence on the effectiveness of assessment centers is extremely impressive. They have consistently demonstrated results that predict later job performance in managerial positions.[5] Although they are not cheap—AT&T, which has assessed more than 200,000 employees, computes its assessment costs at $800 to $1,500 per employee—the selection of an ineffective manager is unquestionably far more costly.

PERFORMANCE EVALUATION SYSTEMS

Would you study differently or exert a different level of effort in a college course graded on a pass-fail basis than one where letter grades from A to F are used? When I ask that question of students, I usually get an affirmative answer. Students typically tell me that they study harder when letter grades are at stake. Additionally, they tell me that when they take a course on a pass-fail basis, they tend to do just enough to ensure a passing grade.

This finding illustrates how performance evaluation systems influence behavior. Major determinants of your in-class behavior and out-of-class studying effort in college are the criteria and techniques your instructor uses to evaluate your performance. Of course, what applies in the college context also applies to employees at work. In this section, we'll show how the choice of a performance evaluation system and the way it's administered can be an important force influencing employee behavior.

Purposes of Performance Evaluation

Performance evaluation serves a number of purposes in organizations (see Table 13–2 for survey results on primary uses of evaluations). Management uses evaluations for general *personnel decisions*. Evaluations provide input into such im-

TABLE 13–2
Primary Uses of Performance Evaluations
(responses from 216 organizations)

USE	PERCENT
Compensation	71.3%
Performance improvement	55.2
Feedback	29.3
Promotion	25.1
Documentation	10.7
Training	8.7
Transfer	7.9
Personnel planning	6.2
Discharge	2.3
Research	1.4
Layoff	0.3

Source: Adapted from A. H. Locher and K. S. Teel, "Performance Appraisal—A Survey of Current Practices," May 1977, p. 246. Reprinted with the permission of *Personnel Journal,* Costa Mesa, Calif.; all rights reserved.

portant decisions as promotions, transfers, and terminations. Evaluations *identify training and development needs.* They pinpoint employee skills and competencies that are currently inadequate but for which programs can be developed to remedy. Performance evaluations can be used as a *criterion against which selection and development programs are validated.* Newly hired employees who perform poorly can be identified through performance evaluation. Similarly, the effectiveness of training and development programs can be determined by assessing how well those employees who have participated do on their performance evaluation. Evaluations also fulfill the purpose of *providing feedback to employees* on how the organization views their performance. Further, performance evaluations are used as the *basis for reward allocations.* Decisions as to who gets merit pay increases and other rewards are determined by performance evaluations.

Each of these functions of performance evaluation is important. Yet their importance to us depends on the perspective we're taking. Several are clearly relevant to personnel management decisions. But our interest is in organizational behavior. As a result, we shall be emphasizing performance evaluation in its role as a mechanism for providing feedback and as a determinant of reward allocations.

Performance Evaluation and Motivation

In Chapter 5, considerable attention was given to the expectancy model of motivation. We argued that this model currently offers the best explanation of what conditions the amount of effort an individual will exert on his or her job. A vital component of this model is performance, specifically the effort-performance and performance-reward linkages. Do people see effort leading to performance and performance to the rewards that they value? Clearly, they have to know what is expected of them. They need to know how their performance will be measured. Further, they must feel confident that, if they exert an effort within their capabilities, it will result in a satisfactory performance as defined by the criteria by which they are being measured. Finally, they must feel confident that if they perform as they are being asked, they will achieve the rewards they value.

In brief, if the objectives that employees are expected to achieve are unclear, if the criteria for measuring those objectives are vague, and if the employees lack confidence that their efforts will lead to a satisfactory appraisal of their performance or believe that there will be an unsatisfactory payoff by the organization when their performance objectives are achieved, we can expect individuals to work considerably below their potential.

What Do We Evaluate?

The criteria or criterion that management chooses to evaluate, when appraising employee performance, will have a major influence on what employees do. Two examples illustrate this:

In a public employment agency, which served workers seeking employment and employers seeking workers, employment interviewers were appraised by the number of interviews they conducted. Consistent with the thesis that the evaluating criteria influence behavior, interviewers emphasized the *number* of interviews conducted rather than the *placements* of clients in jobs.[6]

A management consultant specializing in police research noticed that, in one community, officers would come on duty for their shift, proceed to get into their police cars, drive to the highway that cut through the town, and speed back and forth along this highway for their entire shift. Clearly this fast cruising had little to do with good police work, but this behavior made considerably more sense once the consultant learned that the community's City Council used mileage on police vehicles as an evaluative measure of police effectiveness.[7]

These examples demonstrate the importance of criteria in performance evaluation. This, of course, begs the question: What should management evaluate? The three most popular sets of criteria are individual task outcomes, behaviors, and traits.

INDIVIDUAL TASK OUTCOMES

If it's ends that count, rather than means, then management should evaluate an employee's task outcomes. Using task outcomes, a plant manager could be judged on criteria such as quantity produced, scrap generated, and cost per unit of production. Similarly, a salesperson could be assessed on overall sales volume in his or her territory, dollar increase in sales, and number of new accounts established.

BEHAVIORS

In many cases, it's difficult to identify specific outcomes that can be directly attributable to an employee's actions. This is particularly true of personnel in staff positions and individuals whose work assignments are intrinsically part of a group effort. In the latter case, the group's performance may be readily evaluated, but the contribution of each group member may be difficult or impossible to identify clearly. In such instances, it is not unusual for management to evaluate the employee's behavior. Using the previous examples, behaviors of a plant manager that could be used for performance evaluation purposes might include promptness in submitting his or her monthly reports or the leadership style that the manager exhibits. Pertinent salesperson behaviors could be average number of contact calls made per day or sick days used per year.

TRAITS

The weakest set of criteria, yet ones that are still widely used by organizations, is individual traits. We say they are weaker than either task outcomes or behaviors because they are farthest removed from the actual performance of the job itself. Traits such as having "a good attitude," showing "confidence," being "intelligent" or "friendly," "looking busy," or possessing "a wealth of experience" may or may not be highly correlated with positive task outcomes, but only the naive would ignore the reality that such traits are frequently used in organizations as criteria for assessing an employee's level of performance.

Methods of Performance Evaluation

Three different approaches exist for doing evaluations. Employees can be appraised against (1) absolute standards, (2) relative standards, or (3) objectives.

ABSOLUTE STANDARDS

The use of absolute standards means that employees are *not* compared with each other. Evaluators may write essays describing the employee's strengths and weaknesses. In more elaborate evaluations, the rater may check off "Yes" or "No" responses to a previously prepared list of traits or behaviors that the employee demonstrates.

The common thread through all evaluation methods that use the absolute standard is that the employee is judged against a rigid standard rather than against the performance of other employees. When a college instructor gives grades that are based on 90 and above equaling an A, 80 and above a B, and so forth—and makes no adjustment for how the class does as a whole—an absolute standard approach is being used. This approach avoids problems like trying to rank order five people in a small department whose performance levels are nearly identical. On the other hand, the use of absolute standards tends to result in high evaluations. That is, evaluators lean toward packing their subjects into the high part of the scale. This, in fact, happens in many organizations. Take the case of the U.S. Army captain who could not understand why he had been passed over for promotion. He had seen his file and knew that his average rating by his superior was 86. Given his knowledge that the rating system defined "outstanding performance" as 90 or above, "good" as 80 or above, "average" as 70 or above, and "inadequate performance" as anything below 70, he was at a loss to understand why he had not been promoted, given his near-outstanding performance evaluation. The officer's confusion was resolved when he found out the "average" rating of captains in the U.S. Army was 92!

RELATIVE STANDARDS

The second category of evaluation methods compares employees against each other. These methods use relative rather than absolute measuring devices. For instance, employees may be order-ranked into classification groups such as "top one-fifth" or "second one-fifth." Another approach is merely to rank a given set of employees from highest to lowest. If you are evaluating thirty employees using individual ranking, then only one can be "best" and someone must be relegated to last.

Relative standards overcome one objection of absolute standards in that there can be no bias toward inflating everyone's evaluation. If a department has only five employees, relative standards require that they be compared against each other and ranked. This, of course, can be a major drawback. When the number of individuals being evaluated is small or when there is little actual variability among those being evaluated, relative standards may generate unrealistic appraisals. If, for instance, there are eleven individuals in a department working at different levels of effectiveness, by definition, five of them must be "below average." Ironically, if two of the below-average workers leave, then one of the previously "above-average" performers must fall into the below-average category. Because comparisons are relative, an employee who is mediocre may score high only because he is the "best of the worst." In contrast, an excellent employee who is matched against "stiff" competition may be evaluated poorly when in absolute terms her performance is quite outstanding.

OBJECTIVES

The third approach to evaluation makes use of objectives. Employees are evaluated by how well they accomplish a specific set of objectives that have been determined to be critical in the successful completion of their jobs.

This approach works well where the organization—from the top down—is strongly committed to setting objectives and rewarding people based on their success in achieving their objectives. The use of objectives gives performance evaluation a results-oriented emphasis and provides motivation because employees know exactly what is expected of them.

Potential Problems

While organizations may seek to make the performance evaluation process free from personal biases, prejudices, or idiosyncracies, a number of potential problems can creep into the process. To the degree that the following factors are prevalent, an employee's evaluation is likely to be distorted.

SINGLE CRITERION

The typical employee's job is made up of a number of tasks. An airline flight attendant's job, for example, includes welcoming passengers, seeing to their comfort, serving meals, and offering safety advice. If performance on this job were assessed by a single criterion measure say—the time it took to provide food and beverages to a hundred passengers—the result would be a limited evaluation of that job. More important, flight attendants whose performance evaluation included assessment on only this single criterion would be motivated to ignore those other tasks in their job. Similarly, if a football quarterback were appraised only on his percentage of completed passes, he would be likely to throw short passes and only in situations where he felt assured that they will be caught. Our point is that where employees are evaluated on a single job criterion, and where successful performance on that job requires good performance on a number of criteria, employees will emphasize the single criterion to the exclusion of other job-relevant factors.

LENIENCY ERROR

Every evaluator has his or her own value system that acts as a standard against which appraisals are made. Relative to the true or actual performance an individual exhibits, some evaluators mark high and others low. The former is referred to as positive leniency error, and the latter as negative leniency error. When evaluators are positively lenient in their appraisal, an individual's performance becomes overstated, that is, rated higher than it actually should. Similarly, a negative leniency error understates performance, giving the individual a lower appraisal.

If all individuals in an organization were appraised by the same person, there would be no problem. Although there would be an error factor, it would be applied equally to everyone. The difficulty arises when we have different raters with different leniency errors making judgments. For example, Jones and Smith are performing the same job for different supervisors, but they have absolutely identical job performance. If Jones' supervisor tends to err toward positive leniency, while Smith's supervisor errs toward negative leniency, we might be confronted with two dramatically different evaluations.

HALO ERROR

The halo effect or error, as we noted in Chapter 3, is the tendency for an evaluator to let the assessment of an individual on one trait influence his or her evaluation of that person on other traits. For example, if an employee tends to be dependable, we might become biased toward that individual to the extent that we will rate him or her high on many desirable attributes.

People who design teaching appraisal forms for college students to fill out in evaluating the effectiveness of their instructor each semester must confront the halo effect. Students tend to rate a faculty member as outstanding on all criteria when they are particularly appreciative of a few things he or she does in the classroom. Similarly, a few bad habits—like showing up late for lectures, being slow in returning papers, or assigning an extremely demanding reading requirement—might result in students' evaluating the instructor as "lousy" across the board.

SIMILARITY ERROR

When the evaluator rates other people giving special consideration to those qualities that he perceives in himself, he is making a similarity error. For example, the evaluator who perceives himself as aggressive may evaluate others by looking for aggressiveness. Those who demonstrate this characteristic tend to benefit, while others are penalized.

Again, this error would tend to wash out if the same evaluator appraised all the people in the organization. However, interrater reliability obviously suffers when various evaluators are utilizing their own similarity criteria.

LOW DIFFERENTIATION

It is possible that, regardless of whom the appraiser evaluates and what traits are used, the pattern of evaluation remains the same. It is possible that the evaluator's ability to appraise objectively and accurately has been impeded by social differentiation, that is, the evaluator's style of rating behavior.

It has been suggested that evaluators may be classified as (1) high differentiators, who use all or most of the scale, or (2) low differentiators, who use a limited range of the scale.[8]

Low differentiators tend to ignore or suppress differences, perceiving the universe as more uniform than it really is. High differentiators, on the other hand, tend to utilize all available information to the utmost extent and thus are better able to define perceptually anomalies and contradictions than low differentiators.[9]

This finding tells us that evaluations made by low differentiators need to be carefully inspected and that the people working for a low differentiator have a high probability of being appraised as significantly more homogeneous than they really are.

FORCING INFORMATION TO MATCH NONPERFORMANCE CRITERIA

While rarely advocated, it is not an infrequent practice to find the formal evaluation taking place *following* the decision as to how the individual has been performing! This may sound illogical, but it merely recognizes that subjective, yet formal, decisions are often arrived at prior to the gathering of objective information to support that decision. For example, if the evaluator believes that the evaluation should not be based on performance, but rather seniority, he may be unknowingly adjusting each "performance" evaluation so as to bring it into line with the employee's seniority rank. In this and other similar cases, the evaluator is increasing or decreasing performance appraisals to align with the nonperformance criteria actually being utilized.

Overcoming the Problems

The fact that organizations can encounter problems with performance evaluations should not lead managers to give up on the process. Some things can be done to overcome most of the problems we have identified.

USE MULTIPLE CRITERIA

Since successful performance on most jobs requires doing a number of things well, all those "things" should be identified and evaluated. The more complex the job, the more criteria that will need to be identified and evaluated. But everything need not be assessed. The critical activities that lead to high or low performance are the ones that need to be evaluated.

DEEMPHASIZE TRAITS

Many traits often considered to be related to good performance may, in fact, have little or no performance relationship. Traits like loyalty, initiative, courage, reliability, and self-expression are intuitively appealing as desirable characteristics in employees. But the relevant question is: Are individuals who are evaluated as high on those traits higher performers than those who rate low? We can't answer this question. We know that there are employees who rate high on these characteristics and are poor performers. We can find others who are excellent performers but do not score well on traits such as these. Our conclusion is that traits like loyalty and initiative may be prized by managers, but there is no evidence to support that certain traits will be adequate synonyms for performance in a large cross section of jobs.

Another weakness in traits is the judgment itself. What is "loyalty"? When is an employee "reliable"? What you consider "loyalty," I may not. So traits suffer from weak interrater agreement.

COMBINE ABSOLUTE AND RELATIVE STANDARDS

A major drawback to absolute standards is that standards tend to be biased by positive leniency; that is, evaluators lean toward packing their subjects into the high part of the rankings. On the other hand, relative standards suffer when the number of individuals being appraised is small and when there is little actual variability among the subjects.

The obvious solution is to consider using evaluation methods that combine both absolute and relative standards. This dual method of evaluation, incidentally, has been instituted at some universities to deal with the problem of grade inflation. Students get an absolute grade—A, B, C, D, or F—and next to it is a mark showing how this student ranked in the class. A prospective employer or graduate school admissions committee can look at two students who each got a B in their cost accounting course and draw considerably different conclusions about each when, next to one grade it says "ranked 4 out of 26" while the other says "ranked 17 out of 30." Obviously, the second instructor gave out a lot more high grades!

USE MULTIPLE EVALUATORS

As the number of evaluators increases, the probability of attaining more accurate information increases. If rater error tends to follow a normal curve, an increase in the number of apraisers will tend to find the majority congregating about the middle. You see this approach being used in athletic competitions in such sports as diving and gymnastics. A multiple set of evaluators judge a performance, the highest and lowest scores are dropped, and the final peformance evaluation is made up from the cumulative scores of those remaining. The logic of multiple evaluators applies to organizations as well.

If an employee has had ten supervisors, nine having rated her excellent and one poor, we can discount the value of the one poor evaluation. Therefore, by moving employees about within the organization so as to gain a number of evaluations, we increase the probability of achieving more valid and reliable evaluations.

The U.S. Army has made good use of this technique. For individuals who have been evaluated by ten or fifteen officers during their first five or six years in the service, there is less chance that one or two "slanted" evaluations will seriously influence decisions made on the basis of these performance appraisals.

EVALUATE SELECTIVELY

It has been suggested that appraisers should evaluate in only those areas in which they have some expertise.[10] If raters make evaluations on *only* those dimensions on which they are in a good position to rate, we increase the interrater agreement and make the evaluation a more valid process. This approach also recognizes that different organizational levels often have different orientations toward ratees and observe them in different settings. In general, therefore, we would recommend that appraisers should be as close as possible, in terms of organizational level, to the individual being evaluated. Conversely, the more levels that separate the evaluator and evaluatee, the less opportunity the evaluator has to observe the individual's behavior and, not surprisingly, the greater the possibility for inaccuracies.

The specific application of these concepts would result in having immediate supervisors or co-workers as the major input into the appraisal and having them evaluate those factors that they are best qualified to judge. For example, it has been suggested that when professors are evaluating secretaries within a university, they use such criteria as judgment, technical competence, and conscientiousness, whereas peers (other secretaries) use such criteria as job knowledge, organization, cooperation with co-workers, and responsibility.[11] Such an approach appears both logical and more reliable, since people are appraising only those dimensions on which they are in a good position to make judgments.

TRAIN EVALUATORS

If you can't *find* good evaluators, the alternative is to *make* good evaluators. There is evidence to support that training evaluators can make them more accurate raters.[12]

Common errors such as halo and leniency have been minimized or eliminated in workshops where managers can practice observing and rating behaviors. These workshops would typically run from one to three days, but allocating many hours to training may not always be necessary. One case has been cited where both halo and leniency errors were decreased immediately after exposing evaluators to explanatory training sessions lasting only five minutes.[13] But the effects of training do appear to diminish over time.[14] This suggests the need for regular training refresher sessions.

Performance Feedback

A few years back, a nationwide motel chain advertised that, when it came to motel rooms, "the best surprise is no surprise." This logic also holds for performance evaluations. Employees like to know how they are doing. They expect feedback. This is typically done in the "annual review." But this review frequently creates problems. In some cases, it's a problem merely because managers put off such reviews. This is particularly likely if the appraisal is negative. But the annual review is additionally troublesome if the manager "saves up" performance-related information and unloads it during the appraisal review. In such instances, it is not surprising that the manager may try to avoid addressing stressful issues that, even if confronted, may only be denied or rationalized by the employee.[15] Much of this problem can be avoided by sharing feedback information with employees on an ongoing basis, for example, providing daily output reports with comparative data on actual units produced and the goal for the day or bringing up problems as they occur rather than allowing them to accumulate for the annual review.

Regardless of whether feedback is provided annually or on an ongoing basis, management needs to offer performance feedback to employees. Yet, appraising another person's performance is one of the most emotionally charged of all management activities. The impression the subordinate receives about his assessment has a strong impact on his self-esteem and, importantly, on his subsequent performance. Of course, conveying good news is considerably less difficult for both the manager and the subordinate than revealing that performance has been below expectations. In this context, the discussion of the evaluation can have negative as well as positive motivational consequences. Statistically speaking, half of all employees are below the median, yet evidence tells us that the average employee's estimate of her own performance level generally falls around the seventy-fifth percentile.[16] A survey of over 800,000 high school seniors also found that people seem to see themselves as better than average. Seventy percent rated themselves above average on leadership, and when asked to rate themselves on "ability to get along with others," none rated himself or herself below average, 60 percent rated themselves in the top 10 percent, and 25 percent saw themselves among the top 1 percent! Similarly, a survey of 500 clerical and technical employees found that 58 percent rated their own performance as falling in the top 10 percent of their peers doing comparable jobs and a total of 81 percent placed themselves in the top 20 percent![17]

Accordingly, the subordinate's perception of his or her own performance often overstates the manager's appraisal. Thus, to the extent that evaluation influences the behavior of organizational members, an organization's performance evaluation process can demotivate those employees who perceive the evaluation as unjust.

REWARD SYSTEMS

Our knowledge of motivation tells us that people do what they do to satisfy needs. Before they do anything, they look for the payoff or reward. Because many of these rewards—salary increases, promotions, and preferred job assignments, to name a few—are organizationally controlled, we should consider rewards as an important force influencing the behavior of employees.

Determinants of Rewards

Most organizations believe that their reward system is designed to reward merit. The problem is that we find differing definitions of merit. Some define merit as being "deserving," while to others merit is being "excellent."[18] "One person's merit is another person's favoritism."[19] A consideration of "deserving" may take into account such factors as intelligence, effort, or seniority. The problem is that what is deserving may differ from what is excellent—a problem that is exacerbated by the difficulty of defining excellence. If excellence refers to performance, we concede how unsatisfactory our efforts have been to measure performance. Creation of quantifiable and meaningful performance measures of almost all white-collar and service jobs, and many blue-collar jobs, have eluded us. Thus, while few will disagree with the viewpoint that the merit concept for distributing rewards is desirable, what constitutes merit is highly debatable.

In the next several pages we shall briefly assess the role of performance as a prerequisite for rewards and then discuss other popular criteria by which rewards are distributed. In Chapter 5, we argued that motivation will be highest when performance and rewards are closely linked. But, in reality, performance is only *one* of many criteria upon which organizational rewards are distributed.

PERFORMANCE

Performance is results measurement. It merely asks the question: Did you get the job done? To reward people in the organization, therefore, requires some agreed-upon criterion for defining their performance. Whether this criterion is valid or not in representing performance is not relevant to our definition; as long as rewards are allocated based on factors that are directly linked to doing the job sucessfully, we are using performance as the determinant. For many jobs, productivity is used as a single criterion. But as jobs become less standardized and routine, productivity becomes more difficult to measure, and, hence, the defining of performance becomes increasingly complex.

Yet, for senior managers in corporations or those who oversee distinct business units, there is increased attention being paid to linking rewards (particularly pay) to performance.[20] Companies as diverse as American Broadcasting, Security Pacific National Bank, Sears, Roebuck, and Dow Chemical are measuring the economic performance of their business units, comparing the results against the competition, and awarding rewards accordingly.

EFFORT

It is not uncommon for a report card in grammar school to include effort as one of the categories used in grading students. Organizations rarely make their rewarding of effort that explicit, yet it is certainly a major determinant in the reward distribution.

The rewarding of effort represents the classical example of rewarding means rather than ends. In organizations where performance is generally of low caliber, rewarding of effort may be the only criterion by which to differentiate rewards. For example, a major eastern university was attempting to increase its research efforts and had designated the objective of obtaining grants or funded research as a critical benchmark toward this end. Upon selection of this objective, all faculty members were informed that rewards for the coming year were going to be based on performance in obtaining grants. Unfortunately, after the first year of the program, even though approximately 20 percent of the faculty had made grant applications, none were approved. When the time came for performance evaluation and the distribution of rewards, the dean chose to give the majority of the funds available for pay raises to those faculty members who had applied for grants. Here is a case where performance, defined in terms of obtaining funded research grants, was zero, so the dean chose to allocate rewards based on effort.

This practice is more common then you might think. On the assumption that those who try should be encouraged, in many cases effort can count *more than* actual performance. The employee who is clearly perceived by her superiors to be working less than her optimum can often expect to be rewarded less than some other employee who, while producing less, is giving out a greater effort. Even where it is clearly stated that performance is what will be rewarded, people who make evaluations and distribute rewards are only human. Therefore, they are not immune to sympathizing with those who try hard, but with minimal success, and allowing this to influence their evaluation and reward decisions.

SENIORITY

Seniority, job rights, and tenure dominate most civil service systems in the United States, and while they do not play as important a role in business corporations, the length of time on the job is still a major factor in determining the allocation of rewards. Seniority's greatest virtue is that, relative to other criteria, it is easy to determine. We may disagree as to whether the quality of Smith's work is higher or lower than that of Jones, but we would probably not have much debate over who has been with the organization longer. So seniority represents an easily quantifiable criterion that can be substituted for performance.

SKILLS HELD

Another practice that is not uncommon in organizations is to allocate rewards based on the skills of the employee. Regardless of whether the skills are used, those individuals who possess the highest skills or talents will be rewarded commensurately. Where such practices are used, it is not unusual to see individuals become "credential crazy." The requirement that an individual needs a college degree in order to attain a certain level within the organization is utilizing skills as a determinant of rewards. Similarly, the requirement that an individual has to pass certain skill tasks by demonstrating an acceptable score in order to maintain a particular position in the organization is again using skills as a reward criterion. If it is necessary for a secretary to demonstrate that he or she can take shorthand at 120 words per minute to be eligible for consideration as secretary to a department head, and if department heads do all their dictation into a dictating machine rather than giving it directly to the secretary, we see an example of a skill being utilized as a reward criterion when, in effect, it is irrelevant.

When individuals enter an organization, their skill level is usually a major determinant of the compensation they will receive. In such cases, the marketplace or competition has acted to make skills a major element in the reward package. These externally imposed standards can evolve from the community or from occupational categories themselves. In other words, the relationship of demand and supply for particular skills in the community can significantly influence the rewards the organization must expend to acquire those skills. Also, the demand-supply relationship for an entire occupational category throughout the country can affect rewards.

JOB DIFFICULTY

The complexity of the job can be a criterion by which rewards are distributed. For example, those jobs that are highly repetitive and can be learned quickly may be viewed as less deserving in rewards than those that are more complex and sophisticated. Jobs that are difficult to perform or are undesirable due to stress or unpleasant working conditions, may have to carry with them rewards that are higher in order to attract workers to these activities.

DISCRETIONARY TIME

The greater the discretion called for on a job, all other things being equal, the greater the impact of mistakes and the greater the need for good judgment. In a job that has been completely programmed—that is, where each step has been accorded a procedure and there is no room for decision making by the incumbent—there is little discretionary time. Such jobs require less judgment, and lower rewards can be offered to attract people to take these positions. As discretion time increases, greater judgmental abilities are needed, and rewards must commensurately be expanded.

Types of Rewards

The types of rewards that an organization can allocate are more complex than is generally thought. Obviously, there is direct compensation. But there are also indirect compensation and nonfinancial rewards. Each of these types of rewards can be distributed on an individual, group, or organizationwide basis. Figure 13–1 presents a structure for looking at rewards.

Intrinsic rewards are those that individuals receive for themselves. They are largely a result of the worker's satisfaction with his or her job. As noted in Chap-

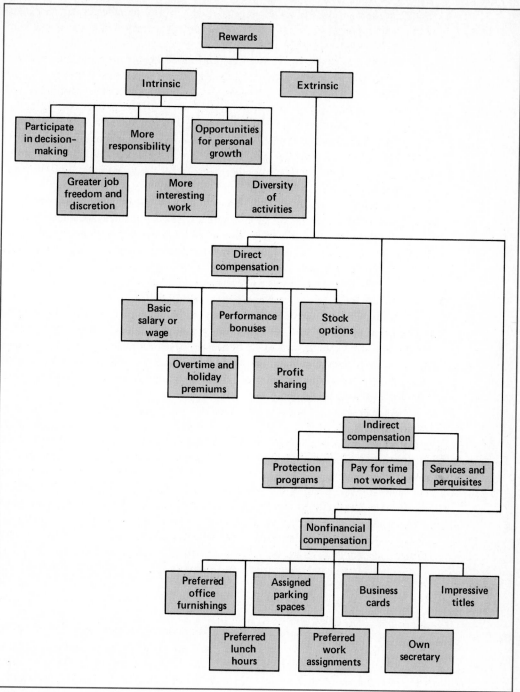

FIGURE 13–1
Types of Rewards

ter 12, techniques like job enrichment or any efforts to redesign or restructure work to increase its personal worth to the employee may make his or her work more intrinsically rewarding.

As previously noted, extrinsic rewards include direct compensation, indirect compensation, and nonfinancial rewards. Of course, an employee expects some form of direct compensation: a basic wage or salary, overtime and holiday premium pay, bonuses based on performance, profit sharing, and/or possibly opportunities to purchase stock options. Employees will expect their direct compensation generally to align with their assessment of their contribution to the organization and, additionally, will expect it to be relatively comparable with the direct compensation given to other employees with similar abilities and performance.

The organization will provide employees with indirect compensation: insurance, pay for holidays and vacations, services, and perquisites. Inasmuch as these are generally made uniformly available to all employees at a given job level, regardless of performance, they are really not motivating rewards. However, where indirect compensation is controllable by management and is used to reward performance, then it clearly needs to be considered as a motivating reward. To illustrate, if a company-paid membership in a country club is not available to all middle- and upper-level executives, but only to those who have shown particular performance ratings, then it is a motivating reward. Similarly, if company-owned automobiles and aircraft are made available to certain employees based on their performance rather than their "entitlement," we should view these indirect compensations as motivating rewards for those who might deem these forms of compensation as attractive.

As with direct compensation, indirect compensation may be viewed in an individual, group, or organizational context. However, if rewards are to be linked closely with performance, we should expect individual rewards to be emphasized. On the other hand, if a certain group of managers within the organization have made a significant contribution to the effective performance of the organization, a blanket reward such as a membership in a social club might be appropriate. Again, it is important to note that since rewards achieve the greatest return when they are specifically designed to meet the needs of each individual, and since group and organizational rewards tend to deal in homogeneity—that is, they tend to treat all people alike—these types of rewards must, by definition, be somewhat less effective than individual rewards. The only exceptions to that statement are those instances where there is a high need for cohesiveness and group congeniality. In such instances, individuals may find group rewards more personally satisfying than individual rewards.

The classification of nonfinancial rewards tends to be a smorgasbord of desirable "things" that are potentially at the disposal of the organization. The creation of nonfinancial rewards is limited only by managers' ingenuity and ability to assess "payoffs" that individuals with the organization find desirable and that are within the managers' discretion.

The old saying "One man's food is another man's poison" certainly applies to rewards. What one employee views as highly desirable, another finds superfluous. Therefore *any* reward may not get the desired result; however, where selection has been done assiduously, the benefits to the organization by way of higher worker performance should be impressive.

Some workers are very status conscious. A paneled office, a carpeted floor, a large walnut desk, or a private bathroom may be just the office furnishing that stimulates an employee toward top performance. Status-oriented employees may also value an impressive job title, their own business cards, their own secretary, or a well-located parking space with their name clearly painted underneath the "Reserved" sign.

Some employees value having their lunch at, say, 1 P.M. to 2 P.M. If lunch is normally from 11 A.M. to 12 noon, the benefit of being able to take their lunch at another, more desirable time can be viewed as a reward. Having a chance to work with congenial colleagues or achieving a desired work assignment or an assignment where the worker can operate without close supervision are all rewards that are within the discretion of management and, when carefully aligned to individual needs, can provide stimulus for improved performance.

Reward Systems in Practice: The Case of Pay

Motivation theory argues for linking rewards to performance. If we accept that pay is a primary reward in organizations, there is little evidence that organizations actually use performnce as the single most important determinant of pay. A more realistic conclusion would be that pay is allocated at least as much for effort as for accomplishment.[21] A survey of nearly nine thousand workers, consisting of management, salaried, and hourly employees, suggests some interesting predictors of pay.[22] For management positions, education proved to be the best predictor of compensation. The job level held and the age of the incumbent were also relatively good predictors of actual pay. "It appears that the better educated, higher level, older managers, who have been with the company somewhat longer, are better paid."[23] Among salaried employees, age was the most closely related variable to pay, closely followed by education and job level. Length of time on the job was the major predictor for hourly workers. Those hourly workers who had been with the company the longest were the highest paid. The researchers concluded:

> One inference that seems reasonable from all these data is that the amount of an employee's pay is likely to be determined by many factors, a large portion of which seem to be from those such as age, education, tenure, and job level. It is possible, however, that such factors have little or no relation to actual effectiveness or job performance.
>
> This finding casts considerable doubt that employee performance is related to pay.[24]

A survey of 493 large manufacturing and service companies provides further evidence to suggest that rewards are not strongly based on performance criteria.[25] As Table 13–3 shows, pay increases in these companies tended to be more influenced by external factors such as the national cost-of-living index and community pay policies than by individual worker productivity.

TABLE 13–3
Ranking of Factors Determining Pay Increases in 493 Companies

FACTORS DETERMINING PAY INCREASES	EMPLOYEE CATEGORY				
	Officers and Executives	Exempt Salaried	Nonexempt Salaried	Nonunion Hourly	Union Hourly
Worker productivity	4	7	5	3	9
Company's financial results	1	2	3	5	7
Company's financial prospects	2	3	4	4	5
Internal equity among groups	6	5	6	6	8
Increases of industry leaders	5	6	8	7	4
Area surveys	3	1	1	1	6
Ability to hire	7	8	7	10	10
National bargaining settlements	9	10	10	8	2
Union demands	10	9	9	9	1
Cost-of-living index	8	4	2	2	3

Note: Importance rating determined by frequency of mentions in first, second, or third place in a ranking from 1 to 10. Sample composed of manufacturing (44%), banking and insurance (38%), utility (15%), and retail (3%) firms.

Source: Adapted from D. A. Weeks, *Compensating Employees: Lessons of the 1970's*, Report No. 707 (New York: The Conference Board, 1976), pp. 12–14.

CAREER DEVELOPMENT PRACTICES

Good employees don't always stay good employees! Their skills can deteriorate; technology may make their skills obsolete; the organization may move into new areas, changing the type of jobs that exist and the skills necessary to do them. Career development or career planning is a means by which an organization can sustain or increase its employees' current productivity, while, at the same time, prepare employees for a future that's different from today.

Career Stages

A career is "a sequence of positions occupied by a person during the course of a lifetime."[26] This definition does not imply advancement or success or failure. *Any* work, paid or unpaid, pursued over an extended period of time, can constitute a career. In addition to formal job work, it may include schoolwork, homemaking, or volunteer work.[27]

Careers can be more easily understood if we think of them as proceeding through stages.[28] Most of us have or will go through four stages: exploration, establishment, midcareer, and late career.

Exploration begins prior to even entering the work force on a paid basis and ends for most of us in our mid-twenties as we make the transition from school to our primary work interest. It's a time of self-exploration and an assessment of alternatives. The *establishment* stage includes being accepted by our peers, learning the job, and gaining tangible evidence of successes or failures in the "real world." Most people don't face their first severe career dilemmas until they reach the *midcareer* stage, a stage that is typically reached between the ages of 35 and 50. This is a time where one may continue to improve one's performance, level off, or begin to deteriorate. At this stage, the first dilemma is accepting the fact that you're no longer seen as a "learner." Mistakes carry greater penalties. At this point in a career, you are expected to have moved beyond apprenticeship to journeyman status. For those who continue to grow through the midcareer stage, the *late career* usually is a pleasant time when you are allowed the luxury to relax a bit and enjoy playing the part of the elder statesman. For those who have stagnated or deteriorated during the previous stage, the late career brings the reality that they will not have an everlasting impact or change the world as they once thought. It is a time when individuals recognize that they have decreased work mobility and may be locked into their current jobs. They begin to look forward to retirement and the opportunities of doing something different.

If employees are to remain productive, career development and training programs need to be available that can support an employee's task and emotional needs at each stage. Table 13–4 identifies the more important of these needs.

Effective Career Development Practices

What kind of practices would characterize an organization that understood the value of career development? The following summarizes a few of the more effective practices.

CHALLENGING INITIAL JOBS
There is an increasing body of evidence indicating that employees who receive especially challenging job assignments early in their careers do better on later jobs.[29] More specifically, the degree of stimulation and challenge in a person's initial job assignment tends to be significantly related to later career success and retention in the organization.[30] Apparently, initial challenges, particularly if they are successfully met, stimulate a person to perform well in subsequent years.

JOB POSTINGS
To provide information to all employees about job openings, job opportunities should be posted. Postings list key job specification data—abilities, experi-

TABLE 13–4
Training Needs within Career Stages

STAGE	TASK NEEDS	EMOTIONAL NEEDS
Exploration	1. Varied job activities 2. Self-exploration	1. Make preliminary job choices 2. Settling down
Establishment	1. Job challenge 2. Develop competence in a specialty area 3. Develop creativity and innovation 4. Rotate into new area after three to five years	1. Deal with rivalry and competition; face failures 2. Deal with work/family conflicts 3. Support 4. Autonomy
Midcareer	1. Technical updating 2. Develop skills in training and coaching others (younger employees) 3. Rotation into new job requiring new skills 4. Develop broader view of work and own role in organization	1. Express feelings about midlife 2. Reorganize thinking about self in relation to work, family, community 3. Reduce self-indulgence and competitiveness
Late career	1. Plan for retirement 2. Shift from power role to one of consultation and guidance 3. Identify and develop successors 4. Begin activities outside the organization	1. Support and counseling to see one's work as a platform for others 2. Develop sense of identity in extraorganizational activities

Source: Adapted from D. T. Hall and M. Morgan, "Career Development and Planning," in K. Perlman, F. L. Schmidt, and W. C. Hamner, *Contemporary Problems in Personnel* (3rd ed.). Copyright © 1983 by John Wiley & Sons. Reprinted by permission of John Wiley & Sons.

ence, and seniority requirements to qualify for vacancies—and are typically communicated through bulletin board displays or organizational publications.

CAREER COUNSELING

One of the most logical parts to career development is career counseling. An effective program will cover the following issues with employees:

1. The employee's career goals, aspirations, and expectations for five years or longer
2. Opportunities available within the organization and the degree to which the employee's aspirations are realistic and match the opportunities available
3. Identification of what the employee would have to do in the way of further self-development to qualify for new opportunities
4. Identification of the actual next steps in the form of plans for new development activities or new job assignments that would prepare the employee for further career growth[31]

CAREER DEVELOPMENT WORKSHOPS

Organizations can offer group workshops to facilitate career development. By bringing together groups of employees with their supervisors and managers, problems and misperceptions can be identified and, it is hoped, resolved. These workshops can be general, or they can be designed to deal with problems common to certain groups of employees—new members, minorities, older workers, and so forth.

PERIODIC JOB CHANGES

Periodic job changes can prevent obsolescence and stimulate career growth.[32] The changes can be lateral transfers, vertical promotions, or temporary assignments. The important element in periodic job changes is that they give the employee a variety of experiences that offer diversity and new challenges.

THE UNION-MANAGEMENT INTERFACE

Labor unions are a vehicle by which employees act collectively to protect and promote their interests. Currently, in the United States, approximately 18 percent of the work force belongs to and is represented by a union. For this segment of the labor force, wage levels and conditions of employment are explicitly articulated in a contract that is negotiated, through collective bargaining, between representatives of the union and the organization's management. But the impact of unions on employees is broader than their 18 percent representation figure might imply. This is because nonunionized employees benefit from the gains that unions make. There is a spillover effect so that the wages, benefits, and working conditions provided nonunionized employees tend to mirror—with some time lag—those negotiated for union members.

Labor unions influence a number of organizational activities.[33] Recruitment sources, hiring criteria, work schedules, job design, redress procedures, safety rules, and eligibility for training programs are examples of activities that are influenced by unions. The most obvious and pervasive area of influence, of course, is wage rates and working conditions. Where unions exist, performance evaluation systems tend to be less complex because they play a relatively small part in reward decisions. Wage rates, when determined through collective bargaining, emphasize seniority and downplay performance differences.

Figure 13–2 shows how a union impacts on an employee's performance and job satisfaction. The union contract affects motivation through determination of wage rates, seniority rules, layoff procedures, promotion criteria, and security provisions. Unions can influence the competence with which employees perform their jobs by offering special training programs to their members, by requiring apprenticeships, and by allowing members to gain leadership experience through union organizational activities. The actual level of employee performance will be further influenced by collective bargaining restrictions placed on the amount of work produced, the speed with which work can be done, overtime allowances per worker, or the kind of tasks a given employee is allowed to perform.

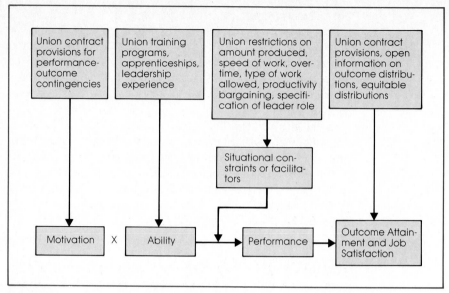

FIGURE 13–2

The Union's Impact on Employee Performance and Job Satisfaction

Source: T. H. Hammer, "Relationships Between Local Union Characteristics and Worker Behavior and Attitudes," *Academy of Management Journal*, December 1978, p. 573.

Are union members more satisfied with their jobs than their nonunion counterparts? The answer to this question is more complicated than a simple "Yes" or "No." The evidence consistently demonstrates that unions have only indirect effects on job satisfaction.[34] They increase pay satisfaction, but negatively affect satisfaction with the work itself (by decreasing job scope perceptions), satisfaction with co-workers and supervision (through less favorable perceptions of supervisory behavior), and satisfaction with promotions (through the lower importance placed on promotions).

IMPLICATIONS FOR PERFORMANCE AND SATISFACTION

An organization's human resource policies and practices represent important forces for shaping employee behavior and attitudes. In this chapter, we specifically discussed the influence of selection practices, performance evaluation systems, reward systems, career development practices, and the existence of a union.

Selection Practices

An organization's selection practices will determine who gets hired. If properly designed, it will identify competent candidates and accurately match them to the job. The use of the proper selection device will increase the probability that the right person will be chosen to fill a slot.

While employee selection is far from a science, some organizations fail to design their selection systems so as to maximize the likelihood that the right person-job fit will be achieved. When errors are made, the chosen candidate's performance may be less than satisfactory. Training may be necessary to improve the candidate's skills. At the worst, the candidate will prove unacceptable and a replacement will need to be found. Similarly, where the selection process results in the hiring of less qualified candidates or individuals who don't fit into the organization, those chosen are likely to feel anxious, tense, and uncomfortable. This, in turn, is likely to increase dissatisfaction with the job.

Performance Evaluation Systems

A major goal of performance evaluation is to assess accurately an individual's performance contribution as a basis for making reward allocation decisions. If the performance evaluation process emphasizes the wrong criteria or inaccurately appraises actual job performance, employees will be over- or underrewarded. As equity theory demonstrated in Chapter 5, this can lead to negative consequences such as reduced effort, increases in absenteeism, or search for alternative job opportunities.

Inadequate or improper feedback was shown to decrease satisfaction and a potential cause of reduced performance. The evaluation of an employee's performance typically impacts the employee following his or her receipt of feedback information (or lack of same) rather than at the time the information is actually being gathered.

Reward Systems

If employees perceive that their efforts will be accurately appraised and if they further perceive that the rewards they value are closely linked to their evaluations, the organization will have optimized the motivational properties from its evaluation and reward procedures and policies. More specifically, based on the contents of this chapter and our discussion of motivation in Chapter 5, we can conclude that rewards are likely to lead to high employee performance and satisfaction when they are (1) perceived as being equitable by the employee, (2) tied to performance, and (3) tailored to the needs of the individual. These conditions should foster a minimum of dissatisfaction among employees, reduce withdrawal patterns, and increase organizational commitment. If these conditions do not exist, the probability of withdrawal behavior increases, and the prevalence of marginal or barely adequate performance increases. If workers perceive that their efforts are not recognized or rewarded, and if they view their alternatives as limited, they may continue working, but perform at a level considerably below their capability.

Career Development Practices

Organizations that provide formal career development activities and match them to needs that employees experience at various stages in their careers reduce the likelihood that productivity will decrease as a result of obsolescence or that job frustrations will create reduced satisfaction.

In today's job environment—with increasing competition for many jobs and limited promotion opportunities in many others—employees will increasingly confront the reality of career plateauing. Out of frustration, employees may look for other jobs. Organizations that have well-designed career programs will have employees with more realistic expectations and career tracking systems that will lessen the chance that good employees will leave because of inadequate opportunities.

Union-Management Interface

The existence of a union in an organization adds another variable in our search to explain and predict employee behavior. The union has been found to be an important contributor to employees' perceptions, attitudes, and behavior.

The power of the union surfaces in the collective bargaining agreement that it negotiates with the organization's management. Much of what an employee can and cannot do on the job is formally stipulated in this agreement. In addition, the informal norms that union cohesiveness fosters can encourage or discourage productivity, organizational commitment, and morale.

POINT

COLLEGE STUDENTS SHOULDN'T BE ASKED TO GRADE THEIR TEACHERS

The evaluation of teacher performance by students is now a fixture of campus life. The results have become an important factor in faculty promotion and retention decisions. In practice, this translates into faculty members with higher student evaluation scores receiving more favorable consideration.

Treating student evaluations as though they were a straightforward measure of good teaching invites abuse. Most important, it fails to recognize the applicability of the "journeyman principle" to college faculty members. This principle acknowledges that those who wish to be practitioners of a skilled trade or profession must undergo rigorous training. Those who complete the training are known as journeymen and are assumed competent to perform satisfactorily the range of tasks ordinarily required. They are not required to prove competence, since journeymen status itself attests to such competence. It is the judgment of incompetence that is made on the basis of special evidence.

Use of this principle would result in a radically different approach to the evaluation of good teaching: It would no longer be important to obtain a fine measurement of the teaching performance of every faculty member. Small distinctions among the ranks of the competent would cease to be important, because they are insignificant with respect to the work. For example, any journeyman plumber can fix your sink, any competent pediatrician can diagnose a child's ear infection, and any competent mathematician can teach calculus. Following the journeyman principle, attention would be focused on identifying those at the extremes. It is important to detect the incompetent—those who cannot be trusted to perform the ordinary tasks properly. It is equally important to detect the exceptional—those who can handle the extraordinary tasks.

Do college faculty members fit the definition of journeyman? There are several reasons to suggest they do. Members of a college faculty have usually successfully completed some amount of graduate training, which may be taken to certify a certain high level of intellectual competence and mastery of subject matter. The ability to present material in a clear and organized fashion is generally a prerequisite for successfully completing a graduate degree. There is, additionally, the process of self-selection: Those who dislike teaching, or feel inarticulate or uncomfortable addressing groups, tend to avoid choosing teaching as a profession.

We may fairly conclude that college faculty members are intelligent, know their subject matter, express themselves reasonably well, and care about teaching. They are a highly selected sample who are, with a few exceptions, clustered at the upper end of the competence continuum. The current idea that it is important to evaluate the teaching performance of every faculty member so as to obtain proof of competence seems to derive from the contrary notion that college teachers are uniformly distributed over the whole continuum of competence.

Adapted from M. J. Rodin, "By a Faculty Member's Yardstick, Student Evaluations Don't Measure Up," Chronicle of Higher Education, *May 3, 1982, p. 63.*

COUNTERPOINT

CHALLENGES TO THE ASSUMPTION OF COMPETENCE

The journeyman principle is thought provoking, but it is vulnerable on at least four points: (1) Teaching students is not like fixing a leaking sink; (2) most college teachers' apprenticeships don't emphasize teaching skills; (3) competence, even if demonstrated at one point in time, need not hold constant for an indefinite time period; and (4) the overt evidence that there is a good deal of bad teaching out there can't be ignored.

Teaching is not a routine task in the way sink repair may be considered routine. Every student is different. A standardized approach isn't likely to succeed in meeting the various learning styles and needs of students.

The successful completion of a graduate degree program is no assurance that a teacher can teach. Graduate study emphasizes research. Most graduate students are not required to teach in order to obtain their degree, and those who do so are evaluated infrequently, if at all. Sure, subject matter competence is needed to complete a graduate degree, but knowledge of a subject is no assurance that one can teach that material.

Even if we assumed that all faculty members were competent teachers at the time they were hired, why should we believe that competence will remain a constant over his or her teaching career? In many fields, subject matter is rapidly made obsolete and displaced. The knowledge held by the teacher of information processing in 1966 would be totally inadequate in 1986. And teaching ability can change over time. Changes in college administrative policy, salary levels, and colleagues can alter the teacher's motivation. The faculty member's interests may also change over his or her career. Thirty years or more of tenure-protected job security (a luxury not offered those in the plumbing profession) can further act to deter a faculty member's motivation to keep up in his or her field or put in the extra effort to make classroom lectures interesting.

Finally, you can't ignore the reality that college teachers *aren't* "clustered at the upper end of the competence continuum." College teachers, like most populations on most competence scales, tend to be distributed along a bell-shaped curve. Some are excellent and some are poor, with most centered around the median. Without student evaluation information, faculty members are deprived of the kind of feedback that is necessary to assess their strengths and weaknesses and work toward reducing those weaknesses.

College faculty, in spite of superior academic qualifications, are not beyond evaluation. To follow the journeyman analogy would suggest, for instance, that a bridge should never be inspected since both the contractor who built it and the architects and engineers who designed it have met the journeyman requirement. The journeyman principle assumes that all teachers are competent when they enter the profession and that that competence is maintained throughout one's teaching career. These assumptions just are not valid.

Ideas expressed here were influenced from "Letters to the Editor," Chronicle of Higher Education, *June 2, 1982, p. 25.*

FOR DISCUSSION

1. What is job analysis? How is it related to those the organization hires?
2. If you were a dean of a college of business, how would you determine which job candidates would be effective teachers?
3. If you were a dean of a college of business, how would you evaluate the performance of your faculty members?
4. What relationship, if any, is there between job analysis and performance evaluation?
5. Why do organizations evaluate employees?
6. How can an organization's performance evaluation system affect employee behavior?
7. Contrast absolute standards with relative standards. What are the advantages and disadvantages of each?
8. If the average employee believes that he is peforming at the seventy-fifth percentile, what does this imply for employee performance reviews?
9. Identify and discuss popular criteria by which organizations distribute rewards.
10. Do organizations reward performance? Do they reward merit? Explain.
11. Some organizations have a personnel policy that pay information be kept secret. Not only is pay information not given out by management but employees are also discouraged from talking about their pay with co-workers. How do you think this practice affects employee behavior?
12. What impact do unions have on an organization's reward system?

FOR FURTHER READING

KERR, S., "On the Folly of Rewarding A, While Hoping for B," *Academy of Management Journal,* December 1975, pp. 769–83. Demonstrates in a lively and thought-provoking fashion numerous instances in which organizational rewards encourage behaviors that management actually seeks to discourage.

KIPNIS, D., S. SCHMIDT, K. PRICE, and C. STITT, "Why Do I Like Thee: Is It Your Performance or My Orders?" *Journal of Applied Psychology,* June 1981, pp. 324–28. Reconciles performance evaluation with leadership and attribution theory to demonstrate how democratic leadership leads to favorable evaluations.

KOPELMAN, R. E., and L. REINHARTH, "Research Results: The Effect of Merit-Pay Practices on White-Collar Performance," *Compensation Review,* Fourth Quarter 1982, pp. 30–40. Reports that all judgmental merit reward systems are not equal. Those that link performance more closely to rewards are likely to generate higher levels of performance, particularly after a year or two.

LARSON, J. R., "The Performance Feedback Process: A Preliminary Model," *Organizational Behavior and Human Performance,* February 1984, pp. 42–76. Outlines a model of the overall feedback process that focuses on the factors that influence supervisors' performance feedback as well as the effects that giving feedback can have on both the subordinate and supervisor.

LATHAM, G. P., and K. N. WEXLEY, *Increasing Productivity Through Performance Appraisal.* Reading, Mass.: Addison-Wesley, 1981. Offers guidance in designing performance evaluation systems that facilitate improved employee performance.

LAWLER, E. E., III, *Pay and Organizational Effectiveness.* New York: McGraw-Hill, 1971. Considers the facts and fantasies underlying the impact of pay on performance; an important book.

NOTES FOR CHAPTER 13

1. E. C. Webster, *Decision Making in the Employment Interview* (Montreal: McGill University, Industrial Relations Center, 1964); and E. C. Mayfield in N. Schmitt, "Social and Situational Determinants of Interview Decisions: Implications for the Employment Interview," *Personnel Psychology,* Spring 1976, p. 81.
2. S. P. Robbins, *Personnel: The Management of Human Resources,* 2nd ed. (Englewood Cliffs, N.J.: Prentice-Hall, 1982), pp. 159–60.
3. M. D. Dunnette and W. C. Borman, "Personnel Selection and Classification Systems," in M. R. Rosenzweig and L. W. Porter (eds.), *Annual Review of Psychology,* Vol. 30 (Palo Alto: Calif.: Annual Reviews, 1974), p. 513.
4. J. J. Asher and J. A. Sciarrino, "Realistic Work Sample Tests: A Review," *Personnel Psychology,* Winter 1974, pp. 519–33.
5. W. C. Byham, "Assessment Centers for Spotting Future Managers," *Harvard Business Review,* July–August 1970, pp. 150–67; and B. M. Cohen, J. L. Moses, and W. C. Byham, *The Validity of Assessment Centers: A Literature Review,* Monograph 2 (Pittsburgh: Development Dimensions Press, 1974).
6. P. M. Blau, *The Dynamics of Bureaucracy,* rev. ed. (Chicago: University of Chicago Press, 1963).
7. "The Cop-Out Cops," *National Observer,* August 3, 1974.
8. A. Pizam, "Social Differentiation—A New Psychological Barrier to Performance Appraisal," *Public Personnel Management,* July–August 1975, pp. 244–47.
9. Ibid., pp. 245–46.
10. W. C. Borman, "The Rating of Individuals in Organizations: An Alternate Approach," *Organizational Behavior and Human Performance,* August 1974, pp. 105–24.
11. Ibid.
12. G. P. Latham, K. N. Wexley, and E. D. Pursell, "Training Managers to Minimize Rating Errors in the Observation of Behavior," *Journal of Applied Psychology,* October 1975, pp. 550–55.
13. H. J. Bernardin, "The Effects of Rater Training on Leniency and Halo Errors in Student Rating of Instructors," *Journal of Applied Psychology,* June 1978, pp. 301–08.

14. Ibid.; and J. M. Ivancevich, "Longitudinal Study of the Effects of Rater Training on Psychometric Error in Ratings, *Journal of Applied Psychology,* October 1979, pp. 502–08.

15. W. F. Cascio, *Applied Psychology in Personnel Management* (Reston, Va.: Reston, 1978), p. 341.

16. R. J. Burke, "Why Performance Appraisal Systems Fail," *Personnel Administration,* June 1972, pp. 32–40.

17. "How Do I Love Me? Let Me Count the Ways," *Psychology Today,* May 1980, p. 16.

18. E. F. Beaumont, "A Pivotal Point for the Merit Concept," *Public Administration Review,* September–October 1974, pp. 426–30.

19. D. Stanley, "The Merit Principle Today," *Public Administration Review,* September–October 1974, p. 425.

20. "Executive Compensation: Looking to the Long Term Again," *Business Week,* May 9, 1983, pp. 80–83.

21. See, for example, L. W. Porter and E. E. Lawler III, *Managerial Attitudes and Performance* (Homewood, Ill.: Richard E. Irwin, 1968), p. 158; and J. R. Schuster, B. Clark, and M. Rogers, "Testing Portions of the Porter and Lawler Model Regarding the Motivational Role of Pay," *Journal of Applied Psychology,* June 1971, pp. 187–95.

22. W. W. Ronan and G. J. Organt, "Determinants of Pay and Pay Satisfaction," *Personnel Psychology,* Winter 1973, pp. 503–20.

23. Ibid., p. 511.

24. Ibid., p. 513.

25. D. A. Weeks, *Compensating Employees: Lessons of the 1970s,* Report No. 707 (New York: The Conference Board, 1976), pp. 12–14.

26. D. E. Super and D. T. Hall, "Career Development: Exploration and Planning," in M. R. Rosenzweig and L. W. Porter (eds.), *Annual Review of Psychology,* Vol. 29 (Palo Alto: Annual Reviews, 1978), p. 334.

27. D. T. Hall, *Careers in Organizations* (Santa Monica, Calif.: Goodyear, 1976), pp. 3–4.

28. See, for example, D. E. Super, *The Psychology of Careers* (New York: Harper & Row, 1957); and E. H. Schein, "The Individual, the Organization, and the Career: A Conceptual Scheme," *Journal of Applied Behavioral Science,* August 1971, pp. 401–26.

29. D. E. Berlew and D. T. Hall, "The Socialization of Managers: Effects of Expectations on Performance," *Administrative Science Quarterly,* September 1966, pp. 207–23; and D. W. Bray, R. J. Campbell, and D. L. Grant, *Formulative Years in Business: A Long-Term AT&T Study of Managerial Lives* (New York: John Wiley, 1974).

30. See Super and Hall, "Career Development: Exploration and Planning," p. 362.

31. J. Van Maanen and E. H. Schein, "Career Development," in J. R. Hackman and J. L. Suttle (eds.), *Improving Life at Work* (Santa Monica: Calif.: Goodyear, 1977), p. 87.

32. H. G. Kaufman, *Obsolescence and Professional Career Development* (New York: AMACOM, 1974).

33. This material was adapted from T. H. Hammer, "Relationships Between Local Union Characteristics and Worker Behavior and Attitudes," *Academy of Management Journal,* December 1978, pp. 560–77.

34. See, for example, C. J. Berger, C. A. Olson, and J. W. Boudreau, "Effects of Unions on Job Satisfaction: The Role of Work-Related Values and Perceived Rewards," *Organizational Behavior and Human Performance,* December 1983, pp. 289–324.

14

Organizational Culture

AFTER STUDYING THIS CHAPTER, YOU SHOULD BE ABLE TO:

Define and explain the following key terms and concepts:

Core values	Prearrival stage
Dominant culture	Rituals
Encounter stage	Socialization
Institutionalization	Strong cultures
Metamorphosis stage	Subcultures
Organizational culture	

Understand:

The common characteristics making up organizational culture
The factors determining an organization's culture
The factors that maintain an organization's culture
How culture is transmitted to employees
The various socialization alternatives available to management

In any organization, there are the ropes to skip and the ropes to know.

—R. R. RITTI and G. R. FUNKHOUSER

*W*hen Henry Kissinger was secretary of state, he asked a young Rhodes scholar on his staff to prepare a paper on a rather esoteric topic. The young man was new and, wanting to impress his boss, sweated over the paper for a full two weeks. However, two days after he submitted it, Kissinger returned the paper with a note scrawled across the top: "This is awful, do it again."

The young man was shattered. But after a lot of hard thought he recognized he could do a better job. Slaving away on the paper for another week, he sent a new version to Kissinger. It was quickly returned with the note, "This is worse than the first version. Can't you do better?"

After a few more days, and a third rewrite, the young man turned in the paper with a note that said, "It may not be good enough and I'm sorry for wasting your time. But this is the best I can possibly do on this subject." In response came Kissinger's note: "I'll read it now."[1]

This episode conveyed to the young man a message about working at the Department of State under Kissinger: Never give anything to your superior unless it represents your best effort. The fact that this story rapidly made the rounds at the State Department attests to the reality that, in every organization, there are appropriate and inappropriate ways to do things. One common attribute held by those organizational members that are perceived as "good employees" is an understanding of "the way things are done around here"; that is, they know their organization's culture.

PRELUDE TO CULTURE: INSTITUTIONALIZATION

The idea of viewing organizations as cultures—where there is a system of shared meaning among members—is a relatively recent phenomenon. Ten years ago, organizations were, for the most part, simply thought of as rational means by which to coordinate and control a group of people. They had vertical levels, departments, authority relationships, and so forth. But organizations are more. They have personalities too, just like individuals. They can be rigid or flexible, unfriendly or supportive, innovative or conservative. IBM offices and people *are* different from the offices and people at General Foods. Harvard and MIT are in the same business—education—and separated only by the width of the Charles River, but each has a unique feeling and character beyond its structural characteristics. Organizational theorists, in the last few years, have begun to acknowledge this by recognizing the important role that culture plays in the lives of organization members. Interestingly, though, the origin of culture as an independent variable impacting on an employee's attitudes and behavior can be traced back forty years ago to the notion of *institutionalization*.[2]

When an organization becomes institutionalized, it takes on a life of its own, apart from any of its members. The Internal Revenue Service, Chrysler Corporation, and Timex Corporation are examples of organizations that exist, and have existed, beyond the life of any one member. Additionally, when an organization becomes institutionalized, it becomes valued for itself, not merely for the goods or services it produces. It acquires immortality. If its original goals are no longer relevant, it doesn't go out of business. Rather, it redefines itself. When the demand for Timex's watches declined, the company merely redirected itself into the consumer electronics business—making, in addition to watches, clocks, computers, and health care products like digital thermometers and blood pressure testing devices. Timex took on an existence that went beyond its original mission to manufacture low-cost mechanical watches.

Institutionalization operates to produce common understandings among members about what is appropriate and, fundamentally, meaningful behavior.[3] So when an organization takes on institutional permanence, acceptable modes of behavior become largely self-evident to its members. As we'll see, this is essentially the same thing that organizational culture does. So an understanding of what makes up an organization's culture, and how it is created, sustained, and learned will enhance our ability to explain and predict the behavior of people at work.

WHAT IS CULTURE?

Organizational culture is one of those topics about which many people will say, "Oh, yeah, I know what you mean," but one that is quite difficult to define in any specific form. In this section, we'll propose a specific definition and review several peripheral issues that revolve around this definition.

A Definition

There seems to be wide agreement that organizational culture refers to a system of shared meaning held by members that distinguishes the organization from other organizations.[4] This system of shared meaning is, on closer analysis, a set of key characteristics that the organization values. There appear to be seven characteristics that, when mixed and matched, tap the essence of an organization's culture:[5]

1. *Individual autonomy*—the degree of responsibility, independence, and opportunities for exercising initiative that individuals in the organization have

2. *Structure*—the degree of rules and regulations, and the amount of direct supervision that is used to oversee and control employee behavior

3. *Support*—the degree of assistance and warmth provided by managers to their subordinates

4. *Identity*—the degree to which members identify with the organization as a whole rather than with their particular work group or field of professional expertise

5. *Performance-reward*—the degree to which reward allocations in the organization (i.e., salary increases, promotions) are based on employee performance criteria

6. *Conflict tolerance*—the degree of conflict present in relationships between peers and work groups as well as the willingness to be honest and open about differences

7. *Risk tolerance*—the degree to which employees are encouraged to be aggressive, innovative, and risk seeking

Each of these characteristics exists on a continuum from low to high. By appraising the organization on these seven characteristics, then, a composite picture of the organization's culture is formed. This picture becomes the basis for feelings of shared understanding that members have about the organization, how things are done in it, and the way members are supposed to behave. Table 14–1 demonstrates how these characteristics can be mixed to create highly diverse organizations.

Culture Is a Descriptive Term

Organizational culture is a descriptive term. It is concerned with how employees perceive the seven characteristics, not whether they like them or not. This is important because it differentiates culture from job satisfaction. Research on organizational culture has sought to measure how employees see their organization: Is it highly structured? Does it reward innovation? Does it stifle conflicts? Job satisfaction, on the other hand, seeks to measure affective responses to the work environment. That is, the former describes, while the latter evaluates.

TABLE 14–1

Descriptions of Two Highly Diverse Organization Cultures

ORGANIZATION A	ORGANIZATION B
This organization is a manufacturing firm. There are extensive rules and regulations that employees are required to follow. Managers supervise employees closely to ensure there are no deviations. People are allowed little discretion on their jobs. Employees are instructed to bring any unusual problem to their superior, who will then determine the solution. Management has no confidence in the honesty or integrity of its employees, so controls are tight. Managers and employees alike tend to be hired by the organization early in their career, rotated into and out of various departments on a regular basis, and are generalists rather than specialists. Effort, loyalty, cooperation, and avoidance of errors are highly valued and rewarded.	This organization is also a manufacturing firm. Here, however, there are few rules and regulations. Employees are seen as hard-working and trustworthy, thus supervision is loose. Employees are encouraged to solve problems themselves, but to feel free to consult with their supervisors when assistance is needed. Employees are also encouraged to develop their unique specialized skills. Interpersonal and interdepartmental differences are seen as natural occurrences. Promotions and other valuable rewards go to those employees who make the largest contributions to the organization, even when these employees are generally acknowledged to have strange ideas, unusual personal mannerisms, or unconventional work habits.

Do Organizations Have Uniform Cultures?

Organizational culture represents a common perception held by the organization's members. This was made explicit when we defined culture as a system of *shared* meaning. We should expect, therefore, that individuals with different backgrounds or at different levels in the organization will tend to describe the organization's culture in similar terms.

Acknowledgment that organizational culture has common properties does not mean, however, that there cannot be subcultures within any given culture. Most large organizations have a dominant culture and numerous sets of subcultures.[6]

A *dominant culture* expresses the core values that are shared by a majority of the organization's members. When we talk about an *organization's* culture, we are referring to its dominant culture. It is this macro view of culture that gives an organization its distinct personality. *Subcultures* tend to develop in large organizations to reflect common problems, situations, or experiences that members face. These subcultures are likely to be defined by department designations and geographical separation. The purchasing department, for example, can have a subculture that is uniquely shared by members of that department. It will include the core values of the dominant culture plus additional values unique to members of the purchasing department. Similarly, an office or unit of the organization that is physically separated from the organization's main operations may take on a different personality. Again, the core values are essentially retained but modified to reflect the separated unit's distinct situation.

If organizations had no dominant culture and were composed only of numerous subcultures, the value of organizational culture as an independent variable would be significantly lessened. Why? Because there would be no uniform interpretation of what represented appropriate or inappropriate behavior. It is the ''shared meaning'' aspect of culture that makes it such a potent device for guiding and shaping behavior. But we cannot ignore the reality that many organizations also have subcultures that can influence the behavior of members.

Strong vs. Weak Cultures

It has become increasingly popular to differentiate between strong and weak cultures.[7] The argument here is that strong cultures have a greater impact on employee behavior and are more directly related to reduced turnover.

A *strong culture* is characterized by the organization's core values being both intensely held and widely shared. As Figure 14–1 illustrates, both dimensions can be envisioned as existing along a continuum from low to high. The more members that accept the core values and the greater their commitment to those values, the stronger the culture is. Consistent with this definition, a strong culture will obviously have a greater influence on the behavior of its members. Religious organizations, cults, and Japanese companies are examples of organizations that have very strong cultures.[8] When a James Jones can entice nine

FIGURE 14–1

Strong vs. Weak Cultures

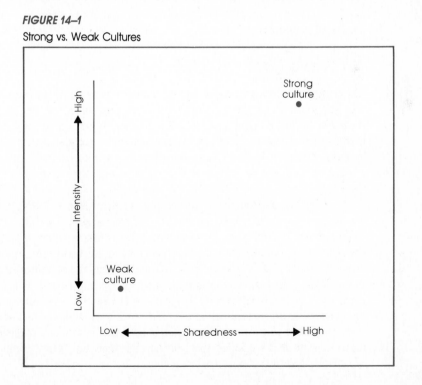

hundred members of his Guyana cult to commit mass suicide, we see a behavioral influence considerably greater than that typically attributed to leadership. The culture of Jonestown had a degree of sharedness and intensity that allowed for extremely high behavioral control. Of course, the same strong cultural influence that can lead to the tragedy of a Jonestown can be directed positively to create immensely successful organizations like IBM, Mary Kay Cosmetics, and Sony.

A specific result of a strong culture should be lower employee turnover. A strong culture demonstrates high agreement among members about what the organization stands for. Such unanimity of purpose builds cohesiveness, loyalty, and organizational commitment. These, in turn, lessen the propensity for employees to leave the organization.[9]

Culture vs. Formalization

A strong organizational culture increases behavioral consistency. In this sense, we should recognize that a strong culture can act as a substitute for formalization.

In Chapter 11, we discussed how formalization's rules and regulations act to regulate employee behavior. High formalization in an organization creates predictability, orderliness, and consistency. Our point is that a strong culture achieves the same end without the need for written documentation. Therefore, we should view formalization and culture as two different roads to a common destination. The stronger an organization's culture, the less management need be concerned with developing formal rules and regulations to guide employee behavior. Those guides will have been internalized in employees when they accept the organization's culture.

Is There a "Right" Culture?

Culture is a descriptive concept. Our position is that all organizations have a culture and that no one set of cultural characteristics are more "right" than others. It should be noted, however, that this position is not universally accepted. The authors of the best seller *In Search of Excellence,* for instance, argue that excellent organizations have strong cultures with common shared values (see Table 14–2).

There is no doubt that firms like Delta Airlines, IBM, DuPont, 3M, McDonald's, and Procter & Gamble are well-managed or "excellent" companies. They also have some cultural characteristics in common. But not all organizations that have these values are successful, and there are many other companies with very different cultures that are just as successful as those described in *In Search of Excellence.* To construe culture as a set of specific shared values implies that there are "right" cultures and "wrong" ones. Such a perspective misrepresents the concept of organizational culture and misdirects attention from *understanding what is* toward *prescribing what should be.* At this time, it is clearly presumptuous to state that we know the cultural characteristics prevalent in "excellent" organizations.[10]

TABLE 14-2
Excellent Companies and Their Common Shared Values

Excellent Companies

Amdahl	Dow Chemical	McDonald's
Amoco	DuPont	Maytag
Avon	Eastman Kodak	Merck
Boeing	Emerson Electric	3M
Bristol-Myers	Fluor	National Semiconductor
Caterpillar Tractor	Hewlett-Packard	Procter & Gamble
Cheesebrough-	Intel	Raychem
Pond's	IBM	Revlon
Dana Corp.	Johnson & Johnson	Schlumberger
Data General	K-mart	Texas Instruments
Delta Airlines	Levi Strauss	Wal-Mart
Digital Equipment	Marriot	Wang Labs
Disney Productions		

Common Values

A bias for action	Hands-on, value driven
Close to the customer	Stick to the knitting
Autonomy and entrepreneurship	Simple form, lean staff
Productivity through people	Simultaneous loose-tight properties

Source: From *In Search of Excellence* by T. J. Peters and R. H. Waterman, pp. 20, 13–15. Copyright © 1982 by T. J. Peters and R. H. Waterman. Reprinted by permission of Harper & Row, Publishers, Inc.

WHAT DOES CULTURE DO?

We've alluded to organizational culture's impact on behavior. We've also explicitly argued that a strong culture should be associated with reduced turnover. In this section, we will more carefully review the functions that culture performs and assess whether culture can be a liability for an organization.

Culture's Functions

Culture performs a number of functions within an organization. First, it has a boundary defining role; that is, it creates distinctions between one organization and others. Second, it conveys a sense of identity for organization members. Third, culture facilitates the generation of commitment to something larger than one's individual self-interest. Fourth, it enhances social system stability. Culture is the social glue that helps hold the organization together by providing appropriate standards for what employees should say and do. Finally, culture serves as a sense-making and control mechanism that guides and shapes the attitudes and behavior of employees. It is this last function that is of particular interest to us. As the following quote makes clear, culture defines the rules of the game:

> Culture by definition is elusive, intangible, implicit, and taken for granted. But every organization develops a core set of assumptions, understandings, and implicit rules that govern day-to-day behavior in the workplace. . . . Until newcomers learn the rules, they are not accepted as full-fledged members of the organization. Transgressions of the rules on the part of high-level executives or front-line employees result in universal disapproval and powerful penalties. Conformity to the rules becomes the primary basis for reward and upward mobility.[11]

As we'll show later in this chapter, who is made job offers to join the organization, who is appraised as a high performer, and who gets the promotions are strongly influenced by the individual-organization "fit"—that is, whether the applicant or employee's attitudes and behavior are compatible with the culture. It is not a coincidence that employees at Disneyland and Disney World appear to be almost universally attractive, clean, wholesome looking, with bright smiles. That's the image Disney seeks. The company selects employees who will maintain that image. And once on the job, both the informal norms and formal rules and regulations ensure that Disney employees will act in a relatively uniform and predictable way.

Culture as a Liability

We are treating culture in a nonjudgmental manner. We haven't said that it's good or bad, only that it exists. Many of its functions, as outlined, are valuable for both the organization and the employee. Culture enhances organizational commitment and increases the consistency of employee behavior. These are clearly benefits to an organization. From an employee's standpoint, culture is valuable because it reduces ambiguity. It tells employees how things are done and what's important. But we shouldn't ignore the potentially dysfunctional aspects of culture, especially a strong one, on an organization's effectiveness.

Culture is a liability where the shared values are not in agreement with those that will further the organization's effectiveness. This is most likely to occur when the organization's environment is dynamic. When the environment is undergoing rapid change, the organization's entrenched culture may no longer be appropriate. So consistency of behavior is an asset to an organization when it faces a stable environment. It may, however, burden the organization and make it difficult to respond to changes in the environment.

CREATING AND SUSTAINING CULTURE

An organization's culture doesn't pop out of thin air. Once established, it rarely fades away. What forces influence the creation of a culture? What reinforces and sustains these forces once they are in place? We'll answer both of these questions in this section.

How a Culture Begins

An organization's current customs, traditions, and general way of doing things are largely due to what it has done before and the degree of success it had with those endeavors. This leads us to the ultimate source of an organization's culture: its founders!

The founding fathers of an organization traditionally have a major impact in establishing the early culture. They have a vision or mission of what the organization should be. They are unconstrained by previous customs of doing things or ideologies. The small size that typically characterizes any new organization further facilitates the founders' imposing their vision on all organizational members. Because the founders have the original idea, they also typically have biases on how to get the idea fulfilled. The organization's culture results from the interaction between (1) the founders' biases and assumptions and (2) what the original members that the founders initially employ learn subsequently from their own experiences.[12]

Henry Ford at the Ford Motor Company, Thomas Watson at IBM, J. Edgar Hoover at the FBI, Thomas Jefferson at the University of Virginia, Edwin Land at Polaroid, Ray Kroc at McDonald's, David Packard at Hewlett-Packard, and Steven Jobs and Stephen Wozniak at Apple Computers are just a few obvious examples of individuals who have had immeasurable impact in shaping their organization's culture. For instance, Watson's views on research and development, product innovation, employee dress attire, and compensation policies are still evident at IBM, though he died in 1956. Polaroid's innovative and risk-assuming culture is a direct reflection of Edwin Land's personal beliefs. McDonald's commitment to the values of quality, service, and cleanliness were originally proposed by Ray Kroc. The formality found today at the University of Virginia is due, in large part, to the original culture created by its founder, Thomas Jefferson. Apple's informal and creative culture was established, and continues to be nourished, by Steve Jobs.

Keeping a Culture Alive

Once a culture is in place, there are practices within the organization that act to maintain it by giving employees a set of similar experiences. For example, many of the human resource practices discussed in the previous chapter reinforce the organization's culture. The selection process, performance evaluation criteria, reward practices, training and career development activities, and promotion procedures ensure that those hired fit in with the culture, reward those who support it, and penalize (and even expel) those who challenge it. Three forces play a particularly important part in sustaining a culture—selection practices, the actions of top management, and socialization methods. Let's take a closer look at each.

SELECTION

The explicit goal of the selection process is to identify and hire individuals who have the knowledge, skills, and abilities to perform the jobs within the organization successfully. But, typically, more than one candidate will be identified who meets any given job's requirements. When that point is reached, it would be naive to ignore that the final decision as to whom is hired will be significantly influenced by the decision maker's judgment of how well the candidates will fit into the organization. This attempt to ensure a proper match, whether purposely or inadvertently, results in the hiring of people who have common values (ones essentially consistent with those of the organization) or at least a good portion of those values.[13] Additionally, the selection process provides information to applicants about the organization. Candidates learn about the organization, and, if they perceive a conflict between their values and those of the organization, they can self-select themselves out of the applicant pool. Selection, therefore, becomes a two-way street, allowing either employer or applicant to abrogate a marriage if there appears to be a mismatch. In this way, the selection process sustains an organization's culture by selecting out those individuals who might attack or undermine its core values.

Bain & Co., a large Boston management consulting firm, originally hired only new graduates from the Harvard Business School. This practice not only provided bright and talented people, it also reinforced Bain's culture. Many of the values instilled at Harvard—competition, verbal dexterity, hard work, ambition—were also core values at Bain. The selection of recent Harvard graduates increased the likelihood of Bain's having poeple who would fit in with Bain's culture and contribute to maintaining it. Other examples of the role that selection plays in sustaining culture are widely evident. Corporations tend to recruit and select management personnel from within their own industry, thus enhancing common perceptions.[14] The top Wall Street law firms still predominantly hire graduates from the prestigious eastern law schools, ensuring homogeneity of both partners and associates.[15] College fraternities and sororities assess potential members' socioeconomic status, personality, and physical appearance to find those "compatible" with the organization's image of itself. Personal contacts or "friends of friends" are a major source of job information for white-collar workers, which increases the likelihood that the organization will hire like-minded individuals.[16] It should not be surprising to learn that a study of the U.S. Federal Trade Commission found that the FTC attached more significance to regional background, old school ties, and political endorsements when recruiting attorneys than to their ability as reflected in grades or in the quality of law schools they attended.[17] These examples all confirm our contention that organizations use their personnel selection process to hire those who will fit in and accept the organization's values, norms, and customs, while at the same time screening out those who might challenge the system.

TOP MANAGEMENT

The actions of top management also have a major impact on the organization's culture.[18] Through what they say and how they behave, senior executives establish norms that filter down through the organization as to whether risk taking is desirable; how much freedom managers should give their subordinates; what is appropriate dress; what actions will pay off in terms of pay raises, promotions, and other rewards; and the like.

SOCIALIZATION

No matter how good a job the organization does in recruiting and selection, new employees are not fully indoctrinated in the organization's culture. Maybe most important, because they are least familiar with the organization's culture, new employees are potentially most likely to disturb the beliefs and customs that are in place. The organization will, therefore, want to help new employees adapt to its culture. This adaptation process is called *socialization*.

All Marines must go through boot camp, where they "prove" their commitment. Of course, at the same time, the Marine trainers are indoctrinating new recruits in the "Marine way." The success of any cult depends on effective socialization. New Moonies undergo a "brainwashing" ritual that substitutes group loyalty and commitment in place of family. New Disneyland employees spend their first two full days of work watching films and listening to lectures on how Disney employees are expected to look and act.

As we discuss socialization, keep in mind that the most critical socialization stage is at the time of entry into the organization. This is when the organization seeks to mold the outsider into an employee in "good standing." Those employees who fail to learn the essential or pivotal role behaviors risk being labeled "nonconformists" or "rebels," which often leads to expulsion. But the organization will be socializing every employee, though maybe not as explicitly, throughout his or her entire career in the organization. This further contributes to sustaining the culture.

Socialization can be conceptualized as a process made up of three stages: prearrival, encounter, and metamorphosis.[19] The first stage encompasses all the learning that occurs before a new member joins the organization. In the second stage, the new employee sees what the organization is really like and confronts the likelihood that expectations and reality may diverge. In the third stage, the relatively long-lasting changes take place. The new employee masters the skills required for his or her job, successfully performs his or her new roles, and makes the adjustments to his or her work group's values and norms.[20] This three-stage process impacts on the new employee's work productivity, commitment to the organization's objectives, and his or her decision to stay with the organization. Figure 14–2 depicts this process.

FIGURE 14–2
A Socialization Model

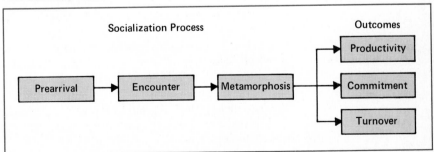

The *prearrival stage* explicitly recognizes that each individual arrives with a set of values, attitudes, and expectations. These cover both the work to be done and the organization. For instance, in many jobs, particularly professional work, new members will have undergone a considerable degree of prior socialization in training and in school. One major purpose of a business school, for example, is to socialize business students to the attitudes and behaviors that business firms want. If business executives believe that successful employees value the profit ethic, are loyal, will work hard, desire to achieve, and willingly accept directions from their superiors, they can hire individuals out of business schools who have been premolded in this pattern. But prearrival socialization goes beyond the specific job. The selection process is used in most organizations to inform prospective employees about the organization as a whole. In addition, as noted previously, the selection process also acts to ensure the inclusion of the "right type"—those who will fit in. "Indeed, the ability of the individual to present the appropriate face during the selection process determines his ability to move into the organization in the first place. Thus, success depends on the degree to which the aspiring member has correctly anticipated the expectations and desires of those in the organization in charge of selection."[21]

Upon entry into the organization, the new member enters the *encounter stage*. Here the individual confronts the possible dichotomy between her expectations—about her job, her co-workers, her boss, and the organization in general—and reality. If expectations prove to have been more or less accurate, the encounter stage merely provides for a reaffirmation of the perceptions gained earlier. However, this is often not the case. Where expectations and reality differ, the new employee must undergo socialization that will detach her from her previous assumptions and replace these with another set that the organization deems desirable. At the extreme, a new member may become totally disillusioned with the actualities of her job and resign. Proper selection should significantly reduce the probability of the latter occurrence.

Finally, the new member must work out any problems discovered during the encounter stage. This may mean going through changes—hence, we call this the *metamorphosis stage*. The choices presented in Table 14–3 are alternatives designed to bring about the desired metamorphosis. But what is a desirable metamorphosis? We can say that metamorphosis is complete, and the entry socialization process, when the new member has become comfortable with the organization and her job. She has internalized the norms of the organization and her work group, and she understands and accepts these norms. The new member feels accepted by her peers as a trusted and valued individual. She is self-confident that she has the competence to complete her job successfully. She understands the system—not only her own tasks, but the rules, procedures, and informally accepted practices as well. Finally, she knows how she will be evaluated, that is, what criteria will be used to measure and appraise her work. She knows what is expected of her and what constitutes a job "well done." As Figure 14–2 shows, successful metamorphosis should have a positive impact on the new employee's productivity and her commitment to the organization and reduce her propensity to leave the organization.

TABLE 14–3
Entry Socialization Options

Formal or Informal? New employees may be put directly into their jobs, with no effort made to differentiate them from those who have been doing the job for a considerable length of time. Such cases represent examples of informal socialization—it takes place on the job and the new member gets little or no special attention. In contrast, socialization can be formal. The more formal the program, the more the new employee is segregated from the ongoing work setting and differentiated in some way to make explicit her newcomer's role. The more formal a socialization program, the more likely it is that management has participated in its design and execution and, hence, the more likely that the recruit will experience the learning that management desires. In contrast, the more informal the program, the more success will depend on the new employee selecting the correct socialization agents.

Individual or Collective? Another choice to be made by management is whether to socialize new members individually or to group them together and process them through an identical set of experiences. The individual approach is likely to develop far less homogeneous views than collective socialization. As with the informal structure, individual socializing is more likely to preserve individual differences and perspectives.

Fixed or Variable Time Period? A third major consideration for management is whether the transition from outsider to insider should be done on a fixed or variable time period. A fixed schedule reduces uncertainty for the new member since transition is standardized. Successful completion of certain standardized steps means that she will be accepted to full-fledged membership. Variable schedules, in contrast, give no advanced notice of their transition timetable. Variability characterizes the socialization for most professionals and managerial personnel.

Serial or Disjunctive? When an experienced organizational member, familiar with the new member's job, guides or directs a new recruit, we call this serial socialization. In this process, the experienced member acts as a tutor and model for the new employee. When the recruit does not have predecessors available to guide her or to model her behavior upon, we have disjunctive socialization. Serial socialization maintains traditions and customs. It is preferred by organizations that seek to minimize the possibility of change over time. On the other hand, disjunctive socialization is likely to produce more inventive and creative employees because recruits are not burdened by traditions.

Investiture or Divestiture? Does management seek to confirm or dismantle the incoming identity of the new member? Investiture rites ratify the usefulness of the characteristics that the person brings to the new job. These individuals have been selected on the basis of what they can bring to the job. The organization does not want to change these recruits, so entry is made as smooth and trouble free as possible. If this is the goal, socialization efforts concentrate on reinforcing that "we like you just the way you are." Far more often there is a desire to strip away certain entering characteristics of a recruit. The selection process identified the candidate as a potential high performer; now it is necessary to make those minor modifications to improve the fit between the candidate and the organization. This fine-tuning may take the shape of requiring the recruit to sever old friendships; accepting a different way of looking at her job, peers, or the organization's purpose; doing a number of demeaning jobs to prove her commitment; or even undergoing harassment and hazing by more experienced personnel to verify that she fully accepts her role in the organization.

Source: Adapted from John Van Maanen, "People Processing: Strategies of Organizational Socialization," *Organizational Dynamics,* Summer 1978 (New York: AMACOM, a division of American Management Associations) pp. 19–36.

Summary: How Cultures Form

Figure 14–3 summarizes how an organization's culture is established and sustained. The original culture is derived from the founder's philosophy. This, in turn, strongly influences the criteria used in hiring. The actions of the current top management set the general climate of what is acceptable behavior and what is not. How employees are to be socialized will depend on the degree of success achieved in matching new employees' values to those of the organization's in the selection process and top management's preference for socialization methods.

HOW EMPLOYEES LEARN CULTURE

Culture is transmitted to employees in a number of forms—the most potent being through stories, rituals, material symbols, and language.

Stories

If you worked at the Ford Motor Co. during the 1970s, you would have undoubtedly heard the story about Henry Ford II reminding his executives, when they got too arrogant, that "it's *my* name that's on the building." The message was clear: Henry Ford II ran the company!

IBM employees tell the story of a plant security supervisor who challenged Thomas Watson, Jr., the all-powerful chairman of IBM's board. The supervisor, a twenty-two-year-old woman, was required to make certain that people entering security areas wore the correct clearance identification. One day, surrounded by his usual entourage, Watson approached the doorway to an area where the supervisor was on guard. He wore an orange badge acceptable elsewhere in the plant, but not a green badge, which alone permitted entrance at her door. Although she knew who Watson was, she told him what she had been instructed to say to anyone without proper clearance: "You cannot enter. Your admittance is not recognized." The men accompanying Watson were taken back. Would this young se-

FIGURE 14–3
How Organization Cultures Form

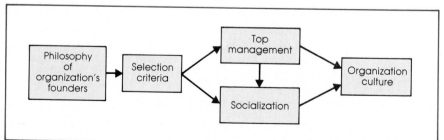

curity guard be fired on the spot? "Don't you know who he is?" someone asked. Watson raised his hand for silence while one of the party strode off and returned with the appropriate badge. The message to IBM employees: No matter who you are, you obey the rules.[22]

Stories, such as these just described, circulate through many organizations. They contain a narrative of events about the organization's founders, key decisions that affect the organization's future course, and the present top management. They anchor the present in the past and provide explanations and legitimacy for current practices.[23]

Rituals

Rituals are repetitive sequences of activities that express and reinforce the key values of the organization, what goals are most important, which people are important and which are expendable.[24]

College faculty members undergo a lengthy ritual in their quest for permanent employment—tenure. Typically, the faculty member is on probation for six years. At the end of that period, the member's colleagues must make one of two choices: extend a tenured appointment or issue a one-year terminal contract. What does it take to obtain tenure? It usually requires satisfactory teaching performance, service to the department and university, and scholarly activity. But, of course, what satisfies the requirements for tenure in one department at one university may be appraised as inadequate in another. The key is that the tenure decision, in essence, asks those who are tenured to assess whether the candidate has demonstrated, based on six years of performance, whether he or she fits in. Colleagues who have been socialized properly will have proved themselves worthy of being granted tenure. Every year, hundreds of faculty members at colleges and universities are denied tenure. In some cases, this action is a result of poor performance across the board. More often, however, the decision can be traced to the faculty member's not doing well in those areas that the tenured faculty believe are important. The instructor who spends dozens of hours each week preparing for class, achieves outstanding evaluations by students, but neglects his or her research and publication activities, may be passed over for tenure. What has happened, simply, is that the instructor has failed to adapt to the norms set by the department. The astute faculty member will assess early on in the probationary period what attitudes and behaviors his or her colleagues want and will then proceed to give it to them. And, of course, by doing so the tenured faculty have made significant strides toward standardizing tenure candidates.

Material Symbols

Bank of America is a conservative firm. Aggressive risk taking is not central to its culture. Its executives drive four-door, American-made sedans. In 1983, Bank of America purchased the discount brokerage firm of Charles Schwab & Sons. In contrast to B of A, Schwab built its reputation on aggressiveness. It sought out and only hired outgoing and what some might call "flashy" brokers. Top executives at Schwab, like those at Bank of America, drove company cars. Only theirs were Ferraris, Porsches, and BMWs. The cars' images fit both the people who drove them and the cultural values Schwab sought to maintain.

Tandem Computers' headquarters in Cupertino, California, doesn't look like your typical head office operation. It has jogging trails, a basketball court, space for dance and yoga classes, and a large swimming pool—all for its employees enjoyment. Every Friday afternoon at 4:30, employees partake in the weekly beer bust, courtesy of the company.[25]

Four-door sedans, Ferraris, and a swimming pool at the office are material symbols that help to reinforce these organizations' cultures. The design and physical layout of spaces and buildings, furniture, executive perks, and dress attire are material symbols that convey to employees who is important, the degree of egalitarianism desired by top management, and the kinds of behaviors (i.e., risk taking, conservative, authoritarian, participative, individualistic, social) that are appropriate.

Language

Many organizations and units within organizations use language as a way to identify members of a culture or subculture. By learning this language, members attest to their acceptance of the culture and, in so doing, help to preserve it.

The kitchen personnel in a large hotel use terminology foreign to hotel people outside this area. Members of the U. S. Army sprinkle their language liberally with jargon that readily identifies its members. Many organizations, over time, develop unique terms to describe equipment, offices, key personnel, suppliers, customers, or products that relate to its business. New employees are frequently overwhelmed with acronyms and jargon that, after six months on the job, have become fully part of their language. But once assimilated, this terminology acts as a common denominator that unites members of a given culture or subculture.

CULTURE IN ACTION

Two recent activities by major corporations allows us to observe, in action, issues related to organizational culture. The first is the purchase of Electronic Data Systems (EDS) by General Motors for $2.5 billion.[26] Both organizations have very different, and very strong, cultures. The second is the breakup of American Telephone & Telegraph.[27] AT&T had a unique culture, heavily influenced by its virtual monopoly over the U.S. telephone system. As it moves away from dependence on its operating telephone companies to become a major force in the telecommunications and computer markets, it will require a significantly different culture if it is to compete successfully. In this section, we look at potential problems when strong cultures collide and when an organization seeks a new culture.

Since the changes that we will describe are relatively recent, they are offered more as problems or challenges to predicting employee behavior rather than after-the-fact analyses of what happened.

GM & EDS: When Cultures Collide

General Motors employs approximately 750,000 employees and generates revenues in excess of $83 billion a year. By any standard, it is a large company, and by most standards, it is a successful one. Its after-tax profits in 1984, for instance, were over $4.5 billion. Success like this is usually accompanied by a strong culture and that's the case of GM. Three core values stand out at GM: (1) loyalty, (2) keeping a low profile, and (3) risk aversion.

GM people are expected to be loyal to their boss and the company. The chain of command is rigidly followed. Employees are expected to defer to those in authority. A number of rituals are carefully preserved to reinforce this value. Those who attack the company—whether from within like John DeLorean or from outside like Ralph Nader—are likely recipients of a strong counterattack.

No GM employee—this, of course, is most relevant in the executive ranks—should be larger than the company itself. Executives should be invisible. The style of Chrysler's Lee Iacocca is the antithesis of a "good" GM executive. This invisibility value is well demonstrated in dress attire. At GM, executives are expected to wear dark suits, fashioned in a full-cut conservative style.

GM has a strong history of risk aversion. Profits came from selling large cars with lots of options. The company's organization structure made extensive use of committees as decision-making bodies. This increased input into decisions. It also reinforced GM's desire not to make mistakes, even if it meant significant delays in decision-making action.

In 1984, General Motors purchased Electronic Data Systems Corp. and merged it into the GM structure. EDS was a relatively new company. It was begun by H. Ross Perot in 1962 to provide complete computer services to organizations. In twenty-two years, it had grown to employ thirteen thousand people and sales of $600 million a year. Ross Perot's initial $1,000 investment had turned him into one of America's few billionaires.

But EDS has its own unique culture. Central to its culture are discipline, determination, competitiveness, aggressiveness, and a twenty-four-hour-a-day commitment to EDS. It is run like a corporate version of the Marine Corps. Its Dallas headquarters resembles a fortified encampment, encircled by barbed wire and patrolled by armed guards. Male employees wear light shirts, ties, and short hair. Beards or tassels on one's shoes are forbidden. To solidify the culture, EDS has a socialization process designed to weed out the uncommitted. Hiring, until the early 1970s, was confined mostly to military veterans. The company still prefers the "lean and hungry" graduates of less prestigious schools rather than Ivy Leaguers. Training for system engineers is intense and lasts for up to two years, with 25 percent of the trainees washing out during this period.

The EDS culture is probably best exemplified in Perot's successful effort in 1979 to free two EDS executives who were being held by the Khomeini regime in an Iranian prison without charge. He put together a team of EDS executives in the United States and snuck them into Iran. The team incited a mob to storm the prison, freeing thirteen thousand prisoners, including the two EDS men. Every EDS employee knows this story within twenty-four hours of joining EDS, and its message is not lost on EDS personnel: EDS takes care of its people. Like a family member, as long as you're giving maximum effort to the company, EDS stands by you through thick and thin. Additionally, it reiterates Perot's belief that no problem is insurmountable.

EDS's merging with GM has been likened to a Green Beret outfit joining up with the Social Security administration. EDS claims its greatest asset is its people, while GM claims its greatest asset is its cars. In a few ways, the cultures are compatible—both, for instance, value loyalty and commitment. But EDS downplays authority and values adventure and risk taking. Ross Perot and EDS are also interchangeable entities—the company is fully a reflection of his beliefs and personality. Can a Ross Perot and an aggressive EDS culture live happily in GM's bureaucracy? Time will tell.

AT&T: Seeking a New Culture

On January 1, 1984, the U.S. government's final step in breaking up the Bell System became reality. AT&T would no longer monopolize the U.S. telephone system. Its operating telephone companies would become independent firms; in return, AT&T would be allowed to compete in the telecommunications and computer markets against the likes of IBM, Xerox, and the Japanese. But this change, if it is to be successful, will require a change in AT&T's culture—from one that is internally manufacturing oriented to an externally focused, market-driven company.

A symbol of AT&T historic culture is the print of Angus McDonald, a nineteenth-century Bell System lineman, fighting to keep the telephone lines open during a blizzard. A long-time feature of AT&T office decor, the print symbolizes the company's commitment to service. But AT&T now faces a very different environment that will require a major shift in its culture. AT&T's culture developed around an incredibly strong service ethic. Employees did what they felt was best for its customers, regardless of what the customers actually wanted. Western Electric, its manufacturing subsidiary, could make phones that would survive falls from 20-story buildings and passed the costs of such phones on to its customers, because it had no competition. This culture strongly influenced the road to the top at AT&T. Operational and technical—rather than marketing—backgrounds were the way up AT&T's corporate ladder.

The challenge at today's AT&T is to alter its culture to be more competitive and aggressive. Its manufacturing-oriented culture encouraged taking too much time to make a product and at too high a price. A marketing culture will be geared to supply customers with what they need quickly, and if that includes lower-quality phones and dozens of options, so be it!

The current challenge of AT&T's top executives is to overhaul its culture for the new competitive battles ahead. This is going to mean changes in its organization structure, the kind of people it hires, and their shared value system. It's also going to impact on employee commitment and turnover rates. AT&T has been dominated by its engineers and most of its employees were committed for life to the security of "Ma Bell." Those days appear to be gone.

IMPLICATIONS FOR PERFORMANCE AND SATISFACTION

Figure 14–4 depicts organizational culture as an intervening variable. Employees form an overall subjective perception of the organization based on factors such as degree of autonomy, structure, reward orientation, warmth and support provided by supervisors, and willingness of management to tolerate conflict. This overall perception becomes, in effect, the organization's culture or personality. These favorable or unfavorable perceptions then affect employee performance and satisfaction, with the impact being greater for stronger cultures.

Does culture have an equal impact on both employee performance and satisfaction: The evidence says "No." There is a relatively strong relationship between culture and satisfaction, but this is moderated by individual differences.[28] In general, we propose that satisfaction will be highest when there is congruence between individual needs and the culture. For instance, an organization whose culture would be described as low in structure, having loose supervision, and rewarding people for high achievement is likely to have more satisfied employees if those employees have a high achievement need and prefer autonomy. Our conclusion, therefore, is that job satisfaction often varies according to the employee's perception of the organization's culture.

The relationship between culture and performance is less clear, although a number of studies find the two related.[29] But the relationship is moderated by the organization's technology.[30] Performance will be higher when the culture suits the technology. If the culture is informal, creative, and supports risk taking and conflict, performance will be higher if the technology is nonroutine. The more formally structured organizations that are risk aversive, that seek to eliminate conflict, and that are prone to more task-oriented leadership will achieve higher performance when routine technology is utilized.

FIGURE 14–4

How Organizational Culture Impacts Performance and Satisfaction

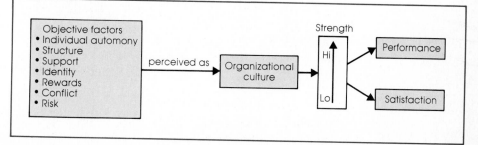

We should not overlook the influence socialization has on employee performance. An employee's performance depends to a considerable degree on knowing what he should or should not do. Understanding the right way to do a job indicates proper socialization. Further, the appraisal of an individual's performance includes how well the person fits into the organization. Can he get along with his co-workers? Does he have acceptable work habits? Does he demonstrate the right attitude? These qualities differ between jobs and organizations. For instance, on some jobs, employees will be evaluated higher if they are aggressive and outwardly indicate that they are ambitious. On another job, or on the same job in another organization, such an approach may be evaluated negatively. As a result, proper socialization becomes a significant factor in influencing both actual job performance and how it's perceived by others.

POINT

THE CASE AGAINST CULTURAL CHANGE

The fact that an organization's culture is made up of relatively stable characteristics would imply that culture is very difficult for management to change. Such a conclusion would be correct.

An organization's culture develops over many years and is rooted in deeply held values to which employees are strongly committed. In addition, there are a number of forces continually operating to maintain a given culture. These would include written statements about the organization's mission and philosophy, the design of physical spaces and buildings, the dominant leadership style, hiring criteria, past promotion practices, entrenched rituals, popular stories about key people and events, the organization's historic performance evaluation criteria, and the organization's formal structure.

Selection and promotion policies are particularly important devices that work against cultural change. Employees chose the organization because they perceived their values to be a "good fit" with the organization. They become comfortable with that fit and will strongly resist efforts to disturb the equilibrium. Those in control will also select senior managers who will continue the current culture. Even attempts to change a culture by going outside the organization to hire a new chief executive is unlikely to be effective. The evidence indicates that the culture is more likely to change the executive than the other way around. Why? It's too entrenched, and change becomes a potential threat to member self-interest. In fact, a more pragmatic view of the relationship between an organization's culture and its chief executive would be to note that the practice of filling senior-level management postions from current managerial employees ensures that those who run the organization have been fully indoctrinated in the organization's culture. Promoting from within provides stability and lessens uncertainty. When Exxon's board of directors selects as a new chief executive officer an individual who has spent thirty years in the company, it literally guarantees that the culture will continue unchanged.

Our argument, however, should not be viewed as saying that culture can *never* be changed. In the unusual case when an organization confronts a survival-threatening crisis—a crisis that is universally acknowledged as a true life-or-death situation—all members of the organization will be responsive to efforts at cultural change. But anything less is unlikely to be effective.

COUNTERPOINT

HOW TO CHANGE AN ORGANIZATION'S CULTURE

Changing an organization's culture is extremely difficult to accomplish, but cultures *can be* changed. In 1963, American Brands was a mature tobacco company, risk aversive, and relying on its high-tar cigarettes for sales volume. A severe drop in its market share, however, led the board of directors to remove its chief executive officer and replace him with an external candidate. Within two years, the firm introduced the first super-low-tar cigarette, within four years it had acquired a major British-based tobacco company, and by the early 1970s, the company had returned to be a major force in the tobacco industry. Lee Iacocca came to Chrysler Corp. in 1978, with the company appearing to be only weeks away from bankruptcy. In five years he took Chrysler's conservative, inward-looking, and engineering-oriented culture into an action-oriented, market-responsive culture.

The following suggestions can lead to cultural change:

1. Have top management become positive role models, setting the tone through its behavior.

2. Create new stories, symbols, and rituals to replace those currently in vogue.

3. Select, promote, and support employees who espouse the new values that are sought.

4. Redesign socialization processes to align with the new values.

5. Change the reward system to encourage acceptance of a new set of values.

6. Replace unwritten norms with formal rules and regulations that are tightly enforced.

7. Shake up current subcultures through extensive use of job rotation.

8. Work to get peer group consensus through utilization of employee participation and creation of a climate with a high level of trust.

Implementing most or all of these suggestions will not result in an immediate or dramatic shift in the organization's culture. Cultural change is a lengthy process—measured in years rather than months. And acceptance of that change will be moderate. But if the question is, "Can culture be changed?" the answer is "Yes!"

FOR DISCUSSION

1. Contrast individual personality and organizational culture. How are they similar? How are they different?
2. What's the relationship between institutionalization, formalization, and organizational culture?
3. What's the difference between job satisfaction and organizational culture?
4. Can an employee survive in an organization if he or she rejects its core values? Explain.
5. What forces might contribute toward making a culture strong or weak?
6. How is an organization's culture maintained?
7. Is socialization brainwashing? Explain.
8. What benefits can socialization provide for the organization? For the new employee?
9. If management sought a culture characterized as innovative and autonomous, what might its socialization program look like?
10. If management sought a culture characterized as formalized and conflict free, what might its socialization program look like?
11. Can you identify a set of characteristics that describe your college's culture? Compare them with several of your peers. How closely do they agree?
12. "We should be opposed to the manipulation of individuals for organizational purposes but a degree of social uniformity enables organizations to work better." Do you agree or disagree with this statement? Discuss.

FOR FURTHER READING

BAKER, E. L., "Managing Organizational Culture," *Management Review,* July 1980, pp. 8–13. Offers techniques for changing cultures.

LOUIS, M. R., "Surprise and Sense Making: What Newcomers Experience in Entering Unfamiliar Organizational Settings," *Administrative Science Quarterly,* June 1980, pp. 226–51. Reviews what we know about the organizational entry experience.

MARSHALL, J., "Organizational Culture: Elements in Its Portraiture and Some Implications for Organization Functioning," *Group and Organization Studies,* September 1982, pp. 367–84. Presents a framework for charting significant elements of organizational culture.

MARTIN, J., M. S. FELDMAN, M. J. HATCH, and S. B. SITKIN, "The Uniqueness Paradox in Organizational Stories," *Administrative Science Quarterly,* September 1983, pp. 438–53. Identifies seven types of stories that occur in a wide variety of organizations.

PASCALE, R., "Fitting New Employees into the Company Culture," *Fortune,* May 28, 1984, pp. 28–42. Describes seven steps of socialization that, the author argues, all successful companies put new employees through.

SCHEIN, E. H., "Coming to a New Awareness of Organizational Culture," *Sloan Management Review,* Winter 1984, pp. 3–16. Develops a formal definition of organizational culture and presents a dynamic model of how culture is learned, passed on, and changed.

NOTES FOR CHAPTER 14

1. T. E. Deal and A. A. Kennedy, *Corporate Cultures: The Rites and Rituals of Corporate Life* (Reading, Mass.: Addison-Wesley, 1982), pp. 65–66.
2. P. Selznick, "Foundations of the Theory of Organization," *American Sociological Review,* February 1948, pp. 25–35.
3. L. G. Zucker, "Organizations as Institutions," in S. B. Bacharach (ed.), *Perspectives in Organizational Sociology: Theory and Research* (Greenwich, Conn.: JAI Press, 1981).
4. See, for example, H. S. Becker, "Culture: A Sociological View," *Yale Review,* Summer 1982, pp. 513–27; and M. S. Schall, "A Communication-Rules Approach to Organizational Culture," *Administrative Science Quarterly,* December 1983, pp. 557–81.
5. Adapted and modified from J. P. Campbell, M. D. Dunnette, E. E. Lawler III, and K. E. Weick, *Managerial Behavior, Performance, and Effectiveness* (New York: McGraw-Hill, 1970), p. 393.
6. See, for example, K. L. Gregory, "Native-View Paradigms: Multiple Cultures and Culture Conflicts in Organizations," *Administrative Science Quarterly,* September 1983, pp. 359–76.
7. T. E. Deal and A. A. Kennedy, *Corporate Cultures;* and T. J. Peters and R. H. Waterman, Jr., *In Search of Excellence* (New York: Harper & Row, 1982).
8. C. A. O'Reilly III, "Corporations, Cults and Organizational Culture: Lessons from Silicon Valley Firms," paper presented at the 42nd Annual Meeting of the Academy of Management, Dallas, 1983.
9. R. T. Mowday, L. W. Porter, and R. M. Steers, *Employee-Organization Linkages: The Psychology of Commitment, Absenteeism, and Turnover* (New York: Academic Press, 1982).
10. For critical evaluations of *In Search of Excellence,* see D. T. Carroll, "A Disappointing Search for Excellence," *Harvard Business Review,* November–December 1983, pp. 78–88; and "Who's Excellent Now?" *Business Week,* November 5, 1984, pp. 76–78.
11. T. E. Deal and A. A. Kennedy, "Culture: A New Look Through Old Lenses," *Journal of Applied Behavioral Science,* November 1983, p. 501.
12. E. H. Schein, "The Role of the Founder in Creating Organizational Culture," *Organizational Dynamics,* Summer 1983, pp. 13–28.
13. G. Salaman, "The Sociology of Assessment: The Regular Commissions Board Assessment Procedure," in *People and Organizations: Media Booklet II* (Milton Keynes, England: Open University Press, 1974).

14. J. Pfeffer and H. Leblebici, "Executive Recruitment and the Development of Interfirm Organizations," *Administrative Science Quarterly,* December 1973, pp. 457–61.

15. E. O. Smigel, *The Wall Street Lawyer* (New York: Free Press, 1964).

16. M. Granovetter, *Getting a Job: A Study of Contacts and Careers* (Cambridge, Mass.: Harvard University Press, 1974).

17. Cited in W. Evan, *Organization Theory* (New York: John Wiley, 1976), p. 162.

18. R. Tagiuri and G. H. Litwin, *Organizational Climate* (Boston: Harvard University Graduate School of Business Administration, 1968); and J. L. Franklin, "Down the Organization: Influence Processes Across Levels of Hierarchy," *Administrative Science Quarterly,* June 1975, pp. 153–64.

19. J. Van Maanen and E. H. Schein, "Career Development," in J. R. Hackman and J. L. Suttle (eds.), *Improving Life at Work* (Santa Monica, Calif.: Goodyear, 1977), pp. 58–62.

20. D. C. Feldman, "The Multiple Socialization of Organization Members," *Academy of Management Review,* April 1981, p. 310.

21. Van Maanen and Schein, "Career Development," p. 59.

22. W. Rodgers, *Think* (New York: Stein & Day, 1969), pp. 153–54.

23. A. M. Pettigrew, "On Studying Organizational Cultures," *Administrative Science Quarterly,* December 1979, p. 576.

24. Ibid.

25. M. Magnet, "Managing by Mystique at Tandem Computers," *Fortune,* June 28, 1982, pp. 84–91.

26. Sources for information on GM and EDS include J. P. Wright, *On a Clear Day You Can See General Motors* (Grosse Point, Mich.: Wright Enterprises, 1979); E. Cray, *Chrome Colossus: General Motors and Its Times* (New York: McGraw-Hill, 1980); K. Follett, *On Wings of the Eagles* (New York: William Morrow, 1983); P. Nulty, "Ross Perot's Raid on Washington," *Fortune,* October 31, 1983, pp. 124–129; and L. P. Cohen and C. F. McCoy, "Perot's Singular Style Raises Issue of How He'll Fit at GM," *The Wall Street Journal,* July 2, 1984, p. 17.

27. Sources for information on AT&T include "Culture Shock Is Shaking the Bell System," *Business Week,* September 26, 1983, pp. 112–16; M. Langley, "AT&T Marketing Men Find Their Star Fails to Ascend as Expected," *The Wall Street Journal,* February 13, 1984, p. 1; M. Langley, "AT&T Has Call for a New Corporate Culture," *The Wall Street Journal,* February 28, 1984, p. 24; and J. Main, "Waking up AT&T: There's Life After Culture Shock," *Fortune,* December 24, 1984, pp. 66–74.

28. D. Hellriegel and J. W. Slocum, Jr., "Organizational Climate: Measures, Research, and Contingencies," *Academy of Mangement Journal,* June 1974, pp. 225–80.

29. Ibid.

30. J. W. Lorsch and J. J. Morse, *Organizations and Their Members* (New York: Harper & Row, 1974).

15

Organizational Change and Development

AFTER STUDYING THIS CHAPTER, YOU SHOULD BE ABLE TO:

Define and explain the following key terms and concepts:

Change

Change agent

Change intervention

Coercion

Cooptation

Intergroup development

Manipulation

Organizational development (OD)

Process consultation

Refreezing

Sensitivity training

Survey feedback

Team building

Unfreezing

Understand:

How change encompasses almost all OB concepts

Why some people resist change

The change process

OD values

The process by which OD operates

The relationship of OD techniques and conflict resolution techniques

The difference between structural and human process techniques

Various techniques available for introducing behavioral change

Most people hate any change that doesn't jingle in their pockets.

—ANONYMOUS

*T*he major U.S. automobile manufacturers like GM and Ford are spending billions of dollars remodeling their plants and installing state-of-the-art robotics to compete more successfully against imports. One area currently receiving attention by these auto companies is computerized quality control. Sophisticated computer-controlled equipment is being put in place to improve significantly the ability to find and correct defects. This new equipment is changing the jobs of the people working in the quality control area, and the management of the auto firms have been seeking ways to reduce the resistance that quality control personnel are showing to these changes.

Innovation is the essence of long-term survival for many companies. At Minnesota Mining & Manufacturing, for instance, management explictly seeks to get 25 percent of the firm's sales from products less than five years old. Such an ambitious goal *demands* the development of a continual stream of new ideas.

The last decade has seen many organizations—both in the private and public sector—in need of shrinking the size of their organizations. These have included such varied organizations as Polaroid, Gulf & Western Industries, B. F. Goodrich, Caterpillar Tractor, and the Los Angeles City School District. The downsizing of an organization can be a difficult experience for employees. There is high uncertainty, key people quit to pursue better opportunities, and morale suffers. Yet, if management fails to help employees cope with this change, productivity and efficiency are sure to suffer.

The foregoing illustrates just three contemporary problems—acceptance of automation, the implementation of innovations, and the downsizing of an organization—that impose changes upon employees. There are all kinds of forces that are making organizations confront the need to adapt and change. Stability may have characterized organizations in the 1950s or 1960s, but the 1980s are a different time. More and more organizations are finding themselves confronting a dynamic environment that requires adaptation. Failure to make that adaptation may threaten the organization's survival. But the topic of change runs wider than merely adapting to a changing environment. The need for change has been implied throughout this text. "A casual reflection on change should indicate that it encompasses almost all our concepts in the organizational behavior literature. Think about leadership, motivation, organizational environment, and roles. It is impossible to think about these and other concepts without inquiring about change."[1] This chapter is about what can be done to make change interventions in organizations more successful.

SOME DEFINITIONS

Let's begin with a few brief definitions. *Change* is concerned with making things different. *Change intervention* is a planned action to make things different. The person or persons who act as catalysts, and assume the responsibility for managing the change process, is the *change agent. Organizational development (OD)* is a popular term used to describe a systems-oriented approach to change. Several of these definitions deserve some elaboration.

Change agents can be managers or nonmanagers, employees of the organization, or outside consultants. For major change efforts, internal management often will hire the services of outside consultants to provide advice and assistance. Because they are from the outside, these individuals can offer an objective perspective often missing from insiders. However, outside consultants are disadvantaged because they usually have an inadequate understanding of the organization's history, culture, operating procedures, and personnel. Outside consultants also may be prone to initiating more drastic changes—which can be a benefit or a disadvantage—because they do not have to live with the repercussions after the change is implemented. In contrast, internal staff specialists or managers, when acting as the change agent, may be more thoughtful (and possibly cautious) because they must live with the consequences of their actions.

Organizational development is a term used for a variety of change-oriented activities. To some, it is merely a sexy name given to small-group discussion methods. At the other extreme, it has been defined in such a general way as to encompass almost the entire management process. For example, OD has been described as "a complex network of events that enhances the ability of organizational members to manage the culture of their organization, to be creative in solving problems, and to assist their organization in adapting to the external environment."[2] Our conclusion is that OD is not really a definable, single concept, but rather a convenient term used to encompass a variety of activities for managing change. We'll come back to discussing OD later in this chapter.

RESISTANCE TO CHANGE

It's been taken as a truism that people resist change. But do they?

Does an employee resist an upward change in pay rate or vacation allowance? Does a homemaker resist the replacement of a cranky old dishwasher for a new one? Does a manager resist an imposed schedule change that requires him to represent his division at an important reception for the new company president rather than finishing his quarterly budget? All these changes are likely to be welcomed warmly and to be implemented with great cooperation from the people concerned. What distinguishes these changes from the changes that people resist strongly is the fact that their nature and effects are relatively well-known and are enthusiastically desired. The degree of people's resistance to change depends on the kind of change involved and how well it is understood. What people resist is not change but loss, or the possibility of loss.[3]

People are likely to resist change for one of two reasons: loss of the known and tried or concern over personal loss.[4]

Changes substitute ambiguity and uncertainty for the known. Regardless of how much you may dislike attending college, at least you know the ropes. You understand what is expected of you. But when you leave college and venture out into the world of full-time employment, regardless of how desirous you are to get out of college, you have to trade the known for the unknown. Employees in organizations hold the same dislike for uncertainty. If, for example, the introduction of word processors means that departmental secretaries will have to learn to operate these new pieces of equipment, some of the secretaries may fear that they will be unable to do so. They may, therefore, develop a negative attitude toward working with word processors or behave dysfunctionally if required to use them.

The other cause of resistance is fear of personal loss of something already possessed. Change threatens the "investment" one has already made in the status quo. The more people have invested in the current system, the more resistant they tend to be toward change. Why? They fear the loss of status, money, authority, friendships, personal convenience, or other benefits they value. This explains why older employees tend to resist change more than younger ones. Older employees have generally invested more in the current system and, therefore, have more to lose by adapting to a change. If you have spent twenty years of your adult life as a mail sorter with the post office, you are likely to resist automatic letter sorters more actively than would a recent high school graduate who has been performing the job for only six months. The latter has less personal investment in the old system and is less threatened by automation.

THE CHANGE PROCESS

When resistance to change is seen as dysfunctional, what actions can be taken? Reducing resistance to change can best be understood by considering the complexity inherent in the change process (see Figure 15–1).

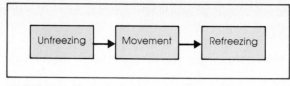

FIGURE 15–1
Change Process

Successful change requires *unfreezing* the status quo, *movement* to a new state, and *refreezing* the new change to make it permanent.[5] Implicit in this three-step process is the recognition that the mere introduction of change does not ensure either the elimination of the prechange condition or the permanence of the change.

The management of a large oil company decided to reorganize its marketing function in the western United States. The firm had three divisional offices in the west, located in Seattle, San Francisco, and Los Angeles. The decision was made to consolidate the divisions into a single regional office to be located in San Francisco. The reorganization meant transferring over 150 employees, the elimination of some duplicate managerial positions, and the institution of a new hierarchy of command. As you might guess, a move of this magnitude was difficult to keep secret. The rumor of its occurrence preceded the announcement by several months. The decision itself was made unilaterally. It came from the executive offices in New York. Those people affected had no say whatsoever in the choice. For those in Seattle or Los Angeles, who may have disliked the decision and its consequences—the problems inherent in transferring to another city, pulling youngsters out of school, making new friends, having new co-workers, undergoing the reassignment of responsibilities—their only recourse was to quit. This actual case of an organizational change will be used to illustrate the unfreezing-movement-refreezing model.

The status quo can be considered an equilibrium state. To move from this equilibrium—to overcome the pressures of both individual resistance and group conformity—unfreezing is necessary. It can be achieved in one of three ways. The *driving forces,* which direct behavior away from the status quo, can be increased. The *restraining forces,* which hinder movement from the existing equilibrium, can be decreased. A third alternative is to *combine the first two approaches.*

Using the reorganization example cited, management can expect employee resistance to the consolidation. To deal with that resistance, management can use positive incentives to encourage employees to accept the change. For instance, increases in pay can be offered to those who accept the transfer. Very liberal moving expenses can be paid by the company. Management might offer low-cost mortgage funds to allow employees to buy new homes in San Francisco. Of course, management might choose to unfreeze acceptance of the status quo by removing restraining forces. Employees could be counseled individually. Each employee's concerns and apprehensions could be heard and clarified specifically. Assuming that most of the fears are unjustified, the counselor could assure the employees that there was nothing to fear and then demonstrate, through tangible evidence, that restraining forces are unwarranted. If resistance is extremely high, management may have to resort to both reducing resistance and increasing the attractiveness of the alternative if the unfreezing is to be successful.

Once unfreezing has been accomplished, the change itself can be implemented. In reality, there is no clear line separating unfreezing and moving. Many of the efforts made to unfreeze the status quo may, in and of themselves, introduce movement. So the tactics for dealing with resistance that the change agent uses may work on unfreezing and/or moving.

Six tactics have been suggested for use by change agents in dealing with resistance to change.[6] Let us review them briefly.

1. *Education and communication.* Resistance can be reduced through communicating with employees to help them see the logic of a change. This tactic basically assumes that the source of resistance lies in misinformation or poor communication: If employees receive the full facts and get any misunderstandings cleared up, resistance will subside. This can be achieved through one-on-one discussions, memos, group presentations, or reports. Does it work? It does, provided that the source of resistance is inadequate communication and that management-employee relations are characterized by mutual trust and credibility. If these conditions do not exist, the change is unlikely to succeed. Additionally, the time and effort that this tactic involves must be considered against its advantages, particularly when the change affects a large number of people.

2. *Participation.* It's difficult for individuals to resist a change decision in which they participated. Prior to making a change, those opposed can be brought into the decision process. Assuming that the participants have the expertise to make a meaningful contribution, their involvement can reduce resistance, obtain commitment, and increase the quality of the change decision. However, against these advantages are the negatives: potential for a poor solution and great time consumption.

3. *Facilitation and support.* Change agents can offer a range of supportive efforts to reduce resistance. When employee fear and anxiety are high, employee counseling and therapy, new skills training, or a short paid leave of absence may facilitate adjustment. The drawback of this tactic is that, as with the others, it is time consuming. Additionally, it is expensive, and its implementation offers no assurance of success.

4. *Negotiation.* Another way for the change agent to deal with potential resistance to change is to exchange something of value for a lessening of the resistance. For instance, if the resistance is centered in a few powerful individuals, a specific reward package can be negotiated that will meet their individual needs. In the oil company's reorganization, acceptance of the transfer and reshuffling of duties by several highly valued middle managers was "bought" by providing them with larger staffs in their new jobs and by allowing them to live on company expense for nearly six months while they and their spouses "looked" for acceptable permanent housing accommodations. Negotiation, as a tactic, may be necessary when resistance comes from a powerful source. Yet one cannot ignore its potentially high costs. Additionally, there is the risk that, once a change agent negotiates to avoid resistance, he or she is open to the possibility of being black-

mailed by other individuals in a position of power.

5. *Manipulation and cooptation.* Manipulation refers to covert influence attempts. Twisting and distorting facts to make them appear more attractive, withholding undesirable information, or creating false rumors to get employees to accept a change are all examples of manipulation. If corporate management threatens to close down a particular manufacturing plant if that plant's employees fail to accept an across-the-board pay cut, and if the threat is actually untrue, management is using manipulation. Cooptation, on the other hand, is a form of both manipulation and participation. It seeks to "buy off" the leaders of a resistance group by giving them a key role in the change decision. The leaders' advice is sought, not to seek a better decision, but to get their endorsement. Both manipulation and cooptation are relatively inexpensive and easy ways to gain the support of adversaries, but the tactics can backfire if the targets become aware that they are being tricked or used. Once discovered, the change agent's credibility may drop to zero.

6. *Coercion.* Last on the list of tactics is coercion, that is, the application of direct threats or force upon the resisters. If the corporate management mentioned in the previous discussion were really determined to close the manufacturing plant if employees did not acquiesce to a pay cut, then coercion would be the label attached to their change tactic. Other examples of coercion include threats of transfer, loss of promotions, negative performance evaluations, or a poor letter of recommendation. The advantages and drawbacks of coercion are approximately the same as those mentioned for manipulation and cooptation.

Assuming that a change has been implemented, if it is to be successful, the new situation needs to be refrozen so that it can be sustained over time. Unless this last step is taken, there is a very high chance that the change will be short lived and that employees will attempt to revert to the previous equilibrium state. The objective of refreezing, then, is to stabilize the new situation by balancing the driving and restraining forces.

How is refreezing done? Basically, it requires systematic replacement of the temporary forces with permanent ones. It may mean formalizing the driving or restraining forces, for instance, a permanent upward adjustment of salaries or the permanent removal of time clocks to reinforce a climate of trust and confidence in employees. The formal rules and regulations governing behavior of those affected by the change should be revised to reinforce the new situation. Over time, of course, the group's own norms will evolve to sustain the new equilibrium. But until that point is reached, the change agent will have to rely on more formal mechanisms.

OD'S VALUES AND OBJECTIVES

Organizational development was previously described as "a systems-oriented approach to change" and "a variety of activities for managing change." All *change* activities would not necessarily be subsumed under the OD label. In this section, we want to elaborate more fully on why all change activities aren't part of organizational development by clarifying OD's values and objectives.

OD interventions are typically built on humanistic-democratic values. The change agent may be directive in OD; however, there is a strong emphasis on collaboration. Concepts like power, authority, control, conflict, and coercion are held in relatively low esteem among OD change agents. The following briefly identifies the underlying values in most OD efforts:

1. *Respect for people.* Individuals are perceived as being responsible, conscientious, and caring. They should be treated with dignity and respect.

2. *Trust and support.* The effective and healthy organization is characterized by trust, authenticity, openness, and a supportive climate.

3. *Power equalization.* Effective organizations deemphasize hierarchical authority and control.

4. *Confrontation.* Problems shouldn't be swept under the rug. They should be openly confronted.

5. *Participation.* The more that people who will be affected by a change are involved in the decisions surrounding that change, the more they will be committed to implementing those decisions.

OD programs focus primarily at the level of the whole organization, department, or work group. As we will show, OD interventions emphasize improving group effectiveness, intergroup relations, and the health of the overall organization. Efforts to change individual behavior alone, while occasionally part of OD programs, tend to get less attention. Table 15–1 summarizes the positive outcomes that can result from successful OD interventions.

TABLE 15–1
Ten Positive Results from OD

---

1. Improved organizational effectiveness (increased productivity and morale; more effective goal setting, planning, and organizing; clearer goals and responsibilities; better utilization of human resources; and bottom-line improvements)
2. Better management from top to bottom
3. Greater commitment and involvement from organizational members in making the organization successful
4. Improved teamwork within and between groups
5. A better understanding of an organization and its strengths and weaknesses
6. Improvement in communications, problem solving, and conflict resolution skills, resulting in increased effectiveness and less wasted time from communications breakdowns, game playing, and win-lose confrontations
7. Efforts to develop a work climate that encourages creativity and openness, provides opportunities for personal growth and development, and rewards responsible and healthy behavior
8. A significant decrease in dysfunctional behavior
9. Increased personal and organizational awareness that improves the organization's ability to adapt to a continuously changing environment and to continue to grow, learn, and stay competitive.
10. The ability to attract and keep healthy and productive people

---

Source: *MODMAN: Managing Organization Change and Development* by D. D. (Don) Warrick, p. 10. Copyright © Science Research Associates, Inc., 1984. Reprinted by permission of the publisher.

OD AND ORGANIZATIONAL CULTURE

OD values are not compatible with every organization's culture! OD embraces the values of collaboration, confrontation, authenticity, trust, support, and openness. These, however, are at odds with cultures that are characterized as high in structure, low in support, intolerant of conflicts, and risk aversive.

OD is clearly more compatible with organic structures and Theory Y assumptions (see Chapter 5) about human nature than mechanistic designs and Theory X assumptions. Of course, a large proportion of organizations in North America are bureaucratically structured, with extensive formalization and centralized decision power. These organizations might benefit most from having OD programs yet, paradoxically, they are also the type of organizations that are also most likely to resist OD values and make interventions difficult, if not impossible. Our point is that OD success is, to a large degree, dependent on the mesh between OD's values and those of the organization. Efforts to impose OD values in an alien culture are very likely to result in failure.

OD INTERVENTIONS

What are some of the OD techniques for bringing about change? In this section, we'll review the more popular intervention techniques. For simplicity and clarity, they have been categorized as either structural or human process.[7]

Structural Techniques

The OD techniques that fall within the structural category affect work content and relationships among workers. To review these techniques in detail would repeat concepts discussed previously, but a quick overview may be helpful.

Planned changes in the organization's formal structure—that is, altering its degree of complexity, formalization, and centralization—represent structural OD interventions. For instance, departmental responsibilities can be combined, vertical layers removed, and spans of control widened so as to make the organization flatter and less bureaucratic. The number of rules and procedures can be reduced to increase employee autonomy. An increase in decentralization can be made to speed up the decision-making process.

Job redesign options—job rotation, work modules, job enlargement, job enrichment, integrated and autonomous work teams, quality circles, the compressed workweek, and flextime—all are structural OD techniques. They could have just as accurately been discussed in this section rather than as redesign options in Chapter 12.

Human resource programs in training and career development might also be broadly interpreted to be structural OD techniques. Finally, efforts to modify an organization's culture—through creating new rituals, redesigning socialization processes, or changing the reward system—could be labeled as structural interventions.

Human Process Techniques

The vast majority of OD intervention efforts have been directed at changing the attitude and behavior of organization members through the processes of communication, decision making, and problem solving. The five most popular techniques are sensitivity training, survey feedback, process consultation, team building, and intergroup development. For the most part, each emphasizes participation and collaboration.

SENSITIVITY TRAINING

It can go by a variety of names—laboratory training, sensitivity training, encounter groups, or T-groups (training groups)—but all refer to a method of changing behavior through unstructured group interaction. Members are brought together in a free and open environment in which participants discuss themselves and their interactive processes, loosely directed by a professional behavioral scientist. The group is process oriented, which means that individuals learn through observing and participating rather than being told. The professional creates the opportunity for participants to express their ideas, beliefs, and attitudes. He or she does not accept—in fact, overtly rejects—any leadership role.

The objectives of the T-groups are to provide the subjects with increased awareness of their own behavior and how others perceive them, greater sensitivity to the behavior of others, and increased understanding of group processes. Specific results sought include increased ability to empathize with others, improved listening skills, greater openness, increased tolerance of individual differences, and improved conflict resolution skills.

If individuals lack awareness of how others perceive them, then the successful T-group can effect more realistic self-perceptions, greater group cohesiveness, and a reduction in dysfunctionnal interpersonal conflicts. Further, it will ideally result in a better integration between the individual and the organization.

SURVEY FEEDBACK

One tool for assessing attitudes held by organizational members, identifying discrepancies among member perceptions, and solving these differences is the survey feedback approach.

Everyone in an organization can participate in survey feedback, but of key importance is the organizational family—the manager of any given unit and those employees who directly report to him or her. A questionnaire is usually completed by all members in the organization or unit. Organization members may be asked to suggest questions or may be interviewed to determine what issues are relevant. The questionnaire typically asks members for their perceptions and attitudes on a broad range of topics—such as decision-making practices; communication effectiveness; coordination between units; and satisfaction with the organization, job, peers, and their immediate supervisor.

The data from this questionnaire are tabulated with data pertaining to an individual's specific "family" and to the entire organization and distributed to employees. These data then become the springboard for identifying problems and clarifying issues that may be creating difficulties for people. In some cases, the manager may be counseled by an external change agent about the meaning of the responses to the questionnaire and may even be given suggested guidelines for leading the organizational family in group discussion of the results. Particular attention is given to the importance of encouraging discussion and ensuring that discussions focus on issues and ideas and not on attacking individuals.

Finally, group discussion in the survey feedback approach should result in members identifying possible implications of the questionnaire's findings. Are people listening? Are new ideas being generated? Can decision making, interpersonal relations, or job assignments be improved? Answers to questions like these, it is hoped, will result in the group agreeing upon commitments to various actions that will remedy the problems that are identified.

PROCESS CONSULTATION

No organization operates perfectly. Managers often sense that their unit's performance can be improved, but they are unable to identify what can be improved and how it can be improved. The purpose of process consultation is for an outside consultant to assist a client, usually a manager, "to perceive, understand, and act upon process events" with which he or she must deal.[8] These might include work flow, informal relationships among unit members, and formal communication channels.

Process consultation (PC) is similar to sensitivity training in its assumption that organizational effectiveness can be improved by dealing with interpersonal problems, and in its emphasis on involvement. But PC is more task directed than sensitivity training.

Consultants in PC are there to "give the client 'insight' into what is going on around him, within him, and between him and other people."[9] They do not solve the organization's problems. Rather, the consultant is a guide or coach who advises on the process to help the client solve his or her own problems.

The consultant works with the client in *jointly* diagnosing what processes need improvement. The emphasis is on "jointly," because the client develops a skill at analyzing processes within his or her unit that can be continually called on long after the consultant is gone. Additionally, by having the client actively participate in both the diagnosis and the development of alternatives, there will be greater undestanding of the process and the remedy and less resistance to the action plan chosen.

Importantly, the process consultant need not be an expert in solving the particular problem that is identified. The consultant's expertise lies in diagnosis and developing a helping relationship. If the specific problem uncovered requires technical knowledge outside both the client and consultant's expertise, the consultant helps the client to locate such an expert and then instructs the client in how to get the most out of this expert resource.

TEAM BUILDING

Organizations are made up of people working together to achieve some common end. Since people are frequently required to work in groups, considerable attention has been focused in OD on team building.[10]

Team building can be applied within groups or at the intergroup level where activities are interdependent. For our discussion, we shall emphasize the intragroup level and leave intergroup development to the next section. As a result, our interest concerns applications to organizational families (command groups), as well as communities, project teams, and task groups.

Not all group activity has interdependence of functions. To illustrate, consider a football team and a track team:

> Although members on both teams are concerned with the team's total output they function differently. The football team's output depends synergistically on how well each player does his particular job in concert with his teammates. The quarterback's performance depends on the performance of his linemen and receivers, and ends on how well the quarterback throws the ball, and so on. On the other hand, a track team's performance is determined largely by the mere addition of the performances of the individual members.[11]

Team building is applicable to the case of interdependence, such as in football. The objective is to improve coordinative efforts of team members which will result in increasing the group's performance.

The activities considered in team building typically include goal setting, development of interpersonal relations among team members, role analysis to clarify each member's role and responsibilities, and team process analysis. Of course, team building may emphasize or exclude certain activities depending on the purpose of the development effort and the specific problems with which the team is confronted. Basically, however, team building attempts to use high interaction among group members to increase trust and openness.

It may be beneficial to begin by having members attempt to define the goals and priorities of the group. This will bring to the surface different perceptions of what the group's purpose may be. Following this, members can evaluate the group's performance—how effective are they in structuring priorities and achieving their goals? This should identify potential problem areas. This self-critique discussion of means and ends can be done with members of the total group present or, where large size impinges on a free interchange of views, may initially take place in smaller groups followed up by the sharing of their findings with the total group.

Team building can also address itself to clarifying each member's role in the group. Each role can be identified and clarified. Previous ambiguities can be brought to the surface. For some individuals, it may offer one of the few opportunities they have had to think through thoroughly what their job is all about and what specific tasks they are expected to carry out if the group is to optimize its effectiveness.

Still another team building activity can be similar to that performed by the process consultant, that is, to analyze key processes that go on within the team to identify the way work is performed and how these processes might be improved to make the team more effective.

INTERGROUP DEVELOPMENT

A major area of concern in OD is the dysfunctional conflict that exists between groups. As a result, this has been a subject to which change efforts have been directed.

Intergroup development seeks to change the attitudes, stereotypes, and perceptions that groups have of each other. For example, in one company the engineers saw the accounting department as composed of shy and conservative types, and the personnel department as having a bunch of ''smiley types who sit around and plan company picnics.'' Such stereotypes can have an obvious negative impact on the coordinative efforts between the departments.

Although there are a number of approaches for improving intergroup relations,[12] a popular method emphasizes problem solving.[13] In this method, each group meets independently to develop lists of its perception of themselves, the other group, and how they believe the other group perceives them. The groups then share their lists, after which similarities and differences are discussed. Differences are clearly articulated, and the groups look for the causes of the disparities.

Are the groups' goals at odds? Were perceptions distorted? On what basis were stereotypes formulated? Have some differences been caused by misunderstandings of intentions? Have words and concepts been defined differently by each group? Answers to questions like these clarify the exact nature of the conflict. Once the causes of the difficulty have been identified, the groups can move to the integration phase—working to develop solutions that will improve relations between the groups.

Subgroups, with members from each of the conflicting groups, can now be created for further diagnosis and to begin to formulate possible alternative actions that will improve relations.

EVALUATING OD EFFECTIVENESS

Do OD interventions work? Let's first review the research results and then look at the quality of the research that the findings are based upon.

Review of the Research

Consistent with the previous section's emphasis on human process techniques, we'll focus our attention on how effective these techniques are in achieving their objectives.

SENSITIVITY TRAINING

Research investigations into sensitivity training indicate that it can effectively change individual behavior. However, the impact of these changes on performance is inconclusive,[14] and the technique is not devoid of psychological risks. There have been cases reported of personality damage to those who were not adequately screened prior to participation. One study found that 19 percent, almost one out of five, of group participants suffered from negative psychological effects some six to eight months after the group met and nearly one out of ten had suffered serious psychological harm.[15]

"The evidence, though still limited, is reasonably convincing that T-group training and the laboratory method do induce behavioral changes in the 'back-home' setting."[16] But behavioral change means little unless we know what kind of change will be achieved. It has been argued by some, for instance, that there is no "typical" pattern of change; rather, there is a unique response for each individual.[17]

> If this is true, the present lack of knowledge about how individual differences variables interact with training program variables makes it nearly impossible for anyone to spell out ahead of time the outcomes to be expected from any given development program. That is, if training outcomes are truly unique and unpredictable, no basis exists for judging the potential worth of T-group training from an institutional or organizational point of view. Instead, its success or failure must be judged by each individual trainee in terms of his own personal goals.[18]

To summarize the results from sensitivity training, we find that the process changes behavior. Just specifically what that change means, however, in terms of on-the-job behavior, is still the subject of considerable debate.

SURVEY FEEDBACK

What does the general evidence demonstrate about survey feedback? We find that survey feedback meetings can lead to attitudinal changes by participants. Satisfaction, positive attitudes toward work and one's supervisor, and involvement in the organization have been shown to increase as a result of group discussion surrounding the survey results.[19] However, the manager of the organizational family can undermine the process. If the results are perceived as threatening, it has been suggested that managerial peer groups be formed to review and discuss findings before meeting with their subordinates in family groups.[20]

While the survey feedback approach changes attitudes, long-term changes in behavior have not resulted from mere group discussion of the results. There is, in fact, "little evidence that survey feedback alone leads to changes in individual behavior or organizational performance."[21] Discussion and involvement will not bring about the desired changes if the discussion fails to initiate follow-up actions.[22]

PROCESS CONSULTATION

A review of six applications of the process consultation intervention found strong, but not overwhelming, support.[23] One of the applications achieved highly positive results. Three obtained mixed results; however, there was a definite balance to the positive side. The remaining applications split between "not appreciable effects" and a "negative impact." So while the effects ranged from highly positive to negative, two-thirds of the interventions demonstrated positive results.

TEAM BUILDING

A review of fifty-six team building interventions found encouraging results—90 percent of the interventions obtained positive effects.[24] Other reports indicate that team building is effective in increasing member involvement and participation in group activities and in improving the effectiveness of meetings.[25] While participant attitudes are affected by team building, researchers suggest that it is unclear "what effects group development has on actual task performance."[26]

INTERGROUP DEVELOPMENT

The final intervention, intergroup development, shows generally positive effects—better than 83 percent of these interventions got favorable evaluations—but 11 percent were negative.[27] Most of the positive results relate to attitudes, and we need to be careful about concluding the effects of intergroup development activities on individual behaviors or organization performance.[28]

Is the Research Tainted?

While the previous research is generally positive in its evaluation of OD interventions, there is growing concern that the research studies have not given a balanced appraisal of OD's effectiveness. The focus of this concern has essentially been directed at the diversity of methodological rigor used in the research reports. This has led one reviewer to argue that the more rigorous the research, the more likely the results are to show negative findings.[29] In other words, one of the possible explanations for most of the positive findings regarding OD interventions may be the predominance of weak or loose methodologies.

Evaluations of OD programs can be categorized as either "hard" or "soft" depending on the criteria used to assess effectiveness. Hard criteria are quantitative measures of job behavior or organizational performance. In contrast, soft criteria include anecdotal data, observational information, and measures of job satisfaction. Soft criteria appear to be more widely used in evaluation of OD programs, which can have the effect of biasing the results toward the positive side. It may well be that OD's success record is based more on the tendency of OD change agents to evaluate the results of their efforts by using anecdotes and attitude measures than the actual value of the interventions themselves.

If it's true that there is a bias toward positive findings in OD research, what's the cause? OD efforts may be more readily connected to satisfaction than hard measures of performance. Change agents may favor soft-positive results rather than hard-negative ones because they want to continue to sell their OD programs to clients, and positive results are a lot easier to sell. Still another possibility is that the bias lies in what gets published. Papers reporting positive findings are more likely to be published even if they contain some methodological shortcomings, while studies finding nonsignificant or negative results need to demonstrate a strong design to be considered for publication.[30]

Further investigation of this positive-bias phenomenon is certainly necessary. In the meantime, it's probably a good idea to look critically at the results of OD interventions to assess how these results were achieved and, specifically, the effectiveness criteria chosen in evaluating the changes.

IMPLICATIONS FOR PERFORMANCE AND SATISFACTION

Changes occur outside organizations that require internal adaptation. Deregulation in the banking industry, for example, is dramatically changing the rules of the game at places like Citicorp and Bank of America. Cable television is rapidly producing new competitors for the three traditional television networks: ABC, CBS, NBC. If organizations fail to implement changes to adapt to their environments, their future survival can be at stake. Similarly, internal forces—like modifications in the organization's strategy, the makeup of its work force, or the introduction of new equipment—requires the implementation of planned change. Employees must adapt to these changes or their performance will suffer.

We've discussed, in this chapter, structural and behavioral techniques for bringing about change, as well as offering suggestions on how organizations can better process change. Unfortunately, a lot of the evaluative studies of OD interventions lack rigor—relying heavily on case studies and anecdotal data for support. If we acknowledge that research in this area is far from flawless, what *can* we say about OD in its relation to behavior and attitudes? First, let's look at structural techniques. A review of a number of studies found 62 percent and 43 percent showed significant improvement for absenteeism and turnover, respectively. Quantity of productivity was significantly higher in 40 percent of the studies.[31] In regards to human process approaches, 71 and 57 percent of these studies showed significant improvement for absenteeism and turnover, respectively; with half showing major gains in productivity.[32] Another review of studies found overall employee satisfaction improved 38 percent of the time with human process interventions, although there were greater changes appearing in satisfaction with the organization, security, and pay than in the job itself.[33]

Maybe one of the strongest cases for the effectiveness of OD values is a review of more than five hundred studies, covering tens of thousands of employees, where change agents moved organizations from having authoritarian to participative climates.[34] One to two years after the change, productivity and earnings in the organizations improved 15 to 40 percent, while control organizations that didn't undergo the change interventions failed to generate such improvements.

POINT

OD IS A ONE-TECHNIQUE SOLUTION

Organizational development concentrates largely on having people express themselves to each other about their mutual working interests and problems, on working together on the resolution of common problems, and on having people weigh out loud and with each other their organizational aspirations and goals. Much of OD seems to hinge on one device—confrontation—for all problems. Further, it is presumed that the same general methods will apply to all organizations.

As any skilled clinician knows, not all patients will prosper equally well with the same therapy. The skilled clinician has a range of therapies and chooses the one that best fits the problem. He diagnoses the problem and selects the solution that is most appropriate. Little of what is presently called organizational development involves anything like formal diagnosis.

A formal diagnosis requires a comprehensive examination of the client's system. Unfortunately, formal diagnosis does not seem to be an intrinsic part of contemporary OD. There are a number of reasons why this is so. There is no systematic body of professional knowledge about organizational development. Most techniques are ad hoc, with limited rationale. Many, if not most, people who work with OD have had limited training. Many lean heavily on psychological clichés or slogans derived from practices used in psychological research, without refining these practices into formulations that create the conditions for intervention. Finally, as already stated, much of OD hinges on confrontation as the single device to solve any problem. In that sense, it has become merely a gimmick.

The state of affairs described here inevitably leads to certain kinds of failures, disillusionments, destructive consequences, and other negative outcomes. This, in turn, will ultimately cause organizations and managers to think unfavorably of organizational development and to withdraw their support from change agents who advocate OD. A couple of examples will support the point.

A major division of a large corporation hired an OD consultant to "open things up" to foster group cooperation. The change agent's efforts led to the removal of the division head when it was discovered that he had manipulated and exploited his subordinates. The consultant had only made employees in this division more potentially vulnerable to exploitation. He would have been better off to have taught these people to be more guarded and protected.

Another effort in a company to "open people up" utilized encounter experiences that involved having the executives get closer to each other. Two executives, who had latent homosexual impulses could not tolerate the closeness, had breakdowns, and had to be hospitalized.

Adapted from H. Levinson, "The Clinical Psychologist as Organizational Diagnostician," Profes-sional Psychology, Winter 1972, pp. 32–40. With permission.

COUNTERPOINT

IN DEFENSE OF OD PRACTICES

It's a gross overgeneralization to assert that much of OD hinges on a single device—confrontation. While it is true that some very successful OD change agents rely on one preprogrammed "game plan," it is far from accurate to assert that any one technique dominates the field. One need only examine the literature to see this. One set of researchers described in detail a successful OD program that included only one sensitivity training intervention, at an early stage, and utilized a great variety of very different techniques and interventions. An excellent review of the wide range of OD techniques included such diverse methods as group therapy, survey feedback, and the balancing of the social with the technological system. Recently developed strategies, such as management by objectives, and human resources accounting can properly be called innovations in OD methodologies. If any single factor in OD practice is most clear it is that an effective OD practitioner is familiar with and can use a variety of techniques, selecting appropriate interventions on the basis of good diagnosis of the system.

It is not difficult to cite "horror stories" where a failure to diagnose or an inaccurate diagnosis led to results damaging to the client system and sometimes to the OD practitioner. There is no argument that diagnosis is a crucial phase in an OD intervention. But the argument that "little of what is presently called organizational development involves anything like formal diagnosis" is debatable. It certainly is not proven by a few case histories. The same is true, of course, for the opposite assertion. A few case histories involving extensive, well-designed diagnostic procedures will not prove that most OD involves formal diagnostic efforts. But numerous cases demonstrate that OD change agents make use of formal diagnostic methods and choose their intervention technique to reflect the uniqueness of the problem and situation.

Adapted from M. Sashkin, ''Organization Development Practices,'' Professional Psychology, *May 1973, pp. 187–94. With permission.*

FOR DISCUSSION

1. What is the relationship between OD and organizational adapatability?
2. Describe the change process.
3. Why do people resist change?
4. What differentiates OD from any change activity?
5. Describe four benefits that would accrue from a successful OD intervention.
6. What impact does an organization's culture have in determining whether OD will be successful?
7. What is sensitivity training? How effective is it in changing attitudes and job behavior?
8. Contrast survey feedback, process consultation, and team building.
9. Are some organizations more likely to require planned change interventions than others? If so, why?
10. Who plays the role of change agent in an organization?
11. What can a change agent do to deal with change resistance?
12. What criticisms might you lodge against those who argue that there are numerous research studies to support the effectiveness of OD interventions?

FOR FURTHER READING

BOWERS, D. G., "Organizational Development: Promises, Performances, Possibilities," *Organizational Dynamics,* Spring 1976, pp. 50–62. Notes that promises of OD have generally gone unfulfilled; its performances are spotty. Suggests what went wrong and what should be done for OD to reach its potential.

FAUCHEUX, C., G. AMADO, and A. LAURENT, "Organizational Development and Change." In M. R. Rosenzweig and L. W. Porter (eds.), *Annual Review of Psychology,* Vol. 33, pp. 343–70. Palo Alto, Calif.: Annual Reviews, 1982. Updates OD literature and expands review to include thinking and research outside North America.

FRENCH, W. L., and C. H. BELL, JR., *Organization Development: Behavioral Science Interventions for Organization Improvements,* 3rd ed. Englewood Cliffs, N.J.: Prentice-Hall, 1982. Reviews OD theory and practice. This popular introductory text includes a section that assesses research on OD.

MIRVIS, P., and D. BERG (eds.), *Failures in Organization Development and Change: Cases and Essays for Learning.* New York: John Wiley, 1977. Collection of cases and essays where OD failed. Also includes an analysis of why each OD effort failed and what was learned as a result.

WARRICK, D. D., and J. T. THOMPSON, "Still Crazy After All These Years," *Training and Development Journal,* April 1980, pp. 16–22. Notes discrepancies between traditional OD values and theories and what happens in practice.

WOODWORTH, W., G. MEYER, and N. SMALLWOOD, "Organization Development: A Closer Scrutiny," *Human Relations,* April 1982, pp. 307–19. Examines the conceptual roots of OD theory for their ideological bias; highlights value problems confronting the OD practitioner; and discusses resulting implications for OD.

NOTES FOR CHAPTER 15

1. P. S. Goodman and L. B. Kurke, "Studies of Change in Organizations: A Status Report," in P. S. Goodman (ed.), *Change in Organizations* (San Francisco: Jossey-Bass, 1982), pp. 1–2.
2. W. French, *The Personnel Management Process,* 3rd ed. (Boston: Houghton Mifflin, 1974), p. 56.
3. W. W. Burke, *Organization Development: Principles and Practices* (Boston: Little, Brown, 1982), pp. 51–52.
4. Ibid.
5. K. Lewin, *Field Theory in Social Science* (New York: Harper & Row, 1951).
6. J. P. Kotter and L. A. Schlesinger, "Choosing Strategies for Change," *Harvard Business Review,* March–April 1979, pp. 106–14.
7. This categorization was adapted from F. Friedlander and L. D. Brown, "Organizational Development," in M. R. Rosenzweig and L. W. Porter (eds.), *Annual Review of Psychology* (Palo Alto, Calif.: Annual Reviews, 1974), pp. 313–41.
8. E. H. Schein, *Process Consultation: Its Role in Organizational Development* (Reading, Mass.: Addison-Wesley, 1969), p. 9.
9. Ibid.
10. See, for instance, K. P. DeMeuse and S. J. Liebowitz, "An Empirical Analysis of Team-Building Research," *Group and Organization Studies,* September 1981, pp. 357–78; and S. J. Liebowitz and K. P. DeMeuse, "The Application of Team-Building," *Human Relations,* January 1982, pp. 1–18.
11. N. Margulies and J. Wallace, *Organizational Change: Techniques and Applications* (Glenview, Ill.: Scott, Foresman, 1973), pp. 99–100.
12. See, for example, E. H. Neilsen, "Understanding and Managing Intergroup Conflict," in J. W. Lorsch and P. R. Lawrence (eds.), *Managing Group and Intergroup Relations* (Homewood, Ill.: Irwin-Dorsey, 1972), pp. 329–43.
13. R. R. Blake, J. S. Mouton, and R. L. Sloma, "The Union-Management Intergroup Laboratory: Strategy for Resolving Intergroup Conflict," *Journal of Applied Behavioral Science,* No. 1 (1965), pp. 25–57.
14. J. P. Campbell and M. D. Dunnette, "Effectiveness of T-Group Experience in Managerial Training and Development," *Psychological Bulletin,* August 1968, pp. 73–104.
15. M. A. Lieberman, I. D. Yalom, and M. B. Miles, "Encounter: The Leader Makes a Difference," *Psychology Today,* March 1973, pp. 69–76.
16. J. P. Campbell, M. D. Dunnette, E. E. Lawler III, and K. E. Weick, Jr., *Managerial Behavior, Performance, and Effectiveness* (New York: McGraw-Hill, 1970), p. 323.

17. D. R. Bunker, "Individual Applications of Laboratory Training," *Journal of Applied Behavioral Science,* April–June 1965, pp. 131–47.
18. Campbell et al., *Managerial Behavior,* p. 323.
19. See, for example, D. G. Bowers, "O.D. Techniques and Their Results in 23 Organizations; the Michigan ICL Study," *Journal of Applied Behavioral Science,* January–February 1973, pp. 21–43; L. D. Brown, "Research Action: Organizational Feedback, Understanding, and Change," *Journal of Applied Behavioral Science,* November–December 1972, pp. 697–774; and J. M. Nicholas, "The Comparative Impact of Organization Development Interventions on Hard Criteria Measures," *Academy of Management Review,* October 1982, pp. 535–36.
20. C. P. Alderfer and R. Ferriss, "Understanding the Impact of Survey Feedback," in W. W. Burke and H. A. Hornstein (eds.), *The Social Technology of Organizational Development* (Fairfax, Va.: NTL Learning Resource Corp., 1972), pp. 234–43.
21. Friedlander and Brown, "Organizational Development," p. 327.
22. M. G. Miles, et al., "The Consequences of Survey Feedback: Theory and Evaluation," in W. G. Bennis, K. D. Benne, R. Chin (eds.) *The Planning of Change,* 2nd ed. (New York: Holt, Rinehart and Winston, 1969), pp. 456–68.
23. R. T. Golembiewski, C. W. Proehl, Jr., and D. Sink, "Estimating the Success of OD Applications," *Training and Development Journal,* April 1982, p. 91.
24. Ibid.
25. Friedlander and Brown, "Organizational Development," p. 328.
26. Ibid., p. 329.
27. Golembiewski, et al., "Estimating the Success of OD Applications."
28. Friedlander and Brown, "Organizational Development," p. 330.
29. D. E. Terpstra, "Relationship Between Methodological Rigor and Reported Outcomes in Organization Development Evaluation Research," *Journal of Applied Psychology,* October 1981, pp. 541–43.
30. B. M. Bass, "Issues Involved in Relations Between Methodological Rigor and Reported Outcomes in Evaluations of Organizational Development," *Journal of Applied Psychology,* February 1983, pp. 197–99; and R. J. Bullock and D. J. Svyantek, "Positive-Findings Bias in Positive-Findings Bias Research," *Proceedings of the Academy of Management,* New York: August 1983, pp. 221–24.
31. J. M. Nicholas, "The Comparative Impact of Organization Development Interventions on Hard Criteria Measures," *Academy of Management Review,* October 1982, pp. 531–42.
32. Ibid.
33. J. I. Porras and P. O. Berg, "The Impact of Organization Development," *Academy of Management Review,* April 1978, pp. 249–66.
34. R. Likert, "Past and Future Perspectives on System 4," *Proceedings of the Academy of Management,* Orlando, Florida, 1977.

CASE IVA

DIFFERENT WAYS FOR HANDLING A CUTBACK

The recession of 1982 brought hard times to many companies, especially those in old, mature manufacturing industries, such as autos, steel, and rubber. This case illustrates how two Pennsylvania steel companies—we'll call them Acme and World—handled a common problem.

The problem was a significant decline in the demand for basic steel products. To keep losses to a minimum, both Acme and World Steel's management realized the necessity to cut costs. One of the major areas for cost cutting was direct labor. Both companies were nonunion, so labor costs were controllable by management. In the fall of 1982, when the cutback was considered, both firms employed approximately three thousand people.

Acme's management concluded that current production needs required only about eighteen hundred employees. A careful analysis of skill requirements, performance evaluation records, and seniority data led to a list of all of Acme's personnel, ranked by "dispensability." Given that 40 percent or twelve hundred employees were appraised as redundant, management advised the bottom twelve hundred on this list that they were being fired. Pink slips were enclosed in each's pay envelope on October 20. They were given two weeks' notice, plus one week of additional pay for each year of service.

World's situation was almost exactly the same as that of Acme. Forecasts of future demand indicated they were significantly overstaffed—with a reduction of 40 percent being the figure management has ascertained was necessary to match personnel needs with production demands. However, World's management had long advocated a no-layoff policy. Management believed that the firm had an obligation to its employees to provide long-term, stable employment. But costs had to be reduced. The solution was to impose an across-the-board cut in all employees' hours. The standard forty-hour week was reduced to twenty-four hours, thereby requiring everyone to suffer equally during this recessionary period. More important, from management's viewpoint, no one had to be laid off. The cost of World's decision was a bit higher than Acme's because of the continuance of payments for fringe benefits. The fringe benefits—insurance, sick leave accruals, and so on—were eliminated for those who were fired at Acme, but all of World's employees continued to receive their full benefits even though their hours were cut 40 percent. On the other hand, when or if business improved, World had all its employees on hand and ready to meet increased demand.

Questions

1. For which company would you have preferred working? Why?
2. How do you think each company's decision would impact employee (a) productivity, (b) absenteeism, (c) turnover, and (d) satisfaction?

3. Would your answers to Question 2 change if employees had had a voice in the decision? If so, how?
4. Why don't more firms use World's strategy for dealing with redundancy?

CASE IVB

THE NEW SWEAT SHOP

Davida Gabriel makes $9.00 an hour as a claims approver for Equitable Life Assurance Society's regional claims processing office in Syracuse, New York. She has recently voted, along with the majority of her co-workers, to join the Service Employees International Union. Her complaint is that her job, which is to key information into video display computer terminals and approve the release of payments to policyholders, has become extremely stressful.

"We call this place a sweat shop. Oh, it may look real nice here—clean and modern—but this place is like a nineteenth-century factory. When I begin every morning, they start clocking me. I have to follow rigid procedures. The computer keeps track of how many claims I process. Every minute of my work time is accounted for. I sit in front of this terminal for six hours a day, except for one fifteen-minute break. My back hurts after a few hours. I get sore arms, sore wrists, and my shoulders ache. My eyes get tired. But all the time I'm thinking about the pressure to hit my goals. At the end of every day, my supervisor gets a printout of my output. It shows my actual productivity against the time it should have taken. The computer also compares the two figures to produce a productivity score calculated to the second decimal point. The company is now planning to use these data in some formula that will determine our performance ratings and wage rates."

A spokesperson for Equitable claims that this automated system has tripled the productivity of some employees. He added: "This is the office of the future. We're automating everywhere we can. As a case in point, we've recently introduced a computer-controlled system for our telephone account specialists. Their job is to answer questions about accounts using video display terminals. We expect these people to pick up a call by the third ring. We've got a program that can hunt down the slowpokes for special attention from their supervisors."

Questions

1. What could management have done, if anything, to avoid these employees joining a union?
2. Could the selection process have reduced employee dissatisfaction with these jobs? Discuss.

3. Review Davida's job in terms of the job characteristics model. Could the job be improved upon?
4. How do computer-controlled jobs increase stress? Can this be reduced?
5. Is this situation appropriate for an OD intervention? Discuss.

CASE IVC

IT'S PERFORMANCE APPRAISAL TIME

Dana Ruff, manager for women's lingerie at the Macy's department store in San Francisco, always dreads November 1. That's the day that all managers are required to turn in performance appraisals on their employees. These appraisals become the major determinant of salary increases, decisions that are made in December and go into effect January 1.

"I can't think of any activity I dislike more in this job than doing the annual performance reviews," Dana related. "I see them as a no-win proposition. My poor performers fight the evaluations. They complain that I'm prejudiced, unobjective, overly picky. You name it, I've heard it all. They want to put the blame on anyone but themselves. And since I make the appraisals, I'm usually the target for most of the bitching. My good performers know they're doing a good job. There is nothing positive I can tell them that they don't expect. Their complaints are usually that I don't give them *enough* recognition. So, like I said, I can't win."

One of Dana's newer employees is one of her biggest problems. Shannon Hersch has been working for Dana and Macy's for seven months. In that short time, she has openly argued with Dana on a number of occasions, has bad-mouthed Dana within the department, and has made two formal complaints to the personnel office about the way Dana has treated her. As self-protection, Dana has taken to keeping a daily diary describing both the good and bad behaviors Shannon exhibits on the job.

Dana has been getting complaints from several of her people about Shannon. They say she is disruptive. She's negative about her job and even comments negatively on Macy's as a place to work. But Shannon has several friends in the department and she appears to be having an impact on them. Based on what she sees and hears down on the floor, Dana believes that Shannon is developing a coalition of marginal workers—those who have received negative appraisals. She notices that Shannon and three peers in the department regularly take coffee breaks and lunch together.

Dana is aware that her boss is watching her more closely as a result of the complaints made to personnel. She has eight full-time and ten part-time employees. It's October 25. Dana's appraisals of her employees are due within the week. Of course, Dana's own appraisal by her boss is due at the same time.

Questions

1. How do performance appraisals effect behavior?
2. Should Dana talk with her boss?
3. Should Dana talk with Shannon?
4. What do you think Shannon's strategy is?
5. How can Dana find out what impact Shannon is having on departmental performance and morale?

CASE IVD

IBM'S CORPORATE CULTURE

IBM's sales exceed $45 *billion* a year. Its worldwide operations employ in excess of 380,000 people. IBM's product lines range from $800 electric typewriters to data processing systems that sell for more than $100 million. It controls 40 percent of the worldwide market for computing equipment. The company is generally acknowledged to be one of the most successful and best managed corporations in America. Of course, it didn't achieve its stature solely on luck. The company obviously does a number of things that work. The following describes a few of the qualities that make IBM the unquestionable leader in its field.

Employee behavior at IBM is the product of its founder's philosophy. Thomas Watson had rules for almost everything. Dark business suits, white shirts, and striped ties were "the uniform." Drinking alcoholic beverages, even off the job, was prohibited. Employees were expected to accept frequent transfers—insiders liked to say that IBM stood for "I've Been Moved." Today, the rules are a bit less severe, but the conservative image is still there. Male sales personnel are expected to wear suits and ties when meeting customers, but shirts no longer have to be white. All employees are also subject to a 32-page code of business ethics.

IBM has always demonstrated a strong commitment to its employees. People get fired, but it has never laid off anyone to cut costs. Redundant employees are retrained and then reassigned. But this commitment is two way: IBM carefully screens job candidates to identify people who will grow with the company. New employees are expected to spend their working careers with IBM. Of course, it doesn't always work that way. Many employees leave voluntarily. The computer industry is largely made up of former IBM-ers. They fill senior executive slots at many of its competitors, and former IBM people are frequently the corporate decision makers who choose which computer system will be installed in their company.

Salaries and benefits at IBM are highly competitive. In several communities, IBM has its own country clubs and makes memberships available to employees for $5 a year. It is not surprising that this concern for its employees has led to a strongly committed work force. As a case in point, IBM has never had a union vote in any United States facility.

Part of IBM's success is also undoubtedly attributable to its commitment to service. Its sales personnel are the envy of the industry. They are thoroughly trained and highly knowledgeable. Most new employees spend much of their first six weeks in company-run classes. Managers are required to take at least forty hours of additional instruction.

Every year, IBM spends more than $500 million on employee education and training. Customers can feel confident that if they have a problem with IBM equipment, its sales and services personnel will be able to solve it.

The commitment to service is strongly customer focused. IBM spends heavily to acquire comprehensive and up-to-date market research data on potential customer needs. In contrast to many of its competitors, which have allowed technology to drive their product line, IBM has sought to let the customers determine what it will produce and sell.

But maintaining a successful record also requires change. IBM has recently demonstrated that it can and will adapt to changing conditions. Between 1981 and 1983, to foster innovation and flexibility, it set up fifteen small independent units within the company to investigate such fields as robotics, specialized equipment, and analytical instruments. Maybe its most significant departure from past tradition has been related to its commitment to compete in the personal computer market. The IBM PC is built largely from parts bought from outside suppliers, making its technical specifications available to other firms in order to stimulate compatible software and peripheral equipment, and is sold through retailers like Sears and Computerland—all of which are major departures from the IBM way of doing things. The company has even begun to offer discount prices to stimulate sales.

Questions

1. Describe IBM's structure. Does this structure inhibit (a) employee motivation, (b) employee innovation, or (c) organizational flexibility?
2. Describe IBM's culture.
3. How does IBM's selection criteria, socialization techniques, and reward system act to maintain its culture?

CASE IVE

IN SEARCH OF A 50 PERCENT INCREASE IN EFFICIENCY

Bill Richards was beaming. An organizational analyst for a major oil company, he had just put the finishing touches on a report he was sure would save the corporation a lot of money and give him the kind of visiblity at the head office that he felt he deserved.

Bill's proposal argued that the current usage of secretaries at the head office was inefficient. The report showed that in 1984, the corporation had 1,440 secretarial positions. This category had four subclasses—from entry-level typists (Secretary I) earning $810 to $1,240 a month, up to executive secretaries (Secretary IV), which paid $1,930 to $2,525 a month. The breakdown within classes found the following numbers at each level: Secretary I, 685; Secretary II, 517; Secretary III, 210; and Secretary IV, 28.

The total compensation cost, in 1984, for Secretary I through IV positions was $23.8 million. Bill's proposal basically restructures the use of secretaries. Secretaries III and IV would continue to be assigned to individual executives, but the first two levels would be reassigned from individual managers to a secretarial pool. Bill's analysis shows that a pool would increase efficiency by 50 percent. Specifically, he argues that the same amount of work could be handled by fewer than half of the 1,200 individuals currently at Secretary I and II levels. In dollars and cents, he calculates that the company would save between $8 and $9 million a year.

Bill's proposal and recommendations were received by his superiors with great enthusiasm. A three-month timetable was established in which the restructuring would occur. Consistent with company personnel policies, every effort would be made to protect all employees with more than one year of service. They would be offered transfers to one of the six production facilities or two marketing offices located within thirty miles of the company's head office.

Rumor of what soon became known as "The Richards Report" spread rapidly. Before top management even approved the document, detailed word of the report's contents had reached every secretary. The response by the secretaries was less than enthusiastic. Some said they would quit before being relegated to a secretarial pool. Many commented on losing the continuity of working for a single manager. Those with the lowest seniority complained of not wanting to be transferred to openings in the company's facilities out in the suburbs.

A year after restructuring began, Bill Richards submitted a follow-up report that included the following information:

Secretarial compensation had been reduced by $8.7 million a year.

625 Secretary I and II employees were transferred or voluntarily resigned during the first three months of the program.

Absences increased from an average of 0.7 days per employee per month before the restructuring to 1.8 afterward.

Voluntary turnover increased from 1.7 per 100 employees per month before the restructuring to 6.1 afterward.

Comments from management indicate no significant loss in quality of secretarial support, but a definite improvement in the speed in which requests are completed.

Questions

1. The savings due to restructuring are far less than $8.7 million. What other costs must be deducted to get a truer figure? Estimate these costs and compute the actual savings.
2. Explain how changes in technology may be able to offer insights into the secretaries' behavior.

CASE IVF

WHAT HAPPENED TO TEAM EFFORT?

Republic Avionics designs and manufacturers sophisticated electronic devices for aerospace use. More than 90 percent of Republic's work evolves out of subcontracting for major aerospace firms like Boeing, General Dynamics, Lockheed, and McDonnell Douglas. Founded in the late 1940s, the company grew to fifteen hundred employees by the mid-1960s and has been stable at this size ever since.

Republic's organization is designed around projects. When a contract is obtained, it is assigned to a project manager who, in turn, is supported by one or more assistant project managers. A typical project manager may oversee five or six projects at a time. The actual manufacturing of the electronic devices is done in the company's manufacturing division, which is headed by the director of manufacturing, Frank West. The director of manufacturing and project managers all report to a common boss—the vice-president of operations. Currently the vice-president of operations is Rob McDowell.

If each contract is to meet its time and quality objectives and come in within budget, the project manager must work closely with manufacturing. The importance of each is recognized at Republic. While the vice-president of manufacturing's annual salary of $120,000 is well above the average project manager's salary of $70,000, project managers earn more than second-level managers in the production function responsible for the manufacturing of the various components.

John Wilson had been hired by Republic in August 1984 to be a project manager. An engineer by training, he had established an impressive research record in the aerospace industry and Republic's top management considered itself lucky to have hired Wilson away from Zaron Industries, where he was a senior researcher in its electronic laboratories. Wilson was charged at Republic with supervising a number of projects, including a multimillion dollar subcontract for General Dynamics. Wilson was supported by Dave Brown, a twenty-six-year-old industrial engineeer with an M.B.A. who had recently been hired out of a prestigious graduate school of business. Dave Brown impressed a large number of people at Republic as being bright and extremely ambitious.

In February 1985, Rob McDowell was informed by the auditing department that Wilson's project for General Dynamics was well behind schedule and running 14 percent over cost estimates. When McDowall confronted Wilson, the latter was obviously surprised. "I've had no knowledge that the project is off schedule. My assistant, Dave Brown, has mentioned that he's had to stay on top of the production people to make sure our project gets high priority. In fact, he's written several rather strong letters under my signature to Frank West to keep him aware of our concern. But Dave's always said everything was O.K. and that he just had to push those guys over in manufacturing a bit more than they have become accustomed to." An inquiry by McDowell to Frank West got a curt reply, "Tell John Wilson to get off my rear. I've got over three dozen manufacturing projects to get done and his letters and those nasty phone calls from his assistant have caused my people to give his projects lowest priority.''

Questions

1. What is Wilson's responsibility? Has he done anything wrong?
2. What is Brown's responsibility? Has he done anything wrong?
3. How might organizational culture explain part of the current problems with the General Dynamic's project?
4. What can McDowell do to deal with the current problem?

EXERCISE IVA

Bureaucratic Orientation Test

Instructions. For each statement, check the response (either mostly agree or mostly disagree) that best represents your feelings.

	MOSTLY AGREE	MOSTLY DISAGREE
1. I value stability in my job.	——	——
2. I like a predictable organization.	——	——
3. The best job for me would be one in which the future is uncertain.	——	——
4. The U.S. Army would be a nice place to work.	——	——
5. Rules, policies, and procedures tend to frustrate me.	——	——
6. I would enjoy working for a company that employed 85,000 people worldwide.	——	——
7. Being self-employed would involve more risk than I'm willing to take.	——	——
8. Before accepting a job, I would like to see an exact job description.	——	——
9. I would prefer a job as a freelance house painter to one as a clerk for the Department of Motor Vehicles.	——	——
10. Seniority should be as important as performance in determining pay increases and promotion.	——	——
11. It would give me a feeling of pride to work for the largest and most successful company in its field.	——	——

12. Given a choice, I would prefer to make $30,000 per year as a vice-president in a small company to $35,000 as a staff specialist in a large company. ____ ____

13. I would regard wearing an employee badge with a number on it as a degrading experience. ____ ____

14. Parking spaces in a company lot should be assigned on the basis of job level. ____ ____

15. If an accountant works for a large organization, he or she cannot be a true professional. ____ ____

16. Before accepting a job (given a choice), I would want to make sure that the company had a very fine program of employee benefits. ____ ____

17. A company will probably not be successful unless it establishes a clear set of rules and procedures. ____ ____

18. Regular working hours and vacations are more important to me than finding thrills on the job. ____ ____

19. You should respect people according to their rank. ____ ____

20. Rules are meant to be broken. ____ ____

Turn to page 524 for scoring directions and key.

Source: A. J. DuBrin, *Human Relations: A Job Oriented Approach* © 1978, pp. 687–88. Reprinted with permission of Reston Publishing Co., a Prentice-Hall Co., 11480 Sunset Hills Road, Reston, Va. 22090.

EXERCISE IVB

Rate Your Job's Motivating Potential

Utilizing your current job or one you have held in the past, rate its key dimensions on a scale from 1 to 7 (7 being the highest degree):

1. To what degree does your job require you to perform a variety of different work activities and allow you to use a wide range of your skills and talents? ____

2. To what degree does your job allow you to do something from beginning to end that results in a visible outcome? ____

3. To what degree does your job have a substantial impact on the lives or work of other people? ____

4. To what degree does your job provide you with freedom and discretion to schedule your own work and to determine how it will be done? ____

5. To what degree does your job itself provide you with clear and direct feedback on how effective you are in performing your job? ____

Turn to page 525 for scoring directions and key.

EXERCISE IVC

Rate Your Classroom Culture

Listed here are eight statements. Score each statement by indicating the degree to which you agree with it. If you strongly agree, give it a 5. If you strongly disagree, give it a 1.

1. My classmates are friendly and supportive. ____
2. My teacher is friendly and supportive. ____
3. I expect my final grade will accurately reflect the effort I make. ____
4. My teacher clearly expresses his or her expectations to the class. ____
5. My teacher encourages me to question and challenge him or her as well as other students. ____
6. I think the grading system used by my teacher is based on clear standards of performance. ____
7. My teacher makes me want to learn. ____
8. My teacher would give everyone in the class an A if we all earned it. ____

Turn to page 525 for scoring directions and key.

EXERCISE IVD

Rate of Life-Change Test

Instructions. For each of the following events, circle its corresponding scale value if it applies to you during the past twelve months:

LIVE EVENT	SCALE VALUE
Death of spouse	100
Divorce	73
Marital separation	65
Jail term	63
Death of a close family member	63
Major personal injury or illness	53
Marriage	50
Fired from work	47
Marital reconciliation	45
Retirement	45
Major change in health of family member	44
Pregnancy	40

Sex difficulties	39
Gain of a new family member	39
Business readjustment	39
Change in financial state	38
Death of a close friend	37
Change to a different line of work	36
Change in number of arguments with spouse	35
Mortgage or loan for major purchase (home, etc.)	31
Foreclosure of mortgage or loan	30
Change in responsibilities at work	29
Son or daughter leaving home	29
Trouble with in-laws	29
Outstanding personal achievement	28
Wife begins or stops work	26
Begin or end school	26
Change in living conditions	25
Revision of personal habits	24
Trouble with boss	23
Change in work hours or conditions	20
Change in residence	20
Change in schools	20
Change in recreation	19
Change in church activities	19
Change in social activities	18
Mortgage or loan for lesser purchase (car, etc.)	17
Change in sleeping habits	16
Change in number of family get-togethers	15
Change in eating habits	15
Vacation	13
Christmas	12
Minor violations of the law	11

Turn to page 525 for scoring directions and key.

Source: L. O. Ruch and T. H. Holmes, "Scaling of Life Change: Comparison of Direct and Indirect Methods," *Journal of Psychosomatic Research,* June 1971, p. 224. Copyright 1971, Pergamon Press, Ltd. Reprinted by permission.

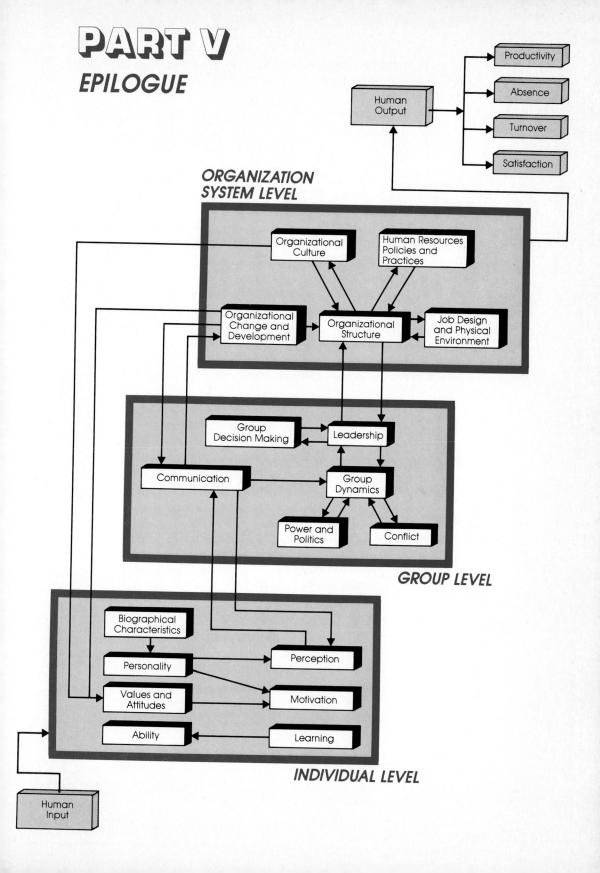

PART V
EPILOGUE

Human Output

Productivity

Absence

Turnover

Satisfaction

ORGANIZATION SYSTEM LEVEL

Organizational Culture

Human Resources Policies and Practices

Organizational Change and Development

Organizational Structure

Job Design and Physical Environment

GROUP LEVEL

Group Decision Making

Leadership

Communication

Group Dynamics

Power and Politics

Conflict

INDIVIDUAL LEVEL

Biographical Characteristics

Personality

Perception

Values and Attitudes

Motivation

Ability

Learning

Human Input

16

Summary and Selected Special Topics

AFTER STUDYING THIS CHAPTER, YOU SHOULD BE ABLE TO:

Define and explain the following key terms and concepts:

Dual-career couples

Individualism

Masculinity

Power distance

Two-tier pay systems

Uncertainty avoidance

Understand:

The primary and secondary variables that predict productivity, attendance, turnover, and satisfaction

The five distinct cross-national categories

The four dimensions inherent in a nation's culture

The U.S. culture using these four dimension

Five trends that impact OB

In our search to explain behavior, we've learned that it all depends. The trick is to know what it all depends *upon.*

—S.P.R.

We wrap up this book with an attempt to integrate what we've learned into some specific models. Then we review two special topics worthy of consideration. First, we look at OB in an international context. Most of the research findings cited in this book are based on U.S. employees. But the behavior of workers in New Delhi can be very different from their counterparts in New York. We'll show how national cultures differ and their implication on such issues as leadership, motivation, and job design. Second, we consider some issues with which the field of organizational behavior may become significantly more concerned over the next half-dozen years.

INTEGRATION

The field of organizational behavior is composed of an array of topics. There seems to be increasing agreement about what makes up the field, but we've made little progress in putting the topics together into some cohesive and logical whole. It's probably accurate to conclude that, at least at the current time, most scholars view the field of OB as being composed of a set of topics that are fragmented and isolated.[1]

We've tried to deal with this problem by developing an integrative model in Chapter 2 and using it throughout the book to show how the various concepts interrelate. We articulated the major objectives of OB—explaining and predicting employee productivity, absence, turnover, and satisfaction—and then proceeded to introduce individual-, group-, and organization system–level concepts that have various degrees of influence on our dependent variables. But we haven't gone far enough. We haven't, for instance, made it very clear which independent variables are primary and which are secondary in explaining and predicting each dependent variable. The reason, quite frankly, is that little research has been undertaken to sort out the strength of various variables in impacting on productivity, absence, turnover, and satisfaction. Any attempt at a comprehensive integration, therefore, would have to include a considerable degree of speculation.

Successful managers know that there is a point in many decisions where, after the data have been carefully reviewed, it is necessary to drop the safety of the facts and venture into the area of making judgments. We have reached such a place in this book. We have carefully scrutinized the research evidence, but there is no comprehensive integrative framework available that rank orders the independent variables we have reviewed. Yet you need such a framework if you are to understand fully the contents of this book. With the clear recognition that any effort to summarize, integrate, and weight our independent variables is fraught with danger, the following models are offered to help you put together the concepts presented in the prior chapters. Keep in mind as you review these models that they represent your author's judgments, derived from the research evidence, as to what variables are *most* relevant. There are other factors that influence our dependent variables but that have been omitted. We're not saying they are irrelevant or unimportant, only that the variables included here appear to offer more powerful explanations and predictions.

Productivity

Let's begin with employee productivity. Which of the independent variables that we have discussed are most important in determining this outcome? Figure 16–1 indicates that the primary determinants of an employee's productivity are his or her own ability and motivation level (shown in bold type). But, in addition, other variables moderate the impact.

At the individual level, we recognize the importance of perception and the personality-job fit as directly influencing an employee's motivation. Everything that happens at work is interpreted by the employee. It is filtered through the employee's perceptual system. Since employees behave based on their perceptions of the world rather than its reality, perceptions are a powerful moderator. Additionally, certain personalities are better matched to certain jobs. A poor match will suboptimize the employee's ability and reduce motivation. Group factors can aid or hinder an employee's productivity. The group's norms can stimulate employees to higher levels of outputs or restrict that output. The strength of these norms to impact behavior, however, will depend on the cohesiveness of the group. The more cohesive the group, the more influential will be its norms. Is the leadership style used by the employee's superior congruent with the employee's needs? The right leadership style will stimulate higher productivity. Is the conflict level within the employee's work group too high, too low, or at an appropriate level? At the extremes, conflict can hinder productivity.

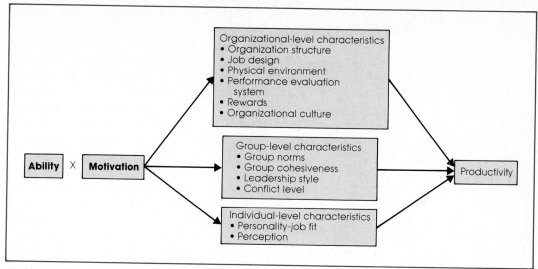

FIGURE 16–1
Explaining and Predicting Productivity

Finally, our model recognizes that the organization's structure, policies, procedures, and culture influence an employee's productivity. When properly conceived, the overall organizational structure, the specific job design, and the physical work environment can facilitate high productivity. Of course, if poorly designed, these same factors can restrict employees from reaching their full potential. The organization's performance evaluation and reward system is a critical element impacting on motivation and eventually productivity. If the evaluation system is seen as unfair, motivation will decline. Similarly, if rewards are not productivity based, they will not reinforce this behavior. Finally, the organization's culture is a strong force influencing employee productivity. Like group norms, the culture conveys to employees the importance placed on productivity.

Attendance

Figure 16–2 integrates what we've learned about the factors that most influence whether an employee attends or absents himself or herself from the workplace. Satisfaction with the job and the incentive/reward system variables are shown in bold type to emphasize their importance. The research demonstrates a consistent inverse relationship between satisfaction and absence. Similarly, the reward system has a strong impact: Do they reinforce attendance? If so, absenteeism should be kept relatively low. But, of course, other factors have been shown to influence the employee's decision to come to work. These include the job situation, employee values and job expectations, personal characteristics, pressures to attend, attendance motivation, and the ability to attend.

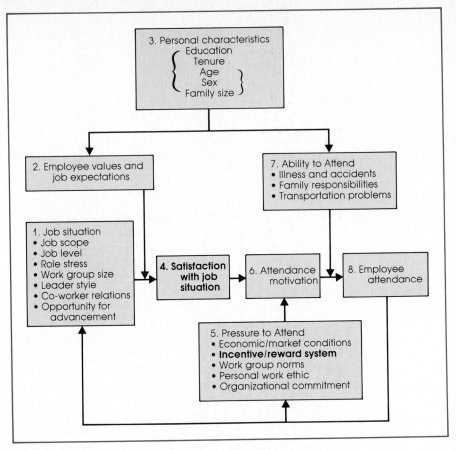

FIGURE 16–2
Explaining and Predicting Attendance

Source: R. M. Steers and S. R. Rhodes, "Major Influences on Employee Attendance: A Process Model," *Journal of Applied Psychology*, August 1978, p. 393. Emphasis made by the author. With permission.

Turnover

The evidence indicates that two attitudes—job satisfaction and intention to turnover or quit—are strongly related to actual turnover behavior. These are shown in bold type in Figure 16–3. This model also tells us things like the following: older, married employees, who have been with an organization for a long time, tend to be more stable. A poor fit between employees' personalities and their jobs will increase the search for alternatives. If the group to which the employees belong is cohesive and friendly, and there are colleagues who joined their work group at about the same time, the employees' propensity to think about quitting will be reduced. Further, the organization's structure, the characteristics of their job, the employees' felt stress, the performance evaluation and reward system, and the de-

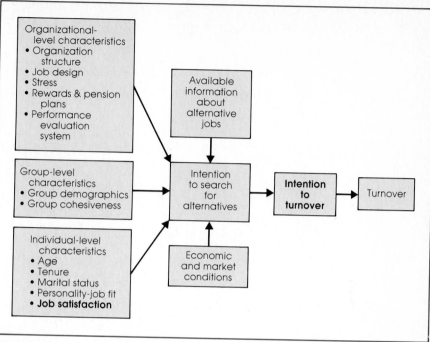

FIGURE 16–3
Explaining and Predicting Turnover

sign of the organization's pension plan will all influence the decision to look for alternatives. Finally, Figure 16–3 acknowledges that the existence of alternative job opportunities impact on the turnover decision. In good economic times, with a labor shortage, and where employees have ready access to information about alternative jobs, the employees' willingness to stay with their jobs—when the other factors are negative—will be clearly reduced.

Satisfaction

Our last dependent variable is job satisfaction. Figure 16–4 reviews the key variables that cause satisfaction. In Chapter 4, we noted the most important factors determining job satisfaction are mentally challenging work, equitable rewards, supportive working conditions, and supportive colleagues. These are represented in our model by job design, rewards, leadership style and the physical environment, and group cohesiveness (shown in bold type).

At the individual level, married employees tend to be more satisfied with their jobs. Additionally, perception is a key determinant. Since job satisfaction is an attitude, its formation is strongly influenced by how employees interpret their work situation. A favorable perception—regardless of actual conditions—will positively impact satisfaction.

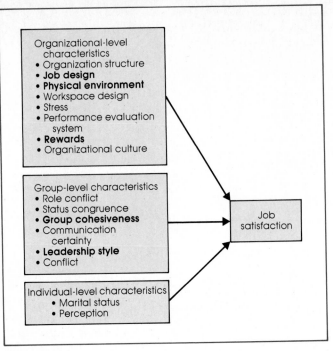

FIGURE 16–4
Explaining and Predicting Job Satisfaction

A large number of group variables have been found to be related to satisfaction. We can predict that satisfaction will be increased where role conflict is low, there is high status congruence, group members are supportive and cohesive, there is a minimun of ambiguity surrounding communications, superiors utilize the appropriate leadership style, and conflict levels are low.

At the organizational level, we would predict satisfaction to be positively influenced when the organization's structure fits the employee's preference for autonomy or certainty, the job scores high on the job characteristics model, the physical environment is supportive, workspace is adequate, job stress is low, the performance evaluation system is perceived as fair, rewards are equitable, and the match between the individual's values and those of the organization are high.

OB IN AN INTERNATIONAL CONTEXT

The vast majority of research studies that have provided the basis for the conclusions made in this book were conducted in the United States with American subjects. If people in all the nations of the world were similar, our U.S. findings would be generalizable to employees in any country. Unfortunately, there is a growing body of evidence to indicate that national cultures differ widely and the result is marked differences in behavior patterns worldwide. A comparison between the United States and Japan can illustrate this point.

American children are taught early the values of individuality and uniqueness. In contrast, Japanese children are indoctrinated to be "team players," to work within the group, and to conform. A significant part of an American student's education is to learn to think, analyze, and question. Their Japanese counterparts are rewarded for recounting facts. These different socialization practices result in different types of employees. The average U.S. worker is more competitive and self-focused than is the Japanese worker. Predictions of employee behavior, based on samples of U.S. workers, are likely to be off target when they are applied to a population of employees—like the Japanese—who prefer and perform better in standardized tasks, as part of a work team, with group-based decisions and rewards.

Cross-national Categories

The world is far from homogeneous. There are cultural differences between countries. Yet, each country is not completely unique. In recent years, considerable progress has been made in the area of cultural analysis. Research has demonstrated that countries can be grouped into meaningful categories or clusters, based on similar employee attitudes and behavior, which can then allow for generalization. Figure 16–5 depicts several cross-national categories—the results of comparative studies of employees in twenty-nine countries.[2] Using self-reported attitudes and expectations, five distinct clusters were established. Several countries—India, Brazil, Japan, and Israel—were found to be independent and, therefore, are excluded. The five clusters and a few representative countries are as follows:

Anglo American: United States, Great Britain, Canada, Australia, New Zealand
Nordic: Norway, Sweden, Denmark
Latin American: Mexico, Argentina, Chile, Peru
Latin European: France, Spain, Italy
Central European: Germany, Switzerland, Austria

These clusters reflect similar characteristics among employees, specifically, common values and attitudes. These, in turn, have been influenced by language similarities and geographic proximity. Based on these clusters, would it be safe to conclude that employees in the commonly grouped countries would behave similarly? The answer is a qualified "Yes." We qualify our answer because there is further research that adds to and modifies these categories.

Key Dimensions of National Cultures

One of the most illuminating cross-cultural studies of similarities and differences among employees has been done by Geert Hofstede.[3] He compared employees from forty countries, all of whom worked for the same large multinational cor-

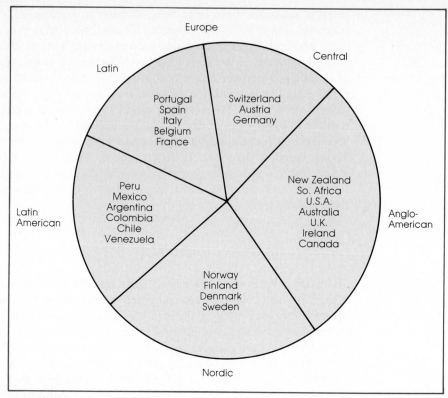

FIGURE 16–5

Cross-national Categories

Source: Adapted from S. Ronen and A. I. Kraut. "Similarities Among Countries Based on Employee Work Values and Attitudes," *Columbia Journal of World Business*, Summer 1977, p. 94. With permission.

poration. What he was looking for was the main criteria by which the national cultures in which these employees worked differed. Hofstede found four such criteria:

Power distance (PD): The extent to which a society accepts that power in institutions and organizations is distributed unequally.

Uncertainty avoidance (UA): The extent to which a society feels threatened by uncertain and ambiguous situations and tries to avoid these situations by providing greater career stability, establishing more formal rules, not tolerating deviant ideas and behaviors, and believing in absolute truths and the attainment of expertise.

Individualism (I): Individualism implies a loosely knit social framework in which people are supposed to only take care of themselves and their immediate families; its opposite is collectivism, which is characterized by a tight social framework in which people expect others in groups of which they are a part—family, organizations—to look after them. In exchange for this, they feel they owe absolute loyalty to the group.

Masculinity (M): The extent to which the dominant values in society are macho or masculine, that is, characterized by assertiveness, the acquisition of money and things, and *not* caring for others or for the quality of life.

Using these four dimensions, Hofstede found some distinct national cultural differences among employees. Before we review these differences, let's review his findings for the United States. We can then use them as a point of comparison.

The U.S. Culture: A Point of Departure

Comparing the forty countries on the four dimensions, Hofstede found the U.S. culture to rank as follows:

> PD = Below average
> UA = Well below average
> I = Highest among the forty countries
> M = Well above average

The results are not inconsistent with the world image of the United States. The below-average score on power distance aligns with what one might expect from a representative type of government with democratic ideals. In this category, the United States would rate below nations with a small ruling class and a large, powerless set of subjects, and above those nations with very strong commitments to egalitarian values. The well-below-average ranking on uncertainty avoidance is also consistent with a representative type of government having democratic ideals. Americans perceive themselves as being relatively free from threats of uncertainty. The individualistic ethic is one of the most frequently used stereotypes to describe Americans, and, based on Hofstede's research, the stereotype seems well founded. The United States was ranked as the single most individualistic country in his entire set. Finally, the well-above-average score on masculinity is no surprise. Capitalism—which values aggressiveness and materialism—is consistent with Hofstede's masculine characteristics.

Contrasting World Nations with the United States

We haven't the space to review the results Hofstede obtained for each of the forty countries, although some examples of extreme scores are presented in Table 16–1. Since our concern is essentially with identifying similarities and differences among cultures, let's briefly identify those countries that are most like and least like the United States on the four dimensions.

The United Sates is strongly individualistic but low on power distance. This same pattern was exhibited by Great Britain, Australia, Canada, the Netherlands, and New Zealand. Those least similar to the United States on these dimensions were Venezuela, Colombia, Pakistan, Singapore, and the Philippines.

The United States scored low on uncertainty avoidance and high on masculinity. The same pattern was shown by Ireland, Great Britain, Philippines, Can-

TABLE 16–1

Examples of Cultural Differences Among World Nations

CULTURAL CRITERION	HIGH	LOW
Power distance	Philippines Mexico Venezuela Yugoslavia	Austria Israel Denmark New Zealand
Uncertainty avoidance	Greece Portugal Belgium Japan	Singapore Denmark Sweden Hong Kong
Individualism	United States Australia Great Britain Canada	Colombia Venezuela Pakistan Peru
Masculinity	Japan Austria Venezuela Italy	Sweden Norway Yugoslavia Denmark

ada, New Zealand, Australia, India, and South Africa. Those least similar to the United States on these dimensions were Chile, Yugoslavia, and Portugal.

Some Selected Implications

The implications of the previous findings are relevant to many of the concepts introduced in this text. To illustrate this point, let's look at how our discussions of personality, motivation, leadership, organization structure, and job design might be modified when attempting to explain and predict the behavior of employees outside the United States.

PERSONALITY

While personalities vary across any population, American employees as a group will tend to be lower on authoritarianism (consistent with a below-average PD score) and higher on risk taking (based on low-UA and above-average masculinity scores) than their counterparts in most countries. In a comparative sense, you could expect to find more authoritarian personalities in Mexico and fewer risk takers in Japan.

MOTIVATION

A good illustration of national differences can be seen through Maslow's hierarchy of needs. The hierarchy argues that people start at the physiological level and then move progressively up the hierarchy in this order: physiological, safety, love, esteem, and self-actualization. This hierarchy, if it has any application at all, aligns with American culture. In countries like Japan, Greece, or Mexico, where UA characteristics are strong, security needs would be on top of the need hierarchy. Countries that score low on M characteristics—Denmark, Sweden, Norway, the Netherlands, and Finland—would have social needs on top.[4] We would predict, for instance, that group work will motivate employees more when the country's cultures score low on the M criterion.

Another motivation concept that clearly has a U.S. bias is the achievement need. The view that a high achievement need acts as an internal motivator presupposes two cultural characteristics—a willingness to accept a moderate degree of risk (which excludes countries with strong UA characteristics) and a concern with performance (countries with strong M characteristics). This combination is found exclusively in countries in the Anglo-American group and in some of their former colonies.[5]

LEADERSHIP

Our review of the leadership literature in Chapter 8 concluded that effective leaders don't use a single style. They adjust their style to the situation. While not mentioned explicitly in our earlier discussion, certainly national culture—as well as the internal organizational culture—is an important situational variable determining which leadership style will be most effective.

National culture impacts on leadership by way of the subordinate. A leader cannot choose his or her style at will: "What is feasible depends to a large extent on the cultural conditioning of a leader's subordinates."[6] For example, a manipulative or autocratic style is compatible with high PD, and we find a high PD in Latin American and Mediterranean countries. PD rankings should also be good indicators of employee willingness to accept participative leadership. Participation is likely to be most effective in low-PD cultures.

The implications of cross-cultural research for predicting leadership style are fairly straightforward. Effective leaders in high-PD cultures will tend to behave more autocratically, while effective leaders in very-low-PD cultures will rely on a participative style.

ORGANIZATION STRUCTURE

Size, technology, and environment were shown in Chapter 11 as major factors influencing the type of structure an organization has. Environment, of course, would include differences across national cultures.

In a country with a large PD rating, people prefer that decisions be centralized.[7] Similarly, UA characteristics relate to formalization. High UA relates to high formalization.[8] Based on these relationships, we find certain patterns. The French and Italians tend to create rigid bureaucracies, high in both centralization and formalization. In India, preference is given to centralization and low formalization. Germans prefer formalization with decentralization.[9]

Cultural differences might also be used to predict the acceptance or rejection of innovative structural designs. For instance, the matrix's dual command structure requires greater tolerance for ambiguity, so cultures high in UA characteristics may be less receptive to this structural design.

JOB DESIGN

As a final thought, we propose that the design of jobs around work teams will be more prevalent in cultures like Japan and less prevalent in places like India.

There are opposing forces operating in the U.S. culture working for and against group designs at the same time. You remember that the United States ranked below average on power distance and very high on individualism. The PD ranking would suggest the use of groups to equalize power, while the high score on individualism would suggest the opposite. In countries such as Japan, where collectivism values are much stronger than those in the United States, employees will prefer work team designs. In contrast, employees in India—where PD values are high—are likely to perform poorly in teams.

A LOOK INTO THE FUTURE

There are economic and social forces currently taking place that present interesting challenges to our further understanding of organizational behavior. In the following pages, we present several of these trends and offer some ideas on how they may impact on our desire to explain and predict organizational behavior.

Technology

"Technology is rapidly changing the way we live" has now become a cliché. Jobs in the 1990s are going to be different because of technology. The issue isn't if there is going to be change but, rather, what those changes might be. Two trends seem directly attributable to new technologies: (1) negative outcomes associated with video display terminals (VDTs) and (2) employees doing their work at home.

Even with improved workstation designs, we can expect increasing complaints from employees who spend their entire work day with video display units. Much is being learned about lighting, terminal support services, viewing distances, and work surfaces, but these jobs create employee discomfort. The result will be negative consequences: eye strain, body aches, anxiety, depression, alienation, and fatigue.[10] There are, in fact, already reports of above-normal absenteeism among VDT users.[11] The reality that more and more employees will be using VDTs will present challenges for job designers. Can the rigid work procedures, routineness, and lack of control in the jobs of VDT users be overcome?

Work, in the pre–Industrial Revolution period, was typically done at home. The Industrial Revolution made the factory economical, so people left their homes to produce goods under a common roof. The early part of this century saw another change: the creation of white-collar "factories"—offices where large numbers of people gathered to process paper. The next step, made possible by computer technology, is a return to working at home. Employees will be increasingly able to do their "paper processing" on computers at home, linked to co-workers and management by modems. It will no longer be necessary for millions of people to commute to work in the morning. They can merely slip into a bathrobe, go into their office at home, turn on their computers, and be "at work." Currently, approximately 2 million people work at home doing things like taking orders over the phone, filling out reports and other forms, and processing information. This is very likely to grow to 20 million by the year 2000. What will this mean for organizing work? Will this change the concept of an "organization"? Will people balk at losing the regular social contact that a formal office provides?

Productivity

There is increasing awareness that significant improvements in productivity are necessary if North American goods and services are to be competitive worldwide. Some of this improvement will result from expanded capital expenditures—new and more efficient machinery and equipment. But a good deal of this improvement will also have to come from better management of an organization's human resources. The fields of organizational behavior and personnel management offer a wealth of such ideas. The well-managed organizations will increasingly look to OB and personnel management research for answers on how to improve employee productivity.

Declining Organizations

The last half-dozen years has seen a dramatic increase in research on declining organizations.[12] The reason would appear to be the recognition that the environment has become more dynamic. The social, economic, and technological changes currently going on is a direct threat to thousands of organizations and, in some cases, entire industries. In the coming years, a number of large and prominent organizations will be forced into retrenchment. The implications for understanding organizational behavior are very real. Employees in organizations that are undergoing retrenchment face increased uncertainty. Are their jobs safe? Who, among their co-workers, might be laid off? Will they get a new boss? Will they have to learn a new job? A number of predictions appear warranted under such conditions.[13] Dysfunctional conflicts will increase as the battle over scarce resources intensifies. Resistance to change will increase as employees fear demotions or layoffs. Motivation will become more difficult as fear of being fired replaces anticipation of pay raises and promotions. Job satisfaction will decline. We would also predict that turnover will increase among the more mobile employees as they pursue jobs in organizations with greater opportunities.

Two-Tier Pay Systems

The search for increased economies in organizations that face retrenchment conditions is creating a new phenomenon—two-tier pay systems.[14]

How would you feel if you were a flight attendant for an airline, with two years' experience and making half the salary of flight attendants with your same airline who have three years' experience? Recent contract negotiations in a number of organizations have resulted in just such situations. To reduce future labor costs, new employees are hired at significantly lower wage rates than are those already employed. This protects employees already hired from pay cuts but still allows management to reduce labor expenses.

Should this practice become widespread, it has clear implications for employee motivation. Equity theory tells us that employees compare their input-outcome ratio against others. One of the most obvious "others" is co-workers. If you're doing the same job as someone else, for significantly less money, yet feel your background and experience are relatively similar, you're not likely to ignore this perceived discrepancy. We would predict that two-tier pay systems are likely to reduce job satisfaction for the lower-paid group and may well negatively impact on their productivity and attendance.

Dual-Career Couples

The majority of married women now have jobs outside the home. There is no reason to believe that this trend—toward the creation of dual-career couples—will lessen in the coming years. There are implications for understanding the concerns and behaviors of both the female and male elements in this arrangement.

The motivation of each party can be influenced by having an employed spouse. Money may be less of an incentive. Promotions that require moves become joint decisions that must consider the total financial implications on the couple and job opportunities for the spouse in the new location. On an individual basis, the working mother may need day care for her children. Organizations that provide such care, in house, will find it easier to acquire and retain women with preschool children. Two careers in one family also changes the responsibility of males with children. Dad is just as likely to stay home with a sick child as is mom! Absenteeism, caused by family responsibilities, will increasingly afflict working fathers as well as mothers.

A FINAL COMMENT

The end of a book frequently has the same meaning to an author that it has to the reader: It generates feelings of accomplishment and relief. As both of us rejoice a bit at having nearly completed our journey through the field of organizational behavior, this is a good time to examine where we have been and what it all means. We have reviewed a lot of theories and, as a noted social psychologist is reported to have said, "There is nothing so practical as a good theory." Of course, we could propose a corollary: "There is nothing so *impractical* as a good theory that leads nowhere." To avoid presenting theories that led nowhere, we offered a three-level, integrative building-block model and a wealth of examples and illustrations to help you see the linkage and practical implications of the theories.

Our major contention has been that organizational behavior is most easily understood by looking at it from three levels: the individual, the group, and the organization system. We started with the individual and attempted to review major psychological contributions to understanding why individuals act as they do. We then looked at groups and argued that the understanding of group behavior is more complex than merely multiplying what we know about individuals by the number of members in the group. We demonstrated that people act differently when in a group than when alone. Finally, we overlaid organizational constraints upon our knowledge of individual and group behavior to improve our understanding of organizational behavior.

Individually, the theories that we have presented offer you some insights into the behavior of people at work. However, together, the theories provide you with a complex system to explain and predict organizational behavior.

FOR DISCUSSION

1. What are the most important independent variables that affect (a) employee productivity, (b) attendance, (c) turnover, and (d) satisfaction?
2. How might the following concepts be modified in Sweden: (a) conflict, (b) reward systems, and (c) decision making?
3. How might the following concepts be modified in Mexico: (a) conflict, (b) reward systems, and (c) decision making?
4. How could you use Hofstede's research if you were an American manager transferred to a foreign country?
5. Describe the U.S. culture in terms of the four major criteria by which cultures tend to differ.
6. In which countries are employees *most* like those in the United States? *Least* like those in the United States?
7. Would you prefer to work at home rather than go into an office five-days-a-week? Explain. Do you think your preference aligns with most people?
8. Discuss how an organization's retrenchment might impact employee behavior.
9. If a two-tier pay system is likely to create perceived reward inequities, why would the management of so many organizations push for such a pay plan?
10. "An employee who has a working spouse is likely to be less motivated than either a single worker or one with a nonworking spouse." Do you agree or disagree with this statement? Defend your position.

FOR FURTHER READING

BLUMBERG, M., and C. D. PRINGLE, "The Missing Opportunity in Organizational Research: Some Implications for a Theory of Work Performance," *Academy of Management Review*, October 1982, pp. 560–69. Argues that explanations and predictions of employee performance must include "opportunity to perform" as well as ability and motivation.

HOFSTEDE, G., *Culture's Consequences: International Differences in Work-Related Values*. Beverly Hills, Calif.: Sage Publications, 1980. Contains comprehensive summary of research comparing national cultures.

KELLEY, L., and R. WORTHLEY, "The Role of Culture in Comparative Management: A Cross-cultural Perspective," *Academy of Management Journal*, March 1981, pp. 164–73. Seeks to link national culture and managerial attitudes, behavior, and effectiveness.

KOEHN, H. E., "The Post-Industrial Worker," *Public Personnel Management Journal*, Fall 1983, pp. 244–48. Reviews implications from shifting worker characteristics and motivations as a result of the United States moving from an industrial to a postindustrial society.

NAISBITT, J., *Megatrends: Ten New Directions Transforming Our Lives*. New York: Warner Books, 1982. Summarizes the major trends in society, several of which have direct implications for organizational behavior and management.

NEVIS, E. C., "Using an American Perspective in Understanding Another Culture: Toward a Hierarchy of Needs for the People's Republic of China," *Journal of Applied Behavioral Science*, Vol. 19, no. 3 (1983), pp. 249–64. Develops a motivational model for the People's Republic of China and shows how an American theory can be applied in another culture.

NOTES FOR CHAPTER 16

1. T. Connolly, "Towards a Reintegration of 'Organizational Behavior,' " *The Organizational Behavior Teaching Review*, Fall 1984, pp. 1–3.
2. S. Ronen and A. I. Kraut, "Similarities Among Countries Based on Employee Work Values and Attitudes," *Columbia Journal of World Business*, Summer 1977, pp. 89–96.
3. G. Hofstede, "Motivation, Leadership, and Organization: Do American Theories Apply Abroad?" *Organizational Dynamics*, Summer 1980, pp. 42–63.
4. Ibid., p. 55.
5. Ibid.
6. Ibid., p. 57.
7. Ibid., p. 60.
8. Ibid.
9. Ibid., and "Europe's New Managers," *Business Week*, May 24, 1982, p. 117.
10. G. Johansson and G. Aronsson, "Stress Reactions in Computerized Administrative Work," *Journal of Occupational Behavior*, July 1984, pp. 159–81.
11. "VDT Users Report Above-Normal Rate of Job Absenteeism," *The Wall Street Journal*, October 19, 1983, p. 27.
12. See, for example, L. Hirschhorn (ed.), *Cutting Back* (San Francisco: Jossey-Bass, 1983).
13. S. P. Robbins, "The New Management: Managing Declining Organizations," paper presented at the Western Academy of Management Conference, Vancouver, B.C., April 1984.
14. "The Double Standard That's Setting Worker Against Worker," *Business Week*, April 8, 1985, pp. 70–71.

CASE VA

ELAINE, THE HARASSED SECRETARY

PART ONE: THE INCIDENT

Sometime, just before noon on a rainy day in April 1981, an attractive twenty-three-year-old secretary named Elaine got up from her desk in a small insurance agency in New England, went up to the office manager's desk and said, "May I go home? I am sick—sick of all this." With a wide sweep of her hand she indicated the office and the women working in it. Without waiting for a reply she spun around and stomped out of the building, jumped into her new light-blue Mercury, and recklessly drove out of the parking lot.

PART TWO: A WOMAN AND HER WORK

Having graduated from high school in 1976, and having completed secretarial school during the summer, Elaine was ready to go to work for the National Mutual Life Insurance Company in their home office by late fall. During the period since her graduation, Elaine had discovered a great deal of extra time on her hands. Although basically energetic, she "wasted" (as she put it) a lot of time in school sitting around talking and visiting with her friends. By the time secretarial school was over and she had gone to work for National Mutual (hereafter NML), she had lost contact with many of her friends. However, she retained a small group of close friends whom she saw frequently during her free time.

Elaine came from a lower-middle-income family and was one of two children. Her older married sister was experiencing personal problems and appeared to be headed for the divorce court. Elaine seldom saw her father for he was constantly on the road. Although she spent a good deal of time with her mother, she was seldom home long enough to talk with her for any great length of time. But her mother followed Elaine's life very closely—incessantly advising, always reading her mail—and was completely involved in a sympathetic but outspoken way in Elaine's social and work life. Elaine, who usually complained when her independence was infringed upon, seemed to accept her mother's behavior as normal and quite permissible.

Although there were many women of Elaine's age at the home office of NML, she rarely joined them in off-work activities. During this period she joined a women's bowling league, but not the one that consisted of NML employees.

In the winter of 1978 she began negotiations with another NML office for employment, and in May 1979 she started work at a new regional office that was in the same town as the home office but located closer to her home. Now, instead of working with a group of thirty to forty women, she found herself working with only nine other women mostly older than she. Instead of lunching in a huge cafeteria, at a table with ten or more women of her own age, she now usually ate alone.

At the home office her work consisted of typing letters in response to certain types of queries by policyholders. These letters were always dictated by the same man. In her new job she typed life insurance estate programs as well as various letters dictated by four different men. Two of these men arrived at the office by 8:30 in the morning and were ready to dictate to Elaine when she arrived at 9:00. Usually she was finished with dictation by 10:30. She took a fifteen-minute coffee break, then came back to run the switchboard. When the men returned at 1:00 P.M. from field work, she would leave for lunch, which she usually had at home.

No formal rules existed regulating hours of employment in the agency, so the days were often either longer or shorter than a typical office job and depended on the work load. Elaine's routine was seldom the same each day. Often there were periods when she would sit and chat with the agents as they related the activities of their day and listened to her stories of things she had done or heard regarding her social life or the company and agency. All in all, Elaine was quite pleased with her new job.

In 1979, Elaine became secretary of her bowling league, and the recording of scores and typing of schedules required about seven hours each week. Four evenings a week she worked as a waitress in a nearby ice cream shop. Between the job at the insurance agency and the work at the ice cream shop, Elaine was earning nearly $300.00 a week. Since she lived at home, her daily expenses were minimal. Thus, with each passing month, her bank account grew larger as she continued to work at two jobs. She lived at home, went out on dates, and ran her bowling league. Elaine, it appeared, not only had a good life but also possessed the abundant energy and vitality with which to enjoy it.

PART THREE: A WOMAN AND HER FRIENDS

Although not a very religious woman, Elaine usually went to church each Sunday, accompanied by two or three of her female friends. These, however, were not the same women with whom she bowled. She rarely saw her bowling friends when she was at parties or on double dates. Her "party" friends were neither school friends nor work associates, although she did spend some of her "fun" time with a few of the young people with whom she worked at the ice cream shop.

Of the nine women in the office, only two others were single. The rest were middle-aged, but they were, in spirit, young and "swingers." Nevertheless, Elaine's relationship with them was one of cordiality and respect but not close. She was not overfond of them as a group, but she indicated that she did not individually dislike any of them. She neither saw nor kept in touch with any of her old associates at the home office and had made few friends in the two years that she was there. Despite the impression this might convey, Elaine was really a gregarious and friendly person. She had a large number of friends drawn from each of her "crowds." Elaine seemed to be leading many different lives at the same time.

When she arrived at the office in the morning, it was not unusual for Elaine to find waiting at her desk one of the four agents for whom she worked. The reason, of course, was that the agents made money out in the field, and not in dictating or sitting behind their desks involved in paper work. Thus their objective was to get their desk work out of the way as soon as possible and then go out in the field. To make a sale, the agent first had to find a name, usually from the existing list; then a standard form introduction letter was sent out. These were sent at the rate of about 25 or 30 a week. He could also have a direct mailing list typed and sent to the home office where form letters were mailed out, then contact these people by phone and attempt to make appointments with them. After an appointment, the agent would send the customer a short note of appreciation with the assurance that he had begun work on his program. After another round of telephone calls and appointments, the sale was made. On the average, if an agent sold two policies a week he would have sent out 90 pieces of mail.

Elaine's work load varied from about 100 to 140 pieces a week. The agents felt that the more they could individually get from Elaine in the way of work, the higher their sales volume would be. Thus they competed for her time, and since there were no set rules governing the amount of work that could be requested, they would usually give her more than she could possibly do and hope that a larger portion would be completed than they had expected. Often they were amazed when all their work was completed. When this happened, however, it was not unusual for them to fail to follow up on it, and Elaine's work would be wasted. Elaine was understandably chagrined by this.

The agents, besides competing for Elaine's time, also competed among themselves, and in many instances Elaine found herself in the middle of a feud. There were also certain months in the year when business picked up markedly. Usually these occurred at the beginning of a year, during the July and November campaigns, just prior to agents' vacations, and before holidays. During these periods, the agents put even greater pressure on Elaine to get the work done. In addition there were occasions when the agents lost large cases or became depressed over extended slump periods, and as a result made extremely unreasonable requests for work from their secretaries. Many times this rush work would be completed and then collect dust on the salespeople's desks for hours, and sometimes days. This further aggravated Elaine who, because of her skill, did most of the rush work.

One day, Elaine was interrupted while typing a letter and asked to do a rush program for one of the usually "rushing" agents. Fifteen minutes later she completed the program and laid it on his desk. During this particular month, with income taxes due, the work tended to slow down a great deal. In addition, the secretaries noticed an increase in requests for favors that usually involved some "special" work or "fast" delivery—which actually were neither so special nor needed so quickly by the agents. When she saw the rush program the next morning, still with the copies attached lying on the agent's desk, Elaine realized that this was one of those "favors."

She was also involved during this time with a greater number of standard preapproach letters but had continually been forced to put them off because of interruptions to do favors. The prospective customers' names would be given to her on Monday, and the letters had to be typed by Thursday evening. She usually spaced the typing evenly each day, but in this case she had to do them all on Thursday.

While she was working at the ice cream shop on Wednesday, her manager called her in and indicated that some of the other waitresses had complained because she was pushing her orders through, that is, placing her orders at the front of the line. He also said that she probably did this because she felt rushed by impatient customers, but that the real problem was that she spent too much time talking and chatting with her friends who often came into the shop. He warned Elaine not to socialize so much. Elaine liked the manager, but felt that he was a little unfair in this criticism in that the other waitresses always talked with their friends too. After work that night, Elaine attended a large party where she soothed her feelings by drinking a bit too much.

The following day, Thursday, the office manager at the agency noticed her talking on the phone while she was typing the standard form letters. Elaine often did this because it seemed to make typing these letters more bearable. The office manager pointed out that some of the agents had complained about her work and that the probable reason for this was her talking on the phone while working.

Elaine's mood that morning was not amenable to such criticism. In the first place, she had a slight hangover from the night before, and this caused her to make mistakes she would not have normally made. Second, she was still somewhat hurt by the criticism of the manager of the ice cream shop—whom she admired a great deal. Third, the weather was rainy and as miserable as she herself felt. None of the agents had shown up for work because of the bad weather and the normal slow operations at this time of the year. This upset Elaine because she wanted to tell them about the party she had attended. In addition the rest of the office staff was also in a bad mood, and her complaining manager, who was a large forty-eight-year-old woman, was just typical of the atmosphere of the day.

By eleven o'clock she felt that she could type the standard letters in her sleep, even though she could not type them correctly. Finally she made one mistake too many, ripped the letter from her typewriter, grabbed her coat, and told the office manager she was leaving. This was a complete surprise to the office manager. She had many times seen women go into the ladies' room to get their problems ironed out by an unscheduled rest, but had never seen someone simply get up and leave. Elaine's actions left her speechless and without a clue as to what her own action should be.

Questions

1. Analyze the factors that led to Elaine's action. Do you think her reaction was typical? Why? Discuss other reactions to pressures on the job.
2. What do you think is going to happen to Elaine next? Do you think she will come back, or will she quit? Why?
3. Do you think that Elaine's relationship with her co-workers was a good one? Discuss. Would Elaine be easy or difficult to work with? Why?

4. Are there any background factors in Elaine's personal life that would have led you to possibly expect such behavior? If so, what are they?
5. Analyze the work flow relationship in the office in which Elaine worked. If you were to make any changes in the organization of the office, what would they be?

Source: R. E. C. Wegner and L. Sayles. *Cases in Organizational and Administrative Behavior,* © 1972, pp 1–7. Reprinted by permission of Prentice-Hall, Inc., Englewood Cliffs, N.J.

CASE VB

EVOLUTION IN THE MAILROOM

Anderson Foods, Inc., employs approximately 700 white-collar workers in its administrative headquarters in the Southwest.

The mailroom where I worked performs the function of routing incoming and intraoffice mail throughout the building and dispatching mail to the local post office twice a day.

Hal Struthers, age forty-seven, is the supervisor of the mailroom and has been with the company in that capacity for nine years. He reports to the office manager, Bert Finnely, who is in charge of all office service departments. In addition to the mailroom, these service departments include the reproduction department, maintenance department, and the stationery and supplies department.

Struthers supervises eleven men who carry out the operations of the mailroom. One of these men, Brian Mancies, is his assistant and officially in charge of the mailroom when Struthers is absent. Mancies is twenty-seven years old and has worked in the mailroom for seven years. The work of the department is divided into two principal functions: the circulation of intraoffice mail and the routing of outgoing mail. The circulation of intraoffice mail is done by four mailboys, each of whom delivers and picks up mail from a single floor. The routing of outgoing mail is performed by three men. One of the men, Carl Peck, is in charge of this operation and reports to Struthers. Peck is fifty-two years old.

At 8:15 A.M. incoming mail was sorted into various pigeon holes arranged by floor. At 9:00 A.M. the four mailboys made their "runs," delivering the mail that was in the pigeon holes to the various offices on their floors. While on their runs, they picked up mail and brought it back to the mailroom. The runs took about twenty minutes. On returning, they sorted the mail into the pigeon holes and placed any outgoing mail on the work table of the outgoing section. These runs were repeated every hour on the hour until 4:00 P.M. The intraoffice personnel finished their day at 5:00 P.M. Struthers also finished work at this hour.

The three outgoing men reported for work at 10:30 A.M. They sorted the outgoing mail into various pigeon holes as it was brought to them by the mailboys. The mail was sealed, weighed, and affixed with postage. They also wrapped cartons and packages for mailing as these were sent down by various departments in the company. The work for the outgoing crew ended at 6:30 P.M. when they "closed up shop" and took the mail to the local post office.

All this work was performed in the same room. Although there was a division in the work performed between the outgoing and intraoffice personnel, there were no partitions in the room. The outgoing personnel had their workspace in one corner of the room, and the rest of it was occupied by the intraoffice personnel. There were only two desks in the rooms, Struthers' and Peck's. The remainder of the furniture consisted of work tables, pigeon hole racks, and postage machines. There were chairs scattered in the room for the personnel to use between runs and during slack periods. The work was usually done while standing, although there were no rules requiring this.

Because of this layout, and the nature of the work performed, there was a lot of conversation and socializing. The work essentially required little attention. The relationship between Struthers and his subordinates was very informal, and usually there was considerable joking and bantering going on throughout the day. Struthers was well liked by his subordinates.

In general, the work situation was characterized by informality and harmony. The two work groups in the mailroom engaged in competition and rivalry both on and off the job. A game that often developed between the outgoing and intraoffice personnel was which group could get ahead of the other in clearing mail off their work tables and into the pigeon holes. The winners had first choice of the most comfortable chairs in the room. A similar game was played within the two groups. In spite of the intensity with which this game was played, there was mutual cooperation and "pitching in" in the instances when the work load became too heavy for one group or one individual.

Off the job, too, there was much socializing. It ranged from eating lunch together and pitching horseshoes during the lunch hour to occasionally getting together and watching a weekend baseball game. Each summer the employees of the mailroom organized an informal picnic that was held at Struthers' home. Generally, all the employees attended the picnics.

In February of my fifth year, a new mailboy was hired to replace one who had been promoted to another department. The new mailboy was Earl Snell. He was twenty-one years old and had been employed twice before by other companies in the area. He took over the first-floor mail run.

Two weeks after Snell was hired, a change was introduced into the mailroom's operation. A data processing system was installed to handle customer accounts from the billing department. The system consolidated billing procedures and was able to print out invoices which showed the amount customers owed Anderson Foods. The bills had previously been handled by secretaries who filled them in, placed them in envelopes, and sent them to the mailroom as they finished them. With the new system this tedious and time-consuming procedure was eliminated, and bills could be processed much more quickly. The bills were sent to the mailroom in stacks, where they were then separated into various regions and inserted in envelopes.

Because of the speed with which the machine processed the invoices, they could be handled efficiently only in large amounts. Hence the billing department ran the accounts off at irregular intervals during the day. The result was that the mailroom often received several hundred bills at a time and at irregular intervals. It was not uncommon to receive over a thousand invoices in one day. Extra help was not hired in the mailroom because it was planned that the mailboys could help in separating and stuffing the bills into envelopes during their free time between runs.

From the onset of this new operation, I noticed a change in the atmosphere of the mailroom. The joking and bantering was not so prevalent; on several occasions, when some of the mailboys began joking while sorting the mail, Struthers was quick to tell them to "cut it out and keep your minds on your work."

The new mailboy, Snell, was a constant topic of conversation among the other employees. Snell always managed to be somewhere else when there was work to be done. His runs were never made on time, and he often took as long as an hour to get around on the first floor. Struthers was constantly receiving complaints from other department supervisors that Snell was socializing with the secretaries on his mail run and interfering with their work. When Struthers asked him where he had been and why his run had taken so long, Snell invariably replied, "I had to go to the men's room." Once Snell said to me: "I get a kick out of Struthers. Every time I'm late, I tell him I had to go to the men's room. The number of times I've told him that I've gone to the men's room would have lasted any normal person a lifetime! He is so harmless, though, that even if he didn't believe me he wouldn't do anything about it."

Snell also irritated the other mailroom employees. He often commented that he couldn't wait to get out of the mailroom and into a better job. He couldn't imagine why anyone would settle for a career in such "meaningless" work. One habit of his particularly irritated the other employees. Snell often arrived just after they had cleared off the work tables and dumped another pile of mail on the table. They would complain to him and tell him to clear the table himself. This happened several times, and finally Snell went to Struthers and told him that he was being picked on. Struthers gathered everyone together and gave a "pep talk" about how everyone in the mailroom was expected to cooperate, help each other out. "I like to think of us in this mailroom as a team," said Struthers, "and not as a collection of individuals with individual jobs."

There were several cynical remarks made after Struthers' talk about "team spirit." The favorite expression became "rah, team spirit," when work had to be done. The rest of the employees decided that since Struthers wasn't going to do anything about Snell's lack of cooperation, they would do something about it themselves. The next time Snell arrived late with his mail, all the other employees told Struthers that they had to go to the men's room—and they left. Struthers then took Snell aside and spoke to him privately. After the conversation Snell left the room in a hurry.

Since I was the only one left in the room, Struthers came over to me. "I can't understand that kid. I've tried so hard to reason with him and get him to cooperate. I've gone out of my way to help him out. He only makes trouble for himself the way he acts, and will never get a promotion at this rate. I'm tempted to give him one, just to get him out of my hair! He's making a mess of this whole operation.''

Later that afternoon Finnely, Struthers' supervisor, came to the mailroom to find out what was the matter. Snell had gone to him and told him that the employees, including Struthers, were picking on him. Finnely was not ignorant of the situation with Snell, for Struthers had mentioned it to him before. Finnely himself talked to the employees and told them that it was ''kid stuff'' to do what they had done in the morning. He said that the answer to the whole problem was to concentrate on work and learn to help each other instead of fighting each other.

But the situation didn't improve. Struthers had trouble getting the mailboys to take it on themselves to help with the invoices as they came in. They resented having to stop what they were doing in order to process the invoices when several hundred came in at a time. Often the invoices arrived late in the afternoon, and several employees would have to stay overtime in order to finish them. They couldn't understand why the invoices came in all at once instead of being spread out during the day. Struthers tried to explain to them that the machine could only process several hundred at a time. But this didn't convince them. Struthers himself often commented, ''I understand their problems in the data processing, but I wish they would understand mine. There ought to be a better way of doing this. This procedure saves the boys upstairs headaches, but gives a lot of them to me.''

The fact that Snell managed to dodge most of the invoice work irritated the other employees. One of them once commented: ''Struthers is so gullible. If I were him, I would fire Snell in a second. I can't understand why he doesn't.''

About this time Struthers revealed another change. For several months discussion had been going on about integrating some of the activities of the mailroom and the reproduction department, which was adjacent to the mailroom. The reproduction department, like the mailroom, was characterized by periods of intense activity and periods of relative quiet. The initial plan was to have the employees who were not busy in one department assist in the other department if they could be of help. Struthers was very concerned that the mailroom employees should cooperate all they could with the plan.

The cooperation never materialized. The employees suddenly found work that appeared to keep them occupied continuously in the mailroom. One employee was seen to empty the mail out of his pigeon holes and sort it back into them again. The cry was often heard: ''Send Snell over to reproduction!'' Struthers was upset over the lack of cooperation and became more and more irritable. He was very concerned because no one was volunteering to help in reproduction, in spite of the fact that on several occasions reproduction had sent workers over to the mailroom.

Toward the end of the summer someone mentioned that nothing had been said about the annual picnic. One of the other employees remarked that it was just as well. The lunchtime horseshoe game, a usual summer activity, had never gotten started and nobody ever bothered to play the game of "who could clear the work tables first" any more.

Questions

1. Describe the jobs of the intraoffice mail personnel and the outgoing mail personnel. In what significant ways were these jobs different?
2. Describe the "games" played by the various personnel in the mail office. Why do employees play such games? What are the positive and negative aspects of these games?
3. What meaning could be attached to the fact that the new mailboy, Earl Snell, and the first organization change occurred very close in time?
4. Why do you think Struthers treated Snell the way he did? Was this good or poor leadership? Why? What effect did his treatment of Snell have on Struthers' relationship with the other employees?
5. Why do you think there was so little cooperation given by the personnel in the mailroom to those in reproduction? What group effects could be operating here?

Source: Wegner and Sayles, *Cases in Organizational and Administrative Behavior,* pp. 111–17.

CASE VC

THE LUGGERS VERSUS THE BUTCHERS

Food Merchandising Corporation had one of its warehouses in a small city in northern New Jersey. The main operation of the warehouse was to stock certain goods and then ship them on order to various stores. The meat department handled packaged meats and wholesale cuts of lamb, veal, and beef. Beef, by far the biggest and most expensive commodity, was generally bought from Mid-western packers and shipped either by railroad or truck. On arrival at the warehouse, the beef was in the form of two hindquarters and two forequarters, each weighing close to two hundred pounds. The problem was to get these heavy pieces of meat off the trucks (or freight cars) and onto the intricate system of rails within the warehouse. Freight was paid by the shipper.

Company and union rules proscribed warehousemen from unloading trucks. It became the function of the general warehouseman (designated "lugger") to assist in the unloading of the trucks, but with no lifting. If, however, the beef was shipped by rail, it became his function to unload the freight cars. After the meat was placed on company rails, it was pushed through the doors into the 35° warehouse where it was placed in stock until it was butchered. The butchery process involved several men. First, the meat went to the sawman. While someone steadied the meat on the rail, the rib, plate, brisket, and shoulder bones were severed. Then it was passed on to the cutters, who butchered it into several smaller wholesale cuts. After that the meat was placed in stock to be shipped out by the night crews.

THE "LUGGERS" VERSUS THE "BUTCHERS"

The operation of the warehouse involved two distinct functions: to unload and stock the beef and then to butcher it. The unloading process was wholly different from the butchering. It required physical strength and coordination to lift 200 pounds of beef all day. Furthermore, when the work load slowed down, the luggers were given different tasks. There was a degree of variety in their work. But the butchering function was very different. The men were geographically confined to the cutting line and performed the same basic operations day after day.

When the warehouse was unionized eight years ago, the men who had most seniority were given first option as to the jobs they preferred. Since many of these men were on the older side, they gravitated away from the more laborious general warehouse work toward the higher-wage butcher jobs. Consequently, two different types of individuals became associated with the two different types of jobs.

The eight butchers were engaged in the skilled practice of butchering meat. Most of them had been with the company for many years. For the most part, they were family men with many off-the-job reponsibilites, were by no means in union affairs, and probably had more loyalty to the company than to the union local. They had a high number of social activities off-the-job such as group picnics, bowling, golf, and the like. The tedious boredom of their job was somewhat mitigated by these mutual activities, and an atmosphere of good humor usually prevailed in their corner of the warehouse.

There were nine luggers, but two of these had been butchers until very recently. More will be said later about these men. A third man usually worked in another section. Thus the term "lugger" referred to a specific group of six general warehouse workers. These workers were younger and generally had less company time than the butchers, but this is not to say that they were young or new. Most of them were married, but treated their home responsibilities differently. For instance, the typical butcher would spend his night at home, and most of the luggers would spend their night working a part-time job.

HANK, JOSH, AND MR. ABRAMS

Hank was the supervisor. When he became supervisor about ten years ago, the men considered him a walking terror but a good supervisor. Now he was considered neither. There were several reasons for this change. First, the coming of the union had made Hank more careful in the way he handled the men. Second, Hank had lost control of the luggers. After several fiery confrontations, he more or less left them alone. When it was necessary to give them an order, great explanations and apologies often accompanied it. His relationship with butchers, however, remained fairly intact. In effect, Hank was afraid of the luggers but not of the butchers. Third, when Mr. Abrams became manager two years ago, it was his policy to use close personal supervision of the men to ensure efficiency. Mr. Abrams, therefore, usurped considerable portions of Hank's responsibility.

Josh was the union representative. He had built up a great friendship with Carl, the shop steward, and the other luggers. His relationship with the butchers, however, was strictly on a business basis. As a consequence, Josh tended to favor the luggers in any controversy. Usually this meant that the butchers complained about the luggers, but nothing really important was done about it.

Mr. Abrams' assistant was Lyle, nicknamed "the Puppy." Lyle used to follow Mr. Abrams everywhere he went, to the great enjoyment of the men. Thus came the nickname "Puppy."

The butchers took the brunt of Mr. Abrams' close supervision, mainly because they were confined to one spot and were easy to observe. Also, this was where the real pressure had to be applied; for if the meat was not butchered, it could not be sent out and stores would run short. Mr. Abrams had the responsibility to ensure that stores were not short. He evidently felt that standing over the men (with the Puppy at his side) would cut down on the little games the men developed to break up their boring routine (i.e., talking, bathroom breaks). The net effect was that the men, being oldtimers, took their breaks anyway but grumbled about being watched over. The luggers were harder to watch, being more spread out, and they also managed to gain some control over Mr. Abrams. He knew that an ill-timed remark or too much supervision would only result in later slowdowns by these men.

A SLOW CHANGE IN STATUS

Six years ago the butcher's job was considered much more desirable than that of the luggers. At that time most of the meat was shipped by railroad. This necessitated a great deal of heavy work. Most of the men would have preferred the cold monotony of cutting meat to lugging 200 pounds of beef from a railroad car to a loading dock. It was at this point that two luggers, Brent and Terry, began to think of developing a system of portable rails that would be adaptable to the large variety of freight cars that came to the warehouse. The rails were successfully designed and developed by the two men. With the passage of time, skill in their use was achieved, and the job of unloading freight cars became quite simple.

The ingenuity of two luggers was widely heralded about the warehouse and in the company, and recognition was given in due proportion. More important, a job that was undesirable before became quite attractive because the chief reason for its undesirability had ceased to exist. The main attractions of the butcher's job were reduced to the companionship of the group, the waning prestige of being a skilled worker, and the higher-wage-more-overtime benefits. This was quite sufficient to keep them satisfied, if not as happy as before.

Hank's supervisory position also suffered. At this date, his position had already been dealt a few blows by the union and the men. Now an innovation was introduced that had no place in his way of doing things. He preferred to completely ignore the rails and allow the luggers to use them as they saw fit. From the company's point of view, the use of rails in freight cars meant very little. Four men were still required in each car. Efficiency remained about the same because it took time to assemble and disassemble the rail system.

If the use of the rails had resulted solely in physical advantages, it is probable that the situation would have gone along unchanged. But the luggers were quick to discover an economic value in their use. The trucks coming in on the front docks had to be unloaded. Since freight was paid by the shipper, the company and union had worked out an agreement in which the trucker was responsible for delivering the meat to the dock. The warehouse workers were only to assist peripherally and were not permitted inside the trucks unless it was absolutely necessary.

The drivers were not happy with their lot of unloading up to 35,000 pounds of beef. Consequently, they often hired warehouse vagrants—men who sat around the warehouse waiting for such opportunities. The going rate was one dollar per 1,000 pounds: between $30.00 and $35.00 a truck. It generally took two hours to unload one truck. The enterprising luggers redesigned the rails for use on the trucks and made it known that a tip of two dollars was in order for anyone who cared to use them. Since the railroad was making more and more use of piggyback services, the number of trucks as well as the amount of the tips began to increase.

A DISPUTE DEVELOPS

Last year, two butchers were given the option of working as luggers. They exercised the option, partly hoping to recuperate some of the wage losses by sharing in the tip money. It was not long before serious arguments developed between the old and new luggers. Beforehand, the luggers had worked out a one-for-you and one-for-me system with the trucks. Such an informal understanding was possible because this tightly cohesive group knew that petty bickering would soon take the problem out of their own hands. The two ex-butchers, however, had no desire to work with the old group. They were in no way amenable to tacit understandings that cut them out. Consequently, when the big trailers turned into the driveway, there began a jockeying for position.

Arguments developed, and other work suffered. When the two ex-butchers turned to the union, they found their upward paths of communication thoroughly blocked. Carl, the shop steward, was a lugger. It was to his disadvantage to press hard on behalf of the two ex-butchers. Josh, the union representative, was much too friendly with the luggers and no progress could be made here. Hank, the supervisor, was worthless in this matter; and Mr. Abrams was too new at this stage to take action. For these reasons, and because of a normal reluctance to push grievances, little pressure was placed on the union.

Early last spring, following a series of flare-ups over equipment usage and truck tips, two "clubs" were formed: Club "Six" and Club "Three." Brent, one of the two rail designers, originated the idea of formalizing the two groups. Each club was given a separate locker for equipment. No exchanges were to take place. Members of Club Three (the two ex-butchers and a third who worked in a different part of the warehouse) were permitted to work a share of trucks proportional to club membership. Members of Club Six (the six original luggers) began a practice of pooling tips and dividing them equally.

At first the formalization of the two groups appeared to be a good solution. There were fewer arguments, and Club Three was reasonably satisfied. However, an unfortunate side effect developed. Previously, the distinctions between luggers and butchers were implicit and the warehouse as a whole was a friendly place. People knew who got along with whom, and friendships often crossed group lines. With the formalization, however, people began to class themselves as "in" or "out." Club Six members began to be more and more isolated among the 25 men who worked in this section of the warehouse. Butchers and luggers constantly complained about each other. Members of Club Six refused to work with members of Club Three, and much ill feeling was generated. But even so, had there been nothing else, these difficulties would probably not have caused any lasting problems. There was, however, something else—the piggyback development.

The railroads were making more and more use of piggyback trucking. This is a system whereby trailers are hauled part of the way by rail, and part of the way by road. As the number of freight cars decreased and the warehouse volume increased, more trucks began coming. These trucks had to be unloaded, and unloading was an expensive and time-consuming proposition. The use of rails on the trucks had cut down the time it took to unload. A good crew could "knock one off" in less than an hour, though the average time was about two hours. The luggers began to move into this very lucrative area. It became quite a steady thing for them to bring home an extra $70.00 or $80.00 per week. Occasionally, if things were slow enough, the luggers would work a truck on company time. Or they would begin setting it up about 3:30, so there would be no delay in getting it started at 4:00.

From the company viewpoint, there was no problem. Trucks were being emptied faster than ever before, even on the rare occasion when a truck came in purposely late. The more usual situation was either that there were too many trucks to unload in the normal day or that the truck was legitimately delayed. At any rate, the rails enabled the ordinary trucks to be unloaded much more rapidly, and the experienced luggers often finished their after-hour trucks in half the normal time. Warehouse efficiency did not suffer.

The butchers, however, were not a happy group. They continued to work the same boring routine in the same 35°. Their income did not change. They watched the luggers develop into a very cohesive group and usurped their status position. They resented the different treatments meted out to the two groups. The luggers were given too much freedom, and the butchers were too closely supervised. The luggers quite often "couldn't" stay overtime, yet they could almost always work a truck. Nothing was ever said when luggers made excuses, but if the butchers did not want to stay, there were given a great deal of grief.

Pressure was applied, and it was not a rare thing to find butchers working three hours overtime for half the money the luggers made in an hour by working a truck. The obvious inequity was deeply resented. The luggers used company time to work trucks, or to set them up, and this violated the union contract. Yet nothing concrete was ever done to stop them. The butchers felt totally frustrated and disenchanted with what they had once considered as high-status jobs. Despite their innate conservatism and procompany attitude they seriously considered a massive walkout to get their grievances heard.

Questions

1. As operations change, status of various groups is often affected. In what way has the status of the luggers and butchers changed over the years?
2. Describe the work flow at Food Merchandising Corporation. Do you think it is efficient? Why? Describe any way in which you think it could be improved.
3. Show how membership in the various groups described affected behavior. Do you think that management effectively utilized the natural formation of these groups to the betterment of operations? Explain.
4. How did the various technological changes in the meat-packing industry affect operations at Food Merchandising? How did the various groups—luggers, butchers, and management—react to these changes?
5. Analyze Mr. Abrams' style of leadership. What effect did this have on the relationships between the luggers and the butchers?
6. Analyze the dispute that led to the formation of Club Six and Club Three. In what ways were the formation of these "clubs" beneficial or deterimental to the operations of the company? If you were a member of management, how would you have dealt with these two clubs?
7. As the case ends, the butchers are threatening a walkout. Can anything be done to avert this? If so, what?

Source: Wegner and Sayles, *Cases in Organizational and Administrative Behavior*, pp. 42–49.

Appendix: Scoring Keys for Exercises

EXERCISE IIA. VALUE ASSESSMENT TEST

Each item in the value assessment exercise is coded in the following manner:

A = theoretical dimension
B = economic-political dimension
C = aesthetic dimension
D = social dimension

Total scores for each dimension are calculated by adding the number associated with the response on the dimension items for each "Yes" response. For example, in the B items (economic-political), if you replied "Yes" only to 31, 34, and 76, your total score on the economic-political dimension would be 23 (5 + 8 + 10). When a sample of 389 females and 352 males was taken, the following percentile norms were developed.

	% PERCENTILE	THEORETICAL	ECONOMIC- POLITICAL	AESTHETIC	SOCIAL
	100	110	110	110	110
	90	74	70	96	96
	80	60	54	88	88
	70	48	46	79	82
	60	40	39	69	77
Female	50	32	32	62	72
(N = 389)	40	25	25	54	67
	30	19	21	46	59
	20	14	17	36	52
	10	8	11	22	39
	1	0	1	3	0

% PERCENTILE	THEORETICAL	ECONOMIC-POLITICAL	AESTHETIC	SOCIAL
100	110	110	110	110
90	85	89	83	90
80	74	76	69	80
70	66	67	60	73
60	54	56	47	65
50	45	49	39	56
40	39	38	32	47
30	31	30	26	39
20	21	21	20	33
10	11	12	12	25
1	0	0	0	4

Male (N = 352)

If you scored high on any dimension, the meaning is indicated below.*

Theoretical. A high score indicates that you prefer and consider most worthwhile those activities that involve a problem-solving attitude and are related to investigation, research, and scientific curiosity.

Economical-political. A high score indicates that you prefer and consider most worthwhile those activities that involve the accumulation of money and the securing of executive power.

Aesthetic. A high score indicates that you prefer and consider most worthwhile those activities that involve art, music, dance, and literature.

Social. A high score indicates that you prefer and consider most worthwhile those activities that involve service and help to people; you exhibit a definite desire to respond and be with people socially.

EXERCISE IIB. DETERMINING YOUR LOCUS OF CONTROL

Add up the total for items 1, 4, 5, 9, 18, 19, 21, and 23. This is your Internal Control score. Totals can range from minus 24 to plus 24. A high positive score indicates that you believe you have control over your own life. Now add up your score for items 3, 8, 11, 13, 15, 17, 20, and 22. This is your Powerful Others score. A high positive total indicates that you believe that others, who have power, affect the outcomes in your life. Finally, add up your score for items 2, 6, 7, 10, 12, 14, 16, and 24. This represents your Chance score. A high positive total indicates that you believe the outcomes in your life are essentially the result of random occurrences.

*The scoring instruction information was taken from J. R. Robinson and P. R. Shaver, *Measures of Social Psychological Attitudes*, rev. ed. (Ann Arbor, University of Michigan, Institute for Social Research, 1973), pp. 510–11.)

People with a high internal locus of control tend to have positive Internal Control scores above 10 and negative Chance scores. A high positive Powerful Others total might indicate that you work for someone else or are significantly dependent on others (i.e., parents, friends) for support. As individuals gain work experience, job expertise, career mobility, and financial and emotional independence, this score tends to decline.

EXERCISE IIC. NEEDS TEST

Growth needs are items 2, 5, 8, 11.
Relatedness needs are items 1, 4, 7, 10.
Existence needs are items 3, 6, 9, 12.

Add the scores for each need set (for example, the summation of your scores on items 2, 5, 8, and 11 represent your growth need total). If you considered all four items within a need category to be very important, you would obtain the maximum total of 20 points.

College students typically rate growth needs highest. However, you may currently have little income and consider existence needs as most important. For instance, one student of mine scored 20, 10, and 15 for growth, relatedness, and existence needs, respectively. This should be interpreted to mean that her relatedness needs are already substantially satisfied. Her growth needs, on the other hand, are substantially unsatisfied.

Note that a low score may imply that a need is unimportant to you or that it is substantially satisfied. The implication, however, is that *everyone* has these needs. So a low score is usually taken to mean that this need is substantially satisfied.

EXERCISE IID. SUPERVISORY ATTITUDE SCALE

	SA	A	U	D	SD
Items 1, 3, 5, 7, 9:	1 point	2 points	3 points	4 points	5 points
Items 2, 4, 6, 8, 10:	5 points	4 points	3 points	2 points	1 point

Add up the total points for all ten items. This is your score. Scores can be between 10 and 50. High scores (above 35 points) suggest supervisory attitudes in line with Theory Y, while low scores (below 25 points) indicate attitudes that fit with Theory X.

EXERCISE IIIA. STATUS-RANKING TASK

The correct ranking is

1. Physicians
2. Lawyers
3. Dentists
4. Chemists
5. Bank officers
6. Airplane pilots
7. Economists
8. Elementary school teachers

9. Actors
10. Real estate agents
11. Automobile mechanics
12. Receptionists
13. Air traffic controllers
14. Funeral directors
15. Bartenders
16. Gas station attendants

Score your individual worksheets by adding up the differences between your ranks and the key, regardless of sign. That is, make all differences positive and add them up. Low scores, of course, are better than high ones. Do the same with the group ranking.

Compute the average score of the individual members and compare it with the group score. Was the group score lower? Relate this exercise (both process and outcome) to the topics of group decision making, status, conflict, and leadership.

EXERCISE IIIB. TEST YOUR MANAGEMENT COMMUNICATION SKILLS*

CORRECT ANSWERS:

1a. Never forget who your boss is—and where your loyalty lies. If you tell him nothing, if you tell him casually, you plant seeds of mistrust.

2c. Honesty and courtesy are the best policies. It's never right to lie. And it's never smart to waste your boss's time.

3b. Keeping appointments and looking your best are basic business principles. No one appreciates a last-minute cancellation of an appointment. You'd be surprised at what good eyes an interviewer has.

4a. Controlling the meeting starts with your setting the ground rules—up front. To feed one person's self-interest is not productive, or fair.

5c. This is the only practical answer. To detail negative observations could lead to legal action; to stress only positive points is to tell a half-truth.

6c. It's best to nip problems in the bud. Procrastination is a sin. And you must first talk with one employee to determine if there's a need to talk with two.

7c. Place the responsibility where it belongs. To be a "good guy" or to leave immediately is not facing up to the problem.

8c. Project a positive thought as you make your position clear. Blaming others is passing the buck; hiding behind a "maybe" meeting is a sign of weakness.

9c. This answer establishes you as an authority

*Communispond, Inc., 485 Lexington Avenue, New York, N.Y. 10017. With permission.

for future stories. To send a gift is unwarranted and tasteless. And to the writer, the story is not "publicity"—it's "news coverage."

10c. Let sleeping dogs lie, particularly on your first day. To ignore the problem is foolish; to initiate conversations is a greater folly. ┼

11b. Keep the conversation on a business level. It's your responsibility to stop office gossip, not encourage it. ┼

12a. This action is prudent and professional. You don't want to embarrass your boss and customer. Nor do you want to be in an awkward position afterward. ┼

EXERCISE IIIC. LEADERSHIP QUESTIONNAIRE

To find your leadership style,

1. Circle the item numbers for items 8, 12, 17, 18, 19, 30, 34, and 35.

2. Write a "1" in front of the *circled items* to which you responded S (seldom) or N (never).

3. Write a "1" in front of *items not circled* to which you responded A (always) or F (frequently).

4. Circle the "1's" which you have written in front of the following items: 3, 5, 8, 10, 15, 18, 19, 22, 24, 26, 28, 30, 32, 34, and 35.

5. Count the circled "1's." This is your score for concern for people. Record the score in the blank following the letter "P" at the end of the questionnaire.

6. Count the uncircled "1's." This is your score for concern for task. Record this number in the blank following the letter "T."

7. Now, refer to the diagram. Find your score on the *concern for task* dimension (t) on the left-hand arrow. Next, move to the right-hand arrow and find your score on the *concern for people* dimension (p). Draw a straight line that intersects the P and T score. The point at which that line crosses the *shared leadership* arrow indicates your score on that dimension.

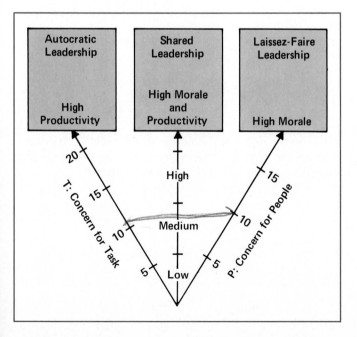

EXERCISE IIID. POWER ORIENTATION TEST

This test is designed to compute your Machiavellianism (Mach) score. To obtain your score, add the number you have checked on questions 1, 3, 4, 5, 9, and 10. For the other four questions, reverse the numbers you have checked: 5 becomes 1, 4 is 2, 2 is 4, 1 is 5. Total your ten numbers to find your score. The National Opinion Research Center, which used this short form of the scale in a random sample of American adults, found that the national average was 25.

The results of research using the Mach test have found that (1) men are generally more Machiavellian than women, (2) older adults tend to have lower Mach scores than younger adults, (3) there is no significant difference between high Machs and low Machs on measures of intelligence or ability, (4) Machiavellianism is not significantly related to demographic characteristics such as educational level or marital status, and (5) high Machs tend to be in professions that emphasize the control and manipulation of individuals—for example, managers, lawyers, psychiatrists, and behavioral scientists.

EXERCISE IVA. BUREAUCRATIC ORIENTATION TEXT

Give yourself one point for each statement for which you responded in the bureaucratic direction:

1. Mostly agree	11. Mostly agree
2. Mostly agree	12. Mostly disagree
3. Mostly disagree	13. Mostly disagree
4. Mostly agree	14. Mostly agree
5. Mostly disagree	15. Mostly disagree
6. Mostly disagree	16. Mostly agree
7. Mostly agree	17. Mostly disagree
8. Mostly agree	18. Mostly agree
9. Mostly disagree	19. Mostly agree
10. Mostly agree	20. Mostly disagree

A very high score (15 and over) would suggest that you would enjoy working in a bureaucracy. A very low score (5 or lower) would suggest that you would be frustrated by working in a bureaucracy, especially a large one.

EXERCISE IVB. RATE YOUR JOB'S MOTIVATING POTENTIAL

Place the scores for questions "1" through "5" into the following formula:

$$\text{MPS} = \frac{a+b+c}{3} \times d \times e$$

A high or low score on "4" or "5" will carry a heavy weight. A total MPS of 200 or higher suggests high motivating potential. Scores beow 50 suggest very low potential.

EXERCISE IVC. RATE YOUR CLASSROOM CULTURE

Add up your score on the eight items. Your score will lie somewhere between 8 and 40.

A high score (30 or above) describes an open, warm, human, trusting, and supportive culture. A low score (20 or below) describes a closed, cold, task-oriented, autocratic, and tense culture.

Compare your score against the ones tabulated by your classmates. How close do they align? Discuss perceived discrepancies.

EXERCISE IVD. RATE OF LIFE-CHANGE TEST

Calculate your total score by adding up all scale values that are circled. Scores below 200 are considered to be low. Scores of 300 or more are considered high. Anything in the 200 range is rated moderate.

The research indicates that high life-change scores are associated with significantly more illnesses—colds, cuts, bruises, headaches, backaches, injuries, and even heart disease. The body's ability to adapt to change is not limitless. Too much change surfaces in stress, illnesses, accidents, and increased absences from work. If your score is 300 or higher, you are about two to three times more likely to have health problems than individuals with scores below 200.

Glossary

Ability. An individual's capacity to perform the various tasks in a job.

Absenteeism. Failure to report to work.

Accommodation. The willingness of one party in a conflict to place his or her opponent's interests above his or her own.

Active listening. The active search for meaning when one listens.

Adhocracy. A structure that is flexible, adaptive, and responsive; organized around unique problems to be solved by groups of relative strangers with diverse professional skills.

Affiliation need. The desire for friendly and close interpersonal relationships.

Assessment centers. A set of performance simulation tests designed to evaluate a candidate's managerial potential.

Assumed similarity. Judging other people to be like you.

Attitudes. Evaluative statements or judgments concerning objects, people, or events.

Attitude surveys. Eliciting responses from employees through questionnaires about how they feel about their jobs, work groups, supervisors, and/or the organization.

Attribution theory. When individuals observe behavior, they attempt to determine whether it is internally or externally caused.

Authoritarianism. The belief that there should be status and power differences among people in organizations.

Autocratic leader. One who dictates decisions down to subordinates.

Autonomous work teams. Groups that are free to determine how the goals assigned to them are to be accomplished and how tasks are to be allocated.

Autonomy. The degree to which a job provides substantial freedom and discretion to the individual in scheduling the work and in determining the procedures to be used in carrying it out.

Avoidance. Withdrawing from or suppressing conflict.

Behavioral theories (of leadership). Theories proposing that specific behaviors differentiate leaders from nonleaders.

Behavioral view (of conflict). The belief that conflict is a natural and inevitable outcome in any group.

Biographical characteristics. Personal characteristics—such as age, sex, and marital status—that are objective and easily obtained from personnel records.

Brainstorming. An idea-generation process that specifically encourages any and all alternatives, while withholding any criticism of those alternatives.

Bureaucracy. A structure characterized by high complexity, high formalization, impersonality, career tracks, employment decisions based on merit, and separation of members' organizational and personal lives.

Career. A sequence of positions occupied by a person during the course of a lifetime.

Career stages. The four steps most people go through in their careers: exploration, establishment, midcareer, and late career.

Causality. The implication that the independent variable causes the dependent variable.

Caused behavior. Behavior that is directed toward some end; not random.

Centralization. The degree to which decision making is concentrated at a single point in the organization.

Change. Making things different.

Change agent. The person or persons who act as catalysts and assume the responsibility for managing the change process.

Change intervention. A planned action to make things different.

Channel. The medium through which a communication message travels.

Classical conditioning. A type of conditioning where an individual responds to some stimulus that would not invariably produce such a response.

Coalitions. Two or more individuals who combine their power to push for or support their demands.

Coercion. The application of direct threats or force upon resisters.

Coercive power. Power that is based on fear.

Cognitive dissonance. Any incompatibility between two or more attitudes or between behavior and attitudes.

Cognitive evaluation theory. Extrinsic rewards allocated for behavior that had been previously intrinsically rewarded tends to decrease the overall level of motivation.

Cohesiveness. Degree to which group members are attracted to each other and share common goals.

Collaboration. A situation where the parties to a conflict each desire to satisfy fully the concern of all parties.

Command group. A manager and his or her immediate subordinates.

Communication. The transference and understanding of meaning.

Communication networks. Channels by which information flows.

Communication process. The steps between a source and a receiver that result in the transference of meaning.

Competition. A situation where one party seeks to achieve his goals or further his interests, regardless of the impact of this behavior on others.

Complexity. The degree of vertical, horizontal, and spatial differentiation in an organization.

Compressed workweek. A four-day week, with employees working ten hours a day.

Compromise. A situation in which each party to a conflict must give up something.

Conflict. A process in which an effort is purposely made by A to offset the efforts of B by some form of blocking that will result in frustrating B in attaining his or her goals or furthering his or her interests.

Conformity. Adjusting one's behavior to align with the norms of the group.

Conformity values. A low tolerance for ambiguity, having difficulty in accepting people with different values, and a desire that others accept one's values.

Consideration. The extent to which a leader is likely to have job relationships characterized by mutual trust, respect for subordinates' ideas, and regard for their feelings.

Contingency variables. Those variables that moderate the relationship between the independent and dependent variables and improve the correlation.

Continuous reinforcement. A desired behavior is reinforced each and every time it is demonstrated.

Cooptation. Acquiring the cooperation of the leaders of a resistance group by giving them a key role in a change decision.

Core values. The primary or dominant values that are accepted throughout the organization.

Correlational design. A research design that seeks to assess potential relationships that may exist between two or more specific variables.

Decoding. Retranslating a sender's communication message.

Delphi technique. A group decision method in which individual members, acting separately, pool their judgment in a systematic and independent fashion.

Democratic leader. One who shares decision making with subordinates.

Dependency. A's relationship to B when B possesses something that A requires.

Dependent variable. The response that is measured; the outcome.

Dominant culture. Expresses the core values that are shared by a majority of the organization's members.

Dual-career couples. Couples in which each member actively pursues a job outside the home.

Dysfunctional conflict. Conflict that hinders group performance.

Effectiveness. Achievement of goal.

Efficiency. The ratio of effective output to the input required to achieve it.

Egocentrism values. The belief in rugged individualism and selfishness.

Elasticity of power. The relative responsiveness of power to changes in available alternatives.

Employee-oriented leader. One who emphasizes interpersonal relations.

Encoding. Converting a communication message to symbolic form.

Encounter stage. The stage in the socialization process in which a new employee sees what the organization is really like and confronts the likelihood that expectations and reality may diverge.

Environment. Anything outside the organization itself.

Equity theory. Individuals compare their job inputs and outcomes with those of others.

ERG theory. There are three groups of core needs: existence, relatedness, and growth.

Existential values. A high tolerance for ambiguity and individuals with differing values.

Expectancy theory. The strength of a tendency to act in a certain way depends on the strength of an expectation that the act will be followed by a given outcome and on the attractiveness of that outcome to the individual.

Experimental design. A research design, containing experimental and control groups, that allows changes in the experimental group's dependent variable to be assumed to have been caused by changes imposed on the independent variable.

Expert power. Influence based on special skills or knowledge.

Externals. Individuals who believe that what happens to them is controlled by outside forces such as luck or chance.

Extrinsic rewards. Rewards received from the environment surrounding the context of work.

Feedback. The degree to which carrying out the work activities required by a job results in the individual obtaining direct and clear information about the effectiveness of his or her performance.

Feedback loop. The final link in the communication process; puts the message back into the system as a check against misunderstandings.

Felt conflict. Emotional involvement in a conflict creating anxiety, tenseness, frustration, or hostility.

Field setting. Research conducted in a real-world environment.

Filtering. A sender's manipulation of information so that it will be seen more favorably by the receiver.

Fixed-interval schedule. Rewards are spaced at uniform time intervals.

Flextime. Employees work during a common core time period each day but have discretion in forming their total workday from a flexible set of hours outside the core.

Formal group. A designated work group defined by the organization's structure.

Formalization. The degree to which jobs within the organization are standardized.

Friendship group. Those brought together because they share one or more common characteristics.

Functional conflict. Conflict that supports the goals of the group and improves its performance.

Functional structure. A structure characterized by grouping similar and related occupational specialties together.

Goal-setting theory. The theory that specific and difficult goals lead to higher performance.

Grapevine. The informal communication channel.

Group. Two or more individuals, interacting and interdependent, who come together to achieve particular objectives.

Group demography. The degree to which members of a group share a common demographic attribute such as age, sex, race, educational level, or length of service in the organization and the impact of these attributes on turnover.

Groupshift. A change in decision risk between the group's decision and the individual decision that members within the group would make; can be either toward conservatism or greater risk.

Groupthink. Phenomenon in which the norm for consensus overrides the realistic appraisal of alternative courses of action.

Growth-need strength. A measure of an employee's desire for self-esteem and self-actualization.

Halo effect. Drawing a general impression about an individual based on a single characteristic.

Hawthorne effect. Workers respond positively to special attention.

Hierarchy of needs theory. There is a hierarchy of five needs—physiological, safety, love, esteem, self-actualization—and as each need is sequentially satisfied, the next need becomes dominant.

Higher-order needs. Needs that are satisfied internally; needs for love, esteem, and self-actualization.

Horizontal differentiation. The degree of differentiation between units based on the orientation of members, the nature of the tasks they perform, and their education and training.

Illegitimate political behavior. Extreme political behavior that violates the implied rules of the game.

Independent variable. The presumed cause of the dependent variable.

Individualism. A national culture attribute describing a loosely knit social framework in which people emphasize only the care of themselves and their immediate family.

Informal group. A group that is neither structured nor organizationally determined; appears in response to the need for social contact.

Informational cues. Words, actions, silence, or inaction that individuals need to derive meaning from communication.

Initiating structure. The extent to which a leader is likely to define and structure his or her role and those of subordinates in the search for goal attainment.

Institutionalization. When an organization takes on a life of its own, apart from any of its members, and acquires immortality.

Integrated work teams. Groups that decide the specific allocation of the tasks assigned to them.

Intellectual abilities. Those required to do mental activities.

Interacting group. The typical group, where members interact with each other face to face.

Interactionist view (of conflict). The belief that conflict is not only a positive force in a group but that it is absolutely necessary for a group to perform effectively.

Interest group. Those working together to attain a specific objective with which each is concerned.

Intergroup development. OD efforts to improve interactions between groups.

Intermittent reinforcement. A desired behavior is reinforced often enough to make the behavior worth repeating, but not every time it is demonstrated.

Internals. Individuals who believe that they control what happens to them.

Intrinsic rewards. The pleasure or value one receives from the content of a work task.

Intuition. A feeling not necessarily supported by research.

Job analysis. Developing a detailed description of the tasks involved in a job, determining the relationship of a given job to other jobs, and ascertaining the knowledge, skills, and abilities necessary for an employee to perform the job successfully.

Job characteristics model. Identifies five job characteristics and their relationship to personal and work outcomes.

Job description. A written statement of what a jobholder does, how it is done, and why it is done.

Job design. The way that tasks are combined to form complete jobs.

Job enlargement. The horizontal expansion of jobs.

Job enrichment. The vertical expansion of jobs.

Job involvement. The degree to which a person identifies with his or her job, actively participates in it, and considers his or her performance important to his or her sense of self-worth.

Job redesign. The changing of job tasks.

Job rotation. The periodic shifting of a worker from one task to another.

Job satisfaction. A general attitude toward one's job; the difference between the amount of rewards workers receive and the amount they believe they should receive.

Job sharing. Two or more people who split a traditional forty-hour-a-week job.

Job specification. States the minimum acceptable qualifications that an employee must possess to perform a given job successfully.

Kinesics. The study of body motions.

Knowledge power. The ability to control unique and valuable information.

LPC. Least preferred co-worker questionnaire that measures task or relationship-oriented leadership style.

Labor unions. A formal group of employees that acts collectively to protect and promote employee interests.

Laboratory setting. Artificial environments in which research is conducted.

Leader-member relations. The degree of confidence, trust, and respect subordinates have in their leader.

Leadership. The ability to influence a group toward the achievement of goals.

Learning. Any relatively permanent change in behavior that occurs as a result of experience.

Legitimate political behavior. Normal everyday politics.

Leniency error. The tendency to evaluate a set of employees too high (positive) or too low (negative).

Locus of control. The degree to which people believe they are masters of their own fate.

Lower-order needs. Needs that are satisfied externally; physiological and safety needs.

Machiavellianism. Degree to which an individual is pragmatic, maintains emotional distance, and believes that means can justify ends.

Management. A field of study devoted to determining how best to attain goals in organizations.

Managerial grid. A nine-by-nine matrix outlining eighty-one different leadership styles.

Manipulation. Covert influence attempts.

Manipulative values. Individuals who value striving to achieve their goals by manipulating things and people.

Masculinity. A national culture attribute describing the extent to which the dominant societal values are characterized by assertiveness, acquisition for money and things, and not caring for others or for the quality of life.

Matrix structure. A structure that creates dual lines of authority; combines the functional and product structures.

Maturity. The ability and willingness of people to take responsibility for directing their own behavior.

Mechanistic structure. A structure characterized by high complexity, high formalization, and centralization.

Message. What is communicated.

Metamorphosis stage. The stage in the socialization process in which a new employee adjusts to his or her work group's values and norms.

Models. Abstractions of reality; simplified representations of some real-world phenomena.

Moderating variables. Abate the effect of the independent variable on the dependent variable; also known as contingency variables.

Motivating potential score. A predictive index suggesting the motivation potential in a job.

Motivation. The willingness to exert high levels of effort toward organizational goals, conditioned by the effort's ability to satisfy some individual needs.

Motivation-hygiene theory. Intrinsic factors are related to job satisfaction, while extrinsic factors are associated with dissatisfaction.

N Ach. Need to achieve or strive continually to do things better.

Nominal group technique. A group decision method in which individual members meet face to face to pool their judgments in a systematic but independent fashion.

Nonverbal communication. Messages conveyed through body movements, the intonations or emphasis we give to words, facial expressions, and the physical distance between the sender and receiver.

Norms. Acceptable standards of behavior within a group that are shared by the group's members.

Observational design. A research design where the researcher observes phenomena and records what he or she sees.

Operant conditioning. A type of conditioning in which desired voluntary behavior leads to a reward or prevents a punishment.

Opportunity power. Influence obtained as a result of being in the right place at the right time.

Organic structure. A structure characterized by low complexity, low formalization, and decentralization.

Organization size. The number of people employed in an organization.

Organization. A consciously coordinated social unit, composed of two or more people, that functions on a relatively continuous basis to achieve a common goal or set of goals.

Organizational behavior. A field of study that investigates the impact that individuals, groups, and structure have on behavior within organizations for the purpose of applying such knowledge toward improving an organization's effectiveness.

Organizational commitment. An individual's orientation toward the organization in terms of loyalty, identification, and involvement.

Organizational culture. A common perception held by the organization's members; a system of shared meaning.

Organizational development (OD). A systems-oriented approach to change.

Organization structure. The degree of complexity, formalization, and centralization in the organization.

Perceived conflict. Awareness by one or more parties of the existence of conditions that create opportunities for conflict to arise.

Perception. A process by which individuals organize and interpret their sensory impressions in order to give meaning to their environment.

Personal power. Influence attributed to one's personal characteristics.

Personality. The sum total of ways in which an individual reacts and interacts with others.

Personality traits. Enduring characteristics that describe an individual's behavior.

Persuasive power. The ability to allocate and manipulate symbolic rewards.

Physical abilities. Those required to do tasks demanding stamina, dexterity, strength, and similar skills.

Physical environment. Physical factors in the work environment such as levels of noise, temperature, and illumination.

Political behavior. Those activities that are not required as part of one's formal role in the organization but that influence, or attempt to influence, the distribution of advantages and disadvantages within the organization.

Position power. Influence derived from one's formal structural position in the organization; includes the power to hire, fire, discipline, promote, and give salary increases.

Power. A capacity that A has to influence the behavior of B so that B does things he or she would not otherwise do.

Power-control (view of structure). An organization's structure is the result of a power struggle by internal constituencies who are seeking to further their interests.

Power distance. A national culture attribute describing the extent to which a society accepts that power in institutions and organizations is distributed unequally.

Power need. The desire to make others behave in a way that they would not otherwise have behaved in.

Prearrival stage. The period of learning in the socialization process that occurs before a new employee joins the organization.

Process consultation. Consultant gives a client insights into what is going on around, within him or her, and between him or her and other people; identifies processes that need improvement.

Production-oriented leader. One who emphasizes technical or task aspects of the job.

Productivity. A performance measure including effectiveness and efficiency.

Product structure. A structure characterized by grouping activities together that relate to a specific product.

Psychological contract. An unwritten agreement that sets out what management expects from the employee, and vice versa.

Quality circles. A voluntary work group of employees who meet regularly to discuss their quality problems, investigate causes, recommend solutions, and take corrective actions.

Reactive values. Individuals who value basic physiological needs and are unaware of themselves or others as human beings.

Realistic job previews. Job applicants receive both unfavorable and favorable information about the job.

Referent power. Influence held by A based on B's admiration and desire to model himself or herself after A.

Refreezing. Stabilizing a change intervention by balancing driving and restraining forces.

Reinforcement theory. Behavior is a function of its consequences.

Reliability. Consistency of measurement.

Research. The systematic gathering of information.

Rigor. A term applied to research where tight control has been held over the variables.

Rituals. Repetitive sequences of activities that express and reinforce the key values of the organization, what goals are most important, which people are important and which are expendable.

Role. A set of expected behavior patterns attributed to someone occupying a given position in a social unit.

Role conflict. A situation in which an individual is confronted by divergent role expectations.

Role expectations. How others believe a person should act in a given situation.

Role identity. Certain attitudes and behavior consistent with a role.

Role perception. An individual's view of how he or she is supposed to act in a given situation.

Scientific management. A body of literature developed in the early 1900s concerned with incentives, selection, training, and the design of jobs to eliminate time and motion waste.

Selective perception. People interpret what they see based on their interests, background, experience, and attitudes.

Self-actualization. The drive to become what one is capable of becoming.

Self-perception theory. Attitudes are used, after the fact, to make sense out of action (behavior) that has already occurred.

Sensitivity training. Training groups that seek to change behavior through unstructured group interaction.

Shaping behavior. Systematically reinforcing each successive step that moves an individual closer to the desired response.

Similarity error. Giving special consideration when rating others to those qualities that the evaluator perceives in himself or herself.

Simple structure. A structure characterized by low complexity, low formalization, and authority centralized in a single person.

Skill variety. The degree to which a job requires a variety of different activities.

Socialization. The process that adapts employees to the organization's culture.

Social learning theory. People can learn through observation and direct experience.

Social loafing. Group size and individual performance are inversely related.

Sociocentric values. The belief that it is more important to be liked and to get along with others than to get ahead.

Sociotechnical systems. A job design philosophy emphasizing both the technical and social aspects of work.

Spatial differentiation. The degree to which the location of an organization's offices, plants, and personnel are geographically dispersed.

Span of control. The number of subordinates who report directly to a manager.

Status. A prestige grading, position, or rank within a group.

Status equity. The degree to which group members perceive that the status hierarchy is equitable.

Status hierarchy. An ordering of individuals by their relative rank.

Sterotyping. Judging someone on the basis of the perception of the group to which that person belongs.

Stress. A dynamic condition in which an individual is confronted with an opportunity, constraint, or demand related to what he or she desires and for which the outcome is perceived to be both uncertain and important.

Strong cultures. Cultures where the core values are intensely held and widely shared.

Subcultures. Minicultures within an organization, typically defined by department designations and geographical separation.

Survey feedback. The use of questionnaires to identify discrepancies among member perceptions; discussion follows and remedies are suggested.

Systematic study. Looking at relationships, attempting to attribute causes and effects, and drawing conclusions based on scientific evidence.

Task group. Those working together to complete a job task.

Task identity. The degree to which the job requires completion of a whole and identifiable piece of work.

Task structure. The degree to which job assignments are procedurized.

Team building. High interaction among group members to increase trust and openness.

Technology. How an organization transfers its inputs to outputs.

Theory X. The assumption that employees dislike work, are lazy, dislike responsibility, and must be coerced to perform.

Theory Y. The assumption that employees like work, are creative, seek responsibility, and can exercise self-direction.

Three needs theory. Achievement, power, and affiliation are three important needs that help to understand motivation.

Traditional view (of conflict). The belief that all conflict must be avoided.

Tribalistic values. The belief in tradition and power exerted by authority figures.

Turnover. Voluntary and involuntary permanent withdrawal from the organization.

Two-tier pay systems. New employees are hired at significantly lower wage rates than those already employed and performing the same jobs.

Type A behavior. Aggressive involvement in a chronic, incessant struggle to achieve more and more in less and less time and, if necessary, against the opposing efforts of other things or other persons.

Type B behavior. Rarely harried by the desire to obtain a wildly increasing number of things or participate in an endlessly growing series of events in an ever-decreasing amount of time.

Uncertainty avoidance. A national culture attribute describing the extent to which a society feels threatened by uncertain and ambiguous situations and tries to avoid them.

Unfreezing. Change efforts to overcome the pressures of both individual resistance and group conformity.

Values. Basic convictions that a specific mode of conduct or end state of existence is personally or socially preferable to an opposite or converse mode of conduct or end state of existence.

Value system. A ranking of individual values according to their relative importance.

Variable-interval schedule. Rewards are distributed in time so that reinforcements are unpredictable.

Variable-ratio schedule. The reward varies relative to the behavior of the individual.

Vertical differentiation. The number of hierarchical levels in the organization.

Work modules. Two-hour time task units, four of which equal an eight-hour day; can be allocated in ways to give workers diverse tasks.

Work sampling. Creating a miniature replica of a job to evaluate the performance abilities of job candidates.

Workspace design. The layout, size, and spacing of an employee's workplace.

Name Index

Berman, H. J., 114
Bernardin, H. J., 426
Binzen, P., 310
Bird, L., 262
Birdwhistell, R. L., 237
Black, J. S., 114
Blackstone, D., 357
Blake, R. R., 244, 245, 259, 264, 265, 309, 473
Blanchard, K. H., 251–53, 260, 266
Blau, G. J., 147, 393
Blau, P. M., 354, 426
Blood, M. R., 238
Blumberg, M., 504
Boal, K. B., 148
Bomers, G. B. J., 309
Borman, W. C., 426
Bottger, P.. 204
Boudreau, J. W., 427
Bowerman, B., 196
Bowers, D. G., 291, 472, 474
Boxx, W. R., 392
Brady, C., 188, 204
Brady, J. D., 155
Brady, M., 155–56
Brass, D. J., 394
Bray, D. W., 427
Brayfield, A. H., 114, 115
Breathed, B., 210, 270
Brenner, S. N., 203
Bridwell, L. G., 147
Brief, A. P., 205, 395
Broadwater, G., 132
Brotherton, C., 355
Brown, B., 238
Brown, C. A., 88
Brown, D., 481
Brown, L. D., 473, 474
Bruner, J. S., 90
Buchanan, B., II, 113
Buckley, W. F., Jr., 213
Bullard, J. H., 355
Bullock, R. J., 474
Bunker, D. R., 474
Burke, R. J., 427
Burke, W. W., 473, 474
Burnham, D. H., 148, 287
Burt, R. E., 394
Byham, W. C., 426

C

Calder, B. J., 112, 148
Caldwell, D. F., 238
Calvasina, E. J., 392
Campagna, A. F., 393
Campbell, A., 114
Campbell, D. E., 394
Campbell, D. J., 148
Campbell, J. P., 114, 452, 473, 474
Campbell, K. M., 148

Campbell, R. J., 427
Capone, A., 269
Capwell, D. F., 115
Cardoza, M., 311
Carrell, M. R., 146, 149
Carroll, D. T., 452
Carson, J., 186
Carter, J., 262
Cartwright, D., 265, 290
Cascio, W. F., 84, 427
Cass, E. L., 200, 203
Cattell, R. B., 89
Chadwick-Jones, J. K., 88
Chandler, P., 319–20
Chandler, R., 371
Chavez, C., 241
Chemers, M. M., 266
Cherrington, D. J., 113
Child, J., 353, 354, 355
Chin, R., 474
Christie, R., 89, 289, 325
Clark, B., 427
Clark, R. D., III, 238
Cohen, B. M., 426
Cohen, L. P., 453
Colby, F. M., 207
Condie, S. J., 113
Connolly, T., 505
Converse, P. E., 114
Coons, A. E., 265
Cooper, C., 391, 394, 395
Cooper, J., 112
Cooper, M. R., 113
Costello, T. W., 90
Costigain, R., 392
Cray, E., 453
Crockett, W. H., 114, 115
Crow, W. J., 85
Croyle, R. R., 112
Culbert, S. A., 291
Cummings, L. L., 14, 112, 147, 148, 204, 291, 355
Cummings, T. G., 202
Cyert, R. M., 290

D

Daft, R. L., 37, 353
Dalton, D. R., 36, 38, 355
Daughen, J. R., 310
Davis, K., 216, 237
Davis, R. V., 114
Davis, T. R. V., 394
Davis, W., 157
Deal, T. E., 452
Dearborn, D. C., 71, 90
de Charms, R., 148
Deci, E. L., 148
DeCotiis, T. A., 394
Delafield, G., 355
Delbecq, A. L., 238, 354

Maier, N. R. F., 204, 238, 310
Main, J., 392, 453
Malatesta, C. Z., 238
Mancies, B., 510–13
Mandel, D., 188, 204
Mangione, T. W., 88
Mann, L., 89
Mannari, H., 88
Mannheim, B. F., 354
Mansfield, R., 354
March, J. G., 290
Marcus, P. M., 291
Margerison, C., 267
Margulies, N., 473
Marsh, R., 88
Marshall, J., 394, 395, 451
Martin, J., 451
Martinko, M., 148
Maslow, A., 122–24, 128, 147
Massengil, D., 392
Maurer, J. G., 291
Mausner, B., 115
Mayes, B. T., 291
Mayfield, E. C., 426
Mayo, E., 38, 179
Meglino, B. M., 87, 115
Meyer, G., 473
Michela, J. L., 87
Michener, J., 117
Miewald, R. D., 352
Miles, M. B., 473
Miles, M. G., 474
Miles, R. H., 353
Mileti, D. S., 354
Milken, M., 276
Miner, J. B., 87, 89, 146, 147, 148, 265, 266, 393
Miner, M. G., 87
Mintzberg, H., 20, 38, 290, 291, 354, 355
Miron, D., 148
Mirvis, P. H., 38, 472
Mitchell, T. R., 87, 146, 149, 237, 238, 266, 267
Moberg, D. J., 291
Mobley, W. H., 87, 115
Moede, W., 204
Mohr, L. B., 15
Molander, E. A., 203
Money, W. H., 266
Moore, L. F., 37
Moorhead, G., 393
Morgan, B. S., 113
Morgan, M., 418
Morris, W. C., 165
Morrow, P. C., 394
Morse, J. J., 453
Moses, J. L., 426
Mouton, J. S., 244, 245, 259, 264, 265, 309, 473
Mowday, R. T., 114, 291, 452
Muchinsky, P. M., 88, 89, 150, 238

Mullin, B. J., 394
Munson, J. M., 113
Murnighan, J. K., 232
Murphy, C. J., 265
Murray, V. V., 289
Myers, D. G., 238
Myers, M. S., 113
Myers, S. S., 113

N

Nader, R., 246, 445
Nadler, D. A., 355, 391
Naisbitt, J., 505
Napoleon, 241
Neilsen, E. H., 473
Nemiroff, P. M., 355
Nevis, E. C., 505
Newman, J. E., 395
Newstrom, J. W., 393
Nicholas, J. M., 474
Nichols, J., 329
Nicholson, N., 88
Nisbett, R. E., 114
Nongaim, K. E., 147
Nord, W. R., 15, 392
Norton, D. D., 392
Nulty, P., 453
Nystrom, P. C., 202, 265

O

Odbert, H. S., 89
Oldham, G. R., 37, 373, 391, 392, 393, 394, 395
Olson, C. A., 427
O'Malley, T., 314–15
O'Reilly, C. A., III, 149, 204, 238, 452
Organ, D. W., 247, 266
Organt, G. J., 427
Osborn, A. F., 238
Osborn, R. N., 265

P–Q

Packard, D., 437
Parasuraman, S., 384, 394
Parker, B., 258
Parker, D. F., 149, 394
Parsons, T., 354
Pascale, R., 452
Patterson, B., 174, 177
Pattiz, L., 371
Pavlov, I. P., 74, 75, 90
Payne, R., 391, 395
Peacock, A. C., 87
Pearson, J., 134
Peck, C., 510–15
Peckham, V., 204
Pedalino, E., 90
Pelz, D. C., 310

Subject Index

Interactionist view of conflict, 295
Interest group, 170
Interests, influence on perception, 64
Intergroup development, 466, 468
Intermittent reinforcers, 78–79
Internal Revenue Service, 430
Internals, 57–58
International aspects of OB, 494–500
Interviews:
  perception in, 69
  selection tool, 398–99
Introversion-extroversion personality, 56
Intuition, 4–5

J

Jargon, 213
Job analysis, 397–98
Job characteristics:
  model, 371–76
  perception of, 224
Job design:
  defined, 359
  future of, 389–90
  group, 200, 365–68
  individual, 201, 362–65
  and performance, 388
  test, 483
Job difficulty, as reward criterion, 412
Job enlargement, 361
Job enrichment, 361, 364–65
Job involvement, 98
Job-personality fit, 60–62
Job redesign:
  defined, 359
  options, 362–71
Job rotation, 362–63
Job satisfaction:
  as an attitude, 98
  as a dependent variable, 30, 105–6, 493–94
  importance of, 110–11
  as an independent variable, 106–8
  measuring, 104–5
  motivation-hygiene theory, 125
  workforce, 105
Job sharing, 371
Job specialization, 359–60
Johnson & Johnson, 435
Judgments, in communication, 234

K

Kinesics, 221
K-mart, 435
Knowledge power, 273
Ku Klux Klan, 242

L

Laboratory studies, 23–24
Language. (see Jargon)

Language, in culture, 444
Language differences, 212–13
Lateral communication, 217
Leader-participation model, 255–57
Leadership:
  behavioral theories, 242–46
  contingency theories, 246–58
  defined, 240
  democratic, 246–48
  Fiedler model, 248–51
  Hersey-Blanchard model, 251–53
  importance of, 262, 263
  influence on behavior, 260–61, 262, 263
  integration of theories, 259–60
  leader-participation model, 255–57
  Managerial Grid, 244–45, 252–53
  Michigan studies, 244
  Ohio State studies, 243–44
  participative, 247–48
  path-goal theory, 254–55
  and power, 271
  situational theory, 251–53
  substitutes for, 258–59
  test, 323–24
  trait theories, 241–42
  Vroom-Yetton model, 255–57
Learning:
  and behavior, 83
  defined, 73–74
  theories of, 74–77
Least preferred coworker (LPC), 248–51
Legitimate power (see Position power)
Leniency error, 405
Levi Strauss, 435
Locus of control, 57–58, 161–63
Los Angeles City Schools, 455
Los Angeles Lakers, 276
Lotteries, 80
Love need, 122
Lower-order needs, 123
Loyalty and perception, 70

M

McDonald's, 97, 434, 435, 437
Machiavellianism:
  personality, 59
  test, 324–25
Macy's, 477
Management and OB, 10
Managerial Grid, 244–45
Marital status, 51
Marriot, 435
Mary Kay Cosmetics, 434
Massachusetts Institute of Technology, 430
Matrix structure, 337–38
Maturity, in leadership, 251–52
Maytag, 435
Mechanistic structure, 332–34
Merck, 435
Mergers, 445–46

Pay, 415–16
Pay equity (*see* Equity theory; Rewards)
Penn Central Railroad, 304
Perception:
  accuracy, 84, 85
  and behavior, 82–83
  and communication, 222–24
  defined, 62–63
  distortion in, 62, 71–73
  factors influencing, 63–66
  of job characteristics, 375
  person, 67–73
  vs. reality, 62–63
  selective, 71, 212
  of structure, 347–48
  training to improve, 84–85
Performance:
  as a dependent variable, 27–30
  as a reward criterion, 410
  satisfaction relationship, 107
Performance evaluation:
  criteria, 402–3
  influence on behavior, 421
  methods, 403–4
  and motivation, 401–2
  and perception, 70
  problems in, 404–6
  purposes of, 400–401
  sharing results of, 409
  standards, 403–4
Personal power, 274
Personality:
  and behavior, 82
  defined, 52–53
  determinants of, 53–55
  as a group contingency, 190
  job fit, 60–62
  and stress, 387–88
  traits, 55–57
Persuasive power, 273
Physical environment, 377–78
Physiological needs, 122
Polaroid, 437, 455
Political science, 8, 9
Politics (*see* Organizational politics)
Position power, 271, 273–74
Positive reinforcement (*see* Reinforcement)
Power:
  bases of, 271–73, 275
  coalitions, 281–82
  coercive, 271, 272
  control, as determinant of structure, 342–43
  defined, 269
  dependency, 270, 275–79
  elasticity, 278–79
  expert, 271, 274
  group, 171–72
  influence on behavior, 285–86
  knowledge, 273
  and leadership, 271
  legitimate, 271

motives, 287
need, 129
opportunity, 274–75
oriented managers, 287
personal, 274
persuasive, 273
position, 271, 273–74
referent, 271
reward, 271, 272
sources of, 271–75
symbols, 273
tactics, 279–81
test, 324–25
Prediction of behavior, 3–5
Prison experiment, 177–78
Privacy, workspace, 380–82
Process consultation, 464–65, 467
Procter & Gamble, 277, 334, 434, 435
Product structure, 336–37
Production-oriented leaders, 244
Productivity:
  defined, 28
  determinants of, 490–91
  and satisfaction, 107
PROSPER, 84
Proximity, influence on perception, 65
Psychological contract, 176
Psychology, 7–8
Punishment, 77

Q

Quality circles, 366–68

R

Raychem, 435
Realistic job previews, 69–70
Reality vs. perception, 62–63
Referent power, 271
Reinforcement, 77–80, 133–34
Relatedness needs, 128
Relational manager, 288
Relationships in a model, 26
Relative standards, in evaluation, 404
Reliability, 20
Republic Avionics, 481–82
Research:
  control groups, 22–23
  designs, 19–23
  evaluation of, 18–19
  purpose of, 18
  rigor, 19
  settings, 23–24
Revlon, 435
Reward(s):
  in culture, 431
  determinants, 410–12
  equity in, 106, 134–37
  influence on behavior, 421